Electronic Government: Design, Applications and Management

Åke Grönlund
Umeå University, Sweden

 **Idea Group Publishing**

 **Information Science Publishing**

Hershey • London • Melbourne • Singapore • Beijing

Acquisitions Editor:	Mehdi Khosrowpour
Managing Editor:	Jan Travers
Development Editor:	Michele Rossi
Copy Editor:	Maria Boyer
Typesetter:	LeAnn Whitcomb
Cover Design:	Tedi Wingard
Printed at:	Integrated Book Technology

Published in the United States of America by
   Idea Group Publishing
   1331 E. Chocolate Avenue
   Hershey PA 17033-1117
   Tel: 717-533-8845
   Fax: 717-533-8661
   E-mail: cust@idea-group.com
   Web site: http://www.idea-group.com

and in the United Kingdom by
   Idea Group Publishing
   3 Henrietta Street
   Covent Garden
   London WC2E 8LU
   Tel: 44 20 7240 0856
   Fax: 44 20 7379 3313
   Web site: http://www.eurospan.co.uk

Library of Congress Cataloging-in-Publication Data

Grönlund, Åke.
   Electronic government : design, applications and management / Åke Grönlund.
      p. cm.
   Includes bibliographical references and index.
   ISBN 1-930708-19-X
      1. Public administration--Data processing. I. Title.

JF1525.A8 G765 2001
352.3'8'02854678--dc21   2001039387

British Cataloguing in Publication Data
A Cataloguing in Publication record for this book is available from the British Library.

NEW from Idea Group Publishing

Electronic Government: Design, Applications and Management

Table of Contents

SECTION II. APPLICATIONS

SECTION III. MANAGEMENT

Acknowledgments

Several people have contributed to getting this book together. First of all, I want to thank the chapter authors–28 people in all–who have not only contributed good pieces of work, but also helped by reviewing other chapters and commenting on the general ideas of electronic government on which the book is based. My colleagues in the Democrit (IT and democratic processes) research programme, in particular Agneta Ranerup, have also been most helpful in responding to different ideas and issues that have been on the agenda over the six months during which the work with the book has been on my desk.

Special thanks are due to Fernando Galindo of Zaragoza University, Spain, who offered me an opportunity to exchange the rainy November of Sweden for a sunny Zaragoza which certainly made the work on the book much more enjoyable, and I believe also more productive.

For help in the final exercise of polishing the manuscript, I want to thank Monica Åström, Thomas Persson and Lars Rönnbäck.

The work on the book was partially supported by STINT (the Swedish Foundation for International Cooperation in Research and Higher Education) and the Department of Informatics at Umeå University, Sweden, where I spend most of my working time. Informatics Umeå is a most exciting place to work, because of the people who work there and because it has expertise in many fields of the broad discipline of Informatics.

Åke Grönlund

Chapter I

Introduction

Åke Grönlund
Umeå University, Sweden

The concept of electronic government (eGov), sometimes electronic governance, is about to emerge from a practitioners' concept to one that also attracts research. Conferences abound, and research scales up from individual researchers and projects to institutes, both those governed by industry, such as IBM's Institute for Electronic Government[1] and those governed by universities, such as the Center for Technology in Government at Albany University.[2] Research and development programs such as the EU Information Society Technologies and Government Online are focusing on developing strategic and transferable IT (information technology) uses in government. Research institutes with the focus on policies and development focus increasingly on IT use, such as the Institute for Development Policy and Management at the University of Manchester.[3] Countries and states establish "Task Forces" in the field, and there is a rich supply of Web pages with titles like "Electronic Government Resources," where electronic services are offered.[4]

It is hard to estimate the amount of effort to implement eGov currently going on around the world. Many things relevant to the field come under different names. Much material is not available on the Web, and even if it is, it is often in other languages than English as it is for use in one particular country rather than intended for the rest of the world to read. Still, an indication of the amount is that a search with Adobe pdf Finder[5] finds 23,308 pdf documents containing the words "Electronic Government," while an AltaVista search finds 44,979 html documents (March 30, 2001). One interesting observation is that not only is research increasingly focusing on developing countries, but also policy documents and implementations come increasingly from countries outside North America, EU and Australia/New Zealand, such as India, Malaysia and Mexico. From a start in the U.S. and the EU, electronic government is increasingly on the agenda worldwide.

eGov generally refers certainly to *more* use of IT, but more importantly to attempts to achieve more *strategic* use of IT in the public sector. History shows emerging uses rather than strategy-based ones (Grönlund, 2000; Norris, 1999), and by now the use is so comprehensive and so diverse that strategies are badly needing in order to get some kind of return on the investment. Typically, so far electronic services have been set up at additional costs (G8, 1999; West, 2000), leaving operations much as they were rather than achieving savings or better services by improved logistics.

eGov is about changes in two related but distinct fields. First, it is about changes in the *internal* government operations that come about as IT is used for automation, cooperation, integration among government agencies and as tools assisting in decision processes. While such IT use has been going on for a couple of decades, the current spark of interest in the field is most of all due to the fact that now, also *external* operations are transformed, as information and services increasingly become available on the Internet. This has meant that government agencies begin trying to organize their operations based on the premise that citizens and companies will to a large extent manage their interactions with the public sector on a self-service basis (See Chapter 15 by Wiberg & Grönlund).

While it is certainly too early to provide other than fragmentary results from research in the field, there seems to be good reasons to investigate the concept of eGov. There are certainly many issues and many experiments that have bearing on the more extensive and more systematic use of IT in the public sector. While many issues are already studied under other banners, I believe there are reasons to consider eGov a research field because the issues must be studied in a context. We will return to some of these issues later, but in short the major reason is that government is not just any business. Many existing research fields have potential relevance for eGov, such as MIS (Management Information Systems), IS (Information Systems) and CSCW (Computer Supported Cooperative Work), but so far these fields have not incorporated the views, concepts and history that make up a democratic government in a way that make them immediately applicable to eGov.

The term "government" covers several aspects of managing a country, ranging from the very form of government, over strategic management to daily operations. Definitions of eGov generally also cover all these areas, and most–but not all!–thus typically contain not only goals of more efficient operations but also of better quality of services and increased and better quality citizen participation in democratic processes.

This book covers the background to eGov, illustrates the situation as of today and brings up some issues for the future that could form the distinguishing focus of eGov research. The authors come from countries across the globe, which is important for giving a comprehensive account of the concept of e-government, and which also provides various angles from which to gain new perspectives and insights.

PERSPECTIVES ON ELECTRONIC GOVERNMENT

To integrate the research from different disciplines and on different topics relevant to eGov, there is a need for defining a context in terms of the public sector model. In simple terms, and at a general level where national differences do not matter, a democratic government is organized as shown in Figure 1.

All too often, an overly simplified view of a democratic system is propagated. In that view, the relationships of the model are presented as straightforward; citizens elect officials, which then go to work in a formal political system containing certain institutions and rules. Their work produces results in the form of directives to the administration, which with blind obedience–without any influence on the political decisions–executes the decisions.

In practice the system is of course much more complex, as Figure 1 intends to illustrate. The political impact administrations can exert by having the expertise necessary to prepare

Figure 1: Basic elements and relations in a democratic government system. Arrows indicate influence, and circles indicate domains of control. Domain intersections indicate "transaction areas" where control is negotiated, such as lobbying and media on the left-hand side, intermediary service deliverers on the right-hand side and professional interaction in government boards and committees on the top side. (Adapted from Molin et al, 1975;16).

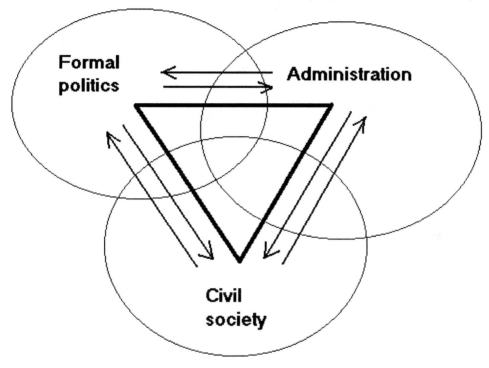

decisions in complicated matters is often acknowledged (Snellen, 2001; Watson et al., 1999). The citizens act in many other ways than by casting votes, for example they organize in many ways, and they lobby. This is not the place for and going into all the various aspects of this, neither to discuss different variations of democratic systems. Let us just observe that there are *a number of relations*, and that each node in the system influences both the others by a number of relationships–*all nodes are interrelated in a complex pattern*. The details of these relations are always under discussion and borders keep changing slightly. Currently, however, they are in a process of profound change in many countries, for several reasons including globalization, economic constraints, changing demographics and the availability of IT. This change can simplistically but effectively be described by two perspectives:

- Omnipresent IT
- Organizational change

There are different backgrounds to both these perspectives, but at this time they collaborate in ways that has given rise to the idea of electronic government. Let me briefly discuss the two.

Omnipresent IT

For a long time, information technologies have been brought to use in various ways in many of the relations of Figure 1. For many years, the use was mainly in the administration node, but now IT is more or less omnipresent (see Figure 2). Moreover, the applications tend to become more sophisticated–e.g. , data warehouses and data mining, simulation tools, decision support systems–and integrated both with each other and in administrative and decision-making procedures. This integration is not trivial (see for instance Chapter 8 by Svensson). It is not simply about making procedures more effective, but can in many cases be about changing values and premises upon which the system was once based. Two examples include the following:

- Use of decision support tools changes the ways in which decisions are made, and how the model and criteria used are understood.
- Use of communication tools may strengthen the role of community networks in relation to cities by making them more effective than other citizens in using public discussion forums for lobbying the administration or the politicians.
- Simulation tools, agents and data mining tools all come with built-in models that are not always explicit, and certainly not understood by all, usually neither complete nor even-handed, and thus intrude in decision-making processes in ways not well understood.

The consequences of this increasing IT-presence are not well known, and as it lies in the concept of (the practice of) electronic government to in fact apply a strategy to integrate all these tools with all these processes in an effective way, it seems a good idea to undertake research to try to understand the role(s) of IT. This has not yet been done comprehensively in a public sector context. While some aspects, such as privacy and technical security, have been awarded some interest, issues of how the balance among these nodes may change have

Figure 2: Examples of ICT uses in relations pertinent to e-government (GIS = Geographic Information Systems; DSS = Decision Support Systems; WMS = Workflow Management Systems; NGO = Non-Governmental Organizations; ICT = Information and Communications Technologies).

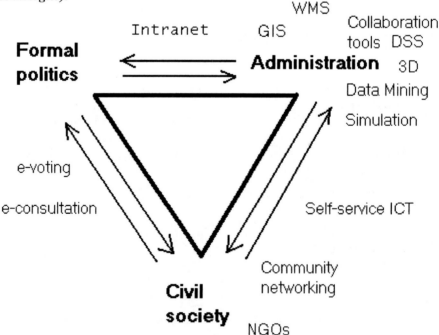

not so far been on the agenda other than in speculative writings. This is, the strategic perspective on eGov is still to be researched. One reason for this lack of comprehensive research may be that while government and its effects are researched by disciplines such as political science and sociology, IT is researched by other disciplines, such as informatics, information systems, computer science, artificial intelligence and others.

We are still in the early phases of the development, and research is still meager. While it is certainly too early to present comprehensive results, at least it is possible to try to bring some early findings from different areas together for the purpose of trying to outline a field of interest that has not yet been formulated. Electronic government has so far mostly been seen as an uncomplicated transfer of IT tools and concepts developed in the private sector into the public one, especially concerned with simple services without considering the policy implications (See Chapter 4 by Lenk et al.).

Organizational Change

As evidenced before, and certainly in some of the chapters in this book, IT has implications for internal change (e.g. Chapter 14 by Nilsson & Ranerup; Chapter 4 by Lenk et al.; and Chapter 15 by Wiberg & Grönlund). A development that currently complicates the picture is the employment of intermediaries in the interactions among the nodes (Figure 3). Several such already exist, both in the field of electronic services and that of facilitating democratic processes (see Chapter 2 by Grönlund for some examples of companies and activities).

The role of these intermediaries is less than clear. They have appeared because the Internet in combination with government outsourcing policies has given rise to new business opportunities. They are currently working in a field where new relations are emerging, not just because of the emergence of e-business, but also because governments across the world

Figure 3: Intermediaries in e-government processes

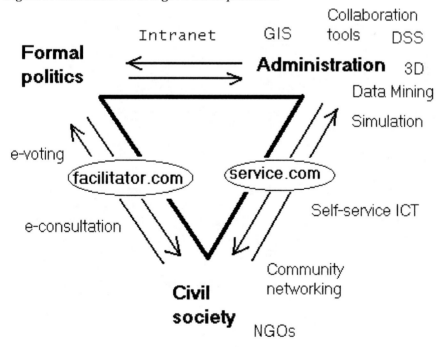

are currently in a process of change for several other reasons. As many of the chapters in this book indicate, pragmatic views based on the result of their operations rather than theoretical or historical views will most likely guide the following development. If so, these new actors will have a potentially important role because they bring to the field the important knowledge about how to use the Internet as a social medium, not just the technicalities of it. They will form the social practices that will guide the policies of electronic government.

The chapters in this book explore some of the relations in Figure 1, and the different ways in which IT is used and plays a role in the fields of tension represented by the domain intersections–the democratic system is constantly re-negotiated in these fields (e.g. concerning how citizen participation should be organized), and by now, IT is also an important player on all these fields.

As one of the fields changes, changes will occur also in the other parts of the model. That is, existing relations between the formal political system, the administration and the civil society change, and new fields of tension will occur, or old ones will be differently charged.

The issues that emerge in the discussions on eGov are of a different nature. Some are "old" issues that have been around for a long time in the discussions of implementation and use of IT systems. They now come in a different light as the systems become more far-reaching (e.g. cooperation among organizations, and between the public and private sectors), enter new use areas and meet new users (e.g. by self-service and an increased Internet population), and as technical uniformity (Internet technology) is leading to both possibilities (e.g. standardization and coordination) and risks (e.g. concerning security and privacy). Some issues are new, like:

- The power and cultural issues concerning the relations between the community networks culture and the formal democracy which come into focus as these two cultures meet on e-democracy arenas.
- The relation between an increasingly international legislation (EU, global) and local independence/self-determination.
- The roles in the electronic service infrastructure currently under development by local, regional, national, international, business, and non-governmental actors (see e.g. the chapter by Anttiroiko).
- The view on decision making (see Chapters 3 and 8 by Janlert and Svensson, respectively).
- The use of advanced tools in such processes (See Chapter 9 by Gates & Nissen).

The chapters in this book develop the perspectives on several of these issues. In doing so, experiences and concepts from other fields are used, but transformed into the public sector setting. Many of these issues have not yet reached the mainstream research agenda, and thus this book should be seen as a way to recognize a research field in its dawning.

The book is divided into three sections: Design, Applications and Management.

In the Design section an introductory chapter by Grönlund gives a general background by investigating the designs of e-government initiatives. Then follows chapters that discuss principal issues pertaining to e-government and in particular to the design of the IT applications used to implement it, issues that distinguish eGov from business. This includes the very idea of decision-making (Janlert), the basic tenets of the public sector (Lenk, Traunmüller & Wimmer), voting and democratic processes (Riera, Sanchez & Torras) and the design of governmental portals (Detlor & Finn).

The Applications section reports and discusses implementations that highlight the issues presented earlier of using new ICT tools. This includes an infrastructure for trust provision (Galindo), different ways of supporting decision making (Svensson; Gates & Nissen), supporting citizens in finding and using electronic public services (Leenes), participating in democratic processes (Macintosh, Davenport, Malina & Whyte) and IT tools for community networks (Gross).

The Management section discusses different challenges to, and perspectives on, management of IT, including a local government strategies perspective (Anttiroiko), a change management perspective (Nilsson & Ranerup), a power distribution perspective (Wiberg & Grönlund), a citizen's perspective (Kieley, Lane, Paquet & Roy) and a perspective from the country most prominently known for its participatory democratic practice, Switzerland (Poupa).

Next follows a brief summary of the chapters.

DESIGN

Electronic Government–Efficiency, Service Quality and Democracy

Åke Grönlund gives a brief overview of the broad range of initiatives and activities that over the past several years have made up the foundations--politically, organizationally and technically--for electronic government.

The Design section overviews the visions and political initiatives, focusing on the EU initiatives such as eEurope, and the current G8 international agenda for the imminent global Internet diffusion. It also reviews a number of definitions of eGov, and finds very different emphases within the omnipresent three-pronged framework including rationalization, service and democracy.

The Applications section gives some working examples of eGov. While in general governments are not making full use of available technology and there are problems in terms of access and democratic outreach, there are indeed examples of organizational change, new partnerships, new intermediaries and reshaped democratic processes. While many of these examples are encouraging and innovative, there are also several severe problems, such as the method of using resale of personal data for financing eGov applications.

So far, the development has been largely unsystematic, which seems to have hampered the development, at least in the short run. This is beause many major leaps that the technology hold potential for, such as organizational integration and major technical investments requiring some advantage of scale, have not been taken, especially not at the local level.

The Management section concludes by bringing up some issues for further eGov research.

One type of issue includes those concerning IT use in general, which become more pressing due to the spread of the Internet to more people, new use areas and new geographic areas. This includes privacy, security, knowledge management, especially informal and not well structured such, and strategic management issues. It also includes the more general issue of how to look upon decision making, and the role of IT tools in decision-making procedures.

Another type of issue has to do with the expansion of Internet use, which raises questions of "digital divides" of different kinds, between rich and poor countries or regions, between groups within one country, cultural differences, etc.

A third type of issue concerns the limits of government. Over the past years, issues of regulation of the Internet, including things like surveillance, key escrow, data transmission, etc. have been on the agenda. While these issues are still relevant, there are other issues emerging. One such pertains to community networking and the current efforts to integrate those with government agendas, locally and internationally. It is not immediately clear what such a dilution of the border between the formal society and the civil one may lead to.

Grönlund concludes that the examples and trends exhibited do not point at a development in some certain direction. Rather they together make up a field in search of a strategy. This points to a need to undertake comprehensive studies on the many facets of electronic government at a time when economic incentives and the technical development work together to increase the investment in technical solutions which are applied with very little respect paid to the complexity of the context in which they are to work, the system of government in democratic states.

Post-Modern Decision Making

Lars-Erik Janlert provides an essay on decision making in the face of profound IT use. The modern ideals for decision and action are hard pressed by doubts on their continued validity and by new difficulties in their implementation that emerge just as old difficulties seem to become more tractable.

The modern ideal for decision and action includes to map out the facts of the matter, make rational deliberations (reasoning, arguing) and choices, do the required problem solving, create an optimal plan and execute the plan.

Doubts about the continued validity of the modern era's model for decision and action have grown stronger during the 20th century, as the information society is described as one in which old ideals of uniformity and predictability are replaced by originality and creativity.

Some old difficulties with the modern model become more tractable through the new information technology. With programming, the gap between plan and execution is bridged. It is easier to make programs cooperate than human beings. Specifically, this improvement applies to "industrialized decisions," that is, decisions made automatically through regulation, formalization, bureaucratization, as a standardizing of "manual," "craftsmanlike" decisions, strongly shaped and tied to time, place and person, in analogy with how industrial machine production superseded manual machine making. Decisions in principle, as for instance laws and ordinances, can be considered as a method of mass-producing decisions. When projects are turned into programs, the rational procedures become more and more possible to conduct with the help of the new information technology. An increased transparency in the forming and the execution of decisions, as well as in the correspondence between implementation and plan, is possible.

It is clear that the new information technology, "IT," is playing a prominent part in these changes. Can it also solve or elude some of the new problems that it creates, or at least is associated with?

Janlert discusses the challenges to decision making in the context of a special case, the problems and possibilities with democratic processes when the technical conditions change.

Tempo and volume are two important delimiting factors in decision-action processes deeply affected by the meeting between new technology and old values. The situation we are facing is that existing decision processes are too slow and that a widespread participation in different decision-making processes takes too much time and effort. Janlert discusses three ways in which this problem can be approached, from practical as well as moral angles.

First, the steering can be moved up to a meta level, where changes happen at a slower pace. Human decision making is concentrated on the automated procedures, the programs that take care of the running decisions at a lower level; automated decision making, the perfection of the industrial decision model. Second, base-level steering could be speeded to match the speed of business and industry activities. Specifically this may appear incompatible with the democracy concept as we now know it, which seems to assume a certain thoughtfulness and reflection, and participation. Third, we could let what happens happen and be content with trying to handle the outcome post fact, compensating and reducing the negative effects of the development in a sort of reactive as opposed to proactive steering.

The Significance of Law and Knowledge for Electronic Government

Klaus Lenk, Roland Traunmüller and Maria Wimmer provide an important caveat to those who overoptimistically advocate a quick e-ification of government using tools and concepts from business environments. They discuss thoroughly the nature of the public sector as a law-based system. Governments are faced with growing demands to organize their work more efficiently and effectively, while public governance structures continue to be necessary.

Currently, eGov focuses on typical front office operations concerning the contact of administrative agencies with citizens. The authors claim this approach misses the point as it ignores that the role of government is not only to provide citizens with services that could as well be provided by commercial firms. The eGov scope should be widened to include all activities of public administration that can be supported by IT. Government covers many processes that are different from the type of processes encountered in retailing, banking or other branches of the economy. Such processes include: complex decision making, processes involving negotiations among various stakeholders, processes of policy formulation (e.g., legislative processes) and democratic participation.

The authors examine these processes from a view of public administration in which law enforcement and the regulation of society through policy implementation are constitutive factors to a much greater extent than the delivery of public services to individuals, and where the role of law and knowledge in reaching administrative decisions has to be explicitly acknowledged.

They sketch a process model of administrative work and distinguish several basic types of processes. They address the problems related to knowledge management, and discuss specific problems of knowledge use and decision making related to four basic process types; routine processes, individualized decision making, negotiations, and democratic deliberation.

They conclude by arguing that a coherent view on e-government should combine four different perspectives:

1) The *addressee's perspective* where the citizen interface of administrative work is particularly prominent.
2) The *process perspective* in which reorganization of processes making use of all kinds of human-machine synergies is paramount.
3) The *cooperation perspective* which complements the process perspective especially by insisting on ubiquitous (tele-) cooperation and on collaborative efforts like meetings, negotiations and deliberations, which do not follow a clear-cut process model and which cannot be fully standardized beforehand.
4) The *knowledge perspective* which highlights the management of information and of knowledge as the major asset in many work situations in the public sector.

In terms of the model in Figure 1, this chapter shows that e-government is not just about the currently addressed service side of government, but rather the core business is on the policy-making side. The authors provide an important contribution by analyzing the complexity and law-bound nature of the processes that IT use is supposed to facilitate. This means that concepts from business management, such as knowledge management, while necessary to introduce in a public sector in the process of rapid and profound reorganization, have to be conscientiously adapted to the public sector environment before they can be successfully brought to use.

Internet Voting: Embracing Technology in Electoral Processes

Andreu Riera, Jordi Sanchez and Laia Torras give an overview of issues in electronic voting over the Internet. Secure Internet voting for public elections, especially remote voting, is currently a heatedly debated issue, from a technological perspective as well as from a socio-political one.

The general requirements for voting turn out to be much harder to implement in an Internet environment as compared to manual polling-station voting:

- *Accuracy*: The final election results must contain all validated ballots cast by eligible voters. It must not be possible to add, delete or alter ballots.
- *Democracy*: Only eligible voters may cast a ballot, and only once.
- Anonymity: It must not be possible for anyone to correlate ballots to the respective voters who cast them.
- *Fairness*: In order to avoid affecting voters' behavior, intermediate results must be secret until the election is completed.
- *Uncoercibility*: To protect the system from automated coercion, vote-selling or extortion, voters must not be able to prove their respective voting decisions.
- *Verifiability*: Either the individual voter must be able to verify that the final tally contains his/her ballot, or some auditing third party must be able to verify the integrity of the whole tally.

This chapter provides a survey of the security hazards pertinent to Internet voting. Previous experiments are presented. The chapter also reviews approaches to solve some of the security problems presented.

Further, the most important socio-political issues regarding the introduction of Internet voting in the public sector are discussed, including digital divide issues, electoral participation, the symbolic aspects of voting, public control of the electoral process and the impact on representative democracy.

The authors conclude computerized methods of voting promise great efficiencies and several advantages over more traditional methods of voting. Still, they believe widespread remote Internet voting in national public elections is some years away, while they believe the use of the Internet to manage the transmission of digital ballots cast at polling places may be applied much sooner.

On the socio-political side, universal use of Internet voting will only be possible if the problems of distrust and unequal access are solved to a satisfactory extent. An incremental approach is suggested as a good strategy for the incorporation of electronic voting systems into the political processes. The authors see Internet voting in the foreseeable time complementing rather than substituting conventional voting methods--an evolution rather than a revolution.

In terms of Figure 1, the discussion on electronic voting highlights the fears and hopes of a radical shift towards more direct citizen participation in decision-making processes, and the concerns about how e-voting should be used. Extensive electronic voting would potentially shift the balance of the system radically, not because of technical security problems, but because voting would be used more or differently.

Towards a Framework for Government Portal Design: The Government, Citizen and Portal Perspectives

Brian Detlor and Kim Finn identify and describe factors that inhibit and promote successful government portal design. These factors are based on a review of recent research on both electronic government initiatives and corporate portal implementations. The result is a generalized framework for government portal design. To test its viability, the framework is used to analyze a portal project led by the Government of Canada to support Canadian youth citizens. The project involved 21 Canadian federal departments in delivering a single Web site integrating youth-related services and information.

The framework offers an effective preliminary construct by which to focus and pinpoint pertinent issues surrounding government portal design.

The primary objective of the chapter is to present a theoretical framework for government portal design that identifies and describes the factors that promote or inhibit successful electronic government. The framework comprises three key perspectives: the *government perspective*, which addresses the organizational factors which affect portal design; the *citizen perspective*, which addresses user concerns that influence the degree to which portals are adopted and utilized; and the *portal interface perspective*, which concerns the extent to which features and functions offered by the portal satisfy both citizen and government information needs.

With respect to the youth portal case, both success factors and challenges are identified. Success factors include the need for a high degree of interdepartmental collaboration to support coordinated on-line service delivery, and a governance structure that involves youth directly in the product development and maintenance processes. Challenges entail balancing government technology standards with youth user demands, supporting universal access, coordinating asymmetric development across various government on-line projects, securing sufficient and sustainable funding, and managing citizen engagement with the project.

In terms of Figure 1, the three-pronged perspective is interesting as it draws the attention to the fact that technology itself can be seen as an actor, requiring certain skills and methods to be best utilized. The "portal design perspective" is an integrative one, important for understanding that focusing on citizens and governments only will not result in a complete requirements description. This is also to say that policy is in fact influenced by the practices pertinent to technology design and use.

APPLICATIONS

e-Government Trust Providers

Fernando Galindo addresses a fundamental problem for the implementation of e-government; trust, a key value in e-commerce, but even more so in e-government. Current developments in the provision of trust, driven by the expansion of electronic commerce, are therefore not sufficient to cater for the needs of electronic government. Trust clearly goes beyond technical functionality, it also involves organizational arrangements. For e-government the services necessary for the provision of trust must also be free for citizens, as they concern exertion of individuals' rights and duties, which have to be available to everyone independently of financial situation.

E-government communications procedures frequently require clear and unambiguous identification of the citizen and the public entity involved before the commencement of relations, otherwise the operation cannot be carried out. Without the relevant data, therefore, relations are restricted to the simple presentation of information to the citizen by public institutions.

Innumerable e-commerce applications exist on the Internet, while applications permitting a real, interactive, legally enforceable relationship to be established between the citizen and government remain scarce.

The weaknesses of Internet use for e-government purposes comprise both problems inherent in the nature of the Net and the difficulties resulting from private ownership of telecommunications networks, as well as the initial adaptation of the infrastructure to the needs of e-commerce. This last limits the field for e-government, which is affected by a wider range of considerations than the optimization of profit.

In particular, this relates to:

- assignation of names and addresses,
- security of communications,
- respect for privacy and other legal principles and
- provision of access to the Internet and other communications networks, as well as telecommunications security services.

Galindo outlines these difficulties and some solutions with in-depth references to the situation in Spain, which is relevant for all of the European Union, as it draws on the Directives of the EU (which are also presented).

The function of trust providers is to create confidence. This chapter outlines the activities of a number of trust providers with reference to the regulation of the Internet and the laws and institutions which engender trust in the democratic state.

E-government trust providers are organizations obliged to respect the guarantees established by law and provide their services to engender trust and the participation of all concerned. The expansion of these services is essential for the further development of e-government. Contrary to the situation with e-commerce, in e-government not any organization may provide trust services. These services must not only meet the requirements established by directives and laws governing digital signatures and compliance with regulations governing the trust provider's services, but they must also be in accordance with the legal principles affecting the use of telematics in e-government.

For the same reason, the authorities are obliged to respect the principle that the user should be free to opt for one out of a number of qualified providers and must therefore take the necessary steps to ensure that trust providers are available free of charge to enable citizens to undertake e-government activities, regardless of their income or specific knowledge.

In the context of Figure 1, this chapter, as that of Lenk et al., points to the fact that introduction of concepts and tools from e-commerce and the private sector in general cannot be done straight-forwardly, but requires adaptation to the requirements of the public sector context.

The Use of Legal Expert Systems in Administrative Decision Making

Jörgen S. Svensson investigates the use of expert systems as support to street-level bureaucrats in Dutch local social services. The background is a very high percentage of decisions made by the street-level bureaucrats that did not comply with existing laws. This is caused by a complex and frequently changing legislation, but also some concerns about the role of the street-level bureaucrats. The large, often unintended, discretion of the street level bureaucrats in decision making raised questions. Was decision making really conforming to central legal principles such as predictability and equality before the law? Against this background, expert systems were introduced. Expert systems may bring about improvements; they support the actual decision-making by providing knowledge, they guard the process of information collection, they improve the quality of decision making and they support effective documentation.

Still, use of expert systems in complex decision-making remains a controversial issue from juridical as well as sociological points of view. An expert system certainly does not guarantee correct decision-making. Use of expert systems may lead to a thoughtless application of formal rules, and factors not known by the system, or hard to formalize unambiguously, run the risk of being ignored, as humans' capability to apply informal methods to find time-saving working solutions by applying experience-based informal rules of thumb is not applied.

Svensson observes that while expert systems certainly can be criticized from many points of view, they are in fact adopted in administrative practice, based on pragmatic considerations. In The Netherlands, over a decade of thinking, experimentation, discussion and actual practice has led to the critics losing ground. Benefits of using these systems have become more concrete, especially when the demand for formally correct decision making is concerned, while the anxiety that expert systems would lead to important drawbacks has not been substantiated.

Svensson concludes the success of expert system support in the social services field was much helped by three factors:
1) The regulation, especially its volume, complexity and completeness; Svensson foresees a trend towards computerizable legislation also in other fields so as to make it possible to roll out the practical successes of expert systems also to these fields.
2) The changing professional status of the general assistance worker; Svensson believes the expert systems have empowered a previously deskilled group with declining status.
3) An increased scrutiny and an increasingly rigorous control structure, rendering municipalities financially responsible for faulty decisions.

In terms of Figure 1, Svensson's chapter clearly illustrates the complex issue of introducing automated tools into the administration. While reasons of economy, equality before the law and openness can be advanced to support the use, there are still a number of issues that speak against it. Especially notable is the shift from theoretical/principal to pragmatic argumentation. This means trust is an important issue. In the Dutch social services, it seems trust in the ICT tools at a certain point in time exceeded trust in the "manual" system.

Agent- and Web-Based Employment Marketspaces in the U.S. Department of Defense

William R. Gates and Mark E. Nissen look into the potential of using software agents in public sector activities. After giving an overview of agent technology, they exhibit a case study involving designing and testing an agent used for job mediation in the U.S. Navy.

Software agents are being developed for advanced applications to enable electronic commerce systems for supply chain automation and support in a business-to-government context, to help improve electricity allocation and pricing decisions, and to facilitate citizen/ government interactions. How far can agent technology go toward automation and support of the public sector?

While literally any public-sector process that involves knowledge and information work offers potential for agent-based performance improvements, the technology remains relatively immature. Caution must be exercised to avoid over-reliance on technology before it has suitably matured into "industrial strength" applications. Although software agents can be developed using artificial-intelligence techniques to exhibit "intelligent" behavior, for many tasks involving creativity, judgment and novel problem-solving behavior, their performance is often inferior to that of people assigned to do the same tasks. Alternatively, for tasks that can be well specified, requiring only modest levels of "intelligence" to perform effectively, agent performance can surpass that of people, particularly in terms of accuracy, speed and cost.

Not all agent designs and designers are equivalent. Some agents developed for a specific set of tasks may greatly exceed the capability and performance of others developed for the same tasks. Which specific tasks and agent designs are most appropriate in any given circumstance remains a matter for empirical investigation. This chapter presents one of the first such empirical investigations of human versus agent performance, addressing the specific problems associated with matching employees with jobs in labor markets.

Two modes of matching people with jobs prevail at present: hierarchical planning and distributed markets. Each has strengths and limitations, but few systems have been designed to exploit strengths corresponding to both. Intelligent agents offer a potential to help both potential employees and employers find one another in a distributed, electronic marketplace. But realizing this potential goes beyond simply changing the rules of internal job matching or making agent technology available to job searchers. Rather, the corresponding markets and technologies must be designed, together, to mutually accomplish the desired results (e.g., efficient and effective matching) and conform to necessary properties (e.g., market clearing). The authors draw from Game Theory results to assess the feasibility of using two-sided matching algorithms to address this market-design problem. They also draw from current agent research to address the information technology dimension of the problem by implementing a multi-agent system to enact, automate and support the corresponding market solution.

This chapter integrates the key economic and technological elements required to design robust electronic employment markets. It also presents preliminary results from a pilot experiment comparing performance for a human-based job assignment process to alternative market designs. These alternative designs can potentially reduce cycle-time and better match employees to job vacancies. However, the human-based process currently provides better rule conformance.

In terms of Figure 1, this chapter illustrates the problems involved with using complex technology in decision making. The introduction is not straightforward, but involves the simultaneous design of the market/the rule system that is to govern the operations of the technology.

The Enschede Virtual Public Counter: Ole 2000—A Case Study

Ronald E. Leenes reports a case study on an attempt to design a one-stop shop for integrated electronic public services in The Netherlands.

In 1995 the Dutch Ministry of the Interior and the Association of Dutch Local Governments initiated an ambitious program to improve public service delivery. The public counters envisioned in the Public Counter 2000 (OL2000) program were to solve some of the problems the public sector was facing, including great fragmentation, both horizontally and vertically, a considerable non-use of facilities and quality problems both as concerns data and decision making.

The aim of the program was to create a nationwide network of one-stop government agencies, providing citizens and business with information and public services. These one-stop government agencies should have both physical and virtual incarnations. The services delivered are primarily those of local government. However, also services from the national levels and from (semi-) private agencies may be incorporated.

In the first phase of the OL2000 program, Enschede was the host of one of 15 pilot projects. This chapter describes the background of OL2000, its results and its future plans. It also focuses on the Enschede pilot, Ole 2000, a virtual, online public counter for a range of local housing and building services. The problems encountered in the project, and some lessons learned, are discussed.

The OL2000 project introduced some new concepts:
- The use of 'demand-patterns' as the binding force between services.
- Including public, semi-public and even private organizations into the concept.
- A (stronger) emphasis on the use of IT to enable service integration.

The author remains positive to the kind of solutions proposed, even though many problems were encountered and the project is still under development. Issues discussed include problematic funding of projects with both public and private partners, organizational cooperation, complexity and technology, redesign of procedures, legal barriers and political support. Though the main problems encountered had to do with organization, the author envisions use of new technology, such as agents, decision support systems, etc., to remedy some of the complexities involved.

In terms of Figure 1, the chapter illustrates the problems of integrating public services: to provide a coherent interface, to achieve usability and to arrange public agencies' procedures so as to achieve efficient services.

Technology to Support Participatory Democracy

Ann Macintosh, Elisabeth Davenport, Anna Malina and Angus Whyte focus on the development, application and impact of ICT on civic representation and participation in democratic processes.

There is a need for many governments at local and national levels to restore public confidence and interest in the democratic process. The chapter gives practical guidance on how parliaments and governments can develop, apply and manage ICT to address this concern and to support the public to participate in setting agendas, establishing priorities and making policies.

The chapter considers the positive and negative effects of technology on democratic processes. A range of perspectives that have provided the impetus for researchers and practitioners to envisage roles for technology in the democratic process are summarized. The authors find that increasingly, theoretical perspectives are becoming informed by practice, as technologies developed for corporate or consumer use are applied in pursuit of collective political ends and to meet needs and demands of individual citizens.

The chapter also considers the issues and constraints that have to be taken into account when designing ICT-based tools for democratic purposes. The major differences and similarities in developing systems that are intended for widest possible accessibility and ease of use, distinguishing from those that are developed to support commerce and entertainment, are highlighted. An example is that e-commerce strategies, like those of government, are increasingly based on the idea of community building.

A significant trend in electronic government as well as in electronic commerce is that consumers adopt roles traditionally taken by producers. While governments may be seen as (electronic) providers of services and deliverers of policy, citizens may choose to seek ownership of service provision and policy making for themselves. Examples in the chapter show that this trend marks out an area of some uncertainty. The ends and means of electronic citizenry may be seen as legitimate and welcome forms of democratic renewal or alternatively as threats to the democratic process, and the prevailing view can change with revolutionary speed.

Working examples of citizen participation in Scotland are described. A Web-based e-democracy toolkit, developed to motivate and facilitate public participation in governance, is described. The tool helps to demonstrate how relatively straightforward computing techniques can be deployed to enhance public participation.

The chapter concludes by highlighting the importance of monitoring and evaluating teledemocracy systems and trials, referring to some recent work in this area and future projects that could support teledemocracy evaluations.

In terms of Figure 1, this chapter observes that policy development is increasingly guided by practice. Both the right-hand side of the triangle–the service side–and the left-hand side–that concerned with public participation–import ICT tools and practices from e-business and community networking, and the practices of use of these tools exert considerable influence over policies.

e-Democracy and Community Networks: Political Visions, Technological Opportunities and Social Reality

Tom Gross discusses IT support for community networks. The chapter reviews requirements for public participation in democratic processes, including forms for public access to information and open discussion participation. The history of community networks is reviewed, and a "generation model" is presented, ranging from community memories and free-nets to the current professionalized community networks.

The current possibilities for technological support for community networking are discussed. This includes tools for sharing information, such as shared global information spaces, annotation systems and social filtering systems, and tools for exchanging information, such as text-based chat tools and virtual environments, combinations of text-based virtual environments and the Web, and tools for sharing the Web.

It is concluded that even though history shows that often the simplest technological solutions are chosen, there are great opportunities to be expected from the more sophisticated tools that are under development.

In terms of Figure 1, this chapter points to the fact that indeed tools used in community networking are beginning to come into use in processes related to the professional politics, as cities arrange online discussion, consultations, etc. Obviously, the technological opportunities are not enough to cater for progress in e-democracy; still they may prove important as more extensive public participation in democratic processes via electronic media will require better tools to facilitate the technicalities of public meetings, including distributing the word, making a statement, expressing shared views, sharing information, collaborating, polling, voting, etc.

MANAGEMENT

Strategic Knowledge Management in Local Government

Ari-Veikko Anttiroiko focuses on the issue of how local governments manage information to cope with an increasingly uncertain and equivocal environment. The success of public organizations depends increasingly on how efficiently they utilize internal and external knowledge resources in adjusting to contextual changes. This requires a special emphasis on strategic knowledge management.

Anttiroiko refers to theoretical work in the knowledge management field for the purpose of considering how organizational design can be used to facilitate the processes in which knowledge is gathered, created, processed, used and demolished in order to build an enriched knowledge base to deal with adjustment and development issues of strategic importance.

The theoretical part of the chapter synthesizes this work into a systematic view of knowledge management and a coherent scheme to be used in local development processes.

Case studies are then presented to illustrate the information needs of city managements, and to illustrate the differences between different kinds of cities. At the "high end" of the cities hierarchy, there are success stories to show how successful cities have managed to position, profile, and differentiate themselves in order to make the best of emerging opportunities and cope with the most severe problems.

At the "low end" of the hierarchy, small rural communities have special requirements in coping with this restructuration process. These are illustrated by the case of the small Finnish town of Himanka. The strategies of small local governments in remote rural areas cannot rely solely on the dialectic in which "quantity becomes a quality," as in the case of growth centers, but quite the opposite, on the quality and flexibility needed in constructing effective adjustment strategies.

Anttiroiko concludes that contextual changes favor an organizational design that relies on interactive mechanisms and enhances communication-intensive processes. The need for 'systemic' knowledge is gradually decreasing whereas the role of encultured and embrained knowledge is becoming decisive in strategic processes. This need cannot be met through the use of formal procedures or even information systems, but by communicative processes. This suggests that uncertainty and ambiguity increased in the last decades of the 20th century, and that local governments need new management tools to respond to this challenge. Anttiroiko finds that one such possibility, use of advanced IT tools for management support, is now spreading to the local governments.

In terms of Figure 1, what Anttiroiko describes concerns all nodes. A basic requirement for success of local government is the successful alignment of forces among city management, local business and universities.

Improvisational Change Management: New Work Forms with Groupware

Agneta Nilsson and Agneta Ranerup study the problems of change with a focus on applying IT to the internal work in municipal administrations. They point to the importance of being able to manage both the process towards intended changes and the situations that occur as the use of technology leads to other, unplanned, changes.

Ranerup and Nilsson investigate internal change work related to implementation of a groupware for managing workflows, a technology that among other things is characterized by its tying together previously detached parts of an organization. The system supports planning and collaboration of common work tasks based on an integrated system for e-mail and shared databases with information. The technology has a potential to change work situations. It also provides a possibility to introduce more process- and collaborative-oriented work forms. The chapter presents experiences from this process of groupware introduction.

One focus in this chapter is to what extent the introduction and use of the information technology has resulted in new forms of work. A second focus is how new ideas and experiences, which are gained from the introduction of groupware, are handled in order to realize the potential of the technology. Finally, groupware is a flexible and open-ended technology allowing for many uses, new, unplanned, uses may occur as users gain experiences. This means there is potentially a tension between the organizational plan and the necessity of an improvisational perspective in the change process. Hence, the third focus is on the role of the organizational plan in an improvisational process of change management.

The discussion takes a point of departure in the Orlikowski and Hofman model of change management. The model describes different types of changes occurring in the organization when groupware is introduced, distinguishing between *anticipated change*, planned changes that occur as intended, *opportunity-based change*, possibilities discovered in the organization, which are taken care of in a deliberative and planned way, and *emergent changes*, such occurring spontaneously among the personnel on their own initiatives and not taken care of in a deliberative manner by the organization.

Both opportunity-based and emergent changes are characterized by not being predictable in detail. The chapter discusses different strategies for meeting these kinds of change. The authors add a fourth type of change in order to make the model more adjusted to the public sector; this is non-occurring anticipated change. This is an important issue in times of grand plans for government change, when consequences of changes must always be seen in the light of basic government principles, such as equality before the law, which will have to be maintained also when business logic demands new solutions for organization.

In terms of Figure 1, this chapter obviously concerns the administration node, as changed forms of work of course most directly concern work situations, work relations and power balances internally. But if IT use results in new forms of work, more process-oriented and more cooperation-oriented, it may lead to the organization becoming less transparent for the citizen-customer, and less controllable and predictable. This might lead to the citizens individually having more trouble in finding effective ways to act in relations with the organization. It also affects the citizens collectively in their role as voters, taxpayers and users of collective resources, that is, also the political bodies may find it harder to affect, or even understand, the work of the administration. This is an illustration of how pragmatically motivated major changes in one of the nodes have potentially important effects on the others.

e-Government in Sweden: Centralization, Self-Service and Competition

Mikael Wiberg and Åke Grönlund study four large government agencies (one of which was later privatized) with operations over the entire country for the purpose of finding out how they used ICT strategically in a regional perspective: how were local branches affected in terms of number of jobs, organization and their role in the overall organization.

The authors find that ICT in the studied organizations most prominently has meant centralization of power. Control was enforced in many ways, by strict economic responsibilities and effective control by weekly assessments of performance of the local branches.

Also, the pressure on the individual professional was increased; areas of responsibilities have become greater, they have to be able to handle more advanced technology, they have taken over parts of the scheduling and work assignments as well as the storemen's work. Another change is that sometimes salary has become partially based on performance.

The development can be characterized as increased individual responsibility, increased central control, and often both broadened and deepened competence on part of the individual professional.

The number of employees has gone down everywhere, but more so in the rural areas. As concerns the customers, the access to service through new technology is considerably better for people in the city than for those in the rural areas. This is because the key issue is access to a computer and knowledge about the information systems that are needed to be able to, for instance, find available jobs. In the rural areas, people have to arrange that by themselves–buy a computer, pay a connection, learn about the information sources–whereas in the cities all this is accessible for free in information centers.

In terms of Figure 1, this chapter considers the "administration" node. The authors point at fundamental restructurings that have considerable consequences at the societal level. There was an increased focus on self-service, and the corresponding–sometimes over-corresponding, as in rural areas self-service opportunities were not introduced–reduced availability of manual service. Together this means new demands on the citizens, both in terms of activities they have to undertake, and in terms of the knowledge they need to acquire. And–where they have to live, if they want to have access to public service.

e-Government in Canada: Services Online or Public Service Renewal?

Barb Kieley, Greg Lane, Gilles Paquet and Jeffrey Roy discuss the nature of e-government and the challenges it brings to management, based on interviews with managers in the public sector in Canada. They claim that moving industrial society government onto a digital platform would simply produce a digitized industrial government—a form of governance that would be increasingly out of step with the changing realities of citizens and businesses alike. The chapter examines the efforts of the Canadian federal government to harness ICT as an enabling force.

E-government takes place within a changing governance context where technology itself may only be one driver, and government must redefine itself for a world of e-governance as this world is being shaped by a variety of forces. The authors discuss what they perceive as the three main forces driving the emergence of e-governance, and the corresponding search for new organizational models:
- Spatial–geography and place
- Digital–communications and time
- Cognitive–education and expectations

For governments, there are inherent contradictions in each that must be recognized. The authors provide a definition of e-government as a government being better enabled to harness new information, communication and social technologies in order to empower the public service of tomorrow. Effective change is premised on the necessary leadership of people, and the collective intelligence of all stakeholders in meeting the potential of a more interdependent world. The definition suggests that any transformation of government must take place in a context of growing interdependence, internally and externally, including partnerships among organizations and collaboration among people across organizational borders.

The chapter reports an interview study among senior public servants across both operational departments and central agencies, asking for views on the likely opportunities and challenges ahead with respect to e-government, including capacities, culture and competencies.

The authors conclude that the promise of e-government is best viewed as an evolving process of learning and adaptation. As digital connectivity grows, a mix of technical and social forces will transform the shape of our public institutions over time. This evolution will likely be neither predictable nor common across all segments of the population. Consequently, digital governance must meet many needs via multiple challenges simultaneously.

E-government must be an engaged and constructive partner in shaping the new governance patterns that will otherwise render it rudderless. These patterns must bridge traditional administrative and political-cultural frameworks to the adaptive and collaborative requirements of a connected and interdependent world–a world that requires a new culture in government, one open and enabled to take advantage of the potential of the digital and information age.

In terms of the model in Figure 1, this chapter is concerned with the problem of making new government policies that can cope with the challenges ahead. Following the authors argument, this policy must be developed in cooperation, not only among government agencies, but also in negotiations with the citizens demanding that the government adapt to the emerging patterns of communications. While this cooperation encompasses all the nodes in the model, an obvious problem is just how the demarcations between execution of law, uncomplicated service and policy-making activities should be upheld, or changed.

Electronic Government in Switzerland: Priorities for 2001-2005–Electronic Voting and Federal Portal

Christine Poupa presents two current Swiss initiatives, electronic voting and the federal portal (virtual office).

Switzerland has a semi-direct form of democracy that is neither parliamentary nor presidential, but is based on consensus and entente: parliament cannot bring down the government, which in turn cannot dissolve the parliament. Swizerland has various and ancient institutions of direct democracy on a federal, cantonal and communal level. Each of the four levels of decision, i.e., the people, the communes, the Cantons and the Confederation, sets store by its prerogatives. Any modification that would be perceived as a loss of control or power is rejected by the echelon concerned.

There is hardly any other country in which the people had such far-reaching rights of co-determination as in Switzerland. But contrary to most other democratic countries, Switzerland works by consensus, and often entente, also on the federal level, where the government coalition introduced in 1891 still exists.

Consensus combined with federalism has consequences on the administration.

The Information Society Project Switzerland is part of the federal strategy for the information society. For three years, the "E-gov" working group has been at work. Other working groups cover topics such as e-commerce, security, culture, education, etc. The main task of the "E-gov" working group was the inventory of existing or future projects, and recommendations to the Federal Council. The participation of people in the democratic process was not central in these thoughts. The emphasis was more on security.

Among urgent measures for the period 2001-2005, CGIS recommends funding the creation of a one-stop shop/virtual office at the federal level and to create a working group about electronic voting.

Switzerland is a federal state. The Swiss cantons have remained, to a large extent, sovereign entities. Consequently, there are 26 legal organizational systems. The administrative procedure can be very different depending on the specific canton. Different languages and different procedures implicate difficulties of implementing a virtual portal in a federal state.

ENDNOTES

1 http://www.ieg.ibm.com/
2 http://www.ctg.albany.edu/
3 http://www.man.ac.uk/idpm/
4 For instance in Texas, http://www.dir.state.tx.us/egov/
5 http://searchpdf.adobe.com/

REFERENCES

Grönlund, Å. (2000). Electronic service management--Local government as a service provider. *Proceedings of E-government in Europe*, March 30-31, 2000, St. James's Court Hotel, London. Access Conferences International, Ltd., London.

Grönlund, Å., Kauranne, T., Hartkamp, F., Kritzenberger, H. and Forsgren, O. (2000). *Managing Electronic Services–A Public Sector Perspective*. London: Springer.

G8. (1997). *Government Use of the Internet*. A Collaborative "fast-track" study by G7GOL and ICA. Available on the World Wide Web at: http://www.open.gov.uk/govoline/ishtml.htm.

G8. (1999). *Government On-Line Project*. Final project report, April. Available on the World Wide Web at: http://www.open.gov.uk/govoline/golintro.htm.

Molin, B., Månsson, L. and Strömberg, L. (1975). *Offentlig Förvaltning*. Bonniers.

Norris, D. F. (1999). Leading-edge information technologies and their adaption: Lessons from U.S. cities. In Garson, G. D. (Ed.), *Information Technology and Computer Applications in Public Administration: Issues and Trends*. Hershey, PA: Idea Group Publishing.

Snellen, I. (2001). ICTs, bureaucracies and the future of democracy. *Communications of the ACM*, January.

Watson, R., Akselsen, S., Evjemo, B. and Aasaether, N. (1999). Teledemocracy in local government. *Communications of the ACM*, December, 58-63.

West, D.M. (2000). *Assessing E-Government: The Internet, Democracy and Service Delivery by State and Federal Governments*. Available on the World Wide Web at: http://www.insidepolitics.org/egovtreport00.html.

Section I

Design

Chapter II

Electronic Government– Efficiency, Service Quality and Democracy

Åke Grönlund
Umeå University, Sweden

The theme of this book is electronic government (eGov). The Introduction briefly outlines the general framework. The following chapters investigate specific issues and cases. In this chapter, I shall give a brief overview of the broad range of initiatives and activities that over the past several years have made up the foundations–politically, organizationally and technically–for electronic government.

eGov concerns both internal and external use of IT, for internal administration as well as for external services. It is about more IT use, better use and more strategic use. In this chapter, we shall focus on the external use, that is contacts between government and citizens and civil sector organizations, government and business, and among government organizations. The reason for this include the fact that this is the novel kind of IT use–internal IT use has been going on for decades, even if the amount and sophistication is now reaching new heights–and the kind that is seen as the most interesting component, and incentive, in restructuring government operations, for instance by increasing cooperation among government agencies and providing self-service facilities to citizens.

Electronic government has not so far attracted a great amount of research. The eGov history contains a number of political initiatives and an IT business that sees government as a white spot on the map, so far underutilizing IT, as compared to businesses as well as to the IT potential. In the overview below, we will therefore find a number of practical examples, but not much research of the kind we find about IT use in the business sector–about management strategies, alignment between IT and organization, knowledge management, collaborative work, power relations, to mention a few things (in the following chapters, though, several of these topics are discussed).

This chapter has three sections, named after the book title: The Design section overviews the visions and political initiatives that have formed the concept and current practices of electronic government. The Applications section gives some examples to show the breadth of the field, and the Management section concludes by bringing up some issues that are important to the field of electronic government, but have so far not been discussed in a coherent manner with bearing on IT use in government.

While the mission of this book is to collect some emerging research in various fields and bring that to bear on the design and management of government, this is clearly possible only to a small extent today. The issues discussed at the end of this chapter thus go beyond what we have been able to achieve in this book, and should be seen as input to an eGov research agenda.

DESIGN

eGov in a Nutshell

Even though it is the rapid increase in Internet use that has sparked the recent hopes for "electronic government," the concept refers not only to more use of IT in the public sector. It is also about governments wanting to become more strategic in their IT use. The need for strategic thinking comes from several developments, including a general trend to restructure government operations by means of deregulation, outsourcing and competition; the advent of a cheap, unifying technology standard; and the increasing use of strategic IT tools in business, e.g., Enterprise Resource Planning (ERP), Workflow Management Systems (WMS) and Data Mining tools.

eGov is usually presented as using IT to:

- Provide easy access to government information and services to citizens and business.
- Increase the quality of services, by increased speed, completeness, process efficiency and other.
- Give citizens opportunities to participate in democratic processes of different kinds.

Focus is typically on external services, but one important idea is to use these to make internal operations more efficient, for instance by relying on self-service.

The Idea of Electronic Government

There are several lines of development behind the idea of electronic government. IT itself is obviously one, but we shall start by taking a look at another important background, the political initiatives and agendas.

As so often when it concerns political initiatives concerning IT use, electronic government has its origin in the USA, dating back to the early 1990s. The ideas were rapidly copied by the European Union, and have since been forming political agendas in Europe in parallel with the U.S. development.

From a North Atlantic perspective, the guiding initiatives are the following:

- The U.S. National Information Infrastructure Initiative, NII, 1993 (NIST, 1996) and Reinventing Government (NPR, 2000[1]). The concept of an information highway was coined and served as a guiding vision for the electronic physical infrastructure.
- The European Bangemann report of 1994 followed suite, translated the information highway into Infobahn and followed the American initiative when the visions of building a fiber infrastructure was concerned. The ideas of reinventing government were, however, not incorporated at that time (European Commission, 1997).

- The EU initiative 'eEurope. An Information Society for All' (European Commission, 1999) establishes a new action plan for Europe, including also a social vision, where there is some place for users (who must be educated) and Government Online (which does not, in the political agenda, require reinvention, only digitalization).

Since that time, initiatives in the spirit of the above-mentioned reports have been formulated in many countries, also outside of the U.S. and the EU. Canada, New Zealand, Australia, the United Kingdom and Sweden are examples of countries that have national manifestos and action plans as well as quite a number of electronic services of different kinds.

We shall now look a little more in detail at the development of a European Union perspective. The focus on Europe is because the USA history has been discussed extensively already, and the European agenda is currently about to reshape government practices across Europe, and electronic government practices and principles are part of this process.

EU Initiatives

The European project "Information Society" started as a reaction on the American NII. The White Paper of 1993, "Growth, Competitiveness and Employment: The Challenges and Courses for Entering into the XXIst Century," is a milestone. The basic idea was to develop an IT infrastructure across Europe as a precondition for growth, European competitiveness, new markets and more jobs.

The European Council formed an expert group, which was to suggest measures to be taken to achieve that vision. The group published in 1994 the so-called Bangemann Report, after its chairman, Commissioner Martin Bangemann: "Europe and the Global Information Society: Recommendations to the European Council" (High-Level Group, 1994). This report made IT officially a part of the EU strategy.

The report emphasizes the importance of competitiveness of European companies. Telecommunications deregulation was one important point for that purpose. Moreover, 10 initiatives to demonstrate the potential of IT were suggested, such as teleworking, distance education, electronic services to small and medium-size enterprises, etc.

The 1996 "The Information Society: From Corfu to Dublin"--The new emerging priorities marked a second phase in the project. The earlier measures to support business competitiveness were complemented by focusing on improvement of the European knowledge base by investing in education and research, social and security issues.

In 1999, a new initiative was presented by the European Commission, "eEurope. An Information Society for All." The "e" was apparently incorporated as a response to the e-commerce boom during the last years of the 1900s. This initiative mentions 10 high-priority areas. Among traditional areas (since the Bangemann Report), like cheap Internet access for all and electronic services in education and health care, there is now also "Government Online" (European Communities, 2000).

In early 2000, the European Council stated the EU strategic goal for the first decade of the 2000s as "to become the most competitive and dynamic knowledge-based economy in the world capable of sustainable economic growth with more and better jobs and greater social cohesion" (Matthews, 2000). A rapid growth of the information society was seen as an important foundation for achieving this.

The Commission presented the eEurope Action Plan in June 2000 (European Commission, 2000b). Compared to the Bangemann Report of 1994, now the attitude towards Internet technology is considerably more open (in Europe, the Internet has until very recently been seen by many as a competitor to other European technologies rather than a de facto world standard). This action plan urges the Member States and the Commission to commit to working to achieve:

- A cheaper (for the users) and more secure and trustworthy Internet.
- Increased user competence.
- Increased Internet use.

This is to be achieved by 2002. The arguably most important incentive is to reduce the gap to the USA; as of early 2001, only 22% of European households have Internet access, while the U.S. figure is some 50% (Anttiroiko, 2001). There is also an even larger gap between northern and southern Europe, with Sweden having more than 50% and Spain some 13%.

For the eEurope subproject Government Online, goals to be achieved already by 2002 are:

- Easy access to important public sector information.
- Consultation via the Internet on major political initiatives (a Web site for that purpose has been established and used[2]).
- Broad citizen access to basic interaction technologies.

The Bangemann Report mirrors mainly the large industry interests represented in the group; deregulation, security, propriety rights, technical innovation and infrastructure. A social dimension on the information society entered later. The digital divide was brought to attention, and was seen as dividing different groups of citizens, different age groups and different regions. There are some reports on social aspects, for instance the Green Paper "Living and Working in the Information Society: People First" (European Commission 1996) and "Building a European Information Society for Us All" (European Commission, 1997b), where inclusion of different social groups and general risks with the information society are discussed.

Still, it seems fair to say that the social dimension is so far subordinated to the technical dimension and–on top of the agenda right now–the urge to achieve more use. Others would express this less cautiously. EU expert Ari-Veikko Anttiroiko concludes:

"The EU seems to adapt a kind of 'asymmetric' IS policy mix in which market-oriented measures were given highest priority, and in which aspects of social cohesion and equality were incorporated to ensure critical mass for the e-economy and e-government. This dual IS policy has been typical of Europe from the very beginning. Usually this duality is expressed in subsequent policy documents by emphasizing that both business and individuals must have easy and inexpensive access to communication infrastructure and a wide range of services. Because of this very tone, European 'citizens' are usually referred to as workers who should learn new skills and become more efficient and effective in their work, or consumers or service users fulfilling their duties in consuming multimedia products and using electronic services effectively, and thus creating critical mass for market-driven IS development." (Anttiroiko, 2001)

G8, Government On-Line and DotForce

There are also integrating initiatives. One such initiative aiming at sharing experiences in order to coordinate the development across countries was the G8[3] Government On-Line Project[4] (GOL). This project engaged some 20 countries across the world, including not only eGov pioneers such as the USA, Sweden, Canada, Finland and New Zealand, but also Korea, India and Mexico.

GOL (completed in 1999) wanted to be a forum for supporting and monitoring the development toward public sector electronic services. Several projects have been completed with the goal to achieve a development with the different countries going in the same directions according to share principles, increase international cooperation to achieve a critical mass for the information society, identify problems at an early stage and exhibit good examples.

One important principle is stimulating cooperation among governments and businesses, universities and–an innovation from the latest G8 meeting in Okinawa–also civil society organizations (NGOs). Among the latter counts now also the Community Networks movement, which is now actually beginning to organize as a global movement.

As for as Government Online is concerned, making government more effective is the main goal–lower costs and better services. There was an urge to replace paper-based transactions with electronic, and to achieve a cultural change in that direction. But GOL has also paid attention to a number of projects focusing on democracy (Östberg et al., 1999), such as the Citizen Offices in Sweden and the civic network Iperbole in Bologna, Italy.

GOL expressed a strong urge to speed up developments. The overarching goal is stated as:

"... to dramatically scale up the use of technology to transform government such that, by the turn of the century, most business will be conducted electronically."
(G8, 1999)

The arguably most important issue at this point is the role of the developing countries in a situation when Internet use becomes a global issue. "DotForce" is an initiative launched at the G8 Okinawa 2000 summit, where the Okinawa Charter on Global Information Society[5] was endorsed (Government of Japan, 2000). This Charter describes how the G8 shall work so as to include the developing countries in the information society. One important part is establishing cooperation with civil society organizations in target countries, and this is why Community Networks are important; they represent NGOs already in the information society and may thus serve as a springboard. DotForce stands for Digital Opportunity Task Force, which is the task force that has started to work on these issues. As of the spring of 2001, this work was started with a consultation phase which is open to anyone at the "dotforce" mailing list (http://www.vcn.bc.ca/), as there is no such thing yet as a global representative for Community Networks.

There are several initiatives in this area, for instance the World Bank "Global Development Gateway"[6] and an upcoming United Nations initiative to prepare the 2003 UN summit in Naples, Italy, where the information society is on the agenda.

eGov: Rationalization, Service and Democracy

The above-mentioned political initiatives express ambitions to employ IT to restructure operations and institutions so as to achieve more efficient processes, better service and more democracy. But both the degree and the nature of change varies. We shall now illustrate that by taking a look at some definitions of electronic government. The following are two typical official definitions (from New Zealand and United Kingdom respectively):

"E-government is a way for governments to use the new technologies to provide people with more convenient access to government information and services, to improve the quality of the services and to provide greater opportunities to participate in our democratic institutions and processes." (NZ eGov, 2000)

"[....] harness ICT[7] to:

- improve the efficiency and effectiveness of the 'executive functions' of government including the delivery of public services;

- *enable governments to be more transparent to citizens and businesses giving access to more of the information generated by government;*
- *facilitate fundamental changes in the relationships between the citizen and the state, and between nation states, with implications for the democratic process and structures of government."* (Hirst & Norton, 1998)

These are two relatively similar definitions, the second one being a little more vague as concerns the citizen influence, as there is no direct mentioning of participation, but rather of possible changes in government-citizen relations. Also the rationalization aspect, a more efficient government, is emphasized, rather than just the citizen-oriented parts.

Some want to emphasize that effects will not come without changes in methods. This is often done by emphasizing changes in leadership. Often when doing so, the term governance is used instead of government:

"Electronic governance involves new styles of leadership, new ways of debating and deciding policy and investment, new ways of accessing education, new ways of listening to the citizens and new ways of organizing and delivering information and services." (Ferguson, 1999)

The two first mentioned definitions contain three elements that almost always recur, with different wording and different emphasis; efficiency (rationalization), quality (of services) and democracy (public participation). It is possible to distinguish different focuses depending on where the emphasis is put. Here we will exhibit three different versions--the economy version, the emancipatory version and the service version.

The Economy Version

While the aforementioned definitions focus on positive effects that are hoped to be achieved, others focus directly on the goals behind the attempts at making services more effective and more easily accessible. One such obvious goal is saving tax money:

"Electronic Government [....] describes the use of new information and communication technologies (ICT) to support the workings of governments and public administrations. Usually there are three main effects expected:
- *better and more efficient services to businesses and to citizens,*
- *greater efficiency and openness of government administration and*
- *cost savings for the taxpayer."* (ITA, 1999)

The Emancipatory Version

Another group of definitions, which also focus on goals rather than the means, emphasize the emancipatory power that they feel, is at hand. Sometimes democracy and a shift of power is focused:

"E-government [...] is not just about service delivery over the Internet [...]. The far more daunting challenge in the years ahead is a revolution in governance itself, a revolution in the fullest meaning of the word—a dramatic shift in the ways that political and social power is organized and used." (Alberta, 2000)

Sometimes radical positive change is attributed to other ideals, and the emancipation is described rather at a technical level, without reference to social goals or expectations:

"Electronic Government is more than a Web site. It is connecting a government with its stakeholders on a scale that until now has been unimaginable. It is leveraging the Internet to simplify government." (EzGov, 2000)

Here, the emancipation is not seen as citizen influence over public decision making, but rather in a cheaper administration craving less tax money. This is a good example of an American view, quite contrary to the European view of government.

The Service Version

While most definitions encompass all the three above-mentioned elements–rationalization, better services and democratic participation in different mixes–there is also a group of definitions that want to limit the scope of electronic government to services only:

> *"What e-Government Is Not: Terms such as 'data resale' and 'digital democracy' are also frequently mentioned within the same breath as 'e-government.' Neither of these terms, however, observes the principle of leveraging the Internet to simplify government. [....] Digital democracy is, in fact, 'e-politics' rather than e-government; that is, leveraging the Internet to simplify the election process (rather than government)."* (EzGov, 2000b)

The definitions are not altogether mutually exclusive. It is possible to be both emancipatory and service focused, for instance. It should also be noted that they are not official government definitions. Still, they give a good illustration to the different ways in which people conceive of e-government.

In summary, electronic government is defined as restructuring processes to achieve better efficiency, better service and more democratic participation. Both the degree and the nature of the changed envisioned differ, but in all cases it is about taking a strategic grip on IT use in the public sector.

A general definition which covers all this–but at the same time misses out on any clear view of the direction to take–is the following:

> *"Digital government initiatives are complex change efforts intended to use new and emerging technologies to support a transformation in the operation and effectiveness of government."* (Pardo, 2000)

APPLICATIONS

After having reviewed some rather ambitious definitions, we shall now take a look at some examples of where electronic government is today. This is only a brief review to cover the breadth of the field. The following chapters will more in depth cover some of the important changes that IT use has brought about, or is about to bring about.

Most examples come from the service area. Also, many of the services that exist are single good examples rather than representative for some quantitative measure of change. Still, there is reason to believe they are precursors of future organization of government activities, as they are well established, work well, are widely appreciated as good examples and seem to have economic and social viability.

A G7/G8 report on 16 national governments' use of the Internet shows that the nature of the use is rather rudimentary. All 16 governments are online, but use the Internet mainly to publish information in a broadcast style; not interactively, not personalized. Web sites are set up at additional costs, they have not replaced any manual operation. Even though email has become widely used within government organizations, the possibilities for citizens to communicate with authorities are limited, for one thing due to the lack of address books (G8, 1997).

Certainly things have happened since 1997, but still government Web sites are mostly about information and simple services. Information is typically static rather that dynamic, and even less interactive services are to be found. It is not even easy to search the information as it is not organized from a citizen perspective but from the point of view of each department (EzGov, 2000) (See the Leenes chapter about the troubles involved in trying to reorganize the information in such a way).

An investigation of a large number of government organizations in the USA yielded the following conclusion:

"In general, we find that e-government has fallen short of its potential. Governments are not making full use of available technology, and there are problems in terms of access and democratic outreach." (West, 2000).

These reports all make the point that the future of electronic services has to be in using the possibilities of self-service and integration among government organizations, not just information on the Web.

To brighten up this rather disappointing view of the current state of the art, we shall now present some examples of services and organizational innovations that can serve to illustrate that it is possible to achieve considerable change. We have chosen examples to illustrate some typically envisioned features of electronic government; self-service, cooperation between government organizations and businesses, new actors, and new forms for citizen-government encounters and democratic processes.

Self-Service and Organizational Restructuring

One way of achieving changes in service provision activities is restructuring operations within one single organization. Two Swedish central government agencies have come a long way on this route by exploiting self-service systems to achieve internal change. These agencies are AMV, the Swedish National Labor Market Agency, which is concerned with helping people finding jobs and educations, and companies finding people to employ, and CSN, an organization administrating government loans to university students.

AMV

AMV (Swedish National Labor Market Agency) has during the latter part of the 1990s left a system where the execution of services centered on the civil servants to one driven by self-service. Many factors have contributed to this change. One of those is that the number of unemployed more than doubled in the early 1990s, which led to the workload on the job agencies increasing beyond capabilities. Other reasons for change include competition from private companies, who in different ways–which very much included use of the Web–started activities very similar to those of the Government Job Offices. This includes a wide variety of organizations, including workforce leasing companies such as ManPower[8] and newspapers[9] (the chapter by Wiberg & Grönlund describes the case of AMV in the context of a new trend in government strategy).

During the 1980s, the encounter between the job seeker and the prospective employer was mediated by the Job Office and the *Job Journal* (Platsjournalen), a printed weekly journal that was the main information source. All free jobs had to be registered with the Job Office, which was then the active link between jobs and job seekers.

During the early 1990s, the Job Offices focused on matching the characteristics of the job seekers with the criteria of the available jobs. The role of the job office was to help the job seeker seeing what jobs that would suit her. IT was the tool for doing this matching, and it much guided the process, as both the job seeker and the Job Officer were dependent on what information was in the system and what matching criteria could be applied.

Today this has changed. The role of the Job Officer is now to point to different media by which the job seeker can help herself, to register job seekers, and to control the activities. There are special information centers, where computers, a wide range of educational and supportive software, and Internet access are provided to the job seekers. These centers are now a link between the job seeker and the job officers. The client-organization encounter is structured by means of a great number of software applications to be used by the job seeker for various tasks (see the Wiberg & Grönlund chapter).

This means that today all the work associated with finding jobs and education options are conducted by the job seeker herself, with considerable IT support. AMV has developed software for a number of activities related to this, such as how to approach an employer, testing of one's interests and qualifications, etc. There is also access to online catalogues of educations, free jobs and CV-databases where the job seeker can make a presentation of herself for any employer out looking for labor to read.

This has led to dramatic changes not only for the job seekers but also for the job officers, who are now only concerned with registration and control, and with helping companies finding a workforce. There are also self-service facilities offered to companies looking for staff, such as the Register of Applicants (Sökandebanken) and the Recruiting Assistant.[10]

CSN

CSN (Swedish National Board of Student Aid) provides loans and grants for education at college and university levels. Most Swedish university students are supplied by such loans. A few years ago, it was almost impossible for them to get in touch with CSN. The main medium was the telephone, and at peak seasons those were typically overloaded. To remedy this situation, CSN built a Web site where students can not only find all information about CSN products and terms, but also make calculations for downpayment schemes and check the status of her own loan.[11] This has meant a huge relief on the staff answering phone calls.

Public-Private Arrangements

AMV and CSN are cases where restructuring of processes has taken place within one single organization. The technology is relatively simple. Codes provide security when such is needed. Only information is processed, no financial transactions are made through the systems. There are other cases where transactions are in fact made, and where the rationalization has been achieved by introducing another party. One such example is ServiceArizona, a public-private arrangement where both the government agency and the company could find incentives.

IBM developed and runs the Web site "ServiceArizona"[12] and the complementary telephone service system. By these systems citizens can renew vehicle registrations. Each transaction costs the government $1.60, a figure to be compared to the $6.60 a manual transaction costs.

As of Fall of 2000, some 12 % of the registrations were renewed through ServiceArizona, which means the governments saved more than $1.5 million, according to IBM's own calculation.[13]

According to the same investigation, ServiceArizona has received appreciation from the users for being easy to use and practical.

Intermediaries

Most of all in the service field, but also in the field of democratic processes, a number of private actors has emerged to work in the intersection between citizens and governments, not only as software provides, but as intermediaries. There are the traditional general consultants, such as IBM, but there are also new actors focusing on providing specialized government services for certain niches. We shall now briefly introduce four of these, three rooted in the services field, one exclusively focusing on democratic processes.

Except for NIC, which was founded in 1991, all these companies are very young, started in 1998 or 1999.

EzGov

EzGov[14] focuses on governments as their customers. Those can buy services from EzGov, such as handling payments of parking tickets. The government will pay per transaction. The cost can be passed on to the individual payer, or it can be covered by the government as a cost to achieve a (bigger) saving, as the associated work will no longer have to be done. According to EzGov, the former method is most common (Manjoo, 2000). This method is supposed to work best at the national or state level, as this is where the large cash flows are to be found.

NIC

A competitor to EzGov, National Information Consortium, NIC[15] currently runs Web sites for 12 American states. NIC builds a portal for the government, free of charge, and the government provides electronic contact with the functions in government that are necessary for operating the service. NIC claims the service is in effect free for the citizen, as only 5% of services charge a fee. NIC's revenue comes from resale of customer data, a business that has been criticized for being immoral. Even if this kind of activity is not new–governments across the world has done that by themselves for many years–the fact that this is now done over the Internet, as an international trade, and that it so obviously is a part of governments' financing has added to its new dimensions.

GovWorks

GovWorks[16] provides services in the USA and in Latin America. In addition to a number of payment services, the company has established a national Web site where information about all U.S. agencies are assembled, and where citizens can conduct their business with government agencies nationwide.

GovWorks is part of the "E-government Alliance," which subscribes to the principles of not reselling data and of openly declaring all fees and ownership details that may affect the trust in the operation. They also declare a commitment to helping bridge the digital divide.

Votia Empowerment

Votia Empowerment[17] is a Swedish company focusing on democratic processes in different contexts. The slogan is "We make e-democracy work." The product is software and help in organizing citizen participation. Customers include the public sector, non-profit, and commercial organizations. The product is described as "integrated services for cost-effective, media-independent dialogue." This includes making information available, organizing individual interaction, summarizing results, etc. The added value for the organization is increased participation and thus enhanced legitimacy in decision making. As concerns the public sector, the company in Fall 2000 organized a very successful first project in the small Swedish town of Kalix (see below).

New Forms for Citizen Participation

The concept of e-democracy (electronic democracy, teledemocracy or digital democracy) is, just like electronic government, a concept that has been given many meanings. Here, we use it to mean use of IT in democratic processes. This is a very wide definition. Often, the term is used much more narrowly to mean electronic voting or polling. This narrow definition is detrimental, as it is obvious that IT can come into use in many democratic processes. Not just directly, such as in consultation, petitioning, information searching and gathering, etc., but also indirectly as IT tools change the workings of the administration. For instance, in GIS systems and data mining tools, a great part of the political rule system is built in, not just the general parts formulated in policies, but also the less published ones invented in local practices to adapt to local conditions, and simply to make things work. The fact that the rules are explicitly stated in these systems affects the opportunities to understand and control the workings of the administration in many ways. On the one hand the rules may become more hidden as they are no longer discussed once they are built into the technical system. In fact, nor are they discussed before they are built in, as this is now part of the administrative nuts and bolts--routines, not of the policy-making agenda. On the other hand they become more inspectable as they are in fact explicitly coded in the programs. Finally, as they are "hardwired," they are not easily changed ad hoc (Snellen, 2001).

In this section we will stick to the democratic processes pertaining directly to the formal politics. In this area, there are currently some interesting opportunities being explored.

Online Politicians

There is a small sample of high-level politicians that the public can consult by email. A well-known example is the Dutch minister Roger van Boxtel,[18] who employs a number of staff to help him answer correctly and responsibly. UK Prime Minister Tony Blair has a communicative function at the Web site "number-10,"[19] Policy Forum on Electronic Delivery of Government Services.

The European Union encourages such practices, and has started to employ it as a part of the Government Online initiative. The idea is to provide consultation about major political initiatives. As an example, on June 5, 2000, Europeans could chat with Commissioner Michel Barnier about the EU enlargement issue.[20]

At the local level there are examples of cities where email consultation with leading politicians has become a regular business. A good example is the Swedish city of Bollnäs,[21] where a reply guarantee on direct mails and frequent politician participation on the local "Dialogue" (email public debate forum) has made the email consultation popular, and local politicians see it as a good way of enlightening the debates in the formal political forums (Nilsson Sträng, 2000).

Expert Panels Online

The Hansard Society for Parliamentary Government[22] has arranged a series of expert panels on the Internet[23] in cooperation with parliamentary committees in the House of Lords as well as in the House of Commons. The panels have resulted in reports within the assignments of the committees. Discussion topics include electronic democracy, domestic violence and the Parliament's information strategies.

Älvsjö Citizen Panel and Citizen Initiative

As a general rule, the use of discussion forums in local governments seems to be less than professionally managed (with some important exceptions!). A Swedish survey shows that while about 15% of the cities/towns have such forums on the Web, most of them are virtually not used (Ranerup, 2001). One reason seems to be that the politicians are not present in the forums–where they are, forums are indeed used (Ranerup, 1999). As concerns electronic voting, a major problem is achieving universal and equal access. Also, the coupling between the debate and the voting is not always very clear.

Älvsjö, a district within the City of Stockholm, is an example of a political organization that has tried to integrate an extended political debate, citizen participation in formal decision making and different communication media. They have arranged a representative citizen panel of 500 people. This panel is consulted by questionnaires (three times during the latter half of the year 2000). The results of the questionnaires are fed into the public debate, but also issues raised in the public debate are fed into the questionnaires so as to get a more representative treatment of them.

Moreover, individual citizens have the right to raise issues in the District Council (which has been delegated a subset of the powers of the City of Stockholm). This can be done by letter or email. All suggestions are responded to in a way proper to the nature of the proposal and the powers of the District Council.

Kalix Consultation

The City of Kalix became known in Swedish media as the most innovative city as concerns e-democracy for the September 2000 "Consultation" (Rådslag) concerning the remodeling of the city center. The consultation lasted for 14 days. Citizens were asked questions regarding general design issues (such as whether they wanted car-free zones or not) by ordinary mail. There was no plan presented; no sketches, no political preferences were stated. Questions could be answered by email, ordinary mail, telephone or by visiting the City Hall. Issues could be debated by email and in chat sessions in which politicians participated.

Every person registered as inhabitant of Kalix, age of 12 or over, could participate. Every person got a password that could be used only once. Those who did not have a computer at home or at work could use public computers at libraries, homes for elderly and such. In the small villages without such institutions, "Internet Cafés" were arranged.

The Consultation was organized and managed by Votia (see above). The company has made an evaluation of the event, and find themselves very happy with the outcome. One-thousand, two-hundred people, 7% of the total population, participated. This can be compared to the handful of comments normally received when city planning sketches and models are exhibited in the City Hall.

So far there has been no independent evaluation of the project, but Votia claims they have been able to reach first-time voters. The use of the Internet seems to have been an important factor in the huge turnout; 86% chose to use email for answering the questions, despite the fact that both telephone and ordinary letters were available (Lepola, 2000).

Electronic Voting

Electronic voting in political elections is a much debated and much criticized opportunity. There have been a few trials during 2000, including the Democratic National Convention; the Youth-e-Vote 2000, an exercise vote for youth and the Arizona Presidential Preference Primary, the world's first legally binding online election involving 40,000 voters (Hoffman & Cranor, 2001; Mohen & Glidden, 2001; Phillips & Spakovsky, 2001). In Europe, examples include test votes made in Germany, and a binding Internet election held by the Umeå Student Association in May 2001.

A few software development projects are underway. In Europe there is for instance Cybervote,[24] a project within the Information Societies Technologies program, which is aimed at performing elections in France, Germany and Sweden (also mobile technology is supposed to be used). Test elections are going to be made in local government contexts in the three countries in 2003.

Alternative technical solutions are already available. SICS, Swedish Institute for Computer Science, is developing a system, and there are programs on the market, for instance from Safevote.[25]

Political elections are technically more complicated, and more value-laden, than opinion polls and bank transactions. No amount of "loss" can be tolerated, privacy must be absolute and the voting situation is a qualitatively different "moment of truth" than an encounter between a customer and a company. There are five basic requirements for a voting system:

- Only a pre-defined set of people, registered voters, are allowed to vote.
- Only one vote per person must be counted.
- Nobody must be able to find out what a certain person has voted for, except herself, even under court order.
- A vote caste must be impossible to change by anyone but the voter herself (who is in fact allowed to change her vote when different options are used, for instance an early vote at a post office can be overruled by a later vote at a voting station).
- Vote counting and distribution of chairs in the parliament must be correct according to the specific rules of each vote.

In practice, systems that do not fulfill all these requirements are today used in local contexts. There are a number of companies in this area, acting as software providers, consultants and/or intermediaries, including the Swedish Votia[26] and Vivarto[27] and the U.S. Votesmart,[28] Election.com[29] and Safevote.[30]

So far, most official recommendations have been against electronic remote voting (see the chapter by Riera et al.). Apart from the social and political issues at stake, there is a very important problem for organizations wanting to employ electronic voting: it requires much expertise to understand beforehand if the voting software actually fulfills what it proposes.

MANAGEMENT

Above, we have highlighted some interesting examples of Internet use in the public sector. We have focused on external use, as this represents the newest step in the development, and as this in many cases serves as the incentive for radical changes in internal procedures, as we saw in for instance the AMV case.

Even if these cases represent pilots rather than a significant mass, there is reason to believe that these are really precursors of some change to come. Even if most government Web sites are not so sophisticated, the number is already impressive. In Sweden, for instance, all local and regional governments, even the very small ones, have Web sites.

The development towards this situation has happened via a combination of strategic initiatives and local entrepreneurship. In the wake of the NII and the Bangemann Report, many countries and states have established national policy statements and agendas. Especially at the local level, the development has been under influence of many other forces than those strategies; that is, the tactical and operational plans have been less than clear (Grönlund, 2001), and successes have typically been partial. Therefore, today many local governments seek to establish strategies tying together already existing, successful, grassroot initiatives with the national (and European) policy agendas.

So far, the development has been driven by a combination of individual champions, the perceived demand pull of the rapidly increasing amount of Internet users, the increasing technical sophistication and reliability of internet technologies, project funds made available by national and EU strategic program, and portal projects driven by various commercial incentives, one of which being to rapidly achieve a large user population, which has meant a lot of "free" services have emerged, including public sector information at commercial sites. Some of these portals include a sort of franchising concept, where cities can rent a standardized Web site instead of building one. One example is Cityguide.[31]

This development is witnessed by many:

"The task for the Government is to build on these individual initiatives and develop them into a comprehensive plan for achieving the benefits of e-government more widely on behalf of all New Zealanders." (NZ, 2000)

Why has the development been so unsystematic? One obvious reason is that it has happened because of the rapid penetration of the Internet, and thus the technical development and the increase in use have been faster than the pace at which plans could be implemented.

Another answer is provided by the EU project Infosond[32] concerned with developing electronic services in a local government perspective.[33] The development was retrospectively described as an ongoing struggle, or negotiation, among different actors, which during different phases affected the ways technology was used (Grönlund, 2000). Initiatives were started by enthusiasts supported by external financial sources. As projects grew and won strongholds in the organization, different departments/institutions tried to control the development. During the whole project period (1996-1999), strategic management never tried to control the situation in any clear way. According to these findings, technology development was no so much the result of one coherent strategy, but rather "drifted" (Ciborra, 1997) as it was negotiated along the road of actors who had different claims on it (Latour, 1999).

The lack of strategy seems to have hampered the development, at least in the short run, as many major leaps the technology hold potential for--such as organizational integration and major technical investments--require some advantage of scale (see also the chapter by Nilsson and Ranerup, which discusses the relation between plans and emergent changes).

Many have observed that neither the technical quality, nor the completeness of the services offered at government sites, are that impressive as a general rule (EzGov, 2000; G8, 1997; Cyprg, 2000). Another common observation is that those that have come the longest way are those that are large enough to bear big investments, and have a large number of transactions (as the CSN above), or work in a field where there is competition (as the AMV above).

When the local level is concerned, the situation is very different. Services are often small-scale, and cross-departmental advantages in other than basic administration seem hard to find. One important issue at the local level, so far not that much discussed, is how solutions involving several partners–partnerships, intermediaries, shared institutions, etc.–of which the government is one, can be built at a local level. There is a need for a local/regional electronic service infrastructure (Grönlund & Ranerup, 2001).

When electronic government is described by software providers, it is natural that the technical opportunities are emphasized. It is perhaps more surprising that the technology focus is so strong also when eGov is described by politicians or EU projects about IT use. One reason is that technical products are more easily described and sold than organizational changes. Another reason is that in Europe, much of the development is organized as projects, which means results have to be delivered within one to two years, and as organizational change takes a long time, other things have to be delivered. As for the EU, transferability is an important issue, and as technical products sefem more easily transferable than complicated issues of organization and use, which have cultural and historical roots that are not easily changed, there is a strong product focus.

There is a lot of literature on social implications of IT use (a prominent example is the "Social Informatics" of Rob Kling, http://www.slis.indiana.edu/SI/index.html), which we shall not review here. Let me just provide a thought figure, which comes from an EU local government electronic services development project.[34] "The Iceberg Model," in Figure 1, illustrates the issues that come up during a typical such project.

The over water part was where the money and effort was spent. It is also what the project reviewers focused on, the "product" (in this case a set of Web pages, a search tool and some services targeting specific user groups). The underwater part lists the issues that came up underway as problems in the organizations where the systems were going to be implemented. The point here is not to go through all these issues. They have to a large extent been covered in the literature in other contexts (Grönlund et al., 2000). The point to be made here is only that the figure illustrates that e-government is certainly in a need of strategy seen through the lenses of development work to date. This need is expressed by many:

>*"Opportunities can be lost because no government organization takes the leading responsibility to oversee and coordinate development of e-government for the benefit of citizens."* (NZ, 2000)

Indeed, but how? We have above mentioned some new actors and new strategies (but strategies can only take you so far; see the chapter by Nilsson & Ranerup). In many places,

Figure 1: Project focus (above the water) and issues that emerge along as the project proceeds (underwater) (Grönlund, 2000)

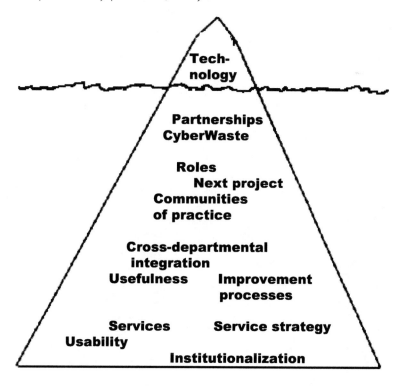

special agencies are set up to oversee the development, local or national. One example is the New Zealand State Services Commission.[35]

Many issues go beyond the scope of any particular government organization, or any individual government. There are general issues that emerge from the new uses of IT that pertain to local, regional, national and international relations among citizen and governments and government organizations. We shall now briefly discuss some of these.

eGov Issues

So far, we have been concerned with issues closely tied to the implementation and use of electronic services from government. There are a number of issues that pertain to electronic government in a more general way, which we believe should be incorporated in an eGov research agenda.

One type of issue concerns IT use in general, which becomes more pressing due to the spread of the Internet to more people, new use areas and new geographic areas. This includes privacy, security and knowledge management, especially informal and not well structured (see, e.g., the chapters by Svensson and Gates & Nissen), and strategic management issues (Wiberg & Grönlund). It also includes the more general issue of how to look upon decision-making, and the role of IT tools in decision making procedures (Svensson, Janlert). Will we, for instance, have more comprehensive and coherent legislation simply because this is necessary to build the computer systems that are needed to make administration more "e"? Will we change our views on good decisions from "principally correct" to "practically working"?

Another type of issue has to do with the expansion of Internet use. This raises questions of "digital divides" of different kinds, between rich and poor countries or regions, between groups within one country differing on social or economic status, age or cultural background, differences between urban and rural areas, etc.

A third type of issue concerns government; where are, or should be, the limits of government? Over the past years, issues of regulation of the Internet, including things like surveillance, key escrow, data transmission, Web publication regulation, etc., have been on the agenda. While these issues are still relevant, there are other issues emerging. The arguably most important issue today pertains to community networks. These have been around for some 20 years as civil society organizations (see the chapter by Gross for a brief history). Currently we see businesses trying to exploit "communities" by addressing people in user groups, "panels" and the like, sometimes solicited as volunteers, but most often automatically selected based on their use habits. One of the important things in the current ambitions to revive local democracy is about trying to (re)create a local (sense of) community based on common issues in a town. One of the means for achieving this may be cooperation with local community networks. It is not immediately clear what a diffusion of the border between the formal society and the civil one may lead to.

While not attempting to review all these issues, just a few words about why they are important to eGov. Briefly put, in terms of the model presented in the Introduction, it is about the tensions between the nodes in the system getting differently charged as IT/ICT gets involved in different ways. The situation can be described as actors in each node so to speak trying to enlarge their respective domain of control, or influence, by means of trying to steer new IT use into directions most favorable to their interests (Figure 2). In the following, we shall look at some examples of this. There is no simple way of assessing the relative strength of the different arrows in Figure 1, as there are so many issues on the agenda that are not well understood. We just want to describe a few of them, and make the point that they are issues

Figure 2: eGov issues with a p otential of changing the domains of control/influence include privacy legislation, use of community network tools in formal politics, self-service to government services and others

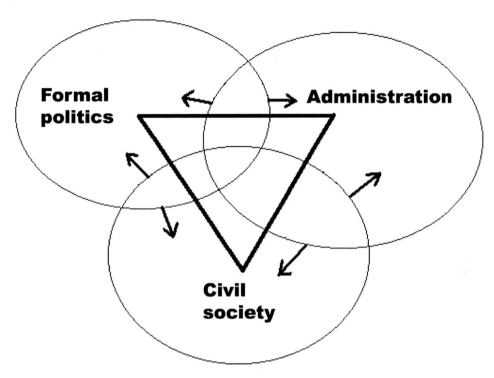

that should be researched within a coherent research field concerning the role of e-government, not just as individual issues.

The Digital Divide

The digital divide is a relatively recent expression, but it has in practice been on the agenda for many years. Yet, now as mass connection to the Internet is happening in the U.S. and the EU, and a few other countries, the issue has attained new dimensions. The question concerns the unequal access to the electronic medium, which seems to reflect traditional divides in society.

There are national agendas for the digital divide debate, about differences in IT skills and use among different age groups, groups of different socio-economic status, different cultural backgrounds, etc. Even though it is sometimes named "the Mercedes Divide" when discussed in countries where already half the population are on the Internet, such gulfs are real and important in every country, something investigations like the U.S. 1999 "Falling Through the Net: Defining the Digital Divide" shows (Department of Commerce, 2000).

As even critics do not doubt that Internet use will increase, there is an obvious risk that government services and democratic processes will be more accessible to some than to others.

There is an international agenda for the debate, currently focusing on the process of integrating developing countries in the information society. This development has many stakeholders; business, for which the not-yet-wired countries represent a huge amount of customers, governments in those countries, citizens in those countries and international development organizations such as the World Bank and the United Nations. Binational support program should also be mentioned. There are many issues on the table, including democracy, national development, international aid, local and international business, and the role of NGOs. This is the light in which initiatives such as the World Bank Global Gateway project[36] and the dotForce task force should be seen.

The further development of these development program is an important item on the eGov research agenda.

Privacy vs. Public Access

Privacy on the Internet is a much-debated issue, one that clearly worries individuals (Engholm, 2000; Cranor et al., 1999), and one where national legislations differ, which makes international trade with personal data profitable. Earlier, the privacy intrusion problem concerned individuals' relations with government, but today it is more a matter of the activities of businesses. A study by the U.S. Federal Trade Commission found 99% of financial Web sites collect personal information about their users; 80% transferred that data to other organizations (BTN, 1998). Government is a player in that game too, as resale of data is sometimes a method of financing government electronic services (see the NIC section above).

When citizen-government relations are concerned, there is a conflict between privacy and public access to official records, and freedom of speech. The European Union is pursuing a strict legislation to enforce privacy, which has led to several cases of individuals facing legal charges for publishing what is often perceived as harmless information on Web sites. In Sweden, for instance, during the period of 1998-2000, 296 cases have been registered at the monitoring agency, the Data Inspection Board (Ågren, 2001). The thrust of the EU legislation is to make information dissemination on the Web a professional matter; journalists are excluded from the strict legislation.

Privacy is sometimes a word used to cover up secrecy. There is a struggle between openness and secrecy going on in Europe, even within EU institutions. In Spring 2000, the Web site www.OpenUpEurope.com was opened. There, some MEPs published documents prior to the EU meetings that were to discuss the documents. The EU rule is that no documents are made public before meetings. By Spring 2001, it seems this initiative has been successful; today the–as yet informal–rule is that the EU allows this publication.

This struggle between the regulatory forces and those promoting openness and a more participatory democracy clearly illustrates tensions among all the nodes in Figure 1–even within the "formal politics" one.

Decision Making, and the Role of IT Tools

Decision support systems have been discussed since the 1980s. They have so far not come to more large-scale use, as there have been many question marks concerning their role, from several points of view other than the technical and practical function: legal, psychological, as well as social. As many of the chapters in this book witness, there seems to be a drift away from such multi-perspective reasoning to a more pragmatic one–"it seems to work." Svensson reports widespread use of decision support systems in the Dutch social services, and forecasts a development towards legislation that is directly formulated to fit into decision support systems. Janlert seeks to capture the way of thinking about decision making that people apply to computer use. Macintosh et al. report the use of community networking style of interaction between government and citizens. These three chapters focus on different lines of development. The Svensson case reports the administrative approach--to make legislation as unified, straightforward and cheap to execute as possible. In the other two cases, the focus is on humans collectively forming meaning and agreements, and doing so without too much adherence paid to the formal democratic processes. This could be called a civil society approach to decision making. Stuck between these two models–which are both well supported by available technology–is the formal political system, which in some way has to deal with the fact that both the other approaches have strong support both technically and socially (from different camps).

This ongoing struggle on harnessing IT for changing the balance between the nodes in the government model is another important item on the eGov research agenda.

From Security to Trust

Trust is one of the three top priorities in the EU Government Online project (see the Design section above). It is also one of the major issues in electronic commerce.

Trust requires technical systems like digital signatures, but goes far beyond those. "Trust providers," such as TRUSTe,[37] BBBOnLine[38] and WebTrust,[39] exist in e-commerce, but they are in their current design incomplete for eGov (see the Galindo chapter in this book). Openness on information policy, "reputation systems" (Resnick et al., 2000), trust seals, etc. are ways by which companies and organizations try to establish customer confidence.

There are limitations to all these solutions. The integrity of trust providers has been challenged as there have been cases where a trust provider has failed to take actions against its customers when they fail to comply with the agreed criteria (Orsak, 2001).

Data resale, practiced by private companies as well as governments, is today arguably a more problematic issue than technical security. Data theft can certainly hurt a few individuals, sometimes hard, but data resale affects not only all of us, but potentially threatens the security of society, as population data, potentially an important tool in information warfare, can now be easily purchased.

On this point, there is clearly a struggle between different countries concerning how to legally handle the threat posed by data resale, as evidenced by recent controversies between online bookstore Amazon and ISP American Online and governments of France and the United Kingdom (Knight, 2000). In terms of Figure 2, this means the politics and the administrative nodes have joined forces utilizing current e-commerce practices–and indeed such organizations, see the NIC section above–for economic reasons, to establish practices that certainly are threatening to individual citizens, and potentially also to governments themselves.

Community Networking and eGov–Cyberspace Landing?

Community Networking (CN) has its roots in "hacker time," but now involves millions of people worldwide. Gurstein (1999) names Community Informatics a research field, but several publications have witnessed and discussed it before (e.g., Rheingold, 1993; Schuler, 1996). Community networks have been around for a couple of decades, under different names, such as (urban) civic networks, freenets, etc. (see the Gross chapter). There is a current effort to organize what has so far been a large number of detached and disparate communities into a global civil movement, which would potentially have considerable size. The first CN World Congress was held in November 2000 in Barcelona with some 450 participants from 25 countries.[40] The yet unformalized "CN Movement" has been approached by influential policy groups such as the G8. The Barcelona organizing attempts should be seen as a way to create a platform for the purpose of being able to act against such groups (Coghlan, 2000).

There are different attempts to define CN. As we are here interested in electronic government, we want to investigate the potential mutual interest between government and CN. Some definitions see CN as purely a civil society issue:

"Community networking provides the means for communities to collaborate amongst and within themselves on a regional level for the betterment of the entire community. The impact of community networks includes social and economic benefits [...] A necessary pre-condition to the development of an effective community network is the inclusion of all citizens within the region served by the community network." (Coghlan, 2000)

Certainly CNs have their roots in civil society, and thus thrive from independence from government. On the other hand, several CNs have political ambitions, and even purely social CNs have interest at stake when governments and business try to utilize CNs for their own purposes, in focus groups, citizen panels and the like.

Some CN definitions focus on their role in a wider societal context:

"Community networks are seen to provide the mechanism for effectively bringing together the interests of the three essential sectors of community: Government, Business and the Civil Sector (volunteer-based organizations, NGOs, etc.)." (Coghlan, 2000)

An important eGov issue, and one with many dimensions, is how this influence is best organized. There are certainly conflicting interests. CN represents civil society and civil organization independently of government. eGov represents governments' problems in handling the relations with the citizens in many aspects. As we have seen above this includes issues of legal regulation and formal democratic processes. In practice, though the two are beginning to meet, for example as local governments apply CN techniques and cooperate with local CNs for the purpose of (re)creating a certain amount of "community" around local government issues (Ranerup, 1999, 2001).

CNs were established before the World Wide Web, and originally simple email techniques were used. In many places, the very attempt to arrange access to the technology was an important founding factor. Today, the situation is different, and thus many see the role of CNs very differently:

"There are potential new opportunities and roles associated with providing 'trusted' current community content and applications, and growing interest in broadband services to homes and small businesses. [....] Community partnerships which focus on the development of locally based and focused content can play a vital role in meeting civic needs and stimulating demand for enhanced services." (Lowenberg, 2000)

There is thus some evidence that CN culture is about to merge with the culture of eGov. This is happening at the global level as well as at the local, by partnerships in projects. While it is too early to say where this cultural clash, or merge, will lead, it is obviously an important field for further studies. In terms of Figure 2, the issue illustrates that tools, techniques, views and practices from the civil sector area (discussion forums, email, membership rather than citizenship as the organizing principle, etc.) are implanted in the practices of local government politics (see the Kalix and Älvsjö examples above). This means elements of one culture are beginning to gain foothold in another. Just how this happens is another item on the eGov research agenda.

The Role of Government

After having discussed some particular eGov issues, we now turn to one more general. One question that may be asked is whether more, and more strategic, use of ICT will make government matter more or less. Will adaptation to e-commerce-inspired operations make government just like any business? Or will government become more powerful in some way? While not all the authors in this book explicitly address this question, it is possible to discern some partial answers.

Lenk et al. see the service parts as things that could be easily outsourced, or, if policy so advises, run by government just like a business would run it. Extensive outsourcing and partnership arrangements seem likely to mean that government would matter less, both in terms of scale of operations and in terms of the ability to maintain procedures very different from (e-)business ones.

But they claim ICT could and should be used also in the "core business" of government, that is the policy making and decision making parts. If ICTs are used successfully in these parts, it might be expected that government policies would become more efficient, and thus make government matter more in the sense being more capable in implementing its policies.

The chapter by Wiberg & Grönlund seems to point in the same direction(s). On the one hand, operations of the government agencies have become more business-like, to the extent of outsourcing. The government Employment Office Web could to most parts be run by a company, the service technicians at Swedish telecom firm Telia work just like any consultant in a private firm and the Job Officers at AMV are just like any clerk as their role as (emancipatory) advisors and mediators has been played down for the administrative and control functions. This means they are easily transferred to the private sector (as Telia in fact has already partly done); only policy can stop that from happening. This seems to say government matters less; it is not different from business. Other factors pointing in the "less" direction is the fact that government abdicated from its role as provider of jobs to regions in need of such. ICT-enabled efficiency thus conquered the regional leveraging policy.

On the other hand, central management has implemented a tight control system, over work, over the economy of local branch offices, over inventory, etc. This means operations are in the hands of policy to an extent they never were before. This seems to say government matters more–is more in control–so long as the operations are kept in the public sector.

Svensson finds that use of decision support systems has made it possible to implement policy better–government matters more. He also finds that solutions are chosen based on practical working solutions rather than theoretical argument. That might indicate that government will rather matter less, as policy will be more influenced by working practice such as e-commerce than by policy. On the other hand, Svensson foresees a development towards more "computerizable" legislation (comprehensive, coherent). This seems to indicate that government at least wants and tries to matter more, by making policy more implementable.

Macintosh et al. hope that government will matter more. They start from the notion that government, at least the political part, today suffers from loss of impact on citizen, and the following declining participation. They hope that new ICT tools for participation will change that, by making it easier to participate and by making governments consider the citizen input more. Thus, government will matter more to people as people discover that they matter more to government.

Anttiroiko, in discussing strategic knowledge management in local government from the perspective of current trends in the changing role of government, finds that their role as institutional mediators becomes harder due to increased international competition. On the one hand this means local government matters less, in the sense they have a less secure situation and their environment is both more uncertain and equivocal. On the other hand their role as a hub for local and regional development increases. As the national governments back off from taking a responsibility for individual regions, their need for information so as to be able to act strategically increases. Also, the dependence on local and "systemic" knowledge is decreasing, while the role of "embrained" (symbolic) and "encultured" knowledge is increasing. Anttiroiko concludes that organizational designs relying on interactive mechanisms and enhancing communication-intensive processes are most favourable for finding and making use of such knowledge. ICT is one of the necessary tools for such processes, and thus ICT should make local government matter a little more than they could without such knowledge.

Based on the above, it seems fair to say that ICT will make government matter differently. A more interesting answer will have to include more knowledge about the further developments in different fields, some of which are discussed at an early stage of development in this book. As the issue clearly reaches beyond what is presented here, it is another important item on the eGov research agenda.

CONCLUSION

This chapter has briefly described the background to electronic government, exhibiting definitions, examples and issues.

The above examples of issues cannot easily be summarized to point at a development in some certain direction. Rather they together make up a field of research currently severely understudied. It is important to start more comprehensive studies on the many facets of electronic government at this time when economic incentives and technical development work together to increase the investment in technical solutions, which are applied with very little respect paid to the complexity of the context in which they are to work, the system of government in democratic states.

ENDNOTES

1 http://www.npr.gov/converse/conversa.html

2 http://europa.eu.int/comm/chat/barnier1/index_en.htm

3 G8 is an extension of the original G7, founded in 1975 as a forum for the leaders of the most important industry nations to discuss strategic economic and political issues of international importance. Original members were France, USA, UK, Germany, Japan and Italy. Canada joined in 1976, the EU in 1977 and Russia in 1998 (http://www.library.utoronto.ca/g7/what_is_g7.html)

4 GOL is presented at http://www.open.gov.uk/govoline/golintro.htm

5 http://www.g8kyushu-okinawa.go.jp/e/documents/it1.html

6 http://www.worldbank.org/gateway/

7 Information and Communication Technologies

8 www.manpower.se

9 E.g., http://www.dn.se and www.vk.se

10 http://www.ams.se/

11 http://www.csn.se

12 http://www.servicearizona.com
13 http://www-3.ibm.com/e-business/casestudy/26261.html
14 http://www.ezgov.com
15 http://www.nicusa.com
16 http://www.govworks.com
17 http://www.votia.com
18 http://www.rogervanboxtel.nl/
19 http://www.number-10.gov.uk
20 http://europa.eu.int/comm/chat/barnier1/index_en.htm
21 http://www.bollnas.se
22 http://www.hansardsociety.org.uk
23 http://www.democracyforum.org.uk
24 http://www.eucybervote.org/
25 http://www.safevote.com
26 http://www.votia.com
27 http://www.vivarto.com
28 http://www.votesmart.com
29 http://www.election.com
30 http://www.safevote.com
31 For instance, http://cityguide.se/karlskrona/
32 (INFOrmation and Services ON Demand, Europeiska kommissionen projekt TAP UR 1017)
33 This answer draws on the more general answer to the question of how technology is developed provided by Actor Network Theory (Latour, 1987, 1999)
34 In the project Infosond, Information and Services on Demand, EU 4PR, project no UR 1017
35 http://www.ssc.govt.nz/siteset.htm
36 http://www.worldbank.org/gateway/
37 http://www.TRUSTe.com/
38 http://www.BBBOnLine.com/
39 http://www.WebTrust.com/
40 http://www.cnglobal2000.org/

REFERENCES

Ågren, P. O. (2001). Is online democracy in the EU for professionals only? *Communications of the ACM*, January.
Alberta. (2000). *The CyberCity Initiative. City of the Grand Prairie, Alberta, Canada.* Available on the World Wide Web at: http://www.city.grande-prairie.ab.ca/ccy_0001.htm.
Anttiroiko, A. V. (2001). Toward the European Information Society. *Communications of the ACM*, January.
BP. (2000). *Studies Project Fast Growth for Electronic Government Goods and Services. Best Practices LLC.* Available on the World Wide Web at: http://www.kmexcellence.com/km/members/hotspot/1999/archive4_2.htm.
BTN. (1998). Using the Web to snare consumers' personal data. In *Bank Technology News*, October, 11(10).

Castells, M. (1996). *The Rise of the Network Society*. Blackwell.

Ciborra, C. (1997). De Profundis? Deconstructing the concept of strategic alignment. *Scandinavian Journal of Information Systems*, 9(1), 67-81.

Coghlan, S. (2000). Community networks: The Oxford County perspective. Meddelande i diskussionsgruppen. *Community Informatics*, December. Available on the World Wide Web at: http://www.vcn.bc.ca/groups/.

Cook, M. E. (2000). *What Citizens Want From E-Government*. Center for Technology in Government, University at Albany/SUNY. Available on the World Wide Web at: http://www.ctg.albany.edu/resources/htmlrpt/e-government/what_citizens_want.html.

Cranor, L. F., Reagle, J. and Ackerman, M. S. (1999). *Beyond Concern: Understanding Net Users' Attitudes About Online Privacy*. AT&T Labs-Research Technical reports. Available on the World Wide Web at: http://www.research.att.com/projects/privacystudy/.

Department of Commerce. (2000). *Americans in the Information Age Falling Through the Net*. U.S. Department of Commerce. Available on the World Wide Web at: http://www.ntia.doc.gov/ntiahome/digitaldivide/.

Cyprg. (2000). Cyberspace Policy Research Group, Arizona University. *Ett antal Publikationer Finns På*. Available on the World Wide Web at: http://www.cyprg.arizona.edu/publications.html.

Engholm, A. (2000). *Krav På Personuppgifter Oroar Nätshoppare*. Computer Sweden 50/2000. Available on the World Wide Web at: http://domino.IDg.se/cs/artikel.nsf/674b84618b948c0cc12567d20050feb7/27e8261bfe501e52802568dd004691fa?.

European Commission. (1994). Europe's way to the information society. An action plan. *COM*, (94), 347.

European Commission. (1996). Green Paper-Living and working in the information society: People first. *COM*, July, (96), 389. Available on the World Wide Web at: http://europa.eu.int/comm/off/green/index_en.htm.

European Commission. (1997a). *The Bangemann Report*. Available on the World Wide Web at: http://www.egd.igd.fhg.de:10555/WISE/globals/ecinfo/general_information/bangeman.html.

European Commission. (1997b). Building the European information society for us all. *Final Policy Report of the High-Level Expert Group*. Manuscript completed in April 1997. Employment & social affairs. European Commission.

European Commission. (1999). *Information Society eEurope*. Available on the World Wide Web at: http://europa.eu.int/comm/information_society/eeurope/background/index_en.htm.

European Communities. (2000). *Government Online*. Available on the World Wide Web at: http://europa.eu.int/comm/information_society/eeurope/objectives/10areas_en.htm.

European Commission. (2000b). *eEurope 2002. An Information Society For All*. Action plan prepared by the Council and the European Commission for the Feira European Council 19-20 June. Available on the World Wide Web at: http://europa.eu.int/comm/information_society/eeurope/actionplan/index_en.htm.

EurLex. (1999). Legislation under preparation Commission proposals Document 599PC0626. Available on the World Wide Web at: http://europa.eu.int/eur-lex/en/com/dat/1999/en_599PC0626.html.

EzGov. (2000). *Realizing e-Government. EzGov White Paper*. Available on the World Wide Web at: http://www.ezgov.com/white_papers_art3_1.jsp.

EzGov. (2000b). *Making Sense of a Revolution. ExGov White Papers*. Available on the

World Wide Web at: http://www.ezgov.com/white_papers_art1_3.jsp.

Ferguson, M. (1999). Developments in electronic governance. The British Council (Rapporten han hämtas i .pdf-format på http://www.britishcouncil.org/governance/edigest.htm).

Foley, K. (2000). The new body politic. NUA analysis, 9 October. http://www.nua.ie/surveys/analysis/weekly_editorial/archives/issue1no147.html.

Government of Japan. (2000). *Okinawa Charter on Global Information Society.* http://www.g8kyushu-okinawa.go.jp/e/documents/it1.html

Grönlund, Å. & Jakobsson, M. (1998). Electronic services to the citizen–Usable and useful? In Karlsson, I. M. & Östlund, B. (Eds.), *Users in Action.* KFB-Rapport 1999:8. Stockholm: KFB.

Grönlund, Å. (2000). Electronic service management--Local government as a service provider. *Proceedings of E-government in Europe.* March 30-31. St. James's Court Hotel, London. Access Conferences International, Ltd., London.

Grönlund, Å., Kauranne, T., Hartkamp, F., Kritzenberger, H. and Forsgren, O. (2000). *Managing Electronic Services–A Public Sector Perspective.* London: Springer.

Grönlund, Å. and Ranerup, A. (2001). *Elektronisk Förvaltning, Elektronisk Demokrati–visioner, Verklighet, Vidareutveckling.* Lund: Studentlitteratur.

Grönlund, Å. (2001b). Building an infrastructure to manage electronic services - Investigating the trajectory of electronic services projects. In Dasgupta, S. (Ed.), *Managing Internet and Intranet Technologies.* Hershey, PA: Idea Group Publishing.

G8. (1997). Government use of the Internet. A Collaborative "fast-track" study by G7GOL and ICA. Available on the World Wide Web at: http://www.open.gov.uk/govoline/ishtml.htm.

G8. (1999). Government On-line Project. Final project report, April. Available on the World Wide Web at: http://www.open.gov.uk/govoline/golintro.htm.

Gurstein, M. (1999). *Community Informatics: Enabling the Community Use of Information and Communications Technologies.* Hershey, PA: Idea Group Publishing.

Hamilton, C. (2000). Mot Attac från Fokpartiet liberalerna; ett pressmeddelande. Medialistan July.

Hart-Teeter. (2000). E-Government: The Next American Revolution. Report prepared for *The Council for Excellence in Government*, September. Available on the World Wide Web at: http://www.excelgov.org/egovpoll/report/contents.htm.

Heeks, R. (1999). *Reinventing Government in the Information Age. International Practice in IT-Enabled Public Sector Reform. Routledge.* Available on the World Wide Web at: http://www.man.ac.uk/idpm/rgiaintr.htm.

Hirst, P. and Norton, M. (1998). *Electronic Government. Information Technologies and the Citizen.* United Kingdom Parliament Parliamentary Office of Science and Technology (Rapporten kan hämtas i pdf-format på http://www.parliament.uk/post/egov.htm).

Henriksson, S. (1995). Datapolitikens död och återkomst. I Infrastruktur för IT-samhället. Nutek rapport B 1.

High-Level Group. (1994). Europe and the global information society: Recommendations to the European Council. ("Bangemannrapporten). *ISPO. High-Level Group on the Information Society*, Bryssel, 26/5. Available on the World Wide Web at: http://www.ispo.cec.be/infosoc/backg/bangeman.html.

Hoffman, L. J. and Cranor, L. (2001). Introduction. *Comunications of the ACM*, January, 69.

Holst. (2000). Teldoks årsbok 2000. Teldok rapport 130.

IT-kommissionen. (2000). Bakgrund. IT-kommissionen 1994-1998. Available on the World Wide Web at: http://www.itkommissionen.se/om/om_bakgrund.html.

ITA. (1999). *Electronic Government--A Link Collection*. Institute of Technology Assessment. Epriwatch project. Available on the World Wide Web at: http://www.oeaw.ac.at/~ita/ebene5/e2-2a18a.htm.

ITLC. (2000). Public sees Internet as a positive force in negotiating the Web of Government, new poll finds. Americans Overwhelmingly Support "E-government," View It As Way to Get More Involved and Better Informed. *Intergovernmental Technology Leadership Consortium*, September. Available on the World Wide Web at: http://www.excelgov.org/techcon/media/pr9_28.htm.

Knight, W. (2000). Shut Amazon down, say privacy groups. *ZD Net UKNews*, December. Available on the World Wide Web at: http://cgi.zdnet.com/slink?68648:14772373.

Latour, B. (1987). *Science in Action: How to Follow Scientists and Engineers Through Society*. Cambridge, Mass.: Harvard University Press

Latour, B. (1999). *Pandora's Hope. Essays on the Reality of Science Studies*. Cambridge, MA: Harvard University Press.

Lejon, B. (2000). En IT-politik för medborgarna. *Dagens Förvaltning. Statskontoret 2000*. Available on the World Wide Web at: http://www.dagensforvaltning.net/artiklar/1122.shtml.

Lenk, K. and Traunmuller, R. (2000). Perspectives on electronic government. In Galindo, F. and Quirchmayr, G. (Eds.), *Advances in Electronic Government. Proceedings of IFIP WG 8.5 Working Conference on Electronic Government*, February 10-11. Faculty of Law, University of Zaragoza, Spain.

Lepola, K. (2000). *Kalix. E-Demokrati Webbarkiv*. Available on the World Wide Web at: http://www.mail-archive.com/e-demokrati@mailinglist.statskontoret.se/.

Liljenäs, I., Grönlund, Å., Brandt, D. and Wiberg, M. (2000). IT i statlig verksamhet–ett medel för landsbygdens utveckling–en fråga om centralisering eller decentralisering? Kfb och institutionen för informatik, Umeå universitet.

Lowenberg, R. (2000). Presentation at the First Global Congress on Community Networking (http://www.cnglobal2000.org/). Citerat från [CI]: Community Networks: The Oxford.

Nilsson Sträng, O. (2000). Telephone Interview. October 15.

Manjoo, F. (2000). Pay those fines online. *Wired News*. Available on the World Wide Web at: http://www.wired.com/news/business/0,1367,38336,00.html.

Marklund, C. (2000). Första SHS-systemen i drift. Öppna system, nr 4/2000, s 25. Stockholm: Statskontoret.

Matthews, C. (2000). *The EU's Lisbon Summit: Gearing Up for the Knowledge Economy*. Available on the World Wide Web at: http://www.ebizchronicle.com/columns/march/chrismatthrew_eeurope.htm. Christopher Matthews är Press Officer and Editor of Eurecom, European Commission (New York)

Mohen, J. and Glidden, J. (2001) The case for Internet voting. *Comunications of the ACM*, January, 72

Molin, B., Månsson, L. and Strömberg, L. (1975). *Offentlig Förvaltning*. Bonniers.

Näringsdepartementet. (1999a). Ett informationssamhälle för alla. Proposition 1999/2000:86. Available on the World Wide Web at: http://www.naring.regeringen.se/fragor/it/lasmer.htm#Informationssamhälle.

Näringsdepartementet. (1999b). Mål och handlingsprogram för IT-politiken. Available on the World Wide Web at: http://www.naring.regeringen.se/fragor/it/handlprog.htm#Prioriteradeområden.

NIST. (1996) United States National Information Infrastructure Virtual Library. NIST, National Institute of Standards and Technology. Available on the World Wide Web at: http://nii.nist.gov/.

NPR. (2000). Conversations with America. *National Performance Review*. Available on the World Wide Web at: http://www.npr.gov/converse/conversa.html.

NZ. (2000). E-Government-A Vision for New Zealanders. E-government Unit of the State Services Commission. Available on the World Wide Web at: http://www.govt.nz/evision/index.php3.

Olofsson, M. (2000). Personlig kommunikation, February. Mats Olofsson är ledarskribent på Västerbottens Kuriren. Available on the World Wide Web at: http://www.vk.se.

Oracle. (2000). *Electronic Government Brochure*. Available on the World Wide Web at: http://e-gov.uk.oracle.com/government/html/gov.html.

Orsak, B. (2001). Do non-profit privacy watchdogs work? *Silicon Alley Daily*. Available on the World Wide Web at: http://www.siliconalleydaily.com/issues/sar02282000.html#Headline3302.

Östberg, O., Clift, S., Götze, J., Logan, G. W. and Richard, E. (1999). Democracy and Government On-Line Services. Contributions from Public Administrations Around the World. *G8 Government Online*. Available on the World Wide Web at: http://www.statskontoret.se/gol-democracy/.

Pardo, T. A. (2000). *Realizing the Promise of Digital Government: It's More than Building a Web Site*. Center for Technology in Government (CTG), University at Albany, State University of New York. Available on the World Wide Web at: http://www.cisp.org/imp/october_2000/10_00pardo.htm.

Phillips, D. (2000). Is Internet voting fair? *Network World*, June. Available on the World Wide Web at: http://www.nwfusion.com/columnists/2000/0626faceno.html.

Phillips, D., Spakovsky, H. (2001). Gauging the risks of Internet elections. *Comunications of the ACM*, January, 69.

Resnick, P., Zeckhauser, R., Friedman, E. and Kuwabara, K. (2000). Reputation systems. *Communications of the ACM*, December, 45-48.

Ranerup, A. (1999). Internet-enabled applications for local government democratisation. Contradictions of the Swedish experience. In Heeks, R. (Ed.), *Reinventing Government in the Information Age. International Practice in IT-Enabled Public Sector Reform*, 77-193. London and New York: Routledge.

Ranerup, A. (2001) Elektroniska mötesplatser för kommunal debatt. In Grönlund, Å and Ranerup, A. (Eds.), *Elektronisk Förvaltning, Elektronisk Demokrati–Visioner, Verklighet, Vidareutveckling*. Lund: Studentlitteratur.

*Rh*eingold, H. (1993). *The Virtual Community: Homesteading on the Electronic Frontier*. HarperPerennial. Available on the World Wide Web at: http://www.monterey.edu/academic/centers/sbsc/sbsc310b/chapter-list.html.

Schuler, D. (1996). *New Community Networks–Wired for Change*. Addison-Wesley

Snellen, I. (2001). ICT:s, bureaucracies and the future of democracy. *Communications of the ACM*, January.

Toppledarforum. (1995). *Lexit Förstudie.Datainspektionen*.

Toppledarforum. (1995b) Gemensamma IT-plattformar för informationsutbyte. Riksförsäkringsverket.

Toppledarforum. (2000). Toppledarforum -En informell samverkansgrupp för förnyelse av offentlig förvaltning med stöd av IT. Available on the World Wide Web at: http://

toppled.nutek.se/omtop.html.

Watson, R., Akselsen, S., Evjemo, B. and Aasaether, N. (1999) Teledemocracy in local government. *Communications of the ACM*, December, 58-63.

West, D. M. (2000). *Assessing E-Government: The Internet, Democracy, and Service Delivery by State and Federal Governments.* Available on the World Wide Web at: http://www.insidepolitics.org/egovtreport00.html.

Chapter III

Post-Modern
Decision Making

Lars-Erik Janlert
Umeå University, Sweden

The modern ideals for decision and action are hard pressed by doubts on their continued validity and by new difficulties in their implementation that emerge just as old difficulties seem to become more tractable. Here I present some questions and reflections on problems and possibilities when the information technological conditions are changed while at the same time modern values are called in question.

MODERN IDEALS FOR DECISION AND ACTION ARE HARD PRESSED BY DOUBTS ON THEIR CONTINUED VALIDITY

The modern[1] ideal for decision and action is well known. In short, the procedure is to map out the facts of the matter, make rational deliberations (reasoning, arguing) and choices, do the required problem solving, create an optimal plan and execute the plan. *Savoir pour prévoir pour pouvoir*. The paradigm for this is the Project. You set up a goal, create a plan to reach the goal and execute the plan. Characteristically, these three stages are separated in time and performed by different categories of people.

From the very beginning many difficulties are associated with this ideal. People do not follow the plan; they misunderstand, they are careless, they cheat, they reinterpret the instructions to suit their own purpose. On the other hand, the plan is never exact enough to be able to work if followed to the letter. To be completely rational puts so high a demand on information collection, reasoning and deliberation that the methods we in practice can afford and have time to use are unacceptable, with the result that it appears unreasonable (irrational) to be completely rational. The project organization—hierarchy, total central control—prevents individuals from exercising and developing their individual rationality; people are misused and the process is suboptimal in terms of human resources. Specializing and division of labor to perform complex tasks (projects) lead to increasing myopia, even for management: what should one take on responsibility for, which facts should be considered, what should be the goals? Local optimization leads to global suboptimization. So-called quality assurance is not about ensuring optimal or even high quality of the result, but about being able to guarantee a highly predictable result (which, in accordance with the theory of quality assurance, should have the lowest quality possible without becoming unacceptable to the customer). An historical example that makes one think is the plan-ruled security work in Stalin's Soviet: each department had to fill (or better, surpass) its centrally allotted quotient of spies and traitors to search out and "disclose" for each period.

Doubts about the continued validity of the modern era's model for decision and action have grown stronger in the 20th century. These ideals may have been fitting for the industrial society, but now (the argument goes) we are entering a new type of society, the information society. Old (that is, modern) ideals of uniformity and predictability are replaced by originality and creativity. Partly it is a matter of an inherent, slowly self-destructive process. Rationality undermines values by weakening the irrational carriers of values, such as religion, heredity, tradition, family, so that eventually irrationality results— since without values reason makes no move. The only values left belong to irrational forces and agents, some of them evil, whose instrument the rational human becomes. Rationality breaks the spell Man has been under, but turns him into a zombie, a tool for the irrational. The postmodern zeitgeist is now telling us—"yes, wasn't it silly to think that pure ratiocination would bring us the good life and the good society? After all, science and rationality is just one perspective among many others, equally valid." Yet, one has to admit that the modernization project by and large has managed to reach its goal. Rationality and the modern project methodology was intended as instruments of freedom, a way of making life better and easier, to escape being worn down and being able to sit in peace and quiet, angling and reading some poetry. But the discipline and the habit of working in project form created a lifestyle that is hard to give up and to find good alternatives to. To fish for pleasure and read poems full time is not quite as alluring any more. Freedom from work has in the late industrial and postindustrial society become a source of anxiety.

NEW DIFFICULTIES IN THEIR APPLICATION EMERGE JUST AS SOME OF THE OLD DIFFICULTIES SEEM TO BECOME MORE TRACTABLE

Some old difficulties with the modern model become more manageable through the new information technology which obviously now plays a driving and paradigmatic role for the growing information society similar to the role played by mechanical and chemical technology in the industrial society. With programming, the gap between plan and execution is bridged. As it is programmed, so it will be. It is easier to make programs cooperate than human beings. Specifically, this improvement applies to "industrialized decisions," that is, decisions made automatically through regulation, formalization, bureaucratization, as a standardizing of "manual," "craftsmanlike" decisions, strongly shaped and tied to time, place and person, in analogy with how industrial machine production superseded manual machine making. Decisions in principle, as for instance laws and ordinances can be considered as a method of mass-producing decisions. When projects are turned into programs, people are no longer thwarted in the projects. Also, the rational procedures become more and more feasible to carry through with the help of the new information technology and its enormous capacity for collecting and processing information. More specific applications give more specific examples of how new information technology can solve old problems. For the methods for deliberation and decision that we call democracy, we may note that many obstacles of a technical nature—e.g., for direct democracy and routine use of referendums—now in principle have been removed. Increased transparency in the forming and the execution of decisions, as well as in the compliance of execution with decision, is feasible.

But information society also brings *new* difficulties for the predominant industrial model for decision and action. The strong increase of pace and volume are two of the more obvious consequences. Traditional planning and steering processes cannot keep pace with the speeded up core activities. The project is outdated and needs major remodeling halfway through or even before it gets started. One example is education. A one-time effort is no longer sufficient to last a lifetime—"life-long learning" has become a necessity. In certain areas the development is so fast that there are problems to deliver an education that is not already obsolete when the students are finished. There is more and more information to consider, leading to information overload. The demands for well-informed decisions and actions become a heavy burden when distributed to the individual. There are more and more specific plans and more explicit decisions to make all the time. Nothing is a matter of routine much longer, because if it is, it will be advantageous to let information technology take over and do it. We get a seemingly more event-driven, unstable and chaotic world. The complex decision and executive structure leads to poor traceability, resulting in the present indistinct-ness and obscurity as to where the operative decisions really are made. The recess of the major ideologies has left the field open for many small and shifting opportunistic ideologies, local, temporary, with a more complex structure. Simultaneously, conspiracy theories flourish, reflecting a wish for simple solutions as well as the increasing virtualization and in its wake the increasing difficulties to convincingly prove that the plot does *not* exist.

It is clear that the new information technology, "IT," is playing a prominent part in these changes. Can it also solve or help to elude some of the *new* problems that it creates (or at least is associated with)? What can be done using information technology to manage, alleviate or evade the difficulties that are at least partially caused by information technology itself?

PROBLEMS AND POSSIBILITIES WITH DEMOCRATIC PROCESSES WHEN THE TECHNICAL CONDITIONS CHANGE

As an important special case that also should give some insights into the more general problem, let us consider democratic decision processes. For this purpose, the simple model depicted in Diagram 1 is used. Here, the box marked P denotes the rules, the directives, the procedures decided upon—while M denotes the members of the body in which decisions ultimately are grounded, and (let us suppose) which also constitute the body of individuals that in principle can be directly affected by the decisions. Let it be open where this is on a scale ranging from direct to representative democracy. Note also the relative independence of the size of the body. Of course, additional requirements on the nature of P, the establishment of P and the application of P are needed to narrow this down to what anyone would want to call "democracy." If we restrict the discussion to the component of insight and understanding, leaving influence and participation aside, we can identify four points (the first three of which are marked in the diagram) where IT gives new or substantially improved possibilities. These concern insight into and understanding of:

A   which the rules, the procedures decided upon, etc. *are* (P)
B   if and how the rules are *followed*
C   if and how rules are *made* and *changed* in the "right way"
D   the *effect*, the outcome of the rules, the result P will have in different cases, under different conditions, contexts, situations, etc.

Concerning A. Storage on computer media and network access together with search tools can improve insight into the rules. In principle, the technical possibilities to give high accessibility of collections and systems of rules have never been better than now.

Concerning B. Computerized inspection tools can make it easier to check that the rules are being followed: one can see *if* the rules are followed, *how* the rules are followed, and one can follow up the circumstances of individual cases in great detail. In principle, the technical possibilities to provide good traceability have never been better than now.

Concerning C. The same goes for checking that rules are made and changed in the proper manner, particularly when rule establishment and amendment is regulated in a similar manner—a reasonable requirement on a democratic system. The model should accordingly be complemented with yet another rule box, as in Diagram 2. (Corresponding arrows have been left out.) Yet another level might of course be introduced (an alternative would be to embed P' in P, but normally one would want to secure a greater inertia in P').

There is obviously a strong tendency to computerize and automate P and the application processes. One motive is better efficiency and economy (fewer bureaucrats), another motive is the increased precision and security already discussed. Computerization can achieve a degree of instrumental *clarity* and absence of ambiguity not possible before, but will most likely also lead to a procedural *complexity* that makes it very difficult to assess what P really means, what its practical consequences are. Add to that a frequently used tactic maneuver to solve or destabilize conflicts that now can be more easily justified: one deliberately complicates the procedures or introduces meta procedures that make the end effects less straightforward. This can be done either as a randomization to obscure the consequences for everybody (useful, for instance, in negotiations where the parties are completely deadlocked in the primary issue of conflict), or as a deliberate move to give the procedure engineer a head start in judging consequences. Generally it does not even have to be very complicated; compare, e.g., Condorcet's paradox and the manipulation of voting order. (There may also be a connection to *deniability*: under the cover of complexity, a representative can more readily depart from the interests he is supposed to represent, by claiming that he was unable to see the final outcome.) Of course, a computer program can be made *enormously* more complicated than written rule systems for bureaucratic handling. More complex procedures are on the other hand obviously an important advantage when being used to achieve greater flexibility. Paradoxically, this perfection of the industrial model of decision making can lead to more flexible, more contextually dependent outcomes. No individual outcome is completely like any other, although the principles remain strictly the same.

The increased difficulty of comprehending programmed procedures seems to imply that some of the gains won with regard to points A, B and C are lost. That makes it extra interesting to study what can be done about the fourth point, D (not marked in the diagram),

Diagram 1:

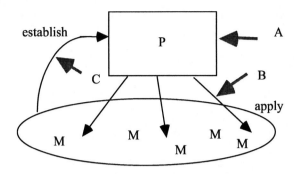

Diagram 2:

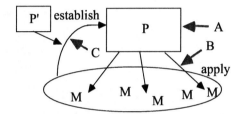

concerning insight into the consequences of P: what you really in effect *do* when you decide the content of P. The new information technology allows us to use interactive simulations, visualizations and virtualizations to study and experience effects—*before* decisions have been made (but also after, to inspect and supervise implementation in a more vivid and accessible manner, and to explore counterfactual possibilities). For example, one could interactively study what different breakpoints in a tax rate schedule would imply in terms of total revenue and tax load distribution, geographically, with regard to income bracket, different lines of trade, etc. Or, one could use a multimedia demonstration, a virtual simulation to give an *experience* of what a proposed expansion of the airport would involve for the residents of the neighboring housing estate.

Such an approach will clearly also introduce new problems. How can one convince oneself that a simulation really corresponds to a certain description, a certain theoretical model? And which are these theoretical models, and what confidence in their validity should one have? When something is explained or demonstrated through a simulation, there are no longer any immediate demands that the underlying theoretical model is simple enough to be understood with a moderate or reasonable cognitive effort (and hence be capable of convincing). There is also a temptation and sometimes an unavoidable technical necessity to add details and circumstances about which the underlying theory or description has nothing to say, thereby leading the decision process astray. As an example: computer-generated reconstruction of the chain of events at a crime or an accident has been used at courts in the USA, causing controversy. We may for instance have a situation where one witness says that the accused had the obtuse object in the hand, but cannot remember whether the left or the right hand. A visual reconstruction can hardly avoid putting the object either in the left or the right hand. One can imagine that such a simulated experience-based decision-making may lead to a new sort of argument or dialogue in which different programs, different computerized models are set against each other. Here, however, we are confronted with a new form of "rhetoric" that we lack experience of and consequently are in a weak position to critically evaluate. Speaking strongly in favor of an increased use of such methods is their obvious popular appeal, their "persuasive" character—who would not want to have a vivid interactive experience rather than to toil with dry, theoretical descriptions? A shift from a purely theoretically based decision making toward a more effect-based decision making is progress, but problematic progress.

Another interesting question is how to view a predictable development where the *citizen*, supported by information technology and the computerization of the rule systems, more actively strives to optimize his advantages and influence on the basis of the given system, rather than being kept within a negatively defined norm. (Companies have obviously long been operated in such an actively law-exploiting mode.) Existing rule systems are hardly designed for such conditions, and it seems that authorities and administrations are well aware that this is the case. One example is the Swedish tax authorities' refusal to give away their (in principle public) computerized tax models to the public.

THE TIME FACTOR: FLEXIBLE COMMITMENTS, CONTINUOUS DECISIONS AND INTERACTION

Tempo and volume are two important delimiting factors in decision-action processes which are deeply affected by the meeting between new technology and old values. New information technology makes the wheels turn faster in industry and society. New information technology helps to generate huge masses of information, expanding decision support indefinitely. The increased connectivity and velocity makes it necessary to take into account ever more remote events and developments. The influence of the surrounding world grows (at least) as the square of the distance to the information horizon. In the past, information about a distant event often reached us long before its concrete repercussions reached us, if indeed the event had power enough to reach that far. There was a margin, time to plan and make preparations. Today we note that the information about events taking place at the Tokyo stock exchange can have practically instant effects on decisions taken in Stockholm. The information has *in itself* become a cause, sometimes with devastating force. The event and the information of the event coincide, there is no gap giving us pause for consideration. Traditional steering processes, like democracy, with human participation and engagement in the heart of the process, will inevitably fail to keep up. The limitation is to be more precise twofold: flow and cycle time. The capacity is not enough; the number of decisions per minute that can be made is insufficient. The time it takes to make a particular decision is too long; the decision is not reached in time to affect the process it was designed to affect in the intended manner. Before even the collecting of the facts of the matter have been finished, while the decision makers are still trying to get a grip on the situation, something decisive will already have happened and conditions have changed radically. The situation we are facing is that existing decision processes are too slow and that a widespread participation in different decision-making processes takes too much time and effort.

What then is there to do when steering is too slow? I can see three main alternatives. First, the steering can be moved up to a meta level, where changes happen at a slower pace. In other words, human "manual" decision making is concentrated on the automated procedures, the programs that take care of the running decisions at a lower level. This is consequently yet a motive for automated decision making, the perfection of the industrial decision model. Second, one could try to somehow speed up the steering at the base level to match the speed of business and industry activities. Specifically this may appear incompatible with the democracy concept as we now know it, which seems to assume a certain thoughtfulness and reflection, time-consuming work to establish support for the idea, consensus-making, participation. The third, least appealing alternative for a person brought up in the industrial society's ideal of order and goal-direction is to give up. Let what happens happen and be content with trying to handle the outcome *post factum*, compensating and reducing the negative effects of the development in a sort of *reactive* as opposed to *proactive* steering.[2] In the last analysis this alternative may imply setting one's hope on some kind of "invisible hand" that in the long term will put things right and lead to, if not optimum, then to some reasonable degree of stability and "progress." The type of invisible hand that currently seems to be in fashion is that of evolution theory, in the generalized form brought forward by Richard Dawkins, Daniel Dennett and others, having its home within the new field of research called *artificial life*.

I will get back to some thoughts also about the second alternative, but first a precursory reflection on the significance of the increased tempo. Higher tempo leads to (more frequent) interaction, which together with cheaper and more easily undoable actions has the effect that the *decision* as a well-defined, substantial, quantum leap of commitment is beginning to dissolve. Old media demand finality for economical reasons. A printed book is a definitive end product for a traditional authoring process. Materially oriented activities put the same demands on finality. The newly built bridge over Öresund will not be torn down tomorrow just because someone has thought of an even better way to build it. The cost relative to the scope of the change is not just high, it is a step function. To even make a very small change is so expensive that you need to accumulate a number of proposed changes and construct a plan that can solve many of these problems at once before you can do anything at all. The initial cost of change sets the height of the steps, hence indirectly the time it takes to accumulate change requirements enough to economically reach up to the next step. Computer-supported media, however, encourage an incremental mode of working, in which version follows version in small steps without ever having to come to a well-defined finish. At the same time the information society brings with it, relatively speaking, a diminishing reliance on material conditions and resources. The accelerated tempo, the shortened lead-time from thought to result, the improved communication and the reduced cost of change serve to invite interaction and cut external pressure to finalize. Traditional one-way processes, part of very long cycles, with large granularity and inertia, tend to be replaced by two-way processes—that is, short interaction cycles with fine granularity opening for faster direction changes and more frequent branching.

As a consequence, also the decision as such is subject to the same interactive exposure, indefinitely extended possibilities to retract and fragmentation. When the finality of the *decision* processes is evaporating, you no longer can tell when it is safe to stop monitoring a particular issue. It seems that we are moving from well-defined decision points, clearly separated in time, to a more or less continuous control, continuous tug of war between conflicting interests. What is the price at this moment? Electronic price tags can change the price as you turn your back, just like the quotations on the digitized stock exchange. Which legislation, which contracts, which agreements are in force at this very moment? Conditional contracts and options appear to be bringing about a state of permanent non-commitment. The disappearance of the large decision points and their replacement with many small, tentative micro-decisions seems to lead in the direction of a merging of the decision process with the implementation: the separation between thought and action is annulled.

Naturally this instills some misgivings that reflection will cease and people will walk around in a constant state of *flow* without being bothered by having to "think." Hegel thought that human beings differ from the animals in their ability to arrest an impulse and reflect on it before it passes into action. The animal cannot interpose anything between an impulse and its satisfaction. This separation between thought and action fits perfectly with the decision-action model of the industrial society.[3] The more tentative and reversible our actions become, the more our thinking is externalized. An illustration is how the writing process changes in the shift from typewriter to word processor. Instead of mentally scrutinizing, walking through, sorting out and making comparative assessments of different formulations in your head, there is now the alternative of letting your fingers run over the keyboard, trying out and *observing* different alternatives, moving words about, etc.—in short, doing the thinking on the screen. In this manner—which is a little disquieting—our inner chaos is moved out into the world.

THE CATEGORICAL IMPERATIVE

The second alternative, speeding up the steering mechanisms, is hardly something that can be realized generally, but maybe we can find new, complementing methods that give some relief. Consider, to begin with, the difference between explicit and implicit methods. To vote on a proposal, to put forward a proposal, to provide arguments for a proposal, to give articulated criticism of a proposal, are some examples of explicit participation in a decision process. To choose product in the store, to join an interest group, to *not* cast one's vote in an election, are some examples of implicit methods of participation. Implicit methods characteristically save time and effort but lack nuances, are difficult to interpret and provide little information. Democracy and market can be taken as the two typical examples of explicit and implicit methods, respectively. The explicit method is articulated, information rich, allows creativity, but is time-consuming for the individual, and the decision process is separated from the processes decided about. The implicit method is obtuse, information poor, cannot go beyond the given frame of choices, but does not take (much) extra time for the individual, and the decision process is integrated with the normal activities.

When I pick an article from the shelf and put it in my cart, I also send a message to the store manager. The message is indistinct but can be interpreted as roughly saying, "I put my vote in favor of having this article in your store." I don't have to think about it but I am not altogether unaware. I can impossibly send the message that I vote for article x, also on the shelf, at the same time as I choose to put article y in my cart—a certain authenticity is inescapable. But what happens if my favorite brand is temporary out of stock, but I need coffee badly and so (reluctantly) pick y? I get frustrated, not just because I do not get the product I really want, but also because I am forced to send a misleading signal. Similarly if an article is taken out of the line. When the store manager drops my favorite brands x, y and z, it may be that my basic motivation for shopping in this particular store is gone, and I stop coming; the store manager will never know why. That kind of information does not get through with these methods. Neither can my shopping actions convey information that I am dissatisfied with an article (the least poor of the available choices) and have articulated criticism and ideas for improvement, that I wish a currently unavailable brand would be on the shelf; or that a completely new and non-existent article would win my approval.

Here is yet another example of implicit method, concerning the construction of walking paths in a new green area. One lays out the green area *without* any paths, waits a few weeks to see where tracks have formed spontaneously and then constructs the paved paths along these vestiges of human choice. The method has its limitations: hillocks and trees are not likely to go away in the process, there is an element of submission to the given conditions, whereas an explicitly planning approach can cut a straight line (blasting rocks and cutting trees). On the other hand, the method does not involve any noticeable extra effort on the part of the pedestrians and contains a very neat selection mechanism of who gets to decide (giving a new meaning to the notion of grassroots democracy). Note also, that this example contains elements of proposal, negotiation and compromise, in so far as the choice of walking direction is affected by visible marks left by earlier walkers. If the area is covered with snow, the effect will be more distinct—any rudiment of a path will offer considerably greater convenience than untouched ground. (There are at least two purposes to take into account: the path as offering more comfortable transport than the surrounding environment; the path as guiding the traveler to some destination.) Again, there is an appealing authenticity to the procedure: as you act so it will be (through some sort of weighted sum of the individual actions). Contrast that with cases such as the local railway line somewhere in the south of Sweden: with great majority it was decided to keep the line, but it turned out that none of the people wanting to keep it were actually willing to travel by train. The railroad cars traveled empty.

The new information technology opens new possibilities of using implicit methods much richer in information, on a grander scale and with more force in the individual footsteps. By well-chosen design of different environments, it is possible to elicit more information. We can vote with our feet, with our *actual actions* in a way never done before. Such methods, like other methods building on more complex analyses of human behavior, should be considered as a sometimes feasible alternative and complement to traditional market processes and democratic processes (and other implicit and explicit processes). But, it has to be action with a certain awareness of the communicative role of the action, to be able to count it as a decision-action method where the individual persons are *participatory* to the decisions. The individual has to be able to know the message emitted by different actions, in practice. For example, we are to some degree generally aware—even if we seldom have reason to explicitly *think* of it—that when we press the brake pedal we also send a message via the brake lights to the drivers behind: "Watch out, I'm braking." (Pressing so lightly on the brake that the brake lights light up without the car braking, or applying the handbrake to brake the car without turning on the brake lights is consequently deceitful conduct, and is so considered.)

There are certainly problems with such an implicit "direct democracy" (given that the particular process satisfies our other requirements of democracy). The quite detailed information about behavior such methods presuppose is sensitive: in wrong hands and used with wrong purpose, the result can be anything but democratic. On the World Wide Web, we can already find advanced attempts to get quite detailed information on individual user behavior. The purpose is of course to sell more. By itself this development is unlikely to give users possibility to become aware of the messages about themselves they are sending when they go clicking around the portals, or to give them greater influence on how this information is to be used. How can we protect ourselves against misuse? How can rightfulness of use be demonstrated? Who should be considered the proper "users" of a facility? It is hardly unambiguous even in the simple park example: those who never walk through the park but take pleasure in watching it from the street or from the window of their apartment. Those who do maintenance work like clearing snow. The question of "proper user" is complicated by the new information technology since user locality no longer coincides with time-space locality. What status should potential users have relative to actual users?

Finally, there is a moral aspect of such methods that is not self-evidently appealing or good. You cannot act without in a sense also expressing that you consider it appropriate to act in this way. As I do, one should do. When you exceed the speed limit it may at the same time entail and commit you to a vote for a raised speed limit. This will put new pressure on us: every step you take, each everyday action you do will have a most tangible moral meaning—think very carefully about what you do at all times! We have heard it before, certainly (by choosing to buy that carpet you will express your support for child labor), but here the moral implications and consequences of your actions suddenly take on a very concrete and indisputable meaning. One may speculate that the effect might be paralyzing and put people in a continuous state of anxiety. Another aspect of the matter is that there may be some advantages in having ideals that differ from reality. To pose as (including acts necessary to keep up the image) and to regard oneself as a better person than you really are can be an effective means both for yourself and for other people to *become* better. Too much authenticity may halt development.

ENDNOTES

1   *Modern* is here used for the line of development that started in the breakthrough of modern science in the 16th and 17th centuries, leading to the growth of industrialism that culminated somewhere in the middle of the 20th century. At this point the modernization project and its industrial society is being gradually phased out and relieved by a post-modern information society.

2   There seems to be a parallel with the discussion in consciousness research about the fact that in a human subject, consciousness about an action appears to come slightly *after* the actual initiating of the action (under certain conditions). At first blush this would seem devastating to the notion that our consciousness controls our actions, and support the infamous old theory that consciousness is just an *epiphenomenon*, as unimportant and irrelevant for the cognitive function of human beings as the heat generated by the electronics of a computer is for the computations going on. But belated consciousness about actions does not exclude the possibility that the after-the-fact consciousness about the action can have an important effect on other, *future* actions. This explanation points in the direction of *pre*conscious procedures on a lower level, adjustable by, controlled by (partly) conscious procedures at a higher level, in analogy with the above decision-action model employing a base level controlled by a meta level. This path takes us back to the first alternative again.

3   One comment about this is, again, that we should not disregard the possibility for *post factum* reflections and analyses that may change our way of thinking (and acting) and hence affect future decision and action. Hindsight has an undeservedly bad reputation, but it is not true that it is particularly *easy* to be wise after the event, if wisdom is something that affects our thinking and behavior.

Chapter IV

The Significance of Law and Knowledge for Electronic Government

Klaus Lenk
University of Oldenburg, Germany

Roland Traunmüller and Maria Wimmer
Linz University, Austria

THE WIDENING SCOPE OF E-GOVERNMENT

Governments at all levels--national, regional and local--are faced with growing demands to organize their work more efficiently and effectively. Moreover, a fundamental reassessment of their agendas has started world wide, which in many cases reduces the role which governments play in serving their societies. Government is considered as a cost factor in the first place, and it has to explicitly legitimize both its standing agenda and the take-up of new tasks. At the same time, it is recognized that public governance structures continue to be necessary to tackle many problems of an ever-changing world. Since newly emerging tasks will demand more and more attention, the existing governmental units are urged to accomplish their core business with only a part of the costs incurred at present.

The use of information technology already has a long tradition in the public sector (Lenk, 1998). Its deployment over more than four decades primarily benefited typical back office operations of a routine type. Less developed is the support of what we perceive as the core activity of public administration, i.e. policy implementation involving complex processes of negotiation and of decision making. These activities shape the business processes of public administration which are the main focus of our attention. To varying extents, these processes are shaped by legal provisions, often to the point that they are chiefly considered as "executing the law." Moreover, they draw on different assets of knowledge which are often situational and implicit. Such processes can only partly be automated, and they have to be carried out by qualified staff. Yet the challenge consists in supporting these activities with IT in innovative ways.

We feel that in the long run, e-Government will only be successful if its scope is widened so as to include all activities of public administration which can be supported by IT. So far, e-Government dealt with some highly visible aspects of the public sector only, in other words with the tip of an iceberg, whilst the hidden part of the iceberg (i.e., the manifold activities of public administration of a more complex nature) did not profit yet from the use of IT in a meaningful sense. In its present form, e-Government puts its focus on typical front office operations concerning the contact of administrative agencies with citizens. It brings about a new quality of citizen-state interaction, but in doing so it tacitly assumes that the back office part of transactions between public agencies and citizens primarily concerns routine processes in the field of service delivery like, e.g., granting drivers' licenses, registering vehicles, etc. Such processes do not exhibit the same level of complexity as administrative decisions which demand sophisticated human intervention.

This tip-of-the-iceberg approach misses the point. It ignores that the role of government is not only to provide services to citizens which could be provided by commercial firms as well. Beyond services in the narrow sense, government covers many processes which are different from the type of processes encountered in retailing, banking or other branches of the economy. Essentially, the difference is to be found at the level of the legal provisions which govern such processes, as well as in the knowledge which is required to make the decisions which are normally the result of the process. Such processes include:

- complex decision making, not only about policy questions but also with regard to operative matters;
- processes involving negotiations among various stakeholders about matters of public interest;
- processes of policy formulation (e.g., legislative processes) and democratic participation.

IT has a great potential to support such processes. In this contribution, we take our start from a view of public administration in which law enforcement and the regulation of society through policy implementation are constitutive factors, to a much greater extent than the delivery of public services to individuals. In this view, the role of law and knowledge in reaching administrative decisions has to be explicitly acknowledged.

We will start by drawing attention to the wide scope of activities of public administration, as well as to the fact that its activities depend on law and knowledge in characteristic ways. Then we will sketch a process model of administrative work and distinguish several basic types of processes. After addressing the problems related to knowledge management, we try to account for the relationship between the process and the results of decision making on one side, and law and knowledge on the other. Finally, we discuss specific problems of knowledge use and decision making related to the four basic process types.

THE SPECIFIC NATURE OF ADMINISTRATIVE ACTION

Starting from the famous expression coined by Wallace Sayre (Jann, 1998), we can say that "public and private management are fundamentally alike in all unimportant respects." The most important aspects which do make a difference are:
- the specific tasks of government,
- the role of law (normative aspects),
- the special significance of knowledge.

Breadth of Public Agendas

There are several matters that distinguish the public sector from private business. To begin with, the extraordinarily complex goal structure of public administration has to be underlined. Government, especially at the national level, is the highest authority to safeguard citizens' life, good and well-being. Public Administration has to guarantee (and enforce) a well-organized, structured and safe society as well as standards of quality of life within a common culture and society. Basic goals of its action include: proper functioning of legislation and jurisdiction, promotion of economic development, protection of principles of civic rights, preservation of nature, emergency management, etc. The goals to be attained are set politically, and they are partly rooted in the national constitution. They are often ambiguous and even in contradiction with other goals, yet public governance has to see to it that its actions do not encroach on rights and vested interests. There are many political demands which public administration has to execute faithfully, which often enough demands the ironing out of potentially contradictory requests made to it.

The Role of Law

Another specific aspect of the public sector has to do with the role of law. The traditional way of implementing political decisions and–at the same time–of observing standards of Rechtsstaat (rule of law) and public safety is legislation. Especially in continental Europe, public administrations are highly regulated by legislation which is enacted on national, regional and local levels. The legal structuring of administrative work has several functions. It can be seen both as a restricting and as a guiding force. In the concept of the Rechtsstaat, norms serve to protect basic freedoms of the citizenry from public interference. At the same time, legal norms are a standard vehicle of communication between government and executive agencies.

Legal norms may be strict and clear, leaving no leeway for interpretation. This is not the rule, however. Contrary to what many observers of European public administration believe, the binding force of many legal provisions is not very strong. Some legal texts do hardly more than communicate goals, which–within the scope of the legal order as a whole– may be attained through policies which the executive agencies are free to develop. Norms may also serve as guidelines, indicating aspects which have to be considered in discretionary decision making. It goes without saying that many micro-political aspects of administrative behavior contribute to determining the outcome of complex processes of decision making. Neither the procedural nor the material law fully determine outcomes.

Knowledge

With regard to complex decision making, knowledge is of particular importance to government. We will less insist on those types of knowledge which are a prerequisite for the internal managing of administrative processes. Management Information Systems is not our prime concern. Rather we will focus on those types of knowledge which are of relevance to the core business of the executive branch of government, i.e., knowledge on which administrative decision making at the operative level normally draws:

- legal knowledge;
- knowledge of the facts given in a special case to be decided upon;
- knowledge about the means for action, which government has at its disposal;
- knowledge about the effectiveness of various measures;
- a "process memory" (Menne-Haritz, 1999) which is gradually built up while working on a decision case.

With regard to these types of knowledge, specific requirements for knowledge management arise. So far, knowledge management is mainly discussed with regard to business environments where knowledge is of importance for promoting innovation. By contrast, we will consider knowledge from the perspective of administrative action. Yet before doing so, deeper insight into the specific features of administrative processes has to be gained.

A BASIC MODEL OF ADMINISTRATIVE PROCESSES

Both, the role of the law and special features of information and knowledge have to be dealt with in the light of what we identified as the core task of public administration, i.e., decision making in non-routine cases. Such decision making exhibits a big variety, according to the complexity and to the circumstances of both the policies at stake and the individual case. This does not mean that it is not possible to construct a basic process model of administrative action. We have developed a process model proper to public administration. It tries to combine two views (Lenk and Traunmüller, 1999, p. 55ff): On one hand, processes can be seen as production processes which obviously is a perspective owing much to Workflow Management Systems (WFMS). On the other hand, there is a decision-making view. It draws on two sources: the classical account of administrative behavior by Herbert Simon (1957) and administrative procedure as it is conceptualized in procedural legislation (e.g., the U.S. [Federal] Administrative Procedure Act or the German Verwaltungsverfahrensgesetze).

Stages in the Administration's Decision Process

Combining the production and decision-making process views, we start from the following process elements:
1.   observing;
2.   thinking (planning, taking decisions);
3.   executing.

Taking a closer look, one can identify the following schema of steps. We will sketch the basic pattern only; more details are in given in Lenk and Traunmüller (1999). The stages are:

- *Observation and Information*: Information has to be gathered from various sources. The behavior of the society or a group of citizens are observed. Such observations can be made for specific purposes (e.g., by the police authority) or for general planning purposes.
- *Substantiating Facts*: The material gained from such observations is evaluated in the light of legal and policy premises. In this way, a "case" is constituted.
- *Decision to Act*: When enough material is collected and combined with the facts, administrators have to make a decision for action.
- *Intervention*: In a typical administrative act, the results of the decision-making process are simply communicated to the addressee. But physical-technical actions can occur as well, such as arresting a person, paying a sum of money, setting up roadblocks, closing of a bridge.
- *Execution*: If some addressees do not comply with the orders, an execution of the order may become necessary. A common example is the forcible way of tax collection.

- *Evaluation*: In the last step it has to be checked whether the action taken had the intended effect concerning the influence on the society. The results of this evaluation should be used for improving both administrative decision making and the rules guiding it.

A closer consideration of the stages listed above underlines the prominent role of information and knowledge. Physical action plays only a minor role. Moreover, the information entering administrative action has a pronounced reflexive character. Every observation made during a process will not only be introduced in the puzzle game of reaching a decision or an agreement, but it will at the same time change the entire texture of the contextual knowledge of the individuals working on the case and hence also of the organization itself. This creates a reflexive memory of the process which is important for the management of this process. Moreover, the result will not be lost with the process coming to an end. It contributes to the gradual constitution of a "domain knowledge"–Dienstwissen, as Max Weber called it in his studies on bureaucracy. This is perhaps the most important source of administrative knowledge to be dealt with in respect to knowledge management.

Limits of the Process Model

Our process model abstracts from many aspects which are quite important in administrative practice:

- Processes are often not isolated but part of a standing relationship between an agency and citizens.
- Processes involve cooperation among actors and with stakeholders in the field to be regulated. Such cooperation often transgresses organizational boundaries.
- Many processes are distributed onto several agencies or institutions for reasons of balancing the use of public power. So, the agencies involved (e.g., police, prosecutors, judges and probation officers) have their own way of thinking and action, and will follow a logic of their own.
- The knowledge aspect is somewhat under-addressed in process thinking. Many observing and information-gathering activities take place without producing tangible results. The collected pieces of information may not be used directly, but these may contribute to organizational learning within an agency. Conversely, actions can be taken without any external information coming in.

Types of Processes

In the field of operational administrative action, a huge variety of different processes can be encountered. A tension exists between fully structured production processes and complex decision processes. Most actual processes fall in between these two extremes. Yet, numerous cases exist where at the moment when a process starts, it is far from clear how complex it will eventually become. Since the later stages cannot be anticipated, such processes will lose much of their quality if they are subjected to strictly defined Workflow Management Systems.

Although many ways exist in which different agencies make their distinct interventions into the social fabric (using regulations, services, transfers, etc.), we use a very coarse-grained distinction of administrative processes:

a) Recurrent and well-structured processes.
b) Processing of cases: individualized decision making.
c) Negotiation processes.
d) Weakly structured processes in the field of policy making including democratic deliberation.

This distinction again emphasizes the difference between "production processes" where almost no choices are to be made and which can often be fully automated, and decision processes which can at best be partly standardized.

Well-Structured Processes

Many recurrent processes are legally controlled in a strict way and formalized to a large extent. They are characterized by a continuous repetition of mostly homogeneous operation steps and give only minor discretion to the persons in charge of each step. An example is the grant of an unemployment benefit:

A citizen applies for unemployment benefit. Her personal data are recorded and her personal job qualification is coded by means of given categories. After completion the data are checked for comprehensiveness. The data include items such as: reasons of unemployment; availability for jobs and constraints (for example care of a child); national insurance identity card and tax card; certificates obtained after prior employment; proof of former employment (when appropriate); entitlements to social benefits of other types. Then, these data are passed on to the service department for executing benefit payment. The service department checks all the data and calculates the unemployment payment. The process ends with the sending of an official statement to the person in question and simultaneously executing the payment order.

From a process point of view, such highly standardized processes may involve several authorities or offices, yet the decision to be taken rests on relatively clear and unambiguous legal grounding.

Individualized Decision Making

Next to the standard processes, one may find processes that are characterized by a high degree of communication with the citizen and by the need to take special situations into account. Typical for individualized case processing is an intense interaction with stakeholders which at the beginning is often not foreseeable in detail. A further characteristic is that the situation can be very complex on factual or legal grounds. The case of a highly indebted single parent asking for social welfare may serve as an example:

A citizen comes to the Social Security office in order to apply for aid supporting the living for herself and her child. In checking the data it becomes evident to the official in charge that more serious problems are looming. This case reveals an unlucky pattern of situations: high debts, threatening loss of housing, water and gas disconnection, problems concerning the upbringing of the child, etc. To solve the acute problem situation means to start several procedures providing help simultaneously. Social aid for living is paid according to the common standards. Yet in other respects, swift action is necessary. This might result in a direct payment to the water and gas supply enterprise. The next step will bring the co-ordination of all necessary measures and services such as granting rent subsidy, assistance in dealing with the threatening flat loss, bringing in a debtor-counseling person, applying for social-pedagogic aids for the child.

Negotiation Processes

Turning to the next process type, we find public administration in a position where it has to combine its traditional role with an involvement in a complex situation. This is an overlapping area between enforcing the law and cooperating with their environment. The classical model of executing the law has to be amended in order to take negotiations into account (Rossen, 1999). To bring negotiation in implies a reasonable amount of discretionary power of the decision maker. But in many instances, it is no longer clear whether a central decision maker with the prerogative of the public power still exists. We give an example in the field of the school administration concerning admission to a primary school.

> *When parents enroll their child in the primary school, the child is examined medically. The medical expert's opinion is then routed to the management of the primary school and might, in some cases, lead to the recommendation (based on medical arguments) to postpone school visit of the child for one year. The school head has discretionary power to follow the expert's opinion and to postpone the child's education for one year. Yet in case of disagreement, parents may bring other medical expert opinions that have to be heard in this case. Although the final decision is with the school headmaster, an intense negotiation process will precede involving parents, medical experts and the school management which strongly influences the final decision.*

Still other negotiation processes may be characterized by features typical of bargaining processes or by sophisticated problems of interpretation.

Weakly Structured Processes in the Field of Policy Making

Policy making and its complex processes represent a special case of weakly structured processing. We feel that such processes present a particular challenge for e-Government and that research on their characteristics is very urgent. Examples are bills of parliament, answers to parliamentary inquiries or complex political decisions. Particularly on the level of ministries, cooperative decision processes are common and extensive. The IT support of non-structured decision processes is only starting, yet promising experiences can be cited. The Information Network Berlin-Bonn (Informationsverbund Berlin-Bonn, IVBB) (Kooperationsausschuss ADV, 1997) is an important case where cooperation at the ministerial level is supported, bridging the distance between Bonn and Berlin. Here, the main concern is the ability to perform work at two government sites (Aden and Gora, 1999). The first outcomes of the IVBB are encouraging and show a wide spectrum of possible applications in the field of CSCW (Computer Supported Cooperative Work).

The negotiated character of policy making permeates all phases of the policy process. It is perhaps not so visible in early phases of policy making like information collection and analysis. During these phases, divergence of interests and positions do not yet reveal themselves very clearly. On the other hand, agreeing on some kind of information and demarcating the search space for further information may pre-empt substantial decision-making which characterizes the ensuing phases of agreeing on some policy and of implementing it.

Most important to policy making activities are meetings. In order to reach adequate support environments, one has to blend conventional data and decision support with collaborative functions. In this way, a set of highly-modular components may be established to handle particular tasks which provides all kinds of knowledge as required and in adequate form. This gives us the catchword for the following discussion on the role of knowledge in administrative action.

KNOWLEDGE AS BASIS OF
ADMINISTRATIVE ACTION

In order to make explicit the special problems which e-Government has to face with regard to the core decision-making functions of public administration, we have start with the characteristics and various forms of administrative knowledge.

What Is Knowledge?

Contrary to many authors–especially in the wake of Artificial Intelligence–we use the term "knowledge" in a narrow sense. In our view, it designates information which is stored in human minds where it is embedded in an already existing context of knowledge. Transforming information into knowledge means that incoming flows of messages and meaning are transformed by amalgamation with the beliefs and commitments of its holder. At first glance, such a narrow definition may make it difficult to account for many aspects of organizational culture and of standard operating procedures which work because shared knowledge of the persons in charge underlies their attitudes and activities. Therefore, we have to stress the huge part of implicit knowledge which human beings hold (Nonaka and Takeuchi, 1995). It is acquired through education, acculturation, experiences or in work practice. Much knowledge acquired on the job (we mentioned "Dienstwissen") is in fact implicit. It is complementing explicit knowledge. While the latter can be passed on in spoken or written language, the information derived from implicit knowledge is passed on on the job and in informal (and non-verbal) ways.

With such a narrow definition, we have to extend the use of "knowledge" in two ways; in order to account for the role of organization and to understand the role of artifacts in human activities:

a)   Strictly spoken, sharing implicit knowledge would not be possible since it is only the underlying information which is transmitted among people. But in a metaphorical sense, we may well talk about organizational knowledge in the sense of pointing to similar or congruent knowledge contents and to similar and congruent beliefs and commitments of their holders. Common culture engenders these similarities. In their efforts to make sense together, people rely on tacit background knowledge which is rooted in socially sanctioned facts of life that anyone knows.

b)   When it comes to activities performed on the basis of knowledge, artifacts often play an important role. Especially when shaped through conscious human labor (e.g., a hammer instead of a raw stone to hit something), they are "informatized" in the sense that they embody the knowledge of the person who made it. Thus, in another metaphorical sense we could say that artifacts embody knowledge as it is seen in Distributed Cognition theory (cf. Cole, 1998; Hutchins, 1995; Nardi, 1995). In the case of a book, beside its role as a storage device for information, we also find the embodied knowledge of generations of book authors and publishers about the way in which books are commonly used. This makes it easier for readers to assimilate the information stored explicitly in the book to their own context of beliefs and commitments.

Administrations Seen as Knowledge Networks

Regarding public administrations as "knowledge networks" is one way of approaching the question of how the knowledge which its individual members detain can be "shared" and brought to bear on problems to be solved and complex decisions to be made. This is more than an expanding demand for information. The idea of a network suggests a qualitative increase and intensification of relevant knowledge. This is particularly the case with regard to introducing tele-cooperation into an organization. Changing the patterns of cooperation is tantamount to changing the distribution of knowledge. The common stock of knowledge is important, because any cooperation presupposes a satisfactory level of commonality (terminology, world views, shared basic understanding of the subject matter at stake). Any redistribution of knowledge must be designed and orchestrated with intent, and managing knowledge becomes a major responsibility for administrators.

Knowledge and the Particular Case of Public Administration

Since knowledge like any other scarce resource should be managed, knowledge management has become an important issue. Several different tasks are commonly included in the management of knowledge: gathering and maintaining of knowledge, preparing and integrating knowledge as well as making use and searching for it. For the general topic of knowledge management in enterprises, we refer to the extensive literature on knowledge management (e.g., Abecker et al., 1998; Probst et al, 1996; Rehäuser and Krcmar, 1996; Roithmayr and Fink, 1997; Schreyögg and Conrad, 1996). Particular treatment on technical support is presented in Borghoff and Pareschi (1998) and Ortner (2000). We will not discuss this body of knowledge here. Suffice it to say that most of the literature on knowledge management is concentrating on typical business problems, most prominently accelerating the rate of (process and product) innovations in a firm. From what we have discussed above, it appears, however, that in building e-Government, additional questions arise.

Some features which are of particular prominence with regard to public administrations have already been addressed: a highly complex target structure, a great variety of tasks, the role of legal regulations shaping structures and processes. In the public sector, however, no tradition exists yet to consider knowledge management as a distinct activity. What is managed so far are information sources: libraries, archives, data banks. The ways in which individual decision makers or groups access these sources and interpret the contents so as to transform their own knowledge is in most circumstances not yet seen as something which can be managed.

The knowledge of decision makers can be considerably improved by large if they could command easy access to information repositories of different types in function of their respective needs. If at the moment of a query, information sources are easily organized into patterns which suit the decision problem at hand, much would be gained in terms of speeding up the process and performing it in a very conscious way. Decision makers tend to use such information which they can easily retrieve in their office instead of operating time-consuming searches in libraries or archives (Bing and Trygve, 1977). This is of particular importance to legal information. But so far, legal documentation is not of great help in this respect. It is organized following types of legal sources and it is left to the decision maker to deduce the applicable norms through interpretation processes which, sometimes, have to take into account many sources. Also, in general, the first steps of reasoning of decision makers concern the search of cases which present similarities. This type of search is even less supported, although proposals in this sense have been put forward very early (Haft, 1973).

Another type of knowledge is gradually built up during a decision process (Menne-Haritz, 1999). A process history grows progressively. It is the continuous choices exerted by decision makers as to the further procedure to be followed which commands both factual and legal information to be accessed and interpreted so as to become case-related knowledge.

THE FUTURE CHALLENGE OF E-GOVERNMENT: KNOWLEDGE AND DECISION MAKING IN A COOPERATIVE ENVIRONMENT

Having discussed both the typical processes in the field of public administration and some of the specific aspects of knowledge relevant for these processes, we will now turn to the problems which have to do with the role of law and knowledge for administrative decision making. Administrative decision making exhibits characteristics which depart from well-structured bureaucratic production processes. In the latter, interpretation of the law plays only a minor role while in a typical decision process, legal premises and knowledge holdings are brought together in ways which often defy their structuring beforehand. The legal premises are themselves objects of knowledge which apply to both the decision content and the process structure in which the decision-making processes evolve.

There is a hard-to-define relationship between law, facts of the case (or a wider "problematique"), knowledge about law and facts, and decision making. This relationship has to be clarified either by a single decision-maker or in a cooperative act: knowledge and law strongly shape the decision and the process in which the decision is reached. Also, co-operative patterns may be of importance if the decision is not taken by a single actor. We account for this complicated situation through the scheme depicted in Figure 1.

In the scheme, well-structured activities which resemble production processes are listed left while the totally unstructured processes and unconstrained decision making are found on the right side. Interestingly, both the right and the left extremes can also be found in private business environments, while the middle ground describes the field where the special characteristics of government loom largest. It is here that the law has a strong impact and that special types of knowledge have to be drawn upon.

The various process types identified above exhibit certain characteristics with regard to the knowledge required in carrying them out. We will not deal exhaustively with all types of knowledge of some relevance for service provision and for administrative and democratic decision making. Rather, we will highlight some typical coincidences. The use of knowledge depends on the type of process. So, typical problems arising in the context of knowledge management and corresponding to the four types of processes are listed in Table 1.

Information and Knowledge Aspects of Well-Structured Processes

The relevant information for well-structured and recurrent production processes is readily available. Much of it can easily be mapped onto electronic media in a similar way as in concepts and solutions used in e-commerce. The legal knowledge required is embodied in automated procedures or expert systems. Therefore, in the back-office part of the processes, human implicit knowledge (know-how) is of less importance. More important is fresh knowledge about the facts of a case which can be gleaned in interaction with citizens

Figure 1: Administrative actions and their relation of knowledge, process, law and cooperation

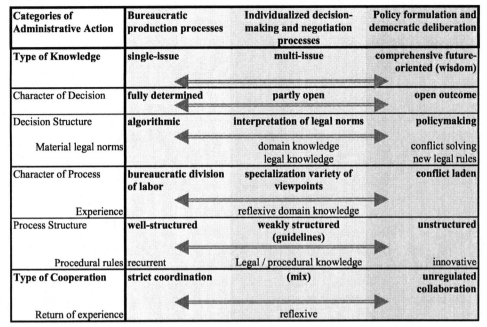

Categories of Administrative Action	Bureaucratic production processes	Individualized decision-making and negotiation processes	Policy formulation and democratic deliberation
Type of Knowledge	single-issue	multi-issue	comprehensive future-oriented (wisdom)
Character of Decision	fully determined	partly open	open outcome
Decision Structure	algorithmic	interpretation of legal norms	policymaking
Material legal norms		domain knowledge legal knowledge	conflict solving new legal rules
Character of Process	bureaucratic division of labor	specialization variety of viewpoints	conflict laden
Experience		reflexive domain knowledge	
Process Structure	well-structured	weakly structured (guidelines)	unstructured
Procedural rules	recurrent	Legal / procedural knowledge	innovative
Type of Cooperation	strict coordination	(mix)	unregulated collaboration
Return of experience		reflexive	

Table 1: Four types of processes

Process type	Issues in Information and Knowledge Management
Routine processes	Knowledge from Interaction and Citizen Information
Individualized decision making	Knowledge of Law and "Process Memory"
Negotiations	Knowledge-Enhancing Platforms for Group Decision Making
Democratic deliberation	Basic Civic Information/Structuring Debates

in the front-office. Such information is often needed to ensure that processes conform to standards of quality. Moreover, lack of knowledge about processes, rights and duties, etc., on the side of the citizen can often present serious problems. Hence with regard to well-structured processes implying citizen-administration interaction, knowledge problems are closely intertwined with front-office interaction.

The management of the relationship between citizen and government can benefit to some extent from standard procedures of Customer Relationship Management. But there are additional exigencies in the public sector concerning identification of the contracting partners, security and reliability of the communication, etc.

The pervasiveness of Internet applications radically changes the communication between administration and citizen. Change enters in two forms: a) as a challenge to deal with modified communication wishes and b) as possibilities to establish a close and constructive relationship. Information demands from the viewpoint of the citizen are quite different from those felt by the administration. For most citizens, administrative contacts occur rarely and are of an exceptional character. So, often, in-depth explanations are required. While the routine processes for serving citizens do not require much information, the situation is different with regard to the position of the citizen.

Citizen information systems for direct consultation via the Internet or for use in one-stop agencies or Call Centers are now being developed in many countries. They contain information which is of help in public life. In principle, such systems are a kind of electronic administration lexicon to answer common questions (Schwabe, 1996; Lenk et al., 1990) which concern:

- basic orientation and referral services ("Where *do I get* what, *and* how?");
- the eligibility for public services and for money transfers, as well as on legal rights and duties;
- the provision of other information of general interest.

The common stock of most citizen information systems are inquiry and referral systems of a practical nature. An example of such a (centrally coordinated) citizen information system is the Austrian system www.help.gv.at. There, a single entrance point (portal) is presented to the citizen and the structure is organized according to life events (Winter, 1998). More advanced are claim information systems which inform about entitlements and duties of citizens in a specific situation. Occasionally, citizen information systems also promote the participation of citizens in the local affairs and establish the transparency of municipal affairs.

Citizen information systems are still far from being perfect. There is generally too much emphasis on technical issues at the expense of content and of consideration for the citizen point of view. All too often the information is given from a supplier's perspective; the view of the administration dominates.

Decision-Making in Individual Cases

Administrative decisions are the result of combining factual and legal information in more or less well-structured processes. A decision can be seen as the result of using different pieces and different types of knowledge. Thereby, its formal structure depends on administrative procedure whereas the content of the decision is influenced by legal norms applicable to the specific problem on which the decision is to be made. Hence the knowledge which enters into a concrete decision comprises knowledge on specific facts of the case, knowledge about the relevant legal definitions as well as knowledge about the process itself.

Let us start with law and its interpretation. The proper task of the law professionals is more to interpret the law and the given case than drawing logical conclusions. Supporting this activity would be an important advantage. If a decision (e.g., on a taxation case, or about granting a retirement pension) is not just a matter of routine, it involves many legal prescriptions which have to be retrieved and read (and interpreted) before they can be applied to the case under consideration. In practice, spotting the applicable regulations is a burdensome task. Astonishingly, IT support is not yet well established here. We now have legal information systems offering legal documentation and information retrieval concerning legal texts and precedents, but without any further elaboration in view of the particular circumstances of the case to be decided. The provision of legal information is still at a level which it already attained three decades ago. What is needed is much more: methods that focus on the process, that are purpose directed and case oriented. Some approaches in that direction are promising but still belong to the scientific realm: case-based retrieval systems are a case in point.

Quite like simple "production" processes, typical complex decision processes are structured over time. But Workflow Management Systems are not of great use for their support, since the actors in a decision-making process need to draw on knowledge and to consult with each other in ways which are mostly not foreseeable. Nor is the extent known to which they can rely on their own knowledge instead of searching for fresh or stored information. This means that the process is not structured beforehand. Administrative procedure legislation affords only weak guidance, mostly in the interest of due process of law and protection of stakeholders from undue interference. Typical decision processes are structured as they unfold, on behalf of the actors participating in them. Such a professional self-regulation does not follow formal patterns, but it has to make reference to past steps of the process itself. Moreover, records of former similar processes are useful. So the self-regulation of decision processes requires the building-up of a "process memory" (Menne-Haritz, 1999). A useful step would be to consider such a gradually evolving process memory together with support for actors in searching for new knowledge, also with regard to upgrading their skills in interpreting information which they obtain from various sources.

Negotiations Drawing on Various Resources

The typical administrative decision is occurring at the operative level and it produces an output to be communicated to citizens or to segments of society. In contrast, management decisions normally concern the internal working of an organization. There is a long line of approaches and systems that have been developed for typical management decisions. But instruments developed for management decisions could support other decisions on the operational level as well. This operational level where administrative services are produced, licenses granted, etc. is characterized by a sequence of choices and options. Now more and more such choices are not made by isolated decision makers, but are the outcome of a negotiation involving typically more than two partners. Increasingly, not only the facts which constitute a case, but also the values to be realized, become an object of negotiation.

The development of platforms which support negotiations in different ways is still in its infancy, despite the fact that for decades already, decision support has been a recurrent theme. A large number of methods and systems has been developed (Bots et al., 1993). The so-called Group Decision Support Systems (GDSS) (Kraemer and King, 1988) explicitly support collaborative processes within a group--e.g., agenda-setting, brainstorming, commenting, voting and documenting the results of deliberations. Groups which use these tools normally rely on a facilitator who structures the debate, both from a technical and from a substantial standpoint. The pros and cons of GDSS are now well known. Results are obtained faster, but perhaps at the expense of a deeper consensus which would promote the implementation of the results obtained. Some of the well-known shortcomings of meetings and of "group-think" may be overcome: the opinions of the most vocal people will not be overrated at the expense of others. Also, a skilful facilitator could often prevent groups from exhibiting extreme forms of behavior which their members individually would not have shown: the greater inclination of groups to take risks and an exaggerated reliance on their power of judgement can be counterbalanced.

The abundance of distinct approaches to supporting management decision calls for some guidance. A rough impression is obtained in considering how the entire field of decision making and their support has changed over time. So early support had a somehow punctual and isolated problem view, and progress afterwards can be interpreted as opening up to a broader perspective. Yet earlier concepts and systems never really faded away. Furthermore, many approaches coexisted with later ones or even were integrated (Lenk and Traunmüller, 1999).

A promising approach would be to develop platforms which support the negotiating parties in their learning efforts by making information available and helping them to build up their own knowledge, about their environment, about consequences of courses of action and about the history of the negotiating process itself. To our knowledge, such platforms do not exist yet.

Democratic Deliberations

Platforms like those just mentioned are also of particular importance to democratic decision making. Instead of dealing with the entire range of policy decisions, we will concentrate here on democratic deliberation in a local environment. Information systems can support and promote citizen participation in public planning as well as in mediation processes in different ways:

- by providing information on a problem and its background also in interactive and multimedia form including "Virtual Reality" techniques;
- by supporting communication processes in different modes and between spatially distant persons ("tele-cooperation");
- by structuring debates;
- by directly supporting decision processes, e.g., through voting.

Concerning information provision, the concept of citizen information has to be enlarged to some extent: basic information needed in executing democratic rights could quite well be provided via the Internet. However, explicit policies are needed to do so in a way which effectively reaches all citizens concerned. One way would be to incorporate it–or provide references to it–in platforms which initiators of a democratic decision process could call upon and make available to all those who want to have a say in the process. We will not deepen this argument here. Rather, for what follows, we concentrate on the second and the third point which are of particular interest for democratic deliberation.

Besides easing access to information, the Internet can help to establish platforms on which democratic debates can happen. The idea of "Issue-Based Information Systems" (IBIS) has been developed by Horst Rittel in 1970, and it has been rediscovered in the late '80s. Such systems can be used to structure debates on controversial issues. The structuring of information is particularly useful in the early stages of the policy process, i.e., for identifying problems and elaborating solutions (Lenk, 1999).

If such platforms are developed, we will soon see innovative systems in which elements of the potential for the supply of information, for the support of communication and for the support of decision-making processes are combined. The design of comprehensive systems for the support of citizen participation can profit especially from developments in the field of CSCW. Access to information and communication support for the participation of citizens are only a precondition for the efficiency of the approach. More complex issues arise at a different stage: structuring debates, allocating rights to raise issues and comment on them. So far, only little experience has been gathered regarding the use of such combined systems which support the structuring of decision making beyond the level of information supply.

An example of new types of participation-enhancing information systems is provided by the GEOMED project (URL, 2001) which was funded by the European Union. It comprises three key issues:

- *Information services*: A wide variety of planning tasks require access to geographical information which is typically represented in maps. Thus, the accessibility of geo-graphical information in heterogeneous GIS systems is established over the Internet. Users are able to access, view and manipulate maps embedded in HTML pages from ordinary WWW client PCs. Other information present in the WWW is accessible, too.
- *Documentation services*: A "shared workspace" is established for the elaboration, storage and retrieval of documents, for messages related to particular geographical

planning projects and for contributions to the debates of a planning process or a mediation procedure. So, in a very convenient way, ordinary users can add information to the documents available.

- *Mediation services* provide assistance to human mediators of a round table. In order to structure interventions, an Issue-Based Information System (IBIS) is provided.

Depending on their design, information systems embody and represent structures which may help to overcome well-known organizational problems related to democracy: the bringing together of like-minded people, the structuring of debates and the embedding of rules which give a better say to people who have difficulty in expressing themselves. Local democracy like any democracy involving more than a small group of people ("seven plus/ minus two") is clearly a problem of organization. Information technologies, beyond their function of supporting telecommunication and providing access to stored information, are technologies of organization. It is important, therefore, that experiments like those described become more numerous and that we gain a clearer impression of the manifold forms which electronic support of citizen participation could take.

CONCLUDING REMARKS

In following some of the lines of argument we developed here, e-Government should be able to dig deeper than just scratching the tip of the iceberg with its present focus on Electronic Service Delivery. In order to do so, specific features of public administration have to be highlighted. Elsewhere (Lenk and Traunmüller, 2000), we have argued that e-Government should combine four different perspectives:

1. the *addressee's perspective* where the citizen interface of administrative work is particularly prominent;
2. the *process perspective* in which re-organization of processes making use of all kinds of human-machine synergies is paramount;
3. the *cooperation perspective* which complements the process perspective especially through insisting on ubiquitous (tele-)cooperation and on collaborative efforts like meetings, negotiations or deliberations which do not follow a clear-cut process model and which cannot be fully standardized beforehand;
4. the *knowledge perspective* which highlights the management of information and of knowledge as the major asset in so many work situations in the public sector.

With our framework, we hope to achieve a fruitful combination of these perspectives. More work is required now to develop specific reference models taking into account not only the various process types, cooperation patterns and knowledge domains, but equally the specific problems of public services like, e.g., social administration, the police and emergency management.

REFERENCES

Abecker, A., Decker, S. and Kühn, O. (1998). Das aktuelle schlagwort: Organizational memory. *Informatik Spektrum*, 21(4), 213-214.

Aden, J. and Gora, W. (Eds.). (1999). *Informationsverbund Berlin-Bonn*. Fossil, Köln.

Bing, J. and Trygve, H. (1977). *Legal Decisions and Information Systems*. Universitetsforlaget, Oslo.

Borghoff, U. and Pareschi, R. (Eds.), (1998). *Information Technology for Knowledge Management*. Berlin: Springer Verlag.

Bots, P., Sol, H. and Traunmüller, R. (Eds.). (1993). *Proceedings of the IFIP TC8/WG8.3 Working Conference on Decision Support in Public Administration*. North Holland, Amsterdam.

Cole, M. (1998). *Cultural Psychology: A Once and Future Discipline*. Belknap Press.

Haft, F. (1973). Juristische Dokumentation mit Computern–Entwicklungsstand, probleme und künftige Möglichkeiten. In Kaufmann, A. (Ed.), *Münchener Ringvorlesung EDV und Recht*, 115-134. Berlin: Schweitzer.

Hutchins, E. (1995). *Cognition in the Wild*. Cambridge, MA: MIT Press.

Jann, W. (1998). Lernen vom privaten sektor–Bedrohung oder chance? Oder: Wer hat angst vor public management? In Edeling, T., Jann, W. and Wagner, D. (Eds.), *Öffentliches Und Privates Management–Fundamentally Alike in All Unimportant Respects?* 11-51. Leske und Budrich, Opladen.

Kooperationsausschuss ADV Bund Länder Kommunaler Bereich (KoopA ADV). (Ed.). (1997). *Handlungsleitfaden IT-gestützte Vorgangsbearbeitung. Schriftenreihe der KBSt Bd. 35*, Bundesanzeigerverlag, Bonn.

Kraemer, L. and King, J. (1988). Computer-based systems for cooperative work and group decision making. *ACM Computing Surveys*, 20, 115-146.

Lenk, K., Brüggemeier, M., Hehmann, M. and Willms, W. (1990). *Bürgerinformationssysteme. Strategien zur Steigerung der Verwaltungstransparenz und der Partizipationschancen der Bürger*. Westdeutscher Verlag, Opladen.

Lenk, K. (1998). Reform opportunities missed: Will the innovative potential of information systems in public administration remain dormant forever? *Information, Communication & Society*, 1, 163-181.

Lenk, K. (1999). Electronic support of citizen participation in planning processes. In Hague, B. N. and Loader, B. (Eds.), *Digital Democracy. Discourse and Decision Making in the Information Age*, Routledge, 87-95.

Lenk, K. and Traunmüller, R. (Eds.), (1999). *Öffentliche Verwaltung und Informationstechnik-Perspektiven einer Radikalen Neugestaltung der öffentlichen Verwaltung mit Informationstechnik*. Decker, Heidelberg.

Lenk, K. and Traunmüller, R. (2000). *Perspectives on Electronic Government, IFIP WG8.5 Information Systems in Public Administration Working Conference on Advances in Electronic Government*, February, 10-11. Zaragoza, Spain

Menne-Haritz, A. (1999). Prozessgedächtnis und Überlieferungsbildung. In Metzing, (Ed.), *Digitale Archive: Ein neues Paradigma?* Beiträge des 4. Archivwissenschaftlichen Kolloquiums der Archivschule Marburg, Marburg, 283-308.

Nardi, B. (Ed.), (1996). *Context and Consciousness: Activity Theory and Human-Computer Interaction*. MIT Press.

Nonaka, I. and Takeuchi, H. (1995). *The Knowledge Creating Company: How Japanese Companies Create the Dynamics of Innovation*. New York: Oxford University Press.

Ortner, E. (2000). Wissensmanagement-systeme und werkzeuge. *Informatik Spektrum*, 23(3), 192-201.

Probst, G., Raub, S. and Romhardt, K. (1996). *Wissen Managen: Wie Unternehmen ihre Wertvollste Ressource Optimal Nutzen*. (2nd Ed.) Gabler Verlag, Wiesbaden.

Rehäuser, J. and Krcmar, H. (1996). Wissensmanagement in Unternehmen. In Schreyögg and Conrad (1996) 1-40.

Roithmayr, F. and Fink, K. (1997). Know-how-unternehmen. *Wirtschaftsinformatik,* 39(5), 503-506.

Rossen, H. (1999). *Vollzug und Verhandlung*. Mohr, Tübingen.

Schreyögg, G. and Conrad, P. (Eds.). (1996). *Managementforschung 6: Wissensmanagement*. Walter de Gruyter, Berlin New York.

Schwabe, G. (1996). Die rolle neuer informations-und kommunikationstechnologie für die Bürgerinformation. *Information Management*, 2, 6-14.

Simon, H. (1957). *Administrative Behavior: A Study of Decision-Making Processes in Administrative Organization*. 2nd Edition. Macmillan, New York.

Geographical Mediation Systems. (2001). EC project description on the Internet. Available on the World Wide Web at: http://arti.vub.ac.be/geomed/geomed.html. Accessed February 22, 2001.

Winter, A. (1998). Die österreichische verwaltung im Internet. *Verwaltung & Management*, 4, 136-138. Available on the World Wide Web at: http://www.help.gv.at-Ein Bürgerinformationssystem.

Chapter V

Internet Voting: Embracing Technology in Electoral Processes

Andreu Riera
SCYTL, Spain

Jordi Sànchez and Laia Torras
Jaume Bofill Foundation, Spain

The 1960 presidential election outcome, its razor-thin margin, and its inaccuracies and slowness of vote count, once again call attention to the antiquated technology of our voting procedures. [...] On Election Day, Mr. Smith goes to his telephone and dials this voter code number. He hears a buzz over the receiver, followed by a recorded announcement that tells him: "The Televoter is now ready to receive your ballot." [...] This Televoter proposal is likely to excite the interest of the producers of electronic computing equipment as well as telephonic companies. It is also likely to be greeted with solid resistance by the producers of contemporary voting machines, printers of paper ballots and political party officials. Among conscientious voters, however, the thought of being in convenient telephonic touch with one's government may be too tantalizing to resist very long.

Public elections in an electronic world
Telephony, Journal of the Telephone Industry, USA, January 28, 1961

INTRODUCTION

Through time, electoral processes have been incorporating more and more technology. The voting methods in the U.S., for example, have evolved from lever machines to punch cards, optical scanning and Direct Recording Electronic (DRE) machines. (A good survey of different voting technologies currently used in the U.S. can be found in Cranor (2001.) Even in those countries where paper ballots and traditional ballot boxes are used, the ballot tabulation process is likely to be using some form of computerized transmission or processing at some point.

The next step in this electoral evolution seems to be Internet voting. This is actually a hot topic these days. After the electoral mess in the state of Florida (US presidential election, November 2000), partly caused by a "user-unfriendly" punch card ballot design, some people rushed to promote Internet voting as the very solution to all the problems of modern democracy.

Internet voting is not so miraculous but still it is promising and, if correctly implemented, it may be helpful in enhancing our democratic processes. Internet voting indeed may offer several potential advantages over traditional methods of voting:

⟨   Reduction in cost for printing, distributing, collecting and tabulating ballots.
⟨   Speed and accuracy of ballot tabulation and ballot recounting.
⟨   Greater mobility of voters.
⟨   Potential increase of voter turnout.

However, the implementation of Internet voting in public elections must be done correctly. Some technical problems have to be carefully studied (and solved) in order to incorporate the Internet as a new medium for casting binding ballots, especially if voters are allowed to vote from any Internet connection instead of using special Internet voting equipment at polling places. Reliability and availability, for example, are basic requirements to ensure voters' franchise and to offer the adequate quality of service. Usability issues are also very important: poorly designed computer screen ballots could easily result in the same type of confusion suffered by many Florida voters. The whole voting infrastructure must also be sufficiently scalable. The existence of adequate contingency plans and the capability of handling recounts are other important requirements.

The list of technological challenges faced by Internet voting is indeed not short. Nevertheless, when discussing the feasibility of Internet voting in the public sector, there is one main concern often highlighted: security (California Internet Voting Task Force, 2000). Of the spectrum of technical issues concerning the use of Internet voting for public elections, security is indeed currently considered the most important one. Internet-based elections must therefore take into account (and fulfill) an extensive list of security requirements to ensure the integrity of the whole electoral process. This chapter explores such fascinating topics, providing an extensive survey of the security hazards faced by the deployment of Internet voting in the public sector. Special significance is given to the case of remote Internet voting (voters casting their ballots remotely from any location) because it is the most challenging option (California Internet Voting Task Force, 2000). The chapter introduces also the most promising approaches to solve some of the security hazards presented.

Not only security and technology issues must be taken into consideration when debating Internet voting. Some social challenges need a satisfactory answer as well. The gradual use of new technologies in the politico-electoral scene must indeed consider the social risks derived from the information society unfolding process (e.g., the digital divide) and from the possible distrust coming from some sectors of the population. For these reasons, the discussion on security issues is complemented in the chapter with an insight into socio-political considerations.

The rest of the chapter is structured as follows. The next section defines Internet voting and the several alternatives to implement it. This section also offers a list of previous experiments of remote Internet voting, which is the most challenging alternative. The third section provides an extensive analysis of the security hazards faced by remote Internet voting. The most promising approaches to solve some of these hazards are also introduced. The next section introduces the concept of cryptographic voting protocol as the core technology that enables the incorporation of security to online elections. The fifth section analyzes the most important socio-political issues regarding the introduction of Internet voting in the public sector. The next section gives our view of Internet voting in the near future, and finally, the last section contains some concluding remarks.

DEFINITION OF INTERNET VOTING

Internet voting is a special kind of electronic voting. There are many examples of electronic voting. Any voting method that involves some electronic device or system could actually be regarded as "electronic." This certainly includes most of the modern democratic elections of the World. Even though voters may not see any electronics, ballots are probably being tabulated (at least, in part) by electronic means. Just like almost everything, today electoral processes involve the use of, to some extent, computers or other electronic equipment.

The growing significance of computer networks in recent years has stimulated the appearance of the novel concept of e-voting. An e-voting system is constituted by a set of protocols, policies, and hardware and software components that jointly allow an election over a computer network to take place, either partially or completely. An Internet voting system is therefore a particular case of e-voting system that uses the data transport infrastructure provided by the Internet. Nowadays, given the Internet's outstanding, e-voting and Internet voting are actually very frequently considered synonym concepts.

Internet voting systems can be classified into two main groups. If ballots are cast by voters from platforms controlled and supervised by election officials or poll workers, we call it poll-site Internet voting. In contrast, if voters cast their ballots unsupervised from a remote location, we call it remote Internet voting. This classification was more precisely defined by the California Internet Voting Task Force, in its "Report on the Feasibility of Internet Voting" (California Internet Voting Task Force, 2000). The Task Force appropriately recommended to gradually phase-in the use of Internet in public elections:

⟨   **Phase One: Internet voting at voter's polling place**. Voters would be required to vote at their home precinct, as usual. The identity of voters would be verified by poll workers at the polling place according to traditional methods already in use. Voters would use computerized equipment connected to the Internet to cast their ballots. The Internet would be used to send the voted ballots to election officials.

⟨   **Phase Two: Internet voting at any polling place**. This is the same as Phase One, except that voters would be allowed to vote at any polling place and not just at their home precinct.

⟨   **Phase Three: Remote Internet voting from distributed computers or kiosks**. Voters could use remote voting places established throughout the community by the elections office. The identity of voters would not be verified by traditional means but instead it would be assured by technological authentication means (e.g., digital signatures.)

⟨   **Phase Four: Remote Internet voting from any Internet connection**. This is the "vote in your pyjama" option. Voters could cast their ballots from any computer terminal with an Internet connection, provided that the security of these platforms could be assured.

Security hazards (and social concerns as well) become more significant along these phases. Consequently, the complexity of the technical solutions required by each of the phases rises. These reasons prevent widespread use in the short term of remote Internet voting (especially systems of Phase Four) for public elections. Complete deployment of systems of Phase Four is really still several years (or decades) away. Nonetheless, some concrete examples have already taken place. In 1998, the Dutch national election saw a trial performed through an e-voting system developed by an academic research group based in The Netherlands. In the 2000 U.S. presidential elections, 250 highly screened military personnel voted online while overseas during an experiment controlled by the U.S. Department of Defense. Those ballots were actually binding. During the same election, a few non-binding trials conducted by private vendors were recorded in some counties of the states of California and Arizona.

In fact, voting remotely over the Internet using systems of Phase Four has already been done with binding effects in elections for political parties and private organizations during the last five years at least. As soon as August 1996, the Reform Party in the U.S. allowed ballots to be cast over the Internet for its presidential primary. (Despite the extensive media coverage of more recent events, this was probably the first time Internet voting was used in a presidential primary in the U.S.) In Europe, the 1997 presidential election of the IEEE Spanish Chapter of Information Theory was performed online using a secure prototype developed by a research group based in Barcelona. On January 2000, several thousand Alaskans living in remote areas had the opportunity to vote through the Internet in the state's Republican Party straw poll. On March 2000, the Democrat Party held its presidential primary election in the state of Arizona in the U.S. About 36,000 individuals voted remotely over the Internet on that occasion.

These, and some other Internet-based elections, have already taken place more or less successfully (this basically depends on whom you ask). What is indisputable is that all these Internet elections had room for improvement. Some of these examples involved not-so-secure Internet voting technology, some led to very low online voter turnout, some had serious technical glitches. However, all these Internet elections have served very well as experiments to tell the experts how Internet voting can (and must) be improved in the future.

SECURITY THREATS TO INTERNET VOTING

The security threats encountered in Internet-based elections are essentially the same as in conventional elections. Ballots can be damaged or lost (either accidentally or on purpose.) Corrupt party officials may wish to modify the election outcome in their favor. Voter registrations can be duplicated and unqualified voters can be registered. Citizens can be coerced, or they can try to sell their votes. Although the nature of all these threats remains the same, the use of the Internet changes the methodology and effects of the corresponding attacks. The Internet as it is today potentially makes attackers harder to track, capture and convict (Schneier, 2000a). There are three main reasons for this. First, the possibility to automate fraud. Second, the possibility to commit fraud at a distance. Third, the ease to propagate attacking tools to have the job done by other people.

This is not to say that Internet voting has to be automatically rejected. The fact that risks exist simply means the risks must be addressed. The lesson here is that elaborate solutions are needed; that Internet voting technology has to be accurately designed, tested and certified; and that the implantation of Internet voting systems has to be done gradually. The development of any Internet voting system must carefully consider a list of security threats and vulnerabilities, and adopt appropriate countermeasures to reduce (or almost eliminate) the chances of any successful attack. These countermeasures include preventive technologies, and appropriate detection and reaction mechanisms as well.

Poll-site Internet voting systems can be protected from most kinds of election fraud far more easily than remote Internet voting systems. Existing security technologies such as IPsec (Kent and Atkinson, 1998) may be used to build a Virtual Private Network (VPN) to securely link the voting equipments at the different polling places to those at the central counting facilities. Voter identification would be done by means of already well-understood conventional methods, and the elections office could more easily control the security of the whole voting infrastructure. Although poll-site Internet voting systems still have to be carefully designed and tested, it is remote Internet voting that raises the most serious security vulnerabilities (Alexander, 2001; California Internet Voting Task Force, 2000; Mercuri, 2000; Phillips and Jefferson, 2000; Rubin, 2000; Schum, 2000). But let's look at the problem of remote Internet voting in more detail.

Remote Internet voting systems basically consist of the following elements:

⟨   **Ballot casting client platforms**: These consist of some hardware device and some software that enable ballot casting. The hardware device might be for example a voting terminal at a government-controlled kiosk, the voter's own personal computer or his/her mobile handset. The ballot casting software may be special-purpose voting software, more generic software such as a Web browser or some combination of both such as a voting plug-in for a web browser.

⟨   **A (number of) ballot-collecting server(s)**: Ballot collecting servers operate in the Internet accepting connections from voters and recording their votes for further tabulation. Ballot-collecting servers may be general-purpose computers running specific voting software. The servers should operate on a well-delimited perimeter with the most appropriate network defenses (firewalls, intrusion detection systems, proactive security administrators and so on) and physical defenses as well.

⟨   **The Internet itself** as the medium to transport voters' decisions from their ballot-casting platforms to the ballot-collecting servers. The Internet is not a very secure network. In contrast with other (more closed) communication networks, the level of physical access needed in the Internet to eavesdrop or inject information is very low. Some crackers are able to remotely gain privileges over poorly administered nodes, routers or Internet Service Provider (ISP) computers, and from there launch a wide variety of attacks.

Given the scenario depicted above, the attacks to the security of a remote Internet voting system can be classified into the following groups (some overlaps do exist):

⟨   Attacks to the transmission of ballots
⟨   Cracker attacks to the ballot-collecting servers
⟨   Attacks to the ballot casting-client platforms
⟨   Attacks by malicious insiders
⟨   Privileged attacks
⟨   Low-tech attacks
⟨   Impersonation of voters
     We will discuss each in turn.

Attacks to the Transmission of Ballots

Ballots have to be transmitted from the ballot-casting client platforms to the ballot-collecting servers. Although a complete Internet voting protocol involves a larger list of security issues (in a later section we will talk more on this), the very transmission of a ballot across the Internet raises by itself three elemental security concerns. These security concerns are confidentiality, authenticity and integrity. Confidentiality of a ballot transmission implies secrecy of the ballot from anyone except at the two ends of the communication. Authenticity of a ballot transmission provides assurance that the ballot received at the destination end was really created at the source of the connection. Integrity of the ballot transmission assures that not even a single bit of the ballot has been modified since it was created.

This kind of security concern may actually be solved by mature transport-level security technology already used to secure e-commerce transactions over the Web. Transport Layer Security (TLS) (Dierks and Allen, 1999), or its predecessor Secure Sockets Layer (SSL) (Freier, Karlton and Kocher, 1996), are the best examples. They have been depurated through the years, and they are hardcoded into any current Web browser.

It is worth noting that authenticity of the ballot transmission has been defined in terms of "the source of the connection" and not in terms of "the person whom the one at the source of the connection claims to be." Security of a ballot transmission is concerned only with the fact that the received ballot has not been injected by a bogus voter in the middle of the connection. A completely different issue is the identification of the voter at the other end of the wire, i.e., the assurance that the person who originated the connection is really who he/ she claims to be. We will explore this topic later.

Cracker Attacks to the Ballot-Collecting Servers

A hacker is an individual with a set of technical skills that allow him/her to explore the limitations of security systems (Schneier, 2000a). The Internet has plenty of hackers. Many of these hackers are benign and not devoted to attacking systems. Unfortunately, however, some hackers are motivated for dishonest reasons (or just backed by people with dishonest reasons). We call them crackers. Some crackers are really good, and they can be surprisingly successful in thwarting many network defenses.

Cracker attacks to a remote Internet voting system will focus on the exploitation of security vulnerabilities of the computers and local networks that host the ballot-collecting servers. The goal of these attacks may be to modify election outcomes, to know how the voting is going or to find out the vote of particular voters. A more easily reached goal would just be to prevent voters from casting their ballots through Denial of Service (DoS) attacks (see Rubin, 2000, for a good discussion about this possibility).

Cracker attacks have to be counteracted in two ways. First, by means of a well-designed voting protocol (see next section.) The adequate security features of the Internet voting protocol may completely prevent crackers from achieving some of the previously listed cracker goals. Second, by means of adequate security administration at the end systems and at their local operation perimeter. In general, all accessible voting services should be hosted by dedicated computers with no other network services enabled, and with a very restricted access. Firewall systems, demilitarized zones, intrusion detection systems, monitoring and logging tools and, in general, the kind of security measures habitually used to enforce the security of servers and intranets, might be helpful to secure ballot-collecting servers. Of course all these tools must be carefully managed by skilled security experts.

Some Internet voting mock tests have already taken place; some of them parallel to the 2000 U.S. presidential election. To date, there have been no successful cracker attacks reported. However, this does not necessarily mean that the protection measures were unbreakable. The tests were non-binding and they involved only a small number of voters.

Allow tens of millions of citizens to cast binding ballots online for a national election, and then you will see really powerful cracker attacks being carried out.

Attacks to the Ballot-Casting Client Platforms

Today personal computers are inherently insecure platforms. Personal computers attached to the Internet are much worse. The operating systems most commonly used today are insecure. The software that implements communication services is insecure. Lots of bugs on all these software programs are discovered every other day. Many of these bugs allow security breaches. The average user is a very bad security administrator of his/her personal computer.

Yes, the ballot-casting platforms are likely to be the weakest link on a remote Internet voting system of Phase Four (Phillips and Jefferson, 2000). Fortunately, this problem does not apply (at least, not to the same extent) in the case of remote Internet voting systems of Phase Three.

The most probable attack against personal computers used as ballot-casting platforms takes the form of a virus or a Trojan horse (a good study of this topic is found in Rubin, 2000). Recent devastating outbreaks of fast-spreading Internet viruses have demonstrated how vulnerable personal computers are to this kind of malware. The ILOVEYOU virus, launched in 2000, infected 10 million computers in the hours before a fix was released (Schneier, 2000a). And it could have been worse if the virus had been designed to be more discrete, to act silently. A virus or Trojan horse could be specially designed to target as many ballot-casting client platforms as possible. Such virus could stay silent until election day, waiting for the voter to initiate the ballot-casting protocol. At that moment, the virus could just "sit" between the voter and the voting software, and do whatever it was designed to. It could record the voter's choice. It could even change it without the voter noticing anything.

There are some ways to protect the ballot-casting client platforms from these threats (Appendix A of California Internet Voting Task Force Report (2000) lists an interesting set of possibilities). The election officials could for example distribute bootable CD-ROMs containing a clean operating system with the required networking and voting software. Other protection measures could be based on the use of additional voting hardware. However, all of these countermeasures impose some inconveniences to voters and would in consequence probably lead to very low online voter turnout. Despite the possible protection measures, we believe that widespread use of Phase Four remote Internet voting in public elections should be allowed only if the security architecture of personal computers and of the most common operating systems sees dramatic improvements.

Of course, the use of devices other than personal computers as ballot-casting client platforms may alleviate this problem. For example, the use of mobile handsets would significantly reduce virus worries (Rubin, 2000). However, the lack of security functionality available at the application layer on these devices opens up other kind of problem at the voting protocol level. In the coming years, we expect both of these two assertions to gradually lose their validity.

Attacks by Malicious Insiders

Let's suppose the ballot-collecting servers are totally secure from cracker attacks. Let's even suppose that the ballot-casting platforms used by voters are secure too. This is just not enough.

The ballot-collecting servers are operated by poll workers who need certain privileges to do their job. The administrator of a computer has in many cases unlimited privileges to manage the computer's resources and behavior. Election officials may also have certain privileges regarding the ballot tabulation process. Any of these people must be considered an insider, with a high level of access to the computing resources and information assets of the voting system. Attacks originated by (or with the collaboration of) malicious insiders are potentially very dangerous, because of the privileged position of the attackers. This type of threat has to be carefully considered when designing any voting system (actually not only those that are Internet based).

Some techniques are helpful in protecting Internet voting systems from malicious insiders. Tamper-proof and special-purpose hardware modules can prevent unauthorized access to data or processes (in this respect it is still worth considering the cautionary notes given in Anderson and Kuhn (1996: pp.1-11)). Secure methods for distributing trust can prevent a single dishonest insider (or a certain number of them) from gaining certain privileges. These two techniques can actually be used simultaneously to provide in-depth security.

There is a particular type of insider that has to be specially considered: the Internet voting system vendor. Given the level of expertise needed, Internet voting technology is likely to be provided by specialized private companies. The problem is that, in contrast with previous mechanical or paper-based voting equipment, Internet voting systems have a lack of transparency (Alexander, 2001). The inner workings of these systems are opaque to the average user, and a superficial look at the system does not give any assurance that it really behaves correctly. As suggested in Waskell (1993), it is not clear the level of trust that a given private company may deserve. Who are the company's members? Who manages the company? In the end, the voting software has been written by individual programmers hired by the company. Who are these programmers?

Malicious programmers could set up very dangerous insider attacks. They could leave "back doors" in the software, which later would allow them to access some data or processes. Back doors could even allow the attacker to shift the behavior of the software at the attacker's will. Malicious programmers could also write "time bombs" and leave them embedded in the voting software. Given a certain condition (for example, a certain number of received ballots), a time bomb would perform some insidious action.

To prevent this kind of attack, Internet voting products have to be extensively audited. In particular, the software source code must pass a rigorous line-by-line examination. There is however some debate on who must do such examination. Some people advocate for forcing Internet voting software to be open source in order to allow public scrutiny by anyone (see for example Alexander (2001) or Mann (1993)). Other people argue that the best examination (from many points of view, including security) would be done by the appropriate security experts, but not by every programmer in the world. Shamos (1993: pp. 3.18-3.25), for example, reports that making the source code open carries some risks and that, on balance, it does not solve the actual problem.

In addition to having the source code scrutinized by the appropriate experts, any Internet voting system intended for public elections must be carefully and independently evaluated to provide assurance of its level of security. See Mercuri (1993) for a discussion about the need of rigorous standards and compliance procedures to be enforced for electronic voting products that target the public sector, and see Shamos (1993: pp. 3.18-3.25) for a possible evaluation methodology of the security measures needed in computerized election systems to compensate the lack of transparency. Actually, extensive and methodical generic evaluation processes have already been defined for IT systems security certification. The best example in this field is the Common Criteria, an international effort that has led to an ISO standard (International Standardization Organization, 1999). This kind of certification is recommended for voting systems in Mercuri (2000).

Privileged Attacks

Although they are not insiders, some people and some organizations have a level of privileges that convert them into dangerous adversaries. Take for example Carnivore, an FBI-promoted law-enforcement tool that is designed to analyze Internet traffic at the ISPs. Of course the motivations behind the use of such tools are supposed to be legitimate, but the fact is that they could be easily used to subvert the outcomes of an Internet election if the voting system was not adequately protected. Even if the deployment of law-enforcement tools like Carnivore does not prosper (apart from being law-enforcement tools, these programs are also magnificent privacy-violation tools), Internet voting has to be protected from the technical workers at the ISPs and at the telecom companies. What is the monitoring capability of a system manager at AOL? How could his/her privileges be used to influence the election outcomes? What effect would the tampering of the DNS server at an ISP have?

Secure Internet voting systems must consider the existence of privileged attackers and must be protected from them. This is not so difficult in terms of the voting protocol itself. However, privileged attackers may be potentially more successful than plain attackers in, for example, launching attacks to the security of the ballot-casting client platforms.

Low-Tech Attacks

A remote Internet voting system can be attacked without using any technological skill or tool. Although these attacks are not so graceful, they might be successful any way.

Low-tech attacks can target the ballot-collecting servers. For example, a group of terrorists could physically assault the building where the ballot-collecting servers are hosted. This attack would of course be very apparent. Nonetheless, depending on the nature of the election, this kind of attack must be taken into account and adequate (physical) security countermeasures have to be adopted. Less apparent, more difficult to prevent and more difficult to catch would be the terrorist that just blows up the electrical supply to the building.

Social engineering is subtler than balaclavas and bombs. Still, it may be very successful. Social engineering is a term that defines a collection of techniques directed to obtain particular information about a system, or to have a certain job done by an employee or privileged user. Social engineering bypasses any kind of technological security measure in place. Because it targets the weakest link of the system (humans), it is surprisingly effective (Schneier, 2000a). For example, an attacker could just pretend to be some election official over the phone, requesting a poll worker to do a certain minor job. More intrusively, an attacker could get into the building, properly dressed as a member of the telecom company's maintenance staff. He/she would eventually be given physical access to certain elements of the voting system. Defenses from social engineering involve proper training of employees and persons responsible for the operation of the ballot-collecting servers, and technical measures to distribute the privileges needed to do some action.

Low-tech attacks can also target the other end, voters and their ballot-casting platforms. If computer kiosks were scattered throughout the streets to allow remote casting of ballots, this equipment would become an attractive target for physical attacks, either destructive or with the aim of tampering them with. Besides that, the very fact of permitting voters to cast ballots from computers at home or computer kiosks on the streets, and especially from the workplace, creates opportunities for extortion and vote-buying (Alexander, 2001). However, it is debatable to what extent this kind of attack is already possible with current voting methods. Social engineering can also be directed to voters. Although the potential effects of social engineering attacks would be less damaging in this case, the chances of success are probably greater.

Finally, low-tech attacks can target the Internet itself. Even though the Internet was initially created to have a high level of fault-tolerance without central points of control, the reality is that some network backbones and some routing nodes are essential for its proper functioning. Destroying or rendering useless one or some of those essential elements would probably cause a major attack to the election in the form of Denial of Service (and huge losses in other sectors). At another scale, preventing access to an ISP would cause Denial of Service to the voters that access the Internet through that ISP.

Impersonation of Voters

In traditional elections, poll workers use physical methods to identify voters. A recent photograph attached to a passport or an ID card, for example, is a valid identification mechanism in the real world. Just as conventional electoral processes, remote Internet voting systems need to reliably identify voters. However, over the Internet, traditional methods are not valid any more. Therefore how can a remote Internet voting system identify the person that is sitting at the other end of a wire?

Identification methods over a computer network may be based on three possible things: something the person knows, something the person has or something the person is. The most obvious example of the former is a password (or passphrase, for increased security). An example of the second is a hardware token (for example, a smartcard, or some small devices that can be connected to a port of a computer). The third method consists of biometrics (fingerprints, retinal scans, iris scans, face or voice recognition, to name a few).

None of these three identification methods is perfect and often the best solutions come by combining two of them (or even all three.) Nonetheless, the real world is not perfect either. In general, the real world relies on biometrics to identify people. We recognize our friends because of their physical appearance. We accept a document as legally binding because it incorporates a handwritten signature. All of these are biometrics. However, biometrics can be falsified. Skilled people can falsify handwritten signatures, or simulate another's voice. In traditional elections, someone can go and vote instead of his twin brother.

Remote Internet voting systems that solely rely on voter identification via the use of a password imply many security hazards difficult to counteract (Phillips and Jefferson, 2000). Authentication protocols that involve digital signatures are more secure. Still, the signature-creation process ultimately requires a password that is used to protect the private key needed to sign. The use of smartcards to store such private keys adds a supplementary level of protection (we are combining something the voter knows –the protection password–with something the voter has–the smartcard). Actually, besides voter identification, some Internet voting systems use digital signatures to assure non-repudiation of some of the actions carried out during the voting protocol, and therefore to ensure long-term accountability. Finally, with regard to biometrics, they are useless when used on the Internet if the identification system is unable to check whether the biometric comes from the person at the time of verification or it is rather a previously used biometric that has been stolen. Moreover, citizens can perceive some kind of biometrics as very intrusive (Alexander, 2001; Phillips and Jefferson, 2000). This would imply low levels of acceptance of the new voting methods.

CRYPTOGRAPHIC PROTOCOLS FOR REMOTE INTERNET VOTING

The previous section has demonstrated the range of threats and attacks that a remote Internet voting system may suffer once it is put in place and operated. The section has also outlined the general security measures that can be used to protect the Internet voting system from those attacks. However, we have said little about the inner construction of the voting software components that constitute the fundamental parts of the Internet voting system. At the very core of a remote Internet voting system lies in fact a voting protocol. This section provides an introduction to the concept of secure voting protocol.

A voting protocol determines with precision the steps and actions involved in casting a ballot remotely, both by the voter and the corresponding ballot-collecting server. These steps incorporate a number of intrinsic security mechanisms (which will mainly remain transparent to the voter). The adequate combination of these security mechanisms is what primarily assures the security features desired for an online election. These security mechanisms must necessarily be of cryptographic nature. Cryptography, the science of secret writing, has been used for centuries to protect the confidentiality of private messages (cryptanalysis has been used for centuries to break this confidentiality, with success in some cases). Cryptography underwent a major change in 1976. The introduction of public-key cryptography (Diffie and Hellman, 1976) meant a radical scientific advance. Since then, the objectives of cryptography have widened from just ensuring secrecy to many other, more complex interaction problems (e.g., digital signing, or remote gambling); and the users of cryptography have spanned from the military to the whole society (especially banking and businesses.)

Nowadays, there are amazing cryptographic protocols to solve a broad variety of security problems, often highly complex, that appear when mutually suspicious peers cooperate over an insecure network (Schneier, 1996). Secure Internet voting is a paradigmatic example of this kind of non-trivial problem that requires elaborate cryptographic protocols to be incorporated into the kernel of the solution. Internet voting protocols are indeed not simple (this is why remote Internet voting is so challenging for cryptographers). The mere use of confidentiality-oriented encryption for securing the transmission of ballots when they circulate the network is not enough. It is an example of flawed voting protocol. Because ballots are deciphered at the ballot-collecting server, anyone with privileges on that server (being an external cracker or just an insider) can easily know the voting decision of every voter. This is of course not acceptable for a public election.

In public elections, anonymity of ballots must be assured while accepting these ballots from well-identified voters. After the event, voters should be able to verify correct treatment of their ballots by the system, and to prove any forgery. Still, they must not be able to prove which were their respective votes. As it becomes obvious, Internet voting security is not just about sending an encrypted ballot from point A to point B. It goes far beyond that. Voting is not like any other commercial or financial transaction (Alexander, 2001; Cranor, 2001). For this reason, the security of an Internet election needs more than just SSL (no matter the number of bits of the session keys). SSL (Freier, Karlton and Kocher, 1996) is the security technology currently used to protect e-commerce transactions on the World Wide Web. SSL indeed would solve the secrecy of ballot transmissions. However, SSL is a general-purpose data transport security protocol. Security services at the transport layer cannot differentiate among the particular security needs and requirements of every application. In other words, SSL has no idea whether the data being transported corresponds to a voting protocol or it is the contents of an HTML page regarding travel services.

To design a valid cryptographic voting protocol for remote Internet voting, first it is necessary to settle the list of security requirements that must be met. The international scientific community has recently reached a certain consensus with regard to the list of security requirements that should ideally be considered when designing cryptographic e-voting protocols (Riera, 1999):

⟨   **Accuracy**: The final election results must contain all validated ballots cast by eligible voters. It must not be possible to add, delete or alter ballots.

⟨   **Democracy**: Only eligible voters may cast a ballot, only once.

⟨   **Anonymity**: It must not be possible for anyone to correlate ballots to the respective voters who cast them.

⟨   **Fairness**: In order to prevent affecting voters' behavior, intermediate results must be secret until the election is completed.

⟨   **Uncoercibility**: To protect the system from automated coercion, vote-buying or extortion, voters must not be able to prove their respective voting decisions.

⟨   **Verifiability**: Either the individual voter must be able to verify that the final tally contains his/her ballot, or some auditing third party must be able to verify the integrity of the whole tally.

One quickly realizes that an ideal Internet voting protocol faces a large number of security requirements that in some cases are contradictory to each other. Consequently, completely satisfactory solutions cannot be reached without the adequate combination of special-purpose cryptographic tools. Some of the requirements even demand strategic trade-offs or the sacrifice of voters' convenience. Nevertheless, we can assume that Internet voting systems must meet the same guarantees currently offered by conventional voting methods, but not necessarily go beyond them.

The scientific community has studied the problem of e-voting during the last 20 years, with the objective of developing secure cryptographic voting protocols. The earliest cryptographic voting protocol was proposed in 1981 by a Dutch scientist, David Chaum (1981). The protocol partially solved the list of security requirements. Since that first proposal, some research groups (mainly academic, but also from private companies) have studied the topic and proposed their own solutions. The objective of these groups has been to attain as many requirements of the previous list as possible, although many times the feasibility of a practical implementation has been considered a secondary concern or it has even been completely omitted. Still, some of the proposals have been implemented, and used in voting trials or even real ballots. (Borrell and Rifà (1996) and Cranor and Cytron (1996) are remarkable examples.)

Even though quite a lot of secure voting protocols can be found in the scientific literature, there is not a widely recognized standard yet (Phillips and Jefferson, 2000). Secure voting protocols can be classified into two main groups (Borrell, 1996): schemes using some derivation of the concept of mixing (the work initiated by Chaum (1981)) and schemes using homomorphic encryption functions (Benaloh (1987) is the starting point in this case). Either group has its own intrinsic characteristics, advantages and pitfalls. Both groups try to minimize the level of trust placed in any of the elements of the system. In any case, any Internet voting system must provide an accurate description of which voting protocol is implemented, since this is the core technology that determines the essential features of the product. Adequate voting protocols can only be constructed by accurately combining a number of cryptographic techniques, and this requires expertise. The designer or vendor of Internet voting technology should clearly explain which of the security requirements of the given list are met, and exactly how. Experience has taught us that security by obscurity means in practice no security. In addition, in the case of public elections, security by obscurity would mean no acceptance.

SOCIO-POLITICAL CONSIDERATIONS

From the mid '90s, some trials of online electoral processes and real ballots have been carried out. In most of these trials the elector had the opportunity to cast his/her vote from a computer terminal situated anywhere in the world. These electoral processes have also been useful for analyzing the impact that they have on society, the political system and the existing legal code. We must assume that in the future we will have new events that will progressively take us to a scene where electronic voting via the Internet will be a fact in any electoral consultation. This possibility is what forces us to analyze the social and political consequences that electronic voting may have.

The debate on Internet voting cannot solely be limited to a reflection on the security technologies and protocols. This is essential but insufficient. Voting in itself is a mechanism that socially legitimates any democratic political system. Whatever the new voting mechanism or procedure is, it has to take into account this fact in order to guarantee that it does not debilitate the political system. This section specifically focuses on these socio-political aspects:

〈   The danger of the digital divide
〈   The possible increase in electoral participation
〈   The symbolic aspects of voting
〈   The public control of the electoral process
〈   The impact on representative democracy

The Digital Divide

The fact that new technologies in general and the Internet in particular are rapidly penetrating our societies is beyond discussion. However, their impact is still unequal and affects only a minority of the population. According to the last European Commission figures, Internet penetration into EU households was 28% in October 2000, while being 18% in March (European Commission, 2000). In any case, Internet users in most western countries were never, in 1999, more than 50% of the respective population, while in the majority of these countries, they were less than 25% (Computer Industry Almanac, 1999; NUA Internet Surveys, 1999). It is true that only the northern countries such as Sweden, Denmark, Finland and Holland had an Internet usage very near or above 50%. In contrast France, Spain, Portugal and Greece were countries that had an Internet penetration of less that 20% in October 2000.

This reflection must be accompanied by other data that helps us measure the unequal proliferation of new technologies in our society. Socially disadvantaged groups (with less economical resources and a lower level of education) as well as older people are the slowest to take up new technologies if at all. In the unfolding of the "information society," there is a risk of a new social fracture, the digital divide. This digital divide can increase the existing socio-economic differences and make them even less surmountable. This text is not the place to refer to the social policies that the governments should boost to overcome this risk of a new social division; however reference to this data is essential in order to evaluate the possibilities and consequences of setting up Internet voting.

Following the facts given by statistics and accepting the resistance to technological changes that exists in large sectors (mainly due to cultural questions) (National Telecommunications and Information Administration, 1999), we can note the following point: the Internet will be condemned for years to be complementary to the traditional procedure currently carried out at polling stations. Presently no one can consider making Internet voting obligatory. This would be to commit an act of social and political irresponsibility that would have devastating consequences for the legitimacy of our democracies.

One of the principal arguments, especially in the U.S., against using Internet in elections is, as the Governor of New York, the Republican George Pataki says (The Brookings Institution, 2000), that there exists a risk of giving an unfair advantage to part of the electorate. Bearing in mind that suffrage is a universal right for all citizens of age, and that there is a low and unequal use of new technologies in our societies, we might ask ourselves if Internet voting violates the equality principle that must always preside in the exercising of suffrage. This is not a minor question as we could even consider the following hypothesis: the results of any election that had the possibility of Internet voting would be advantageous to those who could participate more easily. Everyone agrees that voting from a computer connected to the Internet or having the possibility of voting during a longer period of time, instead of the single voting day, means a lower cost than going to a polling station on a specific date.

We could assume that the incentives derived from the lower costs of exercising the-right-to-vote via the Internet would cause those sectors that had access to the Internet to vote in a bigger percentage than those who did not have these facilities. It is true that the interests of these two segments of society do not necessarily need to be different or polarized, or homogeneous in each sector, but it cannot be guaranteed that it is not like this. Given that the digital divide is proportionally related, for example, to income level, and that income level is an explanatory factor of one's vote, we would need to accept the risk that the results over-represent the interests of those who had bigger incentives to vote (Alvarez and Nagler, 2000).

Arizona's Democratic Party decision to offer the possibility of Internet voting during its 2000 presidential primary election provoked an intense debate on the advantages and disadvantages of this procedure. The association The Voting Integrity Project (VIP) became one of the most active bodies against Internet voting and based most of their criticism on the digital divide. However, in spite of the attempts to legally stop the process in Arizona, the request was refused by the federal judge responsible for the case. He gave his direct assent to the promoters judging that "we haven't restricted anyone from voting, we've just enabled more people to vote." Apart from the pros and cons of the debate (Hoffman and Cranor, 2000), in that presidential primary 35,768 people voted remotely via the Internet and 4,174 voted via the Internet at polling stations (altogether close to one-half of the total participating voters). This is, therefore, a very good first opportunity to examine rigorously and without euphoria the socio-political impact of electronic voting.

Increase in Participation

Another remarkable aspect is that Internet voting may provoke a rise in participation in the electoral process. The possibility that the use of the Internet will permit greater participation is something that should be considered seriously by democracies where the tendency has been a progressive increase in abstention. The reasons for greater participation could be that the new voting method would be more convenient for the voters, would offer greater accessibility for mobile voters and would be more appealing to the younger. The

Arizona experience can give us some clues in this sense. The first analysis was very optimistic from a participation point of view: 85,970 voters in 2000 in contrast to 12,800 in 1996. However, subsequent studies have put doubt on the validity of such a comparison between the primaries of 1996 and those of 2000. The findings argue that the Arizona Democratic Party did not conduct a true statewide presidential primary (Alvarez and Nagler, 2000). In any case, one cannot attribute the rise of participation, if real, to a single factor (in this case Internet voting), and at the moment there is still no sociological study on the impact of distance electronic voting among the electorate.

Also, in this area it is important to be moderately optimistic in light of the tendency to abstain. The best studies on the phenomena of abstention tell us that the main causes are more to do with a lack of interest in politics rather than in the supposed cost that participation represents (Doppelt and Shearer, 1999; Anduiza, 1997). That is to say, Political Science cannot advocate that having more facilities to go and vote would mean a permanent increase in current participation levels. In whichever case, the hypothesis that an increase of electoral participation can be a consequence of utilizing the Internet is perfectly tangible and arguable. It will be important to verify this in successive trials and especially when the Internet stops being a novelty.

The Act of Voting Symbolism

Outside the realms of the digital divide, the possibility of Internet voting opens up other avenues for reflection. The exercising of the-right-to-vote by traditional means, such as in a polling station, carries a certain liturgy: the booth, the selection of voting cards and candidates, the identification of oneself in front of the electoral authorities, the insertion of the ballot paper into the urn, the presence of the supervisors as a guarantee of the clarity of the process.... An extra charge is conferred upon the act of voting for an electoral representative. For many, the fact of voting in a community space is an expression of civil obligation, a form of renewing publicly the adhesion to democratic principles and to grant legitimacy to the governmental institutions.

Internet voting could make this added value disappear and could accentuate a tendency to isolate the individual. This possibility has to be considered as something in the future and framed in a specific socio-cultural dynamic where the effects of digitalization would be increasing. It is important to see that in the near future a huge number of activities, which today we perform in person, will soon be carried out virtually. Like so many other electronic procedures, which are becoming normal, the digital vote via the Internet will be an option. Digital commerce, online administration or education through the Internet are examples. Is this development good news for our society? The answer yes or no depends on our own perception of the consequences of this information society and of new technologies.

It is important to bear in mind, however, that politics is going through a momentous crisis of legitimacy and credibility before digitalization has had an opportunity to show its results (Barber, 1984). The explosion of virtual activities for political action, and in particular the right to vote, does not necessarily have to carry more problems to the political system than those that already exist. One can even argue that keeping the present general systems of political action, in particular the system of voting, could have negative conse-quences for their credibility and vitality. One of the reasons for this would be the increasing presence that virtual realities have in our environment. The risk that politics and its electoral processes are perceived as archaic in contrast to the evolution of other realities could distance certain social segments, for example young people. As said before, it is difficult to categorically state that the use of the Internet automatically means an increase in participation. However, on the other hand it is easier to affirm that to not use the Internet would mean a loss of opportunities for encouraging certain sectors of society to vote.

The Public Control of the Electoral Process

One question which is much more important and difficult to resolve (and especially in those systems of Phase Four) is the difficulty that public powers would have in wielding control over the electoral process. This is a matter of huge importance in order to offer all the necessary guarantees that make the process legitimate. Speaking about the Internet means speaking about new communication and information technology. It is a synonym for liberalization, that is to say, user and private bodies' participation without which the Net would not function. The Internet is laid out as a space where voting can take place. Obviously, this carries with it the acceptance of the private bodies as an essential part that allows the process to work. How could legal guarantees be offered for the correct functioning of the Internet? It should be ensured that no one had his/her voting right limited by the failure of an ISP, for example, or by the temporary saturation of a part of the network. The powers that be are faced with a challenge that cannot be solved by present methods (in other words, the presence or intervention of the police and corresponding electoral authorities). For this reason, a good Internet voting system should guarantee the electronic voter that the digital vote reaches its proper destination. It is worth recalling, however, that the traditional voting methods are not completely infallible. Let us remember, for example, how during the 2000 U.S. presidential election, two absentee ballots containing official votes sent by mail appeared in Denmark.

On the other hand, and especially bearing in mind the example of Arizona, control over specialized private companies that administrate electronic voting must be granted. Presently there exists no legal guarantee on this point (Phillips and von Spakovsky, 2000). It is essential to regulate the profile of these companies as well as the contracting systems before ever using electronic voting for public elections. This is already being done in many countries with companies that deal with the collecting, processing and the diffusion of voting data in traditional voting processes.

Not only do Internet voting guarantees have to be given, but also the citizens must be convinced that they exist. It is beyond discussion, from a sociological point of view rather than legal, that reality is what the citizens believe it to be. Therefore this is a very important area of work without which Internet voting will never be fully implemented. We must also note that this problem is present in e-commerce as well, and that the users' security perception has been gradually consolidating itself, although many of the problems due to insecurity have probably persisted.

The Impact on Representative Democracy

Finally, we must consider the impact that Internet voting may have on the foundations of representative democracy. Digital voting practiced from anywhere in the Internet opens up possibilities for citizens to participate in public affairs discussions and decisions to a degree hitherto unknown. Technical hitches that have often been presented as the reason for not allowing direct participation will lose weight with the implementation of Internet voting. Could Internet voting, then, pose a threat to the survival of representative institutions? This is a question that must be asked by the political-institutional ambits as well as academic ambits without any fear.

We must realize that in the not-too-distant future, there will be voices asking for larger participation levels than those accepted today. It is reasonable to think that there are participation possibilities in the representative systems that could be allowed without going against the liberal democracy principles. Trials on deliberating processes are starting to have a relatively important presence in some of our democracies, even if in many cases they are realized under informal structures that are not legally provided for (Fishkin, 1992). Opting for Internet voting does not necessarily mean defending direct democracy.

It is possible, though, that the incorporation of new technologies causes the current political actors to develop new strategies in their ways of acting. Political parties themselves will need to change from the rigid present structures into something more flexible and open. It would be extreme to say that present political parties will be surpassed by the possibility of citizens' direct participation in the discussion of public affairs. However, one could say that parties have already started to transform and to change themselves into something which is more predisposed to citizen's opinion and are doing so in an agile and immediate way according to each situation. The visiting of Web pages by the main western political parties shows this evolution. We are experiencing a process where existing old political structures have not been put aside but have entered, led by new technologies, a progressive transformation--a progressive transformation with all the risks and opportunities that these dynamics bring into the functioning of the democratic system (Budge, 1996).

In any case, to summarize, it seems beyond discussion that technological advancements will force some rethinking of our democracies. This rethinking will also be impelled by the new characteristics of citizens in our democracies who will enjoy access to information and education in a way never seen before. The final result of this reconsideration does not necessarily mean a break from the democratic practice that our societies have lived with (with more or less fortune) in the last 150 years. The objective of this rethinking must be to incorporate technical advancements to political life, and to give citizens a more central role in the process of decision making and in discussions in collective affairs, while sustaining basic liberal democratic principles. The practice of permanent citizen consultation, shown by Macpherson (1976) to be a characteristic of the participating democracy model, is today closer than ever. In any case, it is no longer science fiction but rather a future political fact. In spite of this, we must take caution with the evolution of electronic voting, whether it be applied to the election of representatives or citizen consultations. Therefore, we have to be cautious and qualify electronic voting without underestimating its future impact.

FUTURE TRENDS

With everything moving into the new digital era, our electoral processes are still often using archaic methods. In most countries of Europe, paper ballots are the rule. In the U.S., one-fifth of the electorate is still using mechanical-lever machines, first introduced in 1892. The machines are 25 to 50 years old, and no company produces them any longer. The problem with the punch card ballots of Florida in November 2000 was predicted more than a decade ago (Saltman, 1988). Still, there are no easy answers yet on how to upgrade the voting technology (Cranor, 2001) and some even believe that secure electronic voting is not achievable at an acceptable cost (Mercuri and Neumann, 2001; Neumann, 1993).

We believe computerized methods of voting promise great efficiencies and several advantages over more traditional methods of voting. Still, widespread Internet voting in national public elections is some years away. Concerns about security, privacy, technical glitches and opportunity of access will delay the introduction of new electoral legislation and the complete deployment of newly certified Internet voting products. Furthermore, the costs associated with the unfolding of national Internet voting infrastructures may be an additional barrier (Cranor, 2001). Internet voting indeed promises to save electoral costs. However, taking into account that Internet voting cannot replace, but it must supplement traditional voting methods, costs could initially increase. See Phillips and Jefferson (2000) for an interesting list of additional costs and potential savings of Internet voting systems.

Still, the electoral evolution has already started. Some governments are studying the feasibility of Internet voting systems, and some non-binding tests parallel to real national elections have already taken place. 2000 has been the year that has spread the debate on Internet voting from the scientific community to the general public. At the time of writing, at least one EU-backed research project has the aim of demonstrating new Internet voting protocols. In the U.S., the National Science Foundation is currently assessing Internet voting at the direction of the White House. As part of this request, the Internet Policy Institute conducted a workshop in October 2000 to examine the issues associated with conducting public elections via the Internet. The California Secretary of State Bill Jones accepted the recommendations made by the California Internet Voting Task Force in January 2000, to initiate a four-stage trial process, starting with Internet voting at polling places and culminating in remote Internet voting. The Gartner Group, a consulting firm, expects that counties in all the states of the US will use some form of Internet voting by the 2004 presidential election. Currently, at least 12 states are considering Internet voting bills.

We believe the introduction of binding Internet voting in the public sector will initially take the form of poll-site Internet voting, perhaps complemented with paper-based backup ballots as suggested in Schneier (2000b). In this way Internet voting will be an alternative method to current conventional voting practices at the polling place. This may happen very soon in some countries (Schum, 2000). At the same time in some places, and later in others, remote Internet voting can be allowed for certain voters (e.g., disabled people and military outside the country). In the end, remote Internet voting can supplement absentee ballots for anyone desiring to vote remotely. More futuristically, secure remote Internet voting could be the first step to frequent popular consultations and referendums. The whole process may take between a few years and some decades to complete, depending on the country.

To be accepted, an Internet voting system does not only need certification by technical experts and standardization committees. Voter confidence is also very important. Furthermore, the support given to Internet voting should not be measured in terms of the potential voters, but rather in terms of the whole electorate. The level of public confidence on our democracies could be undermined if a broad range of voters was not satisfied with the use of the Internet for casting binding ballots. The question is therefore whether voters are slow or not embracing technology. The results obtained by the Online Voting Pilot at Maricopa County, in the state of Arizona, during a non-binding test parallel to the actual 2000 U.S. presidential election show that, in general, the average citizen (at least, in the U.S.) feels quite comfortable with a computerized form of voting. The results are based on 116 responses. All respondents found the computer voting system easy (85% very easy, 15% easy) compared to the current voting system. Those over 55 years were slightly less prone to answer "very easy" (78%) than younger respondents. Only 3% of respondents preferred the existing voting system to the computer system. More than eight in ten (85%) preferred to be able to vote in this way, and the remainder said either way was satisfactory. More than eight in ten believed the computer system was more secure (32%) or as secure (53%) as the current system. Women were twice as likely as men to feel the computer system was less secure. In addition, respondents under 35 years of age were more concerned about security than older ones. Respondents were finally asked: "Assuming the method is secure and that people could vote via the Internet from their home, offices or at a polling place, which would you most likely do?" The results are: 65% would vote from home (Men: 73%; Women: 59%) (Under 35: 67%; 35-55: 61%; Over 55: 78%), 15% would vote from their offices (Men: 8%; Women: 21%) (Under 35: 11%; 35-55: 20%; Over 55: 6%), 19% would vote at a polling place and 1% would prefer not to vote over the Internet.

CONCLUSION

Secure Internet voting for public elections (especially remote Internet voting) represents one of the major challenges for the beginning of the new millennium, both from the technological and from the socio-political points of view.

On the technological side, the design and operation of a secure Internet voting system is a complex matter. Security and privacy issues need elaborate solutions that must be based on a secure cryptographic voting protocol. The job however does not finish after a good voting protocol has been designed. The voting protocol then needs to be correctly implemented. Finally, the Internet voting system has to be properly operated and adequately protected from all the threats we have discussed. It is worth recalling that poll-site Internet voting removes many security hazards of remote Internet voting. Two of these are the identification of voters, and the security of the ballot-casting platforms.

On the socio-political side, the universal implantation of Internet voting will only be possible if we are able to solve the problems of distrust and social fracture that new technologies may cause in our societies. An incremental approach is essential therefore as a good strategy for the incorporation of electronic voting systems into the political processes. The objective is to avoid social perceptions of insecurity with regard to the procedural warranties of our electoral processes. Such kinds of perceptions could generate great opposition to the new voting methods.

We are not living in an ideal world. There is no such thing as a flawless election method, neither using conventional mechanisms nor casting ballots through the Internet. The inaccuracies introduced by conventional systems have been said to lead to error rates in the outcomes as high as 3%-4% (which is quite a big deal). Certainly changing the scenario raises new risks, but it also eliminates others. The apparition of new risks does not mean we have to reject the new scenario. It just means that the new risks must be dealt with. In fact, conventional electoral methods are built in the same way. Risks do exist. The existence of threats is obvious. However anyone perceives electoral processes (in democratic countries) as reliable and secure. What these systems do is to adequately manage the existing risks. Even embracing technological changes, the integrity of our electoral processes still can (and must) be ensured. The trick is to demand standards and rigorous certifications for any new voting method, involving in the process the adequate experts.

In the foreseeable future, Internet voting will not substitute conventional voting methods, but rather it will be introduced as a supplementary method. Internet voting has to be viewed as an evolution, but not a revolution of the current democratic practices. Such evolution must take an incremental approach. The introduction of Internet voting has to be made gradually, through a number of phases that will allow easier public acceptance and the acquisition of experience in the technical field.

The debate is not whether Internet voting will happen or not. The debate is at what speed and in what manner.

REFERENCES

Anderson, R. and Kuhn, M. (1996). Tamper resistance–A cautionary note. *Proceedings of the Second USENIX Workshop on Electronic Commerce*, 1-11, USENIX Association.

Alexander, K. (2001). *Ten Things I Want People to Know about Voting Technology. Presented to the Democracy Online Project's National Task Force*. Washington, DC: National Press Club.

Alvarez, R. M. and Nagler, J. (2000) *The Likely Consequences of Internet Voting for Political Representation*. Paper prepared for the Internet Voting and Democracy Symposium at Loyola Law School, October 26.

Anduiza, E. (1997). *Individual and Systemic Determinants of Electoral Abstention in Western Europe*. PhD Thesis. Florence: European University Institute.

Barber, B. R. (1984). *Strong Democracy: Participatory Politics for a New Age*. University of California Press.

Benaloh, J. C. (1987). *Verifiable Secret-Ballot Elections*. PhD Thesis, Yale University.

The Brookings Institution. (2000). The future of Internet voting. *A Symposium Co-Sponsored by the Brookings Institution and Cisco Systems, Inc.*, January. Event transcript. Available on the World Wide Web at: http://www.brookings.org/comm/transcripts/20000120.htm.

Borrell, J. (1996). *Design and Development of a Cryptographic Scheme to Perform Secure Elections Over a LAN*. PhD Thesis, Autonomous University of Barcelona.

Borrell J. and Rifà J. (1996). An implementable secure voting scheme. *Computers & Security*, 15(4), 327-338.

Budge, I. (1996). *The New Challenge of Direct Democracy*. Blackwell.

Cranor, L. F. and Cytron, R. K. (1996). *Design and Implementation of a Practical Security-Conscious Electronic Polling System*. Technical Report WUCS-96-02, Washington University.

International Standardization Organization. (1999). *The Common Criteria for Information Technology Security Evaluation*, Version 2.1. ISO International Standard 15408.

Chaum, D. (1981). Untraceable electronic mail, return addresses and digital pseudonyms. *Communications of the ACM*, 24(2), 84-88.

Computer Industry Almanac, Inc. (1999). Available on the World Wide Web at: http://www.c-i-a.com/199911iu.htm.

California Internet voting Task Force. (2000). A Report on the Feasibility of Internet voting, January. Available on the World Wide Web at: http://www.ss.ca.gov/executive/ivote.

Cranor, L.F. (2001). Voting after Florida: No easy answers. *Ubiquity: An ACM IT Magazine and Forum*, February, 47.

Dierks, T. and Allen, C. (1999). *The TLS Protocol*, Version 1.0. Request for Comments 2246, January.

Diffie, W. and Hellman, M. E. (1976). New directions in cryptography. *IEEE Transactions on Information Theory*, IT-22, 644-654.

Doppelt, J. C. and Shearer, E. (1999). *NonVoters. America's No-Shows*. Sage Publications.

European Commission. (2000). *Eurobarometer*, April-October.

Fishkin, J. (1992). *Democracy and Deliberation*. Yale University Press.

Freier, A. O., Karlton, P. and Kocher, P. C. (1996). *The SSL Protocol*, Version 3.0. Internet-Draft, November.

Hoffman, L. J. and Cranor, L. (Eds.). (2000). Internet voting for public officials. *Communications of the ACM*, 44(1), 69-85.

Kent, S. and Atkinson, R. (1998). *Security Architecture for the Internet Protocol*. Request for Comments RFC 2401, November.

Macpherson, C. B. (1976). *The Life and Times of Liberal Democracy*. Oxford University Press.

Mann, I. (1993). Open voting systems. *Computers, Freedom and Privacy '93*, Burlingame, CA, March. Available on the World Wide Web at: http://www.cpsr.org/conferences/cfp93/home.html.

Mercuri R. (1993). The business of elections. *Computers, Freedom and Privacy '93*, Burlingame, CA, March. Available on the World Wide Web at: http://www.cpsr.org/conferences/cfp93/home.html.

Mercuri, R. (2000). Voting automation (Early and Often?) Inside risks. *Communications of the ACM*, November, 43(11).

Mercuri, R. and Neumann, P.G. (2001). System integrity revisited. Inside risks. *Communications of the ACM*, January, 44(1).

Neumann, P. G. (1993). Security criteria for electronic voting. *Proceedings of the 16th National Computer Security Conference*, September.

National Telecommunications and Information Administration. (1999). *Falling Through the Net: Defining the Digital Divide*, July. US Department of Commerce.

NUA Internet Surveys. (1999). Avaliable on the World Wide Web at: http://www.nua.net/surveys/how_many_online.

Phillips, D. M. and Jefferson, D. (2000). Is Internet voting safe? *VIP Report*. Available on the World Wide Web at: http://www.voting-integrity.org.

Phillips, D. M. and von Spakovsky, H. A. (2000). Gauging the risks of Internet elections. *Communications of the ACM*, 44(1), 73-85.

Riera, A. (1999). *Design of Implementable Solutions for Large Scale Electronic Voting Schemes*, December. PhD Thesis, Autonomous University of Barcelona.

Rubin, A. (2000). *Security Considerations for Remote Electronic Voting over the Internet*, October. Sunworld.

Saltman, R. G. (1988). Accuracy, integrity and security in computerized vote-tallying. *NBS Special Publication 500-158*. National Bureau of Standards.

Schneier, B. (1996). *Applied Cryptography. Protocols, Algorithms and Source Code in C*, 2nd Edition. John Wiley & Sons.

Schneier, B. (2000a). *Secrets & Lies*. John Wiley & Sons.

Schneier, B. (2000b). Voting and Technology. From the newsletter *Crypto-Gram*, December. Available on the World Wide Web at: http://www.counterpane.com.

Schum, M. (2000). Internet voting: Its perils and promise. *National Workshop on Internet voting*. Washington, DC: Internet Policy Institute.

Shamos, M. I. (1993, March). Electronic voting–Evaluating the threat. *Computers, Freedom and Privacy '93*, March, 3.18-3.25. Burlingame, CA. Available on the World Wide Web at: http://www.cpsr.org/conferences/cfp93/home.html.

Waskell, E. (1993). Overview of computers and elections. *Computers, Freedom and Privacy '93*, March. Burlingame, CA. Available on the World Wide Web at: http://www.cpsr.org/conferences/cfp93/home.html.

Chapter VI

Towards a Framework for Government Portal Design: The Government, Citizen and Portal Perspectives

Brian Detlor
McMaster University, Canada

Kim Finn
Department of Human Resources Development, Canada

This chapter identifies and describes factors that inhibit and promote successful electronic government portal design. These factors are based on a review of recent research on both electronic government initiatives and corporate portal implementations. The result is a generalized framework for government portal design. To test its viability, the framework is used as a lens to analyze a current case study, specifically a portal project led by the Government of Canada to support Canadian youth citizens. The framework offers an effective preliminary construct by which to focus and pinpoint pertinent issues surrounding government portal design.

INTRODUCTION

As means of delivering more effective and efficient government services and encouraging greater democracy and engagement from citizenry, governments around the globe are starting to explore the use of Web-based information technology. For instance, numerous governments are focusing attention on the design and delivery of portals as a major component of government electronic service infrastructures.

Portals are single-point Web browser interfaces used to promote the gathering, sharing and dissemination of information as well as the provision of services to communities of interest. Hagedorn (2000, p. 4) defines a portal as "a site for a particular audience, providing a path to all-encompassing content and services through one access point." As such, portals can be thought of as a launch pad or gateway to information resources via a single point of access, namely through a Web browser interface such as Internet Explorer or Netscape Communicator. It is due to the proliferation of the World Wide Web and the burgeoning success of consumer portal sites such as Yahoo! and AOL (America Online) that portals are perceived by many as having the potential to serve as key enabling solutions for electronic government delivery.

The Government of Canada is set to lead the way in this area by planning to become the government in the world by 2004 that is the most electronically connected to its citizens.[1] Coined Government On-Line (GOL), the vision is "to continually improve the quality of interaction between Canadians and their government by enabling Canadians to request and receive services and information when and where it is most convenient for them, wherever they live" (Government of Canada, 2000). To reach this goal, the Canadian federal government has embarked on the development and implementation of Canada Site[2]—a portal to federal government information resources and services. The benefits of Canada Site are better service, better government and stimulation of electronic commerce activities across the country. As such, the Government of Canada is dedicated to a portal that will complement traditional service channels, protect citizens' privacy and guarantee accessibility.

Governments, like Canada's, are forging new ground. Lessons can be learned from both private-sector enterprises, in terms of the design and rollout of internal corporate portals to service the information needs and uses of employees, as well as the delivery of large consumer portal sites, like Yahoo!, to the general public. However, realizing that governments differ from business in terms of motives and the constituents they serve, governments should be aware that they must tailor portal implementations to address the unique concerns and challenges facing electronic government delivery today, such as the need to protect citizen privacy and the requirement to prevent government misuse of information. Further, due to the relative newness of this technology, there is little empirical research from the academic community to guide or inform the development of electronic government initiatives such as portals. Frameworks are required to help guide research and development in this nascent field.

As such, the primary objective of this chapter is to present a theoretical framework for government portal design that identifies and describes the factors that promote or inhibit successful electronic government. The chapter does this from three key perspectives. The first is the government perspective which addresses the organizational factors which affect portal design. The second is the citizen perspective which addresses user concerns that influences the degree to which portals are adopted and utilized. The third is the portal interface perspective which concerns itself with the extent to which features and functions offered by the portal satisfy both citizen and government information needs.

To reach this objective, background is given on the general benefits, public concerns and challenges of electronic government and the capacity of portals to serve as an enabler of government information and services delivery. From there, a framework for the design of government portals is made based on the above discussion. To test the viability of the framework, a case study is presented within the Canadian context with reference to the delivery of a government Web site for Canada's youth, a specific project within GOL involving 21 Canadian federal departments to deliver a single Web site that integrates youth-related services and information. The goal of this project is to design a Web site for gathering, sharing and disseminating content and services to young Canadians based on their self-identified needs.

One of the strengths of this chapter is that it presents an electronic government framework for portal design that is based on academic research. Further, the chapter applies the framework within the Canadian context which has a federal government with both a strong public and self-directed mandate to become a world leader in the provision of electronic government. It is hoped that the framework can be used to inform and structure future research on this new phenomenon of government portals, as well elicit practical insights on the design and rollout of portals which more closely satisfy citizen needs and facilitate better government.

BACKGROUND

The Nature of Electronic Government

Electronic government refers to the delivery and administration of government products and services over an information technology infrastructure. Overall, there are several benefits, public concerns and challenges facing electronic government today (Great Britain Cabinet Office, 1998; Great Britain Parliament, 1998; Greenfield, 1995; Hwang, Choi, & Myeong, 1999; Nilsen, 1993; Perritt, 1996; Steyaert, 2000).

Two key benefits are: 1) citizen empowerment, namely through provision of convenient and direct communications channels which facilitate greater public participation and interaction with the government; and 2) the delivery of more effective and efficient government information and services, such as increased speed of transactions, greater convenience, and better organization and access to information. These benefits have been recognized for some time. For example, in the mid-1990s it was recognized that the National Information Infrastructure (or super information highway) in the United States, under the governance of then President Clinton and Vice President Gore, was a reliable and accessible open network architecture for disseminating government information and engaging citizens (Perritt, 1996, p. 157; Greenfield, 1995, p. 85).

In terms of public concerns over electronic government delivery, there are several. These include: ensuring confidentiality or privacy in interacting with the government, providing sufficient safeguards against fraud or computer hacking, preventing government misuse of information and guaranteeing universal access to on-line services.

With respect to implementing technical solutions, many challenges exist. These include: designing electronic solutions not built along existing governmental structures, ensuring cooperation among government departments, redefining current work processes and structures, sustaining strong leadership to promote the mission, acquiring adequate funding and retaining sufficient human resources skilled in electronic information services delivery.

A 214-page report written in October 1998 by the Great Britain Cabinet Office offers insights on the benefits, concerns and challenges of electronic government. The report covers research undertaken between November 1997 and July 1998 that explored the extent to which individuals and small businesses were likely to adopt electronic means of interaction with government. Methods of data collection were quantitative surveys and qualitative interviews. Several findings from that study showcase the complexities of delivering electronic government to citizens:

1) Individuals demonstrate very different propensities to adopt new ways of interacting with the government and can be divided broadly into three groups: the first comprising two-fifths of adults who are favourably inclined to adopt new approaches, the second comprising two-fifths of adults who can be persuaded to utilize electronic government services, and the third comprising just under one-fifth of the population who are antagonistic towards such use.

2) In general, propensity to utilize electronic government services increases with social grade and falls with age.

3) The rate of user adoption of electronic government services is highly dependent on how well user needs are understood and incorporated within the design, implementation and support of such services.

4) In terms of delivering new electronic services, it is essential that they improve or enhance existing services (i.e., users are not accepting of new electronic services that simply result in "moving the queue from the counter to a kiosk"). Further the services must be of benefit to users and be cost effective to both users and government.

5) The goals of the delivery of electronic government services are: simplifying procedures and documentation, reducing time taken queuing or waiting, minimizing referrals between officials, eliminating interactions which fail to yield outcomes, extending contact opportunities (i.e., access) beyond office hours and improving relationships with the public.

6) The perceived benefits of electronic government services are improvements in the speed with which transactions are carried out, convenience and access, flexibility in options and hours of service and empowerment (i.e., bringing services closer to the public and allowing them to choose how/when to carry out transactions).

7) The public has concerns over the delivery of electronic government services: ensuring confidentiality or privacy in interacting with the government, providing safeguards against fraud or computer hacking, providing guarantees about government's use of information and providing assistance and support to users.

8) The public has certain perceptions over the delivery of e-Government services: first, they are skeptical about the government's ability to deliver benefits and/or provide reliable assurances about electronic government; second, fairly simple transactions should be a priority, such as the delivery of government information, over the delivery of more complex services, to allow the public to be accustomed to the technology; third, there is no consensus on the best method of interacting electronically with the government (i.e., use of keyboards, touch screens, interactive TV, smart cards).

A report from the United Kingdom Parliamentary Office of Science and Technology provides similar and new insights on the nature and implications of electronic government (Great Britain Parliament, 1998). The report identifies the promise of information and communications technologies (ICTs) in improving the delivery of government services at a cost savings for the taxpayer, helping government become more transparent by providing access to a greater range of information collected and generated by government, and possibly offering deeper effects on society and the nature of democracy by promoting citizen engagement and redefining the role or structure of government itself. Further, the report recognizes that governments face unique concerns in delivering electronic services such as: privacy; vulnerability of a public information infrastructure to crime, acts of war and terrorism; potential abuses of civil rights, and social cohesion versus social exclusion of its citizens—all which must be taken into consideration in the delivery of an electronic government solution.

One of the key challenges facing electronic government delivery identified in the report is the provision of a unified public interface to government information and services not based on departmental hierarchical lines. Overcoming this challenge requires information management and cooperation among government departments to consolidate and redefine current work processes and structures.

The report also addresses the United Kingdom government's intent to work within the seven principles of electronic government stated in its 1996 Green Paper:

1) *Choice*—make electronic delivery of services the preferred option.
2) *Confidence*—safeguard information collected from citizens and business and ensure citizens are made aware of this safeguarding.
3) *Accessibility*—provide services in a format the customer requires them, paying special attention to the needs of people in remote areas, people with limited mobility, and people who do not speak the country's official language(s).
4) *Efficiency*—streamline, automate and integrate government processes so that the boundaries between government departments are invisible or irrelevant to the user;
5) *Rationalization*—share resources for functions and processes which are common to more than one department or agency.
6) *Open information*—make information readily available in convenient and useful forms.
7) *Fraud prevention*—establish measures which check the identity of individuals and organizations dealing with the government and to ensure that information cannot be incorrectly accessed or manipulated.

Other issues raised in the United Kingdom report relating to the delivery of electronic information include the need to create a single window to government information and branding the interface to create a common look and feel. The goal of these actions is to help distinguish official sources from non-official ones which could be providing misinformation. Additional barriers or sources of failure for electronic government initiatives include a lack of clear vision or goal of the electronic solution; a lack of coherent leadership; a lack of information technology skills in the government workforce to implement the solution; poor communication and training of government staff; a tendency to ignore human factors in design of electronic solutions; and loss of expertise to design and streamline government processes, namely through downsizing and removal of middle layers of management in government.

Of related interest is a study by Hwang, Choi and Myeong (1999) on electronic government in South Korea which finds evidence for the need for governments to have a broad vision in rolling out electronic government initiatives. The research team interviewed 69 government officials and found a strong perception by those in charge of administering the electronic "informatization" in South Korea to utilize technology to streamline internal government operations. The team cautions that having a narrow conceptualization of electronic government (i.e., one that places emphasis on technology and internal effects) is both limiting and unbalanced. In response, Hwang et al. stress the importance for government leaders to have an overall well-defined, well-rounded, well-communicated and well-understood vision of their electronic government plans. Specifically, the research team identified a number of themes which can undermine a balanced conceptualization of electronic government:

1) Viewing electronic government as largely an internal operation of government. This can lead to a refurbishing of government to modern technologies but may be limited in its extent to rehabilitate government inefficiencies and operations.

2) Looking at the external benefits of electronic government in terms of what government officials think people want to have. There is a need to promote citizen engagement (not passivity) and to turn away from a "paternalistic administration mentality."

3) Giving greatest weight of electronic government to automation or computerization. There is a hazard in that this may lead to a replication of existing work processes rather than a re-engineering of new ways of doing things within government.

4) Keeping abreast of major developments in information technology and their governmental implications. The authors warn that a preoccupation with complex information technologies is an information highway syndrome.

The findings from the above reports highlight some of the promises and issues surrounding electronic government initiatives today. Together they stress the need to pay attention to the challenges and concerns facing electronic government solutions if the potential benefits of electronic government are to be realized.

Portals and Electronic Government

One specific technology that holds much promise in serving as an enabler of electronic government are portals. These are single-point Web browser interfaces used to promote the gathering, sharing and dissemination of information and provision of services to communities of interest. The primary purpose of a portal is to function as a gateway to information products and services. As such, the goal of a portal is to provide an intuitive integrated view of information products and services. Common portal features include: a classification schema of information categories that help organize information for easy retrieval; a search engine to facilitate more exact and specific information requests; and links to internal and external Web sites and information sources that may be of interest to the targeted community.

A recent model explicates the role of portals as a shared information work space comprising three distinct areas: a content space to facilitate information access and retrieval; a communication space to negotiate collective interpretations and shared meanings; and a collaboration or work space to support work action (Choo et al., 2000, pp. 86-92; Detlor, 2000a). The model could serve electronic government well. An information space within a government portal could provide citizen access to information that the government wishes to disseminate (e.g., press notes, policies, news), information the government collects for itself and makes available for use (e.g., census data, environmental data, economic data) and information that it is required to supply (e.g., public and journalist requests for information). A communication space could enhance democracy and promote citizen engagement. A work space could support on-line transactions between citizens and the government.

To encourage the design and use of government portals in this way, lessons can be learned from the private sector in terms of the success and failures experienced in the implementation of departmental intranets and corporate portals. There seems to be a gap between the anticipated use of these tools and their actual utilization (Lamb, 1999). For example, Newell et al. (1999) demonstrate how organizational structures, decentralized system development approaches and budget constraints can limit the utilization of intranets by employees. In their field investigation of a case study on intranet usage, these authors observe how the mobilization of an intranet initiative as a knowledge management solution, rather than creating a centripetal force integrating individuals across the organization in terms of information sharing and collaboration, ironically created a centrifugal force which reinforced existing functional and national barriers with electronic knowledge silos. Abraham (1998) identifies other constraints that can limit the usability of Web-based systems in organizations, namely: the lack of time by workers to learn the functionality offered in Web-based applications; the failure of upper management to sponsor and publicly support Web information systems; the general dislike of organizational members to share information across departments and groups; the failure of organizations to market and promote new Web information systems; and the preference of potential users of these systems to communicate via traditional telephone and face-to-face encounters.

A recent investigation in a large telecommunications firm by Detlor (2000b) provides further insights on the phenomenon of organizational Web use. Detlor conducted a case study evaluation of Web information systems (WIS) usage. A primary object of that study was the organization's corporate portal. Emphasis was placed on examining the information needs and uses of five major sets of users and the "information ecology" (Davenport, 1997) in which the portal was utilized. Data collection involved a wide variety of techniques, namely interviews, Web tracking, field observations, document review and questionnaires. A modified version of grounded theory (Strauss & Corbin, 1998) served as the primary mode of data analysis; descriptive statistics helped triangulate research results.

The central output of the study was a descriptive model showing the organizational, user and interface factors that promote or inhibit the use of Web information systems. These factors are similar to those identified by Lan and Falcone (1997) in their review and analysis of the literature discussing the contributions, roles and responsibilities of public, non-profit and private sector institutions on the development, maintenance and expansion of the Internet. Lan and Falcone specifically identify institutional arrangements, user preferences and psychological factors, and technical characteristics as being the major factors that influence Internet use in their policy model for electronic government information provision.

In terms of organizational factors, Detlor's model suggests that three key characteristics impact the use of corporate portals: 1) the information politics (Davenport et al., 1992) surrounding WIS development which influence the design of the system itself and impact the adoption and use of the system by users; 2) the development process by which Web information systems are maintained—a perceived slowness or inability to respond to user demands may negatively impact WIS acceptance and utilization; and 3) the information culture of the firm. This last factor speaks to the amount of control the organization places on technical and information content standards in WIS design, the accessibility of the systems to workers and the amount of information hoarding that occurs within the organization. Too much control, lack of accessibility or a high degree of unwillingness to share information results in a decline of or resistance to use of these tools.

With respect to user factors, Detlor's model suggests that four key characteristics impact WIS activity by organizational workers. They are 1) the functional role of users which determine the type of tasks performed on a Web information system; 2) the passion or interest of users in utilizing Web information system technology; 3) the perception of users in terms of the capabilities and potentials of this technology; and 4) the general motivation of users to learn and explore the world around them.

In terms of interface factors, Detlor's model suggests that five key characteristics impact the degree to which such systems are utilized. They are: 1) the ability of the system to tailor or personalize the information content displayed and the applications available for use; 2) the quality of the information displayed—users generally expect the information to be relevant, reliable in terms of its validity and trustworthiness, and timely in that the information is refreshed frequently and is as up to date as possible; 3) the organization of the information in that there are methods by which to navigate and access information quickly in terms of a robust search engine and an elaborate classification schema of intranet sites; 4) the presence of collaborative tools which support the collaboration, sharing of documents and communication; 5) and engagement of these systems in providing an interactive and attractive environment for conducting tasks.

With respect to this last factor, there is specific support in the literature for the need to support interactivity or engagement in the design of government portal sites. Steyeart (2000), in a content analysis of several municipal Web sites in Belgium, finds evidence that Web sites which are highly non-interactive and function as broadcast media for government information reduce the role of the user to that of a customer of government information. Further, such sites do not support possible other roles as voter and/or citizen. Steyeart (p. 3) warns that a lack of interactive possibilities on a government portal neglects the democratic possibilities of the Internet and reduces the potential of the site to that of an "electronic government shop" rather than an "electronic community" as predicted.

Implications can be drawn from Detlor's model on the ways to improve the development and use of government portals. In terms of the interface design, portals can contain features and functions that improve the utilization of these systems. For instance, the portals can contain: 1) a robust search engine and government employee directory to help citizens location information and human experts; 2) a personalization mechanism to modify the portal interface to accommodate individual information needs, uses and preferences; 3) an extensive classification schema of information categories to facilitate improved organization and access to information; 4) collaborative applications such as a shareable document space and a communication area for shared discussions; and 5) links to a wide variety of internal and external information sources on related issues of interest to citizens.

With respect to user characteristics, greater emphasis can be placed on marketing the government portal to citizens and training government workers on its strategic use. Doing so could help showcase the functionality offered in the portal, facilitate a more accurate perception of the features available for use and instill greater interest or passion in use of this technology on a daily basis.

In terms of the government's organizational context, certain steps can be taken to foster the design and development of the portal: 1) a democratic portal steering committee can be established to help promote a portal design that meets the requirements of various internal departments and balance tensions in design between information content and technology perspectives; 2) a more streamlined system development process can be created by which modifications to the portal can be made; 3) universal portal access can become a priority to ensure that all citizens (or as many as possible) have access to the government portal; and 4) control over portal technical standards and information content can be loosened to encourage citizen acceptance and use of these systems.

A DESIGN FRAMEWORK FOR GOVERNMENT PORTALS

By combining current awareness of the characteristics of electronic government with insights from the lessons learned from private industry on portal adoption and use, common themes and issues surrounding government portal design can be identified. The purpose of this section of the chapter is to do just that. The goal is to summarize prior discussion and present a framework for government portal design that describes the more salient factors which impact and influence portal development and use which can be utilized to inform future and existing portal initiatives in the government sector.

Figure 1 below illustrates a high-level vantage point of the factors influencing government portal design gleaned from the discussion above. The framework offers three distinct perspectives on the adoption and use of government portals. The first is the government perspective which addresses the organizational factors which affect portal design. The second is the portal interface perspective which concerns itself with the extent to which features and functions offered by a portal satisfy user and government information needs. The third is the citizen perspective which addresses user concerns that determine the extent to which a portal is adopted and utilized. The framework suggests that bi-directional relationships exist between factors from these three shaping perspectives which impact the extent to which the government portal can support efficient and effective government. The identification of three perspectives aligns closely to the three major entities (i.e., organizational, user and Web information system) defined in Detlor's descriptive model of Web use in organizations.

In terms of the government perspective, there are several factors which affect government portal design and use.

One key factor is information management. As evidenced by prior studies, a success factor in the delivery of a government portal site is the need to facilitate and foster cooperation across the various departments which have a stake in the portal's design. One of the purposes of a government portal is to integrate the various information sources and services that are provided across various government departments. To do this requires that participating departments "buy-in" to this goal and work together to deliver a composite and comprehensive view of information resources and services. This may require a change in work processes for these departments and the need to reach consensus on the ownership and authority of various information sources.

Figure 1: A framework for government portal design

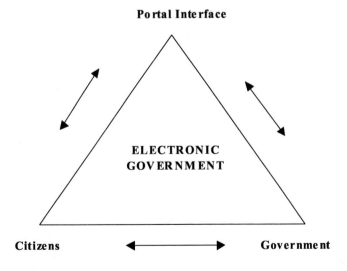

The information systems development process is another government-related factor affecting portal design. This was advocated by Detlor in his model of organizational web use which called for a streamlined approach to portal development, as a perceived slowness or inability to respond to user demands may negatively impact portal acceptance and utilization. The need for a robust development process was also evident in the prior studies of electronic government discussed above which highlighted the necessity of acquiring a sufficient information technology skills base within government to build and rollout an electronic government initiative. Securing adequate funding to support systems development impacts the design of government portals. First, base funding is required to establish a proper information technology infrastructure. Second, long-term funding is required as well. Another concern in the development process is the need to include citizen representatives in the design process. The South Korean study warned of the need for governments not to guess at citizen wants; doing so could jeopardize citizen engagement of electronic government initiatives (Hwang, Choi and Myeong, 1999).

A third factor from the government perspective is policy and leadership. Prior studies have called the need for strong leadership within government to establish policy on electronic government and carry out strategic direction.

With respect to the portal interface perspective, several factors affect government portal design and use. Here, the portal interface perspective is integrative in that it focuses attention on screen design to support both user and government needs. The interface factors are primarily elicited from Detlor's case study investigation of portal use in the private sector.

In terms of tailorability, citizens need to be able to personalize the information content displayed on a government portal so that the information matches more closely to user interests and needs. With respect to information quality, citizens need government portals to provide information that is relevant, reliable and timely so that citizens are satisfied and trust the information that is provided, which in turn, encourages heightened and future use of the portal. In terms of organization and access of portal information, citizens require mechanisms for finding and navigating information, specifically through inclusion of an in-depth taxonomy scheme and a robust search directory. With respect to task-based tools, government portals need to provide features such as discussion areas which help citizens connect with government officials and each other to share ideas and insights. This is a good mechanism by which to promote citizen democracy and empowerment. The portal sites need also to provide a means by which citizens can find government experts on specific areas of interest. In terms of engagement, governments need to provide an attractive, interactive interface as a means of fostering interest and participation in the portal.

With respect to the citizens' perspective, there are user factors which influence the degree to which government portals are adopted and used.

One critical factor, voiced in the discussion on electronic government in general, is public concern over government access and use of citizen information. For instance, the public's desire for universal access was identified as a strong requirement for government portal design. Privacy, security of information and fear of government misuse of information were also advocated as key public concerns in the delivery of electronic government initiatives, primarily from the background information derived from various academic and government-led studies. This suggests that government portal sites need to reinforce and market evidence that steps and procedures are in place which address public concerns. One way of doing this may be the placement of a link to the government's policy on information privacy and security in an obvious and convenient location on the portal site, such as an icon on the site's homepage or as an option from the site's main menu bar.

The management of citizen wants is another factor impacting government portal design. User demand for certain functionality must be weighed against other restraining factors such as the cost of delivering and supporting such services.

The last factor from the citizen perspective is the need to market government portals and train citizens on their use. Detlor (2000b) advocated the need to market and train users on portals as a means of fostering interest in the technology and making users aware of the functionality offered in such systems. This is key in facilitating user adoption of such systems.

Table 1 provides a summary of the factors within each perspective that have the potential to affect government portal design and use. Overall, the framework provides a guideline on the issues and challenges facing government portal design and use.

THE GOVERNMENT OF CANADA'S YOUTH CLUSTER PROJECT

To test the viability of the framework, a case study is presented of a specific government portal initiative within the Canadian context. The goal is to describe the project and then utilize the framework as a lens for analysis of the more salient factors impacting the success of a real-life government portal initiative.

The specific portal initiative in question is the Government of Canada's Youth Cluster project. To describe this project, background is first given on the Youth Cluster and its placement within the Government of Canada's GOL initiative. From there, a description of

Table 1: Overview of the framework's components

Perspective	Factors/Issues Affecting Government Portal Design and Use
Government	-Information management (cooperation across participating government departments, re-engineering of work processes); -Information systems development process (sufficient IT skills, adequate funding, inclusion of citizen representatives); -Policy & leadership (establishment of electronic government policy & strategy, strong leadership to carry out strategic direction).
Portal Interface	-Tailorability of the interface to individual user needs and preferences; -Information quality (provision of relevant, reliable, timely information); -Information access & organization (provision of robust search tools and information classification schemas); -Task-based tools (provision of discussion areas and functions to perform government transactions); -Engagement (provision of an attractive, interactive interface).
Citizens	-Public concerns (universal access, privacy, security, fear of government misuse of information); -Management of citizen expectations in the delivery of electronic government; -Marketing & training of citizens to increase motivation to use the portal and improve their perception of portal functionality.

the history of the project and success factors is provided, as well as a discussion of the strategic considerations, opportunities and challenges facing the Youth Cluster.

Project Context

Under the auspices of the Canadian government's Government On-Line initiative, the Department of Human Resources Development Canada (HRDC) is leading the development of a youth portal or cluster. The Youth Cluster is a key instrument through which quality information and service delivery will be made available to young Canadians providing access to useful, critical information including: employment and career information, education, justice, culture, health, immigration, quality of life, etc. from national/regional and local perspectives.

Government On-Line represents the Canadian government's institutional response to the shift towards knowledge-based economy and advancements in information technology. There are three phases or "tiers" to the initiative, each representing a further evolution towards integrated, client-centered electronic service delivery. Tier One objectives include the establishment of the federal government's on-line presence by December 2000 and the promotion of a client-centred approach to presenting information. Tier Two involves the delivery of key federal programs and services securely over the Internet by December 2004 and the promotion of a client-centered approach to presenting information and services, including clustering and integration. Lastly, Tier Three involves the promotion of inter-jurisdictional electronic service delivery and innovative pilots to improve service to clients.

The delivery of government portal sites addresses all three tiers of the Government On-Line initiative and allows federal departments to proceed along the path towards service integration. The primary purpose is to create a service delivery structure that meets the ever-changing needs of today's technology-savvy citizenry and business communities. The intent is not to replace all other forms of service delivery (i.e., in-person, telephone, fax, kiosk), but rather to add a new mechanism to the mix allowing the public sector to leverage the benefits associated with new technologies and to increase the overall level of service to Canadians and those outside of Canada. The GOL initiative is also perceived as a catalyst for the whole scale transformation of traditional government structures. The hope is that the initiative will precipitate the integration of services to Canadians resulting in a public sector that delivers information, programs and services in a more effective and client-centered manner.

The Government of Canada's Youth Cluster itself directly addresses the commitments made under the auspices of the Government On-Line initiative. The project focuses on government-to-citizen service delivery, representing a new client-centered development model that is fully aligned with GOL Tier Two objectives to:

- deliver key federal programs and services securely on-line;
- encourage end-to-end, electronic service delivery of key federal programs and services; and,
- promote client-centric clustering and integration of information and services.

In addition, due to a highly client-centered development process with which Canadian youth information needs and uses will be identified, the Tier Three objective of inter-jurisdictional electronic service delivery will also be possible. This development approach goes beyond traditional focus group testing by including youth representatives from across the country to participate in the design of the Youth Cluster. The goal is to produce an information taxonomy developed in collaboration with youth clientele for the Web site that will be transferable to information and services provided by provincial, regional and local jurisdictions as well as the non-profit and voluntary sectors.

The portal structure for the Canadian federal government begins with Canada Site. This Web site represents the primary gateway to information and services provided by the Government of Canada to a host of different client groups. This main entryway is then divided into three sub-portals: Canadians, Business and Non-Canadians. Under each of these sub-portals are a number of subject clusters intended to meet the needs of particular client groups by providing access to information and services from various different departments in a seamless and client-centered fashion. Determination of these clusters and their titles was accomplished through focus testing and consultation with groups of individuals across Canada. The Youth Cluster falls under the "Canadians/Individuals" portal along with others such as Health, Jobs, Consumer Information, Financial Entitlements and Travel. Figure 2 below illustrates the hierarchical structure of Canada Site, its sub-portals and their subject clusters (TBSC, 2000).

The Youth Cluster represents a unique opportunity for a number of federal government departments to work together to deliver information and services to young Canadians. The project itself is a pathfinder and builds on investments made through existing policy, program development and communications partnerships. These partnerships will be extended and deepened in order to further develop, market and promote useful and effective youth information and services.

History of the Project

In March of 2000, the Youth Initiatives Directorate within HRDC approached an existing group of senior representatives from approximately 21 federal government departments with the idea of creating a central access point for on-line youth-related information and services. Many federal government departments have existing information on the Internet, however preliminary research done by the Directorate indicated that, at present, this information cannot be easily accessed via federal department homepages and that few of the existing Web sites offered a centralized/dedicated resource for youth information. Repre-

Figure 2: Structure of the government of Canada's portal sites

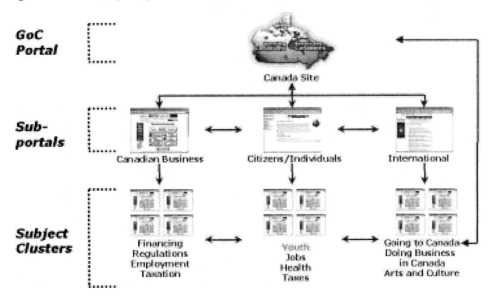

sentatives were receptive to the idea and appointed members from their respective depart-ments to participate in the project.

In May of the same year, a portal learning session for partner departments was hosted by HRDC to initiate dialogue and attempt to begin the process of integrating information and services from a point of common understanding. Shortly after this session, it came to the attention of the Directorate that the government's central agency, the Treasury Board Secretariat, was making funding available to support such initiatives through the Govern-ment On-Line office. Over the next six months, HRDC was given the official lead for the Youth Cluster and directed the proposal-writing process to secure funding from the Treasury Board Secretariat to facilitate the development of the Youth Cluster. While it was under-stood that the need for the tool was great, no individual department was capable of funding the initiative on its own. The Treasury Board at this point in time was allocating funding for a select few projects, deemed "pathfinders" that would be used as pilots or demonstrations for other cluster initiatives over the coming years.

In late October 2000, the Directorate was informed that the project had in fact qualified for funding along with other clusters such as the Consumer Information Gateway, the Seniors Cluster and the Jobs, Workers, Training and Careers Cluster. The amount awarded for the Youth Cluster was $2.4 million (Canadian) covering activities through March 31, 2002, and pending the submission of a detailed business case and Memorandum of Understanding to the Treasury Board Secretariat.

HRDC was given the lead for the Youth Cluster for a number of reasons. As the lead department for Canada's Youth Employment Strategy, HRDC is responsible for a wide range of youth programs and information sources. The department also has strong provincial/territorial and non-governmental links and significant existing intra/interde-partmental relationships and mechanisms in place. These factors, paired with experi-ence in the development of information products and services, made HRDC the most appropriate department to lead this particular project.

Success Factors

There are a number of distinct elements of the Youth Cluster project which bear on the success of the project in delivering a federal government portal that integrates youth-related information and services.

1.   The project hinges on a high degree of interdepartmental collaboration and coordi-nated on-line service delivery.

Horizontal interdepartmental coordination will be critical in the development of this Government On-Line initiative. The design and implementation of this channel will necessitate the involvement of all youth-related departments and agencies, along with many others with less explicit but still important information and services for young Canadians and their families. The project will build on investments made through the existing Youth Employment Strategy policy, implementation, communication and evaluation committees. Partners will explore opportunities for service integration where applicable, based on client-defined needs.

2.   The project plan incorporates a governance structure that involves youth directly in the product development and maintenance processes.

The project will engage young Canadians in the development process in order to ensure that their needs and interests are inherent to the taxonomy and features of the cluster. This represents a unique opportunity for the Canadian federal government to work in collabora-tion not only between departments, but also directly with those clients the product is intended to serve. The benefits of this process are two-fold:

- It will result in a Web-based service delivery mechanism that is truly reflective of and responsive to changing client needs.
- It will provide a tool for youth engagement by involving young Canadians directly in the development process and through interactive feedback mechanisms.

Youth team members will provide advice on design and implementation, issues of concern to youth, ways to reach out to a broader youth audience and programs targeted to youth. Figure 3 below shows the various players comprising the Youth Cluster development team where youth representatives work in association with members of the Canadian federal government's technical, information content and communications teams.

3.   A layered marketing approach will be used to converge existing communications media to maximize reach and user response.

A number of communications and marketing tools currently exist for Canada's Youth Employment Strategy-related information and services at the federal level (Internet, television, radio, 1-800 line, direct mail, events and exhibits, etc.). New research indicates that the youth client group is inherently multi-tasking and that different forms of media drive users from one to the other. The Youth Cluster project represents a unique opportunity to build upon and converge existing communications tools by using a layered marketing approach that links existing forms of media with one another to communicate and promote the Youth Cluster to young Canadians (see Figure 4).

4.   The project plan spans a two-year window.

The development of the cluster is taking place over a two-year period between October 2000 and the end of March 2002. The project plan is ambitious and contains a number of activities as well a series of meetings at various management and operational levels to facilitate decision making, information sharing and learning for participating members of each of the project teams. Tasks include the provision of "learning sessions" to educate and help build relationships between members of the various 21 federal departments involved in the project; the recruitment and orientation of Canadian youth representatives; the identification of cluster information content; the development and implementation of a communications (marketing) plan; the testing and building of a prototype; the full launch and evaluation of the Youth Cluster; as well as continual web site maintenance and the formation of strategic alliances with content partners.

Figure 3: Youth cluster team breakdown

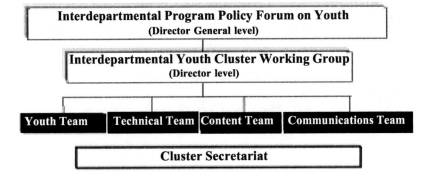

Figure 4: Youth cluster marketing strategy

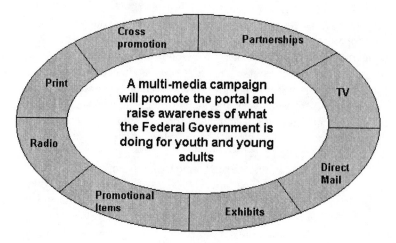

Strategic Considerations, Opportunities and Challenges

HRDC has identified several challenges which impact the development and rollout of the Youth Cluster. These must be taken into consideration in the design and implementation of the final Web site:

1.   Government Technology Standards vs. Youth User Demands

There is a conflicting need to satisfy user information needs and at the same time respect the technology standards put in place by the Government of Canada. This may be a difficult balance to reach given that a significant percentage of youth clients demand that their on-line experiences be high-end and take full advantage of current and emerging technologies. This is not simply a matter of conforming to arcane public sector restrictions on the use of technology. Standards may have to be revisited if existing rules and standards significantly prohibit Youth Cluster usage.

2.   Access

Public-sector institutions are required to ensure that all individuals are able to access programs, services and information. While there are a large number of youth on-line, there are a number of marginalized groups who do not have access to the Internet or the access they have is limited in nature. Providing more upgraded on-line access points, such as public kiosk terminals or Web hook-ups in public libraries may be a partial solution. In all likelihood, traditional means of government access may have to be maintained.

3.   Asymmetrical Development of the Government of Canada Clusters

The development of the Government of Canada's portals or clusters is proceeding in a somewhat asymmetrical fashion. There are approximately 36 different subject clusters under the three sub-portals. Each has a different set of partners, project scope, timeline, level of funding (if any) and progress to date. Some, like the Consumer Information Gateway, have launched; others are planned but work has not yet begun; and still others are in their infancy. There are also differences in the levels of client involvement in each of the cluster development processes. This is not to say that a template approach to cluster development should be adopted. Each represents different client groups and information. A uniform approach may be ideal, but in reality, difficult to achieve.

4.   Funding

Funding for cluster initiatives is also an issue. The Government On-Line process is providing a certain amount of funding to federal departments to assist them in meeting the objectives of each phase or "Tier" of the GOL initiative. This funding process however does not directly address cluster activity. Some cluster groups who were successful in their bids for funding under a special funding opportunity have significantly more resources to achieve the cluster/portal objectives than others do. It is important to note that it is necessary to limit the number of clusters receiving funding given finite resources and an attempt to develop some standards and lessons learned for others to follow. The differences in available resources can make it difficult for some groups to proceed as quickly as they might like.

In terms of funding, there is also the concern of sustainability. While the Youth Cluster project, among others, has received sufficient funding from the Treasury Board for development, there are no funds available to maintain and update the site past March 31, 2002. Given the nature of the client group and the medium, the inability to renew and refresh the Government of Canada's youth Web presence could result in a stagnant source of information that does not engage or retain the attention of Canadian youth.

It will be incumbent on the partners involved in the project to ensure that issues of on-going funding and support are addressed prior to the completion of the prototyping process. The over-arching Government On-Line initiative is providing funds to support the objectives for each stage or 'Tier' discussed previously. This represents the most appropriate source for sustaining funds at present.

5.   Managing the Citizen Engagement Component of the Project

The are a number of fundamental reasons why the project design engages youth directly in the process. Youth is a transitional period in life during which the ties that integrate individuals into society and the working world should be formed. The economic, social and cultural environment of youth is constantly changing; what worked yesterday may not work today; and there is a constant need for re-evaluation. Additionally, youth understand the needs and approaches inherent to the successful design and delivery of youth programs and services. Therefore, projects and programs should arise out of young people's own identification of issues and needs and their chosen response to them (Council of Europe, 1997, p.6).

However, the inclusion of youth citizenry in the design process raises certain strategic and operational considerations. These include:

- identifying parameters for engagement activities given the overarching Government of Canada and HRDC context—this implies developing a certain level of understanding among youth representatives in terms of how government works;
- establishing strategies to manage engagement processes and expectations for both internal and external partners;
- developing clear mandates and foci for engagement activities including various youth constituencies; and,
- balancing the inherent tension between safeguarding the Government of Canada's autonomy and decision making versus successful youth involvement in program and policy development.

ANALYSIS OF THE YOUTH CLUSTER CASE STUDY

The above case study provides a descriptive account of the potential benefits and challenges facing the delivery of a specific Canadian government portal initiative. As a means of identifying and structuring the more salient factors impacting the successful adoption and use of the Youth Cluster, attention now turns to utilization of the chapter's framework for government portal design (refer to Figure 1 and Table 1).

In terms of the government perspective, all three factors identified in the framework are applicable to the Youth Cluster project.

With regards to information management, a success factor in the delivery of the Youth Cluster was the need to foster cooperation across the various departments which have a stake in the portal's design. To facilitate cooperation among the 21 federal departments participating in the project, the Youth Cluster project team provided "learning sessions" to encourage buy-in and cooperativeness among departments. The Youth Cluster project team also established an overarching Working Group for the project comprised of representatives across the participating departments as a means of ensuring that the functionality offered in the portal met the requirements of individual departments and balanced tensions that may occur from different stakeholder groups. In these ways, the Youth Cluster was better able to address information management concerns affecting the portal.

With respect to the information systems development process, there were several examples given in the Youth Cluster case that illustrated the importance of providing a good information system development infrastructure. One example was the Youth Cluster team's concern over the need to secure adequate funding. Specifically, concern was raised over not being able to keep the youth site as up to date as possible once the project's two-year budget had elapsed. It seems plausible that an electronic government initiative would require a dedicated long-term budget to help assure a sufficient and sustained information systems development process. Another example involved the Youth Cluster team's awareness of the need to include citizen representatives in the design process. The Youth Cluster project uniquely addressed this issue by including youth representatives as part of its development team. Though this imposed new challenges in balancing youth representative and government wants, a more adoptable and usable portal is likely to result at the end of the process. A third example evidenced by the Youth Cluster project relating to the systems development process was the expressed need to coordinate activity across other government portal-based initiatives so that final designs were compatible and complementary with other electronic government projects.

With regards to policy and leadership, the Government of Canada is a perfect case in point in the benefits of having strong leadership to establish electronic government policy and carry out strategic direction. Doing so helped in this particular case study to facilitate an overarching, viable plan for electronic government success, namely through Canada Site which provides a single access point to all federal government-related information and services and supports a structure by which to organize and rollout sub-portal and cluster sites tailored to the needs of specific groups.

Due to the early stages in which the Youth Cluster is engaged at the present time of the writing of this chapter, little reference was made in the case study on characteristics of the portal interface. As such, the Youth Cluster could utilize learnings from the framework on the need to incorporate certain functionalities in the portal interface design to facilitate better user acceptance and ameliorate the satisfaction of government information needs. These include: incorporating tailorability or personalization in the portal's design; providing information of high relevance, reliability and timeliness; supplying mechanisms for finding and navigating information, specifically through inclusion of an in-depth taxonomy scheme (as planned in the Youth Cluster project) and a robust search directory; offering task-based tools to perform government transactions and facilitate discussions between citizens and government officials, as well as among government workers; and securing an engaging interface by which to foster interest and participation in the portal by both citizens and government workers.

With respect to the citizens perspective, all three factors identified in the framework are applicable to the Youth Cluster project. For instance, the Government of Canada is well aware of addressing public concerns over the provision of universal access. Specifically, the Youth Cluster project recognized the need to tailor the design of the portal to deemed Web standards that would maximize the reach of the portal site to youth citizens, as well as the necessity of retaining existing and other communication mediums with citizenry so as not to isolate or restrict access to youth-related government information and services to those that did not have a means of entrée to the Youth Cluster. The Youth Cluster project also realized the need to manage citizen wants. In the discussion of the Youth Cluster project, concerns were raised over the need to address high-end expectations in the design of a portal interface for youth citizens, and balance youth demands which may conflict with expectations or issues of importance with the federal government, such as the cost or ability to deliver or streamline certain information services and resources over the Internet. Last, the Youth Cluster project addressed the need to market government portals to citizens. Realizing the importance of user awareness of government portals, the Youth Cluster proposed the need to provide an in-depth marketing media campaign on its government portal and suggested that such an effort could be maximized by linking existing forms of media with one another to communicate the portal to its targeted citizen group.

CONCLUSION

The chapter's framework for government portal design provides a useful lens for analysis of the Youth Cluster project. The framework highlights some of the pertinent issues facing the design, implementation and roll-out of the Youth Cluster government portal and the steps by which the Canadian federal government is addressing those issues. As such, the case study helps illustrate the viability of the framework in identifying salient factors affecting government portal initiatives.

Note that not all aspects of the framework are identifiable from the case study description. This points to the complexity of the task of designing electronic government portals (i.e., there are multiple perspectives to consider in design and many factors under each of these perspectives). This leads to the need for government portal developers to take heed in the framework's contents to ensure that certain factors are not overlooked or remain unaddressed when developing and implementing portal designs. To this extent, the framework can function as an initial checklist of factors to consider in all stages of portal development.

As such, the chapter's framework establishes a preliminary construct by which to organize and describe some of the pertinent issues surrounding government portal design today. These are categorized into three overarching perspectives: government, interface and citizen. It is the hope of the authors that the framework be utilized to shape discussion and direction on the design of government portal sites. Due to the relative newness of the portal phenomenon, there is a lack of theoretical frameworks by which to base further research in this area. The framework is an attempt to bridge this void.

The primary strength of the framework is that it is based on several areas of investigation: past studies on electronic government initiatives and research on portal adoption and use in the private sector. Next steps would be to validate and extend the framework through empirical investigation. Case study investigations of government portal sites would be a likely candidate method by which to gain further insights. By conducting independent analysis of government portal initiatives across various levels of governments in varying nations, key factors and areas of concerns would be more evident, as well as strategies which are successful in bridging such concerns. Doing so can help raise the potential of portals in delivering more effective and efficient government services and encouraging greater democracy and engagement from citizenry.

END NOTES

1 This plan was vocalized by Canada's Prime Minister in his response to the Speech from the Throne in October 1999 (http://pm.gc.cadefault.asp?Language=E& Page=publications&Sub=speeches&Doc=speeches199910131085_e.htm).
2 Canada Site can be accessed at http://canada.gc.ca.

REFERENCES

Abraham, J. (1998). *The Business Values of Intranets: An Exploratory Research Study into the Value of Intranets in Organizations*. PhD dissertation, University of Amsterdam.

Council of Europe. (1997). *The Participation of Young People*. (Research Report). Strasbourg, Germany: European Steering Committee for Intergovernmental Cooperation in the Youth Field, December.

Choo, C. W., Detlor, B. and Turnbull, D. (2000). *Web Work: Information Seeking and Knowledge Work on the World Wide Web*. Dordrecht, The Netherlands: Kluwer Academic Publishers.

Davenport, T. H. (1997). *Information Ecology: Mastering the Information and Knowledge Environment*. New York: Oxford University Press.

Davenport, T. H., Eccles, R. G. and Prusak, L. (1992). Information politics. *Sloan Management Review*, Fall, 53-65.

Detlor, B. (2000a). The corporate portal as information infrastructure: Towards a framework for portal design. *International Journal of Information Management*, 20, 91-101.

Detlor, B. (2000b). *Facilitating Organizational Knowledge Work Through Web Information Systems: An Investigation of the Information Ecology and Information Behaviours of Users in a Telecommunications Company*. Unpublished PhD dissertation, University of Toronto, Ontario, Canada.

Government of Canada. (2000). *Government On-Line: Serving Canadians in a Digital World*. Available on the World Wide Web at: http://www.gol-ged.gc.ca/pub/serv-can/serv-canpr_e.asp.

Great Britain Cabinet Office. (1998). *Electronic Government: The View from the Queue: Comprehensive Research into Potential Customer Take-Up of On-Line Government Services*. Available on the World Wide Web at http://www.citu.gov.uk/research/viewqueue/index.htm: Central IT Unit.

Great-Britain-Parliament. (1998). *Electronic Government: Information Technologies and the Citizen*. Available on the World Wide Web at http://www.parliament.uk/post/egov.htm: Parliamentary Office of Science and Technology.

Greenfield, R. (1995). Electronic government. *NFAIS Newsletter*, 37(8), 85.

Hagedorn, K. (2000). *The Information Architecture Glossary*. Ann Arbor, MI: Argus Center for Information Architecture (Argus Associates).

Hwang, S. D., Choi, Y. and Myeong, S. H. (1999). Electronic government in South Korea: Conceptual problems. *Government Information Quarterly*, 16(3), 277-285.

Lamb, R. (1999). Using intranets: Preliminary results from a socio-technical field study. *Proceedings of the 32nd Hawaii International Conference on System Sciences*, Maui, Hawaii.

Lan, Z. and Falcone, S. (1997). Factors influencing Internet use: A policy model for electronic government information provision. *Journal of Government Information*, 24(4), 251-257.

Newell, S., Scarbrough, H., Swan, J. and Hislop, D. (1999). Intranets and knowledge management: Complex processes and ironic outcomes. *Proceedings of the 32nd Hawaii International Conference on System Sciences*.

Nilsen, K. (1993). Canadian government electronic information policy. *Government Information Quarterly*, 10(2), 203-220.

Perritt, H. H., Jr. (1996). The information highway: On ramps, checkpoints and tollbooths. *Government Information Quarterly*, 13(2), 143-158.

Steyaert, J. (2000). Local governments online and the role of the resident: Government shop versus electronic community. *Social Science Computer Review*, 18(1), 3-16.

Strauss, A. and Corbin, J. (1998). *Basics of Qualitative Research: Techniques and Procedures for Developing Grounded Theory*. (2nd ed.). Thousand Oaks, CA: Sage.

TBSC. (2000). *Client-Centric Service Delivery in the Electronic Channel: Cluster Blueprint*. (Electronic Image): Treasury Board Secretariat of Canada, Government of Canada, October.

Section II

Applications

Chapter VII

e-Government Trust Providers

Fernando Galindo
Zaragoza University, Spain

If trust is a key value in e-commerce, it is much more so e-Government. This is because confidence is essential to the automated, blind relations with government permitted by the new technologies The function of trust providers is thus to create confidence. This chapter outlines the activities of a number of trust providers with reference to the regulation of the Internet, and the laws and institutions which engender trust in the democratic state.

TRUST, E-COMMERCE AND E-GOVERNMENT

Trust

Organized with the help of intermediaries such as Internet service providers who create and provide access to the necessary infrastructure, the spread of the Internet has opened up remote communications between different groups of people. This phenomenon has, in turn, highlighted the need for people and organizations capable of engendering sufficient confidence in relations and communications between Internet users. This is because our senses, together with knowledge and prejudices, are the primary channel generating trust in others and allowing us to expect a predictable response at each moment of the communication process. Thus, when unknown interlocutors enter the communications processes, which is inevitable in a medium such as the Internet, we need both to be aware of their presence and, of course, to place our trust in them.

In this light, it is clear that the creation of trust on the Internet deserves study, since trust is one of the basic motives underlying the actions and behaviour of individuals and society in general, whether or not they personally use the Internet as a communications medium.

Various factors influence trust, or the lack of it. Appearance, modes of speech, ways of dressing, language, membership of a given institution or organization, behaviour patterns, liability and so on are all factors which create trust and influence our expectation of receiving a positive response to our signals.

The Internet and Solutions to the Problem of Trust: The Current Situation

Let us begin by reminding ourselves that the attitudes on which trust is based cannot be brought to bear when the Internet is the communication system used. Although the Internet allows us to establish long-distance relationships with other people, the anonymity of the medium, and our ignorance of the nature and lifestyles of our interlocutors, diminish the trust initially generated by the fact of making instant online contact. This limitation is aggravated by the consideration that neither Internet communications channels nor the intermediaries involved are secure. Thus, we have no guarantee as to the identity of our interlocutors, the integrity of the messages sent and received over the Internet or the confidentiality and secrecy of communications.

Trust is therefore a far-reaching problem for the Internet, and this has stimulated efforts to develop solutions. These may be no more than attempts to patch up the situation described, though considerable work has also gone into resolving these difficulties more completely, as we shall see below.

Some of the proposed partial solutions developed in the field of technology are summarized in a special issue on the question of Internet trust technologies published in *Communications*, The *Journal of the ACM* (December 2000.)[1] Some of these solutions concentrate directly on basic issues such as the diagnosis of trust mechanisms in social relationships, which are involved in the functioning of the Internet and how they affect systems designers, Web pages and Internet access providers.[2] Others propose the use of socially established trust solutions on the Internet—for instance, references to the satisfaction of past customers with the goods and services offered by e-businesses, or to conventional trust providers such as professional organizations, which may provide opinions on products, as well as clear descriptions of a Web site's privacy policy or details of the obligations of buyers and sellers entering into a transaction.[3] Yet others rely on the design of interfaces allowing the expression or representation of important attributes for the creation of trust.[4] There are also those who consider that the Internet has not changed habits already acquired by our society through the use of other communications technologies such as television.[5]

Surprisingly, the proposals put forward in this chapter hardly mention one alternative for guaranteeing trust in communications which institutions, companies, associations and government have all taken up with increasing enthusiasm. This solution is based on promoting the general implementation and use of public key encryption techniques. These mechanisms have been accepted both legally and technically as a method of safeguarding both trust and other principles involved in Internet use, including the basic weaknesses relating to identity, integrity and confidentiality of messages discussed above.

This is the subject of this chapter, which will limit references to trust in the use of the Internet to the field which has come to be known as electronic government to distinguish it from e-commerce. The following paragraphs briefly outline the main differences between these two phenomena.

The use of Internet technology in e-commerce and e-Government is often considered to be a point in common. It would therefore seem that an explanation referring to the features and content of the Internet is sufficient to present the characteristics of both e-commerce and e-Government. This places the specific details associated with the two phenomena in the background, however.

This approach is, therefore, not the most appropriate, since certain features of each area of activity require the creation of reliable organizations and structures capable of adaptation to its specific content. This in turn depends on the set of rights and obligations which could be affected by insecure Internet use in one or the other context. Accordingly, this study will begin with some general considerations regarding the basic features of e-commerce and e-Government.

e-Government

The most significant feature of e-Government is that it frequently does not involve transactions or economic exchange of any kind, which is, of course, the case with e-commerce. The situation becomes clear if we understand e-Government to refer to the relations which may arise between the citizen and the authorities as a consequence of the exercise of rights using electronic tools, and in particular the Internet.

This wide definition implies that the possible relationship has many facets, ranging from requests for information on the bureaucratic procedures relating to personal affairs to the participation of the citizen in the formulation of regulations governing different types of activity or the jurisdiction of the various powers of the State. This might refer, for example, to participation via the Internet in elections for legislative assemblies or parliaments. The Internet could also be used to transmit public opinion on a given matter or proposed solutions for a specific problem to the government or executive, or to local authorities. Evidently, it is the message itself, rather than any economic transaction, which is important here, because it represents the realization of the democratic principle enshrined in the constitution that every citizen is entitled to participate in government through the exercise of political rights.

The acceptance of this definition means recognizing that the authorities and citizens may establish relations using the Internet for the purpose of exercising civil, administrative, social or political rights and obligations established in the constitution or other legislation. For example, this could involve:

- applying for and obtaining a hunting licence or building permits;
- participation in public tenders for the award of a concession to operate a service or perform certain work, and participation in civil service examinations;
- applying for a pension;
- obtaining information on matters falling within the remit of local, regional or national government;
- exercising a political right, such as the election of a parliamentary representative;
- compliance with obligations such as the declaration of taxes or payment of social security contributions;
- bringing an action in the courts in relation to non-performance of a contract by another citizen or company.

These are only a few examples, but all of them have in common that, at least in theory, the citizen could use the Internet in order to exercise a right or comply with an obligation established by law.

Naturally, e-Government is only possible where the legislative, executive and judicial authorities guarantee that the formalities and procedures resolved over the Internet can also be carried out by other, non-computerised, means. This is because the Law recognizes rights and obligations which every citizen may exercise or must comply with through the relevant authorities, whether at the level of municipal, regional or national government, or in the courts, and in accordance with the procedures established in each case.

In this context, procedures mean the formalities or steps establishing the specific course of action to be followed by any citizen exercising a right or complying with an obligation within the relevant sphere of the administration, even where the citizen is not familiar with the details of such procedures.

The problem with this definition and its translation into practical reality is that the normal use of the Internet does not guarantee the minimum legal requirements. As explained above, this is because the identity of persons or organizations sending or receiving messages is not secure, and the contents of a message can be observed, and even modified, by third parties, thus violating the legal principle guaranteeing the confidentiality of communications.

e-Commerce

The situation is radically different when relations arise between two citizens or a citizen and a business or company for the purpose of carrying out an online economic transaction. In this case, it is the exercise of those rights and performance of obligations related to the purchase and sale of goods and services that are significant. The citizen thus obtains a right over another citizen or a company and, in principle, the existence of sufficient funds to settle the transaction is a sufficient basis for action.

This means that any person may make purchases provided he or she has cash or credit to pay for the goods. In the public sphere, on the other hand, each citizen has the right to apply for and obtain services from the authorities, providing that the relevant formalities are completed, regardless of wealth or other considerations, by the mere fact of being a citizen. For example, in the case of elections, the citizen may participate provided that he or she is registered to vote. A hunting licence may be obtained if the applicant is of legal age, is a resident at a fixed address and does not have a criminal record.

The rules of e-commerce are therefore fundamentally based on commercial use and practice, and the trust proper to economic transactions has remained largely unchanged throughout history. Hence, the security weaknesses inherent in the Internet are of less importance in this area than they are to relations between the citizen and the State. In fact, long-standing mail order mechanisms go a considerable way to offsetting the communications problems posed by the Internet. Also, means of payment such as credit cards and cash-on-delivery systems are available to rectify possible abuses due to weaknesses in telecommunications. In this light, it can safely be argued that the crux of the problem of e-commerce is the acquisition and payment of goods and services, while the qualities and attributes of the persons involved are, in general, secondary.

Internet, e-Commerce and e-Government

The foregoing discussion should be sufficient to understand the reasons for the significant differences in the actions and procedures necessary for the deployment in practice of e-commerce and e-Government through specialized applications designed for the Internet.

For example, the basic procedure followed in e-commerce programs consists of proposing the completion of certain dialogues between the buyer and the vendor with reference to the goods or services offered for sale. These dialogues need only be protected against telecommunications weaknesses when the contract is actually made, and it becomes necessary to send payment and exchange transaction and personal data between the purchaser and the vendor.

In e-Government on the other hand, the procedure frequently requires clear and unambiguous identification of the citizen and the public entity involved before the commencement of relations, otherwise the operation cannot be carried out. Without the relevant data, therefore, relations are restricted to the simple presentation of information to the citizen by public institutions.

Perhaps not surprisingly, innumerable e-commerce applications exist on the Internet, while applications permitting a real, interactive, legally enforceable relationship to be established between the citizen and government remain conspicuously scarce.

Trust and Legal Security

We have already mentioned that the solutions to the difficulties described are beginning to appear. The fact that the use of traditional trade guarantees has proved unsatisfactory when applied to global e-commerce has led to a general change in attitude with regard to the use of the Internet in the fields considered here. As a result, the need for the construction of a more secure Internet has been recognized, and to some extent enshrined in recent legislation. This involves the expansion, creation and regulation of new trust mechanisms, basically as follows:

- implementation of the services of certification providers, which are essential institutions for the use of message encryption techniques;
- regulation of e-commerce to establish the identity and specific responsibilities of organizations providing access to communications networks and the Internet;
- creation of legal and arbitration mechanisms and procedures to permit enforceability of regulations governing encryption and the responsibilities of encryption providers.

The results of such measures, the main outlines of which have already been legislated worldwide, will eventually satisfy the formal requirements for effective legal transactions between citizens and government over the Internet or, to put it another way, for secure e-Government.

This chapter describes these matters in the following order:

The first section describes various examples of applications which represent the inception of e-government in practice.

The next section sets out the difficulties inherent in the use of the Internet for e-Government purposes without the adoption of appropriate precautions.

Next, the regulations already in place are presented as a solution to these difficulties.

Finally, a number of examples of appropriate trust services for e-Government purposes are given.

A conclusion follows.

The examples used in the presentation of the issues discussed in this chapter are drawn principally from events in Spain. The use of a case study seems the best approach to highlighting the current situation, because consideration of the use of the Internet in one country sheds light on what is happening, or is likely to happen, in other countries, since the Net is a global phenomenon.

THE USE OF THE INTERNET IN E-GOVERNMENT

This is not the appropriate place to present the possibilities offered by the use of the Internet in e-Government, which are the subject of other chapters included in this book. Suffice it to say that these possibilities are enormous, and that the true potential of the Net for e-Government has yet to be realized.

The starting point is the already high level of computerization at all practical levels of the administration in Spain, which includes habitual use of Web pages by government institutions and agencies to present their activities to the public, informing citizens of their functions.[6] The administration also makes extensive use of intranets open to officials and members of the relevant institutions, though not to the general public.

These intranets are already equipped with the tools and resources necessary for working in remote teams and tele-working. They also permit file sharing, allowing specific procedures to be followed up by various different offices or agencies. In this context, the existence of appropriately designed applications would, for example, allow citizens to obtain information on the state of procedures affecting their interests. The prerequisite for such applications to be implemented, however, is the existence of safe and secure communications. Private citizens, corporate users and officials, or the computers used, must be properly identified and the integrity and confidentiality of in and outbound messages must be guaranteed. Moreover, it is necessary to establish the relevant measures to engender trust in the communications channel with sufficient safeguards for users.

The appropriate telematic procedures should, however, be organized as an additional resource of conventional systems, since the Internet is not universal, but all citizens have the right, for example, to receive information on the stage reached in procedures affecting their interests.

The Internet could also be used in electoral processes, and indeed, pilots schemes and other examples of such use already exist. The problem of generalizing such use of the Net lies in the need for procedures capable of guaranteeing a free, secret ballot for all citizens. This requires the existence of a secure public key infrastructure, in which the choice of certification provider service is free and the service is delivered without charge. It is also necessary to ensure that all citizens have equal rights in electoral processes. At the very least, therefore, the system would have to be compatible with the fact that Internet use is not universal, while the right to vote is. Accordingly, procedures would have to be so regulated as to allow the use of conventional voting systems in elections in parallel with Internet ballots.

These are not the only possibilities offered by the technology and the relevant legal principles, as shown by the existence of schemes such as the E-Europe initiative set in motion by the European Administration in March 2000.[7] This plan establishes short- and medium-term objectives for the implementation of actions proposed by the various European institutions and agencies, which are intended to set up the infrastructure necessary for applications such as those described in the preceding paragraphs to be used in practice.

The Spanish administration has already made progress towards making these projects a reality, particularly in the area of tax declarations and settlements. Since 1998 it has been possible in Spain to file income and other tax returns electronically with an acceptable level of security. The system used is based on digital or electronic signatures and an appropriate public key infrastructure. It is also now possible for citizens and companies to carry out certain electronic procedures with the Social Security authorities. These procedures relate, inter alia, to information on the status of the interested party's contributions. Pilot and partial schemes have also been set up by other government agencies. These activities have been possible because the CERES project has established the Real Fábrica de la Moneda (Spanish Royal Mint) as a certification services provider for electronic communications in activities related to the institutions of government in Spain.[8] This activity will be presented in the fourth section.

At this point, it seems appropriate to explain the nature of the experiences and possibilities outlined in some detail, as well as the technical and legal weaknesses of the

Internet and some potential solutions. These matters provide the framework for the activity of e-Government trust providers and are the subject of the next section.

WEAKNESSES OF THE INTERNET

The weaknesses of Internet use for e-Government purposes comprise both problems inherent in the nature of the Net and the difficulties resulting from private ownership of telecommunications networks, as well as the initial adaptation of the infrastructure to the needs of e-commerce. This limits the field for e-Government which, as we have seen, is affected by a wider range of considerations than the optimization of profit.

In particular, this becomes clear in relation to:
- the assignation of names and addresses,
- the security of communications,
- respect for privacy and other legal principles, and
- the provision of access to the Internet and other communications networks, as well as telecommunications security services.

These difficulties and some solutions are outlined in the following section. Other legal solutions are described in the following section.

The Starting Point... What is the Internet?

The Internet is basically a network for the transmission of programs or data files permitting exchanges between computers located in different places using existing communications infrastructure (basically cable, telephones, satellites and radio waves).

The systems contain text, voice and image data.

Data transmission is possible because messages are exchanged using a standard format, which is a combination of digits, and because they are emitted following the same rules from a client address/computer to a different client address/computer. The messages transmitted are directed or passed on by intermediary computers, servers or administrators whose mission is to deliver the message from the issuer to the receiver in accordance with certain standard orders.

The deployment of the Internet was a consequence of the development of the standard orders forming the IP and TCP protocols in the 1970s. These protocols are sets of technical rules permitting the assignation of addresses or names to the computers involved in message transmissions (IP or Internet Protocol) and controlling file transfers (TCP or Transmission Control Protocol) to the different addresses.[9]

These protocols were initially developed for military purposes, but in a subsequent phase they were picked up, refined and applied by scientific institutions and large corporations, which assigned names and domains to client and server computers. The global computer network called the Internet has been built up on the basis of these names and protocols.

The Net makes it possible to send files, documents and orders practically instantaneously from client computers located anywhere in the world to other client computers elsewhere through transmissions controlled by servers or administrators owned by companies and institutions owning servers which are constantly connected to the network. These organizations are the Internet access providers. The names and domains of the servers are recognized by the authorities responsible for setting standards and administering the Internet.

The servers also store information which can be accessed from other computers. This information may be recorded in the server computer either by its owner or by client computers for the purposes of publication.

The development of effective, user-friendly software such as operating systems and browsers has universalized the use of the Internet. As a result, it is no longer only a small circle of initiates, scientists and engineers who are able to make use of the capabilities of the Internet, as was the case until very recently. Today, any user of a computer can log onto the net, allowing the users of connected systems to share data and tasks with his or her own system. This permits distance working and cooperation between the users of different systems logging on to the Net for similar purposes or having common interests and information needs.

We are now on the threshold of the universalization of these capabilities as a result of the development of applications to facilitate electronic commerce, e-mail services and the inception of what has been called electronic government.

The technology outlined above is what has come to be called the Internet. This technology has made the transmission of messages between institutions, companies and individuals possible in practice. This is something that was already theoretically permitted by the existence of industrial standards and some legal regulations from the moment when it became clear that communications technologies could be used to link computers.

The practical deployment of technological advances before the development of the Internet was, however, hindered by the inflexibility of the techniques used, which were only capable of exchanging highly automated and formalized messages between an issuer and a receiver using specially adapted telephone lines.

Tools such as EDI (Electronic Data Interchange) were used, for example, by automobile dealers to send orders to factories, which led to changes in manufacturing methods and better customer service. Nevertheless, these communications techniques were not appropriate for the huge spread of telecommunications, because they required skilled users with a knowledge of highly formalized programming languages. The Internet, on the other hand, allows the transfer of text, speech and images in digitized messages, but the same data can also be sent using more or less ordinary language.

Technical Problems

In the preceding section, we described the Internet as a network based on the application of technical rules (TCP/IP protocols), specifying the standard formats for the addresses of users sending or receiving messages from personal computers, and using intermediary server computers to route messages. This practice has had certain negative consequences with regard to both the assignation of names and addresses and the use of communications channels, as we shall explain in the following pages. These consequences are, in large part, the causes of the technical problems affecting the Internet which are summarized in this section.

Addresses

The activity of naming and assigning an address to a given location is both ancient and common to all cultures. In the context of the Internet, however, this activity involves the identification of a specific computer using a combination of digits (IP addresses: for example, 155.210.3.20 is the same as tozal.unizar.es), and it has until now been the responsibility of technical and scientific organizations and companies.

These institutions and companies have established technical rules to organize the addresses of computers within the context of a specific culture—that of the United States. At a time of globalization and the increasing use of the Internet for communications, commerce and administrative purposes, it has become necessary to establish institutions which are more respectful of the traditions and legislation of each of the countries to which the Internet has spread than those existing until now. For these purposes, domain and address policy is now being regulated by law. This mission has been entrusted to independent organizations and institutions coordinated by the Internet Corporation for Assigned Names and Numbers (ICANN),[10] the activities of which seem to be more appropriate to the new situation than those of the scientific institutions, such as the National Science Foundation (NSF),[11] and business organizations, such as Network Solutions Inc. (NSI),[12] existing until recently.

One of the objectives of these new bodies is to coordinate the award of addresses and domain names with other organizations responsible for the protection of names, such as the public registries of names, brands and patents which first established themselves in our culture in the 19th century.

The historical weaknesses of the domain name assignation procedure are not without consequences. One of these is that the addresses provided until now are uncertain, and messages can easily be sent anonymously or in the name of another party. This gives Internet users cause for concern, since they know only too well how common it is for the messages received over the Net to contain files which may damage the data already stored in the computer.

The legislation referred to is therefore designed to resolve these problems by establishing rules for the assignation of names and addresses. The Spanish legislation in this area enacted to date is described in the next section.

Communications Channels

The Internet's basic function of automated data exchange is further limited for the user because the communications channels over which the files or messages are transmitted permit the owners or administrators of servers, not to mention hackers, to see, intercept and even modify their contents. These means that confidentiality, which is a fundamental principle of communications in the democratic State, cannot be guaranteed. Moreover, messages can be modified by third parties without the knowledge of either the sender or the receiver. This is a violation of the free exercise of intention and represents a further very significant limitation on the use of the Internet.

These problems do arise in practice, though this is not to say we must accept that they are common. The fact remains, however, that they can be fairly easily caused by anyone wishing to do so, because the necessary technical skills to intercept or modify messages, for example, are easily available.

An Example

The discovery that communications have been illicitly intercepted and acts of industrial espionage committed apparently with the connivance of the security services demonstrates that these are not mere fantasies. The ECHELON telecommunications interception network is a case in point. This network is activated in anti-terrorist and other cases, including commercial matters. Its existence and activities have caused heated debate in the European Parliament and the adoption of a resolution condemning ECHELON in its current form.[13] This measure was directed at the governments of various member States of the European Union and the U.S. Administration.

The European Union has proposed the reform of this telecommunications interception network to adapt its working practices, which are the responsibility of espionage agencies, to the normal legal practices of the democratic countries. The Parliament has also proposed that a code of conduct be drawn up to prevent malpractice and the abuse of rights online. This position has begun to find sympathizers in the US Senate. Among others, the secret services of the United States, the United Kingdom, Australia, Canada and New Zealand form a part of the ECHELON network.

Summary of Technical Problems

The main technical problems related with the use of the Internet are as follows:
The identification of senders and receivers of messages is uncertain and impersonation is easy.

- The integrity of messages is not secure. This is because the electronic messages are sent from computer to computer over an electronic communications network. The owners of computers or of the communications network are therefore in a position to modify the content of the messages without either the sender or the receiver being aware of the changes made.

- Connected with the latter point is the absence of any guarantee that the principle of confidentiality will be respected for the messages transmitted. If the contents of messages can be modified, they can also be observed by the owner of a computer or of the communications network serving as the vehicle for transmission, whatever its nature (cable, fibre-optic, radio waves or general communications channels). Messages can be intercepted and viewed without any trace of the event.

- No sufficiently reliable mechanisms exist with regard to the procedures followed for the transit of messages. Transit thus needs to be assured by regulating the activities of intermediaries and service providers. Independent third parties are needed, for example to certify as accurately as possible the moment at which a message is sent and received by the parties involved in the exchange. Any user knows how easy it is to change the date and time recorded by the computers used in the transmission, sending and receipt of messages.

This is only a brief summary of some problems arising from the mass use of electronic communications. However, it is sufficient evidence to affirm that the possibility of serious violations of the legal principles proper to democratic systems is inherent in the use of the Internet and telecommunications in general.

Such violations could even compromise the guarantee procedures established to safeguard the legal traffic generated when the authorities act to enforce the law or resolve disputes using the Internet as a means of transmitting information and documents. In this context, we should remember that the basic principle in the performance of procedures, and due legal process as a whole, is strict respect for the autonomy of the individual and the declarations made whatever the nature of the proceedings in which statements may be made.

The following section describes some basic principles of the Spanish legal system which are at risk where the Internet is used without due precaution.

Legal Principles at Risk

Legal Certainty

The most basic legal principle to be violated is that of legal certainty, which is recognizes in Article 9.3 of the Spanish Constitution. Any non-compliance with the formalities established by law for any type of private or public documents represents a clear breach of this principle. It is clear that electronic documents cannot even be treated as existing for legal purposes where uncertainty exists in relation to fundamental data such as the name of the person issuing or receiving the document. This is also the case where the contents of documents, and the date of issue or receipt are uncertain.

In accordance with ruling by the Spanish Supreme Court,[15] there can be no legal certainty where "the identity of the person who presented a document appearing in the municipal files is not known, or the date or purpose of presentation is not known...." Similarly, there can be no legal certainty in the case of electronic messages, since the date of issue and receipt are recorded electronically and are not reliable.

Secrecy of Communications

The principle that communications are secret is firmly enshrined in the Spanish legal system, beginning with Article 18 of the Constitution. This is consistent with the principle of freedom of expression proper to all democratic societies. The principle is not respected when messages can be intercepted and viewed, or even modified, by third parties.

The principle of the secrecy of communications may also be violated when solutions established to mitigate the weaknesses of the Internet are based on supervision of secrecy in institutions which are not able to offer sufficient safeguards on their own account.

Privacy

It is not only the principles of freedom of expression and secrecy which may be eroded by the violation of the confidentiality of communications. The right of privacy recognized in all constitutions and modern data protection and privacy legislation is also affected. This has implications for the whole area of ideas, knowledge and intentionality.

Privacy and the secrecy of communications "imply the existence of a private sphere protected from the action and knowledge of all other persons, which in our culture is necessary to maintain a minimum quality of life.[16]"

Activity of Monopolies and Institutions Handling Privileged Information

The legal difficulties are not restricted to the matters described above. A further significant aspect is the privileged position enjoyed by those organizations having sufficient resources and knowledge not only to impersonate issuers or receivers of messages, but also to interfere with messages or learn their contents. These organizations are thus at an advantage compared to citizens, other businesses and institutions.

Citizens, businesses and institutions have, until now, been completely helpless to control the relations arising from the use of computers and communications media and channels at the global level. We have already mentioned the interference resulting from the fight against crime which, apparently because it has not been challenged by law, has now spread to include commercial and industrial espionage.[17]

Crime Prevention

The legal system may still be open to question when the problems noted are solved using the mechanisms we shall describe in the following section. We shall see that one technical solution for these problems is the use of encryption techniques to scramble messages. The application of these techniques is very effective, but they have the disadvantage of hindering the legitimate activities of the security and intelligence forces, whose mission is to investigate and prevent crime. This is because the lack of provision for the legal interception of encrypted messages prevents police action taken "to detect crime and discover and arrest criminals" (Spanish Constitution, Article 126).

The above discussion merely summarizes the point that the legal system as a whole is called into question by the use of the Internet and telecommunications systems without the inclusion of appropriate regulation of security in electronic communications as part of the solution of the problems and difficulties inherent in the spread of the new technologies.

Solutions

Technical solutions capable of at least partially resolving the problems mentioned already exist, which was not the case until very recently. It is also true that these technical solutions are gradually being recognized in new legislation, as a result of which they are also becoming legal solutions.

Other legal solutions refer to the responsibilities of telecommunications and Internet access providers.

The existence of these two types of solutions is a significant matter, because technical measures cannot be deployed in the absence of appropriate regulation establishing the legal conditions for their use. Similarly, legal measures alone are not sufficient to ensure that individuals, companies and government institutions are able to benefit from electronic communications.

The following section presents the main characteristics of technical measures designed to resolve the weaknesses of online communications. Then the chapter presents legal solutions.

Technical Solutions

The use of encryption represents a workable solution for technical problems referring to the identity of the issuers and receivers of messages, integrity of contents, confidentiality and the recording of the date and time messages were sent and received for the purposes of avoiding repudiation. Specifically, the use of public key techniques is required in this area.

Encryption is an ancient technique used especially in military activities. Generals and officers have habitually used and continue to use cryptographic techniques to send orders while ensuring that the enemy is unable to learn the contents of messages even if they are able to intercept the messenger or tap the communications network.

In this section, we shall consider the general changes made to encryption techniques to permit their use in the Internet for the purposes described above. These changes are connected with the development of public key encryption techniques, which we shall discuss below. We shall also highlight the most significant facets of the application of techniques involving electronic signatures and confidential cryptography. Finally, we shall discuss the nature of the institutions it will be necessary to establish if cryptography is to be used to safeguard Internet use—certification providers.[18]

Public Key Encryption

In traditional cryptography, the sender and receiver of the message use the same key to encode and decode messages. Inherent in this procedure is the risk that a third party interested in the contents of messages may obtain the key, allowing him to decode the secrets they contain.

In the 1970s, a new encryption system was discovered which made it more difficult to decode the contents of a message even though the key had been found. This new system was named public key encryption.[19]

The system consists of encoding messages using dual keys, one private and the other public. The key pair is generated by each of the users of the public key encryption system using a number, the private key, which is only known to the owner of the pair of keys. This system permits the encryption of the message by the issuer using the receiver's public key. The receiver is thus the only person able to decode the message using the private key corresponding to the public one used to encode the message. The private key is known only to the receiver

For this mechanism to work, it is necessary for the public part of the key to be known to all those who may wish to send a message to the owner of the private key. Accordingly, the public key needs to be stored in a key deposit containing both the key and the name and main details of its owner, as well as revocations and the reasons for them. At least access to the key deposit must be public.

In view of its importance of its role, it is essential for the entity responsible for custody and administration of the key deposit to be absolutely reliable. This entity is known as a certification service provider, because its main function is to certify that a given public key actually belongs to the specific person or organization claiming to be the owner of the key.

One highly significant feature of the public key system is that it guarantees that knowledge of the public key by a third party will not lead to the discovery of the private key. The size of the numbers making up the private key, and the formulas (algorithms) used to derive the public from the private key, in fact make it practically impossible to work out the private key on the basis of the digits contained in the public key. Obviously, the difficulty of this calculation increases the longer the initial number used to generate the public key. The security of the system rests on safe custody of the private key by its owner in an inaccessible place. A card with a chip is usually considered the most appropriate tool for this purpose.

The public key encryption system is now being used to safeguard the confidentiality of online communications. Specifically, it is being incorporated into the browser software used to send and receive messages over the Internet. In view of the worldwide spread of these facilities, it will be essential to create a network of certification services, whose members will need to coordinate their activities in order to construct a world public key infrastructure to ensure that the technique performs its function.

As is only to be expected, this mechanism has numerous variations and can be applied using a variety of different techniques, the most significant of which are devices and tools to generate and check electronic signatures and those for sending and receiving confidential messages.

Electronic Signatures

One of the most exciting applications of public key encryption in telecommunications is the technique known as digital or electronic signatures, which makes it possible to:
1.   encrypt messages using the private and public keys of the sender and the receiver, in

such a manner that it is possible to identify both as the true owners of the public and private key pairs used to encode and decode the message; and

2.   guarantee the integrity of the message received, because it is possible to verify upon receipt of a message that nobody other than the sender has modified its contents in the course of transmission over the communications and computer networks from the sender's to the receiver's computer.

An essential requirement for the use of digital signatures is the existence of a third party other than the sender and the receiver of the message to certify that the public key used to encode and electronically sign the message is actually owned by the person who encoded and signed it. In view of the function performed, this person is known a certification service provider.

The application of digital signature techniques can therefore solve problems relating to the identification of the sender of the message and its integrity. If the certification service provider has the appropriate mechanisms, these techniques can also be used to certify the date and time at which the message was sent or received.

Confidentiality Encryption

The use of electronic or digital signatures to send encrypted messages does not remove the weakness of online communications in the area of preserving confidentiality, as discussed above. This is because digitally signed messages are sent using open text format and can therefore be read by any third party with access to the communications network or the computers and services used for transmission.

Messages are not normally intercepted in this way because channels can be encoded using other techniques in such a manner that the contents of messages cannot be observed even where they are sent in digitally signed open text format. However, this requires the use of secure channels and computers (i.e. encoded infrastructure).

In any event, when secure channels and computers are not used to safeguard the secrecy and confidentiality of communications to the maximum degree possible, it is also possible to apply public key encryption for confidentiality purposes. This technique ensures that the text of the message is hidden and can only be decoded and read by the holder of the private key corresponding to the public key with which the text was encrypted. This guarantee is greater the longer the key.

Certification and Registration Services

We have already seen that certification services are a vital component of any public key encryption technique.

The main function of these services, as their name indicates, is to accredit or certify that the public key used to encode the message actually belongs to a specific person.

A distinction can be drawn here between certification services and registration services. The role of the former is to certify the assignation of a given key to a given person, while the latter carries out the functions of verifying the identity and attributes of the key's owner, establishing the relationship between the public key and its owner and transmitting the registered data to the certification service.

The storage and publication of public keys and their owners is a vital function of certification services, enabling global communications between persons and businesses resident in different parts of the world. Any person can thus obtain the key and send encrypted messages with the due level of assurance. There can be no doubt that the co-ordination of these services and the use of the same techniques improves the effectiveness of encryption services. This has led to the creation of certification systems associations.

These associations are voluntary systems for the accreditation of certification systems.

The importance of these services for the use of public key encryption is inescapable. They will have an essential role to play in a world where e-commerce and the use of telematics in relations between government agencies and other institutions has spread to the extent augured by market research and opinion polls published by both business and government the world over.

The legal recognition of the solutions provided by public key encryption techniques in the legislation of numerous countries is a clear sign of the need for certification and registration service providers and their increasing prevalence. Nevertheless, such regulation varies from country to country depending on already prevailing legislation governing the organizational principles connected with the use of such techniques.

LEGAL SOLUTIONS FOR E-GOVERNMENT

The development and application of the technical solutions discussed in the preceding chapter has led to the regulation of Internet use in the majority of countries. Although the specific legislation differs from country to country, the main areas of regulation are as follows:

- provision for non-profit institutions working in tandem with government agencies as part of the mechanism for the assignation of Internet names and addresses;
- implementation of certification service providers for online communications;[20]
- definition of responsibilities for all Internet and telecommunications access providers in order to regulate the services provided to the information society, and particularly e-commerce;
- design of legal and arbitration procedures and mechanisms to guarantee the enforceability of the regulations concerning names and encryption, and the liability of service providers.

This section will present the main features of the regulations as regards e-government applications.[21] Once again, Spanish and European legislation has been taken as the basic point of reference. The Spanish experience has been similar to that of other countries both in Europe and worldwide. Also, the basic content of this legislation is generally accepted.

Names

As has already been pointed out, the legislation of names and addresses is essential to progress with the regulation of the Internet. This required the creation of an organization such as ICANN. Spain too has enacted legislation in this crucial area, establishing the rules governing a function which until recently had been left entirely in the hands of the scientific organizations and companies responsible for the administration of the Internet.

Specifically, the regulation of domain names is set out in the Order of the Spanish Ministry of Public Works issued on March 21, 2000. This Order regulates the system applicable to the assignation of Internet domain names under the country code for Spain (.es).

The Preamble to these regulations establishes that the "recently established supranational organization ICANN is responsible for the administration at world level of Internet names and numerical addresses." It is also stated that the function of assigning second-level domain names in Spain under the country code .es will be carried out by the Red Técnica Española de Televisión, a public entity (Resolution of the Secretary General for Communications dated February 10, 2000).

The regulations establish the procedure for the assignation of domain names. The rules are contained in an Annex to the Ministerial Order.

Article 7 is of particular interest, because it establishes the responsibility of the participants in the network for the important function of coordination with conventional registries in the following terms: "The assignation of second-level domain names under the country code for Spain (.es) will be carried out having due regard to coordination with the Central Companies Registry, the Spanish Patents and Brands Office and other public registries, whether national or international in scope. Such coordination will be effected with the maximum celerity using telematic systems wherever possible." The coordination provided for is novel. Until publication of these regulations, domain names could be assigned independently of the registries.

The text of the regulations establishes a structure of agents to take responsibility for maintaining contact with both users and the assignation authority (Article 5) referred to.

This represents a significant step in the regulation of the Internet, particularly once an appropriate system is in place for the coordination of the institutions and companies that have come into being in response to the existence of the Internet with the activities of the legal registries. This will heighten legal certainty as regards the sending of messages, since sound references will exist for the identification of both issuers and receivers.

Security in Communications Channels Used by Government Institutions

The basic regulation of security in communications channels discussed in this section refers above all to digital signatures.

Before going on to describe the regulations, it is worth noting that this is a matter which has attracted attention in Spain for some time now. Indeed, from the beginning of the 1990s, it was predicted that legal precautions would have to be established for the use of telematic techniques by the Spanish government. As we shall see, these precautions initially consisted of warning users of the possibility that basic legal principles could be subject to violations, as explained in the preceding chapter. These warnings were explicitly set out in the Spanish Public Administration Regulation Act, 1992, and the Decree of February 16, 1996, which implements the Act.

Spanish Public Administration Regulation and Common Administrative Procedures Act

The two main articles of interest in the Act (Law 30 of 26th November 1992, amended in 1999)[22] for our purposes are Article 38, which pertains to the amendments made in 1999, and Article 45 (1992 version of the Act), which deals with the incorporation of technological resources.

Article 38 provides that the registers kept by the institutions of government must be recorded on computer formats. The article also specifies that the institutions of government shall have "systems for intercommunication and coordination between registries in order to guarantee compatibility and the telematic transmission of entries, applications, papers, communications and documentation made or presented at any registry."

The incorporation of technological resources was already considered in the first version of Article 45 of the Act, which provided for the use of technology and electronic, computer and telematic systems by government institutions in Spain, as well as the use of such systems by citizens in their relations with government.

The Act requires that users and receivers of documents be perfectly identified in the event that telematic systems are used, and establishes that documents generated using computer systems shall be deemed valid provided their authenticity, integrity and appropriate storage can be guaranteed. These matters are explicitly regulated.

Royal Decree of February 16, 1996

This legislation regulates the use of electronic, computer and telematic technologies by the institutions of the State.[23]

The Royal Decree establishes the regulations implementing the Public Administration Act, 1992, in relation to the use of electronic, computer and telematic technologies.

The Decree establishes general provisions (object of the regulations, rights and constraints applicable to citizens, definitions and general guarantees for the use of electronic, computer and communications, and telematic systems and applications by the institutions of government in Spain); requirements for the use of electronic, computer and communications, and telematic systems and applications (authorized applications, issuance of documents and copies, communications using electronic, computer and telematic systems and applications); and administrative actions (approval and publication of applications and standardization).

The Royal Decree does not directly establish any regulations for the Registries and similar record institutions, though this matter was corrected with the 1999 reform of the Public Administration Act (Article 38), or certification and digital signature services. Various general references are made to security. The regulations establish technical and organizational requirements for authenticity, confidentiality, integrity, availability and storage of information in the case that electronic instruments, communications media and applications are used. These points concern the nature of secure electronic documents. The regulations require that these rules be appropriate to the technology used, the nature of the data and the risks involved.

It is thus clear that these regulations provide a framework of values for the institutions of government in Spain within which subsequent rules would be published in order to safeguard the principles that could potentially be affected by the use of the Internet in e-Government without due guarantees. These regulations require the use of digital signatures.

Digital Signatures

The main objective of the regulation of the security of telecommunications is to provide for the use of public key encryption techniques[24] and certification services to permit the publication of the public key and personal characteristics of its owners. Similar legislation permitting the use of digital signatures has been enacted in numerous countries since 1995.

The main legislation in this area is as follows:

- In the USA the State of Utah Digital Signature Act (1995)[25] and the bill for the Electronic Signatures in Global and National Commerce Act (June 2000)[26]
- OECD guidelines for cryptographic policing (1997)[27]
- German legislation regulating the general conditions of information and communications services (1997)[28]
- Italian regulations concerning the creation, filing and transmission of documents using computer and telematic instruments (1998)[29]
- French cryptography regulations (1998 and 1999)[30]
- UK Regulation of Investigatory Powers, which sets out rules for decryption and confidentiality (2000)[31]

- Spanish Decree Law concerning electronic signatures (Royal Decree 14 of September 17, 1999).
- Various initiatives of the European Union issued from 1997 until the Digital Signatures Directive of December 13, 1999[32]

This chapter is not the place to describe in detail all of the features of this legislation. Nevertheless, references are provided as an aid to anybody interested in the contents of the various acts and regulations. Systematic descriptions are available in a number of published papers.[33]

The contents of regulations can be summarized by saying that the central objectives of the normative models established vary between direct acceptance of digital signature techniques for security in electronic communications and initial recognition of the legal consequences of the generalization of such techniques by treating electronic and manual signatures on an equivalent basis.[34]

The Utah legislation provides a clear example of the implementation of the first model, while the Italian regulations are a partial example of the second. The European Union initiatives are close to the legal solutions proposed.

The activities of the European Union in this area are typified by the approval of the Digital Signatures Directive of December 13, 1999, by the European Parliament and Council.

In the following section, the Directive is briefly outlined as an example of regulation for adoption by all member States of the European Union.

European Digital Signatures Directive

The Preamble (paragraph 4) states that the final objective of the Directive is to contribute to the proper operation of the European Single Market in the area of digital signatures by harmonizing the legal framework for their use within the European Union.

The Directive establishes a series of provisions, based on Section 2 of Article 47 and articles 55 and 95 of the Treaty, by way of a framework for the legal recognition of digital signatures.

The Directive may be summarized in the following terms:

1. It establishes a legal framework for certain certification services available to the public.
2. It concentrates on certification services for public key encryption systems and defines a series of common requirements applicable to the providers of such services and their accreditation.
3. It adopts a technologically neutral stance to permit application to a wide range of digital signature systems.
4. It permits the providers of certification services, in general, to offer their services freely with the need for prior authorization.
5. It allows the member States to introduce voluntary accreditation systems based on common levels requirements and higher level security.
6. It contributes to the harmonization of the legal framework within the EU by granting recognition of digital signatures.
7. It introduces rules applicable to the responsibility of the providers of certification services (basically in order to engender trust on the part of both individual and corporate users of certificates).
8. It includes a series of mechanisms designed to promote cooperation with third countries with a view to world recognition of certificates.

The Directive meets its objectives in a brief regulation comprising a Preamble, 15 articles and four Annexes, which respectively establish the requirements for recognized certificates, for the providers of certification services issuing recognized certificates, for secure devices for the creation of electronic signatures and recommendations for the verification of signatures.

The Directive also includes a special e-Government provision in line with the special nature of the relevant applications. Thus in Article 3.7, "Member States may make use of electronic signatures in the public sector subject to possible additional requirements. Such requirements shall be objective, transparent, proportionate and non-discriminatory, and shall relate only to the specific characteristics of the application concerned. Such requirements may not constitute an obstacle to cross-border services for citizens." A similar provision is made in the Spanish Digital Signatures Decree (Article 5).

There can be no doubt that these regulations represent an important step towards the integration of legal and technical solutions for the lack of security in telecommunications. Nevertheless, this is not sufficient. Following the publication of the EU regulations, legislation must still be passed to establish measures for the adaptation of local law and the implementation of the certification services provided for in the Directive and regulations prevailing in each member State.

This does, however, represent a first step. The regulations currently under consideration (Directive, Article 1, Paragraph 2) do not have the objective of modifying the legislation governing the system of legal principles affected by the use of encrypted or unencrypted electronic communications, as we pointed out in the previous section.

e-Commerce

The legislation discussed is key for the functioning of the Internet, which cannot expand further without such regulations because of the significance of the legal principles affected. If the measures provided are not put into practice, conflicts are bound to arise sooner or later which will prevent the use of the facilities offered by the Internet.

Furthermore, once the preventive regulations are implemented, it will become necessary to regulate the regime governing the activities of all the intermediaries involved in making the Internet work and permitting e-commerce and e-Government. This is the legal regime for the owners of computers/servers providing access to the Internet, transmitting communications or providing any other service necessary for the development of what has come to be known as the information society. The regulations concerning digital signatures do not refer to these institutions, since they only govern the activities of certification services providers for online communications.

European Directive

A start has been made on the regulation of these matters with the publication of Council Directive 2000/31/EC concerning electronic commerce on July 17, 2000.[35] The regulations established in this Directive have yet to be implemented in Spain.

The regulations established by the Directive are of tremendous importance, since they promote the use of the Internet not so much through the application of preventive measures such as encryption, as through the use of measures directly designed to promote use by citizens and access to electronic commerce and the institutions of government. To understand the scope of these regulations, it is necessary to consider the list of services to the information society referred to in the Directive. The contents of the European legislation are now in the process of being incorporated into Spanish Law, and a bill concerning services to the information society and e-commerce is currently being prepared by the Spanish Ministry of Science and Technology (the bill is dated September 29, 2000).

Specifically, Annex B of the aforementioned bill defines the provider of services to the information society as "Any private individual or legal entity providing services to the information society such as online sales of goods and services, the organization of virtual markets, the conduct of commercial communications activities, the supply of online information, the provision of search engines, access, data mining, hosting of information, applications and services, distribution of content on demand and the transmission of information via telecommunications networks."

This list indicates that having solved the problems of security and authentication through the regulation of signatures, the next task is the initial basic regulation of the Internet, which will be essential for the development of electronic commerce. A glance at the list of services contained in the bill shows that their regulation will refer to the legal principles discussed in the preceding chapter as potentially subject to violation if the Internet is used without sufficient guarantees. For example, the bill mentions these principles where it refers to online sales of goods and services, and where it specifies the types of functions which might comprise services to the information society. Clearly, it is essential to respect the identities of buyers and sellers of services in all such cases and to guarantee consumer or user protection. This, then, represents a reference to the legal system taken as a whole, including existing legal mechanisms.

Put briefly, the Directive regulates the following:

1. The free establishment of information society services within the EU.
2. Requirements for the establishment of service providers.
3. The characteristics of commercial communications.
4. Electronic contracts.
5. Liabilities of intermediaries such as communications access providers.
6. Promotion by the authorities of codes of conduct prepared by private individuals and businesses.
7. Acceptance of out-of-court settlements as a means of resolving disputes.
8. Permanence of legal recourse.
9. Co-operation between member States regarding the matters regulated.

Further to the matters dealt with, it should be noted that the regulation of the Internet set out in the Directive gives considerable attention to:

- self-regulatory devices prepared by individuals and companies, such as codes of conduct; and
- the acceptance of arbitration and other out-of-court mechanisms as a means of resolving disputes.

One significant contribution to electronic government made in the Directive is the distinction it draws between the responsibilities of Internet service providers and those providing telecommunications. These responsibilities are clearly similar in the case of e-commerce and e-Government.

The Administration of Justice

The rules and codes described above are, however, insufficient without the creation of appropriate mechanisms to ensure compliance. We have already seen that preliminary steps have been taken in this area in relation to the regulation of information society services, where the use of out-of-court arbitration is provided for. It is of interest to note in this context that provisions have also been made in Spain for e-Government activity in the courts of law and even for the use of encrypted messages sent using telematic systems as evidence. Let us briefly summarize the main legislation in this area.

Judiciary

Article 230 of the Spanish Basic Law governing the Judiciary, as amended on November 8, 1994, establishes the following:

1. The Spanish Courts and Tribunals may use any technical, electronic, computer and telematic systems in the course of their activity and in the exercise of their duties.
2. The documents issued using the aforementioned systems, whether on hard or soft formats, shall be deemed valid and efficacious as original documents, provided that their authenticity and integrity is guaranteed, as well as compliance with relevant trial procedure.
3. Processes undertaken on computer formats must guarantee identification and the due exercise of judicial functions…as well as confidentiality, privacy and the security of the relevant personal data.
4. Persons seeking protection of their rights and interests by the Courts may communicate with the judicial authorities using the technologies referred to in point one provided that such are compatible with the decisions of the Courts and all guarantees and requirements of the relevant procedures are respected.

Various regulations issued by the Spanish General Council of the Judiciary in accordance with the delegation of powers provided for in the Basic Law (Article 230, Paragraph 5) specifically govern the use of computer technology by judges, Courts and Tribunals, secretaries and the officials of the judiciary.

Pursuant to these regulations, an agreement was made on June 19, 1999, between the General Council of the Judiciary and the General Council of Barristers in relation to the implementation of telematic communications between the Barristers of Saragossa. This agreement establishes the framework for the telematic transmission of writs and other documents between the barristers and the courts, first in Saragossa and subsequently in the whole of Spain. It also provides sufficient physical and financial resources for the implementation of the project. This will make it possible to use the module for digitally signed and encrypted writs sent between the courts and the barristers included in the LIBRA developed by the Ministry of Justice for the automated management of proceedings in all of the Spanish courts.

Instruction Issued by the Directorate General of Registries on October 29, 1996

The use of new technologies by the Property and Companies Registrars is now a fact. Indeed, it was already provided for in the Instruction issued by the Directorate General of Registries issued on October 29, 1996, which: 1) regulates the possibility of using computer and telematic systems; 2) provides for new actions and the possible expansion of the use of such systems; 3) establishes rules governing the centralization of systems; and 4) establishes exactly the instruments to be used in fax and e-mail communications between the Registrars and the Central Registry Office. Although data protection is mentioned, no security measures are specified in the Instruction.

Notaries in Spain now also have a range of opportunities to employ the new systems. Thus, the General Registry of Wills has compiled entries using computers since November 13, 1992. Provision has also been made for telematic communication between Notaries and the Registers in regulations issued on December 2, 1992. No specific regulations have, however, been issued in connection with security issues.

Code of Civil Law Procedure

The use of encryption in telecommunications and, implicitly the use of the Internet, are provided for in the Code of Civil Law Procedure.

The New Code of Civil Law Procedure, which was enacted on January 7, 2000, established three fundamental points in relation to the use of the Internet:

1. It explicitly recognized that instruments and tools capable of reproducing words, data, numbers and mathematical operations may constitute evidence (Article 299 and Articles 382 to 384).
2. It provided for the possibility of the communication of processes by means of electronic, computer and similar systems (Article 15.2).
3. It provided for the execution of liabilities accredited by means of documents of any kind or class of physical format, provided they are signed by the debtor or bear his seal, stamp or mark, or any other physical or electronic sign made by the debtor (Article 812).

These regulations form an appropriate framework for the practice of e-Government over the Internet. Indeed, the regulation of the judiciary and related institutions closes the circle of needs opened when the regulation of digital signatures were first issued.

The final section of this chapter will discuss trust providers.

TRUST PROVIDERS

The above discussion shows that the development of e-Government requires the existence of specially qualified, sufficiently independent service providers with a knowledge of the fundamental problems involved and the requirements that must be met before the citizen will be able to use the Internet to exercise their rights and comply with obligations in their relations with the institutions of government.

In Spain, three trust providers have been established whose activities are specifically aimed at electronic government and, where possible, at e-commerce. These providers are the Real Fábrica de la Moneda (Spanish Royal Mint), FESTE and AGACE. Their objectives are as follows:

1. The Real Fábrica de la Moneda is the public key certification service entrusted with facilitating the use of digital signatures in relations established between the various departments and institutions of central government using telematic systems. It also facilities services between the citizen and central government. This latter service is not exclusive and citizens may opt to use other certification services in order to establish relations with central government and other authorities.
2. The Fundación para el Estudio de la Seguridad de las Telecomunicaciones or FESTE (Foundation for the Study of the Security of Telecommunications) is another certification service for electronic communications. Its members are Spanish Notaries and Solicitors, the University of Saragossa (Law Faculty) and one industrial member.
3. The Agencia de Garantía del Comercio Electrónico or AGACE (Electronic Commerce Guarantee Agency) provides a seal of guarantee, which is produced with the participation of consumers, government and companies. The seal certifies compliance by information society systems and services offered in connection with electronic commerce and government with the legal and social principles and values of the democratic state. Accordingly, AGACE recognizes that it is a necessary but not a sufficient condition for such systems and services to meet certain technical standards for the award of its seal.

Public Trust Providers

The acceptance of digital signatures in practice initially took place in Spain as a result of the creation of public certification services such as that offered by the Real Fábrica de la Moneda.

This provided the institutions of the State with the basic legal infrastructure necessary to use telematic systems in their relations with each other and, through specific agreements, with regional, provincial and local institutions and authorities. The regulation of the new technologies has also permitted telematic relations between the citizens and the various institutions of government at all levels.[36]

Spain already has direct experience as a result of the arrangements made for online personal income tax declarations by citizens. The possibility of filing telematic tax returns was first introduced in 1999 for the 1998 income tax declaration, as reflected in the Regulations for the declaration of personal income tax for 1998 using telematic systems. The general conditions and procedure for telematic tax declarations were established in the Order of the Ministry of Economy and Finance issued on April 13, 1999.

Companies were in fact already permitted to file tax returns electronically using a different procedure from that established in the Order. However, the personal income tax declaration introduced the novelty that all mechanisms necessary for the use of public key infrastructure were in place for this scheme. As a consequence, Spanish tax payers have been able to complete and deliver their tax declarations using digital signatures generated using the resources provided by their browsers. The Real Fábrica de la Moneda acted as the certification service provider for this scheme,[37] while the tax offices acted as registry entities.

From a legal point of view, this decision has meant that Spain now has tax regulations establishing the implementation and use of digital signatures. Accordingly, the regulation of the scheme sets a precedent for use in other schemes. Naturally, it will also serve as a point of reference, insofar as it is relevant, for the general regulation of digital signatures in Spain.

The main features of the regulations governing the creation of the State Certification Service and personal income tax declarations are as follows.

Budget Act, 1998

On the basis of the aforementioned precedents, the Spanish Parliament promulgated regulations pursuant to the Public Administration Regulation and Common Administrative Procedures Act, 1992 (Law 30 of November 26, 1992) considered above, and resolved to promote the use of the new technologies by the officials of all of the institutions of government and by citizens in their relations with the State.

As a consequence, and in compliance with Articles 38, 45 and 46 of the aforementioned Act and pursuant to Article 81 of the Budget Act, 1998, the Spanish Parliament authorized the Real Fábrica de la Moneda (FNMT) and the Spanish Post Office (Entidad Pública Empresarial de Correos y Telégrafos) to provide the technical and administrative services necessary to guarantee the security, integrity, validity and efficacy of the issue and reception of communications and documents using electronic techniques and systems. The Public Administration Ministry's Information Technology Board provides advisory services in connection with the technical requirements to be met by the Real Fábrica de la Moneda in the exercise of the functions conferred upon it by law.

This legislation thus authorizes the Real Fábrica de la Moneda to act as certification service provider, following the terminology proper to encryption systems and techniques.

Ministry of Economy and Finance Order Issued on April 13, 1999

The Ministry of Economy and Finance Order issued on 13th April 1999 establishes the general conditions and procedure for the telematic presentation of personal income tax returns.

Structurally, the regulations comprise an explanation of grounds which refers to tax dispositions and the legislation described above in relation with the authorization of the use of telematic technologies by the institutions of government, seven articles regulating the procedure to be followed in making the declaration, two additional provisions and three annexes.

For the present purposes, it is sufficient to note that the regulations contain definitions and procedures setting out the main features of the public key encryption system and the infrastructure necessary for its use.

This infrastructure is provided by the Real Fábrica de la Moneda, acting as the certification service, and of the Tax Administration offices, acting as the registry service for data identifying the users of the system. The regulations also govern the generation of users' public and private keys using Netscape and Microsoft browsers, which allow users to sign their declarations. The electronic signatures are of course capable of verification because the certificate issued by the Fábrica de la Moneda for each user of the system is available electronically.

Article 1 of the Order establishes definitions and concepts referring, inter alia, to keys, certificates, browsers and the position of the Fábrica de La Moneda as the certification service. The technical procedures for the generation and use of digital signatures are set out mainly in the Annexes.

The success of this application has led to the publication of a Tax Administration Resolution (May 3, 2000) concerning the issuance of certificates of compliance with tax obligations and similar documents using telematic systems.

FESTE

Objective

The objective of FESTE was to set up a secure electronic communications network in conjunction with the Spanish Notaries based on the requirements of the legal system. This network is intended for use in the provision of recognized certification services for electronic communications in accordance with the provisions of Spanish legislation governing digital signatures. Once all legal requirements have been complied with, FESTE will form a part of the public key infrastructure needed for the Internet to expand worldwide while respecting the basic legal principles of the democratic State. The resulting FESTE network will be a trust provider for e-commerce and e-Government.

Background

The Fundación para el Estudio de la Seguridad de las Telecomunicaciones (FESTE)[38] was set up following the AEQUITAS report prepared at the behest of the European Commission.[39] FESTE is an institution, incorporated as a foundation, created by the General Council of Notaries, the General Council of Solicitors, the University of Saragossa and the Spanish company Intercomputer. It promotes research into trust networks in electronic communications.

In accordance with FESTE's focus, its objective is to carry out scientific and cultural activities of all kinds contributing, on a not-for-profit basis, to the following matters of public interest: to undertake studies and projects concerning the security mechanisms and instruments necessary for the development and use of information and communication technologies; to collaborate in the design of a legal framework appropriate for the certification of electronic transactions carried out between industry, commerce, banks, government and the citizen; and to act, where possible, as a certification service provider for electronic communications, forming part of the European electronic communications security and trust network.

Outcome

FESTE's object includes the creation of an electronic communications certification service in accordance with the principles of the democratic state. It is also concerned with promoting the use of the new technologies by the legal profession in their day-to-day work.

One of the peculiarities of this Foundation is that Notaries form one of the mainstays of its membership. These legal professionals are responsible for authenticating the credentials presented by individuals and legal entities to identify themselves for a given purpose or in connection with legal acts and contracts made in the presence of the Notary. The profession performed this duty in Spain even before the advent of democracy. Thus the function of the Notary from time immemorial has been just that service rendered by electronic communications certification providers.

Notaries are obliged by law to advise citizens requiring their services of the scope of their rights and the effects of their actions before making any undertaking which could have legal consequences. In this context, FESTE's main objective is to integrate electronic interchange with the professional practice of Notaries and to ensure that such practices are appropriate to underpin the social changes arising out of the expansion of the Internet. This results in the integration of technological resources with society through the action of legal professionals, such as Notaries.

Among the successes of this initiative have been the actions taken to advise the European Commission and the Spanish Government on the drafting of regulations (now in force) concerning the creation of a digital signatures infrastructure in Europe.[40] A further legal consequence of FESTE's activity has been that the statutory regulation of FESTE as a certification service provider, currently in the final stages of preparation, has been drafted with greater attention to Spanish Law than is usual for such organizations, which tend to be governed by US Law.[41]

AGACE

Objective

The objective of AGACE is to establish a seal of guarantee for electronic commerce in conjunction with business and user associations. The aim of the seal is to become a guarantee infrastructure or network for electronic companies launching Internet operations for the first time, and selling or purchasing products online.[42]

The members of this network undertake, as a basic principle for their activity, to respect the general legal principles of the democratic state as described above,[43] and those principles proper to e-commerce services pursuant to the European Directive concerning services to the information society and specifically principles concerning the purchase and sale of goods and services, contracts, consumer and user rights, out-of-court and judicial dispute settlement procedures, and compliance with industrial standards.

To this end, the AGACE seal is in the process of creating a code of conduct for vendors in which consumers will be able to place their trust, and a mechanism for out-of-court dispute settlement in line with European regulations governing dispute arbitration which are currently in the process of preparation. For the purposes of the latter project, AGACE has taken steps to link the seal appropriately to the European Commission's Extra Judicial Network (EEJ/NET).[44]

Background

The non-profit Asociación para la Promoción de las Tecnologías de la Información y el Comercio Electrónico (Association for the Promotion of Information Technologies and Electronic Commerce) or APTICE[45] was created in April 2000. The membership of this Association comprises telecommunications, e-commerce and publishing companies, government agencies and private individuals. One of its main activities to date has been the creation of the Agencia para la Garantía del Comercio Electrónico (AGACE),[46] the e-commerce quality seal.

The Agencia puts into practice the general legal principles underlying the democratic state in that it provides assurance to society in general and, especially to e-commerce companies, consumers and users. The Agency is entrusted with the following functions:
1. Certification of the telematic sales procedures used by creating a quality seal for companies engaged in e-commerce activities.
2. Inspection of the companies certified.
3. Investigation of incidents arising in e-commerce processes.
4. Engendering the trust of buyers.
5. Certification, at the behest of legitimate parties, of the moment at which transactions between buyers and sellers actually took place.
6. Preparation and implementation of arbitration procedures for the resolution of disputes arising as a consequence of e-commerce activities.
7. Preparation and implementation of appropriate regulations for the telematic purchase and sale cycle.
8. Promotion of technical standards to facilitate the expansion electronic commerce.
9. Creation of self-regulatory codes for parties accepting the Agency's seal.

Outcome

The Agency is still at the start-up stage, but it has already succeeded in attaching the following attributes to the seal:
1. It is a quality certificate awarded in connection with compliance with existing standards.
2. It provides interested companies and consumers with up-to-date e-commerce know-how and best practice.
3. It guarantees the rectification of imperfections in transactions carried out.
4. It provides assurance of the reliability of commercial communications.
5. It provides the possibility of carrying out automated consultation of organizations awarded the seal as part of an information society service.

These guarantees will have effect, because the companies and institutions awarded the seal will undertake to comply with a code of conduct enshrining the basic principles of e-commerce best practice, such as:

- Requirements for compliance by the vendor with offers made online.
- The vendor's obligation to provide the consumer with sufficient information concerning the products, the contract or the method of supply.
- Provision of the use of appropriate mechanisms to facilitate problem-free transactions.
- Adoption of measures to guarantee privacy.
- Guarantee of security in telematic transmissions.
- Clear delineation of the responsibilities of the vendor and of the intermediaries involved in e-commerce activities.
- Appropriate definition of quality for the products offered for sale.
- Design and implementation of periodic audit and review procedures.

In the event of any breach of the rules established in the code of conduct, the mechanism for extra-judicial dispute resolution accepted by the parties on making the transaction comes into effect. The precise form and characteristics of this procedure are currently under consideration.

Pilot tests for the implementation of the seal in interested companies have now commenced.

CONCLUSION

As explained in this chapter, e-Government trust providers exist who are obliged to respect the guarantees established by Law and provide their services to engender trust and the participation of all concerned. The expansion of these services is essential for the further development of e-Government. Contrary to the situation with e-commerce, in e-Government not any organization may provide trust services, since those services required to engender the trust of the consumer in carrying out a commercial transaction are plainly insufficient. These services must not only meet the requirements established by Directives and laws governing digital signatures and compliance with regulations governing the trust provider's services, but also they must be in accordance with the legal principles affecting the use of telematics in e-Government.

For the same reason, the authorities are obliged to respect the principle that the user should be free to opt for one out of a number of qualified providers and must therefore take the necessary steps to ensure that trust providers are available free of charge to enable citizens to undertake e-Government activities, regardless of their income or specific knowledge.

Currently, these stipulations take the form of an obligation on the part of the authorities to make e-Government applications available to all citizens as Internet use expands, as follows: free and secure generation of keys permitting authentication and the use of digital signatures in the exercise of any rights using the Internet; and the use of an electronic communications infrastructure offering all guarantees established by the legal system as regards the exercise of all civil, political and social rights and compliance with the obligations of the citizen where the relevant procedures are undertaken using the Internet.

ENDNOTES

1 *Communications of the ACM*, December 2000, vol. 43, 12

2 Friedman, B., Kahn. P. H., and Howe, D. C. "Trust online", in *ibidem*, pp. 34-40

3 Resnick, P., Zechauser, R., Friedman, E., Kuwabara, "Reputation systems," in ibidem, pp. 45-49

4 Casell, J., Bickmore, T., "External manifestations of trustworthinee in the interface," in *ibidem*, pp. 50-56

5 Uslaner, E. M., "Social capital and the net", in *ibidem*, pp. 60-64

6 The Information Technology for Public Administration conference held in October 2000 provides a point of reference for the Spanish experience. The subject of the conference was "Electronic Administration for the 21st Century." Transcripts (in Spanish) of the conference and a number of the papers presented are available at http://www.tecnimap2000.vajesycongresos.com/inicio.htm.

7 See the Communication of the European Council, "E-Europe. An Information Society for All," *European Council of Lisbon,* March 2000 (COM (1999) 687 final).

8 Reports on these schemes are available at http://www.cert.fnmt.es/colabora.htm.

9 For example, see: EVANS, P., WURSTER, T., *Blown to bits. How the new economics of information transforms strategy,* Harvard Business School Press, Boston 2000, pp. 33 ff.

10 See: http:/www.icann.org/.

11 For the objectives of the NSF see: http://www.nsf.org/.

12 See: http://networksolutions.com/.

13 Resolution of the European Parliament concerning ECHELON issued on September 14, 1998.

14 These issues are raised, for example, in the Introduction to the Communications of the European Union Ensuring Security and Trust in Electronic Communication. Towards a European framework for digital signatures and encryption, COM (97) 503, http://www.ispo.cec.be/eif/policy/97503toc.html.

15 Supreme Court 3, S. July 17, 1987, issued by Mr. Martín Herrero.

16 Spanish Constitutional Court 2, S 231 of December 2, 1988, issued by Mr. López Guerra.

17 The Resolution of the European Parliament dated 14th September 1998 states that "[It] considers that the increasing importance of the Internet and worldwide telecommunications in general and in particular the Echelon System, and the risks of their being abused, require protective measures concerning economic information and effective encryption."

18 The proposals set out here seek to clarify a complex issue as far as possible. An interesting explanation is provided in: Information Security Committee, Section of Science and Technology, American Bar Association, "Tutorial," in *Jurimetrics Journal,* vol. 38, 1998, pp. 243-260. COM (97) 503 of the European Union is also of interest in this respect (see *above* note 14).

19 For the history of this encryption system, see the preparatory Reports of the OECD on cryptographic policy at: http://www.oecd.org//dsti/sti/secur/prod/GD97-204.htm.

20 Several examples of certification services providers are: Verisign (http://www.verisign.com/), British telecommunications (http://www.trustwise.com) and Global Sign (http://www.globalsign.net/).

21 A report on the state of the art is at: http://www.ilpf.org/digsig/analysis_IEDSII.htm.

22 The Spanish Public Administration Regulation and Common Administrative Procedures Act, 1992, Law 30 of November 26, 1992. This Act was amended by Law 4 of January 13, 1999.

23 Royal Decree 263/1996 of February 16, 1996.

24 Nevertheless, this does not mean that the legal regulation of electronic signatures does not start with the regulation of other cryptographic techniques. The regulation of certification services for use with electronic signatures is also largely sufficient in the case of confidentiality encryption. That this relationship occurs in practice is shown by the fact that regulations concerning the encryption of signatures always contain provisions that, in some way or other, provide for confidentiality encryption. This is directly the object of the UK regulation of the area (Regulation of Investigatory Powers, RIP). Some reasons for the combined regulation of encrypted signatures and confidentiality are set out in: GALINDO, F., "La conveniencia de una regulación española del cifrado de las comunicaciones electrónicas" in *La Ley,* vol. XX, number 4708, January 8, 1999.

25 For the situation in Utah see: http://www.commerce.state.ut.us/corporat/dsmain.htm.

26 The situation of this legislation is found at: http://thomas.lo.gov. The Bill is H.R. 1714.

27 See: http:/www.oecd.org//dsti/sti/it/secur/prod/GD97-204.htm.

28 See: http://www.iid.de/rahmen/iukdgbt.html.

29 See: http://interlex.com/testi/dpr51397.htm.

30 See, for example: http://www.interenet.gouv.fr/francais/teestesref/cryptodecret99199.htm. An English language summary of several relevant texts is found at: http://jya.ciom/fr-decrees.htm.

31 See: http://www.publiations.parliament.uk/pa/cm199900/cmbills/064/2000064.htm.

32 See: http://www.158.169.51.11/eif/policy/html#digital.

33 For example: REMOTTI, L., "Legal and Regulatory Issues concerning the TTPs and Digital Signatures – Final Report". This paper is found at: http://www.cordis.lu/infosec/sre/stud2fr.htm. *Legal aspects of digital signatures* in http://www.law.kuleuven.ac.be/icri/projects/digisig.eng.htm.

34 This is of course a very general outline of the legislation. For the present purposes, it is sufficient to note that the titles of each piece of legislation already provide a clue as to differences in the treatment of the issue from country to country.

35 Directive 2000/31/EC of the European Parliament and Council issued on June 8, 2000 and concerning certain legal aspects of information society services, in particular electronic commerce in the Internal Market (Electronic Commerce Directive).

36 Law 66 of December 30, 1997, Article 81.

37 Ministerial Order of April 13, 1999 setting out the general conditions and procedures for telematic presentation of personal income tax returns, Article 1, Paragraph 6.

38 http://www.feste.org.

39 The AEQUITAS project stands for "The Admission as Evidence in Trials of Penal Character of Electronic Products Signed Digitally." The project was carried out as a project of the European Commission, General Directorate XIII. The final report is available at: http://www.cordis.lu/infosec/src/study11.htm.

40 These activities are described in GALINDO, F., Las entidades de fiabilidad de las comunicaciones electrónicas. El estado de la cuestión en España, in *Revista Jurídica del Notariado,* NUMBER 26, April–June, 1998.

41 A previous version of this statute is available on the FESTE Web page (www.feste.org).

42 These initiatives have some relation with the example: Truste (http://www.truste.org), A Better Business Bureau Program (http://www.bbbonline.org/), Clicksure (http://www.clicksure.com/) and Web Trader (http://www.which.net/webtrader/index.html).

43 See Chapter II above.

44 Council Resolution of May 25, 2000, 2000/C 155/01 (Official Bulletin of the EC number C 155, 6/6/2000).

45 http://www.aptice.org.

46 A further important function is its teaching activity in conjunction with the CDA-EUSLIP group. See activities at: www.aptice.org. The initiative is supported by the European Commission, Erasmus Programme, Curriculum Development Advanced Modality (number: 28666-IC-1-1998-1-ES-ERASMUS-CDA-2). These activities are co-ordinated by the University of Saragossa and involve Law Faculty staff of Universities in 10 European countries (Austria, Belgium, Finland, Germany, Italy, Lithuania, Poland, Spain, The Netherlands and the United Kingdom). The participating institutions are Erasmus Universiteit, Rotterdam, Facultés Universitaires Notre-Dame de la Paix FUNDP, Johannes-Kepler-Universität,Linz, Katholieke Universiteit Leuven, Lapin Yliopisto Rovaniemi, Lietuvos Teises Universitetas, Queen's University of Belfast, Universidad de Burgos, Università degli Studi di Bologna, Universität Hannover, Universität Wien, University of Warwick, Uniwersytet Mikolaja Kopernika, Uniwersytet Wroclawski, Vaasan Yliopisto and Wesfalische Wilhelms-Universität, Münster.

Chapter VIII

The Use of Legal Expert Systems in Administrative Decision Making

Jörgen S. Svensson
University of Twente, The Netherlands

INTRODUCTION

Welfare states offer their citizens many complex services such as social assistance, (health)care, education and pensions. Generally, such services are tuned to the needs and the circumstances of the citizen in question. This means that the provision of each service requires an individualized administration. During the last century, there has been an enormous increase in the number and complexity of the services provided, as well as in the number of citizens making use of them. The typical modern welfare state has developed specialized institutions, in which numerous bureaucrats are systematically involved in allocating services to individual clients.

A naive perspective on the welfare state and its institutions generally provides an uncomplicated and idealistic picture of this service provision. It is the picture of a democratic political body which determines the services to be provided to citizens in different circumstances, and large administrative bodies which simply administer these legal prescriptions to determine for each citizen whether he or she is entitled to them. However, as indicated, such a perspective is rather naive and does not withstand the scrutiny of administrative practice in most (if not all) street-level bureaucracies. In fact, the administration of welfare state programs is often problematic. Not only do the organizations demand a lot of resources, their functioning as effective administrators of provisions is often criticized. As several studies of "street-level bureaucracies" and "human service organizations" have shown, the practice of bureaucratic service provision is not simply a matter of applying formal regulations to the characteristics of individual cases. Authors like Prottas (1979), Lipski (1980), Hasenfeld (1983) and Van der Veen (1990) point out that the question of who actually gets what is not only determined by the legal statutes. The street-level bureaucrats play a substantial and sometimes questionable role as well. As Prottas argues, much of what will happen to an individual is determined by the preliminary, magical process of turning people into clients to be processed. In his eyes, the street-level bureaucrats who perform this task are like modern-day wizards. Although they seem to be bound by all kinds of formal regulations, they have in fact large discretion in the way they label citizens and consequently in the access people will get to services they may or may not require.

This large, often unintended discretion of the street-level bureaucrat in decision making raises questions. Does this decision making really conform to central legal principles such as predictability and equality before the law? Is there not the danger of bureaucrats abusing their discretionary powers? Can we help street-level decision makers to conform to the formal regulation?

As such questions are asked, different individuals have different opinions. Some argue that street-level discretion is nothing to worry about and may in fact be a very good thing. Some argue that street-level bureaucracies should invest more in the quality of their personnel, that something should be done to reduce the time pressure in these organizations and that street-level bureaucracies should be monitored more closely. Some argue that the rules should be simpler.

As such suggestions are certainly valuable in different situations, there may also be another way to approach the problem of discrepancies between the formal rules and existing administrative practices. Maybe bureaucracies could make a better use of ICT and more specifically, of knowledge-based systems or expert systems to improve their administrative quality?

This chapter investigates the idea that expert systems may be used to improve administrative quality. It does so by looking intensively and critically at one example of knowledge-based system support in street-level bureaucracies, namely that of the use of expert systems in the administration of the Dutch General Assistance Act. In this field the idea of expert system support now exists for over a decade, and it has not only been a topic of scientific research and scientific debate, but it actually has become administrative practice. As I write this, about 40% of the Dutch municipalities use expert systems in the administration of this act.

In my opinion, it also is a very interesting case for three additional reasons:

- The case concerns a sizeable application in a rather complex domain, and thus gives good insight in the possibilities of expert systems.
- The case concerns a rather successful, accepted application in a type of field in which the applicability of these systems has been strongly debated (and contested) by social and legal scientists.
- The case may be viewed as one example of the fact that expert systems are regaining attention as possible tools for modernizing administrative practice.

The chapter will now start with a short introduction into the Dutch General Assistance Act, its administration and the problems concerned with that administration.

Then, I will discuss the idea of expert systems support and present the results of several investigations into the application of expert systems, in this context. Given these results, some have been quick to argue that expert systems are indeed important and valuable tools in the administration of welfare state programs.

The next section will present important arguments against too much optimism. Both from a legal scientific as well as from a social scientific perspective, objections against the use of expert systems have been formulated. On the one hand, these objections have to be taken seriously, because they clearly have some validity, and thus require attention when discussing the possibilities of expert systems. On the other, it is important to notice that these objections have not prevented the introduction of these systems in general assistance in the Netherlands.

As I will then explain, the fact that expert systems are now accepted by the General Assistance administrations, has to do with several specific factors, which really have promoted the use of expert systems in this field. Factors that have to do with the specific role of national regulation, with the professional status of the bureaucrats and with the increased scrutiny under which the administrations now have to function.

In the last section of this chapter, I will draw some conclusions with respect to the general applicability of legal expert systems in service provision and provide some arguments for the idea that expert systems will soon become an important technology in electronic service delivery.

GENERAL ASSISTANCE IN THE NETHERLANDS

To be able to appreciate the possibilities of expert systems for the administration of General Assistance in the Netherlands, it is necessary to understand its context. In this section, I will briefly discuss three aspects of the General Assistance administration: the organization of this service, the development of the formal regulation and the continuing problems in the administration of this regulation. I will conclude this section with the argument that the problems in the administration of General Assistance are at least partly connected to the problematic nature of the regulation and especially to its volume and complexity and to the frequency of policy changes.

The Organization of General Assistance and Recent Developments

The Netherlands' General Assistance Act exists since 1965. Its primary aim is to ensure that every Dutch citizen has access to sufficient (monetary) means for existence. Under this act the Dutch municipalities (just over 500) have the responsibility to organize local assistance administrations to support citizens. This assistance provision by the Dutch municipalities is performed in what is called co-governance (Dutch: medebewind). The provision is not determined by national regulation alone. The municipalities have their own policy responsibilities and can top-up the national provisions with local policy schemes. Moreover, in the General Assistance Act itself, the municipal administrations have been given explicit discretion to deviate from the formal rules when individual circumstances demand this.

Until some years ago the municipal agencies administering the General Assistance were often typified as "benefit factories": places from which many people would receive financial benefits and little else. Recently, however, things have started to change. Within the framework the national program "Structure Administration Work and Income" (Dutch: Structuur Uitvoering Werk en Inkomen) municipalities are now encouraged to work together with public and private agencies to provide services like education and labour market counseling and to form "Centres for Work and Income."

Developments in Formal Regulation

In the initial act of 1965, the amount of national regulation was limited and the implicit assumption was that the municipalities themselves would know how to deal with the small number of General Assistance claims. However, over the years this initial situation has changed.

First, the number of clients has increased from just under 40,000 in 1965 to over half-a-million in the '80s (on a total population of around six million households). Although the number of clients has now again decreased to fewer than 400,000, it is not to be expected that General Assistance will ever become the limited scheme it was in the past.

Second, with the increase in volume in the '70s and '80s, General Assistance has become subject to intensive national regulation. The national government has almost continuously increased its concern with the local administrations, especially in the form of detailed material legislation. Apart from basic rules for the differentiation of client types (single persons, married couples, single-parent families), there are many detailed rules concerning such important details as: the prescription of reduced benefits for recent school-leavers, the application of house-sharing deductions, the determination of maximum debt repayment and even the provision of child allowances to parents living in The Netherlands but working in border countries (to compensate for the fact that these workers do not receive a child allowance in those countries).

Third, apart from the material rules that mostly concern the determination of pecuniary entitlements, there are also many national rules which aim at the realization of sound bureaucratic practices, such as the keeping of client dossiers and the regular checking of client information. In addition, the national government has developed new regulation to promote 'reactivation' of clients over the last few years.

The simple responsibility of financially supporting local citizens in need has developed into a complex Web of national and local regulation. The administrative workers are confronted with formal rules for checking client information, for categorizing clients with regard to their distance to the labour market, for mandatory reactivation activities, for mandatory sanctioning of client behaviour and even for the mandatory reclaiming of benefit payments from former spouses.

A Problematic Administration

The insights offered by scientific observers such as Prottas, Lipski, Hasenfeld and Van der Veen may seem rather academic in the sense that many people will accept that bureaucrats sometimes deviate from the precise regulation, but that this will be nothing to worry about. The Netherlands' General Assistance provision, however, is a case that can hardly be ignored. During the last decades, there has been almost continuous criticism with respect to the actual functioning of the municipal social security agencies.

This criticism reached a height in the 1990s when it was openly admitted that many agencies were practically ignoring their verification responsibilities and that some of the municipalities experienced fraud levels of more than 30% (Bien and Roeders-Veening, 1995).

The (public and political) debate this generated led to the forming of a parliamentary research committee "Administration of the General Assistance Act." In 1993 this committee published its report under the title "Social Assistance an Evident Disorder." As this title suggests, the report passed a harsh judgment on the administrative practice of General Assistance in The Netherlands. It reported that administrative practice had separated itself far from what was prescribed and intended in the law, and that the execution of the General Assistance Act was characterized by inadmissible shortcomings. It also provided some factual insights in the seriousness of the discrepancy between formal norms and administrative practice: in a review of over 3,100 dossiers, hardly any were found which met the legal standards.

Given its findings, this committee advised on improvements to make the execution "a controlled process." Since then, this advice has been taken up and has led to increased emphasis on formality (I will come back to this later in the chapter). However, this new emphasis on formality and administrative quality does not mean that the past problems are now over. The increased pressure on the municipalities to comply with the formal rules has not solved the question of how compliance should be realized. As I write this chapter, there has just been a new investigation concerning assistance and income fraud. Confidential interviews have revealed that of three programs investigated, General Assistance still has the largest level of fraud and abuse: 13% of the persons interviewed admit moonlighting, 5 percent admit official work income which is not registered at the agency, 23% report "smaller jobs," 40% of the beneficiaries admit they consciously send out too few applications for jobs (Letter by the Junior Minister, December 4, 2000).

Connections Between the Regulation and the Existing Problems

As we observe the problems that have surfaced over the years and as we look at the development of the regulation, there is one clear connection between them. In many instances the regulations have followed after certain problems were identified in order to solve those problems. For example, the acknowledgement of the problem of false income specifications by clients was followed by additional rules concerning the verification of those specifications.

However, over the years, it has also become clear that there is a connection in the other direction. As it is observed that street-level bureaucrats deviate from the legal requirements, it is also observed that this deviation is partly caused by the legal requirements themselves and by the limited time allowed for dealing with them. In the case of General Assistance, the rules are not only numerous. They are also complex and interwoven and, to make matters worse, they are very frequently changing. To give an indication: in 1996, just after the major legislative change of that year, municipalities received 88 additional policy documents introducing additional measures (Van Reijswoud, 1998).

It is therefore reasonable to argue that discrepancies between the legal norms and administrative practices are at least partly the result of practical difficulties with the application of this regulation. In General Assistance, the amount and complexity of the material legislation is such that it is simply impossible to know all the ever-changing rules, let alone to apply them correctly.

EXPERT SYSTEM SUPPORT AS A POSSIBLE SOLUTION: TESSEC

It has long been accepted that computers can perform certain symbol manipulation tasks faster and more reliable than humans can. The very development of computing started with the idea that machines could do mathematical calculations for us, and over the years, we have accepted that they can do a lot more than just that. As we live at the beginning of the 21st century, we are used to the idea of using computers to collect, store, process and transmit "data" and "information."

In the field of "artificial intelligence" researchers have long since been trying to go even further. There, the central idea is that computers may be designed to perform even more complicated reasoning tasks: tasks that require "knowledge" and "intelligence." This idea which has been pursued for some decades now has delivered the idea of "expert systems": computer programs, which are able to perform automated reasoning tasks in limited knowledge domains, and which are able to approach and even exceed the quality of decision making by human experts. Already in the 1950s it was argued that such expert systems could also be developed in the legal domain (Bench-Capon, 1991). Legal expert systems would be able to perform legal reasoning tasks and make automated inferences about the legal consequences of a given situation. To make such inferences, these systems would have to contain a formalized model of the legal knowledge considered relevant for that situation. Such a model could consist of a representation of the formal rules in question (rule-based model) or of a database in which a series of exemplary decisions was represented (case-based model). The proponents of these legal expert systems assumed that legal expert systems could be especially helpful in supporting complex legal reasoning tasks. Legal expert systems would help human decision-makers to overcome their personal limitations in knowledge and skills.

From this perspective, the connection with the difficulties in administrative practice is rather straightforward: when it is indeed possible to design such legal expert systems, these systems may be used to support administrative practices. This line of reasoning was also picked up in the specific context of Dutch General Assistance Act. In 1984 the development of the Twente Expert System for Social sECurity (Tessec) was started. The aim was to develop a working expert system and to evaluate its contribution to administrative decision making (Nieuwenhuis, 1989).

The Tessec Expert System

The Tessec expert system, in the design of which I was closely involved myself, was what we may call a straightforward, rule-based system. From an analytic perspective it could be conceived as consisting of three parts.

The core of the system consisted of a representation of "domain knowledge," i.e., the legal and practical knowledge considered relevant for administrative decision making. This model mainly consisted of a large number of if-then rules and text fragments.

The second part was what we called the "inference engine," a computer program that could access the model of the domain knowledge and could apply the rules to perform automated reasoning tasks. This inference engine could systematically check whether the conditions of a rule were met, in which case it would "conclude" that the consequent of that rule applied.

The third part of the Tessec system was the "user interface," a computer program that was designed as a means of communication between the user and the inference engine. On the one hand, this interface handled the "questioning" of the user about the case at hand (i.e., the program could generate questions and collect answers). On the other hand, the user interface used the text fragments in the knowledge model to present (intermediary) conclusions drawn by the inference engine in a readable form. Apart form these basic tasks, the user interface of Tessec could also provide some insight in the reason why certain information was asked (why function) and in the way certain conclusions had been drawn (how function).

Figure 1: Conceptual design of the Tessec expert system: Tessec contains a model of legal knowledge, a module to make inferences using this model and it has a user interface to "communicate" with the user (e.g., a street-level bureaucrat)

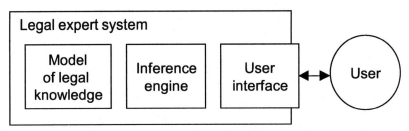

As I realize that this short and technical description is perhaps difficult to follow, Figure 1 gives a schematic presentation in which the central ideas are illustrated.

Designed in this fashion, Tessec as a whole was able to play a question-and-answer game. After it was started, it would consult the user about the case at hand (asking about the age of the client, his/her gender, his/her income, his/her marital status, etc.). Based on this input it would present intermediary conclusions and finally present a complete advice.

An important characteristic of Tessec was that it was primarily designed to support the application of national regulation. In order to achieve this, the knowledge model was primarily based on this regulation: on the General Assistance Act, on the National Standards Order belonging to this act and on royal and ministerial decisions (Svensson, 1988). Nieuwenhuis modelled these formal regulations using a one-to-one (isomorphic) approach in which he tried to maintain a structural correspondence between the regulation and the technical model used in the expert system.

Evaluations of Tessec as a Decision Support System

Nieuwenhuis (1989) did one of the first and most well-known evaluations of the idea of expert system support. He conducted a controlled experiment in which social assistance workers had to make decisions about a series of complicated, fictitious cases. He showed that without the help of Tessec, the workers had great difficulty in reaching formally correct decisions (only two of the 24 decisions proved to be correct). With the help of Tessec, this score was improved to 11 out of 24 in the situation where the expert system was used during consultation with the client. When Tessec was used after that consultation and after an initial judgment by the worker himself, even 16 out of 24 decisions were correct (Table 1).

A second investigation into the impact of Tessec on decision making quality was published by De Bakker and Wassink (1991) and concerned a review of actual decisions regarding housing allowances in one municipality. It was determined that in 1989, before Tessec was implemented, a large number of errors had been made in these allowances (34 errors in 50 investigated cases). In 1990, after the introduction of Tessec, the number of errors almost halved (18 errors in 50 investigated cases).

The results of these inspections are presented in Table 2, where four types of errors are distinguished:
1) decisions in which the existing legal Rules were not applied (error type R);
2) errors caused by incorrect use of a Table (error type T);
3) errors in the input, interpretation and use of Information (error type I)
4) inadequate Verification of the information used in the decision (error type V).

Table 1: Results reached by Nieuwenhuis, 1989

Type of decision	without TESSEC	with TESSEC	
		consultation room	office
Number of decisions made	24	24	24
Number of correct decisions	2	11	16

Table 2: Errors detected in housing allowance decisions before and after the TESSEC module was implemented (source: De Bakker and Wassink, 1991)

	Cases reviewed	Number of errors per error type					Cases with errors
		R	T	I	V	Total	
1989 without TESSEC	50	1	9	16	8	34	24
1990 with TESSEC	50	0	0	9	9	18	17

The investigations by Nieuwenhuis, and De Bakker and Wassink thus clearly demonstrated the possibilities of expert system support in the field of General Assistance. However, despite the results and despite the attention that the investigations received, the implementation of Tessec as an operational system proved to be another thing. As the developers discovered, the social security agencies regarded the system as very interesting but were not easily persuaded to invest in it at the time.

EXPERT SYSTEMS IN ADMINISTRATIVE PRACTICE: MR-SYSTEMS

Tessec was never fully implemented in a standing organization. The commercial firm MR-expert systems, however, carried the same idea further. Over the last decade this firm has developed the idea of expert system support for municipalities and now produces several different systems, which together are used in almost 40% of the Dutch municipalities. Two of these systems are MR-intake and MR-ABW. These systems are remarkably similar to Tessec. They provide almost identical support in collecting information about a client (MR-intake) and in making decisions under the General Assistance Act (MR-ABW).

During the past year, we have examined the use of these systems by the municipalities. We have investigated the motives of the municipalities to adopt MR-expert systems and we have had a new look at the question of whether these systems improve administrative decision making.

Adoption and Reception of the MR-Systems

Over the last two years I have investigated the use of MR-systems (Svensson, 1999; Groothuis and Svensson, 2000). I have interviewed a total of 10 persons in management positions in the municipal administrations. I have had several interviews with managers from MR-expert systems. I have interviewed a well-informed representative from the "Rijksconsulentschap," a body that oversees the municipal administration on behalf of the Ministry of Social Affairs and Employment. I also had more informal discussions with several other people involved in this field of General Assistance. In all these discussions and semi-structured interviews, and also in reading available documentation, I have tried to find out why the municipalities are using the MR expert systems, how the systems are received at the management level and if there are any serious problems in their application.

Concerning the first two questions, I found that the decision to adopt the MR-systems is especially based on the assumption that these systems will improve the quality of decision making, and that they will lead to a better-structured and more standardized process than the manual alternative. I also found that the managers in the municipalities agree that the MR-systems indeed do deliver this quality improvement. In general, the systems are considered pleasant to use. They provide support in making the actual decisions. They function as checklists, so that no important aspects are forgotten. They automatically produce notifications, and the output of the systems can be neatly archived. In sum, the expert systems guard the process of information collection, they improve the quality of decision making and they support effective documentation.

With respect to the question about problems, I found there were surprisingly few complaints. Although there is some criticism, this is generally limited to very practical aspects and incidents. There have been problems with updates and with incorporating specific municipal regulations. In addition, the managers argue that when the MR-intake system is applied, the intake process takes more time than when this is done manually. However, despite these complaints, most respondents are very pleased and they gave no indication of fundamental shortcomings of the approach.

Especially MR-ABW and MR-intake are seen as important tools for improving the administration of General Assistance. Several respondents indicated that their administrations would not be able to function without them and that the systems provide important "guarantees." A strong indication of the level of confidence in the systems is the fact that several municipalities that use MR-ABW have eliminated the step of obligatory testing of each decision from their work processes.

MR-Systems and Juridical Quality

In addition to the gathering of opinions and judgments from people in the field, Marga Groothuis, a trained legal scientist, has recently carried out a juridical evaluation in one municipality which uses MR-expert systems. She has used a checklist to evaluate 30 decisions on a large number of details concerning three aspects:

- *Content of the decision*: are the applicable rules indeed applied and are they applied correctly and with reasonable balance?
- *Wording of the decision*: is the wording of the decision correct, are the legal grounds for the decision explained, has the client been informed about his possibilities to object to the decisions; is the client informed about his duties?
- *Procedure*: is the decision made in accordance with the rules of procedural law, with due care and within the applicable timeframe?

This juridical analysis of the 30 cases, selected at random, reveals two important things (Groothuis and Svensson, 2000; Groothuis, 2001). First, only 18 cases in the evaluation fulfilled all the juridical criteria formulated. In the other 12 cases, Groothuis discovered a total of 25 errors. Second, when the decision making on cases is regarded as existing of a series of partial decisions the number of errors (and also the type of errors) made in different partial decisions, varies with the level of expert system support for that partial decision (Table 3). Where the MR-expert system provides full support, the number of errors is significantly lower than where this support is incomplete or absent. However, it is also important to notice that most errors are present in areas which are incompletely supported by the expert systems.

So, as it seems, the MR expert systems partially support the quality of decision making, especially when we remember that the parliamentary commission in 1993 examined 3,100 cases and found hardly any of them correct. However, from a strict juridical point of view, their use is not unproblematic and having an expert system certainly does not "guarantee" correct decision making.

Table 3: Categorisation of the 25 errors detected in 12 cases in a study of 30 decisions made with the support of MR-ABW

Level of support by MR-ABW	Type of quality criterion			total
	content	wording	procedure	
full support	1	0	0	*1*
incomplete support	5	11	0	*16*
no support	2	1	5	*8*
total	*8*	*12*	*5*	*25*

ARE EXPERT SYSTEMS REALLY DESIRABLE? CRITICISM

So, the idea of expert system support in the administration of General Assistance is at least in part supported by the scientific research on Tessec and by the practical experience with the MR-systems. Does this then mean that expert systems are a good idea and that we should develop and implement them more regularly?

As we look at the scientific literature and follow the discussions, this proves to be another question. In fact the idea of using expert systems in these administrations is criticized and the suggestion that Tessec and MR-systems have proven the case for expert systems is still contested. Legal scientists especially argue that legal decision making is more than just applying formal rules. Social scientists, especially sociologists, point out that administration is more than legal decision making.

The Juridical Objection: Legal Decision Making Is More Than Applying Rules

Although we can find some support for the idea of expert systems in the legal community, many legal scientists are still rather sceptical about the idea of computerised decision making. The scepticism especially concerns two interrelated topics, namely that of differentiation between clear and hard cases and that of law as an open system.

The differentiation between clear and hard cases stems from Hart (1967/1983) and is concerned with the observation that in some situations of administrative life, juridical decision making takes the form of applying predetermined rules to cases, without the necessity of fresh judgment from case to case (Smith, 1994: 17). In such circumstances, we can speak of clear cases. This means that we assume a clear connection between the individual case at hand and the relevant legal rules, and that we therefore accept a simple application of the formal rules will solve the case. However, opposed to these clear cases we find cases in which the straightforward application of existing rules is not considered possible, for instance in circumstances in which no adequate legal rules exist, in circumstances in which conflicting rules–with conflicting outcomes–can be identified, or in circumstances where it is difficult to determine whether the specific case can be brought under a certain existing rule. Such cases are termed hard. In hard cases, it is not possible to make a clear unambiguous or uncontested connection between the case and the legal rules at hand, which means that it is not possible to draw conclusions simply by applying the rules to the facts of a case.

As has been argued by several observers (e.g., Smith, 1994; Leenes, 1999), a fundamental problem of expert systems is that they are essentially designed to treat cases as if they are clear, namely by simply applying the legal rules to each case. Expert systems cannot look beyond their specific programming and principally lack the possibility of a higher order evaluation of the appropriateness of the rules. They thus lack the competence to distinguish those cases for which the rules should not be applied. They lack the human insight necessary to distinguish hard and clear cases.

This means that with the use of expert systems, there is the risk of a thoughtless application of formal rules, even when this demonstrably leads to an outcome which is undesirable from a juridical perspective. Moreover, this inability of expert systems to look beyond their own programming can be viewed as just one problem of the fact that these computer programs are essentially closed systems. They are only programd to accept and process certain input and they will systematically ignore (and refuse to consider) other possibly important factors, which a human decision-maker would take into account.

The Sociological Objection: Welfare Administration Is More Than Legal Decision Making

As discussed earlier, the idea of expert system support firmly roots in the assumption that the problem of correct juridical decision making is primarily a cognitive problem. It is assumed that street-level bureaucrats want to decide in a formally correct manner, but that they simply lack the necessary knowledge and skills to apply all the rules correctly and consistently. This however is a very limited explanation for the gap between formal rules and administrative practice. It ignores other important insights in the practices of such human service organizations.

Social scientists like Prottas and Lipski argue that most street-level bureaucracies are understaffed (both in terms of quantity and quality), which means that they simply cannot comply with the total administrative burden put on them. This is a major reason why the bureaucracies and the people working in them are applying informal methods, namely to find "working solutions." Therefore, when the formal rules require intensive and time-consuming verification of information, street-level bureaucracies can develop informal rules of thumb. Based on their experience, they may decide which cases and which facts will get attention and which cases and which facts will not. In addition, the implicit discretionary powers help street-level bureaucrats to oil the bureaucracy in the interaction with their clients. As bureaucrats unmistakably have these powers, they can use them to sanction client behaviour and in such a way make bureaucratic practice manageable.

Moreover, as Van der Veen (1990: 140) explains, the bureaucratic administration of social programs is based on a double rationality. On the one hand, the bureaucratic apparatus is expected to conform to a legal rationality, in that it takes care of a formally correct administration of the existing legal rules. On the other hand, the bureaucracy is expected to conform to an instrumental rationality. It is expected to adequately address social problems, by making decisions that contribute to the realization of important values. When we look from this broader perspective, the deviations between formal rules and administrative practices cannot simply be categorized as undesirable. They may be necessary for maintaining workable practices in difficult conditions and they may be instrumental in achieving intended outcomes. It then also becomes clear that the introduction of expert systems may harm the functioning of organizations. With the use of expert systems, there will be less room to maneuver and this may undermine the control the organizations and their workers need to tune their practices to varying demands. Following Dennet (1986), it may also be argued that expert systems may undermine the position of the worker, in the sense that these systems will take away valued discretionary elements from their jobs.

Social scientists also object to the closed nature of expert systems. As Scheepers (1991) argues, this lack of openness of computer systems for possibly relevant information should be considered problematic. The use of systems that are not open to unforeseen data could very well result in administrations that are less open to the specific problems of their clients and their specific requests. In the short term, this may negatively affect the service to individual clients whose problems and demands do not always fit in the pre-structured data models. In the longer term, it may also have a negative impact on the system level of these organizations. When computerised systems are only open to the facts anticipated in their programming, they may become blind to the environment in which they are used. They may lose the power of second-order learning and the ability to adapt to their changing environments.

Losing Ground

The objections, from the juridical as well as from the social scientific domain, are certainly fundamental and cannot be denied. As it is, legal expert systems are very limited decision-makers indeed (and by no means "experts"), and there is more to administering welfare than correctly applying the formal rules. However, having said that, where the use of expert systems in Dutch General Assistance is concerned, the above objections seem to be losing ground. Given the results of the Tessec research, given the finding of the parliamentary research committee and given the practical experiences with the MR-systems, there seems to be more and more consensus about the idea that the practical benefits outweigh the more theoretical drawbacks.

More and more critics of the use of expert systems who study this topic seem to give in where the practice of General Assistance administration is concerned. Most open in this respect is Smith (1994), who admits she originally started her investigation of the 'mechanization of legal reasoning' from a rather critical and sceptical position–with the intend to show that law cannot be captured in computer formalisms and thus to show that expert systems will necessarily have serious shortcomings. At the end of her research into this topic, her opinion 'has shifted' (Smith, 1994: 203). She finds that the developments in legal expert systems may 'contribute positively to the quality of legal practice' ("rechtspleging"). This shift in insight is fuelled by an earlier shift she makes–and which she seems unaware of– namely a shift from criticizing the idea of expert systems from a theoretical perspective to a practical, more pragmatic analysis. Given a theoretical perspective, the idea of expert systems can easily be criticized by pointing at some fundamental problems. From a pragmatic perspective, however, a comparison can be made between the two practical options open to social security departments and their clients. What would we prefer? Do we want a situation in which applications are processed by hand, at great costs, where clients will have to wait a long time before they will receive a decision, where this decision will often be unintelligible, and sometimes incorrect? Or, alternatively, do we want a situation with expert system support where a more expeditious processing leads to timely payments and a clear documentation of the decisions and where the possibility of an incorrect decision still exists but is likely to be smaller?

The same changes in thinking can be observed with respect to the "sociological objections," especially with respect to the idea that expert systems would have fundamental negative impacts on the functioning of the bureaucratic organizations as a whole. Those who argue that expert systems have further reaching consequences, in terms of changing power relations and changing flexibility, certainly have a point. However, it is also becoming clear that these changes are not always as negative as predicted. One example here is the idea that the use of expert systems will lead to de-skilling of the street-level bureaucrats, because the expert systems will take over important aspects of their jobs. Although it is clear that the expert system indeed takes over some tasks, it is also clear that this is only part of the story. When we look at the experience with MR-expert systems, we see that in most municipalities their introduction is accompanied with changes in job descriptions and changes in responsibilities, which can hardly be classified as de-skilling or impoverishing. The expert systems are often instrumental in giving the workers broader responsibilities, especially in the context of one-stop shopping initiatives. Moreover, as indicated, several municipalities have lessened the level of supervision.

In sum, given the results of more than a decade of thinking, experimentation, discussion and actual practice, it seems safe to say that the critics are losing ground. On the one hand, the benefits of using these systems have become more concrete, especially where the demand for formally correct decision making is concerned. On the other hand, the anxiety that expert systems would lead to important drawbacks has not been substantiated.

WHY DO EXPERT SYSTEMS WORK FOR GENERAL ASSISTANCE?

As we watch the organizations that now use MR-systems, there is much optimism and there are surprisingly little complaints. Is this then a finding that we can generalize? Can and should we use expert systems more often and in other administrative organizations as well?

In my opinion that is very questionable! As I have witnessed the developments around Tessec and MR-systems, I have become convinced that the success of expert system support in General Assistance was much helped by three particular factors which have made this a rather specific case. These factors are:

- the regulation and especially its volume, complexity and completeness;
- the changing professional status of the General Assistance worker;
- an increased scrutiny and an increasing rigorous control structure.

Volume, Complexity and Completeness of the Regulation

Without a doubt, the major factor in the success of expert systems support in the field of General Assistance has been the existing material legislation. On the one hand, the existence of this regulation, and especially the volume and complexity of it, is still the fundamental source of the core problem that the municipalities face: namely the problem of administering the rules correctly. On the other hand, this same regulation is also an important prerequisite for the development of a working expert system.

Both in the Tessec project as well as in the MR-systems, we find that the large body of national regulation does provide a solid basis for developing expert systems. First, this regulation offers an explicit and well-structured formulation of the central rules in the domain. In other fields such as home-care in The Netherlands, such a complete overview of the rules is simply not available. Second, the regulation does not only provide the rules, but also gives them formal status and legitimacy. Where it is often argued that expert systems can be built, using knowledge provided by human experts, it is questionable that this would be a viable way to develop legal expert systems for administrative purposes. How could we validate the legal knowledge in such systems? What should we do when different "experts" have different opinions of what is legally correct?

Third, connected to this, an important insight is that the regulation of General Assistance in the Netherlands is rather consistent and complete. It is clear that the legislators have gone to some length in making explicit what should be decided under different circumstances and even lacunae left by the legislator are often filled in by explicit regulation on a lower level (e.g., ministerial decisions and or municipal policy).

Fourth, since the national legislation in this field is so extensive and complete, it forms a common core for the functioning of the local administrations. Because all the administrations for a large part administer the same rules, developing expert systems for them is a commercially attractive proposition. The company which is now marketing the MR-systems provides all its municipalities with the same system, and the tuning of that system to local policy is simply done by selecting pre-programd policy options.

Changing Professional Status

Different types of users require different types of expert system support (Bench-Capon, 1991). On the one hand, a non-professional will expect an expert system to provide concrete complete solutions to an actual case at hand. He will not be interested in domain- or theory-level answers. Nor will he be able to deal with incomplete or even contradictory advice, which some knowledge-based systems may offer. On the other hand, a legal professional preparing a case will probably demand the exact opposite. She does not want a system that provides one correct answer to a case. Instead, she expects a system to provide her with all relevant information necessary to make her own decisions. The very idea that a computer program would prescribe decisions would offend her professional prerogative.

Tessec and MR-expert systems both have the typical characteristics of expert systems that aim to provide only one, single solution for each case. They thus are systems that are expected to appeal more to the non-professional than to the legal expert with professional authority and discretion. This raises the question why the municipalities and the street-level bureaucrats working in them accept these systems. Would we not expect them to defend their status as professional organizations with professional workers?

Indeed, I think that is what we would expect, if the municipalities and their workers still had the status of social assistance professionals, as they did some years ago. However, over the years much has changed in this respect. The status of the street-level bureaucrat as a (semi-) professional juridical decision-maker has declined during the last few years. The continuing debate about the quality of their work and about the level of fraud has thoroughly undermined the idea that these workers are real professionals. Moreover, especially the work of the parliamentary commission has definitely destroyed their defense of professional judgment. With respect to determining benefits, the workers have been forced into a new position, namely that of bureaucratic administrators of the rules. This development is especially reflected in personnel recruitment. Most departments no longer hire personnel with a social juridical background but now prefer personnel with education in general administrative tasks.

This de-professionalization–as a result of earlier developments–now facilitates the intro-duction of the MR-expert systems in two ways. First, the systems no longer offend existing professional statuses. Second, as I have argued above, the expert systems seem to support the new status of the consultants. With the help of the expert system, they are able to optimally perform their new administrative tasks, with less supervision. As they can solve more complex problems with the help of expert systems, they are becoming "case managers."

Scrutiny and Control

As I indicated earlier, the crisis and the parliamentary investigation in 1993 led to demands for better scrutiny of the administration and an increased control over the municipal agencies and their workers. This was eventually taken up in the revision of the General Assistance Act of 1996. Under this new act, the formal requirements for the administration of welfare provision by the municipalities have been tightened. A central element in this tightening of the supervision is the introduction of a two-tier system of supervision and with it the introduction of a mandatory accountancy report. With the annual declaration of the costs of General Assistance, the municipalities now have to present an accountancy declaration in which the municipal accountant has to report on his investigation into the validity of that declaration (Article 134 of the General Assistance Act).

Under the new rules, municipalities run the risk that the accountant will reject their declarations, which implies a serious financial risk (the loss of the stately compensation). Therefore the municipalities are now pressed to search for solutions which reduce this risk and which guarantee that the administration accords with the formal regulation. Compared to former days, there is less room for the previous empathic but unverifiable art of decision making. The focus has turned to process control, juridical validity and accurate documentation.

As we have seen above, the implementation of expert systems is a way to improve administrative quality in this sense. It is therefore understandable that several municipalities have adopted this approach, based on their own judgment of the situation. However, that is not all. When I interview representatives from the municipalities, several of those people stated that the use of expert systems is strongly advised by the accountants who now have entered the world of the social service departments. So, as it is, both the legal restrictions and the accountants working within them, now confront the municipalities with a strong incentive to adopt the MR-systems. When a municipality opts for a traditional manual administration, the accountant will insist on an intensive review of the individual dossiers (with the likelihood that errors will be found after they have been made). However, when a municipality applies expert systems, it may get an approval of the administrative process, which implies a more limited review afterwards, and thus a reduction of the risks.

That the increased control is indeed a very important factor in the acceptance of expert systems, is reflected in the sales history of MR-expert systems. Although the systems were already on the market in 1992, the sales strongly increased in 1996 and 1997, directly after the introduction of the new General Assistance Act, in which the new institutional structure was introduced.

CONCLUSION: WHAT CAN WE LEARN AND IS THERE A FUTURE FOR EXPERT SYSTEMS SUPPORT?

As I formulate the above arguments of why General Assistance is a somewhat particular case, I can imagine that some readers may feel disappointed. Tessec and MR-systems have given us concrete experiences of expert system support, but we cannot simply translate these experiences to other domains. Would that be all? In my opinion, that would be a too negative approach. We have learned many things.

First, it should be noted that over the last few years, some other complex legal expert systems have been developed for administrative purposes. For example, De Vey Mestdagh (1997) has build the ESM expert system for administering Environmental Law in The Netherlands, and the SoftLaw Corporation has developed administrative systems for the Department of Veterans' Affairs in Australia. These systems have also been subjected to empirical tests and have proved to enhance decision-making quality. Thus, the experiences with different expert systems have shown us that juridical expert systems do work. They can support administrative workers in a complex juridical practice and they can help to improve the quality of decision making under difficult juridical conditions.

Second, as we review the discussions from the past, we have gathered more insight in the fundamental objections that can be made against expert systems, especially those objections which are related to the idea that expert systems are essentially closed and limited systems. This insight is clearly important when developing new expert systems and when concerning the way these systems may and may not be used.

Third, with respect to the second point, the use of expert systems in General Assistance is an interesting case because here the struggle between practical opportunities and fundamental criticism has been especially strong. On the one hand, we have the very clear problem of maintaining decision quality. On the other, General Assistance, as a social safety net, is still a topic that demands a careful, individualized and open approach. The fact that expert systems with all their limitations are now becoming accepted in such a sensitive area of welfare state provision is very meaningful, in my opinion.

Fourth, as I have argued, we have learned that the implementation of expert systems may be promoted by specific factors--by the existence of a large body of rules (which both was a source of the problem and instrumental in developing this solution); by the changing status of the assistance workers, who lost some of their professional privileges and–crucially in my opinion–by the introduction of accountancy control.

I certainly hope that these insights drawn from the field of General Assistance may be valuable in discussions about the use of expert systems in other fields as well.

A NEW DAWN FOR LEGAL EXPERT SYSTEMS?

About a decade ago, some people working in artificial intelligence and expert systems were talking about the coming AI-winter and, indeed, this winter came. Legal expert systems were a topic of hot debate at the end of the '80s but they did not catch on then and during the '90s interest dwindled. Especially in the Netherlands, many researchers and developers left the field in search for more promising jobs.

At this moment however, I hear more and more people talk about a new dawn for legal expert systems. In The Netherlands and elsewhere, there are several trends which may move us in the direction of legal expert systems applications in other fields as well:

- General Assistance provision is certainly not the only field which has been confronted with increased scrutiny of the street-level bureaucracies. In general, there has come an end to the a priori acceptance of the professional judgments in these organizations and everywhere stricter control structures are set up. Very often these control structures are based on accountancy principles and involve the introduction of actual accountants.
- Where it can be very difficult to model existing regulation, we now see developments into the direction of "computerizable regulation," i.e., regulation which is formulated with the possibility of automation in mind. Well-known examples here are the Dutch tax law which is administered with the help of extensive ICT systems by The Netherlands' tax service (Engers et al., 2000) and the Dutch scholarship system which seems to depend on ICT even stronger and which is administered by the "Information Management Group" (sic.).
- In The Netherlands there is a strong trend towards service integration in front offices and one-stop shops--places where a citizen may find all the services they want at one place and where they will only need to speak to one worker (a case manager). Information and communication technology has been a leading factor in this development, and one of the central ideas is that it will be possible to increase the capabilities

of the case managers in these offices by providing them with computer support (Van der Meer, 1999; Government Report, 1999). Expert systems seem ideally suited to deliver this type of support.

- There is of course the trend of increased "informatization" of service delivery and of e-Government. We are now moving to a situation in which citizens will file electronic requests and expect electronic answers, even on the weekend or in the middle of the night. It may well be that these electronic answers will come increasingly from legal expert systems.

So, although the use of legal expert systems is still limited to a few fields of service delivery, we may see more of them in the future.

REFERENCES

De Bakker, K. F. C. and Wassink, J. G. J. (1991). Development, implementation and impact of the TESSEC expert system. *Presentation at the Conference of the European Group of Public Administration*.

Bench-Capon, T. (1991). *Knowledge-Based Systems and Legal Applications*. London: Academic Press.

Bien, E. A. and Roeders-Veening, C. (1995). *De Uitvoering van de Bijstandswet: Een Vergelijkend Administratief-Organisatorisch Onderzoek Bij zes Gemeenten*. Rotterdam: Stichting Moret Fonds.

Bruinsma, A. and Braam, G. P. A. (1986). Formalisering en evaluatie van besluitvormingsprocessen. *Informatie*, 60, 241-258.

Buchanan, B. G. and Shortliffe, E. H. (1984). *Rule-Based Expert Systems: The MYCIN Experiments of the Stanford Heuristic Programming Project*. Reading, MA: Addison-Wesley Publishing Company.

Dennet, D. C. (1986). Information, technology and the virtues of ignorance. *Daedalus*, 115, 135-153.

De Vey-Mestdagh, C. N. J. (1997). *Juridische Kennissystemen Rekentuig of Rekenmeester: Het Onderbrengen van Juridische Kennis in Een Expertsysteem Voor Het Milieuvergunningenrecht*. Deventer, Kluwer.

Engers, T. van, Kordelaar, P., Jan den Hertog, I. and Glassée, I. (2000). Power: Program for an onthology-based working environment for modeling and use of regulations and legislation. In *Proceedings of Dexa 2000*. Greenwich: IEEE Computer Society.

Government Report. (1999). *De Digitale Delta: Nederland Online*.

Groothuis, M. M. (2001, prep). Forthcoming dissertation. Leiden University.

Groothuis, M. M. and Svensson, J. S. (2000). Expert system support and juridical quality. In Breuker, J., Leenes, R. and Winkels, R. (Eds.), *Legal Knowledge and Information Systems*. Amsterdam: IOS-Press.

Hart, H. L. A. (1976/1983). Problems of the philosophy of law. Reprinted in *Essays in Jurisprudence and Philosophy*. Oxford: Clarendon Press, 88-119.

Hasenfeld, Y. (1983). *Human Service Organisations*. London, etc. Prentice-Hall.

Leenes, R. E. (1999). *Hercules of Karneades: Hard Cases in Recht en Rechtsinformatica*. Enschede: Twente University Press.

Lipsky, M. (1980). *Street-Level Bureaucracy: Dilemmas of the Individual in Public Services*. New York: Russell Sage Foundation.

Nieuwenhuis, M. A. (1989). *TESSEC: Een Expertsysteem Voor de Algemene Bijstandswet*. Deventer: Kluwer.

Prottas, J. M. (1979). *People Processing: The Street-Level Bureaucrat in Public Service Bureaucracies*. Lexington, MA: Heath.

Reijswoud, R. van (1998). Informatievoorziening bij de gemeentelijke sociale dienst. *Een Onderzoek Naar en Stabiliserende Informatievoorziening Bij een Organisatie in Een Veranderlijke Omgeving*. Master's Thesis, University of Twente.

Scheepers, A. W. A. (1991). *Informatisering en de Bureaucratische Competentie van de Burger: Een Onderzoek Bij Sociale Diensten*. Tilburg: Katholieke Universiteit Brabant.

Shortliffe, E. H. (1976). *Computer-Based Medical Consultations: MYCIN*. New York: Elsevier.

Smith, T. (1994). *Legal Expert Systems: Discussion of Theoretical Assumptions*. Utrecht, University of Utrecht.

Svensson, J. S. (1988). Paradigma van het Kennistechnologisch Centrum aan de Universiteit Twente. In van den Berg, E. A.f (Ed.), R.I. Paradigmata. Lelystad: Koninklijke Vermande.

Svensson, J. S. (1999). MRE Kennissystemen voor sociale diensten. *Recht en Elektronische Media*, 4(1), 4-7.

Van der Meer. (1999). *Digitale Dienstverlening: Overheidsloket 2000 & ICT*. Den Haag, Programmabureau OL2000.

Veen, R. J. (1990). *De Sociale Grenzen van Beleid*. Leiden en Antwerpen: Stenferd Kroese.

Chapter IX

Agent- and Web-Based Employment Marketspaces in the U.S. Department of Defense

William R. Gates and Mark E. Nissen
Naval Postgraduate School, USA

Two modes of matching people with jobs prevail at present: hierarchical planning and distributed markets. Each has strengths and limitations, but few systems have been designed to exploit strengths corresponding to both. With evolving information technology, the job-matching process could be accomplished far more equitably and efficiently using Web-based markets within the firm. Intelligent agents offer excellent potential to help both potential employees and employers find one another in a distributed, electronic marketplace. But realizing this potential goes well beyond simply changing the rules of internal job matching or making agent technology available to job searchers. Rather, the corresponding markets and technologies must be designed, together, to mutually accomplish the desired results (e.g., efficient and effective matching) and conform to necessary properties (e.g., market clearing). In this chapter, we draw from Game Theory results to assess the feasibility of using two-sided matching algorithms to address this market-design problem. We also draw from current agent research to address the information technology dimension of the problem by implementing a proof-of-concept multi-agent system to enact, automate and support the corresponding market solution. This chapter integrates the key economic and technological elements required to design robust electronic employment markets. This chapter also presents preliminary results from a pilot experiment comparing performance for a human-based job assignment process to alternative market designs. These alternative designs can potentially reduce cycle-time and better match employees to job vacancies. However, the human-based process currently provides better rule conformance. Future research into Web-based internal job markets should address this shortcoming, among others.

AGENT TECHNOLOGY IN THE PUBLIC SECTOR

In most developed countries, the public sector seems to lag behind private-sector firms and organizations, particularly in terms of adopting advanced technology. Bureaucracy, absence of competitive pressures and other reasons are often cited for this disparity between public- and private-sector organizations, but the novel technology associated with software agents appears to be deviating from this trend; that is, we find evidence of this advanced information technology being developed and applied to military and governmental enterprises at the same rate as—and in some cases ahead of—corporations, businesses and firms.

For example, software agents are being applied to enable electronic commerce systems for supply chain automation and support in a business-to-government (B2G) context (Nissen, 2001), and agents are also being employed to help improve electricity allocation and pricing decisions (Yan et al., 2000). And these applications are well ahead of agent systems in use today in industry, for instance. Other applications (e.g., to facilitate citizen/government interactions) are being conceptualized and developed in advance of private-sector counterparts as well. How far can agent technology go toward automation and support of the public sector? Literally, any public-sector process that involves knowledge and information work (esp. paper-based workflows) offers potential for agent-based performance improvements.

Yet agent technology is not a cure-all for public-sector performance ills. As we describe in greater detail below, agent technology remains relatively immature. And as with leading adoptions of any new or emerging technology, caution must be exercised to avoid over-reliance on technology before it has suitably matured into what can be referred to as "industrial strength" applications (cf. Nissen, 1998). In the case of software agents, to be more specific, although they can be developed using artificial-intelligence techniques to exhibit "intelligent" behavior, for many tasks (e.g., those involving creativity, judgment, novel-problem-solving behavior), their performance is often inferior to that of people assigned to do the same tasks. Alternatively, for tasks that can be specified well, requiring only modest levels of "intelligence" to perform effectively, agent performance can surpass that of people, particularly in terms of accuracy, speed and cost.

Further, not all agent designs and designers are equivalent. For instance, some agents developed for a specific set of tasks may greatly exceed the capability and performance of others developed for even these same, specific tasks. Which specific tasks and agent designs are most appropriate in any given circumstance remains a matter for empirical investigation. This chapter presents one of the very first such empirical investigations of human versus agent performance, and we address the specific problems associated with matching employees with jobs in labor markets.

PROBLEMS WITH CURRENT EMPLOYMENT APPROACHES

Two modes of matching people with jobs prevail at present: 1) hierarchical planning and 2) distributed markets. Patterned after centrally planned (e.g., former Soviet-style) economies and command-and-control (e.g., the military) organizations, the former approach remains prevalent for matching job candidates to jobs within the current enterprise. As an example from the U.S. military, the Navy currently matches sailors to jobs using a centralized, labor-intensive detailing process, one which leaves many parties (e.g., sailors, commands) dissatisfied and results in poor employee morale, performance and retention.

Alternatively, the latter, market-based approach supports unrestricted, point-to-point matching between potential employees and outside employers. As an example from the information technology (IT) environment, technology professionals in nearby Silicon Valley currently have access to a hyperactive job market—characterized by negative unemployment—in which a multitude of job opportunities is available to many people. In this situation, information overload—for example associated with the requirement to search through, screen and filter myriad job opportunities—has become problematic, and employee turnover is now incessant.

Evolving information technology offers great promise for the job-matching process to be accomplished far more equitably and efficiently—for example, using Web-based markets within the firm—and intelligent agents offer excellent potential to help both potential employees and employers find one another in a distributed, electronic marketspace. But realizing this potential goes well beyond simply changing the rules of internal job matching or making agent technology available to job searchers. Rather, the corresponding markets and technologies must be designed, together, to mutually accomplish the desired results (e.g., efficient and effective matching) and conform to necessary properties (e.g., market clearing). The putative performance effects of such marketspace designs merit empirical evaluation.

Through the research described in this chapter, we build upon prior work in Game Theory to assess the feasibility of using two-sided matching algorithms to address this market-design problem. And we build upon prior agent research that created a proof-of-concept multi-agent system to enact, automate and support the corresponding market solution. In this chapter, we begin to empirically evaluate these research advances. The balance of the chapter follows this introduction by discussing employment market economics, after which we summarize intelligent agent technology, including a summary of putative benefits and limitations associated with this emerging technology. We then discuss a specific agent-based employment market design, which is directed initially at an internal, hierarchical-planning employment process. We subsequently discuss empirical results of a pilot experiment using this market design. The chapter closes with a number of key conclusions and an agenda for future research along these lines.

LABOR MARKET ECONOMICS

As background, we draw from what is now textbook understanding of labor market economics (Ehrenberg and Smith, 1997). This discussion reviews market-based labor markets, which are compared and contrasted with hierarchical labor markets. Moving into current economics research, we then discuss two-sided matching games to describe the mechanisms under consideration for incorporation into agent-based labor markets.

Market-Based Labor Markets

Market-based approaches to employee/employer matching rely on the interaction of labor demand and supply (Ehrenberg and Smith, 1997). Figure 1 illustrates labor demand and supply curves for a representative labor market (e.g., manufacturing, software development, clerical support). All units of labor are homogeneous (interchangeable) within a market-based labor market. Jobs that require different skill levels are considered different

Figure 1:   Market-based labor markets

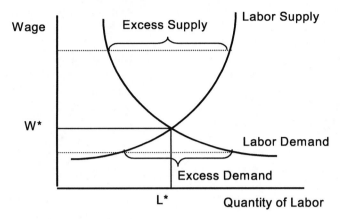

labor markets. The wage rate in this market tends toward its equilibrium value (W*), where the demand and supply curves intersect. The quantity of labor that employers willingly hire at this wage rate exactly equals the quantity of labor that employees willingly supply (L*). Anyone that wants to work in the industry can find sufficient work, and any firm that wants to hire employees can find adequate employees.

If the wage rate is above its equilibrium value, there is an excess supply of labor. At the higher wage rate, employers choose to hire less labor (by reducing output and/or replacing labor with capital), while employees choose to supply more labor (through longer work-weeks and/or new entrants to the industry's workforce). This results in an excess supply of labor. The competition for jobs will force the wage rate to fall until the quantity of labor demanded equals the quantity of labor supplied (i.e., the equilibrium wage rate). If the wage rate is below equilibrium, opposite forces will create an excess demand for labor; compe-tition for employees will increase the wage rate to its equilibrium value.

A subtle but important aspect of equilibrium wage rates involves job amenities (e.g., work environment, geographic location, commute, promotion potential, work content/ challenge, job satisfaction). In weighing employment benefits in one industry relative to alternative time uses (e.g., leisure and other jobs), job amenities are important consider-ations. If job amenities are particularly attractive in one industry, individuals will supply labor to that industry at relatively low wage rates; if job amenities are unpleasant, labor is only supplied at relatively high wage rates (Ehrenberg and Smith, 1997; Moore and Viscusi, 1990). Compensating wage differentials are illustrated by comparing wage rates either across industries (e.g., wage rates for schoolteachers versus garbage collectors or coal miners) or for a particular industry across geographic locations or work environments. Holding other characteristics constant, individuals willing to work in an industry for relatively low wages either receive particularly high benefits from agreeable job amenities or are relatively weakly deterred by objectionable job amenities.

Further developing labor demand and supply provides additional insight into market-based labor markets. Labor demand is determined by the value employers derive from hiring an additional employee (holding the levels of all other inputs constant). In for-profit businesses, the market value of the extra output produced measures labor's contribution. It pays to hire an additional employee as long as the value of the output the employee produces exceeds the cost of hiring that employee (i.e., the marginal value of labor exceeds the marginal cost of labor). Firms hire employees if they value labor at or above the market wage rate; firms (users) that generate values below the market wage rate choose not to hire labor. Thus, market-based labor markets allocate labor to its highest valued (priority) uses; as the market wage increases, lower valued uses drop out, while higher valued uses remain filled.

The labor supply in a particular industry reflects the relationship between the labor employees willingly supply and the market wage rate (i.e., the wage rate implied here reflects total compensation including salary, benefits, bonuses, others). Employees' decisions regarding the labor they will supply for a particular industry encompass both job amenities and the benefits employees receive from the best alternative use of their time, including either their value of leisure or the benefits forgone by not working in other industries. As wages increase for the industry in question, the quantity of labor supplied typically increases. At higher wage rates, the benefits of working in this industry increase relative to the value of both leisure and employment in other industries. Individuals already working in the industry may choose to work longer hours (if institutionally possible), and new employees will choose to enter the industry (by entering the workforce and/or leaving other industries). Thus, market-based labor markets ensure that the employees hired are the most willing to work in the industry. Anyone can find work that is willing to work at or below the market wage rate; individuals demanding higher wages choose to use their time in other ways. As market wages decrease, individuals less willing to work voluntarily leave (either because they have better alternative options or they are relatively less attracted (more put off) by the job's amenities); those most attracted to the industry remain.

Market-based labor markets balance demand and supply, ensuring equality between the quantities of labor demanded and supplied. Moreover, market-based labor markets also allocate labor to its highest valued uses (demand efficiency) and to the uses for which it is best suited (supply efficiency). The demand and supply diagram depicted in Figure 1 only considers a single industry (use) for labor (partial equilibrium). This tends to emphasize the balance between demand and supply; it does not specifically illustrate that labor has other uses. Demand and supply efficiencies become more important as the analysis expands to multiple industries/labor markets (general equilibrium). The information requirements in market-based labor markets also become more evident. To operate efficiently, employees must have complete information about all relevant job opportunities, including salary, benefits and job amenities (e.g., work environment and content, promotion potential, commute).

To mimic the results of market-based labor markets, alternative labor market mechanisms must both balance demand and supply and promote demand and supply efficiencies. The information required to satisfy these conditions is extensive. To ensure demand and supply efficiency, labor assignments must reflect labor's relative value in alternative uses and employee capabilities and job preferences.

Hierarchical Labor Markets

Hierarchical labor markets assign individuals to jobs using a centralized process. Examples of hierarchical labor markets include job assignments within commercial firms, government agencies and the military's labor detailing process. Hierarchical job assignments must rely on administrative procedures to match individual capabilities and job requirements and to reflect both the job's relative priority and the individual's job preferences. There is no mechanism to automatically strike a balance between supply and demand efficiencies, as in market-based labor markets. At one extreme, employers can assign individuals to jobs with little regard to personal preferences. Employees can either accept the assignment or find an alternative occupation. This approach emphasizes the employer's performance (demand efficiency) at the expense of employee morale (supply efficiency). At the other extreme, employers can emphasize individual job preferences relative to job priority and the match between employee skills and job requirements. This emphasizes employee morale (supply efficiency) at the expense of employer performance (demand efficiency). Criticisms against hierarchical labor markets concern their inability to ensure demand and supply efficiencies, inherent equilibrium conditions in market-based labor markets. This inability reflects both information requirements and asymmetric incentives (profits vs. morale).

Demand and supply efficiencies are particularly important for closed systems with a constrained labor supply, such as commercial firms where labor requires significant firm-specific knowledge or the military services and other government agencies. When labor requires employer-specific skills, it is difficult to hire mid-career employees to fill areas of need; employers develop an internal labor force through education, training and promotion, and allocate this labor force across job vacancies. In the military and some commercial firms, wages are uniform across jobs requiring similar skills and experience (no compensating wages). As a result, the cost of assigning labor to one use is the loss of output in the best alternative unfilled use for that labor (opportunity cost); salaries and benefits are irrelevant in measuring labor costs. If labor assignments don't maximize demand and supply efficiencies, the system wastes resources by applying them to less valuable jobs, and reduces job satisfaction, morale and retention by assigning labor to jobs that are relatively less desirable with no compensating wage differential.

U.S. Navy example. To further illustrate the issues involved with hierarchical labor markets, it is useful to briefly describe the U.S. Navy's enlisted distribution system. Because of the Navy's large size, global presence, unique mission and policy of frequent employee job rotation, it is extremely difficult to achieve efficient employee/job matching in this system. The extreme nature of the Navy system makes it particularly attractive for research; if problems with such an extreme system can be solved, then the results of this study should also generalize quite well across many corporations, government agencies and other military branches.

The Department of the Navy (DoN) uses a centralized, hierarchical labor market to match enlisted sailors to jobs (U.S. Navy Bureau of Naval Personnel, 2000; U.S. Navy Commander in Chief, United States Pacific Fleet, 2000). On the demand side, Navy commands (e.g., ships, bases) identify open positions. Job vacancies are compared to projections of available personnel. As the result of military force restructuring in the '90s, the number of positions to be filled generally exceeds the supply of available personnel. Therefore, the Navy develops a Navy Manning Plan that spreads the labor shortage across all commands, on a "fair-share" basis. The Navy then prioritizes job vacancies based on each command's mission, current staffing levels and several other relevant characteristics. This process attempts to distinguish between high and low valued demands for labor, to mimic demand efficiency in market-based labor markets.

On the supply side, available personnel are categorized according to their qualifications (ratings), including skills, experience, education/training, career path and others. Similar skill groups are arranged in communities (e.g., electronics, supply, machinists). Each community has a detailer charged with matching personnel to jobs. Sailors seeking job assignments can express their personal preferences to the detailer. The detailer is responsive to job vacancy priority ratings, but there is some room for discretion in tailoring job assignments to meet the sailors' personal preferences (supply efficiency). Supply efficiency is subordinate to demand efficiency in this process.

DoN's hierarchical labor market is further complicated, because enlisted sailors change jobs every two to three years. Thus, the centralized detailing process reassigns one-third to one-half of the enlisted force every year (e.g., 100,000–150,000 people). This adds a time dimension to the process that is more critical than in typical civilian labor markets. The Navy begins identifying job vacancies and available personnel as early as nine months in advance of planned rotation. Time also affects the job vacancy priority rating. More imminent vacancies receive a higher priority than similar but less-urgent counterparts.

From this brief introduction, it is clear that DoN's centralized detailing process has developed administrative mechanisms to try balancing the quantity of labor supplied and demanded, as well as demand and supply efficiency. DoN fills billets (i.e., jobs) according to a predetermined priority ranking until the labor supply is exhausted, and demand efficiency is emphasized over supply efficiency. In market-based labor markets, equilibrium wage rates automatically perform these functions; wages adjust until there is no excess supply or demand for labor, and employees voluntarily choose their preferred job, considering both relative wages (compensating wage rates) and job amenities. In DoN's hierarchical labor market, wage rates do not increase to limit the demand for labor to the available supply, so commanders are frustrated when they can't fill (even very important) vacant positions. Similarly, wages do not adjust across job assignments to account for job amenities, and assignments do not fully incorporate the sailor's job preferences. Predictably, both commanders and enlisted sailors voice dissatisfaction with the current hierarchical labor market.

Two-Sided Matching Markets

Unlike fast-paced IT firms in Silicon Valley, wage rates for military personnel—and most large corporations—are set by fiat (e.g., by Congress, the Personnel Department) and adjust very slowly to supply- or demand-driven pressures. At least in the short term, the Navy—and most other large organizations—cannot rely on spot labor markets for filling its key jobs with qualified people. Indeed, without its current, hierarchical detailing system, the Navy would find it very difficult to fill many of its important jobs. Yet the Navy—as well as other major enterprises—could also benefit from the efficiencies associated with market-based systems. This conundrum leads us to draw from Game Theory and consider a two-sided matching market (Roth and Sotomayor, 1990). A two-sided matching market assigns individuals to jobs when there are several possible employers and employees. The matching algorithm balances the employers' and employees' preferences, but it can produce assignments that give priority to either employers or employees. As such, the algorithm specifically addresses both demand and supply efficiency. Two-sided matching algorithms are currently used in assigning medical students to residency programs (Roth and Sotomayor, 1990; Roth, 1984; Roth and Peranson, 1997) and pledges to sororities at some colleges and universities (Mongell and Roth, 1991).

The market for medical residents illustrates the two-sided matching system. As U.S. students complete their final year of medical school, they interview for residency positions. Each student interviews with several residency programs, and each program interviews several students. After the interviews, students rank residency programs according to their individual preferences, and programs independently rank students according to their preferences. Students and programs submit their prioritized lists to a central clearinghouse. The clearinghouse compares the lists and assigns students to programs. On a predetermined date, students and residency programs receive their assignments. Each matched student is assigned to one residency program, and each program is assigned students up to the number of available positions. Unmatched students individually seek unfilled positions; programs with unfilled positions can seek either unmatched U.S. medical students or foreign-trained students.

Participating in this centralized assignment process is voluntary. Residency programs and medical students are free to establish individual agreements, but over 90% of assignments are made through this voluntarily, centralized process. To generate this participation level, the matching process must satisfy a few basic conditions. One of the most important conditions is stability: both students and programs must be at least as happy with their assigned match as with any agreement they could reach outside the centralized process. The outcome is unstable if a student and program both prefer one another to the respective program and student with which they are centrally matched. With unstable matches, the student and program would both choose to forgo the assigned match and form their own agreement. If a student is not matched to his or her highest ranked program, the program must have been assigned students that it ranked more highly (i.e., the program would not reject the assigned match). If a program does not receive its highest ranked students, these students must be matched with programs they rank more highly (i.e., the students would not reject the assigned match). Roth (1991) describes the problems encountered when programs don't meet these requirements.

To summarize, as currently implemented for matching medical students with residency programs, the two-sided matching market addresses a number of the differences between hierarchical and market-based labor markets. Most importantly, unlike hierarchical systems, matching markets balance both employers' and employees' preferences. This effectively matches job requirements and employee capabilities, and systematically helps obviate many supply side problems, including employee dissatisfaction, low morale and poor retention. This improves both demand and supply efficiency relative to hierarchical labor markets. Two-sided matching markets also are responsive enough to keep pace with the extreme periodic job rotations effected routinely by the Navy and other military organizations. But such matching markets lack the automatic dynamic response of market-based systems, and the opportunity for side agreements that circumvent the system can be administratively cumbersome. Finally, unlike market-based systems, two-sided matching markets provide some centralized control through the clearinghouse, and periodic matching can dampen the high rates of employee turnover now experienced in high-technology industries.

Despite these positive results, other potential problems must be addressed. The matching algorithm considers both the students' and programs' preferences, but there are generally multiple stable equilibria. Different matching algorithms give different relative emphasis to employer (demand) and employee (supply) preferences. Thus, the balance between demand and supply preferences depends on the matching algorithm (Roth and Sotomayor, 1990, pp. 33-48). Furthermore, the residency-matching program does not distinguish between high and low valued uses in allocating the limited supply of U.S. medical students to residency programs. Programs that might be considered high in priority may fail to match with any students, forcing the program to either contract with unmatched U.S. students, hire foreign-trained students or leave the residency unfilled (Roth and Sotomayor, 1990, pp.143-45). Closed, internal labor markets, such as DoN, cannot fill high priority vacancies with outside labor. Thus, it is important to modify the matching process to recognize job priorities, a function performed by detailers in DoN's hierarchical process. Finally, two-sided matching markets require a significant exchange of information to work effectively. Employees must identify and rank the relevant job opportunities; employers must identify and rank the relevant employees. Mechanisms that help exchange the relevant information can significantly improve demand and supply efficiency. To address this situation, we harness the power of intelligent agent technology and seek to extend current thinking in terms of two-sided matching markets.

INTELLIGENT AGENT TECHNOLOGY

Work in the area of software agents has been ongoing for some time, and it addresses a broad array of applications. Building upon research in the supply chain domain (e.g., Mehra and Nissen, 1998; Nissen and Mehra, 1998; Nissen, 2001), agent technology has particular promise to automate and support electronic labor markets. As computational artifacts, they help overcome human cognitive limitations (e.g., limited memory and processing speed), supporting rapid search and effective filtering through huge numbers of available jobs and potential employees. Further, agents possessing some artificial intelligence (AI) can employ inferential mechanisms (e.g., rules, cases, scripts) to depict and consider diverse individuals' preferences. In a domain with over 100,000 available jobs and prospective employees (e.g., the Navy)—in which both employers and potential employees have specific, idiosyncratic needs and preferences—no other, extant information technology offers the automation and support capability provided by software agents.

In this section, we discuss some representative, extant agent technologies and then outline key capabilities of the Personnel Mall, a proof-of-concept multi-agent system developed to enact, automate and support an electronic employment market. This agent application emerged through research to adapt the Intelligent Mall—its predecessor application for matching buyers and sellers in products and services markets—to focus on matching people with jobs in labor markets. Our focus on this implemented, multi-agent system serves to demonstrate that the kinds of agent-based electronic employment markets discussed in this chapter are not simply concepts of theory or items of speculation. Rather, they build upon demonstrated information technology and provide insight into the kinds of electronic marketspaces that are now becoming technically feasible.

Extant Agent Technologies

Following the literature survey and classification system of Nissen (2001), extant agent applications can be grouped into four classes: 1) information-filtering agents, 2) information-retrieval agents, 3) advisory agents and 4) performative agents. Other groupings from the literature on agents could potentially be used (e.g., Bradshaw, 1997; Franklin and Graesser, 1996; Nwana, 1996; White, 1997), but this classification scheme helps compare various agent capabilities that are applicable to markets and matching processes. Tables 1-4 summarize a number of representative, extant agent applications relevant to markets and matching processes. Specifically, most information-filtering agents (Table 1) focus on tasks such as passively applying user-input preferences to screen and sort e-mail, network newsgroups, frequently asked questions and arbitrary text.

Information-retrieval agents (Table 2) address problems associated with collecting information pertaining to commodities such as compact disks and computer equipment, in addition to services such as advertising and insurance. We also include the ubiquitous Web-indexing robots in this class, along with Web-based agents for report writing, publishing, assisted browsing and other applications listed in the table. Such active information retrieval

Table 1: Information-filtering agent applications (Adapted from Nissen, 2001)

Representative Application	Literary Source
Filter e-mail messages	Maes, 1994; Malone et al., 1987
Filter network newsgroup postings	Sycara & Zeng, 1996
Filter frequently asked questions (FAQs)	Whitehead, 1994
Filter arbitrary text messages	Verity, 1997

Table 2: Information-retrieval agent applications (Adapted from Nissen, 2001)

Representative Application	Literary Source
Collect product/service information	Krulwich, 1996; uVision, 1997; PriceWatch, 1997; Insurance, 1997
Web robots & publication tools	Etzioni & Weld, 1995; Chen et al., 1998; Amulet, 1997; InterAp, 1995
Assisted Web browsing	Burke et al., 1997
Technical information gathering & delivery	Knobloch & Ambite, 1997; Bradshaw et al., 1997
Shopping "bots"	Krantz, 1999

represents an important market task, and many commercial shopping "bots" are being developed to do this in a variety of product and service markets.

Advisory agents (Table 3) provide intelligent advice, and perform something of a classical decision-support role. Examples include recommendations for CDs and movies, an electronic concierge, an agent "host" for college campus visits, planning support for manufacturing systems and other applications listed in the table. More recently, work on agents to provide advice on matching buyers with sellers and decision-support agents have addressed the markets and matching domain directly. Unlike commercial shopping "bots" (i.e., information retrieval agents), agents in this third class decide for themselves what information is needed; then they seek out and use this information to make recommendations for users.

Finally, performative agents (Table 4) are the most sophisticated with respect to the state of the art. They often draw on agent capabilities in other classes (e.g., information filtering, information-retrieval, advisory), but performative agents also perform important knowledge- and information-work activities, changing the state of the external world (e.g., executing binding commercial transactions) through autonomous, deliberate action. In contrast, less sophisticated agents can only support people in performing these activities. Examples of performative agents include marketspaces in which agents can conduct business transactions, auction environments in which agents buy and sell on behalf of their users, and several agent system designs for negotiation. Performative agents also automate knowledge work, such as scheduling, offer an autonomous cooperative-learning environment and provide digital library services.

Table 3: Advisory agent applications (Adapted from Nissen, 2001)

Representative Application	Literary Source
Recommend compact discs & movies	Maes, 1997; Nguyen & Haddawy, 1999
E-concierge services	Etzioni & Weld, 1995
Campus visit "host"	Zeng & Sycara, 1995
Planning support	Maturana & Norrie, 1997; Pinson et al., 1997
Project coordination advice	Johar, 1997
Computer interface assistance	Ball et al., 1997
Military reconnaissance support	Bui et al., 1996
Financial portfolio advice	Sycara, et al., 1996
Buyer/seller matchmaking advice	Freuder & Wallace, 1999
Supply chain decision support	Goodwin et al., 1999

Table 4: Performative Agent Applications (Adapted from Nissen, 2001)

Representative Application	Literary Source
Business marketspace	Chavez & Maes, 1996; Fox et al., 2000; Hu et al., 1999; Mehra & Nissen, 1998; Nissen & Mehra, 1998; Preece et al., 1999
Auction marketspace	Rodriguez-Aguilar et al., 1998; Hu et al., 1999; Sandholm, 1999
Agent negotiation	Bui, 1996; Collins et al., 2000; Guttman et al., 1998; Maes et al., 1999; Sun et al., 1999; Tesauro & Kephart, 2000
Scheduling	Sen, 1997; Walsh et al., 1997
Cooperative learning	Boy, 1997
Digital library services	Mullen & Wellman, 1996

The Personnel Mall is best categorized in the fourth group (i.e., performative agents). It builds upon agent work in other categories, exhibiting behaviors such as information filtering and retrieval. But, it can be used in a performative role as well as an advisory one. Central to the Personnel Mall's potential is its ability to represent a multitude and wide variety of different users—on both the demand and supply sides—to quickly find, retrieve and organize large amounts of market information. Its conformance to market and organizational rules, established for a particular enterprise or circumstance, enables this multi-agent system to automate and support commerce in a broad diversity of electronic markets (e.g., including regulation-laden, hierarchical systems). Such ability suggests the Personnel Mall offers good potential to enact, automate and support the kinds of electronic labor markets addressed through this research.

The Personnel Mall

As noted above, the Personnel Mall is a proof-of-concept multi-agent system developed to enact, automate and support a Web-based marketspace for employee/job matching (cf. Gates and Nissen, 2001). To describe this multi-agent system, we first discuss the Navy enlisted sailor distribution and assignment process, which the multi-agent system is designed to automate and possibly replace. We then describe the Personnel Mall application and outline several putative performance improvements it is likely to effect over the current, hierarchical detailing process. The key is understanding that the Personnel Mall currently automates and supports such matching of products and services along the enterprise supply chain.

The Distribution and Assignment Process

We examine and discuss the basic detailing process and use it for context to describe the Personnel Mall's agent federation in the section that follows. The high-level process delineated in Figure 2 depicts the integration of the command, detailer and sailor along a hierarchical labor market. Notice the distribution and assignment process involves an intermediary (i.e., the Detailer) that matches command needs with available sailors in the marketspace.

The process begins with a command in the organization identifying a need and determining its job requirements (e.g., for an electronics technician, machinist mate). This information is submitted to the personnel command for prioritization. Independently, sailors nearing their job-rotation windows begin conversing with detailers and attempt to convey their job preferences. The detailer then uses this information to match prospective sailors with jobs—looking first to satisfy the needs of the Navy, and second to accommodate sailor preferences—and begins a negotiation process until agreement (or at least consent) is reached with the sailor. The detailer then issues orders, and the sailor reports for duty as specified. The process concludes with the sailor's services being used by his or her assigned command.

Personnel Mall Application

The Personnel Mall is developed for employer/employee-matching enactment, automation and support. Like its predecessor system—called the "Intelligent Mall," which was developed for matching buyers with vendors in products and services markets—the

Figure 2: Basic detailing process

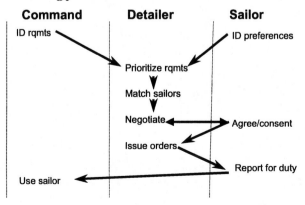

Personnel Mall employs a shopping mall metaphor for employer/employee-matching. In a mall, shoppers (employers) are not expected to know in advance which shops (employees) exist or what products (qualifications) they offer for sale. Neither are the shops (employees) expected to know a priori what other shops (employees) are available or which shoppers (employers) will enter their store.

The Personnel Mall ontology includes entities appropriate for labor markets (e.g., employers [commands], employees [sailors], jobs, wages). However, agent-enabled marketspaces provide a qualitative contrast to physical labor marketplaces; instead of employers and employees searching, matching, hiring and accepting within physical markets, these market and matching activities are performed by software agents that represent employers and employees. The agents—implemented through software objects and methods—communicate and coordinate their activities by exchanging messages with one another. We refer to this application as a "Personnel Mall"—as opposed to the more common "virtual mall" or "cyber mall" names—because it offers more than just virtual shopping. Every entity in this environment possesses (artificial) intelligence, and the agent federation is performative, possessing the capability to autonomously search and match on behalf of commands and sailors alike.

The mall representation presented in Figure 3 shows six intelligent agents representing sailors, three agents representing commands and one command agent's "shopping list" (i.e., input form). The shopping list specifies the jobs to be filled through the marketspace agent federation. This mall is truly virtual; commands and sailors do not reside in any single physical location. Indeed, the commands' and sailors' physical location is irrelevant. What is relevant is that an agent is created to represent every sailor or command interested in participating in this marketspace. Notice there is no agent or explicit intermediary representing the Detailer. Command and sailor agents interact directly through this electronic labor market.

To "launch" a command agent, an officer needs only network access to the agent server (we provide a Web interface for this) and a common Web browser. Any practical number

Figure 3: Personnel Mall screenshot

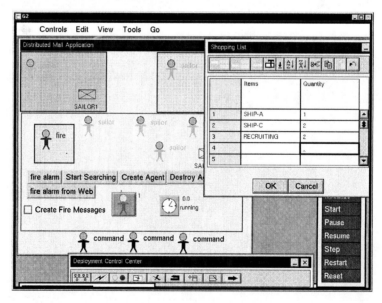

of command agents can co-exist in this mall. Thus, the application offers good potential to scale well to large enterprises such as the Navy. Not apparent in the figure is a special agent called "Host." Command agents register their job openings (e.g., onboard ships at sea, assigned to ships in port, shore positions), and the Host maintains both a "White Pages" and a "Yellow Pages" directory for the mall. Such directories are used to support both sailors' and commands' search through available job listings and applicants, respectively. These directories obviate many human cognitive limitations that impede market efficiency.

A command agent can be specialized to reflect the preferences and priorities of its principal (e.g., Commanding Officer). For example, one command agent can be specialized to search and match based on one officer's preferences for education and training over rank and experience, whereas another's (i.e., identical clone) can be specialized to reflect different (even opposing) preferences. Each command agent can be instantiated with a unique shopping list of job openings. Other knowledge and information—such as user preferences and budget restrictions, product requirements and need dates, and consumer heuristics like price comparison—are formalized through rules for the agents.

As an example, suppose an employer has a job opening. Further, the employer prefers employees with technical backgrounds to those with only managerial experience, but refuses to pay more than $2,000 per week. Finally, the employee must be hired within one week. Using Structured English for explication, two rules to reflect such employer preferences can be written as follows:

Rule 101.

IF	applicant-background(X) = technical
AND	salary(X) < 2000
AND	availability(X) < 1 week
THEN	hire(X) = T

Rule 102.

IF	applicant-background(X) = managerial
AND	salary(X) < 2000
AND	availability(X) < 1 week
THEN	hire(X) = T

Rules 103 – n.

In a top-down rule interpreter, Rule 101 is considered first. If all the antecedent conditions of Rule 101 are satisfied by the applicant, then a decision is made to hire this (technical) individual (i.e., "hire = T" or True). Otherwise, Rule 101 does not hire (i.e., a decision is not made to hire this (technical) individual), and Rule 102 is considered in turn. Likewise, if the applicant satisfies all the antecedent conditions of Rule 102, then a decision is made to hire this (managerial) individual. Otherwise, Rule 102 does not hire, the next rule (e.g., Rule 103) is considered in turn and so forth (e.g., through Rule n). The knowledge engineer develops an appropriate set of rules during the agent-design phase, but individual users (e.g., commands) can modify rules to reflect their particular preferences.

Sailor agents represent sailors wishing to participate in the Personnel Mall. Requirements for launching a sailor agent are similar to those pertaining to command agents. Sailor agents express their intent to participate in the mall (open a shop) by registering with the Host. For instance, sailor agents register individual sailor's attributes in the Host's "White Pages" (e.g., rank, education, training, job skills, availability, community) and search the mall Hosts' "Yellow Pages" to view a complete, current listing of job openings. Sailors use these listings to identify specific assignments that particularly interest them, and they use an input form to convey their relative preferences among this subset of job assignments.

Job preferences and matching. One specific, sailor-agent input form is displayed in Figure 4. Notice the relative preferences listed in Sailor-2's input form. The sailor's first preference is for a job opening on "Ship-C"; the Yellow Pages would include details for this job (not shown in the figure), which might indicate that this assignment involves sea duty onboard a surface combatant scheduled for a tour through a region of potential conflict. Details also indicate this particular assignment provides a good match with the sailor's education, training, skills and experience. Therefore, this particular assignment represents a good career move for this particular sailor. Clearly, other individual sailors will have different and unique preferences and appropriate career moves, which they similarly express through input forms for their personal sailor agents.

Continuing down Sailor-2's ranked list of assignment preferences, this particular sailor would like to attend an advanced training school (e.g., in electronics, computer technology), if not selected by the Ship-C command. Advanced training would also represent a good career move for this sailor, and the Personnel Mall enables each individual sailor to express career ambitions and priorities through job rankings. Still lower on the list, this sailor identifies an assignment on Ship-A, scheduled to remain in port, as a third-priority alternative. Fourth on the list is a position as lifeguard for a Navy swimming pool in California, and the last item represents a recruiting assignment. Using this sailor-specific information, the Personnel Mall explicitly considers each sailor's preferences when matching sailors with job openings, and sailors' agents can work to get matches with the sailor's highest-priority jobs.

The problem with these simple-ranked listings, however, is that they do not reflect relative preferences between different sailors. For instance, suppose Sailor-2 and Sailor-6 both list the same first- and second-ranked job preferences, Ship-C and advanced school, respectively. Sailor-6 may be desperate for this sea-duty tour—and consider attending the advanced school to be a substantially inferior alternative—whereas Sailor-2 may only marginally prefer Ship-C to school. A simple preference ranking would not provide the Personnel Mall with sufficient information to intelligently assign the sailors, based on the relative strengths of their assignment rankings (i.e., assign Sailor-6 to sea duty and Sailor-2 to school). In other words, ordinal sailor preference rankings are sufficient to match the most-desired assignments for any individual sailor, but they do not support rankings based on comparisons across individuals.

The Personnel Mall employs a quasi-price system to support comparisons across sailors. Notice Sailor-2's input form in Figure 4 lists quasi-prices corresponding to the Sailor's relative job preferences. Sailors use quasi-prices to quantify their relative preferences between alternative job assignments. This effectively transforms the matching problem from one relying on ordinal scales (e.g., ranked job alternatives) to one quantifying individuals' relative utility associated with diverse jobs (e.g., using consistent numerical prices, ratings, scores, credits or quasi-pricing instruments). This is comparable to the manner in which a centralized market (e.g., stock exchange) uses relative prices (e.g., price per share) to compare values across diverse products (e.g., securities), or the manner in which employees express their job preferences in market-based labor markets by selecting between jobs based in part on relative wages. This aspect of the Personnel Mall compares favorably with the outcomes of market-based markets discussed above, and expands on the two-sided matching algorithms. The command agent rules in our Personnel Mall currently select the lowest "priced" sailor(s) for each job.

Figure 4: Personnel Mall sailor agent job preferences form

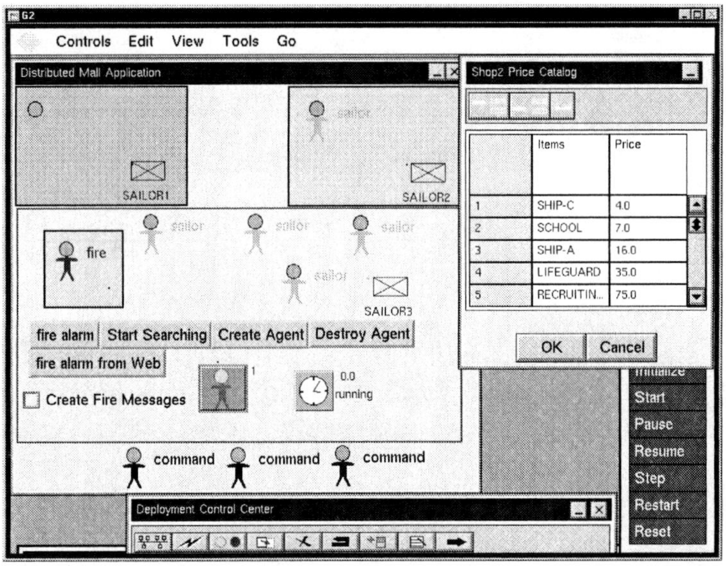

Personnel Mall operation. Figure 5 presents a still-shot of some animated search and match activities. When a command has specified the jobs to be filled (using the Host input form described above), each command agent sends messages to all sailor agents in the Personnel Mall that have expressed interest, through the Host's White Pages, in jobs on its shopping list. Sailor agents wishing to apply for posted jobs reply directly to the requesting command agents, responding separately to each interested command. Each command agent analyzes the messages and determines a preferred sailor for every listed job, based on user preferences (e.g., quasi-prices) and other sailor information (e.g., rank, community, experience).

Each command agent then determines which sailor agents to "visit" (i.e., to negotiate a match), establishes the order in which to visit the sailor agents and consolidates multiple job openings into a single trip. Notice the command agent visiting Sailor-2 is inverted. Such behavior is explicitly required by "regulation" in this mall environment, for instance when sea duty is required. Although humorous, perhaps, this behavior visibly demonstrates that intelligent agents can conform to various personnel regulations (e.g., governing sea/shore duty rotations, experiential requirements, Navy needs). Although difficult to see without animation, the command agent visiting Sailor 1 is currently "jumping" up and down, which represents the local custom when interacting with people in the community of Sailor-1. Similar to the regulation-conforming behavior above, this context-specific behavior demonstrates that intelligent agents can also be sensitive to local customs and variations (e.g., when interacting with sailors from the surface, submarine or aviation communities). The number and kinds of such behaviors specified for intelligent agents are virtually unlimited.

When all discussions have been completed with a given sailor agent, the command agent proceeds to the "exit," where messages are exchanged to extend and accept offers, document the match and issue orders. Each command agent then moves to fill the next job on its list, matches the corresponding sailors and continues in this fashion until all jobs have

Figure 5: Personnel Mall animation

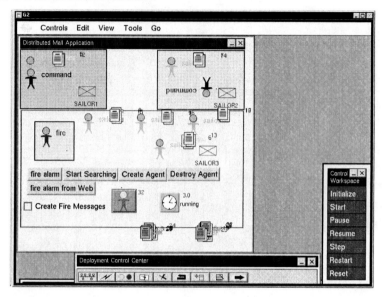

been filled or no sailors are available to fill jobs still on the list. This latter condition reflects one of excess demand for a particular sailor skill/experience set.

Thus, the Personnel Mall is subject to the same market principles and dynamics discussed above in terms of labor markets. As with two-sided matching algorithms, the Personnel Mall appears to offer substantial improvement over hierarchical planning systems (e.g., eliminates the Detailer role, explicitly considers employer and employee preferences) and offers advantages only attainable through electronic markets (e.g., provides access to and helps manage search through abundant, market-wide information, automates many search and matching tasks). The dynamic and emergent behaviors associated with this distributed application are very rich and can be quite powerful—particularly where intelligent, autonomous, persistent agents are free to roam the network and conduct business on behalf of their users.

Putative Benefits and Limitations of the Personnel Mall

To summarize the key points from this discussion, the Personnel Mall is a proof-of-concept multi-agent system developed to enact, automate and support a marketspace for employee/job matching. Based on in-depth knowledge of the Navy detailing process, the Personnel Mall has been instantiated with agents that collaborate in a small federation to perform most search and matching activities required for the marketspace. The application represents and flexibly supports a variety of users and closely integrates commands' and sailors' employment search and matching processes. The Personnel Mall is also designed to conform to policies, rules and regulations that govern personnel, but the job search and matching process and activities it supports represent many hierarchical distribution and assignment systems, in business, government, university, military and other enterprises.

With these capabilities, the Personnel Mall can be used at present to enact, automate and support search and matching in electronic labor markets, just as intelligent malls perform such functions for products and services along the supply chain. Relative to archaic centralized planning systems or crude information-retrieval "bots" used in labor markets today, this innovative application of agent capability is expected to improve performance considerably (e.g., in terms of increased speed, greater information gathering, improved preference matching).

For instance, drawing from analogous performance increases affected through our comparable supply chain multi-agent system (i.e., the Intelligent Mall), benefits begin by disintermediating the distribution and assignment process, obviating the Detailer. As noted and explained above, the Personnel Mall can automatically perform most process activities required to match sailors with jobs—through its federation of intelligent agents—which eliminates the need for an organization of detailing personnel and associated staff. To provide a sense of magnitude, the Navy currently employs roughly 450 detailers and support personnel to perform distribution and assignment activities; some $30M, annually, could potentially be saved annually by implementing a multi-agent application such as the Personnel Mall (Schlegel, 2000).

Additionally, Mall agents perform their search and matching tasks very quickly, gathering and considering substantial information in the process. Pilot experiments in the supply chain domain suggest similar, autonomous agents operate at least an order of magnitude faster than people assigned to perform the same tasks. Agents can also handle information overload, effectively processing much, much larger sets of job/sailor alternatives than their human counterparts. This suggests the lead-time required for assigning sailors to jobs can be reduced, perhaps to an interval so small it approaches just-in-time distribution and assignment. Alternatively, the period between assignments could be extended, simultaneously matching much larger groups of sailors (faces) and jobs (spaces), to improve the quality of fit between faces and spaces. In either case, an intelligent multi-agent system effectively eliminates constraints currently limiting the detailing process (i.e., process time, information overload). Future analysis will determine the detailing process design that best exploits these improvements.

Redesigning the detailing process offers several additional benefits. The Personnel Mall makes all job information available to sailors—and all sailor information available to commands—so personnel can search and rank alternatives from the complete listing of available Navy jobs. This addresses a common complaint from sailors: detailers fail to tell them about more than a handful of the job opportunities that the Navy needs filled. Exit interviews with sailors leaving the Navy suggest the distrust stemming from such behavior represents a significant factor in the decision not to re-enlist (Schlegel, 2000; Short, 2000).

Another putative benefit involves sailors' relative job preferences. Because the Personnel Mall explicitly matches sailors with job assignments based on quantitative preference information, personnel are more likely to be assigned to their preferred commands, which ostensibly promotes better job performance than expected from sailors assigned to less-preferred jobs. Improved job assignments also offer the potential for improved personnel retention, providing a better return on investment in sailors' education and training and increasing the overall level of experience in the Navy. And clearly, increased personnel retention decreases recruiting demands, with potentially many, additional millions of dollars in annual cost avoidance associated.

In contrast, this Personnel Mall application also has potential limitations. As currently designed, it is effectively limited to one-sided matching; job assignments reflect the sailors' preferences, emphasizing supply efficiency (i.e., assignments reflect sailor's preferences as expressed in their quasi-prices). Demand efficiency suffers, because assignments are not based on the sailors' job qualifications and Navy needs. This contrasts to the Navy's current hierarchical detailing system (i.e., matching based primarily on sailors' job qualifications and Navy needs, emphasizing demand over supply efficiency), which suggests that incorporating two-sided matching into the Personnel Mall may offer good potential. A potential to incorporate two-sided matching is briefly discussed in the appendix for the interested reader.

More importantly, the Personnel Mall—and any similar emerging agent technology—is still experimental in nature and not yet mature or ready for "industrial strength" application (e.g., to Navy-wide distribution and assignment). This calls for empirically evaluating how this technology addresses the kinds of distribution and assignment activities required by the Navy, before seriously discussing implementation. Such empirical evaluation represents the focus of the following sections.

RESEARCH DESIGN

The research design involves a pilot experiment that compares detailing process outcomes for human subjects, the Personnel Mall and the two-sided matching algorithm. This pilot experiment is exploratory. We are far more interested in identifying the key concepts, relationships and challenges associated with this domain and marketspace than confirming some set of hypotheses that are well grounded in theory and the literature. Indeed, to date, there is negligible theory and very little literature to address the specific, interdisciplinary problem studied in this investigation.

As such, the experiment involves a common set of detailing tasks that represent the Navy personnel distribution and assignment environment. One group of subjects performs this same set of detailing tasks. The performance of this subject group is compared with that of the Personnel Mall, which performs the detailing tasks automatically, and a two-sided matching algorithm. Performance is measured in terms of quality, cost and cycle time. Each of these research-design aspects is described in turn.

Detailing Tasks

As noted above, detailers match personnel requirements (billets) submitted by various commands with personnel available for periodic job rotation. To some extent, detailers accommodate sailors' assignment preferences through such matching, but the needs of the Navy come first by policy (i.e., demand efficiency is stressed); high-Navy-priority jobs must be filled before lower priority jobs can be offered to otherwise-qualified sailors. In this experimental task environment, each participant is given a list of eight open billets associated with six jobs. This list of jobs and corresponding number of billets is summarized in Table 5, and the experimental instructions are provided in Appendix B for reference. The jobs are ranked in the order of priority established by the Navy.

Notice the heavy horizontal line that bisects the six jobs listed in Table 5. Jobs listed "above the line" represent high-priority assignments; these positions must be filled before any sailors can be assigned to jobs appearing "below the line." This reflects current detailing practice. Deploying sailors aboard ship, both at sea and in port, represents a high Navy priority; recruiting duty also is currently high priority, due in part to the retention problems noted above. All five corresponding positions (i.e., 2 on Ship C, 1 on Ship A, 2 for recruiting duty) must be filled before any sailor can be assigned to the advanced school or serve as either a lifeguard or bartender (these latter two jobs are somewhat fictitious and included for contrast). Every participant in the experiment is given this same list of open billets. Because

Table 5: Jobs requiring assignment

Jobs	Positions
Ship C (deploy)	2
Ship A (in port)	1
Recruiting duty	2
School (advanced)	1
Lifeguard	1
Bartender	1

this task closely resembles those performed by professional detailers in practice, we expect the results of this pilot experiment to generalize well to naval personnel practice.

Participants are also given a list of sailors eligible for assignment to these jobs. For instance, they are have attained the appropriate rank, serve within the applicable service community, due for periodic rotation and have the proper education, training, background, experience, etc. Subjects are also provided with a rank-ordered listing that shows each sailor's preferences for the set of six jobs above. The sailors and rank-ordered preferences are summarized in Table 6. For instance, Sailor 1 would most prefer to be a lifeguard. If this job were not available, Sailor 1 would next prefer assignment to Ship A. Attending school is next on the list, followed by recruiting, sea duty on Ship C, and finally, the bartender job represents this sailor's lowest-priority job. Relative preferences for the other five sailors in Table 6 are interpreted similarly. Every participant is given this same list of sailors and corresponding job preferences.

Each participant is also provided a *unique ordering* in which the six sailors are to be assigned. This reflects the somewhat random sequence and timing associated with matching specific sailors to jobs. In the current distribution and assignment process, detailers match sailors to jobs in relatively small batches (bi-weekly), and the mix of sailors in each batch changes as a function of time. Timing is important, because detailers are required to fill all jobs "above the line" before any sailors can be matched with positions "below the line." This process emphasizes demand efficiency; although detailers try to accommodate sailors' job preferences, the needs of the Navy must be served first. Thus, the relative timing of job openings "above the line" has much to do with any individual sailor's chances of being assigned to a particular job.

This dynamic and policy is reflected in our experiment through randomized orderings of sailor assignments. For instance, Subject-1 may receive the ordering (6,5,4,3,2,1), which indicates that Sailor 6 must be assigned first, followed by Sailor 5, then Sailor 4 and so on. Alternatively, Subject-2 receives a different ordering (e.g., 1,3,5,6,4,2), which indicates Sailor 1 must be assigned first, followed by Sailor 3 and so forth. Final job assignments are expected to vary across participants on the basis of timing between job openings and sailors' availability—just as with professional detailers' assignments. Randomization minimizes any effect that a specific ordering of sailor assignments may have on the results. Because this task closely resembles the professional detailing process, with knowledgeable participants (as described below), we would expect the results of this pilot experiment to generalize well to naval personnel practice.

Table 6: Sailors and job preferences

Sailor	Rank-Ordered Preferences
Sailor 1	Lifeguard, Ship A, School, Recruiting, Ship C, Bartender
Sailor 2	Ship C, School, Ship A, Lifeguard, Recruiting, Bartender
Sailor 3	School, Lifeguard, Ship A, Bartender, Recruiting, Ship C
Sailor 4	Lifeguard, Bartender, School, Ship A, Recruiting, Ship C
Sailor 5	School, Ship A, Ship C, Recruiting, Bartender, Lifeguard
Sailor 6	School, Ship C, Ship A, Recruiting, Bartender, Lifeguard

Subjects

Subjects are drawn from the Manpower Analysis Curriculum at the Naval Postgraduate School, Monterey, California. These students are educated about detailing and many other aspects of naval personnel processes. Indeed, most subjects are familiar with the detailing process. They represent mid-career, professional military officers (e.g., at the O-3 to O-5 level) with roughly eight to 12 years' experience since graduating from college. Because they have personal familiarity with the Navy and understand the detailing process, this group of subjects represents a relatively good proxy for professional detailers.

Experimental Procedure

Procedurally, the participating students receive a seminar-style lecture on the detailing process as part of their graduate school coursework. This ensures the students participate in the study. They are encouraged to perform well, as results are incorporated into their course-grading scheme. The lecture also discusses the Personnel Mall, to familiarize participants with agent technology and its potential application to the distribution and assignment problem, and they are exposed to material concerning labor-market economics and two-sided matching, to familiarize them with the economic and game-theoretic concepts employed in the experiment. Participants are encouraged to ask questions throughout the lecture, and an extended period for questions and answers is included at the end of the lecture.

Following this lecture, participants are told about the rationale for and nature of the experiment, and the experimental procedures are explained. Each participant receives an individualized package of experimental materials (e.g., listing of job openings, listing of sailors to be assigned, rank-ordered sailor preferences, randomized orderings, job-assignment forms), and each item is described. They are, again, encouraged to ask questions.

To make the job assignments, participants are instructed to complete the form included in Appendix B. The form simply lists each sailor and requires the "detailer" (i.e., participant) to fill in the specific job assignment. Participants are reminded about the "above the line" rule, and they are given an opportunity to ask questions pertaining to detailing, the experiment or anything else that may be of concern or confusion. When all materials have been distributed and explained, and all questions have been answered, participants are given a maximum of 10 minutes to complete the detailing tasks. Most participants make the required, six sailor assignments within a few minutes. When finished with the experiment, participants are allowed to take a break, after which they are debriefed on the results of the experiment. Their reactions, comments and questions provide useful validation of the experimental procedures and valuable feedback for future experiments.

Personnel Mall Tasks

As noted above, experimental results for the detailing task are compared with the Personnel Mall for the same set of sailor/job assignments. Because the set of jobs, sailors and relative preferences are known before the experiment, these agent-performed tasks are completed before running the experiment. This allows the researchers to record and compile the Mall performance results for presentation and discussion in conjunction with the experimental results. The Personnel Mall is presented exactly the same information as the human subjects above.

Two-Sided Matching Algorithm Tasks

The two-sided matching algorithm is also used to make sailor/job assignments, and this algorithm is similarly presented exactly the same information as the human subjects above. However, this matching algorithm is run two times. The first run uses a command-oriented bias (i.e., emphasizing demand efficiency), whereas the second run uses the inverse, sailor-oriented bias (i.e., emphasizing supply efficiency). As with the Personnel Mall above, these tasks are also completed before conducting the experiment, and presented in conjunction with the experimental results.

Dependent Variables

Three dependent variables are operationalized and measured in this experiment: 1) assignment quality, 2) cycle time and 3) cost. Briefly, assignment quality represents how well the match reflects the sailors' relative preferences. For instance, if all six sailors were assigned to the highest-ranked job (i.e., job number 1), the average assignment quality measurement would be a perfect 1.00. Conversely, if all six sailors were assigned to the lowest-ranked job (i.e., job number 6), the average quality measurement would be 6.00. Thus, this quality measure reflects matching from the sailors' perspective.

Cycle time measures the length of time required to complete job assignments for all six sailors. This measure is useful to assess the relative efficiency of alternative approaches to the detailing tasks (e.g., manual, agent-based, algorithmic) and offers empirical insight into potential speed enhancements available via such approaches.

Process cost is calculated from sailors' quasi-prices. Costs (i.e., quasi-prices) for the six sailors are summarized in Table 7. For instance, if Sailor-1 were matched with Ship-C, the Ship-C command would have to pay 22 units to Sailor-1. Similarly, if Sailor-2 were matched with Ship-A, the Ship-A command would have to pay 4 units to Sailor-2. Alternatively, if Sailor-3 were assigned to Ship-A, the Ship-A command would have to pay a much-higher 550 units in this case. Process cost simply represents the sum of quasi-prices across all sailor/job matches.

ANALYSIS AND RESULTS

To analyze the comparative detailing process results, we first summarize the experimental results associated with the student participants performing detailing tasks. We then

Table 7: Sailor quasi-prices

Job/Sailor	Sailor 1	Sailor 2	Sailor 3	Sailor 4	Sailor 5	Sailor 6
Ship C	22	16	15	85	10	90
Ship A	28	4	550	100	12	85
Recruiting	26	75	225	135	30	110
School	20	35	14	15	850	150
Lifeguard	24	7	12	18	5	1
Bartender	50	200	100	16	30	110

compare the corresponding benchmark performance measurements with detailing as performed by the Personnel Mall and two-sided matching algorithm.

Human Subject Performance

Experimental data from the 20 subjects are summarized in Table 8. As outlined in the research design above, three performance measurements are recorded for each subject: 1) match quality, 2) time and 3) cost. Match quality represents an average of the six sailors assigned by each subject. Cycle time is measured as total elapsed clock time from the start of the experiment until the subject finishes the six assignments (rounded to the nearest whole minute). Cost is computed as outlined above. Notice no entry appears for Subject 3. One person did not participate in the experiment, due to a schedule conflict, so this subject was dropped. Notice also the time measurement for Subject 11 is listed as "n/a." This subject failed to record the start and stop times for the experiment, so we have no cycle-time value corresponding to this observation. The other performance data associated with this subject are valid, however, so they are used in computing performance statistics.

Mean values and standard deviations across the 20 subjects are presented at the bottom of this table. These values indicate the average sailor is assigned to his or her third (2.99) preference among the jobs, the average subject requires just over three minutes (3.21) to assign the six sailors and the average command cost incurred is 379. Notice the standard deviation for quality (0.37) is relatively small when compared to the mean value of match quality, whereas standard deviations for time (1.18) and cost (273) are quite large in relative comparison. This shows that variation associated with alternative orderings does not produce much variation in terms of the sailor/job matches, but such ordering produces much larger variation in terms of cycle time and huge variation in command cost. These performance data provide a useful benchmark to compare with results from the Personnel Mall and two-sided matching algorithms.

Personnel Mall and Algorithmic Performance

Mean performance data for the human subjects are repeated from above in Table 9 for reference and comparison with corresponding mean data from the Personnel Mall and two variations of the matching algorithm: command-biased and sailor-biased. As suggested by the name, the command-biased algorithm reflects a demand-efficiency approach, in which needs of the Navy are stressed over sailors' preferences. Conversely, also suggested by the name, the sailor-biased approach reflects a supply-efficiency approach, in which sailors' preferences are stressed over needs of the commands.

Table 8: Performance data

Subject	Quality	Time	Cost
Subject 1	2.67	4	476
Subject 2	3.17	2	295
Subject 4	2.67	3	270
Subject 5	3.17	3	280
Subject 6	3.67	3	1376
Subject 7	2.67	3	479
Subject 8	3.17	3	726
Subject 9	3.33	5	487
Subject 10	3.17	2	486
Subject 11	2.33	n/a	177
Subject 12	2.67	2	242
Subject 13	2.50	4	175
Subject 14	2.83	2	193
Subject 15	3.33	4	248
Subject 16	3.50	5	302
Subject 17	2.67	5	274
Subject 18	3.17	2	280
Subject 19	2.67	5	182
Subject 20	3.33	2	297
Subject 21	3.17	2	342
Mean	2.99	3.21	379
StdDev	0.37	1.18	273

Notice the Personnel Mall improves detailing performance across all three dimensions. Specifically, average matching quality improves by almost one order of preference (i.e., from sailors' third choice to their second), the cycle time required to detail the six sailors is reduced by more than 75% and command cost is reduced by over 80%. A 99% confidence interval around the experimental results for match quality (2.78–3.20) indicates the difference in mean performance is significant at an alpha of 1%, as do comparable 99% intervals for cycle time (2.69–3.72) and command cost (260--499). Thus, use of the Personnel Mall appears to dominate the performance of human detailers by a significant margin.

The two-sided matching algorithms also improve performance. In fact, both the sailor- and command-biased matching algorithms produce the same results as the Personnel Mall in this experiment. This reflects the relatively simple experimental design used in this discussion. In particular, both matching algorithms and the Personnel Mall used the same virtual prices to reflect the sailor's job preferences. Furthermore, both matching algorithms assumed that the commands preferred job candidates with lower virtual prices. This command preference ranking guarantees that the sailor- and command-biased algorithms

Table 9: Comparative mean performance data

Approach	Quality	Time	Cost
Human Subjects	2.99	3.21	379
99% Confidence Interval	(2.78-3.20)	(2.69-3.72)	(260-499)
Personnel Mall	2.00	0.75	71
Command-Biased Matching Algorithm	2.00	n/a	71
Sailor-Biased Matching Algorithm	2.00	n/a	71

produce the same outcomes, and that the matching algorithms produce the same outcome as the Personnel Mall. With divergent and more complex sailor and command rankings, the Personnel Mall, Sailor-biased matching algorithm and command-biased matching algorithm could all produce different outcomes. Future analysis will explore these differences.

However, the Personnel Mall and two-sided matching algorithms exhibit a serious flaw not captured in these statistics: two of the high-priority jobs (i.e., those listed "above the line") remain unfilled by their sailor/job matches. Specifically, the Personnel Mall and matching algorithms executed their sailor/job matches as summarized in Table 10. Clearly, with eight job positions to fill and only six sailors available for assignment, some jobs must go unfilled, but none of these automated approaches matched a sailor to the second Ship-C position or the second recruiting position (labeled "Ship C – 2" and "Recruiting – 2" in the table). Instead, the Personnel Mall and matching algorithms assigned sailors to the lifeguard and bartender jobs. Thus, the Personnel Mall and two-sided algorithms, as currently designed, do not conform to Navy rules requiring that high-priority jobs (i.e., those "above the line") be filled first.

For comparison, Table 10 also includes the sailor/job assignments made by Subject-5, whose performance corresponds closely with the mean values for the sample of 20 students; that is, the sailor/job matching performance of Sailor-5 represents that of the average student participant. Notice this participant is able to conform to the "above the line" rule, appropriately leaving unfilled the lower-priority lifeguard and bartender jobs. Thus, we have mixed results from this pilot experiment: the Personnel Mall and two-sided matching algorithm significantly improve performance of the detailing process—across all three performance dimensions—over experimental participants, but only the manual process necessarily conforms to all Navy distribution and assignment rules in this experiment.

For insight into this performance disparity, we refer back to comments made in our introductory remarks, particularly those associated with the relative immaturity of agent technology, as well as wide differences in terms of efficacy associated with agent designs and designers. In the case of the Personnel Mall, it is designed for speed and to automate the basic tasks required for sailor/job matching. Although it considers rules such as the "above the line" job-placement policy from above, a conflict exists between adhering to this rule and making job assignments based on sailor quasi-prices. In other words, where a conflict exists, this agent system is currently designed to serve the sailor's interests at the expense of the command's. Clearly, we can change the rules to have the agents serve commands' interests ahead of sailors' in such cases, but then the sailors would not be as satisfied with the matches. This calls for additional research along the lines of this investigation, for we may be able to develop rules and algorithms that satisfy commands' and sailors' preferences and adhere to

Table 10: Sailor/job assignments

Job\Approach	Personnel-Mall	Command-Bias	Sailor-Bias	Subject-5
Ship C – 1	2	2	2	5
Ship C – 2				6
Ship A	5	5	5	3
Recruiting – 1	1	1	1	1
Recruiting – 2				4
School	6	6	6	2
Lifeguard	3	3	3	
Bartender	4	4	4	

all rules and policies. Through results such as those described from this experiment, that insight into such rules and algorithms is developed.

To summarize, this experiment indicates that the Personnel Mall and two-sided matching algorithm can significantly improve detailing process performance. However, these approaches are currently inferior to human detailers when rule conformance is required. This simple experiment helps shed light on the relative capabilities of people in the distribution and assignment domain, with respect to software-agent and algorithmic approaches. Additional investigation into the Personnel Mall and two-sided matching algorithms is required to address the rules conformance issue.

CONCLUSIONS AND FUTURE RESEARCH

Two modes of matching people with jobs prevail at present: hierarchical planning and distributed markets. Each has strengths and limitations, but few systems have been designed to take advantage of strengths corresponding to both. With evolving information technology, however, the job-matching process could be accomplished far more equitably and efficiently using Web-based markets within the firm, and intelligent agents offer excellent potential to help both potential employees and employers find one another in a distributed, electronic marketplace. But realizing this potential goes well beyond simply changing the rules of internal job matching or making agent technology available to job searchers. Rather, the corresponding markets and technologies must be *designed*, together, to mutually accomplish the desired results (e.g., efficient and effective matching) and conform to necessary properties (e.g., market clearing).

This chapter drew on Game Theory results to assess the feasibility of using two-sided matching algorithms to address this market-design problem. We also drew from current agent research to address the information technology dimension of the problem by implementing a proof-of-concept multi-agent system to enact, automate and support the corresponding market solution. Capitalizing on the best aspects of two-sided matching and the Personnel Mall approaches to the market-design problem, we integrated the key economic and technological elements required to design robust electronic employment markets.

This chapter also presented preliminary results from a pilot experiment comparing performance for the current human-based detailing process to the Personnel Mall and to both sailor- and command-biased matching algorithms. These results indicate that an integrated Personnel Mall/matching algorithm can potentially reduce cycle-time, and improve both supply and demand efficiency. However, the human-based detailing process currently provides better rule conformance, though human-based processes may have a harder time providing rule conformance as the number of rules expands.

Rule conformance requires some centralized control over the labor market; some kind of agent (e.g., human, software) appears necessary to address Navy concerns. Development, implementation and integration of such human or software agents represent an important area for future research, as does continued exploration into the emergent properties and behaviors associated with federations of intelligent (human and software) agents and improving user-interface designs. In addition to such technical research, economic issues—such as constructing and managing variable bonuses to replicate compensating wage differentials, or how to impede user gaming of electronic employment markets—requires near-term attention.

There is clearly much research to be accomplished before robust, electronic employment markets are ready for "industrial strength" implementation in the enterprise. Such research should necessarily be multi-disciplinary and integrative in nature. Economic and technological elements associated with labor-market design are inextricably intertwined; a robust design cannot be achieved without integrating both. This research has taken a step in this direction. We hope to help stimulate future work along these lines.

APPENDIX A–INTEGRATED EMPLOYMENT MARKET AND AGENT DESIGN

Describing potential matching algorithms helps illustrate the issues involved in adapting the Personnel Mall to two-sided matching markets. To simplify, suppose each command (company) requires one sailor (employee) to fill one job vacancy, and each sailor can only fill one billet (job vacancy). Furthermore, salaries are predetermined and invariant for each billet. This one-to-one matching process is equivalent to the "marriage market" (Gale and Shapley, 1962; Crawford, 1988; Harrison and McCabe, 1989; Roth, 1990, pp. 15-121). In a simple job-matching model, salary can be considered a job characteristic that affects sailors' job preferences, along with work environment, promotion prospects, job location/commute, etc. This simplified model provides a convenient starting point. In more complicated two-sided matching models, commands can hire groups of sailors for particular jobs (e.g., several software programmers to develop a new product), and wages vary during the matching process as necessary to balance supply and demand for high-priority undesirable jobs. These extensions will be considered briefly.

In the one-to-one matching model, the matching algorithm begins when commands identify and rank all available sailors qualified to fill a job vacancy. Commands then extend job offers to their highest ranked candidate. Sailors with multiple offers tentatively accept the job proposal they most prefer; sailors reject offers they consider unacceptable (i.e., they would rather not work than accept that offer). Commands that have unfilled billets after this first round extend offers to their second highest ranked candidate, whether or not that sailor has entered a tentative agreement. Again, sailors tentatively accept their preferred offer (potentially rejecting offers accepted in the previous round) and reject less preferred or unacceptable proposals. The process continues through additional rounds until no tentative agreement or newly tendered offer is rejected. In each round, commands with unfilled billets extend offers to their highest ranked candidate that has not previously rejected their offer. After completing this process, some billets may remain unfilled (if all acceptable candidates are assigned to billets the sailors prefer to the unfilled vacancies). Similarly, some sailors may be unemployed (if all acceptable billets are filled with candidates preferred by the commands). However, there are never unemployed sailors if sailors are in short supply, as in today's Navy, and any billet is better than no billet (i.e., unemployment is unacceptable for naval personnel).

Roth (1990) has shown that this matching algorithm produces a stable outcome (there are no commands or sailors who are *not* matched to one another in the final outcome, but who prefer each other to their final assignments). However, this algorithm produces an outcome that emphasizes command relative to sailor preferences (an "command-optimal" outcome). Reversing command/sailor roles generates an alternative stable outcome that favors sailors (a "sailor-optimal" outcome). In this case, candidates offer to work for their preferred command; commands accept their preferred offer and reject unacceptable proposals. As above, the sailor-optimal outcome may include unfilled billets and unmatched personnel. In fact, the unfilled billets and unmatched sailors are the same in both the command-optimal and sailor-optimal algorithms. Both algorithms fill the same billets and assign the same sailors, but different sailors fill different billets.

The iterative nature of the one-to-one matching (marriage) model is the primary difference between this model and current Personnel Mall applications. Furthermore, this iterative process is required to incorporate both demand and supply efficiencies. This iterative process effectively converts the labor market application from a one-sided matching model to a two-sided matching model. Thus, this is one critical extension.

Allowing commands to hire multiple sailors for a particular job (many-to-one matching or the college admissions model) complicates the matching process (Roth, 1985; 1990, pp. 123-186). Commands extend several offers (up to the number of unfilled billets), and tentative matches involve groups of sailors. However, the matching process involves the same iterative nature. This extension is compatible with the Personnel Mall technology. Command agents simply shop for multiple candidates to fill a particular job.

Prioritizing jobs also requires a two-sided matching model/Personnel Mall extension. In competitive markets, priorities are determined by the value of the output that labor produces and reflected in the wages employers are willing to pay. If there are labor shortages, higher valued employers will increase the wage rate to attract sufficient labor; lower valued users will drop out. In closed-system internal labor markets, such as DoN, wage rates do not adjust to reflect labor shortages and job priorities. Hierarchical labor markets use administrative processes to incorporate relative job values (e.g., administratively prioritizing jobs by function/mission). The two-sided matching model/Personnel Mall application just described does not consider job priorities. Thus, the unfilled billets at the end of the matching process may be high-priority, but less desirable jobs.

Variable bonuses (salaries) can be used in a two-sided matching market to reflect job priority. The term *bonuses* suggests that this compensation can take various forms (e.g., wage supplements; benefits, including release time, conference travel; "brownie points" that influence future promotions or job assignments; etc.). Bonuses act as compensating wage differentials in competitive labor markets. In particular, bonuses can be offered for the important but undesirable jobs left unfilled. During the iterative matching process, bonuses can change as appropriate until high priority jobs are "voluntarily" filled with appropriately skilled personnel. In the two-sided matching process, this complicates the matching algorithm (Kelso and Crawford, 1982; Roth and Sotomayor, 1990, pp. 171-86); in the Personnel Mall specification, this requires updating prices before each shopping iteration. And *prices*, in this labor-market context, refer specifically to some kind of variable bonus or compensating wage differential.

One of the critical issues in this extension involves how the bonuses are established (e.g., offered by employers, demanded by candidates or established through a bidding process). Alternative schemes to determine the required bonuses will have implications for how commands and sailors behave (strategic behavior) and the resulting distribution of sailors across billets. If bonuses are pre-announced and never updated, they may not effectively balance demand and supply for high-priority undesirable billets. If bonuses are systematically increased over time until sailors accept the high-priority undesirable billets, sailors have an incentive to delay the match to receive a higher bonus; but they risk someone else filling the billet during their holdout. Finally, bonuses can be determined through a bidding (auction) process designed to identify the minimum bonus that attracts the sailor most willing to accept the assignment in question (Vickery, 1961; Myerson, 1981, 1983; Milgrom and Weber, 1982). Regardless of the mechanism used to determine the bonus, the impact on the matching process/Personnel Mall is effectively the same. (Assignment games provide an alternative approach: Demange and Gale, 1985; Demange, Gale and Sotomayor, 1986; Roth and Sotomayor, 1990, pp. 202-39; Shubik, 1984, pp. 191-225)

This discussion suggests some potential issues in integrating Personnel Malls and two-sided matching models to address labor market issues. The relevant modifications will likely depend on the specific characteristics of the labor market involved. For example, assignment-related bonuses are critical for DoN's detailing process. DoN faces a labor shortage and an institutionally constrained compensation system. Without compensating wage differentials, DoN may have trouble filling high-priority undesirable billets using a two-sided matching model (as opposed to DoN's current one-sided hierarchical matching model). A bonus system might be less relevant for commercial firms with variable wage rates and no labor shortage. Successfully integrating the Personnel Mall and two-sided matching models requires accurately characterizing the labor market and identifying the relevant model modifications. It now remains to investigate a specific labor market, in detail, in order to determine the particular market and agent mechanisms and specifications.

APPENDIX B–EXPERIMENTAL INSTRUCTIONS

Navy Personnel Detailing Task
Profs. Bill Gates and Mark Nissen

Please wait for instructions.

| _____ | _____ | _____ |
| Print your name | Start time | Stop time |

General

You are acting as an enlisted personnel detailing specialist assigned to match a small group of sailors with jobs at several naval commands that need to be filled immediately. The Navy has a policy of first filling the most important jobs (i.e., those listed "above the line"), and although specific job preferences of sailors are important, the needs of naval commands take precedence. Also, you must make assignments on a first-come-first-served basis; that is, assign each sailor in the order noted below (see reverse side of form).

Instructions

The jobs to be filled are listed below. All high-priority jobs must be filled before placements are made to less-urgent jobs. Consider sailors' preferences to the maximum extent practical without jeopardizing high-priority assignments. Assign each sailor according to the specific order shown overleaf in the Specific Order of Sailor Assignments section. Place your name on this form and turn it in when instructed to do so. Also note the start time when instructed to begin, and note the stop time when finished making all assignments.

Jobs to be Filled

Jobs are organized in two categories: 1) high-priority jobs are listed "above the line," and 2) less-urgent jobs are listed "below the line."
Above the line

- Ship A (in port) – 1 job to fill
- Ship C (deploy) – 2 jobs to fill
- Recruiting duty – 2 jobs to fill

_____

Below the line

- Lifeguard (NPS) – 1 job to fill
- School (advanced) – 1 job to fill
- Bartender (NPS) – 1 job to fill

Sailors and Preferences

The sailors and corresponding job preferences are listed below. Jobs are listed in order of preference for each sailor.

- Sailor 1 – Lifeguard, Ship A, School, Recruiting, Ship C, Bartender
- Sailor 2 – Ship C, School, Ship A, Lifeguard, Recruiting, Bartender
- Sailor 3 – School, Lifeguard, Ship A, Bartender, Recruiting, Ship C
- Sailor 4 – Lifeguard, Bartender, School, Ship A, Recruiting, Ship C
- Sailor 5 – School, Ship A, Ship C, Recruiting, Bartender, Lifeguard
- Sailor 6 – School, Ship C, Ship A, Recruiting, Bartender, Lifeguard

Specific Order of Sailor Assignments

Assign sailors in the specific order noted below. For instance, if Sailor 1 has a 3 next to it, you would make this your third assignment, and if Sailor 6 has a 1 next to it, you would make this your first assignment. Write the job assigned next to each sailor below.

_____   Sailor 1: _____

_____   Sailor 2: _____

_____   Sailor 3: _____

_____   Sailor 4: _____

_____   Sailor 5: _____

_____   Sailor 6: _____

REFERENCES

Amulet. (1997). *Amulet Online Description*. Available on the World Wide Web at: http://www.amulet.com.

Ball, G., Ling, D., Kurlander, D., Miller, J., Pugh, D., Skelly, T., Stankosky, A., Thiel, D., Van Dantzich, M. and Wax, T. (1997). Lifelike computer characters: The persona project at Microsoft. In Bradshaw, J. (Ed.), *Software Agents*. Menlo Park, CA: AAAI Press.

Boy, G. A. (1997). Software agents for cooperative learning. In Bradshaw, J. (Ed.). *Software Agents*. Menlo Park, CA: AAAI Press.

Bradshaw, J. M., Dutfield. S., Benoit, P. and Woolley, J. D. (1997). KAoS: Toward an industrial-strength open agent architecture. In Bradshaw, J. (Ed.), *Software Agents*. Menlo Park, CA: AAAI Press.

Bui, T. (1996). *Intelligent Negotiation Agents for Supporting Internet-Based Competitive Procurement*. Working paper.

Bui, T., Jones, C., Sridar, S. and Ludlow, N. (1996). *Decision Support for Reconnaissance Using Intelligent Software Agents*. Naval Postgraduate School research proposal.

Burke, R. D., Hammond, K. J. and Young, B. C. (1997). The find me approach to assisted browsing. *IEEE Expert*, July/August, 32-40.

Chavez, A. and Maes, P. (1996). Kasbah: An agent marketplace for buying and selling goods. *Proceedings of the First International Conference on the Practical Application of Intelligent Agents and Multi-Agent Technology*, April. London, UKl.

Chen, H., Chung, Y., Ramsey, M. and Yang, C. (1998). An intelligent personal spider (agent) for dynamic Internet/intranet searching. *Decision Support Systems*, 23, 41-58.

Collins, J., Youngdahl, B., Jamison, Sc., Mobasher, B. and Gini, M. (1998). A market architecture for multi-agent contracting. In Sycara, K. and Wooldridge, M. (Eds.), *Proceedings of the Second International Conference on Autonomous Agents*, Minneapolis, MN, 285-292.

Crawford, V. P. (1988). Comparative statics in matching markets. *Journal of Economic Theory*, 54, 389-400.

Demange, G. and Gale, D. (1985). The strategy structure of two-sided matching games. *Econometrica*, 53, 873-88.

Demange, G., Gale, D. and Sotomayor, M. (1986). Multi-item auctions. *Journal of Political Economy*, 94, 863-72.

Ehrenberg, R. G. and Smith, R. S. (1997). *Modern Labor Economics: Theory and Public Policy*, Reading, MA: Addison-Wesley.

Etzioni, O. and Weld, D. S. (1995). Intelligent agents on the Internet: Fact, fiction and forecast. *IEEE Expert*, August, 44-49.

Fox, M. and Barbuceanu, M. (2000). The integrated supply chain management project. *Enterprise Integration Laboratory*. Department of Industrial Engineering, University of Toronto. Available on the World Wide Web at: http://www.eil.utoronto.ca/iscm-descr.html.

Freuder, E. C. and Wallace, R. J. (1999). Matchmaker agents for electronic commerce. In Finin, T. and Grosof, B. (Eds.), *Proceedings of the American Association for Artificial Intelligence*, Workshop on AI for Electronic Commerce, July. Orlando, FL.

Gale, D. and Shapley, L. (1962). College admissions and the stability of marriage. *American Mthematical Monthly*, 69, 9-15.

Gates, W. R. and Nissen, M. E. (2001). Designing agent-based electronic employment markets. *Electronic Commerce Research Journal*, Special Issue on Theory and Application of Electronic Market Design (forthcoming).

Gebauer, J., Beam, C. and Segev, A. (1998). Impact of the Internet on procurement. In Nissen, M., Snider, K. and Lamm, D. (Eds.), *Acquisition Review Quarterly*, Special Issue on Managing Radical Change, 5(2), 167-184.

Goodwin, R., Keskinocak, P., Murthy, S., Wu, F. and Akkiraju, R. (1999). Intelligent decision support for the e-supply chain. In Finin, T. and Grosof, B. (Eds.), *Proceedings of the American Association for Artificial Intelligence*, Workshop on AI for Electronic Commerce, July. Orlando FL.

Hammer, M. (1990). Reengineering work: Don't automate, obliterate. *Harvard Business Review*, 68(4), July-August, 104-112.

Harrison, G. W. and McCabe, K. A. (1989). Stability and preference distortion in resource matching: An experimental study of the marriage market. Department of Economics, University of New Mexico, mimeo.

Hu, J., Reeves, D. and Wong, H. S. (1999). Agent service for online auctions. In Finin, T. and Grosof, B. (Eds.), *Proceedings of the American Association for Artificial Intelligence*, Workshop on AI for Electronic Commerce, July. Orlando, FL.

Hu, J., Yen, J. and Chung, A. (1999). A virtual property agency: Electronic market with support of negotiation. In Finin, T. and Grosof, B. (Eds.), *Proceedings of the American Association for Artificial Intelligence*, Workshop on AI for Electronic Commerce, July. Orlando, FL.

Insurance. (1997). Insurance online description. Available on the World Wide Web at: http://www.dmatters.co.uk.

InterAp. (1995). InterAp assigns intelligent agents to the Web. *PCWeek*, June 12.

Johar, H. V. (1997). SoftCord: An intelligent agent for coordination in software development projects. *Decision Support Systems*, 20, 65-81.

Kelso, A. S., Jr. and Crawford, V. P. (1982). Job matching, coalition formation and gross substitutes. *Econometrica*, 50, 1483-1504.

Knobloch, C. A. and Ambite, J. L. (1996). Agents for information. In Krulwich, D. (Ed.), *An Agent of Change*. Andersen Consulting Center for Strategic Technology Research.

Krantz, M. (1999). The next e-volution: BusinessBots could transform corporate commerce, just as the Web transformed consumer shopping. *TIME*, July 12, 47.

Krulwich, D. (1996). *An Agent of Change*. Andersen Consulting Center for Strategic Technology Research.

Maes, P. (1994). Agents that reduce work and information overload. *Communications of the ACM*, July, 37(7), 30-40.

Maes, P. (1997). Pattie Maes on software agents: Humanizing the global computer. *Internet Computing*, July-August.

Maes, P., Guttman, R. H. and Moukas, A. G. (1999). Agents that buy and sell. *Communications of the ACM*, March, 42(3), 81-87.

Malone, T. W., Yates, J. and Benjamin, R. I. (1987). Electronic markets and electronic hierarchies. *Communications of the ACM*, 30(6), 484-497.

Maturana, F. P. and Norrie, D. H. (1997). Distributed decision-making using the contract net within a mediator architecture. *Decision Support Systems*, 20, 53-64.

Mehra, A. and Nissen, M. E. (1998). Case study: Intelligent software supply chain agents using ADE. *Proceedings from the AAAI Workshop on Software Tools for Developing Agents*.

Milgrom, P. R. and Weber, R. J. (1982). A theory of auctions and competitive bidding. *Econometrica*, 50, 1089-122.

Mongell, S. J. and Roth, A. E. (1991). Sorority rush as a two-sided matching mechanism. *American Economic Review*, June, 81, 441-464.

Moore, M. J. and Viscusi, W. K. (1990). *Compensation Mechanisms for Job Risks: Wages, Worker's Compensation and Product Liability*. Princeton, NJ: Princeton University Press.

Mullen, T. and Wellman, M. P. (1996). Market-based negotiation for digital library services. *Second USENIX Workshop on Electronic Commerce*, November.

Myerson, Roger B. (1983). The basic theory of optimal auctions. In Englebrecht-Wiggins, R., Shubik, M. and Stark, R. (Eds.), *Auctions, Bidding and Contracting: Uses and Theory*. New York: New York University Press.

Optimal Auction Design. (1981). *Mathematics of Operations Research*, 6, 58-73.

Nguyen, H. and Haddawy, P. (1999). DIVA: Applying decision theory to collaborative filtering. In Finin, T. and Grosof, B. (Eds.), *Proceedings American Association for Artificial Intelligence*, Workshop on AI for Electronic Commerce, July. Orlando, FL.

Nissen, M. E. and Mehra, A. (1998). Redesigning software procurement through intelligent agents. *Proceedings from the AAAI Workshop on AI in Reengineering and Knowledge Management*.

Nissen, M. E. (1998). Redesigning reengineering through measurement-driven inference. *MIS Quarterly*, December, 22(4).

Nissen, M. E. (2001). Agent-based supply chain integration. *Journal of Information Technology Management* (forthcoming).

Pinson, S., Louca, J. A. and Moraitis, P. (1997). A distributed decision support system for strategic planning. *Decision Support Systems*, 20, 35-51.

Preece, A., Hui, K. and Gray, P. (1999). KRAFT: Supporting virtual organisations through knowledge fusion. In Finin, T. and Grosof, B. (Eds.), *Proceedings of the American Association for Artificial Intelligence*, Workshop on AI for Electronic Commerce, July. Orlando, FL.

PriceWatch. (1997). PriceWatch online description. Available on the World Wide Web at: http://www.pricewatch.com.

Rodriguez-Aguilar, J. A., Martin, F. J., Noriega, P., Garcia, P. and Sierra, C. (1998). Competitive scenarios for heterogeneous trading agents. In Sycara, K. and Wooldridge, M. (Eds.), *Proceedings of the Second International Conference on Autonomous Agents*, Minneapolis, MN, 293-300.

Roth, A. E. (1991). A natural experiment in the organization of entry-level labor markets: Regional markets for new physicians in the UK. *American Economic Review*, June, 81, 415-40.

The college admissions problem is not equivalent to the marriage problem.(1985). *Journal of Economic Theory*, 36, 277-88.

The evolution of the labor market for medical interns and residents: A case study in game theory. (1984). *Journal of Political Economy*, 92, 991-1016.

Roth, A. E. and Peranson, E. (1997). The effects of change in the NRMP matching algorithm. *The Journal of the American Medical Association*, 278, 729-33.

Roth, A. E. and Sotomayor, M. A. O. (1990). *Two-Sided Matching: A Study in Game-Theoretic Modeling and Analysis*. Cambridge, UK: Cambridge University Press.

Sandholm, T. (1999). eMediator: A next generation electronic commerce server. In Finin, T. and Grosof, B. (Eds.), *Proceedings of the American Association for Artificial Intelligence*, Workshop on AI for Electronic Commerce, July. Orlando, FL.

Schlegel, R. J. (2000). *An Activity-Based Costing Analysis of the Department of the Navy's Enlisted Detailing Process*. Masters Thesis, Naval Postgraduate School, Monterey, CA, December.

Sen, S. (1997). Developing an automated distributed meeting scheduler. *IEEE Expert*, July/August, 41-45.

Short, M. M. (1984). *Analysis of the Current Navy Detailing Process*. Masters Thesis, Naval Postgraduate School, Monterey, CA, December.

Shubick, M. (1984). *A Game theoretic Approach to Political Economy*. Cambridge, MA: MIT Press.

Sun, R., Chu, B. T., Wilhelm, R. and Yao, J. (1999). A CSP-based model for integrated supply chains. In Finin, T. and Grosof, B. (Eds.), *Proceedings of the American Association for Artificial Intelligence*, Workshop on AI for Electronic Commerce, July. Orlando, FL.

Sycara, K., Pannu, A., Williamson, M. and Zeng, D. (1996). Distributed intelligent agents. *IEEE Expert*, December, 36-46.

Sycara, K. and Zeng, D. (1996). Coordination of multiple intelligent software agents. *International Journal of Cooperative Information Systems*.

Tesauro, G. J. and Kephart, J. O. (2000). Foresight-based pricing algorithms in an economy of software agents. *IAC Reports* IBM. Available on the World Wide Web at: http://www.ibm.com/iac/papers/ice98_fs/fs_public.html.

U.S. Navy Bureau of Naval Personnel Homepage. Available on the World Wide Web at: http://www.persnet.navy.mil.

U.S. Navy Commander in Chief, United States Pacific Fleet. *Enlisted Distribution System Overview*, undated Power Point Presentation.

uVision. (1998). Available on the World Wide Web at: http://www.uvision.com/.

Verity. (1997). Verity online description. Available on the World Wide Web at: http://www.verity.com.

Vickery, W. (1961). Counterspeculation, auctions and competitive sealed tenders. *Journal of Finance*, 16, 8-37.

Walsh, W. E., Wellman, M. P., Wurman, P. R. and MacKie-Mason, J. K. (1998). Some economics of market-based distributed scheduling. *Proceedings of the International Conference on Multi-Agent Systems*.

Whitehead, S. D. (1994). Auto-FAQ: An experiment in cyberspace leveraging. *Proceedings of the Second International WWW Conference*, 1, 25-38.

Yan, Y., Yen, J. and Bui, T. (2000). A multi-agent based negotiation support system for distributed transmission cost allocation. *Proceedings of the Hawaii International Conference on System Sciences*, Maui, HI.

Zeng, D. and Sycara, K. (1995). *Cooperative Intelligent Software Agents*. Carnegie Mellon University Technical Report NO. CMU-RI-TR-95-14, March.

Chapter X

The Enschede Virtual Public Counter: Ole 2000–A Case Study

Ronald E. Leenes[1]
University of Twente, The Netherlands

INTRODUCTION

In 1995 the Dutch Ministry of the Interior and the Association of Dutch Local Governments (VNG) initiated an ambitious program to improve public service delivery. The aim of this so-called Public Counter 2000 (in Dutch: 'Overheidsloket 2000' or 'OL2000') program was a nation wide network of one-stop government agencies, providing citizens and trade and industry with information and public services. These one-stop government agencies should have both physical and virtual incarnations. The services delivered are primarily those of local government. However, also services of the national level and of (semi-) private agencies may be incorporated.

The first phase of the OL2000 program consisted of piloting. Enschede was the host of one of the 15 pilot projects. This chapter describes the background to OL2000, its results and its future plans. It will then focus on the Enschede pilot, Ole 2000. Ole 2000 is a virtual, online public counter for a range of local housing and building services. This chapter discusses the problems encountered in the Ole 2000 pilot and draws out some lessons to be learned from this project.

The Problem

The public counters envisioned in the OL2000 program are to solve some of the problems the public sector faces. Currently, the public sector is highly fragmented, both horizontally and vertically. The horizontal fragmentation manifests itself in the many sectors in which the public domain is divided (housing, social affairs, trade and industry, etc.) and the fact that each sector has its own institutions, ministries for instance. Each of these institutions itself is subdivided in smaller agencies. Vertically, the Dutch public sector is divided in three layers: national, provincial, and local. On each layer, the horizontal division in sectors of the higher level is more or less replicated. Each level develops policy, aimed at solving the problems of its level. National government makes policy for The Netherlands as a whole, while local governments only develop policy for the local level. With respect to service delivery, the picture is more complex. Services based on national policy and legislation, such as the Inland Revenue, may be delivered on the national level, but also on the provincial or local level, e.g., General Assistance (see Svensson, this volume). This results in a patchwork of service delivery agents. The specialization underlying the fragmentation may be efficient from the perspective of developing policy, it is not from the perspective of the average citizen as a client (Lips, 1998). For simple citizen-government contacts, such as renewing a passport, or applying for rental subsidy, most citizens know where to go and a single visit often suffices. But for more complex problems, such as 'building,' 'moving house' and 'becoming unemployed,' that involve multiple services, the segmentation does pose serious problems. Citizens have to address various offices, desks and counters.

From the perspective of the addressee, the fragmentation of public services is problematic for obvious reasons. The citizen in need of services is sent from pillar to post, often being asked the same questions over and over again. But also from the government's perspective, fragmentation is something to address. Data collection at different locations pertaining to the same individual may lead to erroneous data. The accuracy rate of data collection is relatively low in single-service provision (see for instance Svensson, this volume; Petrie et al., 2000). This problem is amplified when multiple services are at stake. Integrating the intake of services may lead to fewer errors overall, and hence to savings. Also the efficiency of service delivery itself can be improved dramatically. Petrie et al. (2000) describe that customers in the Lewisham One-Stop Shop receive a decision about their combined application for Income Support and Housing Benefit within 48 hours, rather than 8–9 days.

Within the Dutch public administration, there is also another reason to pursue a solution to the problem of fragmentation: the urge to improve policy effectiveness.[2] The Netherlands have an extensive network of services for specific (low-income) groups of citizens. Among these are the National General Assistance, subsidies for exceptional expenditures, remissions of local taxes (council taxes), housing/rental benefits, etc. In many fields, especially in the field of local policy on poverty, there is serious non-use of facilities (e.g., Smolenaars & Van Oorschot, 1993; Algemene Rekenkamer, 1997; Ernst & Young Consultancy, 1999). Smolenaars and Van Oorschot (1993) show that the non-use of Housing Benefits in their sample is between 8% (Nijmegen) and 20%-26% (Rotterdam). The subsidies for exceptional expenditures even show a greater non-use. The non-use varies between 50% (Rotterdam) and 72% (Nijmegen). These studies give rise to the conclusion that target reach of public services in the social welfare domain is insufficient. This is seen as undesirable. It is widely felt that people who are entitled to certain benefits and refunds are supposed to receive these benefits. The fragmentation of services is one of the reasons why target group reach is less than optimal. Other reasons are (Smolenaars & Van Oorschot, 1993; SCO, 1991; Vrooman & Asselbergs, 1994):

- The lack of knowledge about the existence of a particular measure. One survey (SCO, 1991) shows that 38.4% of the respondents mention this to be the source of their non-use.
- Perceived non-applicability. 22% percent of the respondents in the SCO (1991) study report that they (wrongly) thought the measure would not apply to their case.

- Reliance on self-support first. 16.9% of the respondents thought they had to use their own resources before applying for benefits.

A Solution

A solution to many of the problems outlined above is service integration. This idea was acknowledged in the late '80s. It was the basis for the Government Service Centres project (in Dutch: 'SCO project'). The aim of this project was to improve public service delivery and increase the efficiency of government agencies (Spapens, 1995). This goal could be met by bringing related service providers together in one-stop shops (the GSCs), at first without changing the way in which the services were provided.

In 1995 the Ministry of the Interior launched a new program to further improve the quality of service provision (BIOS3, 1995). This program, Public Counter 2000 (OL2000) builds on the experiences of the Government Service Centres project. The OL2000 project introduces some new concepts:

- the use of 'demand-patterns' as the binding force between services;
- including public, semi-public and even private organisations into the concept;
- a stronger emphasis on the use of IT to enable service integration.

The concept of demand-pattern[3] resembles the concept of a life-event as used elsewhere, such as the Australian Maxi system.[4] A demand-pattern boils down to the idea that there is a limited set of complex problems from the perspective of citizens, each consisting of a cluster of sub-problems. Most demand-patterns can be clearly labelled, such as: 'move house,' 'turning 18' or 'becoming disabled,' because they represent identifiable problems for citizens. They relate to actions ('starting an MSE,' 'building a house'), life-events ('marriage,' 'being born') and roles ('immigrant,' 'pressure group,' 'Neighbourhood party organiser'). Since demand-patterns are defined from the perspective of citizens, they may include needs not covered by the public sector, such as wedding rings in the case of 'marriage.' OL2000 aims to integrate all services pertaining to a particular demand-pattern, provided by both public and relevant non-public service providers.

The various integrated service desks each handle a set of demand-patterns typically spanning an area such as 'construction and housing,' or 'health and welfare.' OL2000 primarily aims at restructuring the front-end of government. Whereas in the past each organisational unit that was involved in service provision had its own front-office, the new model implies a separation of front-office from back-office. The back-offices are the traditional organisational units where policy development takes place and where the administrations are kept. The various databases remain the responsibility of these back-offices.[5] The, often newly created, front-offices handle the contacts with the clients and have access to (and possibly modify) the relevant back-office databases.

This model implies that arrangements concerning tasks and responsibilities have to be made between front-office and the various back-offices. The front-office wants to provide a high level of services, not only providing information, but also performing the intake of services and even delivering the service from start to finish (decision making). From the perspective of the customer, this aim is important. It makes little sense to obtain information from the front-office to be sent to a back-office for further services (intake and transactions). The back-office, however, may claim that a particular service requires expert judgment and that the front-office lacks the expertise to make these judgments. Hence, the service level will in practice vary from service to service. It depends on factors such as: complexity of the product, accountability, legal requirements, power of the back-offices, efficiency, cost, etc.

The process of dividing service delivery processes in a front-office and a back-office component of course touches on the power structures and balance within the various organizational units and hence is a serious stumbling block. The prospect of possibly losing power over human, legal and financial resources restrains some heads of agencies from participating in the project altogether (see Hagen & Kubicek, 2000, and the country reports therein).

Integrated service delivery is demanding for the front-office civil servants. Instead of handling a few (sectoral) services, they have to deliver services on a much broader area. Overseeing the whole domain of the integrated front-office is demanding. Especially when we bear in mind that the individual services are often complex in themselves. Training therefore plays an important role in the establishment of integrated service delivery. In Finland this was acknowledged early (in 1993) at the start of the local government service bureau project. The civil servants in these bureaus follow a 180-week study program in three years (Klee-Kruse, 2000). Besides training, ICT can play an important role in the creation of integrated services. IT systems can help increase the level of expertise in the front-office. Expert systems and knowledge-based systems can help the civil servants to make decisions. ICT systems can also help in safeguarding that problems are addressed in a joint-up way. This requires systems that link together individual services on the basis of demand-patterns or life-events. Furthermore, ICT allows services to be brought closer to the client by means of virtual public counters. Thanks to the rapid spread of the Internet in recent years, this idea gained much support. In fact, during the OL20000 program, the emphasis shifted from walk-in integrated service desks to virtual one-stop shops.

The OL2000 Program

The first phase of the OL2000 program, the pilot, ran from September 1996 to January 1998. It was commissioned by the Ministry of the Interior. A steering group consisting of representatives of the participating organisations: the Ministry of the Interior, the Ministry of Public Housing, Town and Country Planning and the Environment, the Ministry of Public Health, Well-Being en Sports, the Association of Dutch Municipalities and the Land Registry managed the project. A task force ('Programmabureau OL2000' in Dutch) was responsible for guiding the actual program.

The OL2000 pilot covered three areas: 'the elderly and disabled,' 'housing' and 'know your civil rights.' Fifteen pilot projects, submitted by (consortia of) municipalities, public and private sector organisations, were carried out (see Table 1). Municipalities were central to the pilots because some 70% of the public service delivery takes place on this level of government (Lammers & Lips, 2000).

Each project received a subsidy from the Task Force OL2000 of up to a maximum of 25% of the project costs, with a maximum of DFL 200.000 per project. The municipality and consortium partners, if any, had to cover the rest of the costs. Each project had to report to the Task Force on a quarterly basis. The Task Force published two review reports describing each project's progress as well as a SWOT analysis.[6] Within each type of pilot project, quarterly meetings were held to share experiences with interested other municipalities.

The first stage of the OL2000 program was relatively successful in the sense that it is clear that the concept of demand-patterns enables a more client-centred approach of service delivery. Some serious IT applications have been developed and some integrated service desks have been set up and tested. Also, and this may be the most important factor, awareness that service delivery can be improved has grown signifi-

Table 1: The 15 OL2000 pilots

Real estate	
Project	**Aim**
Amsterdam region	Virtual real estate information kiosk aimed at businesses.
The Hague	Real estate information at a city district level.
Nijmegen	Virtual and physical integrated desk offering real estate services.
Tilburg	Data warehouse (GIS) to support front-office workers in the city's district counters.
Tytsjerksteradiel	Central integrated desk for real estate information. Tytsjerksteradiel spans a very large area, but has relatively few inhabitants.
Elderly and disabled	
Aalburg	Information Kiosk offering information tailored to elderly and disabled.
Almelo	Integrated service desk in which various semi-public and private service providers in the welfare and well-being domain work together with the municipal welfare department.
Alphen a/d Rijn	A welfare service centre using expert system technology to support the intake of welfare clients.
Eindhoven	Integrated service desk in a local community featuring welfare, building and housing, social affairs services.
Emmen	Integrated desk for housing, welfare and care. At first aimed at public services, later also at semi-public and private services.
Utrecht	Virtual care-counter.
Know-your-civil-rights	
Delft	Integrated counter for immigrants/newcomers to the city of Delft. Cooperation between city, police and immigration services.
Enschede	A virtual counter offering a wide variety of services on the domain of building and housing.
Leiden	A virtual place for youngsters to hang out.
Meppel	City Website and a call centre offering basic information about Meppel public services.

cantly in the Dutch public sector. A study in 1998 showed that 66% of the Dutch municipalities is involved in some project or another the lines of the OL2000 initiative, compared to 33% in 1996 (B&A et al., 1998).

Currently the second phase of the OL2000 program, optimistically called the 'implementation phase,' is under way. The aim is to have 100% of the information and 25% of the transactional services online by 2002 (Ministry of Urban Policy and the Integration of Ethnic Minorities, 2000).

These goals are to be met on three domains: 'construction and housing,' 'health and welfare' and 'business.' On these domains, under supervision of respectively, the Ministry of Public Housing, Town and Country Planning and the Environment (VROM), the Ministry of Public Health, Well-Being en Sports (WVS) and the Ministry of Economic Affairs (EZ), one-stop government shops are implemented.

We now have sufficient background to study one of the 15 OL2000 phase 1 projects in more detail, the Ole 2000 project.

THE ENSCHEDE[7] PILOT: OLE 2000

The history of the Enschede OL2000 project (nicknamed Ole 2000) started some time before the OL2000 programme. In 1995 researchers from the University of Twente and representatives of the city of Enschede decided to jointly develop a virtual kiosk for electronic service delivery. The project built on research carried out by the faculty of Public Administration (legal knowledge-based systems, e.g., Svensson & Nieuwenhuis 1990; see also Svensson, this volume) and on research of the faculty of Computer Science (natural language interfaces for service delivery systems, such as ticket booking systems, e.g., van der Hoeven et al., 1995). The project proposal, in a more modest form, was later submitted for the OL2000 program. In September 1996, the OL2000 task force accepted the proposal and Enschede became one of the 15 OL2000 pilots. The pilot formally started November 1, 1996, and ended in April 1998.

The Ole 2000 project was carried out by a consortium consisting of the city of Enschede, University of Twente, KPN (Dutch Telecom), NIZW (Dutch Institute for Welfare and Well-Being), SightLine (software developers) and BVBijvoorbeeld (Web designers).

The project had a political (the Alderman for welfare and culture) and an administrative principal (the head of the registry general). The daily operations were coordinated by a general task force consisting of a project leader and the heads of the five working groups: concept design, work process design, (Internet) application development, electronic kiosks and evaluation/prototype-testing. The task force held weekly (later bi-weekly) meetings. The working groups met on a more regular basis depending on the needs of the group. The project was supervised by an executive steering committee consisting of members of the city's management team that held monthly meetings. It was responsible for monitoring progress, budget, planning and control. There was also a sounding board consisting of (senior) representatives of the consortium partners. They held quarterly meetings.

The aim of the Ole 2000 pilot was the development of electronic service delivery in the domain of building and housing. This domain features some 150 products and services on a wide range of topics and service levels, such as:

- providing information about zoning plans, waste disposal, local policy (about monuments, the environment, building and housing, zoning, etc.), real estate, public transport;
- delivering permits (e.g., building permits, parking permits, demolition permits);
- granting subsidies (e.g., exceptional expenditures for adjusting houses to accommodate handicapped people);
- supplying goods (e.g., sporting facilities such as rope-pulling ropes);
- accepting complaints (about (street) litter, malfunctioning street lighting, noise, etc.).

Many are information services, fewer are intake services and still fewer are transaction services.

It was clear from the start that the sheer amount of services required an incremental approach to implement them. One service at a time, the transformation from traditional to electronic service delivery had to be made. If we would make services available when ready, this would in a sense run counter to another objective of the project: the joint-up delivery of related services. From this perspective, individual services belonging to a particular demand pattern should not be made available until the whole demand pattern is covered. In other words: no bread is better than half a loaf.

In the task force, we opted for taking on, and delivering to the citizens, one service at a time, while at the same time building the necessary system architecture for the integrated service delivery. Both aspects of the project seemed to be demanding. Building service modules for individual services is a difficult task, because processes have to be transformed into highly automated Web-based processes. The other task, taking care of the integration of services, while at the same time remaining flexible, seemed difficult because we did not have a clear picture of what integrated service provision actually means in practice. The idea is straightforward enough, but when it comes down to the nuts and bolts, it is less straightforward. Questions that arose soon were: Which demand-patterns should we cover? What are the constituent parts of these demand-patterns? How do we interact with users to find out the demand-pattern that matches their needs?

The approach chosen, decoupling developing individual electronic services from taking care of the integration, allowed us to experiment with development strategies.

The order in which services were taken on depended on the complexity of the service, but also on the fact that we needed a demonstrator to show the stakeholders what integrated Electronic Service Delivery (ESD) is all about. This strategy proved important in gaining commitment from higher management in Enschede.

As a result of these considerations, we started with: submitting a bid for a building lot, finding a house for rent and determining the amount of rental subsidy for this house and finally acquiring public green as an expansion of one's garden. The first topic was chosen because it combines text and graphics (maps and photos). A user can browse the system for information and actually apply for a particular building lot. The second topic required cooperation between city and (public) housing corporations. Enschede was to provide maps and general information, while the housing corporations were to provide the available houses on a weekly basis. Users can find houses for rent, information about the neighbourhood, sign up for a house and determine the amount, if any, of rental subsidy they are entitled to. The third topic satisfied a clear demand from the general public in Enschede to extend their gardens with strips of public green. The entitlement to the acquisition of public green was a task suitable for a knowledge-based system.

THE OLE 2000 ARCHITECTURE

We focused on developing a modular framework for electronic service delivery, while at the same time developing individual services. The ESD framework we developed for the Ole 2000 system consists of four conceptual components as shown in Figure 1.

The Gatekeeper

The gatekeeper performs the initial dialogue with the user. Its task is to diagnose the user's problem. The user is instructed to pose a question to the system that describes her need. She does so by making successive selections in a cascading menu, as shown in Figures 2 and 3.[8] After each menu selection, the question, which is shown at the bottom of the screen, is expanded and rephrased in natural language. In Figures 2 and 3, the menu choices are: "I

Figure 1: The Ole 2000 architecture

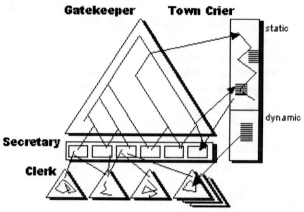

Figure 2: The initial gatekeeper

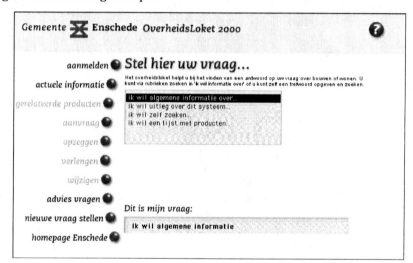

Figure 3: Expanding the question

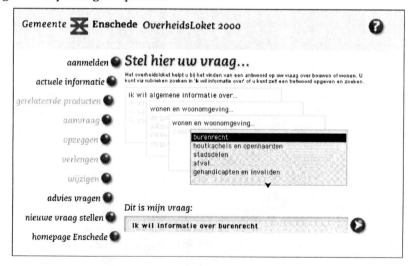

want information", "housing and the (social) environment", "easement". The rephrased question in the end is, "I want information about easement". At this stage in the dialogue, the gatekeeper has determined the appropriate demand-pattern(s) and hands over control of the dialogue to the secretary.

The Secretary

The secretary manages the integrated delivery of the services part of the current demand-pattern. Ideally, it builds a plan of action for the resolution of the current demand-pattern and passes over control to the various specialist modules (the clerks) to solve the sub-problems. The result produced by a specific clerk may cause the secretary to adapt the plan of action. Suppose, for instance, that the secretary has a plan of action for finding housing-related subsidies and that it does not yet know whether the user lives in a rented house or in a privately owned house. It therefore considers a number of services relating to rented houses as well as to privately owned houses to be applicable to the user. Once a clerk establishes the user to live in a rented house, the secretary can update its plan, in this case eliminating the irrelevant clerks from the list. So, ideally, the secretary keeps track of the accomplishments of the system in relation to the user's situation and assigns sub-tasks to be solved by the various clerks.

The Clerks

The clerks are the actual service delivery components. Each of them handles an individual product. Some clerks only deliver information; others also take care of transactions. The parking permit clerk for instance provides the user with information about parking permits, available parking space, cost, the requirements for obtaining a resident's parking permit and it allows people to apply for a permit on-line. The applicant is notified (by email) when he can pick up the permit. The absence of digital signatures, and to a lesser degree, the absence of methods of payment, prevent the system from completing the transaction by electronic means.

The clerks are composed of smaller general building blocks. Examples of these components are: map navigation applets, database retrieval modules, knowledge-based system modules, 'intelligent' intake forms, etc.[9] Instead of designing a basic toolkit of components, they were developed as a spin-off of the development of the individual services. For instance, the parking permit module required a map display that could be manipulated by the user. We therefore developed a map navigation applet. The applet was later generalised, so that it could be used by other services when needed. The map navigation applet is, for instance, also used in the building lot clerk. The clerks share information with other components in the system, such as the town crier, and hence make use of data already available.

Ole 2000 started with a clerk for parking and parking permits and one for land registry. As of March 2001, there were some 30 clerks in operation in the OLE system.

The Town Crier

The town crier is a database with a static component and a dynamic component. The static component provides the basic information for all services of the Department of Building, Housing and the Environment (some 900 entries). For each product or service, a description is available as well as the procedure to follow, the conditions for application and who-what-where information (figure 5). The dynamic town crier contains information about

Figure 4: Land registry information (graphical display)

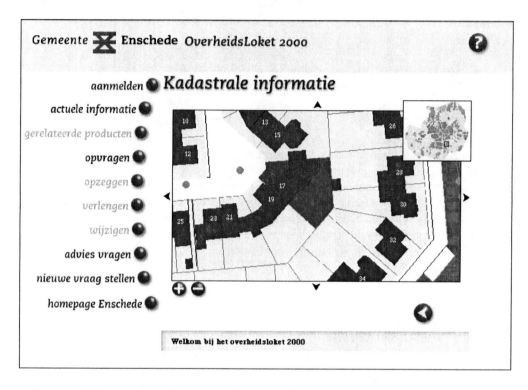

dynamic information, such as recently granted permits (Figure 6), roadblocks and works. Ideally it displays this information when relevant to the user's actions. For instance, when the user seeks a new house, it will get to see that a logging permit for particular premises is granted.

When the user interacts with Ole 2000 and requests information, she will be presented information from the town crier first. If she wants to go into more detail, the product's clerk takes over if there is one.

PROJECT DEVELOPMENT

The modularity of the architecture implies that the various parts, especially the clerks, could be developed independently, and be joined later on in the project. The modules of primary concern were the intake (the gatekeeper), the domain experts handling the services (the clerks) and the integration of service delivery (the secretary). The town crier was thought to be a relatively simple module (the static part), and of later concern (the dynamic part).

Gatekeeper Development

In many virtual public counters, the user is confronted with individual services early on in the dialogue. He is often presented a list of available products and services, grouped according to themes or the organization of the service provider. This approach suffers from a number of drawbacks. First of all, it rests on the assumption that the user knows what he

Figure 5: Static town crier: logging permit

Figure 6: A building permit for the Ruiterkampweg is granted

is looking for in the terms used by the administration. Laypeople typically have difficulties articulating their needs, especially in the proper terms, and hence have difficulty finding the applicable services. Furthermore, this approach depends on manifest needs of the user. The user will most likely only find the services he is aware of, and not the services he is not aware of. These unknown products, corresponding to latent needs, may be relevant to the user just as well; recall the problems relating to non-use of services in the first paragraph. We felt that this product-centred approach is not the way to offer services to laypeople. Instead, we tried to devise a natural way to diagnose the user's needs and stay as close to the user's vocabulary as possible.[10] The diagnosis is then matched to products and services. We have experimented with different approaches and are still not completely satisfied with the results.

Although we still adhere to the approach chosen, we discovered that many users do indeed want to be able to zoom to a single product, instead of being taken by the hand by means of demand patterns. Users are a bit stubborn; they do have a product or service in mind when they address the system. The current incarnation of the gatekeeper allows the user to zoom to the service she deems relevant. Control is then passed on to the clerk covering this particular service. From there, relevant other products, based on the demand patterns the service belongs to, are shown. This is a compromise between a completely guided approach and an approach that gives the user full control. The list of related services should cover the user's latent needs.

Clerk Development

The clerks are central to electronic service delivery. The town crier provides general information services. The town crier informs the user on the conditions for a specific subsidy or permit. The clerks offer the more complex, tailor-made, services. The service depends on the user's situation. This means they have to engage in a dialogue with the user. The building lot clerk, for instance, allows the user to gather information about available building lots. When he is satisfied with a particular spot, he can sign in for this spot. Most clerks provide the intake for services (e.g., the parking permit clerk). Some, such as the change of address clerk, go as far as provide the service completely.[11] It takes the old address and the new address and some proof of identity of the user and changes the citizen's records accordingly.[12]

The clerks perform tasks previously done by civil servants. This means the work processes have to modeled in order to implement them in clerks. Within the task force there has been much debate on the question of back-office involvement in the project. Some wanted to build a system that shows the capabilities of a virtual kiosk, without actually making use of the back-end work processes and systems. This showcase was meant to gain interest for electronic service delivery as a way to improve public service delivery. Integration of the Ole 2000 system in the organisation would be taken on at a later stage. For clerk development this meant that they could be built from scratch, inventing new work-processes on the way.

The opponents of this 'demonstrator-approach' argued that Ole 2000 would only make sense if it were integrated in the actual work processes right from the start. The latter approach won the argument. Hence, the starting point for the development process of each clerk was the actual work process. It required us to describe the current work processes for each service to be implemented. This proved to be a cumbersome task. The people responsible for the various services were reluctant to collaborate in a project that possibly threatens their position. In some cases their task would become redundant, because it can be taken over by the virtual kiosk. Although this behaviour is known from the literature (see for instance Kraemer & King, 1986; and more recent Ciborra, 1997), it proved tougher to handle than expected. For each single service we had to struggle to gain commitment of those responsible. A lesson we learned from this experience is that the relevant stakeholders had to be involved in the process sooner than we did. In most cases the clerks developed did not pose any danger for the people involved, because Ole 2000 only handles the simple (routine) cases for the time to come.

After commitment of the stakeholders was obtained, the work-processes of a service, and the data and the databases involved, could be described. This material was then transformed to procedures suitable for implementation in OLE 2000. The creation of work process descriptions often led to work process redesign. Many existing processes stem from a pre-information systems integration era and make little use of on-line databases. A clear example of a redesign process is offered by the implementation of the parking permit clerk. To qualify for a parking permit in the Enschede city centre, one has to live there and one has to be the owner for the vehicle for which the permit is requested. The applicant had to present proof for these requirements by handing over proof of identity (driver's license or passport), a vehicle registration license and rental agreement or property ownership papers. It turned out these data are available in the authentic registers. They could therefore be retrieved from online databases (the Dutch Municipal Basic Administration (GBA) and the RDW registers). So, instead of having to hand over multiple documents (which the applicant often does not carry on him when visiting the walk-in desk), the checks can now be performed automatically by using back-office databases. The applicant now only has to show proof of identity when he picks up the permit. If digital signatures were available, the permit could be sent to the applicant without him having to visit the walk-in desk altogether. The redesigned services offer an improvement of service provision from the perspective of the user. Services now either involve less physical visits of the client or are speedier.

The analysis and redesign of processes is a cumbersome task. It proved to take up much more time per service than anticipated. Sometimes information about the process is hard to come by because many procedures are not written down or highly outdated. In any case the development cycle for a clerk is considerable (ranging from one to five months) because the procedures as described have to be checked and refined by those involved. Once the work-processes of a service and the interaction are described, the material is handed over to the implementation group. They write the code (in Python and later Java) to implement the service in OLE 2000. After a test period by front-office workers in the walk-in desk, each service is made public in the virtual desk.

Town Crier Development

The development of the static town crier did not have a high priority at first. The town crier was seen as a relatively easy component that could be created along the way. This changed as a result of another project in Enschede. Shortly after the Ole 2000 project started, the Department of Building and Environment began implementing a one-stop walk-in desk for all their services. At first there was little communication between the two projects. However, it soon turned out that the walk-in desk needed extensive IT support. The Ole 2000 town crier proved to be just the kind of support needed. As a result, town-crier development became the primary focus of the Ole 2000 project for some time. Currently the Ole 2000 town-crier module is in operation within the walk-in desk of the Department of Building and Environment.

The main problem in the development of the town crier is maintenance. The town crier basically is a large database with the static information about products and services. In order to keep the data up to date, a scheme had to be devised in which tasks and responsibilities are clearly defined. Central in this scheme are editors, each responsible for an area within the system. They are signalled by back-office civil servants on changes and take an active role in keeping the data current.

FROM OLE 2000 TO OLE 21

The pilot did not achieve its initial goals. Instead of the large number of clerks envisioned, we implemented only three. The gatekeeper was changed several times, but now is more or less stable. The town crier is complete and functions satisfactory. The secretary is partly implemented.

We were too optimistic and ambitious at the outset. This is an experience common to many projects, both in traditional IT implementation (Ciborra, 1997), and in the implementation of electronic service delivery (see Hagen & Kubicek, 2000, for numerous examples). This does not mean the pilot was a failure. The OL2000 task force marked the Enschede pilot as a success, mainly because of the emphasis on demand-patterns as the guiding principle for service delivery and the flexibility of the architecture. Within the city of Enschede, the pilot proved a landmark. The city has acknowledged the need to re-organise service delivery into client-centred integrated service delivery. The pilot formally ended in 1998 and was officially launched for the public in September 1999.[13] Currently a newly created department develops the Ole 2000 for all services in Enschede. This wide-scale adoption within Enschede warrants a new name for the system: Ole 21.

LESSONS LEARNED

In this section I will discuss some lessons and the barriers we had to overcome in the Enschede pilot. They are consistent with those found in other studies (e.g., Hagen & Kubicek, 2000). They are grouped in six key areas:
1. Funding
2. Organizational cooperation
3. Complexity and technology
4. Process Redesign
5. Legal barriers
6. Political support

Funding

Funding appears to be a serious problem in many ESD projects in Europe (Hagen & Kubicek, 2000). This is certainly the case in The Netherlands. The OL2000 project was built on funding by the state government, local government and private enterprises. Most of the funds had to come from the local government. They were supposed to embrace the concepts offered by OL2000. They were also the ones who would profit from the efficiency gains created by electronic service delivery and hence had to carry the main part of the cost of implementing ESD. Furthermore, the development of ESD was more or less seen as an ordinary IT implementation process, something normally not funded by the central government. And finally, the chance of local governments really adopting ESD was deemed higher if it was their own project, based on their own business decision. Investment from private enterprises also seemed natural. The products to be developed could be re-usable. Since there are more than 530 municipalities in The Netherlands, there would be a market for the generic ESD modules.

It turned out differently. Local governments were reluctant to invest or did not have many resources to spare. In the Ole 2000 project, as well as in other OL2000 pilots, the participation of private enterprises proved to be troublesome. They were unwilling to invest in resources (manpower and capital). As a result we had fewer resources than anticipated, and hence a slower pace.

The amount of funding from the central government in The Netherlands is small and for a limited amount of time. This in itself should not be a problem if local governments and/

or the private sector bear the necessary investments. But since they don't, funding is a problem. One of the problems, in my opinion, is that the available funds (both from the central government and the local governments) are distributed over a number of similar projects. All projects are creating service modules for more or less the same products and services. This leads to inefficient development of ESD: local governments are very busy inventing the same wheels. This is a result of the structure of the Dutch public sector. The basic entity for service delivery is the local government. They carry out two types of services: decentralised tasks and deconcentrated/co-governance tasks. In the case of decentralised tasks, parking permits for instance, the local government has autonomy over policy and policy execution, such as service delivery. The differences between municipalities can be considerable. The city of Amsterdam has little parking space available, the village of Vorden has ample space, and hence they differ in parking permit policy. Developing ESD for this kind of service at the local level is sensible. For deconcentrated tasks (housing subsidy for instance), every municipality essentially applies the same rules and procedures. Developing ESD for these services at the local level is not obvious. It would be more efficient to develop these services centrally and distribute them over the various municipalities. A reason why this does not happen is that the principles of real-world service delivery seem to be applied to service delivery in the virtual world. In the real world, service delivery has to be geographically close to the citizen. It does not make sense if one has to travel many kilometres to obtain a passport or parking permit. That is why local government is the cornerstone of public service delivery in The Netherlands. In the virtual world distance no longer is an issue. Yet, local government is taken as the cornerstone of electronic service delivery.

The fact that every local government is developing its own ESD may also be one of the reasons why the private sector does not invest. All local governments seem different, with large differences in services. A solution for a specific municipality therefore does not transfer to another. This prevents private sector players from investing in developing ESD. Local governments cherish the idea of being unique, so that does not help either.

It would help if the central government would develop, or fund the development of electronic service delivery modules for services for which the local governments have limited discretion (deconcentrated tasks). This is actually happening at the moment. The Ministry of Housing, Town and Country Planning and the Environment (VROM), for example, is developing tools for the assessment of housing benefits (the EOS project).

It would also help if local governments would join forces and develop services together. This is a process that may take some time to get going.

ESD may improve government efficiency. Experiences in the UK show that the error rate in electronic intakes can decline dramatically, from 40% to 0% in the IForms project (Petrie, 2000). Also, the quality of decisions may improve dramatically by using IT (see Svensson, this volume). However, in many cases, the return on investment (if at all) is in the far future. One therefore may focus on other important returns on investment such as better customer service delivery, higher customer satisfaction and better target group reach.

Organizational Cooperation

The development of integrated ESD is an organisational change project and not just an electronic front-end to the existing organisation. As I have described in the section on clerk development, building ESD modules often induces process re-engineering. This requires the cooperation of the people involved. Therefore ESD projects are difficult projects. This observation is in line with findings in other studies (e.g., those in Hagen & Kubicek, 2000).

The alignment of technology and organization (Ciborra, 1997) is a process of mutual shaping. It does not help to tell people in the back-offices that ESD is what customers want. Civil servants in the back-offices have their own (self) interests, doubts, disbeliefs, agendas and opinions. They have to be taken seriously. ESD could well pose a real threat to people's jobs. It may also enhance, enrich or alleviate people's jobs. Service delivery currently consumes much time of people in the back-office. Not always is this time well spent. In some instances, the back-office employees, after a phase of reluctance, were glad customers asking the same questions bothered them less. They could now use their time for more demanding jobs. Part of the problem is that for many, in the Enschede pilot at least, the whole concept of integrated electronic service delivery was novel. Many people had no idea what it was all about. This caused disbelief and caution. Seeing may in this respect be believing. Once a mock-up or demonstrator is built, the reality of integrated service provision can be shown and made to live. The first prototypes certainly helped building commitment on all levels of the organisations involved.

Not only cooperation of the various people and departments within the city of Enschede was difficult to establish. The same goes for the outside world. Integrated service delivery crosses the organisational borders. It even crosses the border between the public and private sector. It proved difficult to get external partners (e.g., the housing corporations) to participate in the pilot project. After an initial commitment, they dropped out, only to return when the pilot was about finished. As a result, one of the clerks (finding houses for rent) could not be developed beyond a mock-up. The problems between organisations concern topics such as: who owns the delivery of services, who is responsible for the service, who bears the (development) costs, etc. It is important to sort out these issues at an early stage in the cooperation. Many problems later on turn out to stem from the lack of clarity in respect to goals, requirements, responsibilities, etc. in the initial stages. The problem of not having a clear idea what integrated service delivery is about also plays a role in this area. Again, showing prototypes helped to create support for the plans.

Complexity and Technology

Electronic integrated service delivery in the public domain is complex. We had a vision that the system should be more than a portal to individual services. What this 'more' is was less clear, let alone how to implement it. Developing individual services is one thing; the integration of the services in a way that makes sense to the general public is another. After five years of experimenting in various projects, we still don't have a good model of how to offer integrated services. An important obstacle in this respect is the sheer amount of areas, topics and services. A local government in The Netherlands delivers some 300 different services. These services are part of many demand-patterns that can be defined on the basis of legislation and the structure of the various domains. The demand-pattern building, for instance, consists of all services stemming from rules and regulations regarding the construction of objects (permits, subsidies, etc.). The task of defining demand patterns with their services seems achievable. The integration of the services is more difficult. This requires processes to share data sources and this implies that common ontologies are available. They are not and have to be developed.

The interaction between the various service modules, clerks for instance, is another problem. In the OLE system all interaction was centrally coordinated because the system is basically one application. This does not provide for the necessary flexibility in the longer run. If multiple developers develop service modules, the concept of central control is not very helpful. An alternative to explore is intelligent agent technology (see Sycara & Zeng, 1996; Gates & Nissen, this volume, for instance). The clerks as described in the Ole 21 system, could be intelligent agents that perform various tasks (semi) autonomously for the user. Gates and Nissen distinguish between four classes of agents: information-filtering agents, information-retrieval agents, advisory agents and performative agents. These tasks can also be found in an ESD system. Sycara and Zeng describe how multi-agent systems in which distributed and adaptive collections of information agents coordinate, to retrieve, filter and fuse information for the user can be designed. An important benefit of building ESD modules as intelligent agents is that the central control can be discarded. Instead the plans, beliefs and goals of the agents guide their cooperative efforts to serve the customer. It is also flexible in the sense that agents can be added and removed without having to change the overall system.

The individual service modules vary in complexity. Some are based on complex legislation, others on distributed databases and still others are based on simple PC-based databases. Building service modules for complex regulations requires legal expert systems or knowledge-based systems techniques to be available in a form usable in electronic service delivery. While there is much experience with stand-alone legal expert systems in The Netherlands (the TESSEC and MRE systems described by Svensson in this volume for instance), there are little or no suitable tools for ESD. Currently we are investigating the potential of legal knowledge-based system modules for the Dutch Ministry of Housing, Town and Country Planning and the Environment (VROM) for their services.

Process Redesign

There is much more to the development of electronic service delivery than automating existing processes. What I mean by this is that we have to rethink the whole concept of a service. Sometimes it is not desirable to just automate the existing procedure, but to remove the need for the citizen to interact with the government agency altogether. As an example we can contrast the way vehicle registrations are handled in Arizona and in The Netherlands.[14] In Arizona, car owners can renew their vehicle registration by visiting a Web site where they can pay for the renewal. Shortly afterwards they receive a sticker by mail to put on their number plate. The banner on the Web site touts 'Quicker Sticker.' This clearly marks the main benefits of this service. This service seems a good example of ESD. Instead of having to visit some office to obtain the sticker, one can order the sticker online. In The Netherlands we have gone a step further. The contact between car owner and vehicle registration office, the RDW, is eliminated almost completely. When someone buys a car, he has to register the car with the RDW. After this one-time contact, periodic payments are made by means of electronic bank transfers. So, everything runs automatic apart from the first contact. This is an example of the full potential of ESD. Instead of automating the existing procedure, the Dutch RDW has reengineered the whole process.

Other examples of this kind of fundamental reengineering can be seen in some other countries, such as Finland (Klee-Kruse, 2000) and Sweden.

Legal Barriers

The development of ESD reveals legal barriers. Most services involve rules and regulations. These regulations sometimes prohibit ESD. In the Enschede pilot, land property information form the Land Registry is displayed. This is prohibited by the Land Registry Act (in Dutch: Kadasterwet), but is currently tolerated by the Land Registry.[15] In the Delft pilot a front-office clerk had to be appointed in two public agencies (in one of them as zero fte personnel) in order to be able to follow two procedures simultaneously and reduce the amount of paperwork. In both cases, changes in legislation would help ESD.

In The Netherlands, as well as in other countries (Hagen & Kubicek, 2000), we desperately need digital signatures and digital means of identification. As mentioned, in several places around the country one can register a change of address using a social fiscal number (and sometimes passport number) as proof of identity. In Maassluis one can register one's dog by supplying name, address and date of birth on an on-line form. This means one can give anyone in Maassluis a virtual dog, provided of course that these data are available. This is unacceptable and dangerous. It is fairly easy to write an application that collects these data from the Internet (using an on-line phonebook) to register dogs for these people. The victims of this action will receive a tax form for their virtual dog. Clearly this would amount to much annoyance and extra work to correct the illegitimate applications. This problem has to be addressed by the central government. There is little hope in this respect. The Minister of Urban Policy and the Integration of Ethnic Minorities, who coordinates the e-government affairs in The Netherlands, already said we will not have a digital identity card before January 2003. Many ministries and other agencies are involved in this project, which means delays.

Political Support

Information technology can be an enabler of organisational change. Integrated service delivery proved to be an abstract concept for higher management, especially in its consequences for the organisation. Offering an intelligent form is one thing, processing the form in a man-machine environment is another. Early prototypes of the Ole 2000 system made a valuable contribution to the ESD discussions within higher management. They have now adopted the viewpoint that (electronic) integrated service delivery is desirable from the perspective of the citizen, that it may lead to savings and that it is the way to go.

The support from higher management is essential to overcome the inertia to change on lower levels.

OUTLOOK

In this chapter I have described the cumbersome way we had to go in developing an electronic service delivery system for the city of Enschede. There is far less progress than we hoped for at the outset. On the other hand, there is progress, and it is clear ESD has benefits. More and more citizens gain access to the Internet. The number of Internet users in The Netherlands has increased rapidly over the last couple of years. This is partly due to the fact that some Internet providers have provided free Internet access, only leaving the telephone costs to the customer. We are now approaching critical mass to make serious investments in ESD worthwhile. Citizens call for better service delivery. This does not necessarily mean electronic service delivery in the sense of transactional service delivery. A step in the right direction is the availability of good information pertaining to public services on the Internet. That way people can better prepare themselves for their visit to town hall.

In Enschede, the crossbar is laid higher. The city strives for a system that allows many services to be dealt with electronically. The task force building the Ole 21 system now has some 10 people working on the project full time. Apart from these, many people in the back-offices contribute to the system. The progress is steady and will take some years to reach full bloom. This may not at all be a disappointment, now that we have a more realistic view on what building ESD actually is.

ENDNOTES

1 The author was a member of the Ole 2000 task force.

2 From discussions with researchers from other countries in Europe, I get the impression this reason is hardly felt in other countries, apart from Finland where pro-active service provision is widely accepted.

3 This concept is somewhat unfortunate because it suggests that it consists of subjective problem clusters, whereas it is meant to denote objective problem clusters. Demand-patterns are to solve the problem of latent questions. Subjective problem clusters do not address latent questions.

4 http://www.maxi.com.au

5 The primary focus of OL2000 is on improving the service quality of the public sector, and not on improving the efficiency of governmental operations (see also Lips, 1998). Note that increasing the efficiency and internal and external effectiveness is a primary drive of many other e-Government projects (Lips, 1998; Caron & Bent, 1999).

6 These reports (in Dutch) can be found at http://www.ol2000.nl. A brief description of each pilot can be found in Lammers and Lips (2000).

7 Enschede is a city with approximately 150,000 inhabitants in the east of The Netherlands, some 14 kilometres from the German border.

8 We have experimented with a number of different ways to derive the relevant demand patterns. One of the approaches, based on a dialogue starting with expressions such as "I want…," "May I…," "I am looking for…," "I have…," is described in Leenes and Schaake, forthcoming.

9 See the chapter by Jörgen Svensson in this volume on legal knowledge-based systems.

10 See Leenes and Schaake forthcoming for one of the approaches

11 A service such as the one described is not available in the OLE system, but it is offered in other cities, such as Maassluis; see https://secure.maassluis.nl/adresw.html.

12 Proof of identity (digital signature) is one of the main problems in realizing ESD in The Netherlands. Maassluis and others use the passport number and the social security and fiscal number (SOFI) to identify a citizen. Needless to say that this is not a trustworthy way to establish someone's identity.

13 http://www.enschede.nl/ole2000 and http://www.loket.enschede.nl

14 See http://www.serviceArizona.ihost.com/ for the Arizona version.

15 'Gedoogd' in Dutch is one of the typical Dutch concepts that is so famous that it made it into the English language.

REFERENCES

Algemene Rekenkamer. (1997). *Klantgerichtheid Publieke Dienstverlening.* Den Haag: Sdu Uitgevers.

BIOS-3. (1995). *Beleidsnota Informatisering Openbare Sector 3: Terug naar de Toekomst, (Policy Memorandum Informatisation in the Public Sector: Back to the Future),* Den Haag: Ministerie van Binnenlandse Zaken.

B & A Group and Moret Ernst & Young Management Consultants. (1998). *Naar een Landelijke Implementatie van de Eén-Loketgedachte (Towards a Nationwide Implementation of the One-Stop Government Shops)*. Den Haag/Utrecht.

Caron, D. J. and Bent, S. (1999). *Collaboration in Building Single-Window Projects: The Art of Compromise*.

Ciborra, C. U. (1997). De profundis? Deconstructing the concept of strategic alignment. *Scandinavian Journal of Information Systems*, 9(1), 67-82.

Ernst & Young Consulting. (1999). *Terugdringen Niet-Gebruik van Sociale Voorzieningen: Opsporen en Actief Benaderen*.

Gates, W. R. and Nissen, M. E. *Agent- and Web-based Employment in the U.S. Department of Defense*.

Hagen, M. and Kubicek, H. (Eds.) (2000). *One-Stop-Government in Europe: Results From 11 National Surveys*. Bremen: University of Bremen. Available on the World Wide Web at: http://www.fgtk.informatik.uni-bremen.de/cost/one-stop-government/home.html.

Hoeven, G. F. van der, et al. (1995). SCHISMA: A natural language accessible theatre information and booking system. *Proceedings of the First International Workshop on Applications of Natural Language to Data Bases*, Versailles.

Klee-Kruse, G. (2000). One-stop-government in Finland. In Hagen, M. and Kubicek, H. (Eds.), *One-Stop-Government in Europe: Results From 11 National Surveys*, 209-222. Bremen: University of Bremen.

Kraemer, K. L. and King, J. L. (1986). Computers and public organizations. *Public Administration Review*, 46, 488-496.

Leenes, R. E. and Schaake, J. (1997). OLE2000, A study in questions and demand. *IFIP WG 8.5 Workshop*, Stockholm, 1-21. (revised version to appear in *Information Infrastructure and Policy*).

Lammers. K. and Lips, M. (2000). The Netherlands. In Hagen, M. and Kubicek, H. (Eds.), *One-Stop-Government in Europe: Results from 11 National Surveys*, 401-466. Bremen: University of Bremen.

Lips, M. (1998). Reorganizing public service delivery in an information age: Towards a revolutionary renewal of government? In Snellen, T. M. and van de Donk, W. B. H. J. (Eds.), *Public Administration in an Information Age*. Amsterdam: IOS Press.

Ministry of Urban Policy and the Integration of Ethnic Minorities. (2000). *Contract with the future; A Vision on the Electronic Relationship Between Government and Citizen*. Available on the World Wide Web at: http://www.minbzk.nl/pdf/eo/actie/contract_with_future_5-00.pdf. Accessed May 2000.

Petrie, A., Brewer, N. and Bellamy, C. (2000). England and Wales. In Hagen, M and Kubicek, H. (Eds.), *One-Stop-Government in Europe: Results From 11 National Surveys*, 163-207. Bremen: University of Bremen.

Projectgroep Ole2000. (1998). *Pilot Project Overheidloket 2000: Evaluatieverslagen*. Enschede.

Sociaal Cultureel Planbureau (SCP). (1991). *Avo '91, Aanvullende Voorzieningen Onderzoek 1991*. Rijswijk: Sociaal Cultureel Planbureau.

Smolenaars, E. and Oorschot, W. van (1993). Minimabeleid kampt met effectiviteitsproblemen. *Sociaal Bestek*, (9)11.

Spapens et al. (1995). *Evaluatie Experimenten Servicecentra van de Overheid. (Evaluation of the Experiments with the Civic Service Centres)*. Den Haag: Ministerie van Binnenlandse zaken.

Svensson, J. S. (2001). *The Use of Legal Expert Systems in Administrative Decision Making*.

Svensson, J. S. and Nieuwenhuis, M. A. (1990). TESSEC, an expert system for social security legislation. In Kracht, D., de Vey Mestdagh, C. N. J. and Svensson, J. S. (Eds.), *Legal Kknowledge Based Systems; An Overview of Criteria for Validation and Practical Use*, 87-92. Lelystad: Koninklijke Vermande.

Sycara, K. and Dajun Z. (1996). Multi-agent integration of information gathering and decision support. In Wahlster, W. (Ed.), *ECAI 96, 12th European Conference on Artificial Intelligence*, John Wiley and Sons.

VROM. (1999). *Het Loket Bouwen en Wonen: Op Weg Naar Geïntegreerde Dienstverlening. (Ministry of Housing, Regional Development and Environment: The Service Desk Building and Housing: Steps Towards Integrated Service Provision)*. Den Haag: VROM.

Vrooman, J. C. and Asselbergs, K. T. M (1994). *De Gemiste Bescherming: Niet Gebruik van Sociale Zekerheid Door Bestaansonzekere HuiShoudens*. Den Haag: Vuga.

Chapter XI

Technology to Support Participatory Democracy

Ann Macintosh, Elisabeth Davenport, Anna Malina and Angus Whyte
International Teledemocracy Centre, Scotland

INTRODUCTION

This chapter focuses on the development, application and impact of information and communication technology on civic representation and participation in the democratic process.

Governments, at local and national levels, need to restore public confidence and interest in the democratic process. They need to improve the turn out at elections and, importantly, they need to address the underlying sense that, except during election campaigns, the views of the public are not actively sought or, importantly, listened to and taken into account. This chapter gives practical guidance on how parliaments and governments can develop, apply and manage information and communication technology (ICT) to address this concern and to support the public to participate in setting agendas, establishing priorities and making policies–to strengthen public understanding and participation in democratic decision making. However, the question is still unanswered as to whether ICT will enable more open, democratic and effective government. In this chapter we will explore this question and consider the positive and negative affects of technology on the democratic process.

The first section in this chapter briefly summarizes a range of perspectives that have provided the impetus for researchers and practitioners to envisage roles for technology in the democratic process. Increasingly, theoretical perspectives are becoming informed by practice, as technologies developed for corporate or consumer use are applied in pursuit of collective political ends and to meet needs and demands of individual citizens. Policy makers and analysts have articulated priorities and frameworks which cut across conventional policy-making divisions, making ICT considerations central to their vision and action. At the end of the section we summarize recent developments that are typically considered.

Section two considers the issues and constraints that have to be taken into account when designing ICT-based tools for "democratic" purposes. Specifically it highlights the major differences in developing systems such as these that are intended for widest possible accessibility and ease of use, from those that are developed to support commerce and entertainment. These differences are important, since government operates under quite different conditions. Some similarities bear careful examination though. In commerce, corporate governance and marketing borrows the language and action of politics more and more ('guerrilla marketing' for example). E-commerce strategies, like those of government, are increasingly based on the idea of community-building.

In the third section we focus on a significant trend for policy makers concerned with electronic government that also echoes trends in electronic commerce. A trend for consumers to adopt roles traditionally taken by producers has been evident in commerce for some time. The entertainment industry, as a special case, illustrates dramatic shifts in its symbiotic relations with people as end-consumers on the one hand and producers of popular culture on the other. So while governments may be seen as (electronic) providers of services and deliverers of policy, citizens may choose to seek ownership of service provision and policy making for themselves. As our examples show, this trend marks out an area of some uncertainty. The ends and means of electronic citizenry may be seen as legitimate and welcome forms of democratic renewal or alternatively as threats to the democratic process, and the prevailing view can change with revolutionary speed. We provide examples of ICT-based 'activism' that contrast, in values if not in core technology, with the more commonly reported 'hacktivism' and 'cyberterrorism.'

In the fourth section, working examples of citizen participation, specifically in Scotland, are fully described. The section focuses on the use of the Internet by democratically constituted organizations to gather opinions from citizens and also by citizens to lobby government and public agencies. A Web-based e-democracy toolkit, developed to motivate and facilitate public participation in governance, is described. The International Teledemocracy Centre, working with BT Scotland, developed the toolkit in late 1999. The tool helps to demonstrate how relatively straightforward computing techniques can be deployed to enhance public participation.

In the fifth section, the importance of monitoring and evaluating teledemocracy systems is stressed. Far too many government-related departments are introducing teledemocracy systems without putting in place the mechanisms by which they can assess the impact of the systems on both civic society and the government processes they are meant to interact with. In this section we describe some recent work in this area and future projects that could support teledemocracy evaluations.

BACKGROUND

Towards the end of the 1980s, there was recognition that the world was changing qualitatively and political practices were remote from the electorate (Hall & Jacques, 1989; Wright, 1994). Shapiro and Hacker-Gordon (1999) suggest that "in reality democracy often disappoints" (p. 1). The argument has developed that modern politics needs to renew public trust, and a new shared framework of beliefs and interactive links between state institutions and civil society is required. New social and economic structures are also being articulated in the new millennium, to tackle the opportunities and risks of the 'Information Society.' Democratic governments are forced to re-think the way they undertake their business, deliver services and interact with citizens. This applies to all levels of government--local, regional, national and European--which need to be able to respond to the needs of the people and ensure the business and communities they represent get the best possible service. The importance of developing a creative and participative democracy which involves responsible citizens in the process of government is being widely acknowledged (Malina, 1999a). Some commentators offer moral arguments for shaping democracy (e.g., Sclove, 1995); others outline practical possibilities for more inclusive democracy (e.g., Fotopoulos, 1997); and yet others explain how some democratic practices over others can entitle people to more power over decisions that affect their own lives (e.g., Catt, 1999).

In addition, the arrival of more sophisticated communication technology brings attention to bear on the dialectical relationship between ICT and society (Hague & Loader, 1999). Optimists argue strongly that new digital media of communication provides a virtual space for more democratic human interaction, creating new potential for open interrelationships and more democratic public participation. However, evangelists who argue without empirical information that a more inclusive citizenship can be supported by the dramatic advances in computer and telecommunication technologies are subject to criticism. Kyrish (1994), for example, argues that overly deterministic arguments about new interactive technology produces utopian visions, reviving what he has called the "liberalizing arguments" of "earlier revolutionary technologies." Interest in utilizing electronic instruments for democratic purposes can be traced back to the introduction of the telegraph and telephone, and later radio and cable television. In referring to empirical findings, Wilhelm (2000) argues that social and political problems cannot easily be solved by technology, and to assume this is the case is clearly misguided. Nevertheless, this author indicates it is reasonable to consider further the role of ICT together with the part which could be played by citizens in modifying and extending political interaction in society.

Thompson (1995) considers mass communications historically as "a definitive feature of modern culture and a central dimension of modern societies," and allocates a central role to the development and impact of communication media (p. vii). Laying aside mythical discourses and prolific use of rhetoric which has filtered into the development of contemporary ICTs and virtual environments at all geographic and administrative levels, it may be argued that new societal possibilities are attached to the design of new ICTs. With the proliferation of computerised technology and increased popularity of the Internet and World Wide Web, there is little doubt that the maturation of new forms of human interaction in multiple electronic public spheres provides new potential for articulating social, cultural, political and economic relations and planning in society. Here, the design of new ICTs--at least to some extent--determines potentiality of communication outcomes (Mansell & Silverstone, 1996).

However, it would be wholly inaccurate to suggest that the existence alone of new technology is enough to empower people, since citizens may just as easily be disempowered by unscrupulous power holders and/or inept planners. Moreover, ICT may be used to entrench existing practices rather than to innovate and improve them. Tsagarousianou, Tambini and Bryan (1998) refer to the prospects of electronic democracy in the current historical period, in which great technical change is combined with upheavals in both telecommunications and media industries, a perceived need to find solutions to problems in democracy and at the same time economic requirements to develop new consumer markets for the implementation of new technology. In examining a range of civic networks in the USA and Europe, these authors come to the conclusion that there is much inequality of access, low level of take-up and relative inactivity even when structures are set up specifically to support democratic practices. However, just providing wider provision of access alone may not guarantee useful political activism, according to Tsagarousianou (1999). In this regard,

Gregson (1997) makes the suggestion that even politically active people can find it difficult to transfer activism from real-world contexts to digital platforms. Gregson suggests training and experience is required before people can begin to visualize how the new medium might be useful in a participatory sense. However, Tsagarousianou et al. (1998) argue, participation may also be constrained because many initiatives are actually "executive-initiated, top-down and mostly based on giving more access to information" (p. 174).

Hacker and Todino (1996) differentiate between the concepts of electronic democracy and electronic democratization. Electronic democracy, according to these authors, is the ability to provide practical means, i.e., the provision of instruments which bypass more traditional routes. Electronic features provide a higher degree of citizen involvement in the political process through push-button voting and telereferenda. However, choices do not always take account of minority needs, and responses can easily be limited in the way pre-set criteria are assembled. In addition, voters may be overwhelmed with information, constrained by time and unable to understand the complex issues at stake, particularly if subjected to the political manoeuvring of media specialists. Electronic democratizations is the means of enhancing processes of democracy already assumed to be in place, in ways that "increase the political power of those whose role in key political processes is usually minimized" (Hacker and Todino, 1996, p. 72). Electronic democratization is also dependent on "whether information is packaged as an easily accessible social good or sold as a costly consumer product" (Malina, 1999b, p. 38).

The means of communication has developed faster than the ability of many people to use new ICTs. Therefore there is need to understand aspects of political interrelationships and democratization in the real world and continue to theorize democratic practice using ICT. How can citizen requirements be incorporated into the political process in an egalitarian society, so that more equal consideration is given to them in the formulation of ICT planning and democratic practice? In considering this issue, some commentators suggest teledemocracy--as conceptualized in the notion of the electronic town hall--may not support more deliberative processes (Thompson, 1995). The notion of teledemocracy therefore needs to ensure that the role of communications technology is designed to incorporate more in-depth public participation. Budge (1996) argues that the "challenge of direct democracy is to the limited participation of citizens in their own government" (p. 1). In practice, direct democracy using ICT would involve people in electronic interaction rather than leaving it entirely to electoral processes associated with representative democracy.

Barber (1984) highlights early evidence of the civic use of technology to promote teledemocracy, suggesting new technology and the "electronic enhancement of communication offers possible solutions to the dilemmas of scale " (p.274). While democratic outcomes are not always certain, there is little doubt that new technology offers fresh possibilities to strengthen participatory discussion through small meetings not dependent on time, place or face-to-face presence. In highlighting an argument for more participatory citizenship and promoting the idea of technology constructed along more democratic lines, Barber (1984) and later Sclove (1995) highlight the notion of strong democracy. Strong democracy creates citizen participation where none has existed before. The aim is to find mutual solutions and promote common ends through widespread participatory processes.

Strong democracy is inclusive democracy, according to Fotopoulos (1997), who refers to a broadening of democracy in all public arenas--not just political, but also social, cultural, economic and ecological arenas. According to Fotopoulas, strong democracy includes any area of societal life and human activity where decisions can be taken collectively and democratically. The idea, he suggests, is to equalize the distribution of power and eliminate the idea of domination of one human being over another. For Fotopoulos, a more inclusive democracy means a greater synthesis of historical traditions, merging what is best from classical democracy and social democracy with Green, feminist and libertarian approaches.

There is, then, a broad range of political theory-driven rationales for including citizens directly in the policy-making process. A theme that is common to many and echoed in policy making is an expressed need for transparency around decision making. ICT is commonly seen as means to enhance transparency by providing wider access to decision-making processes and promoting involvement in them, but at the perceived risk of marginalizing groups without the prerequisite access to technology.

Within the European Union, one of the objectives of the Amsterdam Treaty is to ensure full transparency for citizens on the activities and decision making of the EU institutions and further ensure that these decisions are taken as openly as possible. A teledemocracy system inspired by the notion of inclusion must also be sensitive to these issues. In other words, the notion of teledemocracy must be wholly prepared to support the three principles of openness, accessibility and participation in government. Member States and the Commission itself are being encouraged to use the Internet to support consultation and feedback on major political initiatives. The aim is to go beyond simply publishing legislation and white papers on the Web and establish a discussion and feedback forum possibly with independent moderators. Teledemocracy could be designed to be directly supportive of these issues.

Three transforming factors demonstrate the growing importance of teledemocracy at this point in time. Firstly, rapid developments in new technologies–interactive TV, light-weight browsing technology, high bandwidth mobile phones, speech recognition, natural language and other technologies are combining forces to produce powerful future mobile devices. Third-generation mobile (3GM) phones with broadband wireless communications will become available within the next three to five years. Digital TV broadcasts providing access to Web-based services will become increasingly important for governments seeking to reach a wide cross section of the population.

Secondly, there is an increasing uptake and use of technology. The NUA Internet Survey (www.nua.ie) shows that over 300 million people worldwide are connected to the Web, and the number is expected to grow to 500 million over the next two years. Similarly, the IDC Report Internet Usage and Commerce in Western Europe 1998-2003, February 2000, estimates that by 2003 half of Western Europe's population, 215 million people, is expected to have access to the Internet

Thirdly is the growing and urgent requirement to engage people in the democratic process. In Europe the turnout at elections is continuing to decline. There was a 24% turnout in UK for the 1999 European elections, while in May 1999 the turnout for elections for the new Scottish Parliament was 58%. There is a growing belief by people that the way they vote will have little effect on the decision making process of the elected government. Although governments across Europe are attempting to engage people more through opinion-gathering mechanisms such as surveys and consultations, the general feeling by those consulted is that their opinions will not be taken into account.

These transforming factors, which are shaping our view of teledemocracy, demon-strate the need to take a holistic view of teledemocracy. Such a view needs a fusion of ideas from technologists, information scientists and social scientists to ensure teledemocracy has the potential to empower people to participate in setting agendas, establishing priorities and making policies–to strengthen public understanding and participation in government.

Moreover, as noted in the summary of theoretical perspectives we began with, there is nothing inherently democratic about technology. New technologies can bring new forms of exclusion, with 'information have and have nots.' There is a concern that the emergence of teledemocracy as a driver of participation in the democratic process will tend to favour individuals and communities which are already participating, widening the gap between advantaged communities and disadvantaged ones. The importance of developing systems that take into account the disadvantaged has to be an important aspect of teledemocracy work. Access to technology and in particular the Internet currently predominates among individuals with above-average incomes. There is a danger that the digital divide will continue to grow. Therefore, if not designed and deployed carefully, teledemocracy systems could be seen as a threat rather than an advantage to potentially excluded individuals and communities. However, new technological devices are emerging that will produce a situation where many people may have no need for the traditional desktop PC to access the Internet, using instead other devices, for example games consoles, digital TV, Web-enabled phones and other mobile devices.

DESIGN ISSUES

Electronic public services, where services include access to the democratic decision making processes, are starting to be delivered by government organizations. However, e-Government services cannot simply be equated to e-commerce. Although many of the issues associated with e-commerce are also associated with e-Government and consequently problems solved in one area support the other, there is a major difference and this is 'equity.' Governments are charged with assessing a range of competing claims on public resources, setting policy and delivering policy according to procedures by which the public at large can judge them to have done so equitably, for the general public good. People dealing with commercial organizations are typically looking for financial integrity and confidentiality however, when dealing with government agencies, people expect not just integrity and confidentiality but also a level of transparency in the process that ensures trust in the service being provided. This point was highlighted in the recent report by the 'Digital Scotland Task Force' set up by the Scottish Executive to advise Ministers on actions to be taken to ensure that Scotland obtains and retains maximum economic and social advantage from digital technologies (Scottish Executive, 2000). In providing e-commerce services, organizations are providing services to their specific customers whereas government services are for the public at large. Government cannot choose its customers but rather has a duty to ensure access to all services to everyone. E-commerce services are typically focused around single events, e.g., buying a car or opening a bank account, where buyers and suppliers work in an environment that is open to competition. E-Government services are much wider, encompassing a range of events, services and political processes that are by their nature open to contention.

Accessibility, usability and security are widely considered critical issues in the design of systems and services for the general public. The contentious nature of governance means that, in the design of teledemocracy systems, these issues can become more complex. Democratic needs for openness and transparency may conflict with needs for ease of use and simplicity of access. The issues of unequal access to technology and the unequal technical capabilities of citizens demand systems that are simple to use. Similarly the demand for transparency may call for procedures to be streamlined and simplified. However (as the recent U.S. election outcome illustrates) when procedures are seen to fail, demands are made for explanations of why procedures are as they are, and their wider legitimacy may be called into question. Answering such questions calls upon a range of intermediaries trusted to account for and resolve anomalies. So, in seeking to streamline e-democracy processes, care must be taken that a desire to 'cut out the middle person; in the interests of efficiency, does not unwittingly remove human intermediaries trusted to articulate why these processes exist in the first place, to make them happen and to resolve conflicts around their operation.

Transparent networking has provided Internet technologies and protocols that allow access to information regardless of everyday constraints such as time and the physical and social location of the user. Transparency in the democratic process is more often associated with the idea of 'due process,' where representatives and intermediaries must be seen to do whatever they do, in the appropriate place and time. Democratic processes are also founded on geographically based constituencies, in contrast to the Internet norm of anonymity and location independence. So in addition to questions of trust in 'technology' as something that is new (and possibly feared for no other reason), and questions of trust in 'government' as an institution that can deliver 'the public good' (in its broadest sense), teledemocracy systems face additional issues. Establishing trust demands both that government can establish that those who seek access to information, services or decision making have a legitimate right to do so, and that the privacy and civil rights of those who are governed are not compromised in doing so.

An interesting description of the levels of trust needed for digital government has been developed by the Cabinet Office of the UK government (Cabinet Office, 2000a). These trust levels indicate the degree of confidence that will be required in a person's proof of identity submitted before a given digital government transaction can take place. Here they propose that there should be four levels of trust with Trust Level 0 requiring no verification of identity and with Trust Level 3 being the highest level. The question of which services require which level of trust is not addressed; the guidelines state that in allocating transactions to trust levels, departments will need to consider the given definition of each level and the terms 'significant' and 'substantial' in the context of the parties likely to be affected.

From previous experience in developing and managing electronic democracy systems the following design issues and trade-offs need to be explored:
- balancing the need for straightforward access to systems, with the needs to collect personal data and analyze responses;
- balancing the needs for standard, generic, interface features with the need to reflect the expectations of a variety of target audiences;
- balancing how to support easy and flexible navigation through issues;
- deciding how much background information should be provided to assist individuals to be adequately informed on issues and so have the competency to contribute.
  In considering these points there is a need to ask three questions:
- Who do you want to be able to access the system in order to read the information and why?
- Who do you want to be able to access the system in order to not only read the information, but also to participate and contribute to the debate and why?
- How will the system be promoted to these sections of the community?

A fourth question helps organizations answer these questions: "Are the results of the participative action legally binding to government or rather informing the debate on the issue?"

Once these questions have been answered, the type of access method can be designed and the level of security and authentication for user interaction determined.

CITIZENS AS PRODUCERS RATHER THAN CONSUMERS

Research in the United States has led to considerable scepticism that the Web has enhanced participation. Harrison and Stephen (1999), in a survey of 40 networks, found many examples of activity that is oriented towards information access, but "considerably less support for services oriented toward the more participatory conceptions of democracy"(p. 232). Davis (1999) suggests that interactivity on the Web is an illusion. Dahlgren and Sparks (1991) state that often, behind the rhetoric of electronic democracy, what is initiated is a very particular version of publicness, arranged around ordered forms of dissemination of information, in which official political channels decide on the definition of the problem, and the content of the message, and thus strongly influence the direction of the outcome.

There is thus a danger that if 'inclusive democracy' is defined by government primarily in terms of access to services, or reaction to government-led initiatives, many citizens will remain outside the process, as they will not see how they can contribute to the formation of policy. Dutton's (1999) discussion of digital democracy is focused on electronic access to politics and services, with an emphasis on the 'citizen as user.' In this section, we consider what the alternatives to the citizen as user might be (drawing mostly on Internet research in the U.S.), and the extent to which they can be accommodated by an existing apparatus for representative democracy.

A starting point is to explore the notion of citizen as 'producer' of policy, of plans, of political structures. Citizens may be initiators of any of these, or, at least, co-producers with representatives of government, and technology may support both. To initiate activity with any credibility, citizens need to communicate and organize. The effectiveness of such activities can be judged in terms of a number of factors, and a growing body of literature has emerged (e.g., Denning, 1999; Wray, 1998) which monitors and analyses technology-driven 'activism.' The activities described range from joint planning of legislation, to obstructive and damaging Web behaviour; they may be categorized as a continuum from 'activism' through 'hacktivism' to 'cyberterrorism.' Wray characterizes this continuum in terms of a move away from the public sphere model (the 'Habermasian web') to "the Web as a conflicted territory bordering on a war zone."

As our concern in this chapter is with inclusive rather than disruptive technologies and with legitimate organization and participation, we focus here on the Habermasian Web, and the extent to which it may or should be realized in the face of existing cynicism about a Web-based cybersphere. It must be noted that the Habermasian Web may be a complex structure: Dahlgren (1991) suggests, for example, that the concept of one 'public sphere' should be replaced by multiple 'public spheres' that may be nested and networked by means of technology. Participation in these spheres may prepare citizens for democracy in a number of different ways.

Historically, the right to association has been recognized as a signature feature of democracy. Klein (1999) in a discussion of citizen associations on the Internet, describes these in (Habermasian) terms of "the public assent which a number of individuals give to certain doctrines and in the engagement which they contract to promote in a certain manner the spread of those doctrines." Associations allow citizens to both receive and provide education in public affairs, and create centres of political power independent of the State. The downside of association is the danger that politics may become the domain of factions who (and Klein cites Tocqueville here) may "eventually tyrannize an atomized and apathetic citizenry." Klein suggests that a 'Madisonian' solution--to promote such factions, as a healthy democracy depends on the number and diversity of its associations--should guide government attitudes to cyberassociations (though this view is contested). He observes that "a citizen action can be announced on existing listservers in order to attract participants, and a forum can be created quickly at nearly no cost to participants. The same flexibility that computerization has brought to industry can now be realized by associations, with the result that grassroots movements may quickly coalesce in response to emerging issues." Klein provides a positive example of such activity, in a case study of a Boston-based citizen association that formed in 1993 in response to the revision of the U.S. Telecommunications infrastructure.

A comparable case study is presented by Denning (1999), who describes a public forum to foster dialogue and debate about cryptograophy legislation in the UK. Those involved, says Denning, were "motivated by concern that a lack of public discussion and debate in the United Kingdom on cryptography issues was allowing the government to set policies that they believed were not in the interests of the United Kingdom and its citizens." By means of the listserver, the civil servants responsible for policy were actually available to the people who disagreed with them and they had to justify their actions to a small group of geographically dispersed experts. The result was a forum open to an educated community of commentators that offered a fully open review of what government was doing. In the U.S., the process of developing an Advanced Encryption Standard has led to the formation of similar online fora with participation by representatives from the NIST (National Institute of Standards and Technology). Denning concludes that when the Internet is used in 'normal, non-disruptive' ways, it can be an effective tool for activism as it can educate individuals and small groups in how to handle the public and the media, in fund raising, in preparing petitions and alerts, and in planning and coordinating.

Web sites like NetAction, or e-groups are useful starting points, as they make the technology transparent. They cannot, however, inculcate acceptable behaviour, an issue that Dutton considers to be a major inhibitor of successful political organization. In his 1999 monograph, Society on the Line, he identifies two dimensions to this problem: the degree to which regulation of a public forum would inhibit rights to free speech (of paramount importance in the U.S.), and the extent to which participants in electronic forums do not agree among themselves on the norms that should govern dialogue about public affairs. The PEN project in Santa Monica, an early attempt to use the Net to provide comprehensive public input into policy-making at local government level, provides an illustration (Docter and Dutton, 1998) of problems raised by free speech issues--abusive input by some participants alienated large numbers of others and led to the atrophy of the forum.

The adverse effects of unbridled or untutored participation in online fora have been observed in a number of research projects (e.g., Willhelm, 2000) reporting discourse and content analyses of Usenet groups devoted to political issues. In Willhelm's study, there is little evidence of development of joint lines of argument of positions: discussion is dominated by statements which reinforce existing points of view, and the purpose of discussion is clearly to consolidate rather than extend points of view. The study supports Willhelm's contention that access is not the main issue in the development of digital democracy. The resources that individuals and communities can exploit are primary--what Willhelm calls 'resource antecedents.'

It then becomes vital to demonstrate not only how teledemocracy systems meet prior policy objectives. Given the rapidity of change in both the political and technical landscape, objectives may change before any clear relation to outcomes can be established. Moreover the success of teledemocracy systems may both depend on and change current practices in unforeseen ways, and it is important to consider how these changes measure up against those of alternative stakeholders in the political process, including self-organized citizen groups.

We return to the issue of evaluation after reviewing examples of citizen participation in teledemocracy systems that we have recently implemented. Although based on relatively well-established technologies, these straightforward examples illustrate many of the issues already discussed.

WORKING EXAMPLES OF CITIZEN PARTICIPATION

As working examples of citizen participation, this section focus is on teledemocracy in Scotland and lessons that can be learned from these deployed systems. The International Teledemocracy Centre working with BT Scotland has developed a Web-based e-democracy toolkit. The toolkit demonstrates how relatively straightforward computing techniques can enhance public participation in the newly established Scottish Executive and Parliament. The purpose of the e-democracy toolkit on the Centre's Web site is three-fold. Firstly, it gives people, from all over the world, an opportunity to look at, and importantly try out, what such tools offer. Secondly it hosts "live" applications–both on-line petitions and on-line consultations. Thirdly, it allows the Centre to evaluate the use of such tools and use the evaluation results to refine the design of the toolkit and direct research.

Governments have come relatively late to the Internet. "A world full of phoney democracies" published in *The Economist* (June 24, 2000) describes how governments are unable to chose their customers and how services must meet all citizens' requirements. It noted the important need to change working practices in government in order to put in place e-Government and listed four stages of moving to e-Government:
1.   Disseminating information over the Web.
2.   Allowing citizens to use email to pass information to government offices.
3.   Allowing citizens to fill in forms over the Internet.
4.   Integrating a range of user services.

The early e-Government applications were concerned with the delivery of public information but now many are moving towards delivery of electronic forms and e-Government services. However teledemocracy services have been slower to arrive in practice. Even though there has been a plethora of practical experiments over the past decade in many countries, these have tended to remain as experiments. Becker and Slaton, (July 2000) explore the current state and future of teledemocracy initiatives. They consider the initiatives that are designed specifically to move towards direct democracy rather than ICTs supporting the existing representative democracy. Tsagarousianou (1998) gives descriptions of a number of projects explicitly stating what they have not managed to achieve with current technology.

From a democracy perspective, in 1997 notions of devolution had begun to reshape the UK government highlighting opportunities to form new national entities in the regions of Scotland, Wales and Northern Ireland. A 'Yes vote' in the Scottish devolution referendum in 1997 predicated the arrival of a new Scottish Parliament on May 12, 1999. The Scottish Parliament gave devolved power for specific areas of government from the Westminster Parliament in London to a new Scottish Parliament based in Edinburgh. Prior to its emergence, the new Parliament was billed as an opportunity to develop a modern efficient parliamentary network, an open political administration supporting new electronic communications resources, new forms of political interaction and wider participation (The Consultative Steering Group, 1998). From the beginning, the belief was expressed that the citizenry should be able to maximize opportunities presented by an open, accessible and participatory Parliament and new opportunities presented by ICT. Delivery of one-way information from the top down and the danger of developing new structures primarily along fiscal lines were to be avoided. Reflecting this, all documents and debates relating to the business of the Parliament are made available on-line and there is live coverage of the Parliament at www.scottishparliamentlive.com. Also the Scottish Parliament was to assess the scope of ICT for invigorating democratic participation at the local level. The following statement underlines the point in suggesting:

> It will also be important to develop a culture of genuine consultation and participation if people in Scotland, particularly those who do not currently engage in the political process, are to be encouraged to participate. (p. 9)

The new Parliament wanted ICT to be a fully integrated part of its democratic processes rather than an add-on component.

From a technology perspective, ICTs are currently at the point where the people can participate better and more directly in all aspects of democratic decision making. The Scottish working examples in this section use relatively straightforward technology. However the Centre also has a dedicated research program into developing next-generation teledemocracy systems. This research draws on several technical themes:

- Computer-supported collaborative work (Sharples, 1993; Conklin and Begeman, 1988; Jarke et al., 1997; Marker and Pipek, 2000; Shum and Selvin, 2000)
- Adaptive workflow and ontologies (Uschold, 1998; Jarvis et al., 2000)
- Knowledge modelling and knowledge management (Traveen et al., 1995; van Heijst et al., 1997; Stader and Macintosh, 1999; Kingston and Macintosh, 2000)

There is a significant amount of research in each of the technical areas identified above. However, what is lacking is a principled and yet flexible framework for integrating all the different aspects that address the general problem of electronic democracy. The European Commission is attempting to address this though its Fifth Framework Program (FP5) (http://www.cordis.lu/fp5/about.htm) which sets out the priorities for the European Union's research for the period 1998-2002. The thematic program 'Systems and Services for the Citizen' specifically includes R&D projects aimed at on-line democracy.

One such FP5 project is EDEN--Electronic Democracy European Network. The overall objective of EDEN is the improvement of communication between Public Administrations and citizens in decision making processes. The research involves the use of natural-language-based tools to allow people to take part in consultations using a variety of technologies, such as mobile phones, the Web, e-mail and to automatically route their enquiry or point of view to the appropriate government official. It is a collaborative project with local authorities: Bologna, Antwerp, Bremen, Nitzko, Vienna, along with Piacentini Archive and with research partners: Omega Generation, International Teledemocracy Centre, Public Voice Lab--PVL, Telepolis Antwerpen, TZI--Center for Computing Technology at the University of Bremen and Yana Research.

E-Lobbying

The practice of interest groups and individuals lobbying elected representatives is often viewed as running counter to principles of open government, particularly where influence goes unseen and unaccounted for. Nevertheless, if lobbying can be seen as the boundary between formal structures of governance and the informal influence of organized citizenry (Nixon and Johanssen, 2000) then it possible that ICT may help to make this process more transparent. One of the oldest and most transparent forms of lobbying is petitioning. This section focuses on e-lobbying through the use of electronic petitioning. It describes the development of an electronic petitioning system and its application within the Scottish Parliament. The system called e-petitioner is one component of the e-democracy toolkit being developed to motivate and facilitate public participation in governance.

A petition is a formal request from one or more people to a parliament. In many countries around the world, citizens have used petitions for a long time to make their feelings known about issues that concern them. The format of petitions and the way petitions are submitted and subsequently processed by parliaments varies greatly. The Scottish Parliament actively promotes petitions as a means by which the public can effectively lobby Parliament. One of the main documents setting out how the new Parliament should work states that the Scottish Parliament should aspire to use all forms of ICT "innovatively and appropriately" to support its three principles of openness, accessibility and participation. On the issue of petitions, the Scottish Parliament established a dedicated Petitions Committee. The remit of the Public Petitions Committee is to consider and report on whether a public petition is admissible and what action is to be taken on the petition. From July 1999 to November 2000, the Committee received and dealt with approximately 300 petitions.

A paper (Macintosh, 1999) on the development and use of electronic petitioning was submitted to the Scottish Parliament, and in December 1999 the Scottish Parliament agreed to allow an Internet-based petition from the ITC's Web site sponsored by the World Wildwide Fund for Nature (WWF) to be the first electronic petition to collect names and addresses electronically. The Parliament subsequently agreed to allow groups and individuals to submit petitions using the International Teledemocracy Centre's electronic petitioning system for a one-year trial period (Scottish Parliament, 2000). The e-petitioner system is also being used to submit e-petitions to the British Prime Minister at No. 10 Downing St.

The e-petitioner tool can be found at www.e-petitioner.org.uk. This Web-based electronic petitioning tool allows a user to create a petition, add background information and submit the petition. It also allows other users to sign the petition and/or join an integrated electronic discussion forum on the topic. In creating the petition, the sponsor composes the text and provides an address to which all communication should be sent. The sponsor can also provide any amount of background information to provide a rationale for the petition and to better inform those reading it. Members of the public who wish to support the petition can add their names and addresses on-line, and importantly, anyone wishing to raise any issues themselves about the petition can do so on-line through the integrated, on-line discussion forum. The discussion forum is available for anyone to read or send comments to whether they support the petition or not. Persons wishing to add their names or enter the discussion do not require an email account; they can do so from any Internet access point, e.g., a public kiosk, cyber café, community centre or home.

With regard to petition statistics, the number of persons supporting the petition is automatically updated along with the names and areas/countries. This information is available for anyone to view. Full names and addresses are filed for use with, and only with, the petition (unless consent for other use is given by the person adding their name and address) ensuring adherence to data protection requirements. With regard to how much checking of names and addresses is necessary for electronic petitions, this is an important question to address. It would be easy to say that it should match the level currently available for paper-based petitions but that then raises the issue of what level of security checking is actually used for paper-based names and addresses other than manually reading the often illegible handwriting. On the other hand there is always the temptation to say that everything must be checked thoroughly, which is the case for electronic voting but not necessarily for names and addresses on petitions which are not legally binding. The e-petitioner tool provides an adequate level of checking of names. To ensure validity, duplicate names and addresses are automatically removed. Names and addresses are given a "confidence" rating by the system depending on a number of factors, for example, Internet Provider (IP) address and how many times the same IP address has been used to sign the petition. These confidence ratings are closely examined prior to submission of the petition to check for any irregularities. When the petition closes, the petitioner can submit the petition with names and addresses electronically and/or can produce a paper version of the petition for submission.

In designing the system a number of key "democratic" requirements were considered. It was important to ensure that the petitioning process was as transparent as possible while remaining within the data protection standards. It was important that people were adequately informed about the petition issues and therefore could better decide whether to support the petition or not. Participation was important and achieved by incorporating a mechanism for users not only to add their support for the petition but also to comment on it–negatively or positively. The system is implemented using Microsoft SQL and ASP. The Web site does not use frames or contain large graphics files, to ensure that local community centres running slower machines can easily access the system. It is also important that features that might make the system difficult, for the partially sighted are excluded.

It is difficult to draw too many conclusions from these first electronic petitions to the Scottish Parliament. However, it was originally thought that electronic petitioning might let the Internet run wild and thousands of frivolous names and addresses would be collected. Initial evaluation has shown this is not the case. The opposite could be argued. Instead of a pen being thrust into the hand of the would-be petitioner with a request to "sign here," the petitioner needs to be much more committed to the petition cause. They have to: boot up their PCs, log onto the Internet, search the Net for the site and then sign. In this way the names and addresses being gathered could be considered a more realistic representation of those supporting the petition cause. A detailed evaluation of the impact of e-petitioner on participation levels is being funded by the Joseph Rowntree Charitable Trust.

Interest in e-petitions on the site has gradually increased. An e-petition concerning the ocean recovery campaign has over 6,000 names and addresses.

E-petitioner has demonstrated that electronic petitions can be effective and will not necessarily create a large number of frivolous names and addresses. E-petitioner has allowed the organizations raising a petition to better inform the public about their cause. It has also allowed them to better understand the concerns the public has about the petition issues. The figures on the following page show the e-petition screens for the WWF electronic petitions.

E-consultation

Electronic consultations demonstrate how governments, parliaments and other democratically constituted organizations can effectively use technology to gather the opinions of the people they represent.

Electronic opinion gathering can a take a number of forms ranging from very open consultation where the organization merely lists a number of topics and invites discussion on them, to the other extreme where the organization produces a detailed consultation paper and asks specific questions on the policy statements made in the paper. This chapter

Figure 1: E-petition screens for the WWF electronic petitions

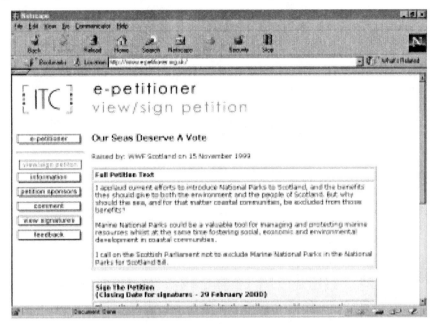

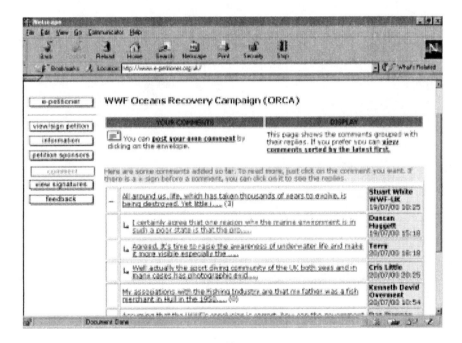

considers two specific examples--one involving a list of topics and the other involving a detailed consultation document.

E-Consultation Based on Topics

The first example is concerned with the development of an electronic consultation system and its use to consult young people in Scotland.

The Scottish Executive published a strategy document (1999) in which the Minister for Children and Education stated he wished to consult widely on an action program for youth which values young people and reflects their own aspirations and needs. Therefore in February 2000, the Scottish Executive asked the International Teledemocracy Centre to run an electronic consultation exercise as part of this Action Program for Youth.

From May 2 to June 4, 2000, any young person with access to the Internet could go to www.e-consultant.org.uk/ScottishYouth, give their opinion on a range of hot topics and vote on which of these key issues they think are the most important facing young people in Scotland today. The Web site, which could be accessed from home, school, cyber café or community centre, provided an opportunity for young people to participate in democracy over the Internet. The results of this six-week on-line consultation exercise formed important input to Scottish Youth Summit 2000--nine separate conferences across Scotland which took place on June 19 and was attended by more than 1,000 young people and Scottish Ministers.

The initial list of hot topics, which included drugs, education, money and homelessness, was identified from responses from about 500 young people aged 11-18 who gave their views to teachers and youth groups, and took part in a survey in *Young Scot* newspaper in March 2000.

The e-consultant tool for young people aimed to:
1. make the site easy to access and use by a broad range of 11-18 year-olds ("users");
2. clearly identify what was being asked of users, and why they were being asked;
3. encourage users to read and respond to comments, using a 'threaded' discussion forum;
4. take account of education authority guidelines on the disclosure of personal information by school pupils, by not disclosing full names;
5. minimize editorial control of the content, except where in breach of stated conditions of use.

The first of these objectives was the most challenging, particularly within time and resource constraints. Only a small minority of young people enjoys easy access to the Internet from home, and school access is normally tied to specific curricular activities. Also it was unlikely that many young people would be able or willing to visit the site more than once during the period.

The consultation was publicized directly to young people through the *Young Scot* newspaper, by leaflets distributed via the Scottish Parliament, and City Council Libraries and Community Education departments. During the consultation period, on-line advertising was initiated by the Scottish Executive, involving the placing of 'banner ads' on two Web sites heavily used by young people in the 15-18 age group.

When young people went to www.e-consultant.org.uk/ScottishYouth, they could:
- read what others thought about the top 20 issues facing young people in Scotland today;
- participate in the discussion on the issues;
- vote for the 10 most important issues.

For each of the issues, they could read any comments that had already been made by young people and view an opinion poll chart showing how important others thought the issue was. Importantly, they could participate by adding their own comment and rating. On the vote page young people were asked to choose up to 10 issues that they thought were the most important ones facing young people in Scotland today. Young people did not have to post comments in order to vote, but this type of participation was encouraged.

To evaluate the consultation exercise, the young people were invited to input their name, gender and age. These personal details were not published on the Web site or anywhere else. Table 1 shows the summary of the numbers taking part.

Electronic consultation is an innovative way to consult young people using the Web. Over 500 comments for an electronic consultation is very high and the figure suggests that young people are comfortable with this mode of communication. It is encouraging to see roughly equal male and female participation. The difference between the upper and lower age range participation is due to the timing of the exercise; during this period the majority of 15 to 18 year olds were on exam leave from school.

The comments input by the young people can be characterized as uninhibited either by fear of technology or adult censorship. Below are some typical comments on the issues 'crime and trouble.' Most of those who commented felt that the police unjustly target young people on the basis of their age, where they live or relatively minor past offences. The comments have not been corrected for spelling or grammar.

Crime and Trouble

Police should not just assume that kids on the street at night r causing trouble. Discrimination in the police force should be stopped. Mike, 3/5/00

We don't think it's fair because the council build parks etc for us. but when we make use of the parks someone always complains and then we get shifted on by the police. Kirsty and Kathryn, 5/31/00

Why must the youth of today always be blamed for every single crime that happens?!?!?! No matter what happens we are always the first a policeman will come to and the last to be ruled off the list of suspects! What ever happened to equality? Although the police aren't always to blame. Security guards are just as bad. Peolpe I know were searched by a security guard just for LOOKING suspicious. They hadn't stolen anything and the security guard just walked off. It is amazing that stuff like this still happens in the 21st century!!! Pam, 6/1/00

The five issues Alcohol, Smoking, Sex, Drugs and Schools received the most comments. With respect to the voting, for both age groups Drugs was voted as the most important issue. For the 11-14 age group this was followed by Bullying, Smoking, Alcohol and Crime. For the 15-18 age group Drugs was followed by Alcohol, Sex, Schools and Crime.

The full results and an evaluation report can be found at www.e-consultant.org.uk. Responses to the on-line evaluation questionnaire were very positive. They showed that most

Table 1: Summary of numbers taking part

Total number of Comments	**587**
Total number of Votes	**279**
Number of male voters	146
Number of female voters	133
Number of voters in age group 11-14	178
Number of voters in age group 15-18	101

young people found the site easy to use, and thought they would use it again for other consultations. However a significant minority thought it too text-oriented and lacking a rich and colourful page style. Presentation aspects aside, the most frequently mentioned 'like' was the opportunity to vote and express an opinion, and the most disliked aspect was the inability to add to the range of issues. Most thought that Web sites were generally a "good way to voice your opinion." There were a few concerns about entering personal details, but the most frequently voiced general concern was that the comments would not "make a difference."

E-Consultation Based on a Consultation Document

Much of the work of parliament and government relates to the preparation of policy documents that require widespread discussion and consultation. These documents typically set out views regarding the nature, importance and aims of policy, and as such encapsulate a large amount of knowledge (both explicit and implicit), exhibit considerable structure and are often constructed from disperse data, information and knowledge sources. It is important that the consultation reaches all the people and organizations it might affect or who have a genuine interest in the issue. The responses from the consultation are critical in refining and developing policy further.

There is a high cost of failure in this process from both the government and the organization perspectives. From the point of view of the government, if subsequent actual policy provokes feedback that should have been generated by the consultation, the cost ranges from embarrassment to the cost in time and effort to amend or remake the policy. Testament to the high cost of failure from the point of view of the organization is the amount of money that large organizations spend on legal teams whose sole task is to scan proposed policy for issues that may affect their business.

However, the escalating number of consultations taking place increases the problems:

- increasing the burden on policy developers both to author clear, well-structured consultation documents and to analyze responses from the consultation exercise;
- increasing the burden on those individuals and organizations being consulted to respond such that their response is complete and representative of the entire organization;
- increasing the burden of analysis for the policy developers.

Therefore there is a need to make it easier for individuals and organizations to respond to consultation documents and to make it easier for policy developers to provide feedback to clearly show they have dealt with the responses.

Much research has been conducted on how to conduct consultations. A code of practice has been developed by the UK government on written consultation (Cabinet Office, 2000b). Written consultation is considered the classic form of consultation, even though now it is increasingly read in electronic format rather than print. This switching to electronic document handling is perhaps facilitating dissemination but is not in itself materially affecting the other issues.

This practical example of an e-consultation based on a consultation document is work by the International Teledemocracy Centre for the national advisory body for education in Scotland (Learning & Teaching Scotland). It concerns the development of an innovative approach to on-line consultation focusing on the 'Education for Citizenship' curricula material for 3 to 18 year olds in Scotland. The Web-based e-consultant tool integrates the consultation document with the questions in it, allowing people to respond quantitatively and qualitatively on-line. The e-consultation was launched on December 15, 2000, with responses closing on March 16, 2001, allowing three months for the on-line consultation exercise to take place.

Learning & Teaching Scotland used several approaches to obtain the views of the target audiences:

- formal responses using the distributed consultation document, available both on paper and electronically;
- feedback from a number of conferences and events planned in conjunction with various partners;
- responses from young people in schools and youth forums using youth consultation material focusing on the document;
- electronic consultation.

The e-consultant approach addressed the need to collect responses from the wider community and informal responses generally. The on-line consultation can be read by any Internet user, but only users who register can comment on the Education for Citizenship consultation paper. The registration process is relatively quick and easy, capturing the user's name, address and email address.

The outline structure of e-consultant comprises five main sections. The Overview section informs users about who wants the consultation done, who they want to consult, why the consultation is taking place, how the results will be used and provides a timetable of events. The Information section informs users how they can contribute and provides Web access to each section of the consultation document with hyperlinks to allow users to respond to each question as it arises in the document.

The on-line consultation takes place through the Comments section. The Education for Citizenship paper is explicitly structured around the consultation questions, organized under four main headings:

- What is "citizenship" and why is "education for citizenship" important?
- What should education for citizenship seek to achieve?
- Effective education for citizenship in practice
- Implications and next steps.

Accordingly, the comments are organized around these questions and issues, and the system emphasizes the ability to link to and from the corresponding on-line text of the consultation document. Users are able to give quantitative ratings to some of the consultation questions, and to comments made in response to these. There are three types of questions: open questions: e.g., "what is your view?"; partially closed questions: e.g., "how far do you agree;" and closed questions: e.g., "do you agree." The most interesting are the open questions where the user can type in their own response to the question; read the responses from others, type in their response to an existing response and rate how highly they consider others' responses to the debate.

The Feedback section allows Learning & Teaching Scotland to provide a statement of how they will respond to the consultation. The Contributors section shows name and country of the users who have entered a response. For research purposes and to assist with the evaluation, there is an on-line questionnaire for registered users to complete before they exit from the site.

The figures below show sample screens from the e-consultant tool. The first screen shows the information pages with the hyperlinks to the questions. The second screen shows the comments pages with appropriate links to the text of the consultation document.

THE IMPORTANCE OF EVALUATION

Governments, at local, regional and national levels, are increasingly introducing technology to support the democratic processes. Email, on-line discussion forums and

Figure 2: Sample screen showing the information page with the hyperlinks to the questions

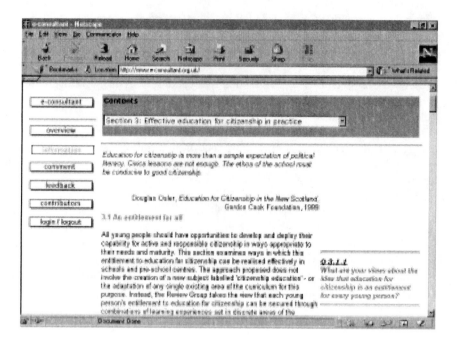

Figure 3: Sample screen showing the comments page with appropriate links to the text of the consultation document

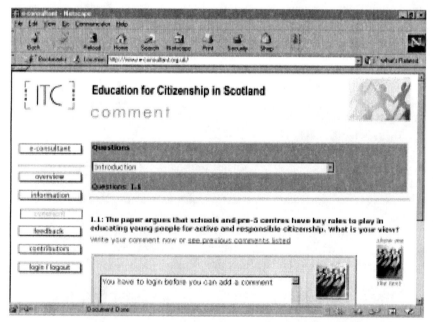

bulletin boards are now appearing on a large number of government-related Web sites along with the associated claims that government is now much better at reaching out to the public they represent and gathering their views and opinions. However, these claims have not, as yet, been substantiated. Links between developing the technology, civic inclusion and participation in the democratic process have not been explored systematically or comprehensively, although it is often assumed in the statements of policymakers. Our own work on the evaluation of the systems described in this chapter is still ongoing (a summary report on the Scottish Youth Summit e-consultation is available at www.e-consultant.org.uk), but we can offer a general description of this work below.

Evaluation is required to establish whether the system works as specified, i.e., quality assurance. However as pointed out, evaluation also needs to consider wider questions of accessibility, usability, security and transparency. It should also address:

- whether to continue to use a selected e-democracy system, and if so:
- how to improve the design;
- any feasible and desirable changes in how the system is promoted and deployed.

If the answers to these questions are to be transferable as 'best practice,' evaluation should also assess what local circumstances had a bearing on the success or failure of the implementation. A critical issue is the analysis of similarities and differences between e-participation and real-life/traditional participation.

There is no accepted methodological framework to measure the uptake and use of teledemocracy services. Such a framework needs to evaluate teledemocracy from the integrated perspectives of "technology and democracy." Our research therefore also addresses wider questions of the impact of developed teledemocracy systems on democratic decision making processes. Although these questions will vary in their detail according to project objectives, some high-level questions being addressed are:

- To what extent and in what ways can ICTs make government information accessible and understandable to citizens?
- Do such ICTs contribute to more openness and accessibility in local administrations?
- Will such ICTs encourage and assist the public to participate in government and facilitate consultation?
- How can such ICTs enhance the participation capability of the socially excluded?

To address these questions we aim to identify and validate metrics which clearly demonstrate and measure the impact and benefits of advanced ICTs on the democratic processes. These metrics will combine both quantitative and qualitative assessments.

The specific tasks are as follows:

- to develop a classification framework for "technology-supported democracy" metrics and identify metrics for the evaluation of democratic processes;
- to determine the effect of the introduction of ICTs to support the democratic process through monitoring the identified metrics;
- as a result of the above, develop and validate methods to enable governments to successfully manage the implementation of advanced software tools for the support of the democratic process.

The results of our research will, potentially, support government by providing them with the methods necessary to quantify the impact of ICTs in both democratic and business terms and as a result justify investment in this area. The work will also support the software developers by identifying where the tools being developed could be enhanced to directly support the above monitoring of "technology-supported democracy" metrics.

CONCLUSIONS

The tools described in previous sections are very much '1st-generation' support tools for teledemocracy in the UK. The next generation is likely to exploit the affordances of networked technology to a greater extent, and capture more of the collective processes that underlie democracy. One way forward, for example, may be to provide extensions of the consultancy tool described above that will allow the deliberations of groups to be made available where an individual who has participated in a consultation has done so as a representative of a group. If access to such deliberations are to contribute to improved understanding of the democratic process, issues relating to the quality of online collective deliberation need to be addressed.

The recent initiative on Education for Citizenship may be seen as moving towards the '2nd-generation' of teledemocracy in the UK. The initiative offers an opportunity to move from a citizen as user of services to a citizen who can influence policy. An important part of this is an improved understanding of how to comport oneself online in the presence of others and how technology can facilitate the development of collective position statements by means of shared argumentation.

Finally, technology is emerging as a tool not just to disseminate information and inform people but also to provide them with the capacity and competency to participate in democratic debate and influence decision making. It is very important that the systems which are developed for this area are sensitive to the needs and wants of the users. The user group includes those users with disabilities, those who are elderly and those have no experience of interacting with technology.

REFERENCES

Barber, B. (1984). *Strong Democracy: Participatory Politics for a New Age*. Berkeley: University of California Press.

Becker, T. and Slaton, C. (2000). *The Future of Teledemocracy*. Westport, CN. LC.

Budge, I. (1996). *The New Challenge of Direct Democracy*. Cambridge: Polity Press.

Cabinet Office. (2000a). *Trust Levels and Government Transactions*. Available on the World Wide Web at: http://www.citu.gov.uk/iagc/guidelines/authentication/trustlevels.htm. Accessed November 2000.

Cabinet Office. (2000b). *Code of Practice on Written Consultation*, draft, April, London.

Catt, H. (1999). *Democracy in Practice*. London and New York: Routledge.

Conklin, J. and Begeman, M. L. (1988). GIBIS: A hypertext tool for exploratory policy discussion. *ACM Transactions on Office Information Systems*, 6(4).

Dahlgren, P. and Sparks, C. (Eds.). (1991) *Communication and Citizenship: Journalism and the Public Sphere*. London: Routledge.

Davis, R. (1999). *The Web of Politics: The Internet's Impact on the American Political System*. New York: Oxford University Press.

Denning, D. (1999). *Activism, Hacktivism and Cyberterrorism: The Internet as a Tool for Influencing Foreign Policy*. Available on the World Wide Web at: http://www.nautilus.org/info-policy/workshop/papers/denning.html. Accessed December 13, 2000.

Docter, S. and Dutton, W. H. *The First Amendment Online: Santa Monica's Public Electronic Network,* 125-151

Dutton, W. H. (1999). *Society on the Line: Information Politics in the Digital Age*. Oxford: Oxford University Press.

Fotopoulos, T. (1997). *Towards an Inclusive Democracy*. London: Cassell.

Gregson, K. (1997). Community networks and political participation: Developing goals for system developers. In *Proceedings of the ASIS Annual Meeting*, 34, 263-270.

Hacker, K. and Todino, M. (1996). Virtual democracy at the Clinton White House: An experiment in electronic democracy. *Javnost/ The Public*, 3(1), 71-86.

Hague, B. and Loader, B. (Eds.). (1999). *Digital Democracy: Discourse and Decision Making in the Information Age*. London: Routledge.

Hall, S. & Jacques, M. (Eds). (1989). *New Times: The Changing Face of Politics in the 1990s*. London: Lawrence & Wishart Limited.

Harrison, T. and Stephen, T. (1999). Researching and creating community networks. In Jones, S. (Ed.), *Doing Internet Research*. Thousand Oaks, CA: Sage.

Jarke, M., Jeusfeld, M. A., Peters, P. and Pohl, K. (1997). Coordinating distributed organizational knowledge. *Data and Knowledge Engineering*, 23, 247-268.

Jarvis, P., Moore, J., Stader, J., Macintosh, A. and Chung, P. (2000). Harnessing AI technologies to meet the requirements of adaptive workflow systems. In Filipe, J. (Ed.) *Enterprise Information Systems*, 163-170, Kluwer Academic Publishers.

Kingston, J. and Macintosh, A. (2000). Knowledge management through multi-perspective modeling: Representing and distributing organizational memory. *Knowledge-Based Systems Journal*, 13(2-3), 121-131, Elsevier Science.

Klein, H. (1999). Tocqueville in cyberspace: Using the Internet for citizen associations. *The Information Society*, 15, 213-220.

Kyrish, S. (1994). Here comes the revolution again. In *Superhighway Blues, Media Information Australia*, November, (74).

Macintosh, A. (1999). Electronic petitions and the Scottish Parliament. Paper presented to the *Public Petitions Committee of the Scottish Parliament*.

Malina, A. (1999a). Third way transitions: Building benevolent capitalism for the information society. *Communications: The European Journal of Communication Research*, 24(2), 167-188.

Malina, A. (1999b). Perspectives on citizen democratization and alienation in the virtual public sphere. In Hague, B. and Loader, B. (Eds), *Digital Democracy: Discourse and Decision Making in the Information Age*, 23-38. London: Routledge.

Mansell, R. and Silverstone, R. *Communication By Design*. New York: Oxford University Press.

Nixon, O. and Johansson, H. (1999). Transparency through technology: the Internet and political parties. In Hague, B and Loader, B. (Eds.), *Digital Democracy: Discourse and Decision Making in the Information Age*, London: Routledge.

Märker, O. and Pipek, V. (2000). Computer-supported participation in urban planning from the viewpoint of communicative planning theory. Paper presented at *Working Conference on Advances in Electronic Government*, Zaragoza, Spain, February.

New York University. (2000). *Projects on NYU Web*. Available on the World Wide Web at: http://www.nyu.edu/projects/wray/wwwhack.html. Accessed December 13, 2000.

Sclove, R. E. (1995). *Democracy and Technology*. New York: Guildford Press.

Scottish Executive. (1999). *Making it Work Together–A Program for Government*. Available on the World Wide Web at: http://www.scotland.gov.uk/library2/doc03/miwt-00.htm. Accessed December 2000.

Scottish Executive. (2000). *Report by the Digital Scotland Task Force*. Available on the World Wide Web at: http://www.scotland.gov.uk/digitalscotland/report.htm. Accessed December 2000.

Scottish Parliament. (2000). *The Report of the Meeting of the Public Petitions Committee on 14th March, 2000 to Trial Internet Petitions*. Available on the World Wide Web at: http://www.scottish.parliament.uk/official_report/cttee/petit-00/pumop0314.htm. Accessed December 2000.

Shapiro, I. and Hacker-Cordon, C. (1999). *Democracy's Value*. New York: Cambridge University Press.

Sharples M. (Ed.). (1993). *Computer-Supported Collaborative Writing*, Springer-Verlag.

Shum, B. J. and Selvin, A. M. (2000). Structuring discourse for collective interpretation, distributed collective practices 2000. Paper presented at *Conference on Collective Cognition and Memory Practices*, Paris. Available on the World Wide Web at: http://www.limsi.fr/WkG/PCD2000. Accessed December 2000.

Stader, J. and Macintosh, A. (1999). Capability modeling and knowledge management. Paper presented at *Applications and Innovations in Expert Systems VI, Proceedings of ES 99, the 19th International Conference of the BCS Specialist Group on Knowledge-Based Systems and Applied Artificial Intelligence*, Cambridge, December.

Terveen, L. G., Selfridge, P. G. and Long, M. D. (1995). Living design memory–Framework, implementation, lessons learned. *Human-Computer Interaction*, 10, 1-37.

The Consultative Steering Group. (1998). Shaping Scotland's Parliament. *The Scottish Office*, December.

Thompson, J. (1995). *Media and Modernity*. Oxford: Polity Press.

Tsagarousianou, R., Tambini, D. and Bryan C. (Eds.). (1998). *Cyberdemocracy: Technology, Cities and Civic Networks*. London and New York: Routledge.

Tsagarousianou, R. (1999). Electronic democracy: Rhetoric and reality. *Communications: The European Journal of Communication Research*, 24(2), 189-208.

United Kingdom Parliament. (1998). *Electronic Government–Information Technologies and the Citizen*. Available on the World Wide Web at: http://www.parliament.uk/post/egov.htm. Accessed December 2000.

Uschold, M. et al. (1998). The enterprise ontology. *The Knowledge Engineering Review*, 13.

Van Heijst, G., van der Spek, R. and Kruizinga, R. (1997). Corporate memories as a tool for knowledge management. *Expert Systems with Applications*, 13, 41-54.

Wilhelm, A. (2000). *Democracy in the Digital Age*. London and New York: Routledge.

Wray, S. (1998). Electronic civil disobedience and the World Wide Web of hacktivism: A mapping of extraparliamentarian direct-action net politics. A paper for the *World Wide Web and Contemporary Cultural Theory Conference*, Drake University, November.

Wright, T. (1994). *Citizens and Subjects*. London: Routledge.

Chapter XII

e-Democracy and Community Networks: Political Visions, Technological Opportunities and Social Reality

Tom Gross
Institute of Applied Information Technology, German National Research Center for Information Technology, Germany

Political systems and technology are interdependent and influence each other. On the one hand, political systems and political leaders aim at influencing technological development and benefiting from technological progress; on the other, technological development has a considerable proportion of its own dynamics and potential to influence society and political systems. This chapter particularly focuses on electronic democracy and virtual communities and accordingly discusses recent ideas and plans of political leaders, derives requirements for technology, presents systems and prototypes, and reports cases demonstrating how and what technology is really used.

INTRODUCTION

The interdependence of political systems and technology is unquestioned. In various initiatives of single countries and associations of countries' visions for changes and improvements are tightly coupled to technological development. The 'eEurope 2002—An Information Society for All' initiative of the European Union (EC, 2000) or the 'National Partnership for Reinventing Government' (NPR, 2001) and the 'National Information Infrastructure' (NIST, 2000) of the USA are good examples. In fact, one of the objectives of eEurope is for Europe to become the "most competitive and dynamic economy in the world" (EC, 2000). And in the USA it is claimed that the NII "can help unleash an information revolution that will change forever the way people live, work and interact with each other" (NPR, 2001).

Many of these governmental initiatives offer huge incentives—in general, in the form of research funding—and therefore have the potential to highly influence the technological development. Nevertheless, the actual technological development and progress is hard to predict and even harder to control. The history of information and communication technology can be seen as a path where for some steps the development could be controlled and for other steps it could not. The Internet and all the services and applications that have become available on top of it are an essential basis for today's information society, e-government and e-democracy. And yet, its development has neither been foreseeable nor controllable. For instance, the ARPANET and TCP/IP were developed by the Department of Defense of USA; whereas applications like Internet Relay Chat, Multi-User Domains, Internet Gopher or the World Wide Web were not developed in governmental organizations (Leiner et al., 1997). The controllability of social development and social change through technology is also unclear. In many cases technological development is stimulated by the social changes, and technological development itself entails social changes (Coleman, 1999).

It is obvious that these interdependencies are very complex and cannot be analyzed in one book chapter. This chapter focuses on electronic democracy and community networks. In the next section political ideas and plans concerning information and communication technology are discussed and requirements for technology are derived. Then electronic communities—virtual communities and community networks—are introduced and their technological requirements are derived. Systems and prototypes providing functionality for e-democracy and community networks are introduced. Finally, we will discuss the actual use of systems.

ELECTRONIC DEMOCRACY

Electronic government can be seen from the addressees,' from the process, from the cooperation, and from the knowledge perspective (Lenk & Traunmueller, 2000). The same holds true for e-democracy. This chapter primarily focuses on aspects related to the cooperation between the public sector and the citizens, and among citizens, as well as the support for cooperation by modern information and communication technology. The public awareness and desire for e-democracy have been there for years. Already in early 1994 MacWorld magazine polled 600 randomly selected adults and found that more than half of the respondents said that online voting in elections is the most desirable service; that 60% of the respondents had a moderate or strong interest in participating in online polls; that almost 60% liked to take part in interactive, electronic town-hall meetings with political leaders and other citizens; and that almost half of the respondents would like to have electronic contact to elected representatives (Piller, 1994).

Subsequently, requirements for e-democracy are discussed. Basically, citizens need to be able to access information and to discuss political issues, and to vote electronically.

Public Access to Information

In order to take active part in democratic processes, citizens need various types of information. They need information with respect to elections—that is, only well-informed citizens guarantee that good and adequate decisions are taken. Furthermore, they need information about possibilities of their own involvement in policy discussion and decision making. Examples of information about current policy making are information about current and future committee meetings and votes, text and status of pending bills and regulations, position papers and background research material on current issues. Examples of information on the output of current governments are scientific research results, legal documents, surveys, reports and public announcements. Frankenfeld (1992) calls this the right to knowledge or information.

On a whole the information can come from the public sector via information gatekeepers or directly from citizen to citizen. Figure 1 shows an example where the citizens access information provided by the political-administrative system. The case where no information gatekeepers are in place can be referred to as disintermediation (Bonchek, 1997). From a technological point of view, this means that citizens need to be able to retrieve information and documents, which others have stored. This goes far beyond concurrency, access control or transaction scheduling. During democratic processes citizens have to take many decisions based on information that was produced by others. Therefore, they often have to proof the validity of the information. They require transparent information sharing, which shows the creators of the information and the motivation that led to the information. Also knowledge of the perspective that led to the solution and that caused the information and decision, and that served as a basis for further information production and decision making is essential. Ideally the system presents the relationship between the conceptual frame, the knowledge and the information produced or the decision taken (Robinson, 1991). Furthermore, the information consumers should be able to correlate their share of knowledge and their points of view to a problem. This allows them to consider alternative perspectives on the respective subject. A holistic representation of the problem sphere, of the relations among the different perspectives on the problem space and on possible solutions that can be matched to the solutions are necessary.

Open Discussion Participation

Open discussion and the citizens' possibility to take part in them is the second major requirement for e-democracy. Open discussion has to take place in a top-down direction—that is, citizens need possibilities to contact elected representatives and directly interact with

Figure 1: Public access to information from the political-administrative system

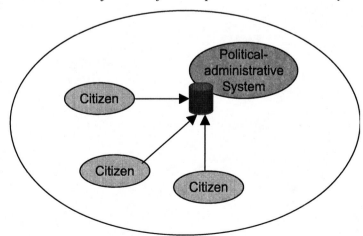

them. Furthermore, the bottom-up direction—that is, discussions among citizens—is equally important. These latter discussions can be held among two individuals, between one person and a large number of other citizens, or among the broad public. Figure 2 illustrates this citizen-citizen communication and citizen–political-administrative system communication. Frankenfeld (1992) calls this the right to participation.

Through open discussion the citizens can broaden their understanding by exchanging information, views and feelings with other citizens. From a technological point of view, support for communication among citizens can take place through the exchange of symbolic messages or through the exchange of non-symbolic messages like changes of states, communication can support the processing of results of one step, the planning of steps, or the discussing and evaluating of results. Communication can take two forms: the distribution of messages to certain people and the aimed interpersonal communication in a particular work arrangement. Communication is a key requirement for e-democracy. Effective communication requires a mutual understanding of the subject of conversation, a common language, shared references to things that are known to all communication partners and so forth. Clark and Brennan (1991) call this mutual understanding 'common ground.'

Efficient technological support for communication among citizens does not only provide functionality for information exchange, but also provides the citizens with information about the other citizens. In traditional town hall meetings, this information can be captured by the participants automatically. In electronic systems that are used by geographically dispersed citizens, this information has to be provided by the system. In particular, information about the presence of other citizens in the system, the availability of other citizens and the attention, interest and emotional state of other citizens is important for smooth discussions—this is often referred to as group awareness (Gross, 1997b).

Anonymity is a very tricky aspect, because on the one hand it is often good and important to identify individuals and to make them responsible, but on the other hand there are several situations where it is desirable and legitimate to stay anonymous. Another trade-off can be identified between free speech and censorship. However, a thorough discussion of these aspects would go beyond the scope of this chapter.

As a result of information sharing and open discussion, citizens can establish a shared knowledge—community memory—over time. Marshall and associates (1994) emphasize

Figure 2: Open discussion among citizens and between citizens and the political-administrative system

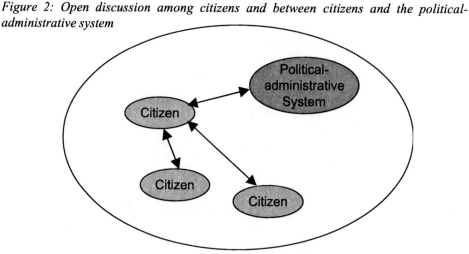

the importance of community memory for online communities and argue that it is important for the participants to construct and maintain a shared understanding "of what they are doing: the task, the pertinent body of material, preliminary findings, progress and methods." In order to create, maintain and increase community memory, systems have to support the acquisition and continual updates of the contents and the structure of the community memory and the identification of the relevancy of material found. The authors further argue that the Internet is an effective vehicle for communication and for collections of materials and that community memory has the capacity to greatly extend the reach of the individual.

COMMUNITY NETWORKS

In general, community networks are communication and information systems that aim at enhancing community and enriching lives; they are often based locally and driven locally (Miller, 2000). According to the Association for Community Networking (Gonzalez, 2001), community networking projects bring together local people to discuss and decide upon community issues. These projects explicitly focus on the whole community—they particularly want to include those who are traditionally left out (e.g., low-income groups, minorities, senior citizens). They, therefore, often provide information and training concerning general computer skills, the Internet and basic research skills. And they include inexpensive public access to libraries, schools, businesses and non-profit organizations. Figure 3 shows a community network where the citizens and the political-administrative system are part of the network. In contrast to Figure 1 and Figure 2, here the citizens are really part of the system—in many community networks the members feel as part of the community and are prepared to contribute their time and effort for the other members.

Rheingold (1993) argues that virtual communities have the potential to revitalize democracy. In fact, community networks have the potential to vastly influence e-democracy initiatives. Kubicek and Wagner (1998) have analysed the evolution of community networks and argue that their role has changed drastically. They distinguish four generations of community networks. It started with community memories in the 1970s—a public forum, where everybody could freely publish their opinion electronically. In the 1980s free-nets

Figure 3: Community network consisting of citizens and political-administrative system

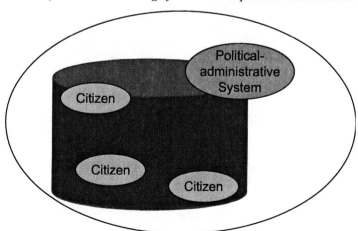

were the first publicly accessible information and communication systems; they provided free email and Internet access for their users. Since the 1990s, the perspective of community networks like the Boulder Community Network changed. As most people have a private email account and access to the Internet, these systems mainly focus on providing public access terminal for less privileged people and on providing all kinds of local information about the community for people within and without the community. More recently, a fourth generation of professionalized community networks can be identified, where the basic assumption is that more and more users of community networks take the perspective of customers and consequently expect professional services (e.g., professional contents) and do not necessarily want to contribute themselves. The Digital Cities project of AOL, the Sidewalk project of Microsoft Network and the New York Today project of the *New York Times* are examples. During these decades the nature of community networks has changed considerably. The first two generations aimed at a dissemination of information and power. In the fourth generation concentration might increase again—the decisions of what kind of information, in which format and so forth are taken by professional providers. The third generation—that is, the current community networks—can be seen as an intermediate form. This scenario contrasts several assumptions underlying new communities, which are described as "fundamentally devoted to problem-solving" with "principles based on equity," and so forth (Schuler, 1996).

De Cindio and others (1997) did a similar analysis of the evolution of community networks. They call the early attempts of community networks civic networks, which provided members of the local community with access to a vast amount of resources and bi-directional communication. Later, civic networks split into community networks or citizen networks, which were often based on bulletin board systems; civic nets, which were often promoted by local administrations and offered residents information and contacts to city officials; and city nets, which served as 'window-shows' for the public administration with hardly any interaction with the users. According to the authors the first two types (i.e., Civic and Community Networks) clearly emphasized bi-directional communication and user involvement, whereas the third type (City Nets) offers less interaction.

Whereas Kubicek and Wagner see these developments as mutually exclusive, De Cindio and others do not. Rather the different types of community networks are seen as complementary. On a whole, De Cindio and others are more optimistic concerning the democratizing power of community networks. They argue that "instead of reducing interactive communication to a new broadcasting medium, we need to transform it in the tool of choice able to sustain the local community—intended not as a mere recipient of electronic services offered by public and private organizations, but seen as a great resource for social development."

With respect to the underlying information and communication technology today, often the term community informatics is used (Gurstein, 2000). Community informatics refers to the very general use of information and communication technology in order to foster online communities among citizens. It is emphasized that through computer-mediated communication, normally disparate individuals who share interests rather than geographical proximity can form communities. In these communities individuals can interact socially, economically and politically. Furthermore, community informatics also covers the use of information and communication technology to support local communities of people who might even know each other before starting to interact electronically. On a whole the notion of community informatics is considerably broader than the terms discussed before.

TECHNOLOGICAL OPPORTUNITIES

In this section we will present systems that can be used to support e-democracy or community networks. We will include both systems that have been designed and developed specifically for e-democracy and community networks and systems that have initially been designed for other purposes, but offer adequate functionality.

Sharing Information

Public information systems can be technically based on email for personal communication, email distribution lists for announcements and so forth, newsgroups for discussions, the WWW for any type of multimedia information. Some more specific systems are shared global information spaces, annotation systems and social filtering systems.

Shared Global Information Spaces

Global Internet-based information systems like the WWW provide basic mechanisms for information sharing between the public sector and citizens, but mainly among citizens. Shared global information spaces offer additional functionality such as access and concurrency control, meta information on the shared artefacts and on their current state. Two very prominent examples are the BSCW system and Lotus Notes.

The Basic Support for Cooperative Work (BSCW) system offers functionality for information sharing via the WWW (Bentley et al., 1997). Being implemented as Web server extension, it can be accessed from any standard Web browser without extra installation. The BSCW information space is structured into workspaces containing any kind of objects (e.g., text documents, spreadsheets, links). Different services are offered for the objects such as versioning, notifications about changes and so forth. Access to workspaces is restricted to workspace members. Figure 4 shows a screenshot of a BSCW workspace. Icons to the left of the objects indicate the file type; icons to the right of the information objects indicate changes (in this case read events).

Lotus Notes provides similar functionality for sharing and exchanging information (Lamb, 1995). It does require proprietary clients and servers, but they are available for any platform. The information is also presented in workspaces. Objects are stored in a special database and can therefore be edited concurrently—the system later on tries to merge the changes. For close cooperation among users, the system also offers a shared calendar and an integrated email system. For instance, Lotus Notes can be used as an intranet, and via the Internet integration in Domino, which allows the automatic generation of Web pages from workspaces, information can be provided to the public.

Annotation Systems

Annotation systems allow users to comment Web pages. So, Web pages can either be commented by governmental organizations or by citizens and the citizens then can read the Web pages and its comments, and comment again. HyperNews, the W3 Document Annotator and ComMentor are interesting annotation systems.

HyperNews allows users to annotate and comment on Web pages as well as annotate and comment annotations and comments at an arbitrary depth (LaLiberte, 1995; 2001). It is based on an extended Web server and can be accessed with any standard Web browser without installation. Annotations and comments are stored along with the name of the author and the date of creation and are kept persistently, so they can be accessed anytime. Figure 5 shows a Web page with HyperNews annotations and comments. On the left of the

Figure 4: BSCW workspace with objects

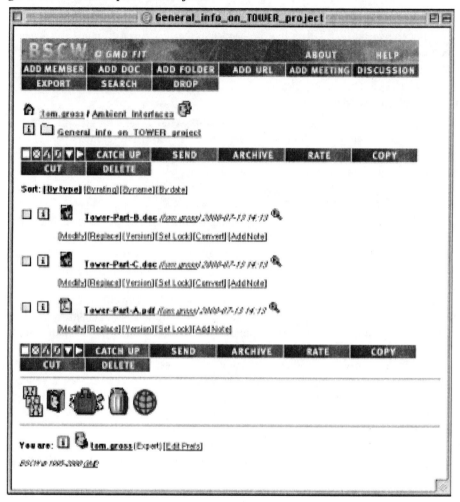

annotations and comments, the type (e.g., a question mark for a question, an exclamation mark for a statement) is indicated; on the right author and creation date are added.

The W3 Document Annotator (WDA) offers functionality that is similar to HyperNews. Whereas in HyperNews annotations and comments can only be added on the bottom of the respective page, WDA allows addition of comments in any paragraph of a Web page. Comments and annotations are represented by a little icon, that represents a hyperlink to the comment. WDA can be accessed from any standard Web browser (Schenk, 1995).

ComMentor is also similar to HyperNews. As opposed to HyperNews and WDA, comments are not stored on the same Web server as the base Web page. Therefore, in ComMentor any Web page can be annotated—the author of the base Web page does not even have to know that the page is annotated. However, ComMentor can only be used with special browsers; standard Web browsers cannot display the annotations and comments (Roescheisen & Mogensen, 1999; Roescheisen, Mogensen & Winograd, 1995).

Figure 5: HyperNews with annotations and comments

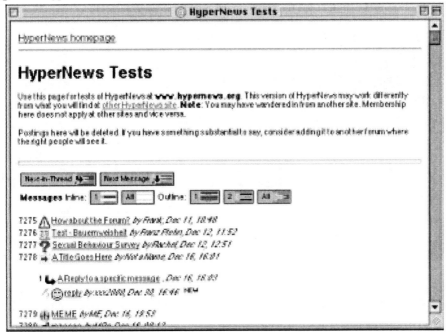

Social Filtering Systems

The filtering and rating of information by humans is often referred to as social filtering. Systems supporting social filtering are called social filtering systems or recommender systems and can either be active or passive (Resnick & Varian, 1997). In active social filtering systems, the users who find information with potential interest to another person actively send it to them (Maltz & Ehrlich, 1995). In passive social filtering systems, the interested users have to query for recommendations (Goldberg, Oki, Nichols & Terry, 1992). Interesting examples such as GroupLens are briefly described on the following pages.

GroupLens is an example of a passive social filtering system (Konstan et al., 1997). It was initially developed for social filtering of Usenet newsgroups. Users who have read an article rate its relevancy. Users who come later are not only provided with the new articles, but also with the other users' ratings. Figure 6 shows the MovieLens system, an adaptation of GroupLens for the recommendation of movies.

Examples of further social filtering systems that are based on similar principles are the Self-Enriching Library Facilities (SELF) project (King et al., 1994) and Group Asynchronous Browsing (GAB) (Wittenburg, Das, Hill & Stead, 1995).

Exchanging Information

Open discussions are often explained with the metaphor of an electronic town hall meeting. Benjamin Barber (1984) claims that a strong democracy requires "a form of town meeting in which participation is direct yet communication is regional or even national." In the 1970s most electronic town meetings were based on two or more media. Often the meetings were advertised by newspapers and then broadcasted by TV and citizens could

Figure 6: MovieLens

participate using the telephone. Therefore, there was not a feeling of a real meeting among citizens. Since the 1980s computers have been increasingly used for the communication.

Text-Based Chat Tools and Virtual Environments

These systems are purely text-based and consequently only have very limited hardware and network requirements for the users and can be used by a broad public. The Internet relay chat and multi-user domains are presented as relevant examples.

The Internet relay chat (IRC) is a multi-user multi-channel chatting network that allows people all over the Internet to talk to one another in real time. Users of IRC are known to the other users and the system by their nickname. The IRC structure is built up of channels—virtual places, usually with a topic of conversation. Nicknames have to be unique per channel. Channels can have three different modes: public mode—this is the default mode where the user can be seen by all other users and anyone can join the conversation; private mode—this means that anyone can see that a person is logged in, but not the person's channel; and secret mode—this means that the person's name is not displayed on the list of active users (Fryatt, 1996; Harris, 1995; Lowe, 1996).

Multi-user domains (MUDs) are network-accessible virtual realities for multiple participants who can freely extend them. The user interface is entirely textual. Users have the appearance of being situated in a place, which is artificially constructed and contains all users who are connected at the same time. The first MUDs in the 1980s, were multi-user adventure games where users were fighting each other. By the end of the 1980s several MUDs for social interaction were developed. For instance, the TinyMUD was developed in 1989 to invite people to hang around, chat, meet friends and discuss a variety of topics. In TinyMUD, players can create their own rooms with their own interior. TinyMUD users can get help from Colin, a robot that answers questions that are directed to it via messages. Colin gives information about the universe of the MUD such as players or rooms, provides maps for roaming, and delivers and forwards messages between players (Mauldin, 1994). An example highlighting the use of MUDs and MOOs for serious purposes is the tele-education, which is offered at the Diversity University in the interactive classroom. Users can enter the interactive classroom via Telnet and choose one of the classrooms (e.g., a class room with a course on C++). As in any MOO, users can navigate by typing textual commands and receive textual descriptions of the environment they are in. Examples of commands users can submit are look list to receive a list of other participants who offer help, map to receive a map of the Diversity University and objects to receive detailed help about the objects and possible actions in a room (DU, 1996).

Combinations of Text-Based Virtual Environments and the Web

These systems combine the strengths of text-based virtual environments such as MUDs and the strengths of Internet-based information systems such as the Web. Often the room-based structure of the MUDs is used to allow users of the Web to have social encounters and communication with other users of the Web such as in WAXWeb and WWW-MUD.

The WAXWeb system, for instance, is a cooperative hypermedia system (Meyer & Hader, 1994). The system particularly aims at supporting groups of authors or scientists or students to write and publish hypertext documents. In a MUD-based shared workspace, hypertext documents can be shared among users. These hypertext documents are immediately available on the WWW. The users of WAXWeb can create their own documents, comment on the documents of other users, discuss documents with other users who are logged in at the same time or participate in online seminars and workshops.

The WWW-MUD integration is a tool for tele-education (Newberg & Rouse III, 1995). Teachers and students interact in a MUD—they can exchange ideas and knowledge and send them in text format or picture format to other users. The system can also be used for presentations.

Sharing the Web

Systems that allow the common navigation through the WWW basically inform users of the WWW about the presence and current locations of other users and allow them to move through the WWW together. Interesting examples are CSCW3 and Virtual Places.

The CSCW3 prototype is an extension of the WWW and offers a broad range of extensions to the standard WWW (Gross, 1997a). Users can send their bookmark lists to other users, users can have shared bookmark lists where they can collect and manage bookmarks together, users can annotate Web pages and users can exchange electronic business cards with contact information and so forth. In an IRC-like chat tool, they can chat with other visitors of the Web page. And they can couple their Web browsers—so, a specific user can guide others through the Web. Figure 7 shows the CSCW3 main window and the room view with a list of current and past visitors of the Web page.

Virtual Places extends the WWW with user presence (GNN, 1996). Virtual Places can add presence to any Web page; however, users have to use the Virtual Places browser to have the presence information visualized. Small avatars of the present users are overlaid over the unmodified Web page. Users can contact other users by clicking on the respective avatar—depending on the hardware equipment, a text chat or an audio conference is started automatically. Furthermore, Virtual Places allows users to synchronize their Web browsers—a user can lead other users through the WWW.

Besides the above-mentioned systems that offer specific functionality for sharing and exchanging information, for discussions and for voting, some toolkits that allow users to share single-user applications are available. Examples of application-sharing toolkits are NetMeeting, Timbuktu and VNC. NetMeeting (Microsoft, 2000) allows users to share any

Figure 7: CSCW3: (a) main browser window; (b) room view with other visitors

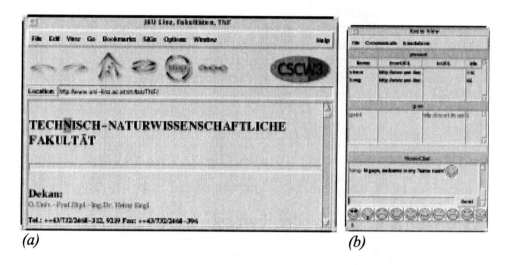

(a)   *(b)*

office applications and offers video and audio conferencing, a shared whiteboard system and so forth. So, for instance, NetMeeting could be used to share a Web browser and at the same time communicate with the integrated video conference system. Timbuktu (Netopia, 2000) and VNC (AT&T, 2000) offer similar functionality and are available for various operating systems.

Furthermore, new and upcoming types of technology are currently influencing e-democracy initiatives and will certainly do so in the future. Examples are mobile and nomadic systems that will be available for users anytime and anywhere (Gross, 2000). Other examples are context-aware systems—that is, systems that are able to analyze the current situation such as physical environment, other persons in the vicinity and so forth. This information is then used to adapt the information and services for the user. For instance, an e-government application could then only provide the users with confidential information about his income and taxes when the person is in a private environment without other persons (Gross & Specht, 2001).

DISCUSSION

This section discusses public access to information, open discussion participation and community networks: the systems that are currently used and the technological potential of the systems described above.

Public Access to Information

Most public access initiatives aim at (1) supporting citizens who cannot afford to be online with an online connection and (2) providing the information via Web sites and via personal email or email lists. Concerning the connection per se, there are still some big differences among different nations. The Center for Democracy and Technology has presented a survey of Internet access in Central and Eastern Europe (CDT, 2001). The survey shows that among the East-European countries, Slovenia with more than 500

Internet users per 10,000 inhabitants is doing far best; the next countries are the Czech Republic, Slovakia, and Latvia with less than 200 Internet users per 10,000 inhabitants respectively. The situation is worst in Moldova and Belarus with less than one Internet user per 10,000 inhabitants. So, overall Internet connection per se cannot be taken for granted. In South America and particularly in Argentina, the situation is not much better (Finquelievich, 1999).

Concerning the contents, Doctor and Ankem (1996) have studied several hundred systems and the contents they provide. They have developed a three-dimensional taxonomy. On the first dimension situational (or subject) categories are introduced such as education, governmental process, social services. On the second dimension the type of help is distinguished including advocacy, counselling, directional, factual and interactive communication. The last dimension takes into account socio-economic identifiers such as age group, educational level, gender or income. Applying their matrix they found that directional and factual help dominated and that most of the systems targeted towards middle and upper middle income.

Concerning the underlying technology none of the systems presented above are used. In particular, public access to information could be facilitated with shared global information space systems. They allow set up of shared community spaces that can only be used by the members of the community spaces. This particular feature could be used for the administration of semi-official information. By semi-official information we mean information about a city of a country that should be only accessible for citizens from the city or country. With shared global information spaces this functionality could be provided easily. The only disadvantage for citizens is that they have to type their user name and password anytime they want to access the documents.

Open Discussion Participation

Open discussion and citizens' participation in it are supported by mailing list and bulletin board systems. Occasionally, Usenet newsgroups are used. The use of chat varies considerably—whereas in some systems it is used, some authors of guidelines to set up public commons explicitly recommend not to use chat, because it is not suited for the purpose of public political discussions. It is rather argued that the Web should be used for providing information and mailing lists should be used additionally in order to also have a push channel (Clift, 2001).

Concerning the systems presented above, annotation systems and social filter systems offer useful functionality for supporting open discussion participation. With annotation systems citizens are able to annotate and comment on existing material. For instance, with a system similar to ComMentor, it would be possible for citizens to annotate and comment on information on any Web server. Such a system would allow citizens to comment on and annotate the official information from political-administrative systems. So, citizens have the advantage of receiving the original information plus the annotation and comments. The price is that the download of the material is slower, because anytime the material is accessed, the comments and annotations are also downloaded.

Social filtering systems would allow citizens to rate information they read and then provide the rates to citizens who read the information later on. Active social filtering systems allow citizens to easily send the information they discovered to other interested citizens they just discovered. If organized by topics and interest, such a system could work as follows: citizens can subscribe to topics of interest; citizens who discover an interesting document can then send the information to an email server with the topics that the document included as keywords; the email server could then automatically forward the new document to the citizens who have subscribed to the respective topic. Some challenges for the citizens with this approach are the additional effort for the sender of sending the recommendations and the potential disturbance of citizens who receive recommendations they do not need.

Community Networks

Community networks, in general, offer a broader functionality and try to integrate citizens into a community and set up a community memory. Often community networks integrate functionality related to public access to information and related to open discussion participation. The Milano Community Networks, for instance, offers email in the form of mailing lists and as Web mail, electronic forums for discussions and interactive real-time chat tools (De Cindio et al., 1997). Hecht did a great survey of community networks in the USA (Hecht, 1999). Hecht distinguishes the following service types: community involvement, educational services, economic development, government and democracy, health and human services, quality of life information, technology training and telecommunications access.

Concerning the systems presented above, community networks already use a broad range of systems. Besides standard technology such as the Web, email and Usenet newsgroups, text chat such as IRC and MUDs are also used (Smith & Kollock, 1998). In the digital city of Amsterdam, for instance, an annotation system (HyperNews) is used for annotating and commenting on the Web pages contained in this virtual city. The digital city of Amsterdam as of today has more than 150,000 inhabitants heavily using it (DDS, 2000). Nevertheless, applications for navigating the Web in groups are not yet used. Such applications would add some interesting new opportunities for the citizens of digital cities like Amsterdam. They could navigate the digital city together and citizens who know some areas well could guide others through these areas. Also, social encounters would then be possible. So, in fact, the digital city would get several strength back that normal cities are having. However, citizens might feel uncomfortable if other citizens can constantly see where they are navigating and if other citizens can approach them anytime. And, as Sclove argues: '[e]ven hypothetical new media (e.g., advanced virtual realities), conveying a dimensionally richer sensory display, are unlikely to prove fully satisfactory substitutes for face-to-face interaction.' However, if community networks are—at least to some extent—built around local communities, citizens can meet in both the electronic space, but also the physical space (Sclove, 1995). Finally, Doheny-Farina (1996) argues that community networks entail the danger that citizens do not meet any more in real life and that unplanned encounters will hardly happen any more. As this work was published back in 1996, it could be argued that with today's technology this danger is reduced. For instance, if combinations of text-based virtual environments and the Web or shared Web applications are used, these social encounters can and do happen electronically— citizens can meet incidentally on Web pages on communication channels, and so forth and have spontaneous chats.

CONCLUSIONS

In this chapter we have mainly focused of technological opportunities for e-democracy. For obvious reasons progress in e-democracy does not only depend on technology and technological development.

For instance, in the USA e-democracy was used as an argument for the creation of the new National Information Infrastructure (NII). Miller (1996, p. 212) writes that '[o]ne of the most powerful arguments for the creation of the new National Information Infrastructure (NII) is that it will strengthen democracy.' At the core of the NII lies a universal service for everybody in the USA, but similar ideas and approaches are spreading quickly in other countries as well. A universal service can, according to Miller, be defined as 'eliminating barriers so that everyone has the opportunity to use our evolving telecommunications systems for meaningful and effective participation in all aspects of society.' For several years now the technological basis for the NII has been available.

Nevertheless, there remain several non-technical challenges. A particular challenge of a universal service lies in the fact that the training, experience and resources vary considerably among citizens. Furthermore, preferences and interests are different. In fact, universal service does not mean that everybody can and should be able to do the same things in an equal way. Rather, the minimal level of service that is needed for meaningful participation should be defined. Miller enumerates five requirements for a universal service. Although he primarily focuses on the situation in the USA and challenges relating to the NII, the requirements are general and can be applied for other countries as well. A universal service should provide access to the service from anywhere, create an adaptive and adaptable interface for the service, offer flexible training and support, support systems and services for personally and socially meaningful tasks and make sure that the universal service is affordable.

The challenges do not only concern the citizens, but also the persons in the public services. Coleman (1999) reports an interesting case in this respect about the Westminster Parliament. According to Coleman the Westminster Parliament has witnessed at least two what he calls 'information revolutions.' The first information revolution was the rise of the printing press, which allowed printing bills in the sixteenth century. Before that, bills had to be read aloud. Coleman reports that this was only accepted with resistance of some members of parliament arguing that the secrets of the parliament should not be disclosed. The second information revolution of the Westminster parliament was the rise of telegraphy, radio and television. Until 1954, BBC was the sole broadcaster and BBC was forced to broadcast discussions only 14 days after the discussion really took place. Only in 1978 radio microphones were allowed and only in 1985 cameras were allowed in the House of Lords.

On a whole this chapter is mainly driven by technological opportunities; it presented systems and prototypes that offer functionality with a potential to improve and facilitate e-democracy. Although, we also glanced at some challenges with technology as well, this was not the primary aim. We, therefore, also did not address the issue of functional overload of systems.

REFERENCES

AT&T. (2000). *VNC--Virtual Network Computing*. Available on the World Wide Web at: http://www.uk.research.att.com/vnc/: AT&T Laboratories Cambridge. Accessed January 8, 2001.

Barber, B. (1984). *Strong Democracy: Participatory Politics for a New Age*. University of California Press.

Bentley, R., Appelt, W., Busbach, U., Hinrichs, E., Kerr, D., Sikkel, S., Trevor, J. and Woetzel, G. (1997). Basic support for cooperative work on the World Wide Web. *International Journal of Human-Computer Studies*, 46(6), 827-846.

Bonchek, M. S. (1997). *From Broadcast to Netcast: The Internet and the Flow of Political Information*. Unpublished PhD thesis, Harvard University, Cambridge, MA.

CDT. (2001). Bridging the digital divide. *Center for Democracy and Technology*. Available on the World Wide Web at: http://www.cdt.org/international/ceeaccess/index.shtml. Accessed March 17, 2001.

Clark, H. H. and Brennan, S. E. (1991). Grounding in communication. In Resnick, L. B., Levine, J. M. and Teasley, S. D. (Eds.), *Perspectives on Socially Shared Cognition*, 127-149. Washington, DC: American Psychological Association.

Clift, S. (2001). *Democracies Online—Commons*. Available on the World Wide Web at: http://www.e-democracy.org/do/commons.html. Accessed March 17, 2001.

Coleman, S. (1999). Westminster in the information age. In Coleman, S., Taylor, J. and van de Donk, W. (Eds.), *Parliament in the Age of the Internet*, 9-25. Oxford, UK: Oxford University Press.

DDS. (2000). *De Digitale Stad Amsterdam*. Available on the World Wide Web at: http://home.dds.nl/. Accessed March 17, 2001.

De Cindio, F., Sonnate, L. and Cannada Bartoli, V. (1997). From the milano community network to the association of civic networking in Lombardia. *First European Community Networks Conference--ECN'97*, Milan, Italy, July 3-5.

Doctor, R. D. and Ankem, K. (1996). An information needs and services taxonomy for evaluating computerized community information systems. *Americal Society for Information Science 1996 Mid-Year Conference. The Digital Revolution--ASIS'96*, San Diego, CA.

Doheny-Farina, S. (1996). *The Wired Neighborhood*. New Haven, CT: Yale University Press.

DU. (1996). *Diversity University East Campus-Web Gateway*. Diversity University. Available on the World Wide Web at: http://moo.du.org:8888/. Accessed November 20, 1996.

EC. (2000). *eEurope 2002—An Information Society for All. Council and European Commission*. Available on the World Wide Web at: http://europa.eu.int/comm/information_society/eeurope/pdf/actionplan_en.pdf. Accessed January 8, 2001.

Finquelievich, S. (1999). *Community Informatics: The Slow Argentinian Wap. University of Buenos Aires*. Available on the World Wide Web at: http://www.scn.org/tech/the_network/Proj/ws99/finquelievich-pp.html. Accessed March 17, 2001.

Frankenfeld, P. J. (1992). Technological citizenship: A normative framework for risk studies. *Science, Technology and Human Values*, 15, 226-243.

Fryatt, M. (1996). *Synchronous Communications*. Available on the World Wide Web at: http://www.oise.on.ca/~mfryatt/synchcmc.htm. Accessed October 27, 1999.

GNN. (1996). *Welcome to Ubique's Place on the Web*. Global Network Navigator, Inc. Available on the World Wide Web at: http://www.vplaces.com. Accessed November 20, 1996.

Goldberg, D., Oki, B., Nichols, D. and Terry, D. B. (1992). Using collaborative filtering to weave an information tapestry. *Communications of the ACM*, 35(12), 61-70.

Gonzalez, M. (2001). *Association for Community Networking (AFCN): What Is Community Networking?* Boulder Community Network. Available on the World Wide Web at: http://bcn.boulder.co.us/afcn/cn/definition.html. Accessed January 8, 2001.

Gross, T. (1997a). The CSCW3 prototype—Supporting collaboration in global information systems. *Conference Supplement of the Fifth European Conference on Computer-Supported Cooperative Work-ECSCW'97*, Lancaster, UK. September 7-11, 43-44.

Gross, T. (1997b). Towards flexible support for cooperation: Group awareness in shared workspaces. *Proceedings of the Eighth International Workshop on Database an Expert Systems Applications-DEXA '97*, Toulouse, France. September 1-2, 406-411.

Gross, T. (2000). Towards ubiquitous cooperation: From CSCW to cooperative Web computing to ubiquitous computing. *Proceedings of the Eighth International Information Management Talks-IDIMT 2000*, Zadov, Czech Republic, September 20-22, 145-162.

Gross, T. and Specht, M. (2001). Awareness in context-aware information systems. *Mensch & Computer-1*. Fachuebergreifende Konferenz, Bad Honnef, Germany, March 5-8, 173-182.

Gurstein, M. (Ed.). (2000). *Community Informatics: Enabling Communities with Information and Communication Technologies*. London, UK: Idea Group Publishing.

Harris, S. (1995). *The IRC Survival Guide--Talk to the World with Internet Relay Chat*. Reading, MA: Addison-Wesley.

Hecht, L. (1999). *U.S. Community Networks and the Services They Offer*. Available on the World Wide Web at: http://www.internetpublicpolicy.com/communitynetworks.html. Accessed March 16, 2001.

King, G., Kung, H. T., Grosz, B., Verba, S., Flecker, D. and Kahin, B. (1994). The Harvard Self-Enriching Library Facilities (SELF) project. *Proceedings of the Digital Libraries Workshop-DL '94*, Newark, NJ, May 19-20.

Konstan, J. A., Miller, B. N., Maltz, D., Herlocker, J. L., Gordon, L. R. and Riedl, J. (1997). GroupLens: Applying collaborative filtering to usenet news. *Communications of the ACM*, 40(3), 77-87.

Kubicek, H. and Wagner, R. M. M. (1998). Community networks in a generational perspective. *Designing Across Borders: The Community Design of Community Networks at the Participatory Design Conference-PDC '98*, November 14.

LaLiberte, D. (1995). Collaboration with hypernews. *Workshop on WWW and Collaboration at the Fourth International WWW Conference-WWW '95*, September 11-12.

LaLiberte, D. (2001). *About HyperNews*. NCSA, National Center for Supercomputing Applications. Available on the World Wide Web at: http://www.hypernews.org/HyperNews/get/hypernews.html. Accessed January 8, 2001. University of Illinois.

Lamb, R. (1995). Using online information resources: Reaching for the *.*'s. *Proceedings of the Digital Libraries Workshop-DL '95*, Austin, TX, June 11-13, 137-146.

Leiner, B. M., Cerf, V. G., Clark, D. D., Kahn, R. E., Kleinrock, L., Lynch, D. C., Postel, J., Roberts, L. G. and Wolff, S. S. (1997). The past and future history of the Internet. *Communications of the ACM*, 40(2), 102-108.

Lenk, K. and Traunmueller, R. (2000). A framework for electronic government. *Proceedings of the Eleventh International Workshop on Database and Expert Systems Applications-DEXA 2000*, Greenwich, UK, September 4-8, 271-277.

Lowe, J. T. (1996). *Internet Relay Chat-Information*! Undernet. Available on the World Wide Web at: http://www2.undernet.org:8080/~cs93jtl/IRC.html. Uxbridge, UK. Accessed November 20, 1996.

Maltz, D. and Ehrlich, K. (1995). Pointing the way: Active collaborative filtering. *Proceedings of the Conference on Human Factors in Computing Systems-CHI '95*, Denver, CO, May 7-11, 202-209.

Marshall, C., Shipman, F. M. and McCall, R. J. (1994). Putting digital libraries to work: Issues from experience with community memories. *Proceedings of the Digital Libraries Workshop-DL '94*, Newark, NJ, May 19-20.

Mauldin, M. L. (1994). Chatterbots, TinyMUDs, and the turing test: Entering the loebner prize competition. *Proceedings of the Twelfth National Conference on Artificial Intelligence-AAAI'94*, Seattle, WA, August 1-4, 16-21.

Meyer, T. and Hader, S. (1994). A MOO-based collaborative hypermedia system for WWW. *Proceedings of the Second International World-Wide Web Conference-Mosaic and the Web-WWW'94*, Urbana-Champaign, IL, October 17-20.

Microsoft. (2000). *NetMeeting Home*. Microsoft Corporation. Available on the World Wide Web at: http://www.microsoft.com/windows/NetMeeting/default.ASP. Accessed January 8, 2001.

Miller, M. (2000). *What Is a Community Network?* Available on the World Wide Web at: http://www.si.umich.edu/Community/faq/What.html. Accessed January 8, 2001. University of Michigan, School of Information, Community Networking Initiative.

Miller, S. E. (1996). *Civilising Cyberspace: Policy, Power and the Information Superhighway*. New York: ACM.

Netopia. (2000). *Netopia-Timbuktu Remote Control and Systems Administration*. Netropia Corporation. Available on the World Wide Web at: http://www.netopia.com/software/. Accessed January 8, 2001.

Newberg, L. and Rouse III, R. (1995). *Integrating the Two Most Exciting Internet Applications: The World Wide Web and Multi-User Domains*. Phoenix Project, University of Chicago. Available on the World Wide Web at: http://www.bsd.uchicago.edu/Staff/Web_Notes/MOO-WWW.html. Accessed November 20, 1996.

NIST. (2000). *National Information Infrastructure General Information*. National Institute for Standards and Technology. Available on the World Wide Web at: http://nii.nist.gov/nii/niiinfo.html. Accessed January 8, 2001.

NPR. (2001). *Vice President Gore's National Partnership for Reinventing Government*. Available on the World Wide Web at: http://www.nrp.gov. Accessed January 8, 2001.

Piller, C. (1994). Consumers want more than TV overload from the information superhighway. *MacWorld*, October.

Resnick, P. and Varian, H. R. (1997). Introduction to special issue on recommender systems. *Communications of the ACM*, 40(3), 56-58.

Rheingold, H. (1993). *The Virtual Community*. Reading, MA: Addison-Wesley.

Robinson, M. (1991). Computer-supported cooperative work: Cases and concepts. *Proceedings of the Conference on Groupware-Groupware'91*, Utrecht, NL, 59-75.

Roescheisen, M. and Mogensen, C. (1999). *ComMentor-Scalable Architecture for Shared Web Annotations as a Platform for Value-Added Providers*. Stanford Univerisity Program in Human-Computer Interaction. Available on the World Wide Web at: http://hci.stanford.edu/commentor/. Accessed January 8, 2001.

Roescheisen, M., Mogensen, C. and Winograd, T. (1995). Short paper: Interaction design for shared World Wide Web annotations. *Conference Companion of the Conference on Human Factors in Computing Systems-CHI'95*, Denver, CO, May 7-11, 328-329.

Schenk, M. (1995). *W3 Document Annotator*. Ecole des HEC, University of Lausanne, Switzerland. http://eliot.unil.ch:8085/docs/wda-Article.html. Accessed August 23, 1996.

Schuler, D. (1996). *New Community Networks: Wired For Change*. New York: Addison-Wesley.

Sclove, R. E. (1995). *Democracy and Technology*. New York: Guilford Press.

Smith, M. and Kollock, P. (1998). *Communities in Cyberspace*. London: Routledge.

Wittenburg, K., Das, D., Hill, W. and Stead, L. (1995). Group asynchronous browsing on the World Wide Web. *Proceedings of the Fourth International WWW Conference-WWW'95*, Boston, MA, December 11-14, 51-62.

Section III

Management

Chapter XIII

Strategic Knowledge Management in Local Government

Ari-Veikko Anttiroiko
University of Tampere, Finland

The success of public organizations depends increasingly on how efficiently they utilize internal and external knowledge resources in adjusting to contextual changes. This requires a special emphasis on strategic knowledge management. Referring to the theoretical and empirical works of Nonaka, Blackler, Daft and Lengel, this contribution considers how organizational design can be used to facilitate the processes in which knowledge is gathered, created, processed, used and demolished in order to build an enriched knowledge base to deal with adjustment and development issues of strategic importance. This theme is discussed with special reference to local government. The main conclusion is that uncertainty and ambiguity increased in the last decades of the 20th century, and that local governments need new management tools to respond to this change. The challenge of knowledge management in local government is to manage knowledge processes concerning ICT-based information provision, interaction and transactions. They are needed to form an enriched knowledge-intensive orientation base that serves the strategic adjustment and trend-making processes in the context of information society development.

INTRODUCTION

The success of public organizations depends increasingly on how efficiently they utilize internal and external knowledge resources in adjusting to contextual changes and in creating 'new trends' by innovative and proactive actions. This requires a special emphasis on strategic knowledge management.

Remarks on Knowledge Management Studies

Knowledge is a fundamental factor in all our orientation and action processes. This is why it appeared in organization and management theories at the very inception of these theories. Yet, since the 1960s increasing attention has been paid to strategic planning and environmental scanning. Very soon 'knowledge' became a focal concept in management literature. It emerged as a strategic resource and a key to competitiveness. Thus, the present discussion on knowledge management has its roots in theories and concepts presented several decades ago.

Certain new trends have changed the preconditions of knowledge management. First, the role assigned to information society in leading nations and public and private organizations since the early 1990s has provided a new perspective on growth, competitiveness and wealth creation. Secondly, related to IS development, the increasing role of new technologies has changed certain aspects of interaction, communication and value creation, and provided new tools for managing knowledge resources and processes. And lastly, know-how, knowledge intensiveness, learning capabilities and core competences have become key elements of competitiveness bringing socio-cultural factors to the foreground of national, regional and local development strategies.

Knowledge management is that branch of management in which attention is paid to managing organizational knowledge and knowledge processes. Three perspectives have prevailed in this field. Traditionally both theory-building and development activities have dealt with data and information management and information systems design. Since the 1980s discussion expanded to knowledge creation with special emphasis on the value of knowledge, particularly on innovations and intellectual capital. Thirdly, more contextual issues that are at the very heart of strategic knowledge management have also been discussed, the emphasis being on such themes as adaptation to the changes in external environment, managing knowledge of strategic importance, performing environmental scanning, managing network and governance relations, and creating and utilizing different forms of social capital.

Even if all these thematic areas have been recognized in the studies on public management, we still have much to do if we wish to understand the nature of knowledge processes in public organizations, and how they should be developed in the context of new forms of governance, globalization and information society development.

The Purpose of this Contribution

This chapter aims at building a coherent framework to be used in studying how organizational design can facilitate the processes in which strategic knowledge is gathered, created, processed, used and demolished in local governments. In the second section local governments' contextual relations are presented as the point of departure. On this basis local government is seen as a mediator between the broader context and local conditions.

In the third section attention is paid to the core concepts--knowledge and knowing--and their meaning for organizations. After this the discussion moves on to strategic knowledge processes.

After discussing contextual changes, the mediating role of local government and strategic knowledge processes, a new dimension is introduced, organization structures that can be used in facilitating knowledge processes. This section ends with a brief synthesis, a contextual model of strategic knowledge management adapted to local government.

Next the empirical findings of selected Finnish cases of strategic knowledge management are presented. They focus on strategies of medium-sized high-tech cities and small local governments in rural areas. Managers' information needs are moreover outlined. After this, the discussion progresses to electronic government and the informationalization of local government's knowledge processes, including the use of computer-based information systems. In the last chapter the core findings are briefly summarized.

LOCAL GOVERNMENT IN A CHANGING WORLD

The status and role of local governments vary from country to country. Yet, in most of the western countries, they enjoy constitutional recognition as self-governing bodies in charge of wide a range of administrative, service, developmental and political functions. Their practical role in most post-industrial societies has become more and more important.

Local government in general is assuming a higher profile and greater autonomy. This implies more freedom in making local choices. The decentralization trend, however, is only one side of the coin. The other one is very different, related to such megatrends as globalization and regionalization. These trends are in a dialectic relationship with each other, and help to understand why local governments' fundamental role is to seek optimal ways of utilizing global contextual changes and minimizing related side-effects for the benefit of a local community. This kind of strategic view emphasizes the need to understand the external changes, to utilize local development potential and to strike a creative balance in their dialectic relationship.

Focusing on Contextual Changes

One of the basic assumptions of strategic management is that we need information on external environment and changes therein in order to be able to adapt to or create new opportunities from these changes. For this purpose we should gather information on forces and trends, key resource controllers, and actual and potential competitors and collaborators (Bryson, 1995, p. 24). This kind of information is needed in order to position the organization and to map out its opportunities and threats, thus picturing the external dimensions of widely applied SWOT analysis (assessment of an organization's Strengths, Weaknesses, Opportunities and Threats).

Forces and trends are usually broken down into PESTs (political, economic, social and techgical trends). A more detailed description of categories of particular importance to the public sector is provided by Emmert, Crow and Shagraw (1993; cited in Bryson, 1995, pp. 88-89) that are in a slightly modified form:

1. Social and organizational complexity, i.e., technological change, globalization and increased interdependencies and interconnectedness which pose a challenge to institutions, those that were usually designed in a much more stable and regulated environment.
2. Privatization and increased interaction among public, private and non-profit sectors along the lines of the ideas of new public management, public choice theory and the conceptions of reinventing government.
3. Continuation of technological change that affects directly and indirectly organizations' functions, processes and resource allocation patterns. One of the apparent consequences in organizations is a need for 'business process reengineering.'
4. Limited public-sector resources and growth: one of the challenges of all public organizations is to deal with the problem of 'limits to growth' and the need for greater productivity and effectiveness.

5. Diversity of the workforce, customer base and citizenry including various racial, ethnic, gender and cultural forms. This differentiation will certainly complicate governance relations, service design, recruitment, management and related issues.

6. Individualism, personal responsibility and civic republicanism as a broad category refers to changes which imply that reliance on large institutions is gradually being usurped by self-reliance and greater individual responsibility.

7. Search for quality of life and sustainable development has long been recognized as an emerging megatrend, including such areas as post-materialist values, green politics, women's movements, health care issues, security issues, etc.

8. Transitions with continuity, not revolution, is a universal dilemma in the sense that there is less and less reliance on revolutionary movements, on the one hand, and emerging legitimation of 'muddling through' strategy, which counts on our chances to achieve gradual improvements in institutions' performance and economic life on the other. Yet, we are still puzzled by the paradox that typically it has been difficult to initiate major institutional change in the absence of a crisis.

In the early 21st century, it seems clear that both globalization and information society development will continue to be the most prominent megatrends for years. They are sources of changes that on many occasions simply force organizations to make the best of their knowledge processes.

Local Government as an Institutional Mediator

Indicators of such megatrends as information and knowledge intensification, networking, globalization, the Internet revolution and virtualization with their localizing aspects need to be identified utilizing both external and internal sources (see Skyrme, 1999; Choo, 1998). In this new situation local actors may create networks in order to be able to represent their locally defined interests not only at local but also at national and even international levels. In addition, new strategies and working methods are needed to anchor their policies and actions on a strong commitment to local community or local civil society. This is the context in which the dimensions of strategic knowledge processes are becoming visible, as illustrated in Figure 1 (cf. Castells, 1989).

Figure 1 provides a macro theoretical view of the context in which local government must play its role as a key institutional mediator. It is not the only actor with this kind of task, but it is nonetheless the actor with a legitimate coordinating role in promoting local development activities, strengthening democratic processes and ensuring the welfare of citizens. How to design the strategies that serve these functions is, of course, at the core of strategic management in local government, and strategic knowledge management is likewise about how to gather and create relevant information, how to facilitate and structure knowledge processes, and how to take care of implementation and evaluation.

Local Trend-Making and Adaptation Strategies

Increased interaction, interdependency and volatility on a global scale have changed both local governments' external environment and their community characteristics and organizational orientation bases as well. Local authorities and major cities in particular have gone through a profound transformation since the 1980s. They are more and more competitive and streamlined organizations with a global orientation.

In recent years local governments have shown an increasing tendency to improve their capacity to adapt to megatrends by means of resource coordination, selective intervention and disciplined support. They are becoming 'catalytic local states' seeking to achieve their

Figure 1: Local government as an institutional mediator

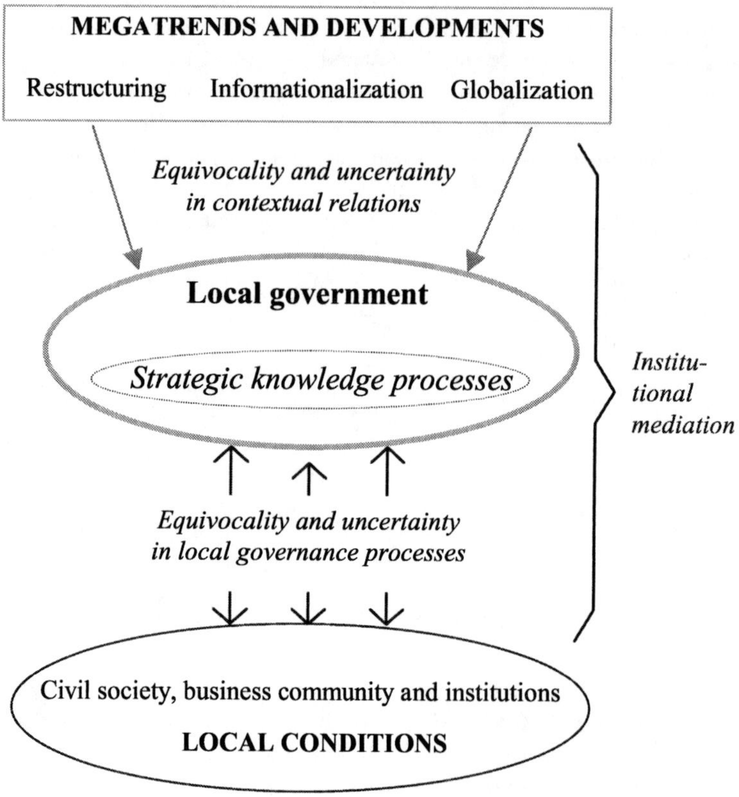

growth-oriented goals not only by relying on their own resources but also by assuming a dominant role in growth coalitions and networks, and attracting global flows of various forms of capital (cf. Weiss, 1999). During the last 20 years, new globalism has made local governments more market-oriented. At the same time disparities between localities and regions have become wider and are likely to become wider still in the years to come (Savitch, 1996).

Due to the catalytic policies referred to above, local governments are less and less restricted to their locally determined resources, even though their locational and physical characteristics still matter. New ICTs, in particular, are altering the significance of specific locations in many respects (Blakely, 1994). Where the specific local conditions still matter relate to skilled labor, technological milieu, security and pleasant environment. They are, in fact, becoming more important than proximity to energy sources, marketplace or transportation terminals. Knowledge concerning local conditions and their relational characteristics is of strategic importance for local authorities seeking to influence firms' locational decisions and to be attractive to global flows of goods, services, capital, information, know-how and people.

Big cities have always been an integral part of the world economy and international politics. Now it seems that the scene of the contemporary world is becoming more dynamic than it has ever been before in human history, with implications for global geography. This means that the "urban hierarchy" with its delocalizing and relocalizing processes is changing urban dynamism and cities' competitive positions. At the top of this hierarchy, there are the much discussed 'world cities' or global cities like New York, London and Tokyo, which benefit from the new global order. Then there are some second order world cities such as Los Angeles, Paris and Osaka, and many old industrial conurbations which struggle to restore their position in the new world order (Atlanta, Detroit, Pittsburgh, Birmingham etc.), threatened by growing metropolises of new information and service industries, especially those of the Asian cities and city states (Wu, 1996, pp. 126-129). If we look at this urban hierarchy from a European perspective, we find that London and Paris, and perhaps Berlin, are in a class of their own. In a lower rank there are europolies with some international functions (Amsterdam, Brussels, Frankfurt, etc.) and a number of more or less specialized cities, with locational, cultural, industrial or other strengths. At the bottom of the hierarchy there are thousands of remote, sparsely populated rural areas with poorly resourced local governments. They hardly can achieve long-lasting results from an attempt to attract footloose industries in growth sectors, but rather, may make the best of their situations by designing flexible adaptation strategies by utilizing local creativity and social capital, and concentrating on areas which are based on their local and regional potentials and resources. As to the rationale of local development, there is a need to point out that not every locality or region needs to try to be a 'growth machine.' On the contrary, sometimes the allocation of resources at regional, national and macro-regional levels is much more efficient if the development of remote areas is based on creative adjustment orientation.

It seems that in this global competition cities, if they wish to remain competitive or to gain some benefits form a new global order, need to design some kind of 'globalization strategies' comparable, to a degree, to those designed by companies when they start internationalizing their activities. What they need to do is sketched in the following figure.

It goes without saying that neither formal or institutional information nor the information produced by operative systems of the city government are enough in this kind of strategic positioning and adjustment process. Two special extensions are needed: more visionary information on megatrends on the one hand, and more action-oriented and dynamic view of knowledge processes on the other. These will be discussed in more detail in the following pages.

Europe is full of good examples of this kind of reorientation and restructuring in which high hopes are placed on the utilization of new ICTs and creation of competitive industrial clusters. This is evident in such cases as Barcelona in Spain, Bologna in Italy, Ennis in Ireland, the London borough of Brent in the UK, Tampere (eTampere) and Virtual Helsinki in Finland, and such European networks as the four motors for Europe (Lombardy, Baden-Württemberg, Rhônes-Alpes and Catalonia), Telecities and ERISA regions (Bremen, Shannon, Murcia, Schleswig-Holstein, Blekinge, Tampere, Västerbotten, North Karelia, etc.). (see Voyer, 1998; Anttiroiko, 1999; Borja & Castells, 1997). Positive developments have in many cases been driven by export-oriented industries in growth sectors that are dependent on know-how and advanced technology. This is why technical universities and technology centers, for example, have proved to be essential for cities' globalization strategies.

KNOWLEDGE IN ACTION

Knowledge is a key element in increasing productivity, making profits, producing services cost effectively and promoting local or regional development. What is essential is that a new informational logic of development is 'radicalizing' this underlying relation. The most characteristic feature of this logic is that knowledge intervenes in the knowledge process itself. Thus, contrary to agrarian and industrial modes of development, new sources

Figure 2: Rational model of a city's globalization strategy process (cf. Elcock, 1996, p. 50)

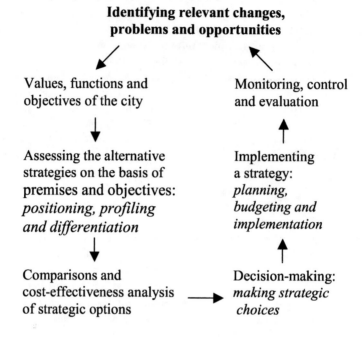

of growth and productivity revolve around knowledge and communication processes (Castells, 1989). This is why knowledge, innovations, intellectual capital, learning, new ICTs, knowledge work, knowledge management and knowledge-intensive organizations have attracted so much attention in the management literature since the 1980s (see, e.g., Crainer, 1998).

A Concept of Knowledge

From the viewpoint of value addition incorporated in the chain of informational processes, it is important to make distinctions between data, information, knowledge and wisdom. Data is composed of an encoded body of elementary variables or 'value signifiers' presented within a specific value space. Information is a kind of enriched data usually in the form of a flow of messages applicable to or relevant for a specific practice or situation. Knowledge, in general, is an enriched form of information possessed by a human being in his or her cultural context facilitating self-reflection as well as individuals' or organizations' relationships with fellow men, physical entities and socio-cultural environment. And lastly, wisdom, which is the most problematic category, refers to an individual's understanding of fundamental questions of humanity and life based on essential knowledge associated with value judgments and a high level of reflection. Even though the distinctions between these are not clear-cut, they imply that there are some content-specific differences between data management (e.g., Levitin & Redman 1998), information management (e.g., Rowley, 1998; Palmer & Weaver, 1998; Earl, 1998) and knowledge management (e.g., Blumentritt & Johnston, 1999).

Nonaka (1994, p. 15) builds his theory of organizational knowledge creation on a view that knowledge is created through a continuous dialogue between tacit and explicit knowledge. Explicit knowledge refers to codified knowledge that is transmittable in formal language, whereas tacit knowledge is characterized by personal quality and context-specific commitment, which causes difficulties in those cases in which someone is trying to formalize and communicate it. Interplay between these two epistemological dimensions can have four modes. These forms of knowledge conversion, sometimes abbreviated to SECI, are socialization (from tacit to new tacit knowledge), externalization (from tacit to explicit knowledge), combination (from explicit to new explicit knowledge) and internalization (from explicit to tacit knowledge). In organization theories these aspects have been emphasized in studies on organizational culture, information processing, knowledge creation and organizational learning respectively (see also Nonaka, Toyama & Konno, 2000, pp. 8-9.)

Nonaka argues that the interactions between these dimensions will tend to become larger in scale and faster in speed as more actors in and around the organization become involved. He also claims that a failure to build a dialogue between tacit and explicit knowledge may cause problems. In brief, in organizational knowledge creation all four modes of knowledge creation need to be organizationally managed to form an iterative cycle. These transformational aspects are both theoretically and practically most challenging in this model. As to the theory, Cook and Brown (1999, p. 385) have claimed that tacit knowledge cannot be transformed into explicit knowledge, and visa versa. Nonaka, Toyama and Konno (2000, pp. 9-13) for their part have shown convincingly how this can happen and how it can be facilitated. Even if it remains unclear whether these processes are strictly speaking about conversion in the sense that one mode of knowledge is actually 'extracted' from another mode of knowledge, this framework is heuristically appealing and sound from the point of view of common sense experience.

Core processes in this cycle can be found where shifts between different modes of knowledge conversion take place. Socialization starts characteristically when a team or field of interaction is built to facilitate the sharing of members' experiences and perspectives. The core element in this kind of knowledge conversion process (from tacit to tacit knowledge) is 'empathizing.' Externalization is triggered by successive rounds of meaningful dialogue that can be used in communicating tacit knowledge. A key precondition of this process is articulation, in which tacit knowledge becomes explicit knowledge. Combination in dealing with explicit knowledge is facilitated by coordination between team members and other parties and by the documentation of existing knowledge. Its characteristic feature is the act of connecting explicit knowledge with other explicit knowledge. And lastly, internalization can be triggered by experimentation, which relies on iterative processes of trial and error. In this process explicit knowledge becomes embodied and thus transformed into tacit knowledge (Nonaka, 1994, pp. 19-20; see also Nonaka & Konno, 1998, pp. 42-45; and Nonaka & Toyama & Konno, 2000, pp. 9-13.)

Blackler (1995, pp. 1023-1025) provides a more comprehensive classification. He identifies five images of knowledge in the literature on organizational learning: embrained, embodied, encultured, embedded and encoded knowledge. The first one, embrained knowledge, refers to knowledge dependent on conceptual skills and cognitive abilities. It is associated with abstract knowledge which has been claimed to have a vital role in Western culture. Embodied knowledge is more action oriented, situational and implicit. Encultured knowledge is about achieving a shared understanding in a given cultural context. This is an important aspect in studies on organizational cultures. Embedded knowledge is inherent in systemic routines and institutional arrangements, thus highlighting the relationships between technologies, roles, formal procedures and emergent routines. This may be seen as a sub-category of encultured knowledge with special emphasis on systemic and institutional aspects. Lastly, there is a distinct category termed encoded knowledge. This category has a more technical nature as compared to the above-mentioned. It refers to information conveyed by signs and symbols, including everything from traditional books to electronic data. In the information age encoded knowledge and related decontextualization and recontextualization processes have proved to be vital for practically all types of organizations (see Järvinen, 1999).

Processual View to Knowledge

According to Blackler (1995, p. 1033), Nonaka's distinction between tacit and explicit knowledge is rather conventional and has some serious limitations. Extension of the knowledge categories presented above is only an initial step; more profound revisions are needed. This motivates Blackler to suggest two methodological principles to guide the analysis further. First, rather than discussing knowledge as such, it is more appropriate to focus on knowledge as a process, that is, on knowing. Cook and Brown (1999, p. 382) have addressed the same point, stressing that there is need to bridge the knowledge we possess and the epistemic dimension of our actions (knowing) within organizations on the basis of an epistemology of practice. Secondly, old dualisms, like individual vs. community or social vs. technical, should be replaced by new approaches which make it easier to conceptualize the multi-dimensional processes of knowing and doing. Blackler's own suggestion is to develop a theory which is based on a contextual activity theory perspective of the process of knowing. He relies on Engeström's model when operationalizing this proposal. The basic idea is that we need to model the dynamics of knowing in order to contextualize knowledge. Knowledge emerges in an activity system which is in a state of constant flux (Blackler, 1995, pp. 1035-1039). This relates to the fact that knowledge creation cannot be managed in the traditional sense of 'management.' Rather, controlling the flow of information is only one part of the picture. The other one is managers' ability and willingness to provide conditions which stimulate active and dynamic knowledge creation within the organization (Nonaka, Toyama & Konno, 2000, p. 22).

An important advantage of activity theory is that it defines activity in its social-cultural context, as emphasized by Ruohonen and Higgins (1998, p. 383). This view suggests that knowing should be seen as socially embedded activity, that is, as mediated, situated, constructed and pragmatic activity. There are, however, some noteworthy remarks concerning the extension of this approach, for it is claimed to be inadequate with respect to the relationship between knowledge and power. The fundamental problem is that in activity theory all the elements of a social system are treated as if they were of equal analytical significance. Thus, with a view to power relations, domination and subordination, knowing is also more or less contested activity. This means that, for example, globalization, informationalization, post-Keynesian public policies and other trends that affect the capitalist system are continuously transforming the activity systems operating within this wider context (Blackler, 1995, pp. 1039-1040). It also provides some evidence of the necessity and feasibility of contextualizing the action-based socially embedded knowledge processes.

What Do We Need Knowledge For?

So far we have conceptualized knowledge as an abstract phenomenon. The next step is to ask for what purposes organizations need information or knowledge. In a rather simplistic sense, this may be described as a process in which data is gathered and processed, then it is selectively enriched, specified and interpreted, thereby transformed into information, and finally this information is combined in a creative and synthesizing process that brings out new organizational knowledge. But knowledge for what? Answers to such general questions are as varied as one may expect. Yet, in management literature two influential explanations can be identified: knowledge is needed to reduce uncertainty on the one hand, or to reduce equivocality or ambiguity, on the other (Daft and Lengel, 1986, pp. 554-557). The basic argument goes like this: as an organization has to tackle problems posed by its environment, understanding these changes helps in adjusting to them. Because managers try to look into the future in order to create strategies for coping with it, uncertainty is always there. This forms the following challenge: the less uncertainty and the more it can be reduced, the better predictions can be made and the better strategies can be designed (Elcock, 1996, p. 52).

There is an important difference between equivocality and uncertainty. Uncertainty is in a sense an external aspect of informational relations referring to the absence of answers to explicit questions, but equivocality originates in ambiguity and confusion. Thus, uncertainty can be said to be a measure of the organization's ignorance of a value for a variable in the space, whereas equivocality is rather about whether such a variable exists at all. Choo (1998, p. 246) clarifies this distinction by stating that equivocality as a lack of clarity causes opaqueness that has more to do with the confusion of multiple, plausible meanings than with the absence of sufficient quantities of information. We may further divide equivocality into two types. Communicative equivocality originates in the lack of knowledge of relevant actors' understanding, opinions, commitment or goals, whereas thematic equivocality refers to vagueness of contextual issues or abstract phenomena, including such more or less institutionally or politically occasioned changes as the impacts of the doctrine of new public management, new forms of multi-level governance, levels of taxation, or de jure regionalization or such dynamic contextual phenomena as information society development or globalization of the economy.

In order to define strategies and design structures to meet the knowledge process requirements, there is a need to identify the sources of organizational uncertainty and ambiguity. In a tentative sense these sources can be classified into three broad groups: technology, internal relations and external environment. Technology includes knowledge base, tools and techniques used to transform inputs into organizational outputs. The organization's internal relations, and interdepartmental relations in particular, are about the need for integration across the units of an organization. Our focus here is on the third factor, external environment, which causes uncertainty and equivocality as described in a previous section. Uncertainty relates to organizational intrusiveness and activeness in data collection. In short, the more stable and noncompetitive the environment, the fewer incentives there are to gather data on environment. Ambiguity in an organization's knowledge-based relationships to external environment can be operationalized on the basis of analyzability in terms of causality (Daft & Lengel, 1986, pp. 563-567). Another, slightly different way of conceptualizing the sources of uncertainty is to pay attention to uncertainty about environment, about values and about organizations, which require investigations, policy guidance and coordination respectively (Elcock, 1996, p. 53). Whatever classification is used, it is important to identify the sources of uncertainty in order to be able to focus adequately on those areas which are actually or potentially causing the most critical changes affecting the organization's fate.

STRATEGIC SENSE-MAKING AND KNOWLEDGE PROCESSES

In this section we provide a process-oriented view of knowledge. Knowledge processes contain all the elements of the conceptual hierarchy of knowledge (data, information, knowledge). Our focus is only on strategic knowledge processes. For analytical purposes it is divided into two discrete forms. We begin by discussing an overall strategic knowledge process at a high level of abstraction, referring to it as a sense-making process. It is an epistemic view of strategic adaptation process thus emphasizing the general aspects of the relationship between an organization and its environment (cf. the strategy process described earlier). More concrete, 'formal' and procedural aspects of this process are simply referred to as knowledge process. This includes not only the formal procedural aspects of knowledge-related activities but also the most concrete data and information management functions, even though the latter are not discussed explicitly in this chapter.

Sense-Making Processes

In the early organization theories for public administration, knowledge was predominantly conceptualized within the internal administrative processes, thus to be conceived of bureaucratic procedures, rationalization of work processes, identification of administrative functions and aspects of decision making. New perspectives emerged around the 1960s. This was the time when H. Igor Ansoff developed his ideas of strategic planning and Francis J. Aguilar (1967) introduced the concept of environmental scanning, to name just two examples. The most influential book at that time was probably Ansoff's *Corporate Strategy*, published in 1965, followed by *Strategic Management* in 1979. As a part of emerging agenda in business life, increased attention was paid to how companies seek and process information of strategic importance, for the view of strategic management relied on strategic diagnosis and rational strategic planning process (Crainer, 1998; Anttiroiko & Savolainen, 2000). Even if strategic management in its original form became too formalized and removed from reality, as Henry Mintzberg and many others claimed, its fundamental insights have remained valuable for management science. Such new concepts as Michael Porter's theory of competitive advantage, Mintzberg's analysis of managerial work, and Norton and Kaplan's concept of Balanced Scorecard are facing the very same dilemma: how to determine the importance of knowledge and to acquire cost-effectively the knowledge of strategic importance.

One of the basic observations in strategic management literature is that the organization's capacity relates to the degree of environmental change or turbulence. In a stable environment routine functions are easy to perform without much sensitivity to contextual changes. This, however, is no longer the kind of world we are living in. Even public organizations are operating in an increasingly dynamic environment with greater demands and requirements. Also, the ideas of public choice and new public management have changed our views of public sector and the way it performs and how it should perform its functions. Thus, public organizations need new tools in order to form coherent and 'informationally' rich orientation base which is, ultimately, about sense-making.

This sense-making process can be conceptualized in alternative ways, but all the models contain some basic elements. Let us look at them briefly. The process starts when some dramatic changes take place in the organization's environment. In a challenging situation emerging, managers and other people involved have to try to map out what this is all about and how significantly it can affect the organization's life. This process continues with constructing conceptions and definitions that help to conceptualize the change and trace its sources and causes. After this there is a need to take a closer look at those phenomena that are most relevant for the organization. This helps to identify the most promising ideas and interpretations and go further in assessing and analyzing them (cf. Weick, 1995).

In the third phase of this sense-making process, organization has to deal with choices and selections. The point is that observations and raw data must be assessed on the basis of previous experiences. What needs to be decided is whether this particular change can be understood within the framework of existing explanatory and interpretative models or whether totally new ones must be constructed. All this is needed in a final decision-making phase of the process. The last phase of the process is about retention, in which successful sense-making processes and results are stored into the organizational memory. This creates an 'epistemic warehouse' which is utilized when new changes and challenges are faced in the future. The function of sense-making is to offer means to solve ambiguous problems by sharing information and knowledge and using them in building collective orientation base for the organization (cf. Weick, 1995).

Operationalizing the Strategic Knowledge Process

Nonaka (1994, 32) pays attention to an organization's ability to deal with the task of acquiring, creating, exploiting and accumulating new knowledge. This formulation takes us very close to how the knowledge process can be operationalized. More comprehensive classification is provided by Pertti Järvinen (1999), who concludes that with regard to the lifecycle of knowledge, there are four main processes: creation, use, store and demolish. Following these ideas the **knowledge process** can be defined as a collective process in which information is collected, created, processed, used or demolished in order to form an enriched knowledge-intensive orientation base for taking care of an organization's knowledge management tasks. Strategic knowledge processes are those aspects of knowledge processes which have the most profound and far-reaching impact on an organization's adjustment to contextual changes and its capacity to create new trends.

In the contemporary world the operating environment of institutions or organizations is relatively complex, characterized by varying degrees of interdependencies and various forms of systemic and governance relations. In order to manage the interactions and transactions in this kind of environment, a sufficient level of empirical knowledge and theoretical understanding is needed to guarantee an organization's success. This leads to two conceptual clarifications. First, strategic knowledge is in its most essential sense embrained knowledge. Secondly, strategic knowledge is to a large extent explicit knowledge, as opposed to tacit knowledge, and its characteristic form of knowledge conversion is combination. Thus, new strategic knowledge that helps in the organization's adaptation and trend-making processes can be created by reconfiguring and accumulating embrained knowledge through sorting, adding, recategorizing and recontextualizing (Järvinen, 1999, p. 6). Suffice it to say here that these are meant to show only some essential features of strategic knowledge, and thus are not to be taken categorically.

As to the organization's knowledge-based relation to environment, there are changes in which complexity relates in an essential sense to symbolic and cultural mediation processes. What this implies leads to another conceptual aspect: strategic issues in their most challenging forms concern equivocality. Related to this we may specify that strategic issues belong to a domain in which the structural characteristics of the organization for reducing 'uncertainty' relate primarily to embrained knowledge and likewise for reducing 'equivocality' to encultured knowledge. Accordingly, we end up in a situation in which successful organizational design favors the qualities of symbol-analyst-dependent and communication-intensive organizations.

With regard to embrained and explicit knowledge, the main activities are **collecting** and **processing** information and synthesizing it. But, as Nonaka (1994) and many others point out, this is not enough when dealing with knowledge creation. Consequently, comprehension, imagination, insights and innovations have a vital role to play in the knowledge-**creation** process, especially when dealing with problems of equivocality. This is how a specific form of tacit knowledge, that which is very close to intuitive and visionary activities, comes into the picture. This is why one-dimensional or formal concepts of strategic knowledge need to be redefined by introducing more contextual and action-oriented dimensions. (On a model of knowledge creation see, Nonaka & Toyama & Konno, 2000.)

Successful sense-making and knowledge processes do not end when the organization has been fed by the information that is expected to serve the organization's management and decision-making functions. This is, in fact, just the beginning, for the ability to utilize and apply information is the key to successful action and interaction. **Use** of knowledge covers several activities, such as representing, managing, measuring, retrieving, utilizing and disseminating knowledge. These are also closely associated to tacit knowledge, socialization and learning by doing. Combining explicit and tacit knowledge requires more or less integrated approaches, as suggested in a theory of competence-based strategic management (see Järvinen, 2000, pp. 157-160).

The last category of knowledge process refers to actions with intentions for getting rid of useless information or harmful orientations. Accordingly, **demolishing** knowledge is present in all these phases reflecting a need to dispense with useless data, to cope with information overload, to give up convictions or beliefs that have proved to be false and to unlearn harmful habits (cf. Järvinen, 1999).

Sense-Making and Knowledge Strategy

In the strategic knowledge processes, the organization seeks information on environmental changes and utilizes it in strategy formulation. A basic model of the organizational knowledge-based adaptation process is presented in the figure on the following page.

Figure 3 illustrates that knowledge forms an integral part of the organization's overall sense-making process. Knowledge processes are needed to create information that supplies the constantly changing 'epistemic warehouse' which can be utilized in different phases of reactive adaptation and proactive trend-making processes. Along with this, the model shows that beside the actual knowledge processes–collecting, creating, processing, using and demolishing information–both knowledge sharing and communication processes are of central importance. These social dimensions must be designed by introducing general communicative principles and information system solutions for the organization.

What is essential here is that the relevance of knowledge and knowledge systems is dependent on type of organization, industry or field of operation and the broader environment. Thus, there is no single success strategy in this. For a specific organization in a challenging situation, it may be vital to develop the human resource-based knowledge strategy, whereas in other conditions the sustainable success of an organization may require the building of organizational techniques that support more routinized knowledge processes. Thus, strategic competence management may vary on the basis of the importance of, let us say, organizational capabilities, technological arrangements, human capacity and knowledge assets for an organization's competitive advantage. According to Kirjavainen (2000), there are such competence strategies as:

- capability of managing knowledge, know-how and competences;
- having specific kinds of knowledge or competencies;
- having exceptional transformational capacity;
- having strengths in the human dimension: learning, creativity, motivation, etc.

Figure 3: Strategic knowledge process of the organization

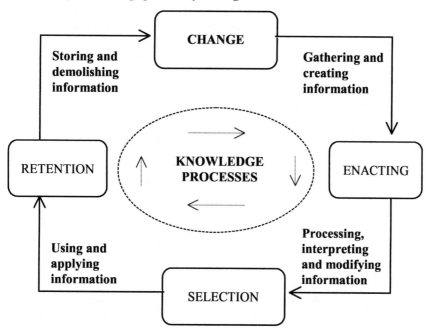

In this way knowledge is combined with knowing at a strategic level. This is not, ultimately, so much about new techniques but about change in organization and management culture.

ORGANIZATION TYPES AND STRUCTURES

The last element in our framework for strategic knowledge management in local government is about organization structure. All the basic themes discussed so far–external environment, knowledge and knowledge processes–have much to do with organizations and their design. In this section the discussion deals with how contextual changes and especially increased knowledge-intensiveness affect organizations in general. After this a more detailed description is provided of why and how these tendencies have to be taken into account in organizational design. And lastly, all the elements are synthesized into a model of knowledge management in local government.

Knowledge-Based Organization Typology

Organizational needs and competencies vary greatly on the basis of the mission and function of an organization, its position in the institutional field and the arrangement of its internal relations. All these have direct and indirect connections to the organization's relation to its external environment.

Mintzberg (1993) has proved convincingly how organizational structure tends to relate to external environment. Blackler (1995, pp. 1026-1030) takes this further by adding to this a third dimension, knowledge. He classifies organizations by focusing on whether an organization has to deal with routine problems or unfamiliar issues, and whether its capacity is determined by the insights of key individuals or more collective efforts. These and the four knowledge types (those presented in a previous section except for encoded knowledge) provide conceptual tools for systematizing this field, as presented in Figure 4.

Blackler's argument is that because of certain contextual changes, organizational forms develop towards symbolic-analyst-dependent organizations and communication-intensive organizations in particular. We may legitimately claim that these forms express the reflexive appropriation of knowledge rooted in reflexive and dynamic aspects of modernization (see Giddens, 1997). It is likely that changes that feed ambiguity will determine the institutional and organizational adjustment process and thus transform the aspects of organizational design and knowledge processes. In accordance with this, the trend seems to be away from dependence on embodied and embedded knowledge, and towards more intensive creation and use of embrained and encultured knowledge.

Figure 4: Knowledge-based organization typology (Blackler, 1995, p. 1030)

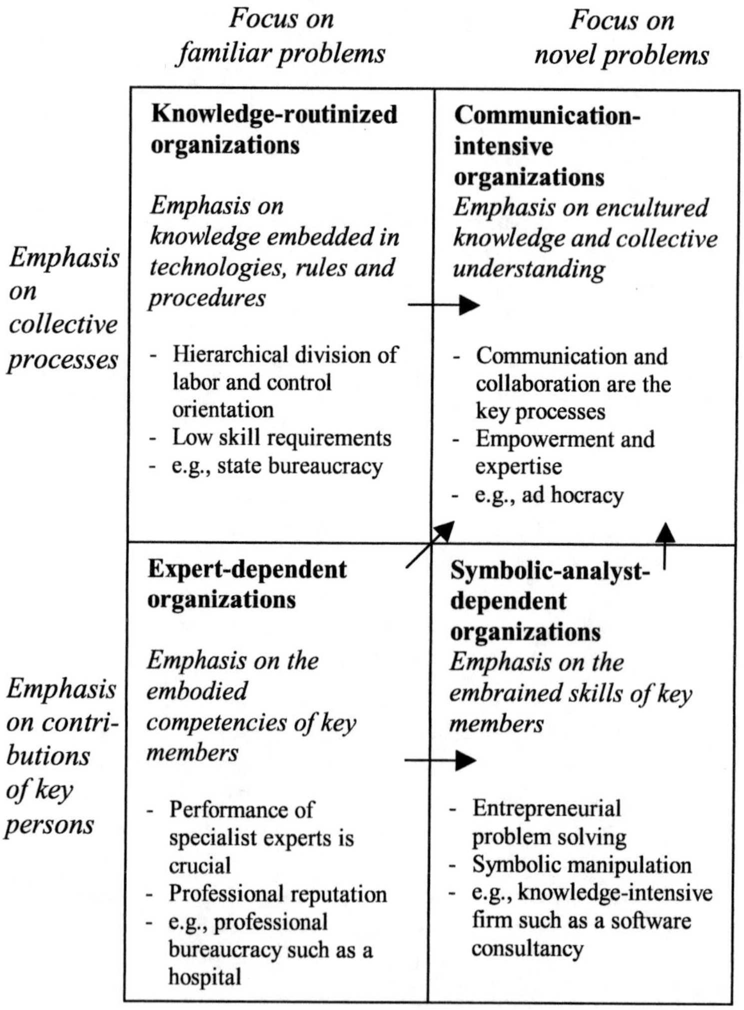

	Focus on familiar problems	*Focus on novel problems*
Emphasis on collective processes	**Knowledge-routinized organizations** *Emphasis on knowledge embedded in technologies, rules and procedures* - Hierarchical division of labor and control orientation - Low skill requirements - e.g., state bureaucracy	**Communication-intensive organizations** *Emphasis on encultured knowledge and collective understanding* - Communication and collaboration are the key processes - Empowerment and expertise - e.g., ad hocracy
Emphasis on contributions of key persons	**Expert-dependent organizations** *Emphasis on the embodied competencies of key members* - Performance of specialist experts is crucial - Professional reputation - e.g., professional bureaucracy such as a hospital	**Symbolic-analyst-dependent organizations** *Emphasis on the embrained skills of key members* - Entrepreneurial problem solving - Symbolic manipulation - e.g., knowledge-intensive firm such as a software consultancy

Design of the Organization Structure

Following Daft and Lengel (1986, p. 559), we may ask how organization structures and support systems should be designed in order to meet the need to reduce uncertainty and equivocality. As the previous discussion suggests, in order to reduce uncertainty, an organization has to provide sufficient information; and to deal with equivocality, it is information of suitable richness and its usefulness in sense-making that matters. Thus, in respect to uncertainty, well-designed organization structure facilitates the amount of information needed for management control, coordination and decentralization, and as to reducing equivocality, structural design may help to enable debate, clarification and enactment, thus providing tools for finding solutions to ambiguous dilemmas.

Daft and Lengel (1986, pp. 560-561) propose seven structural mechanisms that help to deal with both uncertainty and equivocality issues in varying degrees. These are presented in Figure 5. The idea is that these form a continuum starting from tools to be used to tackle well-defined problems and thus to reduce uncertainty, and proceeding towards more communicative and sensitive mechanisms designed to facilitate the process of reducing equivocality.

Daft and Lengel's model shows illuminatingly how the nature of a problem relates to both the nature of media used and the content of knowledge. Thus, if we only have to know how to act in a simple situation, provision of formal procedures can help us to cope with the situation. If we want to reduce uncertainty, we may use formal information systems which rely on four sources of information: (a) internal operative information gathered from financial and other systems; (b) internal normative information sources, like mission statements, objectives and principles of action; (c) external information sources such as special reports of various organizations, databases and mass media; and lastly relatively seldom utilized sources of (d) systematically arranged personal or group information. This is why some simple problems of uncertainty can be solved by making regulations or at least by utilizing formal information systems such as MIS, DSS or EIS. These systems have their limitations even if they provide access to a single database where all current financial and operational data on an organization can be found. This may be a part of the reason why in

Figure 5: Structural elements in reducing uncertainty and equivocality (Daft & Lengel, 1986, p. 561)

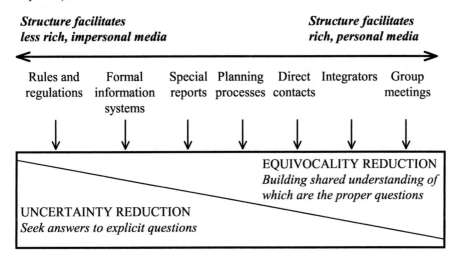

practice executives have tended to use other managers and informants and also their own experiences and intuitions as their primary information sources (Leidner & Elam, 1993). As Daft and Lengel's model reveals, there are unanalyzable and non-routine tasks and problems that cannot be solved by using formal systems. If we wish to specify the mission of an expert organization, we need 'rich' media that facilitates communication and helps us to find shared understanding. These problems are more 'qualitative' in nature and have more to do with collective and also broader normative aspects than those of more structured problems (cf. Markus & Robey, 1988, p. 587).

Appropriate organizational design may help an organization's ability to create and utilize new knowledge. Nonaka (1994) has paid special attention to how this kind of design can improve the knowledge-creation process, i.e., how to improve an organization's strategic ability to acquire, create, exploit and accumulate new knowledge continuously and repeatedly in an iterative process. He uses the term hypertext organization to indicate such an organizational design. The core feature of such an organization is "the ability to switch between the various 'contexts' of knowledge creation to accommodate changing requirements from situations both inside and outside the organization," as expressed by Nonaka. In principle, the challenge is to combine the efficiency and stability of a hierarchical organization with the dynamism of the flat, cross-functional task force organization. It is a process of orchestrating different rhythms or 'natural frequencies' generated by the hierarchical organization and dynamic teams (Nonaka, 1994, 32-33).

Synthesis of Knowledge Management in Local Government

In order to strengthen local capacity, there is a need to develop organization structure and mechanisms that support local governments' strategic adjustment and trend-making processes. The first task in doing so is to understand the local preconditions and their relation to contextual changes. Local government is seen as an institutional mediator in this process. When this is integrated with applied knowledge-based organization typology and organizational mechanisms, we have all the necessary elements for building a contextual model of strategic knowledge management applied to local government, as illustrated in Figure 6.

This model suggests that local governments have to reconnoiter the task and service branch-related environments they have to cope with, and ascertain the knowledge requirements of each in order to understand what organizational structures and mechanisms are needed to facilitate their knowledge processes. In this model Blackler's four-fold typology is used tentatively to differentiate between departments or units of a city. When this is combined with Daft and Lengel's description of basic facilitation mechanisms, we get a picture of how local governments' top management may group their organizational units and facilitate their knowledge processes so that their knowledge-based resources and potentials can be identified and utilized in the best possible way.

KNOWLEDGE-BASED STRATEGIC MANAGEMENT–EMPIRICAL FINDINGS

What is essential in local government is its constitutional or legal framework, territorial dimension and political nature. It is also a multi-contact organization and multi-sectoral service provider with huge and diverse knowledge requirements. What characterizes local government is the institutional framework that mediates subjects, objects and working

Figure 6: Contextual model of strategic knowledge management in local government

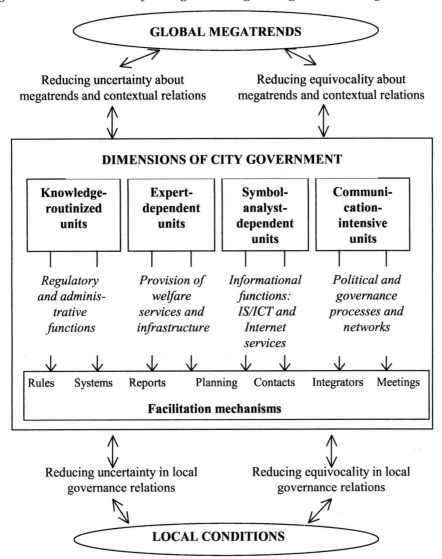

arenas in various activity systems (education, health care, social welfare, industrial policy, etc.). There are remarkable differences between the core elements of these activity systems depending on their organizational settings, positions, functions and environmental relations. These preconditions suffice to indicate that there is a risk of repeating the besetting sin of old-fashioned strategic planning: trying to tackle too many issues, analyze too much information or appease too many conflicting interests. This is why some have suggested that in the public sector managers should aim to achieve a series of 'small wins' as steps towards more ambitious goals instead of a rational once-for-all 'big win.' This requires a selective approach to making strategic choices (Elcock, 1996, pp. 51-52).

The most typical organization types in local government with regard to knowledge are knowledge-routinized and expert-dependent organizations, the latter holding mainly for specialized service units, such as hospitals. A shift towards communication-intensive forms of organization has occurred since the early 1990s. Certain symbol-intensive processes are also on the increase. Emerging informational logic of service provision, formation of virtual cities, increased use of management support systems, much discussed new forms of teledemocracy and new working methods and governance relations which are based on networking, partnership and cooperation, all these reflect contextual trends and have a vital impact on knowledge processes in local government (see Grönlund, 2000; Anttiroiko & Savolainen, 1999).

As regards local authorities' responses to uncertainty and increased complexity, the trend has clearly been towards a more active role in data collection and more sophisticated methods of environmental scanning. At the same time the problems of defining information needs and providing accurate and relevant information are becoming much more critical than they have been in a more stable and predictable environment. As presented in the framework, increased ambiguity causes problems of a special kind. In local government's knowledge-based relationships to the external environment, this sense-making requirement is likely to strengthen internal entrepreneurship and empowerment as well as project-based coordination and management of governance relations.

What follows is a brief look at selected empirical aspects of knowledge management in local government. The discussion begins with local success strategies and continues to top management's information needs and utilization of computer-based management support systems.

Strategies of Finnish High-Tech Cities

Helsinki, the capital of Finland, and its surrounding area have a unique position in Finnish economy and social life as the unchallenged information metropolis of the country. However, as a unique case it is not discussed here. Instead, we focus on certain growth centers with an industrial heritage and a dynamic economy, cities that have formulated strategies to cope with the new geography of the information age. The cities of Tampere, Oulu and Jyväskylä in particular with their strong global and developmental orientations have designed and implemented strategies that have been successful, or at least improved their image. They share an ability to form a functional 'golden triad' of developmentally oriented city government, proactive universities and leading business partners like Nokia Corporation. In comparison cities like Lahti in the interior or Pori in the costal area have suffered from having no university and being too dependent on domestically oriented labor-intensive industries. University cities like Kuopio in Eastern Finland or Vaasa in the costal area are hard pressed to keep pace with change. What explains these differences? Let us look briefly at what characterizes the three growth centers and their sense-making processes.

Tampere is an old industrial city that has become one of the leading high-tech cities in Finland. It has almost 200,000 inhabitants, being the second largest regional center in Finland. The city adapted new policies relatively quickly after the advent of the Internet in Finland in the early 1990s. In 1997 the City Council endorsed the Tampere City Strategy entitled *Information is the Key to the Future* that defined guidelines for developing the city in partnership with other agencies. One of the key objectives was to become a hub in the information society while maintaining a role as one of the leading industrial centers in Finland (Anttiroiko & Savolainen, 1999).

The story does not end here. On the contrary, in December 2000 the city launched the eTampere program, being at the moment the most ambitious development plan in Finland, and expected to make Tampere a key city within the global information society by strengthening the knowledge base, generating new business and creating new electronic public services available to all citizens. The program includes the establishment of the Information Society Institute (ISI), the Research & Evaluation Laboratory (RELab), the eEconomy Business School, the eTampere Business Accelerator, the Technology engine programs and the Infocity program focusing on the city's online services. The eTampere program is in line with the European Union's eEurope program launched in December 1999 (eTampere 2000; see also European Commission, 1999).

Even if the plan appears a bold venture, a five-year development project with a budget of some 130 million euros and requiring a huge amount of venture capital, it has three important mainstays. First, its strategic lines are in accordance with the megatrends of our age. Second, Tampere already has proved to be one of the leaders in the high-tech industry. For example, Communicator was developed by Nokia in Tampere. In addition, key players from the city government, universities and business hold stakes in the project and the implementation is decentralized. Yet, the eTampere program is coordinated along the lines of 'management by contract' by the city government (see http://www.tampere.fi/etampere).

The City of **Oulu** is the largest city in northern Finland. The population of the City of Oulu itself is over 120,000 inhabitants, and the whole Oulu Region has almost 200,000 inhabitants. Nowadays Oulu is well known for its technology. This high-tech growth started after the establishment of the University of Oulu in 1958. In the region there are two science parks, Technopolis and Medipolis. In addition, there is a technology center known as Ii Micropolis and several research institutes. The region is well known for its rapidly growing high-tech industry, which sells its products throughout the world. The most famous company in this field is Nokia. As to the diffusion of innovations, Oulu set up the first science park in Scandinavia in the early 1980s and also the first municipal web site in Finland in the early 1990s (see http://www.ouka.fi).

The most recent Finnish "success story," the City of Jyväskylä, is a good example of how the city that faced an economic depression in the early 1990s was able to recover and restructure its industrial base relatively quickly. Jyväskylä is located in the lake district of central Finland. It is a lively university town with about 80,000 inhabitants and 35,000 students.

In the 1990s the City of **Jyväskylä** gained a reputation as a highly dynamic and business-friendly city. It has been widely recognized that the City Manager, Pekka Kettunen, had a pivotal role in this process. As to the strategic action lines, a key to this development seems to be, more than anything, decisive and strategically well-grounded investments in targeted and high-quality ICT education which ultimately attracted one of Nokia's R&D units and other companies to the city. Jyväskylä's strategic choice plus its compact city structure, pleasant environment and entrepreneur-friendly city policy, have given it good chances to survive in the competition with other medium-sized technocities in Europe (cf. Väyrynen, 1999, pp. 178-179).

In the city strategy of Jyväskylä entitled *Towards the City of Know-How Through Shared Growth* (in Finnish, *Osaavaan Jyväskylään Yhteisen Kasvun Kautta*), the city's point of departure has been the ability to react quickly and with the right strategic choices to contextual changes. And what it takes is functional and effective partnership policy and a management that aims at constant renewal.

In a 'municipal contest' in 1999, Jyväskylä was acclaimed the most business-friendly town in Finland. In a study published in Spring 2000, the most attractive places to move in Finland were Tampere, Jyväskylä and Turku. Jyväskylä's strength is also its pleasant environment, as evidenced in some surveys. This all reflects the image of Jyväskylä as an active and creative city (see http://www.jyvaskyla.fi).

What seems to be common to these successful, innovative and forward-looking cities is the well-managed governance relations and high level of social capital (including partnerships between city government, universities and business), early diffusion of innovations related to IS development (as in the cases of Oulu and Tampere in particular) and strategically targeted measures designed to create preconditions for high-tech industries and certain other growth sectors.

Realities in Rural Areas—The Case of Himanka

Realities in small rural municipalities are very different from those of leading high-tech cities. We look at this side of the picture through the empirical case of municipality of Himanka (see Anttiroiko & Savolainen, 2000).

Himanka is a small rural local community in central Ostrobothnia with some 3,300 inhabitants. It is located in the coastal area of the Gulf of Bothnia. Just like other small municipalities, Himanka was afflicted by the severe depression that spread throughout Finland in the first half of the 1990s accompanied by a government policy shift towards a more streamlined competitiveness policy emphasizing the role of urban centers as the engines of growth. What we discuss here is how one of the key figures of the municipality of Himanka, Administrative Manager Pirjo Mansikkamäki, sees the present situation (she was interviewed by the author in April 2000). The idea is to show the realities small municipalities have to cope with when making their strategic choices.

First of all, it is worth stressing that planning orientation is almost the opposite to what it was in the 1970s. The age of 'planning enthusiasm' in Finland and other Nordic countries, characterized by administrations able and willing to produce a huge amount of comprehensive planning documents, is over. Planning and administrative officials conceded that this system produces long-term plans that have less and less relevance in a dynamic environment. This implies that instead of drafting rationally constructed comprehensive planning documents, emphasis is put on a minimalist but focused strategic planning and management process. It also seems that the trend extrapolations or even scenarios are losing part of their relevance as tools of strategic management. In short, uncertainty has increased dramatically since the early 1990s and there are no simple tools for use in sense-making processes.

In practice, small municipalities are still very dependent on information from the wider institutional system that affects their service provision and financial position. Thus, decisions taken by central government are considered to be important. The supranational decision making of the European Union also has a growing impact on local communities, on their economic life and agriculture in particular. On both of these higher institutional levels, decisions and policy lines have a tendency to increase uncertainty at the local level. It is relatively commonly believed in the municipalities in rural Finland that EU enlargement will reduce the support for rural and remote areas in advanced member states of the Union. This bodes profound changes in rural areas all over the country.

Not only the information on decisions and plans of key institutional actors, but also research and statistical data have a relevance in managing small municipalities. The biggest problem so far seems to be the way this information is presented: it should be more clear and concise in order to be useful. What is needed is the kind of information that helps local politicians and officials assess the expected impacts and consequences of different solutions and make the best possible choices between them. Knowledge of causal relationships, even in a rather schematic form, is considered to be the most useful, though it is at the same time the kind of information that is difficult to produce.

As to the content of information, in strategic planning in small municipalities, among the most important indicators are jobs and inhabitants. Changes in population can very soon be seen in such areas as basic education, vocational education and services designed for elderly people. It goes without saying that all kinds of economic information is vital for decision making, too. In allocating, monitoring and controlling financial resources, the use of the municipality's own operational information system is generally assumed to be particularly useful (cf. Kraemer et al., 1993). Comparative data is also important, though it does not help much in actual decision making after all (cf. Anttiroiko & Kallio, 1999; Anttiroiko, 2000, p. 27; for broader empirical evidence on these, see Kraemer et al., 1993; Hasan & Hasan, 1997).

What is strategically one of the most decisive elements in many local communities is the general objective to maintain their independence and local autonomy. The municipality of Himanka, for example, wishes to continue to be an independent local authority even if its chances of coping with emerging challenges and external pressures are rather limited. This is a clear value stance that does not gain much support from the outside world. Yet, this both compels and motivates the development of local community, and gives at least one locally shared value judgment that can be used in assessing strategic options. And why is this local autonomy important? This is simply because it makes genuine local choices possible. (cf. Stewart, 1986).

Present local conditions and contextual changes have led to a situation in which small local authorities are forced to be rather reactive. This means simply that the local authority reacts after the problem has actualized. This does not mean, however, that the only strategy adapted is one of resignation. For example, in the municipality of Himanka, top management has developed a sort of pragmatic model of strategic choices in which strategic thinking is built into the operational solutions. Accordingly, due to limited strategic planning capacity as well as increased uncertainty, comprehensive strategy documents or municipal plans may not be the most efficient ways of communicating local strategies. Instead, strategic lines are to be found implicitly in strategic actions. Administrative Manager Mansikkamäki describes this situation in the following way: "Instead of objectives and measures written down in a comprehensive local development plan, reactions to changes in environment are constructed in quick decisions and actions. For example, in the municipality of Himanka, in the early 1990s, certain posts that were not in the area of provision of basic services were withdrawn, necessary investments in ICTs were made, and welfare and health services were reorganized by establishing decentralized and more flexible service solutions. All these actions were, in fact, based on decision making that was proactive and was based on prediction of the directions of change."

Himanka's action lines are very similar to those made in other parts of Europe in which local authorities have showed some responsiveness to external pressures and challenges and started to reform their organizational structures, processes and cultures. Chris Moore (1991) identified four kinds of responses to change in Britain in the 1980s: resignation, resistance, radical reform and more pragmatic reformism. The Municipality of Himanka seems to follow the lines of 'pragmatic reformism' just like most of the other Finnish rural municipalities which try to adapt to environmental constraints but reject, to a degree, the policy lines of the Finnish "Rainbow Government" led by social democrats and a conservative national coalition.

What Mansikkamäki emphasizes is that even a reactive approach contains some elements that stimulate strategic thinking. It forces decision makers to consider new challenges and short-term solutions on the basis of their long-term consequences. And, even more important, these reactions require some degree of efficiency and organizational capacity. If local communities did not have competent administrative and service organizations, they would not be able to adapt even to short-term changes. This is how municipalities contribute to strengthening state capacity and building locally designed adaptation strategies.

Managers' View of Their Information Needs

Success strategies cannot be created without a proper knowledge base. One of the key questions that relates to strategic knowledge management is what kind of knowledge the top management of local government needs.

We concentrate here on the need for information on the external environment. These questions were touched upon in a survey on the uses of management support systems in local government in Finland (Anttiroiko & Kallio, 1999; Anttiroiko, 2000). It was conducted electronically in June 1998. E-mail and a link to the survey site were sent to 55 municipalities to be distributed to the organization (to the top management, heads of department and chief information officers). Within set time limits 72 officials from 37 municipalities responded to this e-survey. Most of them were from cities with more than 20,000 inhabitants. What is essential to point out here is that the questionnaire was 'qualitative' in the sense that informants had to construct their answers by themselves having no predetermined options or answer categories.

In the e-survey in question, informants' information needs concerning external environment were elicited. Answers are presented in Table 1.

What city managers see as vital is the comparative information on other municipalities, especially with those in the same size category or in the same region. This reveals how benchmarking and related ideas have taken root in present-day local government. The need for this kind of information is exceptionally important in education, social welfare and health care, and central administration as well. It is obvious from the answers given that city

Table 1: Information needs in external environment in Finnish cities

Managers' need of information on external environment	Total % (n=72)
Comparisons with other municipalities	39
Demographic trends and developments	29
Employment	29
National economy–present state and future prospects	19
Central government's decisions and measures	19
Changes in legislation	14
The EU and European policies	10
Taxation and estimates on tax revenues	7

management is not satisfied with the present situation: comparative information is not properly available and it is gathered too haphazardly.

Another important area of information need concerned the population trends. This is vital for resource allocation and marketing services. Equally important was the information on employment and unemployment trends. Both these areas were considered important especially by top managers in the central administration of municipalities, financial and planning officials, and managers in social welfare and health care sectors. As to the availability of such information, on the basis of the answers given by informants, the present information systems seem to serve these information needs relatively well. Other information on external environment concerned national economic conditions, government decisions, legislation, the European Union and general information on tax revenues, as presented in Table 1.

If these are basic information needs, how do managers obtain this information? Information on external environment must usually be gathered from various external sources. Let us take a closer look at the sources the management of central administration and financial and planning officials have considered to be most important. In the Finnish context the main sources are The Finnish Association of Local and Regional Authorities, Statistics Finland and mass media (newspapers, radio, TV). In a number of answers the Internet (or WWW in particular) was also mentioned.

What seems obvious from this study is that the most clearly identified information needs of city managers are in the area of explicit information on the changes of environment (comparisons, population, employment, economy). Thus, using Blackler's typology, this is about strengthening the organization's capacity to acquire embrained knowledge.

Another observation is that the information on 'dynamic processes,' such as employment or population, is considered to be more important than that of 'institutionally constructed' information (government, legislation, the EU, taxation), the latter being rather systemic in nature. This reveals that a profound transformation has already taken place in the sense that city managers are more and more interested in dynamic contextual factors.

A NEW DIMENSION: KNOWLEDGE MANAGEMENT OF E-GOVERNMENT

The discussion about electronic government reflects a transition to a new technological trajectory in public administration (see Bellamy 1996; Bellamy & Taylor, 1998). Even though we are able to construct a rather schematic picture of what public administration will look like 10 years from now, changes in knowledge processes can be expected to be profound. The basic assumption behind this is that IS development is characterized by increased technological mediation in social action and interaction, which affects the future development of government at every institutional level. One concrete expression of this is the emergence of computer-based information systems, which are touched upon as an example of this trend.

Towards Electronic Government

One of the hot topics in discussions about IS revolves around electronic government (e-Government), or online government. This new concept refers to the use of the Internet in order to guarantee easy access to public sector information, provide a wide range of electronic public services, enhance citizen participation through electronic means and use ICTs in taking care of internal procedures and external relations of administrations. In Europe the EU has been active in developing this aspect of IS. The EU's perspective emphasizes easy access to public sector information for European citizens and businesses with the aim of increasing the number of Internet users and promoting IS development. Another emphasis is on the use of government services and increasing interaction and participation that are expected to ensure better transparency (European Commission, 1999).

A good example of national government's commitment to e-Government comes from Britain. Namely, as Modernising Government (1999) as one of the most ambitious policy documents of the 1990s reveals, in Britain by 2002 it should be possible to accomplish some 25% of dealings with government electronically, this figure to increase to 50% by 2005 and to reach 100% by 2008. Local authorities are expected to set their own targets for electronic delivery.

The following 10 points show what the British government considers to be vital for the electronic government (quoted from Modernising Government, 1999):

1. Household access to electronic services through developments such as interactive TV. But there will also be a very wide range of public access points, with advice on hand.
2. Much more user-friendly, inexpensive and multi-functional technology such as TV, telephones and broadcasting converge.
3. As part of this, less dependence on keyboard skills as remote control pads, voice command, touch screens, video-conferencing and other developments make it easier for users to operate and benefit from new technology. But other skills will be built up in schools, in the workplace and across the community.
4. Continuing dramatic increases in computing power, and in the power of networked computing, together enabling government services to be delivered more conveniently, accurately, quickly and securely.
5. Wide-scale take-up of multi-purpose smartcards, with which citizens can identify themselves, use services, safeguard their privacy and, increasingly, make and receive payments. Cards will also evolve into still more powerful technologies.
6. Government forms and other processes which are interactive, guided by on-line help and advice, and collect all the necessary information in one go.
7. Smarter knowledge management across government, which increasingly enables government to harness its data and experience more effectively, and to work in new ways.
8. Use of government Web sites and other access points as single gateways, often structured around life episodes, to a whole range of related government services or functions.
9. Repackaging of government services or functions, often through partnerships with the private sector, local government or the voluntary sector, so that they can be provided more effectively.
10. Flexible invest to save approaches, where the huge potential of new technology to increase efficiency is used imaginatively to fund better-designed processes.

In all, this view of the information age government reveals what dramatic changes are likely to take place in the near future.

Knowledge Processes in e-Government at the Local Level

The electronic government at the local level may be conceptualized in different ways depending on the criteria used. From a relational viewpoint there are the following basic electronically mediated governance relations:

- Authority-to-Citizen e-Government (A2C)
- Citizen-to-Authority e-Government (C2A)
- Authority-to-Authority e-Government (A2A)
- Business-to-Authority e-Government (B2A)
- Authority-to-Business e-Government (A2B)

This basic model can be extended and further divided into more detailed descriptions. For example, citizen-oriented perspectives can be extended to include the whole local civil society, and A2B can be widened to apply to market regulations and thus to Authority-to-Market e-Government (A2M). These themes will not be elaborated here.

From a functional point of view, local e-Government can be divided into two main areas: use of ICTs in performing basic administrative, service and democratic tasks, on the one hand, and strategic IS development policies and related citizen/user-oriented assessments, on the other. The first of these, basic e-Government functions, contains three elements as follows:

- *Electronic service provision*: information about services, interaction and communication related to the provision and use of services (including public service portals), and various kinds of electronic service transactions.
- *Electronic democracy*: information about relevant actors and issues, forums for communication, discussion and participation, and teledemocratic transactions such as online voting.
- *Electronic administration*: internal organization of public administration, inter-departmental information flows, computer-based administrative procedures (including the use of e-documents, databases and electronic archives), information systems and organizational IT management functions.

Strategic IS development policies are about how to utilize ICTs in dealing with contextual relations and in working with stakeholders. This contains three management areas. *Network management* is about utilization of ICTs in networking, creating partnerships and managing governance relations. *Strategic IS management* focuses on local IS strategies, development policies and related actions. Lastly, as an instance of IS strategy, *technology management* is needed to address local and regional ICT and telecom issues (including access, security, interoperability and competition) (cf. Alabau, 1997). An additional dimension to be mentioned is *citizen/user-oriented assessment* of development policies, which is about *demand, access, privacy, usability* and *costs*. These are needed not only to assess whether development plans are realizable, but also to consider whether these new systems provide real benefits for both communities and citizens in their everyday lives.

As to knowledge management, this all means that knowledge is created, transferred, processed, utilized and stored increasingly in digital form, which in turn requires sophisticated information management tools and competencies. Secondly, informationalization of administrative, service and democratic processes, at least if it is meant to increase efficiency and flexibility, requires reengineering or even e-transformation throughout the local government organization. The same holds to a certain extent for knowledge processes. Local government units must be able to provide sufficient information, provide electronic services, create electronic forums and portals, and conduct electronic transactions through integrated systems (Grönlund, 2000).

We may say that at the very core of knowledge management in electronic government are knowledge processes which are based on the informational logic of local government. In practice this refers to ICT-based information, interaction and transaction processes which are designed to serve the local government's administrative, service and democratic functions. When the concept of knowledge management is contextualized with this new logic, we arrive at the conclusion that the key function of knowledge management in the context of e-Government is to manage knowledge processes concerning ICT-based information provision, interaction and communication and different forms of electronic transactions in order to form an enriched knowledge-intensive orientation base. This helps in taking the lead in IS development and in utilizing the potentials of a structural transformation of society.

Computer-Based Information Systems in Local Government

The design of strategies requires a process in which all the relevant knowledge resources, both internal and external, are utilized optimally so that managers obtain the information they need. There are many facilitation mechanisms as described in previous sections. In this section we take a closer look at one of the structural mechanisms, computer-based information systems (CBIS) that could be seen as e-governments' management tools *par excellence* (see Anttiroiko & Lintilä & Savolainen, 2001). As a facilitation mechanism these systems are characteristically designed to reduce managers' uncertainty about selling, financial position and similar measurable aspects of organization's performance (see Daft and Lengel, 1986, p. 562.)

CBIS includes such applications as management information systems (MIS), decision support systems (DSS), executive information systems (EIS) and data warehouse (DW) systems. The basic aim of these is to provide managers with the information they need in decision making and in other management activities. Recent trends have created a totally new context in which to apply these systems. Even if senior managers have traditionally been slow in taking up CBIS at work, a major long-term trend is an increased dependency upon computing and CBIS at every managerial level in public organizations (Hasan & Hasan, 1997, p. 4; Kraemer et al., 1993).

It is a widely shared belief among chief information officers (CIOs) that information technology can provide a competitive advantage, even though there are evidently several obstacles to instituting such a system (Kini, 1993). There is a range of benefits which may make these more attractive to senior managers provided the overall costs are reasonable. For example, according to the study by Leidner and Elam (1993), EIS use was positively and significantly associated with problem identification speed and decision-making speed, as well as with the extent of analysis in decision making (cf. Mohan et al., 1990).

According to Helen and Suzanne Hasan's (1997, p. 3) empirical survey on EIS in local governments in two Australian states, 22% of all local governments reported they had EIS with a further 10% considering one. Almost all EIS had been planned and implemented some three to four years before the conduct of their survey, and only two of them were in place before 1991. As the situation is very much the same in many other Western countries, local government can be fairly said to be living an initial phase in introducing advanced management support systems.

The areas in which EIS have evidently benefited managers include financial modeling, budgeting and reporting. Moreover, applied systems contain graphic representations of performance data and other data such as property management and human resources. In fact, many studies show that the information obtained through CBIS is more valuable for allocating, monitoring and controlling financial resources than for taking care of the management of operations (Kraemer et al., 1993).

Hasan and Hasan (1997, p. 3) have concluded that one result of the introduction of these systems has been greater awareness of information as an organizational resource. Even if several officials in Australian local government said it was too early to list any effects relating to the use of the EIS in their organization, many had found such benefits as improvements in the ease of communication, timely reporting leading to better decision making and organization-wide sharing of information that had previously been departmental.

Kraemer and others (1993) have reported interestingly that managers who are most satisfied with the usefulness of CBIS are those CBI consumers-type managers who use support staff to mediate their CBI environment, rather than 'knowledge executives' who use the computer to access information directly. This suggests that indirect use of computing might be appropriate for many senior managers, for hands-on use of computing requires considerable amount of time and expertise. Thus, managers must develop a substantial level of computing expertise in order to make effective use of most of the software and databases from which they might generate the information they need.

CONCLUDING REMARKS

Contextual changes favor an organizational design that relies on interactive mechanisms and enhances communication-intensive processes. The need for 'systemic' knowledge is gradually decreasing whereas the role of encultured and embrained knowledge is becoming decisive in strategic processes. To put it simply, we need to know more about other people, other cultures and novel phenomena and trends, which requires rich information. This need cannot be met through the use of formal procedures or even information systems, but by communicative processes. One way of modeling this is presented in Figure 6.

Our selected case studies showed that it is important for a city management to identify its information needs. This is of particular importance in city strategy process in which every city should position, profile and differentiate itself in order to make the best of emerging opportunities and cope with the most severe problems. This has been successfully done in such Finnish medium-sized high-tech cities as Tampere, Oulu and Jyväskylä.

Small rural communities have special requirements in coping with this restructuration process, as shown by the case of Himanka. One way to meet this challenge is to create a model in which strategic thinking is built in the operational solutions. The strategies of small local governments in remote rural areas cannot rely solely on the dialectic in which "quantity becomes a quality," as in the case of growth centers, but quite the opposite, on the quality and flexibility needed in constructing effective adjustment strategies.

What the theoretical part of this chapter provides for the practices of local governments is a systematic view of knowledge management and a coherent scheme to be used in local development processes. In addition, the informational logic of local government requires that ICT-based information, interaction and transaction processes are designed to serve the local government's administrative, service and democratic functions. This is indisputably an area that needs to be studied more thoroughly if we wish to create a local government system capable of meeting the challenge of the global information age.

REFERENCES

Aguilar, F. J. (1967). *Scanning the Business Environment*. New York: Macmillan.
Alabau, A. (1997). Telecommunications and the information society in European regions. *Telecommunications Policy*, 21(8), 761-771.
Ansoff, H. I. (1965). *Corporate Strategy*. New York: McGraw Hill.

Ansoff, H. I. (1979). *Strategic Management*. London: Macmillan.

Anttiroiko, A. (1999). *The Informational Region. Promoting Regional Development in the Information Age*. University of Tampere. Department of Local Government Studies. Publication Series 3/1999.

Anttiroiko, A. (2000). Strateginen tietojohtaminen kunnallishallinnossa. [Strategic knowledge Management in local government]. *Hallinnon Tutkimus [Administrative Studies]*, 1, 19-32.

Anttiroiko, A. and Kallio, O. (1999). *Johdon Tietojärjestelmät Kunnallishallinnossa. [Management Support Systems in Local Government]*. Tampere: Tampereen yliopiston julkaisujen myynti, TAJU.

Anttiroiko, A., Lintilä, L. and Savolainen, R. (2001). Information society competencies of managers: Conceptual considerations. To be published in Pantzar, E., Savolainen, R. and Tynjälä, P. (Eds.), *Information Society for People*. Tampere: Tampere University Press.

Anttiroiko, A. and Savolainen, R. (1999). The role of local government in promoting IS development in Finland. *Finnish Local Government Studies*, 27(3), 410-430.

Anttiroiko, A. and Savolainen, R. (2000). Kuntien strategiset tulkinta- ja tietoprosessit. [Strategic interpretation and knowledge processes in local government]. In Pantzar, E. (Ed.) *Informaatio, Tieto ja Yhteiskunta*. *[Information, Knowledge and Society]*. Tampere: Information Society Research Center. The Academy of Finland, Reports of the Information Research Programme of the Academy of Finland, 4.

Bellamy, C. (1996). Information and communication technology. In Farnham, D. and Horton, S. (Eds.), *Managing the New Public Services*. Second edition. Macmillan.

Bellamy, C. and Taylor, J. T. (1998). *Governing in the Information Age*. Buckingham: Open University Press.

Blackler, F. (1995). Knowledge, knowledge work and organizations: An overview and interpretation. *Organization Studies*, 16(6), 1021-1046.

Blakely, E. J. (1994) *Planning Local Economic Development. Theory and Practice*. 1989. Second Eedition. Thousand Oaks: Sage.

Blumentritt, R. and Johnston, R. (1999). Towards a strategy for knowledge management. *Technology Analysis & Strategic Management*, 11(3), 287-300.

Borja, J. and Castells, M. (1997). *Local and Global. The Management of Cities in the Information Age*. United Nations Center for Human Settlements, UNCHS (Habitat). London: Earthscan.

Bryson, J. M. (1995). *Strategic Planning for Public and Nonprofit Organizations. A Guide to Strengthening and Sustaining Organizational Achievement*. Revised Edition. San Francisco: Jossey-Bass Publishers.

Castells, M. (1989). *The Informational City. Information Technology, Economic Restructuring and the Urban-Regional Process*. Oxford: Blackwell.

Choo, C. W. (1998). *The Knowing Organization. How Organizations Use Information to Construct Meaning, Create Knowledge and Make Decisions*. Oxford: Oxford University Press.

Cook, S. D. N. and Brown, J. S. (1999). Bridging epistemologies: The generative dance between organizational knowledge and organizational knowing. *Organization Science*, 10(4), 381-400.

Crainer, S. (1998). *Key Management Ideas. Thinkers that Changed the Management World*. 3rd Edition. Pitman Publishing. London: Financial Times Management.

Daft, R. L. and Lengel, R. H. (1986) Organizational information requirements, media richness and structural design. *Management Science*, 32, 554-571.

Earl, M. J. (Ed). (1998). *Information Management. The Organizational Dimension.* First published 1996. First published in paperback 1998. Oxford: Oxford University Press.

Elcock, H. (1996). Strategic management. In Farnham, D. and Horton, S. (Eds.), *Managing the New Public Services.* Second edition. First edition 1992. Second edition 1996. London: Macmillan.

Emmert, M. A., Crow, M. and Shangraw, R. F., Jr. (1993). Public management in the future: Post-orthodoxy and organization design. In Bozeman, B. (Ed.), *Public Management: The State of the Art.* San Francisco: Jossey-Bass.

eTampere. (2000). *Program Plan.* City of Tampere, December.

European Commission. (1999). *eEurope. An Information Society for Us All.* Communication. Available on the World Wide Web at: http://europa.eu.int/comm/information_society/eeurope/index_en.htm.

Giddens, A. (1997). *The Consequences of Modernity.* Original printing 1990. Last reprint 1997. Stanford, CA: Stanford University Press.

Grönlund, Å. (2000). *Managing Electronic Services. A Public Sector Perspective.* With contributions from Tuomo Kauranne et al. London: Springer.

Hasan, H. and Hasan, S. (1997). Computer-based performance information for executives in local government. *Australian Journal of Public Administration*, September, 56(3), 24-29. (EBSCOhost print: Database, 7 p.)

Järvinen, A. (1999). Facilitating knowledge processing in a workplace setting. *Research Work and Learning Conference.* Leeds 10-12, September Proceedings.

Järvinen, P. (1999). On processes concerning knowledge. Draft May 31, 1999. *Knowledge Exploration in Contexts (KECO Group).* Tampere: The University of Tampere.

Järvinen, P. (2000). Atk-toiminnan johtaminen. (Management of IT activities). Opinpaja Oy.

Kini, R. B. (1993). Strategic information systems. A misunderstood concept? *Information Systems Management*, Fall, 10(4), 44. Web source: EBSCOhost database.

Kirjavainen, P. (2000). *Strateginen Osaamisen Johtaminen.* [*Strategic Competence Management*]. Miten teen osaamisesta yritykseni kilpailuvaltin? Moniste. Käytetty 14.12.2000.TuKKK/Johtamiskoulutusinstituutti. Turun kauppakorkeakoulu.

Kraemer, K. L., Danziger, J. N., Dunkle, D. E. and King, J. L. (1993). The usefulness of computer-based information to public managers. *MIS Quarterly*, June, 17(2), 129-148. (EBSCOhost print: Database, 26 p.)

Leidner, D. E. and Elam, J. J. (1993). Executive information systems: Their impact on executive decision making. *Journal of Management Information Systems*, Winter, 10(3), 139-155. (EBSCOhost print: Database, 16 p.).

Levitin, A. V. and Redman, T. C. (1998). Data as a resource: Properties, implications and prescriptions. *Sloan Management Review*, 40(1), 89-101.

Markus, M. L. and Robey, D. (1988) Information technology and organizational change: Causal structure in theory and research. *Management Science*, May, 34(5), 583-598.

Mintzberg, H. (1993). The structuring of organizations. In Asch, D. and Bowman, C. (Eds.), *Readings in Strategic Management*, 322-352. Published in 1989. Last edition 1993. London: Macmillan.

Modernizing Government. (1999). Presented to Parliament by the Prime Minister and the Minister for the Cabinet Office by Command of Her Majesty, March. UK: The Stationery Office. Consulted in March 23, 2001. Available on the World Wide Web at: http://www.official-documents.co.uk/document/cm43/4310/4310.htm.

Mohan, L., Holstein, W. K. and Adams, R. B. (1990). EIS: It can work in the public sector. *MIS Quarterly*, December, 14(4), 435. (Print: Database, 15 p.)

Moore, C. (1991). Reflections on the new local political economy: Resignation, resistance and reform. *Policy and Politics*, 19(2), 73-85.

Nonaka, I. (1994). A dynamic theory of organizational knowledge creation. *Organization Science*, 5(1), 14-37.

Nonaka, I. and Konno, N. (1998). The concept of 'Ba': Building a foundation for knowledge creation. *California Management Review*, 40(3), 40-54.

Nonaka, I., Toyama, R. and Konno, N. (2000). SECI, Ba and leadership: A unified model of dynamic knowledge creation. *Long Range Planning*, 33, 5-34.

Palmer, S. and Weaver, M. (1998) *Information Management*. Team Leader Development Series. Oxford: Butterworth-Heinemann.

Rowley, J. (1998). Towards a framework for information management. *International Journal of Information Management*, 18(5), 359-369.

Ruohonen, M. and Higgins, L. F. (1998). Application of creativity principles to IS planning. In Watson, H. J. (Ed.), *Proceedings of the Thirty-First Hawaii International Conference on System Sciences. Volume VI: Organizational Systems and Technology Track*. Los Alamitos, CA: IEEE Computer Society.

Savitch, H. V. (1996). Cities in a global era: A new paradigm for the next millennium. In Cohen, M. A., Ruble, B. A., Tulchin, J. S. and Garland, A. M. (Eds.), *Preparing for the Urban Future. Global Pressures and Local Forces*, 39-65. Washington, DC: The Woodrow Wilson Center Press.

Skyrme, D. J. (1999). *Knowledge Networking. Creating the Collaborative Enterprise*. Oxford: Butterworth-Heinemann.

Stewart, J. (1986). *The New Management of Local Government*. Institute of Local Government Studies, University of Birmingham. London: Allen & Unwin.

Voyer, R. (1998). Knowledge-based industrial clustering: International comparisons. In de la Mothe, J. and Paquet, G. (Eds.), *Local and Regional Systems of Innovation*, 81-110. Boston, MA: Kluwer Academic Publishers.

Väyrynen, R. (1999). *Suomi Avoimessa Maailmassa. Globalisaatio Ja Sen Vaikutukset*. [*Finland in the Open World. Globalization and its Impacts*]. Suomen itsenäisyyden juhlarahasto Sitra 223. Taloustieto Oy.

Weick, K. (1995). *Sense-Making in Organizations*. Thousand Oaks, CA: Sage.

Weiss, L. (1999). *The Myth of the Powerless State. Governing the Economy in a Global Era*. First published in 1998. Reprinted in 1999. Cambridge, UK: Polity Press.

Wu, W. (1996). Economic competition and resource mobilization. In Cohen, M. A., Ruble, B. A., Tulchin, J. S. and Garland, A. M. (Eds.), *Preparing for the Urban Future. Global Pressures and Local Forces*, 123-154. Washington, DC: The Woodrow Wilson Center Press.

Chapter XIV

Improvisational Change Management: New Work Forms with Groupware

Agneta Nilsson and Agneta Ranerup
University of Göteborg, Sweden

INTRODUCTION

In Sweden, an increasing number of the municipal administrations are introducing groupware for case and document management. During 1996, the municipal administration in this study began the introduction of a platform for case and document management based on Lotus Notes Domino. This system supports planning and collaboration of common work tasks based on an integrated system for e-mail and shared databases with information. It is obvious that this platform has a potential to change the work and work situations for the employees. More specifically, this platform provides a possibility to introduce more process- and collaborative-oriented work forms. In this chapter, we present experiences from this process of groupware introduction. In the organizational plan, one of the formulated objectives of this change process is to achieve new process and collaborative ways of work (ADB-kontoret, 1997). Therefore, a first focus in this chapter is on to what extent the introduction and use of the information technology has resulted in new work forms.

Our discussion takes its point of departure in an improvisational model of change management introduced by Orlikowski and Hofman (1997). This model describes different types of changes occurring in the organization when groupware is introduced. The model distinguishes between planned changes on the one hand and changes that emerge over time as people gain more experience of the technology and its potential on the other hand. It is important to provide people in the organization with knowledge about the potential of the technology as well as time to experience the technology in order to shape it according to their own needs (Mambrey & Pipek, 1999). We are interested in how to obtain desired changes in the change process both in terms of planned changes and in terms of changes that emerge through experience of the technology. This chapter will discuss how to manage a change process of groupware introduction in order to result in process and collaborative ways of work. Therefore, a further focus is on how new ideas and experiences, which are gained from the introduction of groupware, are handled in order to make use of the potential of the technology.

One important point of departure for the change process is the previously mentioned organizational plan with the intentions and objectives of the introduction. However, groupware is flexible, which means that people must get the possibility to gain experiences in order to see its potential (Orlikowski & Hofman, 1997). In their improvisational model they argue for the value of a flexible plan and enabling conditions. Ciborra's (2000) theory about technological and organizational change advises against any form of control. The tension between the organizational plan and the necessity of an improvisational perspective in the change process creates the background to our last question: what is the role of the organizational plan in an improvisational process of change management?

Our research contribution is an indepth analysis of groupware introduction in the public sector using an improvisational perspective. Previous studies of such processes have mainly been conducted in the private sector (e.g., Orlikowski, 1993; 1996). Our contribution is also to focus on the role of the organizational plan in an improvisational change process. We mean that previous studies have not sufficiently dealt with this. Therefore, it is our hope that these experiences can be of value in other processes of groupware introduction in public sector environments.

We will in the following chapter mainly deal with the change process from the perspective of the municipal administration. Naturally, both citizens and politicians will indirectly be affected by the introduction of groupware, since the introduction may change the work at the municipal administration. They might also be affected more directly in their interactions with the administration. This raises new and interesting questions about the consequences of the introduction for citizens and politicians, which we bring forward at the end of this chapter.

The specific contribution of this chapter is the indepth analysis of change management of groupware introduction in the public sector. Therefore, the chapter will continue with a thorough description of the case in the study followed by a section describing the method used in the empirical study. Next there is a section introducing the research field to which our research pertains, namely computer support cooperative work. This is followed by a more detailed description of the theoretical model used in this study, the improvisational model of change management (Orlikowski & Hofman, 1997). Subsequently the empirical results are discussed in terms of the theoretical model. The chapter continues with a discussion based on our experiences in light of theories concerning improvisational change management. The aim is to contribute in the development of theories for improvisational change management within the public sector. The chapter is closed with our conclusions and future issues.

BACKGROUND

The Public Sector

A typical feature of the public sector is the fact that it has to handle goals like the proper functioning of legislation and jurisdiction (Wimmer et al., 2001), but also in a very concrete way handle goals and associated activities related to providing services. As a consequence, in many cases work is being performed which cannot be conducted directly using computer technology. Typical examples of this phenomenon are childcare and education as well as care for elderly. The employees at the organizations studied have a relatively low level of previous experience and knowledge about computer technology. This phenomenon is known from previous research into public sector environments, and has been defined as a barrier to understanding the strategic potential of information technology (Heeks & Davies, 1999). The lack of experience and knowledge about computer technology, sometimes combined with the distance between the operative work and the use of the technology, often led to difficulties for employees to see the individual benefits of using the technology. This does not characterize the public sector in general since there are many organizations within the public sector with both long experiences of and indepth knowledge about computer technology. Even so, it is worth emphasizing that there is a considerable amount of organizations in the public sector, as well as parts of organizations, where this characterization is valid. Therefore, we mean that the difference in knowledge levels is an important aspect to consider when introducing new technology.

There is a further phenomenon of interest to our study. In Sweden, like in many other countries, there has been a process of decentralization in local government, that among other things resulted in the creation of local government districts in many cities including the 'big three': Malmö, Göteborg and Stockholm. Put simply, the aim of the decentralization was twofold; one was to increase democracy in local government, another was to increase efficiency and accountability (Ranerup, 1999). Irrespective of the actual consequences of the decentralization and the associated local government districts, the creation of local government districts added to the complexity of the already complex administrative processes of local government (Wimmer et al., 2001).

The Case

Our discussion in this chapter is based on an empirical study evaluating the introduction of groupware in the municipal administration of Göteborg in Sweden, a city with a population of approximately 460,000 inhabitants. We have studied the experiences of the introduction at three local government districts and at the central administrative unit. The study investigated what changes had occurred when the groupware system was introduced according to the participating interviewees from the organization.

The local government districts are semi-autonomous administrative units of the municipal administration. In total, the municipal administration of Göteborg comprises 21 local government districts. The districts have their own councils, with the authority to decide how to spend their budgets within a framework of centrally set economic, political and legal limits. The work performed at these local districts varies, yet maintains a clear focus on public service (schools, social services, childcare, etc). Every council is responsible for social services in one of 21 geographic areas of Göteborg. The central administrative unit is responsible for overarching administrative tasks.

The introduction of groupware in the municipal administration is an ongoing process extending over several years. In 1996, one of the participating local government districts and the central administrative unit introduced the system while the other two districts introduced the system in 1998. The decision to introduce this particular groupware system in the local government districts was taken at the central management level of the municipal administration. The semi-autonomous districts decide themselves when and how they want to introduce the technology and how they want to proceed. Each district formed local project teams to conduct these introductions, including structuring the various databases and the other components available in the system. This means that the system mainly looks the same in the whole city but with some differences in structure and choice of components.

The organization in charge of the introduction formulated the intentions with the introduction of the groupware system in an organizational plan (ADB-kontoret, 1997). In the plan one of the intentions was that the technology should result in improved collaboration between the employees phrased as "collaboration in the virtual work group independent of time and space" (translated from ADB-kontoret, 1997, p. 1). This objective also includes the desire that the technology should result in new organizational forms where employees share knowledge. The exchange of knowledge enabled by the technology was regarded as a value in itself. The introduction of groupware also aimed to reduce the processing time for handling cases, or in other words to obtain a rationalization of work (ADB-kontoret, 1997).

The Groupware System

The groupware system at interest in this study is an adjustable standard system for case and document management based on the platform of Lotus Notes Domino. The system consists of several components all integrated by the e-mail function (ADB-kontoret, 1997). The components are the Diary, the Electronic Archive, the Work-Group-Databases, the Project-Team-Databases, the Common Information Databases, the Handbook Databases, the Notice Board, the Web Publication and the Discussion Databases.

The core of the system is the Diary and the Electronic Archive. Together these components are the center of the process of case- and document management and contain all these documents in the organization. In the databases for a Work-Group, the main work is performed. New cases from the Diary are received here and distributed among the person in charge of the matter. Alternatively, databases for Project-Teams can be set up for a project supporting collaboration and information sharing within the team. Further, the members of the organization can use Discussion Databases to discuss different subjects independent of time or place. The other components of the system, i.e., various Common Information Databases and Handbook databases, serve as the organizations collective memory and support the day-to-day activities. The system also provides utilities for updating the organizations Web Publication and an electronic Notice Board.

Method

The empirical study described in this chapter applies an ethnographic approach (Hammersley & Atkinson, 1995) using interviews and feedback sessions to collect the empirical material. We started our fieldwork by participating at sessions aimed to introduce and educate employees in the use of the system. After these introductory sessions, we began the interviews focusing on how the interviewees experienced their work situation and the use of the new technology.

The interviews were semi-structured and covered questions on: the impacts of the system on the work situation, patterns of communication and collaboration and changes in the information flow in the organization. The interviews were conducted during the period of April to June 1999. In total 20 semi-structured interviews were conducted and taped, each lasting for about one hour.

The empirical data is an attempt to reflect a longer period of experience from the groupware introduction. Therefore the local government districts were chosen in consideration of when they introduced the system. The interviewees represent two different groups of users. One group has three years of experience of using the system and the other group has less than a year of experience.

The interviewees in the study are civil servants and represent several areas such as school, care for elderly, childcare and various administrative units. They represent a broad span of professional competence and experience within the municipality. In addition, they represent a broad professional hierarchy since both secretaries as well as managers were interviewed. The interviewees were selected in collaboration with a contact person at each local government district. The rationale was the need for local knowledge, i.e., to select people who actually use the system. In order to avoid bias in the selection, the contact persons were instructed to select interviewees representing the broad span of attitudes towards and experiences of the technology. All interviews were handled confidentially.

As a complement to the interviews, four sessions for feedback were arranged. During these sessions, the interviewees participated providing a possibility for us to present feedback as well as to confirm the tentative analysis. As thus, the sessions have provided a means to triangulate the result in order to assess its validity (Silverman, 1993).

The collected material has been analyzed and compared with the improvisational model of change management (Orlikowski & Hofman, 1997). Our motive has been to compare an empirical pattern with a predicted one, as suggested by Yin (1984). In this way we have been able to describe experiences that are in accordance with the model, but also to detect discrepancies between our experiences and the model. The reflections presented here from applying the model concern the management of change processes in public sector environments as well as the model itself. We have analyzed the tension between theories promoting traditional normative change processes verses theories supporting improvisational strategies. In our analysis we have especially focused on the role of the plan in improvisational change management.

Computer-Supported Cooperative Work

The following piece of research pertains to the research field of Computer-Supported Cooperative Work, abbreviated CSCW. This research field has a history of more than a decade and mainly focuses on the use of computer support for collaborative work among white-collar workers, administrators and other professionals. The research field as such has evolved through conferences on both American and European basis. A recent example is the European Conference for Computer-Supported Cooperative Work (ECSCW'99) held in Copenhagen, September 1999 (Bødker et al., 1999). The CSCW field deals with collaboration and coordination of common work tasks using computer support. Common information spaces are often used to enable collaboration. These are usually shared databases containing both formally structured information as well as unstructured information.

The simplest form of existing groupware is the kind supporting e-mail. A common groupware is Lotus Notes with a more multi-facetted functionality. The functionality of the latter includes shared databases and e-mail to facilitate collaboration and coordination. This means that this technology to a higher degree facilitates new collaborative work forms compared to the simplest form of groupware consisting of only e-mail.

The majority of the conducted studies concerning the introduction of groupware and groupware-enabled change processes have been carried out in the private sector (Bikson & Eveland, 1996; Karsten & Jones, 1998; Orlikowski, 1993, 1996; Vandenbosch & Ginzberg, 1997). However, the use of groupware involves an increasing number of public-sector environments, each of these has their specific characteristics. There are a few examples of studies conducted in the public sector of these new experiences. One example is Pipek and Wulf's (1999) study that focuses on the lifecycle of a groupware system, from its introduction to its removal in a government organization. Researchers such as Macredie and Sandom (1999) have studied the introduction of groupware in a military organization with a special focus on the adoption and use of a workflow system.

These studies, within the private and the public sector alike, focus on the process of introduction, albeit at a rather general level. According to many authors, the user's understanding of groupware evolves gradually over time (see, e.g., Orlikowski & Hofman, 1997). This implies that users cannot anticipate future possibilities of use in advance. Consequently, the focus in previous studies has been on the appearance of emergent organizational and technological changes rather than on organizational visions and plans with the introduction. This means that the issue of managing such processes has received less attention.

Another common feature of these studies is the persistence of an improvisational perspective on the process of introduction as such. A change management perspective on the process of introduction and use of the technology seems to be absent in previous research. Ciborra (2000) argues that it is impossible to control groupware introduction. However, we mean that the need and possibility to manage this process is dependent of the context, and therefore active change management can play an important role in the public sector. As a contrast to this focus in previous research, a perspective that combines an improvisational perspective on the technological change process with more active planning ambitions is largely absent (Macredie & Sandom, 1999). Due to the specific work environment in the public sector, there is a need for further studies addressing these issues and the particularities of groupware-enabled change processes in this particular kind of environment.

In this chapter we will not focus on theories concerning collaboration, coordination and common information spaces, i.e., theories from the research field of Computer-Supported Cooperative Work. The reason is that we are not concerned with the development of groupware but focus on the process of change when introducing groupware. Our focus thereby concerns technological and organizational change management. However, the theories we use are not general theories of technological and organizational change management. Instead, the theories we use emanate from research concerned with the introduction of groupware (Orlikowski, 1993, 1996; Orlikowski & Hofman, 1997). We regard this as an argument for the relevance of the theories we use in our research and the problems we deal with.

Improvisational Model of Change Management

Our point of departure for this chapter is the improvisational model of change management as outlined by Orlikowski and Hofman (1997). In her research, Wanda Orlikowski has focused on the introduction of Lotus Notes mainly in the private sector (Orlikowski, 1993, 1996), a work that among other things resulted in this model. The authors (Orlikowski & Hofman, 1997) claim their model to be descriptive, i.e., it illustrates the changes occurring when introducing groupware, and they discuss how to manage these processes.

Traditional models for technological and organizational change management have a weakness according to Orlikowski and Hofman (1997). They mean that these models present an idealized picture of what happens in groupware introductions. The core of their model is the contrast between on the one hand planned changes and strategies and on the other hand changes and strategies developed gradually against the experiences of the change process as such.

The model rests on two major assumptions: "First, the changes associated with technology implementations constitute an ongoing process rather than an event with an end point after which the organization can expect to return to a reasonable steady state" (Orlikowski & Hofman, 1997, pp. 12-13). This is a way of arguing against traditional models that depicts technological change as a three-stage process that includes unfreezing, changing and refreezing with a fixed beginning and end of the process (Lewin, 1958). This means that traditional Lewinian models imply that technological change is an event that should be managed during a specific period as a contrast to being viewed as an ongoing event (Dawson, 1994; Lewin, 1958). Such models are inappropriate to describe the introduction of groupware according to Orlikowski and Hofman (1997). A reason for this is that groupware facilitates collaboration, coordination and common information spaces, which can develop over time in various ways. The potential of groupware in practice is more complex and difficult to grasp compared to traditional forms of information technology.

Groupware is usually more flexible and adjustable than traditional information technology. It has an open architecture that enables the users to shape the technology according to their own needs. This means that the users need to experience the technology in order to understand its potential. Consequently, there is a second assumption in the improvisational model of change management that: "...all technological and organizational changes made during the ongoing process cannot, by definition, be anticipated ahead of time" (Orlikowski & Hofman, 1997, p. 13). The traditional perspective on change processes, with a fixed beginning and end based on an organizational vision with planned objectives, is not sufficient when dealing with groupware.

Characteristics of the Three Types of Change

Orlikowski and Hofman's model distinguishes between three kinds of changes that may occur when introducing groupware. A first kind of change induced by the introduction of technology is the 'anticipated change,' according to Orlikowski and Hofman (1997), which are planned changes that occur as intended.

A second kind of change is 'opportunity-based change,' a concept that refers to possibilities discovered in the organization, which are taken care of in a deliberative and planned mode of action. This means that some people discover a new possibility to use Lotus Notes. If this possibility is believed to be of value for a larger group of people, it is distributed to relevant groups of employees through for example seminars or workshops.

A third kind of change is the 'emergent change.' Emergent change is characterized by occurring spontaneously among the personnel on their own initiatives. This kind of change is not taken care of in a deliberative manner by the organization. This feature mainly distinguishes this kind of change from the opportunity-based change described above.

Both opportunity-based and emergent changes are characterized by not being possible to predict or describe in advance. As shown in Figure 1, according to the model the three types of changes might appear in an arbitrary order. In other words, there is no planned or logical order between these changes.

Critical Enabling Conditions

In the article where the model is outlined, the authors (Orlikowski & Hofman, 1997) present various kinds of critical enabling conditions of importance to the process. One of the critical enabling conditions is that dedicated resources exist with the capacity to take care of ideas and

Figure 1: The improvisational model of change management over time (Adapted from Orlikowski & Hofman, 1997)

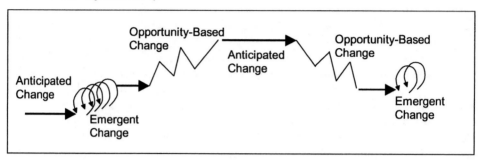

possibilities that occur during the process. Especially the opportunity-based changes depend on being recognized and handled in a purposeful manner. In other words, it is necessary to take care of and make use of the constructive ideas that appear over time. Orlikowski and Hofman mention examples of enabling conditions like technological staff dedicated to support users, meetings and various workshops and seminars (Orlikowski & Hofman, 1997). In addition, the arrangement of seminars and workshops requires resources. Even if an organization conducts the introduction using an improvisational perspective, it is not certain that the organization has invested in resources for these forms of enabling conditions.

Another form of critical enabling conditions presented has a focus on organizational features. This concerns the interdependent relationship between the organization, the technology and the change model (Orlikowski & Hofman, 1997). Orlikowski and Hofman's research suggested that these key dimensions must ideally be aligned or at least not in opposition. More specifically, "A flexible change model, while likely to be problematic in a rigid, control-oriented or bureaucratic culture, is well suited to an informal, cooperative culture…" (Orlikowski & Hofman, 1997, p. 18).

Orlikowski and Hofman outlined their model mainly based on experiences from the private sector rather than the public sector. They claim that informal, collaborative cultures are more likely to be successful using the improvisational model of change management in change processes. However, the authors claim the opposite concerning rigid, control-oriented organizations and mean that the model would not be applicable there to the same degree. As mentioned previously, it is argued that there must be alignment between the type of organization where the model is used and the model itself.

A common notion is that public-sector organizations usually are more hierarchical and bureaucratic and therefore less open to improvisational changes. According to a recent characterization of public sector organizations, several features distinguish the public sector from the private one (Wimmer et al., 2001). One feature is the complex goal structure that includes the proper functioning of legislation and jurisdiction, but also in a very concrete way to handle goals and associated activities related to providing services like childcare and care for elderly. Another feature is the high degree of legal structuring of administrative work that strongly affects the shaping and running of public administration. A further feature is that administrative decision making in the public sector usually involves many people (Wimmer et al., 2001). This would then make the improvisational model of change management less harmonized, albeit not incompatible, with public-sector organizations.

However, there are studies conducted in public-sector environments where the model has been applied. For example, Macredie and Sandom (1999) reported experiences from a study where the model was applied in such a traditional and hierarchical environment as a military organization. Macredie and Sandom (1999) showed that improvisational changes do occur in hierarchical public sector organizations and, consequently, improvisational models of change management are applicable to this kind of environment. We mean that previous studies such as the one by the Macredie and Sandom (1999) have shown that the model was found not only possible but also useful to apply in such environments. Therefore, we applied the model in spite of the characteristics of the environment in the study. Our aim with this was to use the specific characteristics in the environment in the study and the model to discuss improvisational change management in the public sector. More specifically, we bring forward aspects in order to adjust the model to the public sector.

An additional rationale for applying the model is that the process of groupware introduction in the municipal administration of Göteborg was immediately characterized as improvisational. This, since it had been an ongoing process for several years, beginning in 1996. The conducted introductions in some of the local government districts enabled other districts of the municipal administration to gain from the experiences. Similar to the research by Orlikowski and Hofman, the introduced groupware system is a Lotus Notes Domino platform that is highly adjustable.

IMPROVISATIONAL CHANGE MANAGEMENT

Anticipated Changes

Several anticipated changes have occurred in the municipal administration (Nilsson et al., 2000). One of the most apparent changes is the use of e-mail, which has had a significant impact on the work situation. The interviewees expressed that the change to e-mail as a communications medium enabled more efficient work performance. This is opposed to the earlier medium, the telephone, which is associated with difficulties of getting a hold of people and therefore being time consuming.

As mentioned above, the interviewees in the study represent two different groups concerning the length of the use of the groupware system. The group that has used the system longer is referred to as 'old' users and the other group is referred to as 'new' users. A difference between old and new users is that old users have advanced from e-mail use towards an increased use of the databases. The rationale for this is the need for shared databases with up-to-date information available for everyone. Another reason was the need to evolve from an extensive use of e-mail, described as a misuse of e-mail, to a more direct use of databases.

Another change of significance concerns the information flow in the organization. The introduction of the groupware system made common information available on-line in various databases. This has affected meetings, which have changed from being a session for information dissemination to a session for discussion in particular among the old users. Employees are now required to keep themselves informed of summoned meetings and to arrive at meetings well prepared to take part in discussions.

Moreover, the users can access the information they need at any time, which both old and new users perceive as an advantage. The users described this as enabling efficient work with a constructive effect on the individual work situation. The access to information independently of time and space as well as other co-workers has simplified the individual work situation.

Lastly, the structure of the case process has constructively been affected by the introduction of the system. Standardized templates for documents have simplified the process of the formal checking procedure both internally in the local government districts as well as externally in the political boards within the municipal organization. The system allows personnel in charge of a matter to follow the cases via the system, which the users emphasize as an advantage in work.

Opportunity-Based Changes

The introduction of the groupware system has so far mainly involved changes concerning the medium employees use to collaborate in the organization (Nilsson et al., 2000). This change is an ongoing process and the use has not yet advanced to the full potential of the groupware system. One important factor for this process to advance is to support changes occurring in the organization by deliberative actions. If the organization takes care of potential changes by deliberative actions, they would be characterized as opportunity-based changes according to the improvisational model of change (Orlikowski & Hofman, 1997).

We have found some opportunity-based changes in the municipal administration. The use of discussion databases in the groupware system is a change that is characterized as both emergent as well as opportunity-based. The intention with these databases was to support employees' ability to discuss and exchange knowledge and experiences. However, these are rarely used and the interviewees questioned the need for such forums in the form they currently exist. These forums are set up for the employees within a local government district. According to the interviewees, the geographic proximity of the employees makes the electronic alternative to physical meetings less attractive, which turns the edge of the need and usability of the discussion forums. The interviewees recognized the potential for these forums when they were set up across organizational boundaries. The discussion forums were also used more actively in situations where they had been changed into a pure information dissemination forum.

The findings from the empirical study indicate that there are several ideas for potential changes that could be realized. This is in turn highly dependent on the ability of the organization to take care of these opportunities.

Emergent Changes

Other changes occurring due to the introduced groupware system were not anticipated. In the improvisational model of change management (Orlikowski & Hofman, 1997), these are referred to as emergent changes, i.e., changes that occur without deliberative actions in the organization.

Our study shows that after the groupware system was introduced, the employees work both electronically and in parallel maintain the manual paper-based routines (Nilsson et al., 2000). There are various reasons for this but one obvious reason is the fact that not all employees have access to the system yet. Consequently, many documents need to be distributed via paper-based media. This concerns particularly the communication with the politicians in various boards and committees in the municipal organization. A consequence from this is duplication of work.

Another reason for duplication of work is the filing regulations in the organization. Existing regulation only deals with paper-based media and does not sufficiently correspond to the introduced electronic system. Due to the lack of adequate directives, manual procedures for paper-based archiving are maintained resulting in duplication of work. Both old and new users perceived this as resource consuming and out of fashion.

The new users also tend to cause duplication of work themselves by working locally on their computer. This is mainly due to the lack of trust in the technology, caused by events where employees, by simple handling mistakes, have lost documents without receiving any understandable warnings from the system.

Another example of emerging changes is the use of the system as an enabler for the employees to take part in work and information of other employees. The users described this as something that occurred early in the change process. However, due to the lack of time, this was later limited to situations with a direct need in connection with a specific work task.

The Change Process in the Municipal Administration

The potential of the groupware system to have an impact on the user's work situation is large. The results from this study illustrate several areas where the effects of the use of the system are apparent. Particularly the individual work situation has benefited from the technology, supporting both information and communication dimensions for the employee to perform work. An example of this is that work routines have in different ways been simplified and made more efficient or disappeared.

The use of e-mail enabled communication between people in the organization in an easy way. The access to information via the groupware system has contributed in a constructive way to the work situation. The communication in the organization is efficient. Information is accessible. The process of handling a case is regulated and efficient and the common electronic archive keeps all documents neatly filed. These were all anticipated changes and achieved through the introduced groupware. However, our results show that the introduction of the system has not changed the organizational ways of work towards collaborative work as intended.

One important rationale behind the objective to change towards collaborative work was to achieve efficient work in the organization. This included reducing existing duplication of work as much as possible from the organization, reducing lead-time for case handling and facilitating sharing of knowledge and experiences (ADB-kontoret, 1997). All these intentions can be realized using the potential of the groupware system. We would here like to emphasize that the actual realization is dependent on the organization's choice of to what extent it wishes to exploit the system. Our intention in this discussion is therefore to point out enabling conditions that can support the change process towards collaboration in order to advance further.

Collaborating with other people in the organization has become possible in a new and easier way supported by e-mail and databases. However, it becomes apparent that it is the medium used to collaborate (i.e., using e-mail and databases) that is the main change from the groupware introduction. The use of the groupware system seems so far to have had a limited impact on any patterns of collaboration that regulate whom to work with and concerning which work to collaborate on. The groupware system with all its components seems to be regarded firstly as an information channel rather than a process-oriented work tool supporting collaboration. However, the potential of the groupware system for collaboration is recognized and the use of the system can evolve further.

The interviewees expressed that they have not experienced any concrete changes neither concerning whom to collaborate with nor concerning what work. Nevertheless, the interviewees express that they are convinced of the potential of the groupware system. They believe they can develop more collaborative work forms and they regard this as a gradual process. However, they mean that this requires both time and support, and it is essential that the groupware system becomes a natural part of the employees' daily work. It is necessary that the individual use and benefits from the groupware system become apparent for each user of the system.

The users acknowledge the potential of the groupware system for collaboration across organizational boundaries in the municipal administration of Göteborg. They especially believe that the groupware system can support employees of the same profession to exchange knowledge and experiences.

In summation, introducing a groupware system does not automatically lead to changes in work (Orlikowski, 1993; Karsten & Jones, 1997) but is dependent on many factors such as support and training as well as organizational culture, basic procedures and reward systems in an organization. In terms of the improvisational model by Orlikowski and Hofman (1997), these are all enabling conditions of importance. The previous discussion about the characteristics of public-sector organizations, such as the complex goal structure, the high degree of legal structuring of administrative work and the many people involved in administrative decision making in the public sector (Wimmer et al., 2001), are typical features of organizational culture and basic procedures.

Collaboration in the Municipal Administration

By looking closer at how the enabling factors provided in the organization were arranged, we can learn valuable lessons from our study. The three factors identified in our study concern 1) the communication of the organizational plan and visions, 2) the focus of the training provided and 3) the arrangement of the training provided. A further necessity in order to make use of the groupware system is that it requires a certain amount of people to have access to the system. This is referred to as critical mass (Grudin, 1994). In the discussion about duplication of work, the fact that not everyone in the organization has access to the system has been mentioned. This will be discussed further in the section about the role of the plan in change management.

The first factor concerns the communication of the organizational plan and vision with the introduction of the groupware. Many of the interviewees expressed that the organizational objectives with the introduction were unknown to them. The fact that many of the interviewees were unfamiliar with the organizational vision and objectives with the groupware introduction seems to have affected the outcome of the process negatively. The employees' unawareness of the organizational visions has limited their understanding of the technology and its potential.

The second factor concerns the focus of the provided training. The training focused largely on the technical aspects of the use of the system, leaving the organizational issues of changed work procedures without discussion. In the beginning of an introduction of groupware, it is generally very difficult for users to imagine the potential of the technology. There is a need for employees to learn about the new ways of work which focus more on collaboration (Mambrey & Pipek, 1999).

Ciborra and Lanzara (1994) address a similar phenomenon using the words of 'formative context.' This refers to both organizational and cognitive dimensions influencing employees' understanding of the current work situation as well as limiting their ability to imagine new ways of work. This phenomenon seems to be valid and an even more serious problem for employees in the municipal administration due to limited experience of technology.

An effect of the lack of discussing the new ways of work during the training provided was that employees were learning a very limited part of the system, focusing strongly on the technical functions. This is an additional argument for communicating the organizational vision enabling people to understand the intentions and the potential of the introduced groupware system. We mean that this is particularly important for the employees in organizations such as the municipal administration considering its bureaucratic tradition where the structure of laws and regulations strongly affects the shaping and running of public administration. According to the organizational structure and organizational principles in the public sector, people from several agencies and levels are involved in a process where an administrative decision is taken (Wimmer et al., 2001). We mean that the need to communicate the organizational vision is further emphasized in this environment due to the phenomenon of formative context (Ciborra & Lanzara, 1994) and the general need to learn and discuss the potential of the groupware system (Mambrey & Pipek, 1999). In addition, the employees also have to deal with the restrictions and conditions in the existing structure in the forms of legislation (Wimmer et al., 2001).

The third factor concerns the arrangement of the provided training. It is equally important to support the employees in the use of the groupware system as well as fundamental computer skills. The municipal administration conducted the training in larger groups comprised of individuals with varying competencies in both fundamental computer skills and the groupware system, which made it difficult for the employees to fully take advantage of the training. One point of view put forward was the need for adjusted training. The interviewees expressed that they would prefer shorter individual sessions at their own workplace to better enable the individual to comprehend the potential of the groupware system in relation to the individual's work situation. They also emphasized the need for continuity concerning support and training. The employees expressed this as an infinite need in the ongoing process with new needs constantly appearing as the individual progresses.

Based on experiences from our study, we emphasize the need for enabling conditions in order to achieve expected changes, as suggested by the model (Orlikowski & Hofman, 1997). We mean that these enabling conditions need to be provided at an early stage of the process as well as continuously during the process. The identified need for continuous support and training can for example be provided at various spaces for knowledge transfer, training sessions either individual or in small groups, workshops or similar activities (Mambrey & Pipek, 1999). The provision of continuous support concerning both the use of the technology as well as the potential of the groupware system in relation to the organizational vision may function as an important part of the enabling conditions in order to achieve desired outcomes of the change process.

Theories for Improvisational Change Management

In the specific environment of the public sector where we conducted our study, it is apparent that the employees' experiences from information technology is relatively low. This is our main argument for emphasizing the importance of enabling conditions. The employees' low level of experience hinders their ability to imagine new ways to work and use the technology (Heeks & Davies, 1999). Ciborra (2000) advises against any form of control and management of change processes. However, this is when studying change processes in knowledge intensive or high tech businesses dealing with innovation. Based on the findings in our study, we are not arguing against emergent changes and innovations. Instead, we argue for enabling conditions for both planned and emergent changes to occur in this particular organizational environment of the public sector. In organizations where the level of experience from information technology is considerably higher, our argument may be less valid. Instead, Ciborra's (2000) view is likely to be more applicable in such organizations where the absence of control enables innovative thinking among the employees with the capacity to see the use and benefits of the technology themselves.

The improvisational model (Orlikowski & Hofman, 1997) argues for the value of a flexible plan and enabling conditions. Ciborra's (2000) theory about technological and organizational change advises against any form of control. A question worth raising is whether these theories are in opposition to each other. Are these theories different views on the process or different phenomenon in the process at focus? A possible interpretation is that Orlikowski and Hofman's view of the process is a wider perspective including anticipated, opportunity-based and emergent changes while Ciborra's view is more limited, focusing on the phenomenon of the emergent changes and innovations.

If the different theories mainly concern the difference of scope and focus, and therefore are complementary for different purposes, we argue that the decisive aspect to consider is the organizational context in the particular situation. We mean that in an organization, such as the municipal administration in the study, there is a strong need for enabling conditions for changes to occur at all, be it planned, opportunity-based or emergent.

From a historical perspective, it appears to be a stronger inertia in the public sector concerning changes towards new ways to work, as we discussed in the previous section. The difficulty people have in general in understanding the potential of the technology and its capacity to change work forms as discussed above is further intensified by this factor. Therefore, we mean that the specific characterization of these public-sector environments makes the provision of enabling condition crucial in order to achieve results in a change process.

The Role of the Plan in the Improvisational Change Management

In our study we have established that certain planned changes occurred while others did not. These experiences served as a reason to analyze a dimension of the improvisational model of change management by Orlikowski and Hofman (1997), which has not been treated previously. Orlikowski and Hofman (1997) claim that their model describes how changes actually occur in such a change process rather than to provide an idealized picture of the process. In other words, their model is an illustration of what is actually happening. In a similar model of a change process outlined by Mintzberg (1978), he distinguishes between on the one hand intended strategies and on the other hand emergent strategies in a way that is relevant for our discussion. Both Orlikowski and Hofman's model and Mintzberg's model are based on empirical experiences of change processes and are characterizd as descriptive. It is worth noticing that the model outlined by Mintzberg contains an interesting aspect not represented in the other model. The intended strategies can be realized as intended (see Figure 2). However, in the model it is also represented that intended strategies for one or another reason are not realized. This type is called 'Unrealized Strategy' and has been emphasized in bold text and arrow in Figure 2. Supported by the model of Mintzberg and based on our experiences, we mean that the model by Orlikowski and Hofman (1997) can be further developed by the addition of type of change. We relate this to Orlikowski and Hofman's own discussion about the plan, which we have seen a possibility to evolve.

Based on this we mean that there is a general value in following up the plan in a more active way than described by Orlikowski and Hofman (1997) also in an improvisational change process. The authors (Orlikowski & Hofman, 1997), emphasize that the plan should be a guide rather than

Figure 2: The types of strategies (adapted from Mintzberg, 1978)

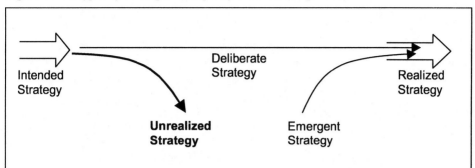

a blueprints but they do not discuss further how this should be handled in practice.

A more active plan utilization has the advantage of allowing the manager of the change process to follow the ongoing process. In a plan there might be anticipated changes not occurring in practice that are well worth following up. This could actively support the realization of the anticipated changes. The improvisational model, in its current form, does not support this.

It is, however, equally important to maintain a flexible attitude towards the plan. If experiences gained during the ongoing process show that the anticipated change is actually an unrealistic objective or an undesirable change, this implies revision of the plan. This is what we mean by a flexible plan. In other words, we argue that the plan itself is a necessity that should be used actively to support the process and provide guidance to the ongoing process. Nevertheless, we also stress the necessity to handle the plan in a flexible manner, allowing for revisions based on experiences from the ongoing process of change.

Adding the 'non-occurrence of anticipated changes' to the model increases the versatility of the model since it can now be utilized in the situation when the organization sees that desired changes which have not occurred would in reality have led to undesirable results (Nilsson et al., 2001). In such situations, the model helps manifest the fact that the choice not to take action (not to correct the non-occurrence) is a conscious choice to revise the plan rather than a serendipitous lack of activity. In this manner, the organization can make a deviation from the plan explicit, in contrast to an indecisive non-occurrence without any further notice in the organization.

An attempt to illustrate our ideas is shown in Figure 3, where we have elaborated on Orlikowski and Hofman's improvisational model of change management by adding the type of change "non-occurring anticipated change." In the figure two types are added, labeled A and B. A refers to non-occurring anticipated changes that after consideration are determined as "still desired" and worth following up. It may become an occurring anticipated change if handled with deliberative actions and further support. This is illustrated by the loop (A). On the other hand B refers to non-occurring anticipated changes that after consideration are determined as "undesired," for instance due to unrealistic expectations or misjudgments about the environment. This way the model supports both the reintroduction of changes deemed desirable, as well as the flexibility to revise the plan discarding undesirable changes.

Improvisational Change Management–From Plan to Action

In an essay on organizational change, Czarniawska and Joerges (1996) discuss the interesting issue of how plans, visions and ideas created on one level of an organization turn into action in new localities. They emphasize how organizational studies tell us rather little about the issue of how ideas turn into changes. Czarniawska and Joerges argue that all ideas, organizational visions or plans must be translated to be received by local levels in order to materialize into concrete actions and changes. Naturally, the translation as such is pursued by people: "... there seem to be 'idea-bearing' organizations and professional roles which deal mainly with translations" (Czarniawska & Joerges, 1996, p. 36). We have found that this perspective on the role of the organizational plan in improvisational change processes can be useful and say something about the complex problems that exist in public sector environments like the one we have studied.

In our case, a computer support company called ADB-kontoret, owned by the city of Göteborg, has played an important role in the process (Nilsson et al., 2001). During the process of implementation, as well as afterwards, this organization had an overall responsibility of handling and supporting the implementation process at large. They have also been the main providers of training in the groupware system. In addition, they formulated the organizational vision in association with the implementation process against the background of the IT policy of the city of Göteborg. Lastly, they have been the organizational unit with the main responsibility of disseminating organizational visions and plans. Consequently, the computer support company in our case can be characterized as the idea-bearing organization.

Another important role is that of the professional translators (Czarniawska & Joerges, 1996) who have closer links with the various districts or organizational units. The municipal administration of Göteborg, as described above, comprises of 21 local government districts with certain autonomy concerning economical and organizational issues, and is managed by district managers. In our study, the district managers have played the role as translator of the plan to local context rather than the computer support company. As argued by Czarniawska and Joerges, ideas must take root in local knowledge to materialize into action: "As more and more people are persuaded to translate the idea for their own use, it can be materialized into collective action...The idea is enacted: other people are persuaded to join in, decisions are formally made" (Czarniawska & Joerges, 1996, p. 44).

It is here interesting to note that the actual decision to use this particular groupware system was a central level issue of the organization. However, the local administrative districts through their district managers were in a position to decide when they want to commence this process as well as how they want to proceed. Each district established local teams to conduct the groupware introduction, which then functioned as the link between the

Figure 3: Elaborated improvisational model of change management

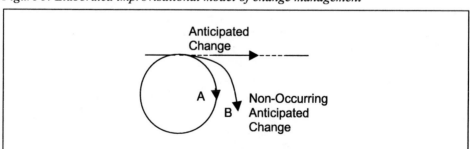

local government district and the computer support company. Experiences from our study show that there were diverging views among the district managers regarding fundamental aspects such as the level of diffusion of the groupware system in the organization at large, as well as in various parts of it. We here touch upon the previous discussion about how the number of users actually using the groupware system affects the usability of the groupware system, i.e., the issue of a critical mass (Grudin, 1994). We found district managers who in a more active way than others supported these teams in their effort to promote the use of the groupware system in order to change to new work forms (Josefsson & Nilsson, 1999).

An example of this is how e-mail is appropriated by various parts of the organization. During an early phase, some of the interviewees experienced an excessive use of e-mail for all sorts of work and the duplication of e-mail messages was substantial as have been described earlier. In some districts, this led to directives with the intention to increase the use of databases as a way of redirecting the use of e-mail towards the use of databases. In other words, the collaborative capacity of the technology as outlined in the organizational vision has materialized into concrete instructions here. Our experiences clearly indicate that the change process has been more successful in districts where the district managers played a more active role to promote such changes (Josefsson & Nilsson, 1999). In addition, this has helped to solve the problem with the e-mail. In other words, the combination of autonomy where each district can decide when the groupware system should be introduced and how it should be used, combined with the necessity of translating the plan to local context, raises further complexity in this kind of organizations, which has not been dealt with previously in the research concerned with groupware.

Finally, to realize plans and organizational visions in practice, knowledgeable actors must act upon them (Olesen & Myers, 1999). Such actors might be situated on higher levels of the organization as senior managers (Olesen & Myers, 1999), on lower levels as super users (Essler, 1998; Ranerup, 1996) as well as on intermediate levels as in our case, i.e. district managers. This is in line with our research, as well as with the research of Czarniawska and Joerges (1996). A complicating factor in our case is that these actors might possess certain levels of independence in relation to the organizational visions and plans behind the process. For example, some of our actors played a more proactive role in order to promote collaboration than others. This refers primarily to the district managers, who we found were a central driving force for the evolution of the use of the groupware system in this setting (Josefsson & Nilsson, 1999).

By this, we do not wish to question the appropriateness with for example local government districts as the organizational structure of the municipal administration. As described previously, the introduction of local government districts is a consequence of trends towards decentralization in the public sector that adds to the complexity of an already complex organizational structure. Instead, we wish to emphasize a consequence local government districts can involve concerning processes of groupware introduction. To achieve changed work forms in processes concerning groupware introduction, it is necessary to take care of the possibilities and good ideas that appear in the organization. Our experiences show that the role of the organizational plan should be used more actively, although with awareness of the problems with autonomy that might exist in contexts such as these. We mean that the phenomenon of autonomy concerning the translation of plans must be treated in a more open manner than has actually been the case.

In summation, we have here treated a further aspect of importance for the result of the use of the groupware system, compared to technological (Macredie & Sandom, 1999) and cultural aspects (Karsten & Jones, 1998; Orlikowski & Hofman, 1997). As our case shows this aspect might, if not handled properly, limit the change towards collaboration compared to the potential and plans.

FUTURE ISSUES

We will now briefly introduce some future issues against the background of our experiences and our previous discussion. The first such issue is related to the relatively limited experiences of and knowledge about information technology that was an aspect of significance in the case in the study, as well as in many other similar environments. A consequence from this lack of knowledge and experiences is that enabling conditions in the form of training, workshops, etc., are of strategic importance for the employees to imagine both how to use the groupware system as well as new ways of work.

An interesting question is what will happen in the relatively near future when large groups in these organizations will have substantially deeper knowledge and more experiences of information technology in general and groupware in particular. Will it be possible for them to imagine new ways of work as well as to actually change the organizational structure to a more informal and collaborative one? In other words, our conclusions from our study might largely be dependent on the current state regarding knowledge and experiences of information technology, which then can be characterized as temporal.

On the other hand, these new ways of work are a drastic change as compared to the present bureaucratic organizational structure in which formal rules and regulations have provided the grounds for activities. Changing to an organizational structure characterized by process and collaborative ways of work was one of the aims with the introduction of the groupware system according to the plans (ADB-kontoret, 1997). In a discussion about the potential to change the public-sector administration towards this direction, the difficulties with doing so is emphasized (Lenk & Traunmüller, 2000). The advantages that are associated with such new ways of work are also significant. To what extent such changes actually are possible as well as in which circumstances such changes can be achieved are interesting issues for further studies.

Our study as well as our previous discussion has been carried out from the perspective of the employees within the local government. This as opposed to other groups that might be influenced by the introduction of groupware such as politicians and citizens. Public-sector organizations as the one discussed in this chapter can be characterized as bureaucratic, hierarchical and heavily affected by rules and regulations. However, this also means that their work forms are established and formal, and thus in a way, transparent to for example citizens. This compared to more informal, collaborative and flexible but at the same time not as transparent forms of organizations.

Another issue is what will happen in the future to the transparency from the perspective of citizens and politicians. With the introduction of groupware and new ways of work: "The accessibility of public administration authorities will decrease, not only for the citizen but also for public and political bodies. The partition walls within the public administrations may become more permeable, but the outer walls may become thicker and more massive" (Snellen & Wyatt, 1993, p. 291). An interesting issue is to what extent this actually seems to be the case, as well as what measures should be taken to remedy the situation from the perspective of citizens and politicians.

CONCLUSION

In this chapter, we have described the change process related with the introduction of groupware in a Swedish municipal administration. In our analysis and discussion, we have used the improvisational model of change management by Orlikowski and Hofman (1997). Based on the experiences from the study, we have brought forward some aspects, which can contribute to improve the results in similar change processes in comparable organizational environments in the public sector.

Firstly, we would like to emphasize the importance of communicating the organizational plan and vision. We found that the employees' unawareness of the organizational visions limited their understanding of the technology and its potential.

Secondly, we stress the significance of providing support and training for the personnel concerned. We discussed this from two different views both concerning the focus the training ought to have as well as concerning how the training in practice ought to be arranged. We found that the lack of discussing the new ways of work during the provided training limited the employees' learning. For the employees to fully take advantage of the training is important to provide adjusted and continuous support.

Thirdly, we would like to add a type of change in order to make this model more adjusted to the public sector, namely the type non-occurring anticipated change. The argument for this is based on both the experiences from our study as well as previous research concerning characteristics of the public sector (Heeks & Davies, 1999; Wimmer et al., 2001) and Mintzberg's (1978) research about change management. A consequence from these is the common results of anticipated changes not being realized. The addition of this type of change facilitates a more active management of this phenomenon.

Fourth, we would like to emphasize the necessity of translating the organizational plan into local context and we have discussed the complexity local autonomy can involve. As such, local autonomy is a consequence of public sector reform towards decentralization.

Our study has confirmed what previous research has put forward concerning the importance of enabling conditions in order to reach collaboration when introducing groupware (Orlikowski & Hofman, 1997). In addition, our study showed that this is particularly important in organizational environments within the public sector where the level of knowledge and previous experiences of technology is low. The bureaucratic culture, the complex organizational environment (Wimmer et al., 2001) and the low level of knowledge and experiences (Heeks & Davies 1999) together complicate the process of change. The discussed enabling conditions in forms of the communication of the plan, adjusted training, arenas for knowledge transfer, work groups, seminars, etc., are necessary in order for the organization to make use of the full potential of the groupware system. These enabling conditions serve an important role enabling the organization to realize planned changes and to take care of the changes that emerge over time in the change process.

ACKNOWLEDGMENTS

We would like to thank ADB-kontoret in Göteborg, Sweden, the local government districts for their participation and the Swedish Council for Work Life Research for funding our research.

REFERENCES

ADB-kontoret. (1997). LIS--The virtual work group, independent of time and space (LIS Den virtuella arbetsgruppen, oberoende av tid och rum, in Swedish), *Internal Report*. Göteborg: ADB-kontoret.

Bikson, T. K. and Eveland, J. D. (1996). Groupware implementation: Reinvention in the sociotechnical frame. In *Proceedings of CSCW'96*, Cambridge MA, USA, 428-437.

Bødker, S., Kyng, M. and Schmidt, K. (Eds.). (1999). *ECSCW'99 Proceedings of the Sixth European Conference on Computer-Supported Cooperative Work*, September 12-16, Copenhagen, Denmark. The Netherlands: Kluwer Academic Publishers.

Ciborra, C. U. (2000). Drifting: from control to drift. In Braa, K., Sørensen, C. and Dahlbom, B. (Eds.), *Planet Internet*, 185-195. Lund: Studentlitteratur.

Ciborra, C. U. and Lanzara, G. F. (1994). Formative contexts and information technology: Understanding the dynamics of innovation in organizations. *Accounting Management Information Technology*, 4(2), 61-86.

Czarniawska, B. and Joerges, B. (1996). Travels of Ideas. In Czarniawska, B. and Sevón, G. (Eds.), *Translating Organizational Change*, 13-48. Berlin: Walter de Gruyter & Co.

Dawson, P. (1994). *Organizational Change: A Processual Approach*. Newcastle: Athenaeum Press Ltd.

Essler, U. (1998). *Analyzing Groupware Adoption: A Framework and Three Case Studies in Lotus Notes Deployment*. Dissertation. Department of Computer and Systems Science, Stockholm University/Royal Institute of Technology, Stockholm.

Grudin, J. (1994). Eight challenges for developers. *Communications of the ACM*, 37(1), 93-105.

Hammersley, M. and Atkinson, P. (1995). Ethnography. *Principles in Practice*. London and New York: Routledge.

Heeks, R. and Davies, A. (1999). Different approaches to information age reform. In Heeks, R. (Ed.), *Reinventing Government in the Information Age. International Practice in IT-Enabled Public Sector Reform*, 22-48. London and New York: Routledge.

Josefsson, U. and Nilsson, A. (1999). The progress of groupware use in local government. In *Proceedings of the 6th European Conference of Information Technology Evaluation*, 159-166. Uxbridge, UK: Brunel University.

Karsten, H. and Jones, M. (1998). The long and winding road: Collaborative IT and organisational change. In *CSCW'98*, 29-38. Seattle, Washington, USA.

Lenk, K. and Traunmüller, R. (2000). Introductory presentation: A framework for electronic government. In Tjoa, A. M., Wagner, R. R. and Al-Zobaidie, A. (Eds.), *Proceedings of the 11th International Workshop on Database and Expert Systems Applications*, 271-277. California: IEEE Computer Society.

Lewin, K. (1958). Group decisions and social change. In Maccoby, E. E., Newcomb, T. M. and Hartley, E. L. (Eds.), *Readings in Social Psychology*, 197-211. New York, Rhinehart & Winston.

Macredie, R. D. and Sandom, C. (1999). IT-enabled change: Evaluating an improvisational perspective. *European Journal of Information Systems*, 8, 247-259.

Mambrey, P. & Pipek, V. (1999). Enhancing participatory design by multiple communication channels. In *Proceeding of the International Conference on Human-Computer-Interaction, HCI'99*. Lawrence Erlbaum.

Mintzberg, H. (1978). Patterns in strategy formation. *Management Science*, 24(9), 934-948.

Nilsson, A., Josefsson, U. and Ranerup, A. (2000). Towards public-sector networking: Change management introducing groupware. In Svensson, L., Snis, U., Sørensen, C., Fägerlind, H., Lindroth, T., Magnusson, M. and Östlund, C. (Eds.), *Proceedings of Information Systems Research in Scandinavia conference 2000, IRIS'23*, 1345-1357.

Laboratorium for Interaction Technology, University of Trollhättan Uddevalla.

Nilsson, A., Josefsson, U. and Ranerup, A. (2001). Improvisational change management in the public sector. In *Proceedings of the 34ᵗʰ Annual Hawaii International Conference on Systems Science*. Alamitos, CA: IEEE.

Olesen, K. and Myers D. M. (1999). Trying to improve communication and collaboration with information technology, an action research project which failed. *Information Technology & People*, 12(4), 317-332.

Orlikowski, W. (1993). Learning from Notes: Organizational issues in groupware implementation. *The Information Society*, 9(3), 237-250.

Orlikowski, W. (1996). Evolving with Notes: Organizational change around groupware technology. In Ciborra, C. (Ed.), *Groupware & Teamwork*, 23-59. J. Chichester: Wiley & Sons.

Orlikowski, W. and Hofman, D. (1997). An improvisational model for change management: The case of groupware technologies. *Sloan Management Review*, Winter, 11-21.

Pipek, W. and Wulf, V. (1999). A groupware's life. In Bødker, S., Kyng, M. and Schmidt, K. (Eds.), *Proceedings of the Sixth European Conference on Computer-Supported Cooperative Work, ECSCW'99*, 199-219. The Netherlands: Kluwer Academic Publishers.

Ranerup, A. (1996). *User Participation with Representatives (Användarmedverkan med Representanter*, in Swedish). Dissertation. Department of informatics, Göteborg University.

Ranerup, A. (1999). Internet-enabled applications for local government democratization. Contradictions of the Swedish experience. In Heeks, R. (Ed.), *Reinventing Government in the Information Age. International Practice in IT-Enabled Public Sector Reform*, 77-193. London and New York: Routledge.

Silverman, D. (1993). *Interpreting Qualitative Data. Methods for Analysing, Talk, Text and Interaction*. London: Sage Publications.

Snellen, I. and Wyatt, S. (1993). Blurred participation but thicker walls. Involving citizens in computer supported cooperative work for public administration. *Computer-Supported Cooperative Work (CSCW)*, 1, 277-293.

Vandenbosch, B. and Ginzberg, M. J. (1997). Lotus Notes and collaboration: Plus ça change. *Journal of Management Information Systems*, Winter, 13(3), 65-81.

Wimmer, M., Traunmüller, R. and Lenk, K. (2001). Electronic business invading the public sector: Considerations on change and design. In *Proceedings of the 34ᵗʰ Annual Hawaii International Conference on Systems Science*. Alamitos, CA: IEEE.

Yin, R. (1984). Analyzing case study evidence. In Yin, R. (Ed.), *Case Study Research. Design and Methods*, 105-115. Beverly Hills, CA: Sage Publications.

Chapter XV

e-Government in Sweden: Centralization, Self-Service and Competition

Mikael Wiberg
University of Göteborg, Sweden

Åke Grönlund
Umeå University, Sweden

The Internet has often been envisioned to have decentralizing effects. Not only should the technology in theory have the potential for making it easier to live and run companies in rural areas, but also this is in fact supposed to happen on such a scale that the countryside would achieve a development similar to that in urban areas. In Europe, and certainly in Sweden, governments–long before Internet use became widespread–established policies to help development in rural areas. It seems then that the Internet would come as a welcome gift, as it is supposed to facilitate such policies; indeed rather make them obsolete if it in fact were true that Internet use would inherently lead to decentralization.

This chapter reviews a study concerned with how Swedish government agencies used IT during the period of 1985-1999–to centralize or to decentralize?

The reason for studying government agencies is that the Swedish policy in support of regional development is meant to balance other developments that are negative for the region, such as the long way to markets, negative population growth, etc. This policy competes with other goals, such as economic goals and incentives for the individual government organization. The study was undertaken to see what the practical result of all these different policies is.

In this chapter, we first briefly review the background, which includes a shift in attitudes for government agencies towards more of economic incentives, a generally more business-like approach. We go on to present our research questions and hypotheses. The results are then illustrated by a review of one of the four organizations studied, the AMV (the Swedish National Labor Market Agency), which is the organization officially celebrated as the e-Government role model for the future. Finally, we present our conclusions (which come from all four organizations studied, with AMV being the most prominent example).

GOVERNMENT AGENCIES, REGIONAL POLICY AND BUSINESS DEVELOPMENT

Over the past 15 years, the role of Swedish national government agencies has changed dramatically. Agencies converted to government-owned companies, privatization and deregulations have meant that size, tasks and the terms of operations have changed fundamentally. In particular, the possibilities to use government agencies as actors in the regional policy have become less open. Previously, starting in the 1970s, relocation of government agencies to promote employment in regions where private business move out or is generally weak was an often-used measure.

There were two main reasons for the relocation strategy. The first was to slow down the expansion in the capital area, for the purpose of achieving a more balanced development nationwide. The second was that the government wanted to achieve positive effects for the recipient cities. By relocating government agencies, it was hoped that also other organizations that had close cooperation with those agencies would follow, thus increasing the positive effect (Statskontoret, 1989, pp. 9-21).

Since the early 1990s, the government sector has gone through dramatic change. Work has been rationalized and central government tasks have been decentralized to a regional or local level. Management by goals and results rather than by detailed instruction has been implemented at all levels. Government organizations have been reorganized or closed, government-owned companies have been privatized. Due to the severe financial crisis in central government, encountered in the early 1990s, efficiency has been emphasized. The goal of the regional policy is now to support growth in all regions for the purpose of contributing to the national growth (Reko 1997, p. 9).

In the late 1980s, the Ministry of the Interior emphasized three basic goals and incentives that would permeate the reform of the administration. At the ideological level, civil servants were to work more flexibly with a customer focus, rather than strictly abiding by the regulatory framework. There was an ambition to getting rid of the civil servant hallmark as a highly formal red-tapist. By focusing on the customer, government could fulfill the second goal, a service spirit permeating the organization. Complementing these two goals was an economic one; improved efficiency on the part of the civil servants. This was to be achieved by computerization and organizational change (Stjernberg, 1989, pp. 25-26).

In conclusion, the current goals replace detailed government control by customer service and efficiency.

AIM AND RESEARCH QUESTIONS

The overall goal of the research project "IT in Government Administration–A Means for Centralization or Decentralization?" was to investigate how IT use has affected regional and local branches of central government agencies: localization, organization, employment and individual workplaces' role in local, regional and national networks. We studied:

- Changes in organizational structure concerning geographic localization of departments and tasks, changes in transportation of information and people.
- The way these changes had affected individual workplaces' work functions, work content and role in local, regional and national networks.
- How the changes had affected service quality and accessibility.

Hypotheses

Given the situation described above, where efficiency and service have become more important than regional development as incentives and drivers for the national government agencies, our main hypothesis was that the rural areas were largely impoverished by the implementation of the new policy. We believed IT was used mainly to make organizations more effective, which typically means fewer people at the operational level and more centralized control. We believed that not only would employment decrease in rural areas, but also–most of all–there would be a change in work content. We hypothesized that highly skilled work was centralized whereas low-skill jobs would remain in the rural areas, or be relocated to such areas, for instance in call centers. This would mean the rural areas would become impoverished also socially, as jobs would be less diverse with a heavier emphasis of low-end jobs, which would lead also to services and culture not only shrinking in volume, but also becoming less diverse.

A potential modification of this very negative hypothesis, we believed, was that a number of centers would be established, and that in that sense a decentralization would have occurred, namely from the Stockholm area to a number of regional centers.

As for service quality, we expected to find diverse developments. On the one hand, we expected to find manual services replaced by electronic ones, thus decreasing the service supply immediately available locally. On the other hand we thought that at least the IT-educated and IT-equipped part of the population would see an actual increase in service quality as the number, content and quality of services via automated telephone services and the Internet would grow.

By another note, we believed that the reduction of (physical) service points would mean that the local human networks become thinner. The sum of all this, we believed, would be that the negative consequences for the rural areas outweigh the positive ones that individuals may experience from some better individual services.

More strictly, our main hypothesis--that the rural areas were impoverished--was operationalized in the following sub-hypotheses:

Hypothesis 1: The number of jobs decreases in the rural areas, or decreases more there than in cities or in places within commuting distance.

IT use in, for instance, the banks has had that kind of effect, and we expected to see a similar development in the national government sector.

Hypothesis 2: Highly skilled jobs are centralized while low-skilled ones are decentralized.

Recent development has seen routine jobs such as call centers allocated to rural areas because of the low salaries and government subsidies available there, while qualified jobs concerned with control and product development are centralized, among other reasons for the purpose of making services and activities across the country more similar.

Hypothesis 3: The cities' function as a "brain" is reinforced by centralizing units for control and decision making.

Also on this point the banks may serve as the role model. Telephone banks and Internet banks are central units operating across the country. There are examples of banks operating nationwide having only one single office, in Stockholm.

Hypothesis 4: A number of regional centers are developed.

This hypothesis is an alternative modification to the above three. It means the centralization is not directed towards one single city, but to a number of cities. These could be regional centers, or they could be national headquarters situated in places other than Stockholm.

Hypothesis 5: Manual services decrease.

This hypothesis is modeled, again, after the bank example, where the ambition to achieve efficiency (by means of ATMs, mail service, telephone banks, Internet banks) has led to a substantial decrease in the number of local offices and the number of staff at the remaining offices. We expected a similar development when government agencies were required to rationalize their operations.

Hypothesis 6: Service quality increases.

This may sound as contradicting Hypothesis 5, but it is not. We hypothesize that electronic services in fact in many cases deliver better services than manual ones, for instance by increased availability (24 hours, 7 days, over distances, etc.), quicker response, more complete information and services, new action spaces opening up to customers, etc.

This may certainly not be true for all people, but for those who are "wired" and have the necessary knowledge to navigate and utilize public services that are not always straightforward.

METHOD AND DELIMITATIONS

The research project was a cooperation between the departments of Informatics and Social and Economic Geography.

There was a literature study part and a case study part. The literature study part included studies of available documents, such as employment data, yearly reports, government strategy documents and interviews with people in key positions.

The case study part focused on the region of Västerbotten. We visited 19 local offices, conducted interviews and studied facilities and activities. The offices were selected to cover three types of areas: cities, rural areas within commuting distance from cities and remote rural areas (more than 40 kilometers from a city).

Four government agencies were studied; Telia (Swedish Telecom, previously 100% government owned, now partly privatized), AMV (National Labor Market Agency), the Police (which in Sweden is a national agency) and the Social Insurance Office.

The offices studied were situated in Umeå, Vännäs, Vindeln, Lycksele, Vilhelmina and Dorotea. These places were selected for population and geographic localization.

In the rest of this chapter, we present the results of the study as a whole, but for lack of space, the examples are taken from only one organization, the AMV.

Some Key Concepts

Remote and Commuting-Distance Rural Areas

This study made the typical distinction between remote rural areas and commuting-distance ones. The difference between the two is that commuting-distance areas are situated within 40 kilometers from a city with a population over 3,000 people. The choice of 3,000 people is because this is the size of a town expected to be enough for maintaining a basic public and commercial service supply (Nutek, 1997, p. 4). The 40 kilometers distance is chosen because this is the distance people are expected to commute daily to jobs or shops (for Sweden as a whole, this distance is set to 30 kilometers, but in the Västerbotten region, being largely rural, people are expected to cover more distance). A population over 50,000 marks a "city."

Centralization, Decentralization, Concentration and Distribution

Spatial relocation of activities tends to change the distribution of important functions. Typical terms for this are *centralization* and *decentralization*.

Decentralization literally means "from the center," and centralization of course the opposite. The concepts are used in many contexts, but the strict definitions have to do with the authority of decision making, not just geographical relocation of activities. Centralization and decentralization thus have to do with the distribution of power being shifted, either towards or from some center (which can be differently defined according to the focus of the study). Decentralization then means that the local level increases its power (Engellau, 1982, p. 11).

Centralization consequently means that the top of a hierarchy strengthens its position with respect to control and decision making. In this case this would mean the national government becomes strengthened at the expense of the regional and local levels, or the regional one at the expense of the local.

Decentralization means strategic decision making and control over operations would be shifted to a lower level in the hierarchy, from central level to regional or local, or from regional level to local.

There is yet another dimension to decentralization. According to Selle (1991, p. 107), "Decentralization means the degree of autonomy in geographically delimited political-administrative units with respect to their relations to a central national power." This is to say the national government can delegate tasks to regional or local governments, for instance towns. In this study, however, we limit the view to national government agencies.

The Swedish government is hierarchically organized. It is comprised of several levels with well-defined administrative borders, a fact that does not inhibit those borders to be changed over time.

The Swedish regional policy has had the ambition to leverage regional differences. One means to that end has since the 1970s been relocation of government agencies. This has been called decentralization, but in fact the concept of deconcentration is more appropriate. Deconcentration occurs when different functions, such as execution or responsibility, are distributed over a larger geographical area or down a hierarchy, but the control remains centrally. The difference between decentralization and deconcentration is thus one of control and decision making: decentralization requires some amount of those items (usually together) to be shifted down the hierarchy.

A relocation of an activity does not necessarily mean decentralization as long as power does not come with it. A government organization moving out from Stockholm remains centralized as long as the organization remains highly hierarchical and power is not delegated downwards. Geographical relocation is thus better named deconcentration. The Swedish terminology is less clear on this point than, for instance, the French, from where influences have been found to the Swedish development (Andersson, 1989, p. 107; Arell, 2000).

AN EXAMPLE–THE LABOUR MARKET AGENCY

We will now illustrate our study by presenting an example from AMV (the Swedish National Labor Market Agency). AMV is chosen because it in many ways represents the spearhead of the Swedish development. Officially celebrated as the avant-garde for electronic government (Ekroth, 2000), the AMV has been very ambitious in introducing self-service over the Internet and accompanying electronic systems to support customer activities in job searching. Other government agencies are following, most importantly the Social Insurance Office, which is currently on the track for a similar development. AMV is thus a role model for the Swedish development towards electronic government.

Computerization at AMV

The computerization at AMV (then AMS, Arbetsmarknadsstyrelsen) started in the early 1980s, with an intense period in the mid '80s. At that time, computer support for searching for jobs and labor and matching between available jobs and job seekers was built. There were two basic systems. One was the Job List System (Platslistsystemet), which produced lists of available jobs. This system comprised functions for registration and production of statistics concerning available jobs as well as job seekers.

The other system was the Job Mediation System (Platsförmedlingssystemet), which made searching the Job List from terminals possible, and which contained functions for observation, that is on an ongoing basis searching for matches between jobs and people. The system was run nightly against the Job List Systems. The system required regional computers for registration and searching, a central computer for matches and nationwide communication between the regional and central computers, and to each office where terminals were installed. In 1980, some 20 terminals were connected, but during the '80s the system was expanded to cover the whole country.

During the 1990s, computer use in the AMV has changed fundamentally. By the early 1990s the above-mentioned Job Mediation system was fully implemented. The administrative routines were run on a new AMV mainframe computer, which meant the organization no longer had to rely on outsourcing to private service bureaus.

Each regional AMV office had its own computer for administrative systems. The Job List, in the early 1980s produced at five locations, was in the early 1990s produced at only two. By then, the Job Mediation system was run at the regional computers. But the major change during the 1990s concerns the use of an intranet and of the Internet, implemented during the second half of the decade.

The Job Mediation system (called AF-90) contains information about every person registered as job seeker at any Job Office in Sweden. There is personal data, data about education, what job(s) the person is looking for and job experiences. The information is confidential (Arbetsmarknadsstyrelsen, 1982, p. 3). For the AMV staff, there are different levels of access. The so-called assistant access level, for instance, is only about registering information about available jobs, and registering information about job seekers at the actual office where the assistant works. The access system is centralized, which means an assistant can perform her work at any workplace (Arbetsmarknadsstyrelsen, 1982, p. 3).

The nationwide Mediation system is today the most important tool for the Job Officers, and it is heavily used. There are about 5,000 concurrent users, and the number of transactions in the system is about 50 per second. This translates to a daily number of transactions sometimes in excess of 1,700,000.

In the Mediation system, AF-90 is used for a number of tasks. In the communication with employers, it is used for instance to find suitable candidates to direct[1] to available positions, to exhibit to the employers the available workforce so as to give them an idea of what competence can at all be found. In communication with job seekers, the system is used for instance to search jobs, provide information about the situation at the labor market and to follow up the result of job applications. Information about the job seeker can be entered for the purpose of automatic observation. Automatic matching of the job seekers' competence profile against available jobs is then done every night when the database is updated in a batch mode. Positive results (match found) are sent to the job seeker.

The AF-90 also contains a complementary system where the requirements of free jobs are matched interactively with the competence and preference profiles of the job seekers. AF-90 is a part of the European system EURES, which contains information about available jobs EU-wide.

The major difference between the system of the 1980s and that of today is that today, the searching and matching activities can to vital parts be conducted by the job seeker herself by means of Internet use. Access to the systems that make this possible was previously a Job Officer exclusive right. Job seekers had to wait until the information on free jobs were published in the Job List, or until they got a message from a Job Officer telling about the result of a matching operation.

To complement the job mediation functions, the AF-90 also contains some administrative tools to help the staff, for instance automatic alerts.

As the AMV has applied management by goals and controls for over a decade, the systems that are used to follow up on activities are indispensable. There is a management information system named Leda, by which statistics are collected and analyzed weekly or monthly. Activities are analyzed by region as well as overall for the whole country. The information is available on the AMV intranet, which means that not only managers at different levels, but also the individual Job Officer can check the statistics for her own office each week. The original data comes from the AF-90 system (Arbetsmarknadsstyrelsen, 1982, p. 9).

The AMV system for economy control is named Presto. This system is used for budget planning and follow-ups on the activities at the local offices. The system makes it possible to study the whole chain of events from decision (on some unemployment benefit) to payment. The regional offices (LAN) use this system for control of the activities at the local offices within each LAN's jurisdiction.

The system for production of statistics is named Händel. This system, too, collects the basic information from the AF-90. Then it constructs long time series, containing job seeker histories. This information is anonymized, and is used for planning, for instance to identify which groups are likely to encounter problems at the job market in the future.

In addition to the Job Officer support tools in the AF-90, there is a range of administrative tools for the staff's daily use. One of these tools is VIS, the AMV information service on the intranet. VIS contains selected management information from the Leda system. The staff also has access to a personal mailbox, several tools such as the AMV Rulebook, catalogues on educations, electronic forms and rules for economic support to individuals.

There is also an economy system used for administration of the different unemployment financial subsidies, reporting job seeker activities (it is compulsory to visit information events, attend assigned courses and so on) and time reports.

Table 1 summarizes the administrative tools available.

New Terms During the 1990's

By the end of the 1990s, the AMV was radically reorganized. In 1996, the organization was subject to considerable demands of reducing costs. This led to the fact that most part of the regional districts' administration was transferred to a new organization, AMV Services (AMV-tjänster). Districts were redefined geographically. The aim for the reorganization was to make the internal administration more effective. To reach that end, the traditional regional organization, based geographically on the towns and the political regions, was abandoned.

Table 1: IT systems for use by the job officers

System	Function
AF 90	Registration of job seekers and job offers. Links to the Social Insurance Agency, the Internet Job List and a service for printing the paper version of the Job List
AIS	Guide on how to handle the job-seeking process
Blankett	All forms used at AMV are available electronically for filling in and/or printing out
Diva	Database on available educations and descriptions of professions
Lilla Lila	Advising system, containing guides for the Job Officer on what to ask a job seeker during the interview
Regelboken	The AMV Rule Book
Resetjänst	Travel bookings
Email	Send email to job seekers, and internal messages
VIS	Intranet

AMV in Västerbotten

The regional AMV office, the Länsarbetsnämnden (LAN), residing in the regional capital Umeå, is the administrative center and management organization for the local Job Offices in Västerbotten. Locally, the management body is the AMV committee, one in each town (kommun).

At the local level, there are Job Offices, one in each town except for the hub towns of Umeå, Skellefteå and Storuman, which have more than one office each. In addition to the ordinary job offices, there are in Umeå and Skellefteå what is called "special offices," for instance information centers (Infotek) containing, among other things, computers and Internet lines for self services. Other special offices include AF International (jobs abroad) and AF Culture and Media. In the other towns, the ordinary offices have to cover all fields.

At the local level there are also so-called Labor Market Institutes (LMIs). In Västerbotten, such a body exists in five towns; Umeå, Skellefteå, Lycksele, Malå and Vilhelmina. Table 1 shows the number of AMV employees at the local level in 1993 and 1999.

In addition to at least one office in each Västerbotten town, there are also two itinerant offices, in Tärnaby and in Burträsk. As Table 2 shows, the number of employees at job offices and LMIs has shrunk by on average 15% (20% for men, 14% for women), or a total of 437 people.

Since the mid-80s, each job office has a budget responsibility. The local offices receive their money from the regional LANs, which in turn get their funding from AMV. The local offices have one budget for operations and one for "actions" (activities for or financial support to job seekers). There is also a special budget for complementary actions directed towards disabled people.

Local managers make up a budget and distribute funds on the available set of actions, the goals of which are set at the national and regional levels. All since the 1980s, the possibilities to decide on the daily operations have been increasingly up to the individual office. As of today, there is virtually no LAN involvement in daily operations at the local offices. The idea is that the LAN is first of all a managing unit, but also a service organization supplying guidance to the local offices. The latter function, however, is today about to be lost due to the considerable reduction of staff at the LANs and to the general AMV restructuring.

Table 2: Number of AMV employees at the local level in Västerbotten (Source: LAN Västerbotten)

Town	1993			1999			1993-1999
	Men	Women	Total	Men	Women	Total	Change
Robertsfors	1	4	5	3	3	6	20%
Umeå	65	102	167	66	99	165	-1%
Skellefteå	56	66	122	40	63	103	-16%
Storuman	3	7	10	4	4	8	-20%
Sorsele	2	3	5	2	2	4	-20%
Norsjö	2	10	12	2	7	9	-25%
Nordmaling	5	3	8	3	3	6	-25%
Åsele	3	5	8	2	4	6	-25%
Dorotea	1	6	7	1	4	5	-29%
Malå	2	8	10	2	5	7	-30%
Lycksele	13	21	34	6	16	22	-35%
Vännäs	4	4	8	2	3	5	-37%
Vindeln	2	8	10	1	5	6	-40%
Vilhelmina	11	14	25	6	9	15	-40%
Burträsk	3	3	6	1	2	3	-50%
Total	173	264	437	141	229	370	-15%

Changes in the Internal Work

By 1980, AMV (then AMS) tried to establish better routines for job mediation. There was an ambition to better utilize resources. Computerization was one means, already initiated.

The deployment of computer terminals across the country aimed at providing job seekers with better–more complete, more up-to-date, searchable–information. From 1979-80, computer use was expanded. In 1981, a new organizational plan was established, valid as of July 1. The staff was divided into two groups, mediators and advisors. At least 50% of the staff was to do mediation (Arbetsmarknadsdepartementet, 1982, p. 19). The goal of the advising was to "...make it possible for the job seeker to find, get, and keep a job. The advisory service is available to those who do not have clear goals in terms of what job to look for, people with work hindering disabilities and those who have a job but look for another" (Arbetsmarknadsverket, 1988:10).

A marked change in the internal work at AMV was the transition from the paper-based journals of the '80s–where files were transported by car from one office to another as people moved, for instance, to the AF-90 system. Due to the availability of AF-90 and the Internet, information can now be disseminated in parallel to several or all offices. This has changed the work of the Job Officers. While previously local knowledge was key, and a sufficient requirement, today the staff has to be knowledgeable about a wide variety of matters, including local employers and those in nearby towns, potential markets for job seekers, options for studies abroad, university and distance education, and distant employers.

Another important change is the effect in the early 1990s dramatically increased–by more than 100 %–unemployment. Today, a Job Officer spends very little time advising. The key is job seeker self-service, and for the job seeker herself to come up with the initiatives on what to do. The staff is now focusing on making the job seeker as "visible" as possible in the AF-90 database, for instance by helping her to define her best possible competence using the predefined keywords of the database. They are also working actively with employers, asking for specifications of requirements for new staff, describing the AMV educations and discussing what measures in terms of education could be taken for, as the term is, "dress up" the unemployed so as to make them better match the employers' demands.

Customer Encounter and Customer Service

Over the past two decades, considerable changes in the customer encounter at AMV have taken place. This has led to the job seeker's part becoming more active, including increased responsibilities. Following dramatically increased unemployment, the role of the Job Officer has become less active concerning the actual job mediation, and a change towards a more goal-oriented behavior, where the number of activities (people getting a job, an education or similar) is a key.

A parallel development is the abandonment of the government monopoly on job mediation, which has led to a number of new agents in the field, including intermediate employers such as ManPower and regional or national dailies such as Västerbottens Kuriren (www.vk.se) and DNnet (www.dn.se). Another factor affecting the way work at the Job Office is done is the rapid increase in Internet use, which has meant self-service is in fact possible.

AMV is an example of a government agency that has put considerable effort into providing computer support for self-service, now including not only lists of jobs and educations, but also multimedia tools for learning how to apply for a job, for writing a CV, for learning about the content and requirements of different professions, and a number of other things (see Table 3).

The Information Offices (Infotek) are places where all these tools are available to the job seeker. The fact that these tools are available has meant the job seeker is now required to work her way through the full set of tools, giving her a lot of more work as compared to in the 1980s. On the positive side, she has a considerable amount of options at her hands, not only the rich set of tools and information provided by the government job offices, but also the services of the new actors in the job mediation market.

The following summarizes the development since the early 1980s, which has taken two major leaps: from paper to computerized system, and from focus on the Job Officer to focus on the job seeker as the key actor in the job-seeking process.

1980

In the early 1980s, the encounter between the job seeker and the employer was mediated by the Job Officers and the (paper) Job List, which was the main information source. The Job Officer was the link between available jobs and available job seekers. The Job List was the job seekers' only guide to the complete job supply.

1990

In the early 1990s, computerized matching between job seekers and available jobs, based on profiles for qualifications and requirements respectively, was the focus. This

Table 3: Software applications designed and supplied at the job offices by AMV to support the job seeker (Liljenäs m fl, 2000, p. 82)

System	Function
1. Structuration support	
Struktur	Support for development of job-seeking action plan
2. Orientation support	
Pejling	Register of available educations and descriptions of a large number of professions
Yrkesguiden (Job Guide)	Advising by means of descriptions, multimedia presentations and films about jobs and educations.
Diva	Another register of available educations and descriptions of a large number of professions
Stöd & Stipendier (Support & Grants)	Information about how and from where to apply for grants
Steget (The Step)	Teaches a number of things you need to know for starting your own business: budget calculations, planning of financing, tax regulations, etc.
Frida	Information about non-government schools
Dialog	Searching for educations and professions by the type of activities and tasks involved, to help the job seeker find jobs with appropriate content
3. Support for learning about yourself	
Impuls	An interactive tool designed to help answering questions such as "What do I want to do?" "What are my strengths?" "What are my dreams?"
Max i Jobblandet (Max in the Job Land)	Description of jobs and categories of jobs by typical tasks; cheerful approach, bordering to that of a cartoon

matching was initiated by the Job Officers, who held a key position. The role of the Job Office was to support the job seeker in describing her qualifications properly, for the purpose of being able to identify the most suitable jobs. IT was the key factor, as both the job seeker and the Job Officer were dependent on the matching possibilities, which depended on the contents of the database and the job-seeker qualification description.

1999

By 1999, the role of the Job Office is to help the job seeker help herself. This is done by providing tools for learning about the job market, about how to approach employers and about how to acquire the skills necessary for getting a desired job. An intermediary institution, the Infotek, loaded with IT tools, has become an important tool for reducing the workload on the Job Officers. Here, job seekers are kept busy with helping themselves without much assistance. The encounter between the job seeker and the Job Officer is well prepared by the job seeker first having to go through several IT tools to compose a clear plan for her job-seeking odyssey, including a well-structured description of her own skills and desires, a reasonable list of potential jobs, a plan for how to get there, including for instance suggestions for appropriate education as preparation, etc.

In conclusion, over the past 20 years, the main information source for the job seeker was the printed Job List. In the early 1990s, the computerized Job List and matching system

AF-90 was fully deployed, which made job seeking national rather than local, and which gave the job seekers the opportunity to search by themselves. By the late 1990s, there were a lot of electronic information sources available to the job seeker, and the searching and matching activities are largely delegated to her, leaving the Job Officer with registration and control duties.

Changes in Transportation of Goods, Information, and People

From the above description it should be clear that AMV has used the IT systems over time to provide more and more information to the client-organization encounter. This was done in two distinct phases. In the first phase, the Job Officer was provided with new tools for searching and matching to complement. In the second phase, these tools, reshaped and in combination with other information on professions, educations, etc., were made available directly to the client, the job seeker.

The job-seeking process, and the roles of the client and the Job Officer respectively, have thus changed considerably over the two decades described here. The series of pictures below illustrates this.

In the early 1980s (Figure 1), the job seeker went to the Job Office to read the Job List and to talk to a Job Officer (by appointment), who acted as a sort of counselor. As the information was paper based, the whole system was mainly local. Interaction among offices was complicated and thus rare, as was looking for jobs in other cities.

The job-seeking process was initiated by a job seeker registering at the Job Office. She was interviewed, and a paper document was filed (at the local office only), providing a job-seeker profile. The job seeker had to rely on the Job Officer for the further process. On rare occasions, another office required information about the available workforce, or about an

Figure 1: Early 1980s. Printed media prevail

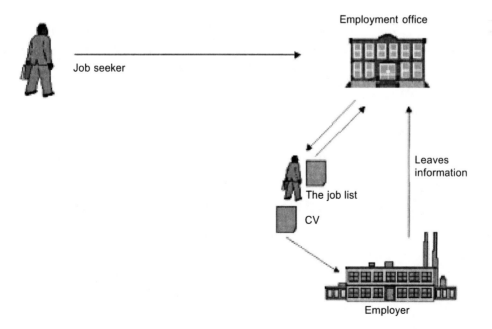

individual. In such cases, the appropriate files were sent by car to that office. Contacts between offices were maintained by telephone as necessary.

The Job List was printed weekly, and covered the whole country. One problem was that positions often were quickly filled, and thus the list was often obsolete already a few days after it was printed.

By the late 1980s (Figure 2), the AF-90 was implemented. This meant the job seeker could search the whole country for jobs and for labor. There were self-service terminals at the Job Offices, which meant part of the process could be handled by the job seeker herself.

By the late 1990s (Figure 3), self-service was the main idea. There are two new institutions, the information and services available on the Internet, and the "Infotek," a place where all these services are made available for those who can't access them from home, and where several other IT tools, developed by AMV to guide the job seeker, are available.

The job seeker is required to first go through a number of these tools. After that, she meets with a Job Officer to go through the result so produced, to register and to discuss the plan for action.

There are also several systems for use by the Job Officers (Table 1). These systems are partially integrated with other systems, for instance that of the Social Insurance Agency and the Internet Job List (www.ams.se, an outsourced service), and the AMV regions. The hub in the system is the computer on which the AF-90 is run.

At a typical encounter between the job seeker and the Job Officer, the former has already become knowledgeable (from her work at the Infotek) about what education or other service she is interested in. In such cases, only the AF-90 is used, possibly in combination with Resetjänst (for instance if a trip to a potential employer is required). In other cases, when the Infotek sessions have not yielded the intended result and if the Job Officer believes only relatively small measures have to be taken, systems like Diva are used to support a discussion on potential educations and services to support the further process (during this discussion, the Job Officer is constantly assessing the situation with the AMV budget and goals in mind).

Figure 2: Late 1980s. Computerized searching and matching

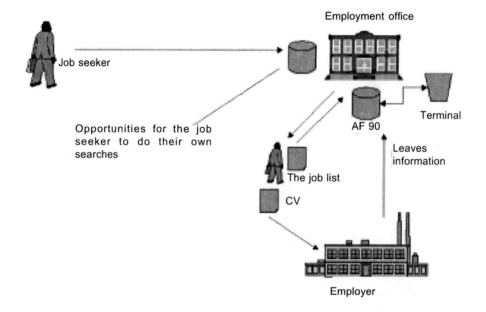

Figure 3: 1999--Self-service prevails

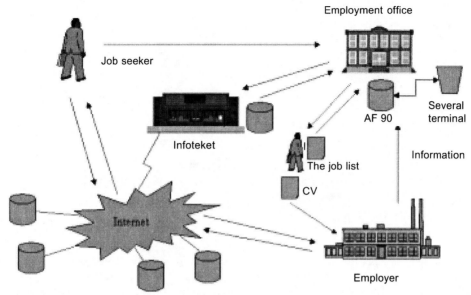

Job seeker

Employment office

Infoteket

AF 90

Several terminal

The job list

Information

CV

Internet

Employer

Virtual and private employment offices

Differences Between Cities and Rural Areas

It is clear that the supply of AMV services, manual and electronic, is better to people living in cities. First, the city offices provide a more diverse supply (e.g., the specialized services on jobs and educations abroad). Second, the Infoteks, the IT centers open to job seekers, exist only in the cities. Job seekers from the rural areas within commuting distance can, and do, use these facilities, whereas people in remote areas have to make do with the local supply. This means not only that the vast supply of support tools is not available, but often also that Internet access is not provided, or is provided only at a low quality over a modem. This means job seekers have to do without, or have to subscribe to an Internet service to their home, and at their own expense buy a computer, a modem, etc.

SUMMARY: CENTRALIZATION OR DECENTRALIZATION?

The development described above cannot simplistically be described as either centralization or decentralization. There are many ingredients in the development, and there are examples of changes in both directions. Also, the development has not been going straight in one direction; different periods have exhibited different traits. A summary of the most important ingredients for our purposes reads as follows (numbers refer to Figure 4).

The 1980s

1)   Concentration of management functions at regional offices and AMV.
2)   Responsibility for achieving the goals was delegated from AMV to the regional offices (LAN) and onwards to the local offices. The LANs were assigned responsibility for

managing the job-mediation work within each region (county), and each local Job Office was assigned responsibility for following the budget.

3)   Power was shifted to the LANs and the AMV away from the local offices, as the goals for the (local) activities were set at the LAN and AMV at the same time as the responsibility for achieving them was delegated to the local managers.

4)   The ability of AMV to control lower levels in the organization was improved as the central databases replaced the paper files.

The 1990s

1)   Control over activities is centralized as the computer systems allow better overview and analysis.

2)   A number of routine activities have been decentralized to the local offices, such as decisions on financial support for attending courses and travel support.

3)   The local Job Officers are constantly informed about how their activities relate to the stated goals, which has led to the staff realizing their contributions are constantly measured against the goals, and they are required to fulfill those. At the same time, they have no control over how the available funds are allocated across different activities. Taken together this means power is centralized (or at least shifted upwards--sometimes only to the LANs) while decisions on routine matters are decentralized.

4)   Power is shifted from the regional level to the central one as direct links between the local and central levels have been created by the increased IT use, e.g., the reporting systems and the intranet. By these systems, the central level can follow up on local activities, and disseminate information directly to the local offices. This way, the LANs have lost their earlier monopoly on information and control in their respective geographic area.

5)   Decentralization: the job seeker is now something of her own agent by having to use the self-service systems rather than having a Job Officer acting on her behalf. The Internet is the key enabler for this development.

CONCLUSION

Our aim was to investigate how IT use has affected the local and regional activities of government agencies in terms of localization, organization and employment, and individual workplaces' function in local, regional and national networks. The conclusions presented below concern all organizations studied, not just the AMV presented as an example above.

Our main hypothesis was that the rural areas were largely impoverished by the new policy, implemented to a large extent by means of IT use.

We studied four government agencies during the period of 1980-1999 (one of these organizations became a government-owned company during the period). We found three distinct stages in the development, here described by the AMV case:

Period 1, Before circa 1985

IT is used for mass production of simple products, such as the printed Job List. Mediation is mainly manual.

Figure 4

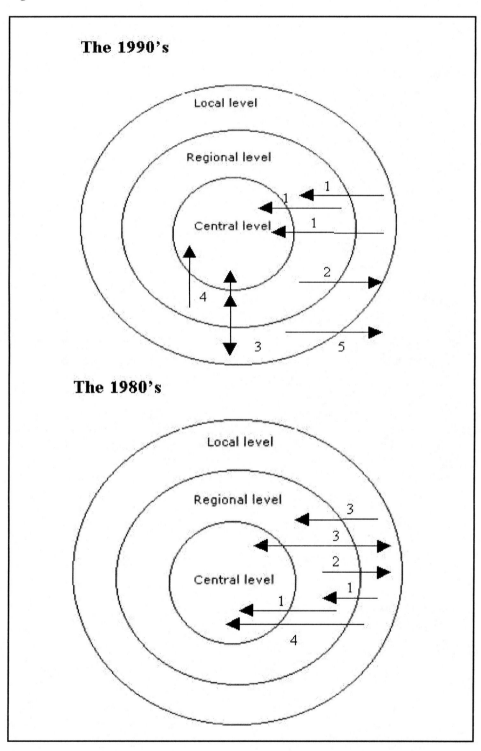

Period 2, 1985-1995

IT is used to support the Job Officers, who get more advanced possibilities, new information sources and tools for searching and matching. Mediation is now computer supported, and the Job Officer is the key actor in the job-seeking process.

Period 3, After circa 1995

IT is now frequently and increasingly used for self-service. The role of the Job Officer in the job-seeking process is reduced to administration, monitoring and control.

IT is used for central control of the performance of local entities' and individual Job Officers. An intranet is used for weekly result reports.

The years for transition from one stage to the next vary among the organizations. AMV is the most advanced, by now completely in Stage 3 when cities are concerned, less so in rural areas (which are largely seen as lagging; the efforts are spent on the new self-service policy). The Social Insurance Agency is currently in Stage 2, with strong ambitions going to Stage 3 in a few years time.

Put simply, we have seen that IT use in the organizations studied has meant centralized power. Management by goals, distributed responsibilities and efficient monitoring and control–for instance weekly reports on performance–are used very strategically by AMV and Telia. At the same time, the pressure on the individual employee has increased; she has to be able to manage more and more advanced technology, areas of responsibility have been widened and sometimes salary has become related to performance. In summary there was:

- increased individual responsibility;
- increased central control;
- often both widened and deepened competence on the part of the individual.

Comparing cities, commuting-distance countryside and remote rural areas, the following development was found:

The number of jobs has decreased everywhere, but most so in the rural areas. The availability of the new IT-based services is decidedly better in the cities than in rural areas. This is because the key issue is access to a computer, support tools, data communication and the skill to know where and how to search for information. In rural areas, the individual job seeker is often left to supplying this for herself, whereas in cities, technically well-equipped self-service offices are available.

Services have become more comprehensive, more versatile and more readily accessible when making use of IT, while manual services have not kept up with this development. This is currently to the detriment of people in rural areas in many cases. There are situations when no IT service can replace the presence of a real policeman when it comes to providing citizens with a feeling of security, for instance.

Review of Hypotheses and Findings

Were our hypotheses confirmed? The answer is both yes and no. Let us briefly review our hypotheses in the light of our findings:

Hypothesis 1: The number of jobs decreases in the rural areas.

Confirmed. The number of jobs has decreased everywhere, but most so in rural areas.

Hypothesis 2: Highly skilled jobs are centralized while low-skilled ones are decentralized.

On this point, the development is not so clear. On the one hand, jobs in rural areas are lost. On the other hand, the remaining jobs have become more qualified than before. They now require use of complicated IT, enlarged areas of responsibility, etc. At the Social

Insurance Office, some offices have been specialized to handle certain tasks and thus special competence is retained or concentrated to these offices, some of which are situated in rural towns. At the Job Office, Job Officers have had to learn about the Internet and about other sources to information than those provided by AMV so as to being able to assist the job seekers. On the other hand, their professional identity as advisors has been played down, and their efforts have been shifted towards administration and control.

Hypothesis 3: The cities' function as a "brain" is reinforced.

This seems to be the case. Control, in terms of detailed decision making, such as budgets for individual offices and the ability to monitor and follow up on activities, have been centralized. But at the same time, the individual professionals have been allowed greater freedom in terms of how to organize the daily work–under strict control by result, but not by schedule. The service technicians at Telia can choose whether to actually visit a customer or advise her over the phone on how to help herself. The daily planning is negotiated among technicians rather than assigned by a dispatcher, and technicians can exchange tasks among themselves at will. In summary, while the center has become more in control by goal and result, there is more room than before for some entrepreneurship at the grassroot level. It seems the detailed instruction style of the industrial paradigm has shifted towards the information society style of freedom under (quite heavy!) individual responsibility.

Hypothesis 4: A number of regional centers are developed (rather than just one).

This was not seen happening. In the case of one of the organizations, the Social Insurance Agency, there was indeed an organization where special assignments were distributed among a number of offices. But this organization was special for the region of Västerbotten, and it is already about to be abandoned for an AMV-style model, that is, self-service via the web, automated telephone systems, call centers and considerably reduced manual service at local offices.

Hypothesis 5: Manual services decrease.

This is already the case at AMV and at Telia. The "Vision 2005" initiative at the Social Insurance Agency will implement a similar model. As the number of employees has been reduced most heavily in the rural areas, this tendency is most visible there. But as electronic and telephone services become increasingly sophisticated, and promoted, the same development can be seen in cities, even if offices are still there.

There is also a change in the nature of the manual services. As service functions with human competence and technical support are maintained at very few locations, perhaps "Help Desk" is a more adequate word.

Hypothesis 6: Service quality increases.

Our conclusion is that this hypothesis is indeed confirmed, but with the important qualification "for some." What is clear is that the individual's access to information and services has increased considerably during the latter half of the 1990s. The number of information sources has increased. Examples include the online databases on jobs and educations at AMV. So-called service telephones–automated telephone systems–have made the routine matters at the Social Insurance Agency, such as ordering of forms and certificates, available around the clock. Many things that formerly only employed staff could do are now open and easily accessible to the client/customer/citizen, including searching for jobs in databases using self-developed requirement profiles, searching an unlimited amount of jobs, calculating social benefits, taxes, etc. using automated tools and so on.

But this has come at a price. It costs time, education and money. Users have to learn to handle the new information sources. Not just the medium, which is the simple part, but how to use search terms, where to search, how to write a CV, how to introduce yourself to a prospective employer, to name a few things from the AMV area.

Also, a computer is necessary, and there is a cost for using data communications. In the cities, facilities are provided as replacement for the closed or harder-to-access offices, but in rural areas, people are often left to their own initiative and their own financial resources. In that sense, rural areas have been impoverished by the current development, and are likely to become even more so. As an example, the current investment in broadband communications to the home seems unlikely to reach rural areas, as the investment is made on a for-profit activity by private investors, unlike previous important infrastructures like roads, railroads and television networks, which were built or subsidized by the government.

Our main hypothesis was that IT use in government agencies had largely contributed to impoverish rural areas. Our findings show that this was indeed the case, but not quite the way we had expected. The impoverishment is not due to deskilling of jobs in rural areas and concentration of highly skilled jobs to the cities. In fact, many jobs in rural areas have rather become more high skilled than before. What is clear is that the number of jobs has decreased more in rural areas than in cities, and that the central control over operations has increased dramatically. Local offices as well as individual employees are much more controlled than they were before. Government agencies have acted on business economic incentives rather than on the goals of the regional policy. This way the government role as guarantor of jobs in rural areas has decreased, if not been abandoned altogether, and the impoverishment that follows from the fact that a shrinking population is less able to motivate services like post offices, schools and shops has taken yet a step in a negative direction. The government organizations' role as an instrument in regional policy has thereby been reduced.

ACKNOWLEDGEMENTS

This work was supported by the Swedish Transport and Communications Research Board (KFB). The work was undertaken in cooperation with the Department of Social and Economic Geography at Umeå University. Thanks are due to our partners there, Ingrid Liljenäs and Daniel Brandt.

ENDNOTE

1 "Direct" in this context means that the Job Office tells a candidate to apply for a particular job. Failure to apply leads to reduction in unemployment benefits.

REFERENCES

Andersson, P. (1989). *Informationsteknologi I Organisationer: Bestämningsfaktorer Och Mönster.* Linköpings Universitet. Linköping.
Arbetsmarknadsdepartementet. (1982). *Verksamhetsberättelse,* 1981-1982.
Arbetsmarknadsdepartementet. (1988). *Verksamhetsberättelse,* 1987-1988.
Arbetsmarknadsstyrelsen. (1982). IT inom arbetsmarknadsverket. *AMS Informerar.* Ain, 2.
Arell, N. (2000). Franska förhållanden–om decentralisering, dekoncentration, stat, region och samhällsplanering. *GERUM Rapport.* Umeå Universitet.

Ekroth, S. (2000). *Core Values of Public Adminsitration in Sweden*. Öppna System 2/2000. Stockholm: Statskontoret.

Engellau, P. (1982). *Strategier för Decentralisering: Att Effektivisera Offentlig Förvaltning*. Stockholm: Liber.

Nutek. (1997). Utveckling i landsbygd och glesbygd–regioner på väg mot år 2015. Stockholm: Nutek och Glesbygdsverket.

Reko. (1997). *Regionalpolitik för HeLa Sverige*. Reko-stat-utredningen, Betänkande.

Selle, P. (1991). Decentralisering–Ett troll med minst två huvuden. Rotstein, Bo, I. (Ed.), *Politik Som Organisation: Förvaltningspolitikens Grundproblem*. Stockholm: SNS Förlag.

Statskontoret. (1989). Omlokalisering av statlig verksamhet: Utvärdering av utflyttningen på 70-talet. *Rapport*, 8A.

Stjernberg, T. (1989). Kompetens i fokus: Lärande som strategi inom statsförvaltningen. Stockholm, Allmänna förlaget.

Chapter XVI

e-Government in Canada: Services Online or Public Service Renewal?

Barb Kieley and Greg Lane
Deloitte Consulting, Canada

Gilles Paquet and Jeffrey Roy
University of Ottawa, Canada

Moving industrial society government onto a digital platform would simply produce a digitized industrial government—a form of governance that would be increasingly out of step with the changing realities of citizens and businesses alike.[1]

INTRODUCTION

This chapter examines the efforts of the Government of Canada to harness information and communication technology (ICT) as an enabling force. Various forms of e-Government are now clearly on policy and managerial reform agendas of the public sector. The extent to which the challenges are well understood, however, is the source of much debate. Some managers and politicians remain particularly sceptical in the face of spectacular claims of external commentators that the Internet is a revolution in both citizen expectations and service delivery.

Yet, e-Government is expanding. As online activity grows across private, public and civil spheres of organizational life, and as governance transformations impact organizations across these sectors, governments are not immune. The more relevant question is whether they can orchestrate change by fostering adaptive capacities, or whether change will be imposed.

This chapter begins from the premise that e-Government presents a real transformation in democratic governance, including design, decision-making and service delivery capabilities. Importantly, e-Government takes place within a changing governance context where technology itself may only be one driver–as people debate the extent to which it is a tool for improving current systems or a key for redefining them. Whatever the balance here, the struggle is that government must redefine itself for a world of e-Governance, even as this world is shaped by a variety of dynamic forces.

As we move forward, we provide some definitional parameters around governance and government and the relevance of the now omnipresent "e." The next section looks at the centrality of partnerships in this new context. We then examine the impacts on people–particularly within government, and draw from extensive interviews with senior public servants and reports on how they interpret the challenges that lie ahead. The next section builds on this reporting and offers a forward-looking assessment of the likely evolutionary scenarios that lie ahead. We end with conclusions.

DEFINITIONAL CHALLENGES–GOVERNANCE AND GOVERNMENT

As a starting point, governance may be defined as effective coordination in an environment where both knowledge and power are distributed. Every organization is built on governance, whether formal or informal, ineffective or successful.

The rise of e-Governance refers to new processes of coordination made possible or even necessary by the advent of technology–and the spreading of online activities in particular. As a result, e-Government (a term that we further define below) in the broadest sense refers to an IT-led reconfiguration of public sector governance–and how knowledge, power and purpose are redistributed in light of new technological realities.

In summarizing what has been written about the information age and/or digital world to date, our perspective is that there are three main sets of inter-related forces driving the emergence of e-governance and the search for new organizational models across all sectors:

   Spatial - geography and place

   Digital - communications and time

   Cognitive - education and expectations

Globalization drives new spatial considerations that are changing our notion of place, as economic and, to some degree, social and political forces for integration create new interdependencies beyond national borders. As a result, identity and community are less bound by geography, with new and far more complex networking patterns emerging (Paquet, 1997a).

More instantaneous communicating and changing perceptions of time are related considerations–as the expression "Internet time" redefines many organizational activities in the private sector, and in government as well. A digital world implies instantaneous decisions and accessibility, and speed and responsiveness become the hallmarks of performance (Guillaume, 1999; Tapscott and Agnew, 1999).

Changing cognitive capacities are the third set of final contextual forces driving change–as the rapid expansion of both information and education empowers populations to become less passive and better educated. Organizations struggle to define and retain the right mix of competencies in a knowledge-based workforce increasingly characterized by mobility, diversity and assertiveness (Rifkin, 2000; Rosenau, 2000).

These simultaneous forces are at the heart of the struggle to adapt to a new governance environment. For governments, however, there are inherent contradictions in each that must be recognized.

New notions of place mean that e-Government emerges not within a traditional order of national processes, rather within a more complex picture of both globalizing and localizing pressures. e-Government, at the national level, means interfacing with the new global possibilities and pressures, while empowering cities and regions with the tools to act collectively in order to prosper. Governance, in a digital world, is bound to encompass a growing number of multi-level processes, heightening the need for coordination and learning across traditionally separate public-sector systems.

New notions of time also result in contradictory pressures for government. While "Internet time" stimulates service delivery and the desire to be more customer-oriented, public interest considerations and more citizen-oriented government often heighten complexity and time requirements. Using technology to engage citizens in more deliberative forms of democracy may well require more time--and more patience.

Similarly, demographic trends signal new challenges as an emerging knowledge society takes shape. Driven by the so-called Internet generation, the citizenry is becoming less homogenous, less passive and accepting of traditional forms of authority and representation, and more contradictory in its demands (Thorton, 1998). Government will be challenged to not only respond, but to also redefine the social contract of the new millennium--meaning both the rights and responsibilities of a connected citizenry.

The struggle to define a vision of e-Government reflects our search for better ways to adapt in order to meet new spatial, digital and demographic realities. As the initial quote above implies, e-Government cannot simply be derived from the imposition of new technology on existing organizational models. As the public sector adapts itself to a new environment, it must also serve as a catalyst for guiding all stakeholders toward a common path. e-Government is intertwined with the broader governance transformations reshaping and joining our economy, our society and our polity.

Within such parameters there is a struggle with terminology. We suggest that the term, digital government, reflects a partial re-configuration of the public sector through new information and communication technologies (ICTs). As such, digital government is quite close to Government On-Line (GOL). The critical mission is to improve service-delivery capacities through the potential of a new digital platform.

This new digital architecture is a crucial component of the e-Government challenge--but it is also incomplete. It is crucial since the investments made into ICTs will lay a foundation for a less hierarchical and more flexible organization.

However, it is incomplete since hardware and software alone cannot ensure better performance and ongoing learning. New social technologies are also required, meaning the new skill sets, mindsets and approaches to leadership. A definition of e-Government that encapsulates a broader agenda of renewal and multi-dimensional technological change may prove more helpful:

e-Government is a public sector better enabled to harness new information, communication and social technologies in order to empower the public service of tomorrow. Effective change is premised on the necessary leadership of people, and the collective intelligence of all stakeholders in meeting the potential of a more interdependent world.

This definition suggests that any transformation of government must take place in a context of growing interdependence–both internally and externally. We continue the conceptual investigation of e-Government by further probing what we believe to be two of the most critical dimensions of this path: partnerships and people.

PARTNERSHIPS

e-Governance creates pressures and opportunities for new partnerships--internally and externally. Within government, ICT fosters new horizontal opportunities by shifting away from traditional bureaucratic structures toward alternative delivery arrangements. The growing possibilities for consultations with both stakeholders and the citizenry are also expanded with new technologies. Moreover, on-line delivery implies integrative channels within government, linking external users across sources and systems internally.

These trends mean ICT forces are both dispersing and centralizing–fostering a need for integrative action. Put another way, these forces create tensions between vertical governance of traditional government and the horizontal governance implied by digital government. The emergence of digital government will therefore require actions and strategies at the level of individual departments and agencies; but such efforts must be orchestrated within the parameters of government-wide leadership and coordination.

Accountability is a key element of such a balance. The manner by which accountability is perceived and exercised by government leaders will determine the degree to which it embraces more collaborative models of governance. Traditionalists invoke the underlying principle of Ministerial Accountability based on a clear and rigid view of vertical control and risk-minimization in order to serve and protect the interests of the publicly accountable political leader.

The rise of e-Governance, with its pressures for a variety of initiatives introducing alternative models of decision making and service delivery, implies a sharing of accountability. The need for collaboration, partnerships and joint ventures grows within government, and often between private and public organizations.

There are also important debates around the issue of whether accountability is at risk when external partners become involved in the governing and shared delivery of government programs and services. According to some, new governance arrangements threaten to undermine key institutions and practices of democratic accountability (Globerman and Vining, 1996).

This camp believes that any change to the existing system of ministerial accountability will damage the integrity of the system. There is some question as to whether the ad hoc nature of the ever-increasing number of partnership arrangements between sectors challenges accountability mechanisms or can be absorbed in traditional models of decision making with adaptations to risk mitigating strategies.

An alternative view is that collaborative arrangements can make government more accountable (Armstrong and Ford, 1999). The proponents of collaborative arrangements insist that involving external stakeholders strengthens accountability to citizens by virtue of the addition of partners. In particular, private and civic sector partners bring additional pressure for accountability to customers or clients. Notwithstanding legitimate concerns about new ways of doing things, it is difficult to conclude from these debates that the virtues of traditional accountability, namely their clarity and simplicity, can serve as justifications for their extension into an e-Governance era.

These tensions shape ties between governments and the vendors of ICT systems and solutions. ICT solutions, however, are more pervasive in demanding closer collaboration between private vendors and public sector clients (Mornan, 1998). The complexity and sophistication of such solutions produce many strategic choices for governments about how to deploy ICT both in and across public-sector operations. Yet, a critical distinction across business and government remains, namely the relative emphasis on results in the former case, and the relative importance of process in the latter sphere.

Contracts Versus Partnerships

Any move toward ICT outsourcing, meaning a reliance on external service providers, most often found in the private sector, is likely to be both controversial and consequential for government, particularly from a human resources perspective. The advantages of outsourcing ICT and its management to external parties are derived from the opportunity to leverage the competencies of specialists. The disadvantages are rooted in concerns about control and performance measurement, while underlying questions of cost often become the resulting sources of friction.

The main challenge is relational: new collaborative capacities are required. Partnerships require shared purposes and agendas, as well as trust and an integrative mind set. The implication here is that the skill sets of the individuals involved and the mechanisms guiding their relational activities must both be conducive to such an effort. The main challenge facing all parties engaged in today's increasingly complex forms of ICT partnerships is that despite a recognition of the need to work together in new ways, most organizational processes and most people reside within the realm of contracting, with an emphasis on both cost and control. Although common to all sectors, this point is particularly prevalent in the public sector, as the extra burden of transparency and fairness, the basis of traditional assurances of public accountability, loom large.

Current examples of outsourcing are a case in point, as any such decision by a government department is bound to be strategic and controversial. The transfer of assets, including people, is a process with potentially huge consequences on government's capacity to act in the public interest. In a world of markets and contracts, the outsourcing path is fraught with risks and uncertainty: the response is often a quagmire of control efforts and validation. Moreover, even if such agreements are forged operationally, public-sector approval requires additional scrutiny and explanations to public chambers--and it should come as no surprise that many deals are unable to withstand such pressures.

Recently, the state of Connecticut in the United States spent millions of dollars and over three years negotiating one of the most ambitious outsourcing deals of a government ever, only to see the deal collapse before completion. Both parties (the government and the primary vendor) provide amicable, though contrasting, explanations for the deal's demise. While no single factor is evident, it is fair to conclude that the requisite mix of political acceptability and profitability could not be achieved in an adequate fashion due, in part, to a tremendous emphasis on contracting specifications, objectives, terms and conditions--a process fundamentally at odds with the trust and collaboration required to partner on such a massive scale. A federal public servant in Canada commented privately that in his mind, profit always wins out over partnership in such cases.

Nonetheless, perhaps due to the strengthening pressures of e-Governance, the trend toward outsourcing-type arrangements grows unabated. Tying itself directly to the experiences of Connecticut, the San Diego County government is now six months into the largest municipal outsourcing experience. While these experiences are unique in scope, they present elements common to all governments, at all levels, as IT becomes a strategic imperative for effective governance. Such tensions have led to growing calls for partnerships in place of contracts. The differences may be subtle in terms of words, but the consequences of this contrast are far reaching. Poupart and Austin compare two modes of relationships:

Partners respond to a need in a changing world by sharing control in the context of an assertive relationship to offer a future that facilitates innovation in a world of possibilities.

Contractors respond to a request in a procurement world by giving up control in the context of a collaborative relationship to provide help, assistance, pairs of hands that facilitate project management in a world of deliverables (Jelich et al., 2000, p. 52).

Our premise is that the realization of e-Government remains at odds with a traditional public-sector apparatus firmly rooted in hierarchical traditions. The resulting challenge of shifting from incremental procurement reform to genuine collaboration lies in the need to rebalance purchasing safeguards with partnering opportunities. Equally important are the new skill sets of public managers and leadership requirements that result.

PEOPLE

The need for e-Governance rises hand in hand with the knowledge workforce. Conceptually, Rifkin envisions growing ranks of knowledge workers who will forge new communities of interest, only some of which are likely to resemble traditional employee-employer relationships of the past. He argues that "people of the twenty-first century are as likely to perceive themselves as nodes embedded in networks of shared interests as they are to perceive themselves as autonomous agents in a Darwinian world of competitive survival" (Rifkin, 2000, p. 12).

How will public-sector organizations deal with what Rifkin sees as a new human archetype where people are more autonomous, better educated, more mobile and less rooted by traditions of place (either geographically or organizationally)? These conceptual issues intimately link the workforce challenges of digital government with those of cultural reform (in an organizational sense). Whereas Westminster systems continue to emphasize vertical accountability, government on-line is (correctly) being pursued in a horizontal fashion.

An international study by Essex and Kusy (1999) underlines the views of executives from both government and industry, for whom an increasing reliance on the external workforce is a significant trend. They report that from 1997-2002, leaders are expecting an increase from 10% to 25% in non-core (meaning non-traditional full-time, or external) workers. This crescendo of the external workforce may well accelerate with the technology-induced pressures for organizational innovation and flexibility. The result is a complex mix of agendas and incentives that explains the growing emphasis on interpersonal skills such as negotiation, facilitation and consultation.

These skills are forming the basis of "new public servant," one who is much more collaborative and comfortable with technology, and the consequences of these shifts for human resource in management in government will be profound (Moritz and Roy, 2000). Thus, government is becoming both more fluid internally and more networked externally, as distributed governance models drive the move toward a flexible and modular workforce.

As a result, the role of the public servant must adapt; governments must effectively couple new forms of community-wide strategies that are both horizontal and potentially centralizing, with recent trends toward empowerment and flexibility--and the decentralizing nature of such pressures (i.e., agencies seeking greater autonomy). Governments must learn to benefit from heightened worker mobility–viewing such trends as strategic imperatives for public-service innovation.

In doing so, a challenge for many governments lies in more direct competition with industry. In the Canadian government, for example, the Computer Systems (CS) Community is based heavily in and around Ottawa-Hull, the National Capital Region (NCR). In 1999, 67% of all CS employees were located in the NCR, compared to 34% for the entire PS. As

CS employment increases, more workers are located in the NCR which gives rise to new managerial challenges–namely, an intensifying labor market that also serves as a common pool of competencies for both industry and the government.

Consequently, a major challenge of digital government lies in this competition for human capital, a dynamic particularly acute in national capitals such as Washington, DC and Ottawa, which seem to couple growing professional mobility and inter-sectoral proximity.

The governance implications of such trends are perhaps contradictory: a paradoxical impact of IT may be that, while it enables more organizational flexibility and decentralization across the public sector, particularly with respect to service delivery, leadership patterns also have centralizing tendencies. This factor could impact both the presence and effectiveness of national governments operating across their country, and their ability to recruit specialized workers in limited urban centres (particularly national capitals) where labour markets are most competitive.

In a world of e-Governance, an appropriate response by government in meeting this dynamic must be based on the understanding of both the complexity and contradictions at work. On the one hand, the move toward greater usage of PPPs suggests that labour mobility and geographic proximity could complement one another, and create a common environment more conducive to trust and collaboration. On the other hand, the very real danger is that the most entrepreneurial employees will leave the public service, seeking either higher compensation or more flexible work environments than government is able to accord to them.

As important as the technology itself, government must address the people and performance challenges of digital government in the next few years. Adapting the role and profile of the public servant is critical to realising the needed administrative cultural shift associated with horizontal governance and collaborative partnerships.

E-GOVERNMENT IN CANADA– RHETORIC AND REALITY

In Canada, the foundation for the e-Government movement has been established by three key policy documents put forward by the Management Board of the Government (Treasury Board of Canada Secretariat):

1. A Blueprint for Renewing Government Services Using Information Technology (1994)
2. Strategic Directions for Information Management and Information Technology: Enabling 21st Century Services to Canadians (April 2000)
3. A Framework for Government On-Line (February 2000)

This movement was inspired and prioritized by the October 12 Speech from the Throne in which the federal government vowed that by 2004, it would be known around the world as the government most connected to its citizens. This e-Government initiative has been labelled "Government On-line" (GOL) in Canada--although on-line service delivery is just one of the many components of GOL. A high level committee of senior public sector executives was subsequently created to act as the senior advisory and oversight committee ("champion") for GOL.

In terms of implementation, the leadership or oversight role was given to the Chief Information Officer Branch (CIOB) in the Treasury Board Secretariat. Within this Branch, an Office for Government On-Line was established to coordinate GOL efforts across the federal government. The office determined three key areas of implementation: technology, people and business processes.

The backbone of the technology component is the Strategic IM/IT Infrastructure Initiative (SII) aimed at developing a federated architecture for the federal government. Other technology projects include the GoC Public Key Infrastructure (PKI) and the Secure Channel (SC) Project aimed at providing a secure electronic environment for GOL. In addition, a Shared Systems Initiative (SSI) was initiated to provide common departmental internal systems. Lastly, the development of a new government-wide portal is underway to provide an eventual basis for seamless, single-window service delivery to Canadians over the Internet.

In speaking with a cross-section of senior public servants across both operational departments and central agencies, we probed them on their views about the likely opportunities and challenges ahead with respect to e-government.[2] Specifically, this dialogue was guided by three broad directions: i) capacities–the overall vision and approach requirement; ii) culture–the adaptive challenges, the new decision-making approaches and the changing leadership requirements; and iii) competencies–the necessary skill sets and human resource considerations for managing people.

Capacities

The short-term vision for the federal government is to ensure that all government services are on-line by the year 2004. According to government leaders, this vision must be viewed as the realization of an environment where citizens have a choice of delivery channels. And if they are using the electronic channel, services must be organized in such a way that on-line engagements are meaningful and accessible through a single window.

For many senior managers, the rapid acceleration of technological innovation is challenging government's capacity to adapt in an unparalleled manner. For instance, the government put in place major telephone call centres roughly 25 years ago, and even today issues arise as to their effective utilization. In a digital world, planning for the next three years will be a challenge, to say nothing of achieving a coherent forecast of the world in 10 years time.

Another emerging challenge for e-Government lies in the balance between corporate direction and departmental flexibility. Federal executives accept that flexibility is crucial in order to facilitate innovation at the department level. At the same time, they believe that new capacities are required on a government-wide basis, as departments need to have a shared approach to common objectives, much like integrative Y2K efforts.

One result is that on-line government means taking a government-wide approach to agenda setting. Infrastructure is key to enabling such inter-connectivity and responsiveness at a government-wide level. The notion of a federated architecture model is meant to be sensitive to the difficult balancing act at play by achieving government-wide coordination in a fashion that equally respects departmental flexibility and front-line innovation.

Industry is also a critical reference point for the emergence of e-Government, and business may have multiple roles to play. The extent to which the private sector is a competitor, a model or a partner of government is an issue of strategic importance.

Executives believe that the constant pressure to respond to a changing marketplace also forces government to become more innovative itself. The main reason lies in public expectations, shaped by a variety of service delivery experiences that create points of comparison between private and public models. Thus, innovation being spurred by electronic commerce translates into higher public expectations toward government.

In terms of contrasts, however, others suggest that adopting a business case approach with the sort of return on investment tests prevalent in the marketplace may not be the most appropriate route for government. In the short run, much of the effort in fostering a digital architecture may not carry such returns, and what is required is a business case accounting for this form of strategic investment. In this sense, government's mission is partly distinct from business in serving broader questions of the public good, such as infrastructure, in a digital era.

The shared view across executives is that complementarity is more important than commonality. There was broad agreement that there is much to be gained from bringing private-sector people into government—adding that creativity, rather than conformity, should be encouraged. The uncertainty so prevalent in a digital environment also challenges relations between business and government. If the public sector possessed a clear blueprint of what it wanted to achieve, with few unknowns, then it would be relatively easy for industry to be able to promise to help reach specified targets. The absence of any such certainty makes collaboration a challenge.

In terms of realizing new forms of private-public partnerships, some respondents point out that the public sector carries unique attributes that may augment the complexity of forging such arrangements. The greater role of public scrutiny, for example, may make it difficult to foster a culture conducive to risk. As a result, there is a need for collective education—including all stakeholders and the public in order to learn to better acknowledge when a certain amount of failure must be tolerated.

Culture

Many respondents stressed that in a world of greater electronic connectivity, aligning leadership is a critical challenge. The key is to provide leadership that ensures an integrative strategy of technology, people and performance. Providing a culture that unleashes creativity and focuses on outcomes must be a key priority of public-sector leadership today.

In terms of the new type of leadership required for e-Government, not everything is new however. Clear direction and sound judgment remain critical success factors, although the systems within which they are being applied are rapidly changing. A unique challenge in government is the lack of clear equivalent to the CEO and Board of Directors of a private sector company, which means that the politicians and the public are key stakeholders.

Government's complex agenda, along with the uncertainty of how to couple bottom-line considerations with what is in the public interest, may well increase the risk associated with IT investments. A holistic assessment of government requirements is necessary, both to provide adequate funding for the digital foundation of e-Government and to better guide decision making as layers are built upon this base.

A major leadership challenge will be to find ways to create momentum for such innovation and creativity, and to guide this momentum in a coherent direction. An additional role for an e-Government leader is to ensure that all components of the organization (corporately or at the department level) understand the ramifications of new technology for every aspect of decision making, policy formulation and service delivery. Building this understanding requires a culture of learning. This need for multiple forms of direction and accountability creates a particular challenge for senior public-sector managers at the Deputy and Ministerial level. Leadership means blending specific targets and mandates with horizontal agendas, and IT is a critical driver in this regard.

New forms of trust will be required across government, and this type of connectivity, often much more horizontal than in the past, cannot be easily rooted in hierarchy. One government executive estimates that on a scale of organizational complexity, Y2K may be viewed as perhaps a 4 out of 10. Subsequent phases of on-line government and digital governance, in contrast, should be viewed as more akin to an 8 of 10. Y2K was largely remedial; these next steps are about process realignment and designing something entirely new.

In terms of information flows and transparency, many of the executives agree that the explosion of information is altering government decision making in far-reaching ways. As one example, much of the legislative framework adopted for an industrial era, designed to protect and control information flows, may no longer be appropriate in an era of information sharing and knowledge management.

However, many see this shift, at least, in a potentially positive way. As information becomes more readily available, there is greater transparency across government, and the public will not only demand more, they will also know more. The result will be that people will feel a higher sense of value for their investments in government, and if the value is not there, a more informed public means greater accountability.

Practically, the growth of information also carries enormous consequences for workflows within government. Responding to electronic mail, maintaining adequate records and learning to separate data that is largely noise from strategic information, are all organizational challenges of an unprecedented magnitude in a digital era.

For the time being, these challenges may raise more questions than answers. Government managers must ask themselves—how much do you negotiate and how much do you dictate, when do you devolve and when is centralization necessary?

Flexible balance is a crucial theme. Some individuals point to a careful, but strategic role for central agencies to assist in this transition, although it must be one of facilitation rather than dictation. Central agencies may be best positioned to provide a neutral forum for cross-departmental learning and sharing strategic advice.

Yet, central agencies must prepare for this role by becoming a focal point of relational knowledge as to how government interacts with other stakeholders—citizens, businesses and social groups, and other levels of government. Here again, a new federated approach to governance requires a balance of autonomy and coordination.

How are these changes sustained? According to several executives, there must be an organizational culture that empowers ownership to those taking decisions. In turn, accountabilities are multiplied, and the central management challenge is to link individual and collective performance. The latter must also be a part of people's accountabilities, and it must be measured.

Some respondents foresee a more networked model of government where technology both empowers public servants with more information and connects them to their clients in a much more direct fashion. This shift entails a much greater need for partnering within government, as well as between government departments and their external agents in the network.[3]

Competencies

Executives link the renewal of leadership with a focus on people; they also point to the need to start with the most senior managers across government. One individual underlined that since the background of a significant proportion of Deputy Ministers is in policy, their sensitivity to the impact of a digital transformation may be limited.

Government must invest more in training, and think about systemic ways to reward those who promote innovation and risk in a manner that recognizes government's uniqueness, rather than being captured by it. A new balance between performance and process is required, and e-champions must be nurtured to lead the way. Once again, others are equally insistent on the responsibility of senior management, suggesting that there should be a basic IT proficiency test for potential EX candidates.

The risks and rewards associated with IT and e-Governance are also important factors in managing staff. One leader comments that IT failures are often more visible than those in policy or program areas, and there must be attention accorded to this point. Similarly, traditional governmental processes may not support the same types of rewards for success in a highly charged IT environment than those found in industry.

The result is that government must pay closer attention to its human resources efforts, and in particular, to its capacities to train and retain highly skilled workers. The public sector, according to many, has much to offer in terms of interesting work and flexible work styles.

Fostering a dynamic and supportive work environment is as much a part of the foundation for digital government as technology itself. The digital transformation is all encompassing; it is therefore necessary that the process of reform be as open as possible. While communications tools are one component, the process must also involve consultation, listening and dialogue.

The challenge extends to all layers of the public sector. For example, program managers in government have not traditionally thought about electronic service delivery and its various dimensions, such as the need for horizontal governance. These types of issues are indicative of the ongoing challenge facing public servants.

PROSPECTS

Overall, four main drivers emerge from discussions with executives, and while their order may be arguable, each is important. The first and most recent policy driver is the 1999 Speech from The Throne and its pledge to ensure that all government services will be on-line by 2004. This type of political support creates somewhat of a burning platform to make things happen.

The second key driver is the government-wide priority of improving service delivery to citizens and businesses, electronically or otherwise. The strategic challenge here involves embracing a citizen-centric model based on a single window, enhanced accessibility and efficiency, reliability and security. This logic sees clients shaping governments, and the expectation is a growing client base moving on-line.

The third driver is part of the overall strategy to modernize government—a process in which technology is now recognized as a key factor. Fourthly, the federal executives suggest that a successful evolution toward e-Government will yield synergies with the private sector, increasing their competitiveness internationally. There is broad agreement that the 21st century context of globalization and digitization accelerates the importance of each of these points.

In terms of inhibitors, a key consideration is cost. In fact, there are huge amounts of resources required to create a digital infrastructure. Yet, cost may also be perceived incorrectly if bottom-line considerations are not weighted properly against a complete picture of government's agenda. Since strategic investments into digital government play an important public interest role, carrying many spin-off benefits for industry and communities alike, there can be no simplistic return on investment calculations.

Another challenge of moving to e-Government is the issues of acceptance and accessibility. Several executives pointed out that, on average, connected Canadians are probably better off citizens, and the danger of a growing digital bias is an issue not only for government, but rather for all stakeholders in our society.

Thus, certain segments of our population will require special efforts in order to develop the skills necessary to benefit from the promises of a digital world. At the same time, a service provider government must be prepared to offer the necessary advice and support for aspiring users of on-line channels.

Although all executives concur with the dangers of a digital divide, some also perceive a strategic opportunity for government. Electronic channels, and innovative approaches to deploy them may allow governments to become more creative in reaching out to these same Canadians, demonstrating a commitment to both connectivity and cohesion.

The Path Ahead

The effectiveness of any government in responding to its digital agenda is clearly multi-faceted and highly strategic and central to the public sector's relevance in the millennium. We summarize our observations into three rather intuitive scenarios for the road ahead for any government, and then provide a set of key variables likely to determine the relative likelihood of each path emerging.

The three scenarios include: resistance or regressive deployment; status quo or incremental action; and radical adaptation for a digital world.

In the first instance, the most dangerous possibility does not lie in traditional public servants and politicians rejecting IT as a significant force (as it is practically impossible to do so). Rather, more subtle forms of regressive behaviour would emerge if IT is viewed as largely a mechanism of control and automation, rather than enabling. This form of control can be pursued either at the operational level of government, by managers over subordinates, or politically by leaders who, by reflex, look to IT to centralize and control both power and information. Such attempts will likely prove futile, further weakening the public sector--as its credibility and performance steadily erode.

In the second scenario, some change is accepted but incremental strategies are formulated to achieve it. The potential for this scenario lies with traditionalists, whose cautionary claims may be partially legitimized by making a case that government is not private enterprise; as such, e-Governance and promises of Internet speed may not be fully appropriate for serving the public interest.

The resulting caution in IT planning and an emphasis on contracting over partner-ships in outsourcing arrangements are likely to limit government's capacity, with arguments for the preservation of clear public accountability used to justify inaction. The media may also contribute to the traditionalist's cause, as the British government discovered recently when it was (somewhat unfairly) profiled in *CIO Magazine* (cio.com) for alleged failures in its IT initiatives.

An important lesson of the digital age is the interdependence of these first two scenarios: the more defensive, cautionary or manipulative a government appears, the more hostile the media reaction is likely to be, creating a vicious circle of paranoia and defensiveness.

The third scenario is perhaps uncomfortable, given that it carries risks. Yet, those public managers and political leaders who have it right are those who claim that the risk of inaction is greater than moving forward boldly. The key to this scenario is a fundamental renewal of administrative culture in order to better learn how to share accountability, to better coordinate activities in a more flexible and more effective way, and to better empower public servants and their partners, allowing new solutions for come forward in a dispersed and open matter.

This latter point may well be the secret to the digital transformation–that is to say, nobody can claim to have a clear road map of public-sector renewal in this scenario. Acceptance of this point, publicly as well as privately, will mark members of those espousing such change.

Our two sets of explanatory factors will be central in terms of how governments respond. First, partnerships and the emergence of new collaborative dialogues within government, between governments and across sectors are a critical dimension. The second and quite related variable lies in the necessary leadership of people–new skill sets and new leaders will be required to both empower knowledge workers and defend experimental action.

This new leadership must also be political in order to engage the public in this new journey, challenging them to be constructive and raising the collective intelligence of all stakeholders, including the citizenry. The real danger of subsequent experiments in digital government becomes enhanced. Costly mistakes, created and magnified by the built-in inertia of traditional governance systems, could re-enforce the position and power of those resisting change.

CONCLUSION

What are the lessons to be drawn? First, realizing the promise of e-Government is perhaps best viewed as an evolving process of learning and adaptation. As digital connectivity grows, a mix of technical and social forces will transform the shape of our public institutions over time.

Yet, precisely how this transformation will occur depends greatly on the citizen, and the manner by which public expectations are shaped by collective education and experiential learning. This evolution will likely be neither predictable nor common across all segments of the population. Consequently, digital governance must meet many needs via multiple challenges simultaneously.

For this reason, the federal executives understand the need to move beyond the somewhat simplistic comparisons of the old and the new model of governing. The holistic challenge is to seek innovation while recognizing that redesigning governance requires buy-in and ongoing support, as much from public servants working in government as from clients of the services they provide.

A related and quite important message emerging from both the literature and our respondents is that governments will operate with heightened interdependence. Partnerships are now central to public management, and it must be a priority for all governments to foster and strengthen capacities for collaborative action.

In a digital world, relationship management will become a core competency of the new public servant. The digital infrastructure must be complemented by human ingenuity, and trust among all partners becomes an essential ingredient in order to navigate an environment of heightened change and uncertainty.

In sum, there is a need for expanding, deepening and sustaining dialogue—across all stakeholders and the citizenry. e-Government must be an engaged and constructive partner in shaping the new governance patterns that will otherwise render it rudderless.

These governance patterns must bridge traditional administrative and political-cultural frameworks to the adaptive and collaborative requirements of a connected and interdependent world–a world that requires a new culture in government, one open and enabled to take advantage of the enormous potential of the digital and information age.

ENDNOTES

1 Harris, B. (2000). "E-Government: Beyond Service Delivery" in *e.gov* (supplement to *Government Technology* magazine, Spring Issue: egov.govtech.net).

2 The primary set of interviews took place over the winter of 2000, during the adoption phase of the GoL agenda. Follow-up interviews also took place in the fall of 2000.

3 The Government of Canada has recently launched a renewed portal which features three "clusters" or streams of services, integrated across functions for separate clients groups (citizens, businesses and non-Canadians). For many observers, such a step marks the tentative beginning of reorganizing government internally to better orient information, services and functionality externally.

ACKNOWLEDGEMENT

The research assistance of Paul Faya and the input of Professors Barb Allen and Luc Juillet are greatly appreciated.

REFERENCES

Armstrong, J. (1998). Reflections on alternative service delivery models. *Optimum*, 28(1).

Bellamy, C. and Taylor, J. (1994). Introduction: Exploiting IT in public administration-- Towards the information polity. *Towards the Information Polity? Special Issue of Public Administration*, Spring, 72.

Boston, J., Martin, J., Pallot, J. and Walsh, P. (1996). *Public Management: The New Zealand Model*. Auckland: Oxford University Press.

Browning, J. (1998). Power to the people-Government isn't disappearing. It's being disintermediated. *WIRED Magazine*, January.

Canadian Defence Industry Association. (1999). *CDIA Procurement Committee, Industry Proposals for DND Procurement Reform*. Available on the World Wide Web at: http://www.cdia.ca/committee/procure.htm.

Carr, G. (1998). *Public-Private Partnerships: The Canadian Experience*. Speech to Oxford School of Project Finance. Available on the World Wide Web at: http://home.inforamp.net/~partners/oxford.html.

Center for Technology in Government. (1998). *Making Smart IT Choices*. Albany. Available on the World Wide Web at: http://www.ctg.albany.edu/resources.

Center for Technology in Government. (1999). *Using Information in Government Program*. Albany. Available on the World Wide Web at: http://www.ctg.albany.edu/projects.

Chief Information Officer's Branch (CIOB). (1995). Treasury Board of Canada Secretariat. *Blueprint for Renewing Government Services using Information Technology*. Ottawa. Available on the World Wide Web at: http://www.cio-dpi.gc.ca.

Chief Information Officer's Branch (CIOB). (1997). Treasury Board of Canada Secretariat. *The CIOB Strategic Direction Priorities: 1997 to 1999*. Ottawa. Available on the World Wide Web at: http://www.cio-dpi.gc.ca.

Chief Information Officer's Branch (CIOB). (1998). Treasury Board of Canada Secretariat. *Supporting Electronic Government: The Government of Canada Public Key Infrastructure*. Ottawa. Available on the World Wide Web at: http://www.cio-dpi.gc.ca.

Corden, S. (1997). The Australian government's industry commission examines competitive tendering and contracting by public sector agencies. *Public Administration Review*, March/April, 57(2).

Duff, A. (1997). *Outsourcing Information Technology--Human Resource Implications*. IRC Press, Industrial Relations Centre, Queen's University, Kingston.

Essex, L. and Kusy, M. (1999). Fast forward leadership--How to exchange outmoded leadership practices for forward-looking leadership today. *Financial Times*, Prentice Hall.

Ferris, N. (1999). CIOs on the go. *GovExec.com*, March. Available on the World Wide Web at: http://www.govexec.com/features.

Ford, R. and Zussman, D. (Eds.). (1997). *Alternative Service Delivery: Sharing Governance in Canada*. Toronto: KPMG and IPAC.

Gagnon, Y. and Dragon, J. (1998). The impact of technology on organizational performance. In Galliers, R. D. and Baets, W. R. J. (Eds.), *Information Technology and Organizational Transformation*. Toronto: Wiley Series in Information Systems.

Globerman, S. and Vining, A.R. (1996). A framework for evaluating the government contracting-out decision with an application to information technology. *Public Administration Review*, November/December, 56(6).

Guillaume, G. (1999). *L¢empire de réseaux*, Paris: Descartes & Cie.

International Council for Information Technology in Government Administration. (1998). Procurement study group report. *An International Journal on Information Technology in Government*. Available on the World Wide Web at: http://www.ica.ogit.gov.au.

International Council for Information Technology in Government Administration. (1997). ICA information sharing within and between governments study group report. *An International Journal on Information Technology in Government*. Available on the World Wide Web at: http//www.ica.ogit.gov.au.

Jayes, D. (1998). Contracting out information technology services at the UK inland revenue. *OECD, Contracting Out Government Services*. Paris: OECD=s Public Management Occasional Paper No. 20.

Jelich, H., Poupart, R., Austin, R. and Roy, J. (2000). Partnership-based governance: Lessons from IT management. *Optimum*, 30(1), 49-54.

Kobrin, S. J. (1998). You can't declare cyberspace national territory: Economic policy-making in the digital age. In Tapscott, D., Lowy, A. and Ticoll, D. (Eds.), *Blueprint to the Digital Economy: Creating Wealth in the Era of E-Business*, McGraw-Hill.

MacDonald, H. (1997). *Information Technology Projects--A Review of the Treasury Board Enhanced Framework for the Management of IT Projects*. Working Paper 97-42, Faculty of Administration, The University of Ottawa.

Mascarenhas, R.C. (1993). Building an enterprise culture in the public sector: Reform of the public sector in Australia, Britain and New Zealand. *Public Administration Review*, July/August, 53(4).

Moritz, R. and Roy, J. (2000). Demographic insight on Canada's federal information technology workforce: Community renewal and tomorrow's leadership imperative. *Canadian Government Executive*, July.

Mornan, B. (1998). Results-based procurement: A model of public-private sector collaboration. *Optimum*, 28(1).

Nelson, M. R. (1998). Government and governance in the networked world. In Tapscott, D., Lowy, A. and Ticoll, D. (Eds.), *Blueprint to the Digital Economy: Creating Wealth in the Era of E-Business*. McGraw-Hill.

New Zealand Public Service. (1997). *Information Technology Stocktake*. Wellington: State Services Commission.

Newcombe, T. (1998). Multistate on-line procurement project under way. *Government Technology*, October. Available on the World Wide Web at: http://www.govtech.net/publications/.

OECD. (1997). *Information Technology as an Instrument of Public Management Reform: A Study of Five OECD Countries*. Available on the World Wide Web at: http://www.oecd.org/puma/gvrnance/it.

OECD. (1998). *Contracting Out Government Services*. Paris: OECD's Public Management Occasional Paper No. 20.

Papows, J. (1998). *Enterprise.com--Market Leadership in the Information Age*. Reading: Perseus Books.

Paquet, G. (1997a). States, communities and markets: The distributed governance scenario. *The Nation-State in a Global Information Era: Policy Challenge*. Queens University Bell Canada Conference.

Paquet, G. (1997b). Alternative service delivery: Transforming the practices of governance. In Ford, R. and Zussman, D. (Eds.), *Alternative Service Delivery: Sharing Governance in Canada*. Toronto: KPMG and IPAC.

Public Works and Government Services Canada. (1998). Benefits-driven procurement. *A Paper Presented to the Ninth International Public Procurement Association*. Avaliable on the World Wide Web at: http://www.pwgsc.gc.ca/sos.

Rifkin, J. (2000). *The Age of Access--The New Culture of Hypercapitalism*. New York: Jeremy P. Tarcher/Putnam.

Rosenau, P.V. (2000). *Public-Private Policy Partnerships*. Cambridge, MA: The MIT Press.

Scott, G. (1996). *Government Reform in New Zealand*. Washington, DC: International Monetary Fund.

State of California Department of Information Technology (DOIT). Various. Available on the World Wide Web at: http://www.doit.ca./.

Tapscott, D. and Agnew, D. (1999). Governance in the digital economy. *Finance and Development*, December, 84-87.

Tapscott, D., Lowy, A. and Ticoll, D. (1998). *Blueprint to the Digital Economy: Creating Wealth in the Era of E-Business*. McGraw-Hill.

Thorton, K. (1998). *Living in the Information Society--Rethinking Government*. Available on the World Wide Web at: http://www.ibm.com/ibm/public.

Weill, P. and Broadbent, M. (1998). *Leveraging the New Infrastructure--How Market Leaders Capitalize on IT*. Cambridge, MA: Harvard Business School Press.

Yankelovich, D. (1999). *The Magic of Dialogue--Transforming Conflict into Cooperation*. New York: Simon and Schuster.

Chapter XVII

Electronic Government in Switzerland: Priorities for 2001-2005–Electronic Voting and Federal Portal

Christine Poupa
Institute for Advanced Studies in Public Administration, Switzerland

This chapter presents some reference points about institutions of direct democracy in Switzerland and electronic democracy in Switzerland. It will then focus on two projects: electronic voting and federal portal (virtual office).

INSTITUTIONS OF DIRECT DEMOCRACY IN SWITZERLAND

The rules and institutions of direct democracy in Switzerland have to be presented, in order to understand the situation of Switzerland as far as electronic government is concerned.[1] Switzerland is a federal state. The Cantons are attributed far more responsibilities than the Confederation, including education–also at the university level–the police, religious services and health services. Justice and taxes are areas shared between the Confederation and the Cantons. The collection of taxes is the responsibility of the Cantons.

Switzerland has a semi-direct form of democracy that is neither parliamentary nor presidential, but is based on consensus and entente: parliament cannot bring down the government, who in turn cannot dissolve the parliament. It has various and ancient institutions of direct democracy on a Federal, Cantonal and communal level. Each of the four levels of decision, i.e., the people, the communes, the Cantons and the Confederation, sets store by its prerogatives. Any modification that would be perceived as a loss of control or power is rejected by the echelon concerned.

Federal Level

On a Federal level, Switzerland recognises (Mockli, 1993):

- the compulsory constitutional referendum for the total or partial revision of the Constitution, since 1848;
- the optional legal referendum, since 1874;
- the popular initiative for the partial revision of the Constitution, since 1891;
- the referendum on international treaties, since 1921 and enlarged since 1977;
- the annulment referendum regarding urgent Federal decisions, since 1949.

The referendum, an institution initiated from either top or bottom according to precise rules, has a conservative role, i.e., to reject a form of evolution by constituting a means of veto. The referendum refers to a project developed by the political class: administrative, executive or parliament. The popular initiative has an innovative role. It is initiated by civilian society, and can also serve to short-circuit the decision-making process. The official reaction of the political class to a popular initiative is called a counter-project. The results of the consultations can be compulsory or optional. Parliamentary decisions are therefore not definitive or obligatory since a group–and including an extra-parliamentary one–can ask to consult the people directly, by means of an initiative. Among the tools available to the people, we should also mention the petition, which can be submitted to any authority but a response is not compulsory.

The citizens must collect a certain number of signatures within a limited time. (Mockli, 1993, Papadopoulos, 1994): on a Federal level, since 1977, this number is 50,000 signatures (previously: 30,000) from citizens or from eight Cantons, within a time limit of 100 days in order to initiate a referendum, and 100,000 signatures (previously: 50,000 signatures) in 18 months for an initiative. The time limit runs from the publication of the title and the text proposed by an initiative committee of at least seven persons in the official Federal Journal.[2] An initiative can take place if sufficient bona fide signatures are collected within the time limit laid down. The Federal Council[3] then has 24 months to submit a message to the Federal Assembly and a request for a popular initiative. The time limit is 30 months if the Federal Council chooses to submit a counter-project to the Federal Assembly. The Federal Assembly, in turn, has four years in order to decide whether or not it approves the initiative.

If, as is often the case, the Federal Assembly rejects the initiative, it must be submitted "to the people and the states for adoption or rejection."[4] It is therefore possible that it takes up to seven years between the submission of an initiative and consultation of the public.

In order for a referendum to be adopted, it must obtain the majority of electors' votes. For an initiative to be adopted, it must obtain a double majority: that of the electorate and that of the Cantons. In such cases, the small rural Cantons, each with 15,000 to 120,000 inhabitants, have as much weight as the urban Cantons such as Zurich with 1,175,000 inhabitants. This double majority is aimed at preserving the rights of the rural minorities.

If we refer to the period 1970-1987 (Papadopoulos, 1994), the citizens have by no means always approved and accepted decisions made by the government and the parliament. There have been 98 federal votes, not counting the initiatives. The acceptance rate by the people stands at 84.5% for issues submitted to a compulsory referendum, 61.5% for issues submitted to an optional referendum and 64.3% for counter projects. The Swiss people therefore have the real power to influence the policy of its elected representatives, government or parliament.

Cantonal Level

Each Canton has its own legislation, and decides–for instance–on its taxation rate for Cantonal taxes, on the training and recruitment of teachers, and on the organisation and establishment of the police, etc. The tools of political expression available to citizens also differ greatly from one Canton to another since each Canton has its own constitution.[5] Most of the Cantons recognise referendums and popular initiatives, covering an even wider range of subjects than on a Confederation level, for example a compulsory referendum in the case of a project to modify taxation rates.

Two Cantons[6] still exercise the most visible form of direct democracy: the "Landsgemeinde,"[7] an annual meeting of all the citizens on the voting roll of a Canton with the right to vote on the public square, where they express their position on each subject submitted to a vote by raising their hands.

A "Landsgemeinde" existed in all the small Cantons in the German-speaking area.

However, Schwyz (127,500 inhabitants and 30 communes) has abandoned its Landsgemeinde, Uri with 36,000 inhabitants and 20 communes has also abandoned. Nidwald with its 38,000 inhabitants and 11 communes abandoned its "Landsgemeinde" at the end of 1996. Appenzell Ausserrhoden (54,200 habitants, 20 communes) abandoned its Landsgemeinde by secret vote on September 28, 1997.[8] Obwald (32,000 inhabitants, seven communes) decided to abandon it in 1998, also by secret vote.

The way the Landsgemeinde functions differs from one Canton to another. Appenzell Ausserrhoden simply allowed its citizens to approve or reject an issue submitted to a vote. Appenzell Innerrhoden allows each citizen to intervene during the "Landsgemeinde," in order to ask a question, to propose a new candidate for an administrative post, etc. During the vote, the raised hands are not counted. An estimate is made: a majority in favour or a majority against, or a second ballot if no majority is visible to the naked eye. If a second vote is required, the people must vote again. If, after several votes (up to 10), no clear majority is revealed, the vote is declared negative (status quo).

Communal Level

The communes also recognise various forms of democracy (Walti in Kriesi, 1993, p. 36), directly linked to the Constitution of their Canton. We can distinguish four different cases:

- direct democracy without communal parliaments in the traditional rural Cantons of Appenzell Innerrhoden, Glaris, Nidwald, Obwald, Schwyz and Uri;
- direct democracy with communal parliaments in the towns for the following Cantons: Aargau, Appenzell Ausserrhoden, the two semi-Cantons of Basel, Bern, Graubünden, Luzern, St. Gallen, Schaffhausen, Solothurn, Thurgau, Valais, Zug and Zurich;
- representative democracy except in the small communes in the cantons of Fribourg, Vaud and Ticino; and finally
- representative democracy in every commune in the cantons of Geneva and Neuchâtel.

Our task here is not to carry out an exhaustive study of these different forms of direct democracy within Swiss communes. Moreover, comparisons are hazardous, since quite different authorities can be designated by the same name in two different Cantons, whereas the same authority can take different forms within a single Canton according to the size of the commune. The Communal Council in the Canton of Vaud is the highest legislative body within a commune, elected for four years via proportional representation or by a majority according to the communes. In the Canton of Fribourg, however, a Communal Council is an executive body. The executive authority is termed the Municipal Council in the Canton of Vaud. The municipal council, elected for four years, elects a "syndic" (Major) as its head, also for four years. Still in the Canton of Vaud, the small communes[9] have a General Council made up of all citizens of the commune on the electoral roll[10] as a legislative body. This General Council elects the executive body but takes all decisions concerning voting on the budget, on taxation, on communal regulations, on auditing and on the communal accounts directly, at an assembly.

"As the General Council has nearly the same composition as the Assembly of the Commune, there are no referendums against its decisions" (Chevallaz, 1984, p. 17). "The communes of the Canton of Vaud do not have laws, and therefore they have no legal power" (Ethenoz, 1996, p. 19), contrary to certain communes in the Canton of Valais.

How Direct Democracy Actually Functions in Switzerland

The participation rate at elections is in continual decline in Switzerland. The majority of the population manifests less and less interest in political life (whether as a candidate or an elector).[11] Compared with the rest of Europe, Switzerland has the lowest average rate,[12] often well below 50% (Mockli, 1993, p. 9).[13] One reason for this is the number of elections and votations.

For example in 2000, the people had to vote four times at the Federal level, each time on many different subjects, plus often cantonal and local topics (March 12: five federal objects, participation rate 42%, May 21: one federal object, participation rate 48%, September 24: four initiatives and two counter-projects, participation rate 45%, November 26: five federal objects, participation rate 40.5 to 41.5%, depending on the object). In 2001 the people will have to vote again on three occasions at the federal level (March 4: three federal objects, participation rate between 51.1 and 55.3%, June 10: three federal objects participation rate between 39.7 and 41.9% and December 2).[14]

Although formally it is the people who decide, there are often a handful of politicians or interest groups that decide finally on the subjects voted upon, their presentation, the formulations and the arguments, etc. This type of functioning is more typical of representative democracy.

Moreover, we should not lose sight of the fact that in Switzerland, often quoted as a model of direct democracy, a large proportion of the population does not have, or has not always had the right to be heard; this applies to foreigners and women.

Foreigners

Foreigners represent 19 to 20% of the population in Switzerland. The blood law is applied: children born in Switzerland of foreign parents remain foreigners, unless lengthy and unpredictable proceedings are undertaken that were–until recently–also costly. The naturalisation process is somewhat dissuasive: 12 years residence in Switzerland, impromptu visits to the candidate's home by the authorities during the entire duration of the procedures, which can last several years, and the cost fixed according to the annual income.

You can find in Switzerland "third-generation foreigners" (foreigners whose grandparents came to Switzerland). Only certain communes and Cantons have now begun to grant the right to vote (in Jura, Neuchâtel and partially in Appenzell Ausserrhoden), and sometimes the eligibility to be elected (in Neuchâtel, Jura) to certain categories of foreigners–and then only for questions strictly concerning local matters.

On March 4, 2001, in the Canton of Geneva (about 40% foreigners), the people rejected the right to vote and to be elected at the communal level to foreigners residing in Switzerland for at least eight years, by 51.98%. The canton of Schaffhausen rejected by 70.2% the modest project to allow the communes to grant the right to vote to foreigners at the communal level.

Women

On a Cantonal level, women had the right to vote for the first time in Switzerland, in the Canton of Vaud in 1959. However, they had to wait until much later before being granted the right to vote in certain Cantons: in Appenzell Ausserrhoden, this was in 1989. They were therefore able to vote on Cantonal issues for the first time in 1990! On a Federal level, women were granted the right to vote in 1971. This right, granted so belatedly to women compared to other western democracies, partially explains the relative indifference of women vis-à-vis politics, as noted in studies referring to the period 1970-1990. The latest estimates, however, seem to indicate equal participation of men and women.

Given the high number of those involved and the complexity of the decision-making process, work and evolution within the Swiss political system are therefore slow and the results are modest. Could electronic democracy–and electronic voting–help the Swiss people to take part more frequently in the political debate?

ELECTRONIC DEMOCRACY IN SWITZERLAND: TOWARDS ELECTRONIC VOTING

Very Favourable Conditions

There is hardly an other country in which the people have such far-reaching rights of co-determination as in Switzerland. But contrary to most other democratic countries, Switzerland works by consensus, and often entente, including on a Federal level, where the government coalition introduced in 1891 still exists: the parties allocate the seats prior to the elections.

Consensus combined with federalism has consequences on the administration, as we will see in the section dealing with the creation of a federal portal (virtual office).

Public administration and government should be a powerful user, influencer and precursor of information technology innovations. But as far as electronic democracy is concerned, there is a Swiss paradox (Poupa, 1998, p. 137).

Switzerland is a rich country, where the majority of households own personal computers, and with access to the Internet among the highest in the world.[15] It is also often quoted as a model of direct democracy. But Switzerland–or at least a major part of its political class–has been reticent towards information technology and has hesitated to acknowledge the potential assistance of new technologies in political debates and decision-making processes.

In February 1998 the Federal Council issued a strategy for the information society in Switzerland "to promote in a positive manner the open and democratic character of society." One of the nine domains concerned was electronic administration, "to verify in which way technologies could be used to enlarge the public political scene and reinforce the participation of people in the democratic process of decision making."

The debate on e-Government took place in ISPS[16] (Information Society Project Switzerland), which was coordinating the group on the information society (CGIS) as part of the federal strategy. For three years, "E-gov," one of the working groups on the information society, has been working on e-Government. The CGIS coordinated other working groups: e-commerce, security, culture, education…These working groups had no money to allocate. Interesting projects were postponed because of lack of resources (money and people: the federal administration is not allowed to hire new employees to limit public expenses). The main task of the "E-gov" working group was the inventory of existing or future projects, and recommendations to the Federal Council.

The participation of people in the democratic process was not central in these thoughts. The emphasis was more on security (electronic signature, e-commerce...). Online democracy, electronic assembly, political forums and chats are not–yet?–very popular in Switzerland. Most of the initiative committees create Internet sites with information and arguments, but not with interactivity (no forums or empty ones, etc.).

How One Can Vote in Switzerland

Traditional political communication is extremely predominant in Switzerland with meetings, radio and television debates, extensive choice of media, posters, distribution of pamphlets in letterboxes. For the vote, each citizen receives, at his domicile and several weeks prior to the date of the vote, all the necessary material:
- voting forms and envelopes for voting by mail;
- an information brochure from the Federal Council (or the canton or the commune–depending on the matters to decide).

In addition to the title and the full text of each subject to be voted upon, this brochure contains the arguments by those initiating it, those by the Federal Council, the result of Parliament's vote on this issue and the recommendations for voting by the Federal Council.

Each citizen may then vote:
- by mail (several weeks before the closing date of the vote);
- by anticipation (in advance several days prior to the vote at certain voting stations about which information is displayed in each commune by public posters); or
- on the actual date of the vote at his usual voting station.

To vote by mail is not available by default in every canton. This way to vote is sometimes available only on demand (Vaud, Neuchâtel until 2001…). When generalized, the vote by mail is very popular and tends to increase the participation rate. For example, in Geneva over 90% of voters use the mail.[17] But the participation rate at elections is in continual decline in Switzerland (see previous paragraph, "How Direct Democracy Actually Functions in Switzerland.")

Interest in electronic voting is rising: why not–especially for the "fifth Switzerland," the Swiss people living abroad–trying to test this new procedure to vote?

Electronic Voting in Switzerland

The second report from the CGIS for the Federal Council is dated May 16, 2000 (OFCOM, 2000). Among urgent measures for the period 2001-2005, the CGIS recommends to fund the creation of a one-stop shop / virtual office (see "**Administrative Portal**," p. 364) at the federal level and to create a working group about electronic voting. For the first time, a budget has been allocated to fulfill these objectives.

Milestones

Tele-voting by the Internet is not yet allowed in Switzerland, despite several interpellations on the part of socialist and ecologist representatives that were made several years ago:
- on a Federal level on June 19, 1996 (postulate to the National Council by Jean-Niels de Dardel, a socialist from Geneva);

- on a Cantonal level, in Geneva, in 1997, two members of Geneva's Greater Council, the Canton's legislative body, submitted a proposal (motion from the Ecologist Vesca Olsommer and the Socialist René Longet: "Could the Web be used to vote or to sign for popular initiative or referendum?")

On August 14, 1996, the Federal Council refused to examine the question of the "feasibility of exercising political rights via the Internet and its social consequences" proposed by the de Dardel postulate. The Federal Council did not want to enter into the issue, and the postulate was rejected: no one within the Confederation was ready, at the time, to deal with the matter in depth: they lacked knowledge about the implications, concerning technical issues, infrastructures or data processing security.

Today, Swiss law on political rights does not allow the use of electronic signatures within the political framework. Collecting signatures within the framework of a popular initiative or a referendum must continue in paper form, while the Swiss banks, including the Cantonal banks–controlled and managed by the Cantonal authorities–have recognised the validity of electronic signatures for several years.

A working group about electronic voting has been created on the recommendation of the CGIS. This working group, with representatives from the Cities, the Cantons and the Federal Chancellery, now exists under the direct supervision of the Federal Chancellery. Its mandate was defined in June 2000 in a decree signed by the federal chancellor (Huber-Hotz, 2000):

- August 2001: delivering a report (preliminary analysis, and first propositions).

The working group will disappear at this stage. A new procedure will be used for the next stages:

- September 2002: conception of solutions
- December 2005: detailed specifications
- 2004-2007: discussion with the Federal Assembly and decision
- December 2010: official introduction of electronic voting in Switzerland

The objectives are to give electors the choice to vote (or to collect signatures for referendum or initiatives) via electronic communication or by usual means (traditional mail or polling station). These usual means are planned to remain accessible during a transitional period of a few tens of years.

Electronic voting should be accessible before 2010 in specific ways or locations:

- downloading forms to collect signatures,
- voting electronically at the polling station....

According to the Federal Chancellery, experiments of a more local nature, on a Cantonal level or in some larger towns are planned in the near future.

The Parliaments should be convinced first and use electronic voting. At the Federal level, electronic voting is used by the Federal Assembly during the sessions. But the system is not very reliable: one can vote from his seat for his absent neighbour. The second chamber implemented a more secure system that requires both hands to vote.

In cantonal parliaments, most of the time people have to a raise hand or stand up to vote. A few cantons have adopted electronic voting in Parliaments (Berne, Vaud, Fribourg...). Geneva has voted a budget of 500,000 CHF to adopt electronic voting. The system should be available to vote during parliamentary sessions starting in 2002.

Possible Consequences of Electronic-Voting in Switzerland

The participation of citizens in a vote or in a referendum is not something that can be improvised. Only a long public debate (via the media, public meetings, etc.) allows the electorate to gain a grasp of the subject, to form an opinion or to become motivated to vote. People need time to think over and to make up their minds. The Internet is often thought as an instant tool, where everything has to go fast. Speed and thought are not always compatible. The electorate particularly needs time in the case of new topics or new forms of voting.[18]

The form of voting is also psychologically significant: going to the voting station remains a ritual. The act of voting at the voting station seems to give more responsibilities to the citizen–and a sense of belonging. At the opposite, electronic voting–especially from home–seems to minimize the weight of this civic act, making it "virtual". The mere fact to quickly announce the results of a vote on the Internet, as it is now often the case in Switzerland, has de facto suppressed the traditional gathering in town halls where the people used to come and wait for the results. This used to be an important moment of the political life. The results where commented, the crowd was there, materializing the notion of people.

The Internet also affects two sensitive points within Swiss political life: the weight of the traditional parties, and the relative weight of certain parts of the electorate. The traditional political parties have a somewhat hierarchical culture. The intensive use of the Internet would, for them, represent a small revolution. The traditional voters in Switzerland are rather older and rural. The official introduction of the Internet in political life as a means of political communication, electronic voting or the collection of electronic signatures would probably lead to increased participation by younger, urban members of the electorate and students in particular.

I do not believe that the overall participation rate would be significantly changed by a possible introduction of new tools. However, there could be–as each time there is a change to voting rules–a shift of voters. One of the last examples to date was when women were granted the right to vote on a Cantonal level in the Canton of Appenzell Ausserrhoden. Many men deserted the "Landsgemeinde" and therefore no longer voted on a Cantonal level. They felt that the "spirit" of the "Landsgemeinde" had been distorted.

Confidence and Security

Generally, electronic voting is viewed with caution, even in countries where electoral fraud is not common: by definition, the information is not tangible, and control by the citizen is almost impossible.

Acceptance of electronic voting is a question of confidence (confidence in the government, the officials and in the computer system, etc.). "Security and trust are even bigger concerns for government than for the private sector."[19] The CGIS is considering creating a "passport for the Internet" using a smart card combined with an electronic signature.

As far as security is concerned, a "public key infrastructure," considered as a starting point for electronic democracy in Switzerland, has been elaborated. The order RS 784.103[20] fixes since May 2000 the legal framework to authorise providers of certification services (i.e., electronic signatures).

The primary qualities required of information on the Internet must be availability and accessibility. This, however, poses a problem that has not yet been resolved within Switzerland: that of the confidentiality of personal data. Several administrative bodies, from the Confederation to the communes, have circulated sensitive information at some time or other, despite clear legislation on the protection of data and to the consternation of those affected. This ranges from a new address to the date of a divorce transmitted by the registry of inhabitants of certain communes to financial establishments, to information on the health of certain unemployed persons distributed inadvertently by the Confederation on a badly protected Intranet. Unless the "passport for the Internet" fully resolves this type of problem, the more systematic and larger-scale use of the Internet may still be delayed.

The Swiss Confederation plays a major role in the definition of infrastructure and technical specifications, but invests very few resources and time in thinking about the sociological usage and impact of new technologies in the political field. What about the administrative field?

ADMINISTRATIVE PORTAL IN SWITZERLAND: http://www.ch.ch

Milestones and Goals

The Federal Chancellery is also in charge of this project since September 2000.[21]The Confederation intends to fund the creation of this administrative portal at the federal level (estimation 20 to 30,000,000 CHF for 2001-2002). The terminology is not yet defined: the official documents mention indistinctly Virtual counter, Single counter, (permanent) Federal Portal, Virtual office(s)...But in contrast to electronic voting, the work concerning the virtual office has already quite advanced.

The Federal Chancellery issued a draft convention[22] at the end of the year 2000 for a rapid consultation: the Cantons had six weeks (until the December 1, 2000) to comment this convention between the Confederation and the Cantons.

This convention organises the relationship and cooperation between the Confederation and the Cantons to create a one-stop shop/virtual office at a federal level to fulfill the needs of Swiss citizens.

Cooperation Between the Confederation, Cantons and Communes

The convention has been approved by all the Cantons at the beginning of 2001. The agreement between the Confederation and the Cantons (together with their communes) in relation to the development of a federal portal organizes the cooperation:

- **The consultation group** is a forum for specialists to exchange information. It will form the first circle of test groups. It's a large body with representatives of the Federal Administration, all the Cantons and numerous communes. The first meeting took place in February 2001 and gathered more than 50 civil servants.
- **The management committee** counts four or five members from the Federal Administration and a more or less equal number from the Cantons, as well as one representative from the Association of Cities and Association of Communes respectively.

The administrations are beginning to co-operate horizontally with one another, but there will be no changes to the order of competence:

"The project to establish a 'Guichet virtuel' is based wholly on the existing order of competence in Swiss federalism. The consultation group will nevertheless set out guidelines for the standard content of the topics, the technical aspects such as links and ensure quality is monitored. In order to provide support for all this work, the Federal Chancellery will set up helpdesks on behalf of the cantons and communes. The Confederation will place the multilingual and technical platforms at their disposal and will also ensure that the necessary security infrastructure is established within the framework of the project. (...) The Confederation aims to guarantee a coordinated approach. For the future operation it is planned that the costs will be shared between the Confederation and the cantons.[23]

The convention previously mentioned organises the relationship between the different parties. The participation of cities will not be compulsory but encouraged by the cantons. The first virtual counters should be accessible by the end of 2001. The goals of this virtual counter are presented in a report: Virtual Counter: The Electronic Communication with the Administration, the Parliament and the Courts.

The main idea is to create an access gate to the Internet, whose presentation is structured differently from the mode of organisation of the administration and does not conform to the official procedures but presents information according to situations of the everyday life of an individual or a company. This Internet site will not replace existing ones, whether from the Confederation, the cantons or the cities, but it will add a new way to access the right information at the right time.

Thanks to the Internet one will soon find an answer to all kinds of questions and will not have to recall any more if such or such service is provided by the Confederation, the canton or the city. A Portal will very quickly give access to the needed information by means of key words like "taxes" or "marriage." That means for example that a couple eager to marry will seek information through the DFJP, the OFJ then the cantonal department of justice to reach finally the local Registrar's office and to find there–in best case–the address and the opening hours. That does not mean either that the couple in question will have to search the Civil code and the cantonal laws, a legal arsenal which is pure nonsense for the non-lawyers.

To visit a virtual counter means that the couple in question will arrive at the "form on the preparatory procedure" while selecting successively two or three Internet links which could be named "marriage"/"conditions." Maybe this form must be brought personally to the Registrar's office or it can be electronically signed and sent electronically; this depends on the way the virtual counter is designed (and of the legal framework).

The first pilot projects have been chosen according to the interest of the administrations: the information had to be already widely available on the Internet at the federal, cantonal and local level to minimise the cost and the amount of work. The selected themes are: taxes, marriage, living abroad, how to create a company.

Difficulties of Implementing an Administrative Portal in a Federal State

Switzerland is a federal State. The Swiss cantons have remained, to a large extent, sovereign entities. Consequently there are 26 legal organisational systems. The administrative procedure can be very different depending on the specific canton you live in. The Cantons have much more attributions than the Confederation. So, the Cantons (and the cities) have much more contact with the citizen than the Confederation.

The dissemination of administrative information is consequently of fundamental importance in Switzerland. Unfortunately, up to now, Internet sites do not fulfill this role of dissemination of administrative information. Two inquiries[24] led to the conclusion that Swiss citizens are often unable to find the appropriate information on the Internet (in 1998, 72% never found the needed information on official sites; in 2000: only 4% always found the information, 22% most of the time).

Transparency, clarity, accessibility are not the first keywords one thinks of to characterize the (Swiss) administrative information, despite the success of the Internet: the Confederation's official site www.admin.ch is the most popular Internet URL in Switzerland.

However www.ch.ch has been chosen as the new address of the federal portal. This address appeared to be easy to pronounce, to understand and to identify.[25] This is a choice by default: no consensus could be found around intelligible keywords, due to the different official languages. In Switzerland, information has to be available for each of the three official languages (French, German, Italian).

Different languages and different procedures thus this implicate even more difficulties of implementing a virtual portal in a federal State.

CONCLUSION

When we observe messages addressed to the Webmasters of existing sites, we realise that these are genuine requests for information (Poupa, 1997): "Who should I approach to find a job?," "What permits are necessary to live and work in Switzerland?," etc. The role of the virtual administrative portal should be to reply to these questions immediately on the Internet via a search engine, linked ideas and appropriate vocabulary. Citizens also appreciate e-mail with personalized response within a few hours, but very few administrations are able to deliver this service.

The promotion of on-line administration now receives large support–including financial support–in Switzerland. But Switzerland is a Confederation, where each level of the administration adheres jealously to its prerogatives. Everything that could appear to interfere in other levels of administration is extremely badly perceived and leads to attitudes of rejection. Redesign of procedure and/or a new repartition of responsibilities between different administrative levels[26] may become an accepted solution in the future: with the growing use of the Internet, more and more people will be aware–through the Swiss Administrative Portal–of the difference of treatment in Switzerland (taxes, education, naturalisation,[27] etc.).

The portal model favoured in Switzerland is the Austrian one[28] : general information at the national level, and links to local sites where the presence and quality of relevant information is not granted. In an archetypical centralized State like France, the approach is different: the portal[29] gives access to hundreds of official formularies and detailed information about nationally standardized procedures. The links to other official national sites (laws, public reports, etc.) and to international public sites are presented for information only. That means, you don't rely on them to get the information to calculate and pay your taxes, for example.

The more standardized procedures are, the less information you need (you know the information is the same from one part of the country to the other). And the easier it is to spread this information (top-down). The more decentralized the State is, the more effort and coordination you need to gather the right information (bottom-up).

Many people were exited about the idea of using the Internet to improve democracy and participation. But despite some theories it is not easy to get people to express themselves, to debate and to build a consensus to take decisions via the Internet on a regular basis. In Switzerland, you will find only very limited examples–limited in time and scope. Last but not least, manipulation is very easy on the Internet. A degree of fraud may be tolerated as far as money is concerned. The tolerance zero is the only acceptable when it comes to ballot in democratic election. When will electronic voting–remote internet voting–offer this level of security?

At the moment, the Swiss Confederation focuses its efforts on infrastructure, security and technical specifications. The time should come to think about the sociological significance of the usage (or rejection) of new technologies in the administrative and political fields.

ENDNOTES

1 This is an updated extract from Poupa, (1998) that also presents the rules and institutions of direct democracy in Switzerland.

2 http://www.admin.ch/ch/f/ff/index.html.

3 The Federal Council is the Swiss government. It consists of seven Federal Councillors elected by the Federal Assembly, i.e., the State Council and National Council together, for a duration of four years, and renewable almost tacitly. The President of the Confederation, elected for one year by the Federal Assembly among the Federal Councillors, is a "primus inter pares," i.e., a first among equals. By rotation, each Federal Councillor in principle becomes the President of the Helvetic Confederation. As such, he chairs the meetings of the Federal Council and assumes certain representative functions.

4 Federal Constitution, Article 121, 6.

5 These constitutions are in the process of being modified in several Cantons. For example, the Canton of Vaud, after the positive outcome of a popular consultation in 1998, instituted a "Constituante" that should lead to propositions of modification of its constitution, and to the adoption of a new constitution in 2003/2004.

6 At the beginning of 2001, only two Swiss Cantons have preserved their "Landsgemeinde": Appenzell Innerrhoden (15,000 inhabitants, six communes), Glaris (38,500 inhabitants, 29 communes).

7 For historic and political information about the "Landsgemeinde," see Küng (1990).

8 Result of the vote: abandon of the "Landsgemeinde" desired by 54% of the electorate. The April 1997 session was therefore the last "Landsgemeinde" in Appenzell Ausserrhoden. Participation in the voting of September 28, 1997, was particularly high in Appenzell Ausserrhoden: 61%.

9 In the Canton of Vaud, a small commune is considered as one with less than 800 inhabitants. There are exceptions, however: certain communes with less than 800 inhabitants have the same institutions as larger ones, i.e., a communal Council.

10 An assembly of all citizens, whether on the electoral roll or not, in both small and large towns of the Canton of Vaud, is called the Assembly of the Commune.

11 There are exceptions. It depends on the matter that is voted on (see Note 8).

12 We should, however, moderate this judgment: the reference figures are not the same from one country to another. In France, for example, reference is made to the number of persons who have voluntarily registered on the electoral rolls, and not to the number of citizens with the right to vote, as is the case in Switzerland.

13 Example of the participation rate at the legislative elections: 1947: 72.6%, 1987: 46.5%, 1991: 46%. Participation rates between 20 and 30% are frequent for Cantonal elections or votes.

14 The federal calendar of votes, with dates, subjects and results is available on the Internet: http://www.admin.ch/ch/f/pore/va/liste.html.

15 Access to the Internet: 44%, PC at home: 57% (Baromédia 2000).

16 http://www.isps.ch/.

17 The Canton of Geneva generalized the vote by mail in 1995 and now has a participation rate above the Swiss average rate. See the study "Enquête sur le vote par correspondance": http://www.admin.ch/ch/f/pore/va/doku/pdf/enquete_bsa.pdf.

18 For example, in Brazil, the electronic vote was generalized in the mid '90s. This is now the only way to vote. In a recent poll, in an urban area, 70% of the votes could not be

taken into account, because they were not validated properly by the voters. (Reported to the author by a Brazilian official present at this polling station)

19 "Government and Internet" in *The Economist*, June 24th 2000, p. 4.

20 "RS 784.103 Ordonnance du 12 avril 2000 sur les services de certification électronique (OSCert)" http://www.admin.ch/ch/f/rs/7/784.103.fr.pdf.

21 http://www.admin.ch/e-gov/dok/einsetzungsverfugung_guichet_fr.pdf.

22 http://www.admin.ch/e-gov/dokZusammenarbeitsvertrag_Entwurf_Vernehmlas sung_f.pdf> with comments.
  http://www.admin.ch/e-gov/dok/Erlaeuterungen_Vereinbarung_f.pdf.

23 The Federal Portal "Guichet virtuel"– a Project of the Confederation, the Cantons and the communes: http://www.admin.ch/e-gov/e_gov_english.doc.

24 Two inquiries by Olivier Glassey, HEC Lausanne (1998 and 2000): http://uts.unil.ch/questadmin/.

25 The Federal Chancellery asked Isopublic, a private company, to study this question with representatives from all the linguistic areas.

26 This has already happened between cantonal and local levels, in some areas.

27 You can apply for citizenship after 12 years of residence in Switzerland (with some additional conditions). But you have to apply at the local level: you become a Swiss citizen because you have been recognized to "originate" from a Swiss commune. A city (and a canton) can decide that you have to live, for example, five years in the city and eight years in the canton before being eligible, regardless of the time you have been living in Switzerland. So, if you had to move a few times, you may live in Switzerland (or even in a canton) for over 20 years and not being eligible for citizenship. The local and additional conditions of eligibility differ widely from one canton to the other, from one commune to the other.

28 http://www.help.gv.at.

29 http://www.service-public.fr/.

REFERENCES

Chancellerie Federale. (2001). *The Federal Portal "Guichet virtuel"–A Project of the Confederation, the Cantons and the Communes*. January 9, 2001. Available on the World Wide Web at: http://www.admin.ch/e-gov/e_gov_english.doc.

Chancellerie Federale. (1999). *Enquête Sur le Vote Par Correspondance*. Available on the World Wide Web at: http://www.admin.ch/ch/f/pore/va/doku/pdf/enquete_bsa.pdf.

Chevallaz, G. A. (1984). *Brève Initiation à la Vie Civique*. Lausanne: Payot.

Ethenoz, P. (1996). *Le Pays où je Vis: Institutions Politiques et Histoire de la Suisse*. Morges: Commission consultative Suisses-étrangers

Huber-Hotz, A. (2000). Décision concernant l'institution du groupe de travail "avant-projet vote électronique" chargé de cerner les problèmes que pose la mise au point du vote électronique, Chancellerie de la Confédération suisse: Berne, June 30, 5. Available on the World Wide Web at: http://www.admin.ch/e-gov/dok/ einsetzungsverfugung_evoting_fr.pdf.

Kappeler, B. (1997). Rapport du Groupe de Réflexion "La Suisse et la société de l'information" à l'intention du Conseil fédéral suisse): Berne, June. Available on the World Wide Web at: http://www.intro.ch/groupedereflexion/fr/.

Knüg, J. (1990). Landsgemeinde–Demokratie im Wandel der Zeit, Innerrhoder Geschichtsfreund (33.Heft).

Kriesi, H. (Ed.) (1993). Citoyenneté et démocratie directe: Compétence, participation et décision des citoyens et citoyennes suisses. Zurich: Ed. Seismo Sciences sociales et problèmes de société.

Les Teleprocedures: Vers Une Administration Electronique Citoyenne? (2001). La Lettre d'information du groupe de coordination societe de l'information (GCSI). *Isps.Ch Newsletter*, June, (7), 6-8. Available on the World Wide Web at: http://www.isps.ch/newsletter/isps.ch_newsletter_7_fre.pdf (french version) and also http://www.isps.ch/newsletter/isps.ch_newsletter_7_ger.pdf (german version).

Mockli, S. (1993). Démocratie directe: Un moyen pour remédier aux défauts fonctionnels de la démocratie représentative? St. Gallen: Hochschule St. Gallen-Institut für Politikwissenschaft (n° 203) (version remaniée d'un exposé tenu le 12 janvier 1993 à Paris devant la sous-commission sur la démocratie participative de l'assemblée parlementaire du Conseil de l'Europe).

OFCOM. (2000). 2e rapport du Groupe de coordination Société de l'information (GCSI) à l'intention du Conseil Fédéral du 16 mai 2000, Bienne, 64 p. (Office fédéral de la communication). Available on the World Wide Web at: http://www.isps.ch/fre/stored_documents/PDF/302.pdf.

OFCOM Groupe de coordination Société de l'information (GCSI). (2000). "Guichet virtuel": La communication électronique avec l 'administration, le Parlement et les tribunaux, June 9, 37. Available on the World Wide Web at: http://www.isps.ch/fre/stored_documents/WORD/312.doc.

Papadopoulos, Y. (Ed.) (1994). Elites politiques et peuple suisse: Analyse des votations fédérales 1970-1987. Lausanne: Ed. Réalités sociales.

Poupa, C. (1997). Services en ligne, services publics et utilisateurs: réflexions, réalisations et projets (exemple du répertoire des sites Internet du secteur public suisse), ACE 2000 (Advanced Communications for Europe), November 19, Paris, p. 7. Available on the World Wide Web at: http://www.comunicon.ch/cp/ace2000.htm.

Poupa, C. (1998). Démocratie directe et cyber-démocratie en Suisse, Idheap: Chavannes, 35 p. (Discussion paper de l'Idheap n° 12), May. Available on the World Wide Web at: http://www.comunicon.ch/cp/discno12.pdf.

Poupa, C. (1998). Direct democracy and cyberdemocracy in Switzerland. In Snellen, I. T. M. and van de Donk, W. B. H. J. (Eds.), *Public Administration in an Information Age: A Handbook*, 579, 137-157. Amsterdam: IOS Press.

Poupa, C. (1999). La publication électronique des informations juridiques suisses. In *Annual Conference of the European Group of Public Administration (EGPA) "Delivering and Managing Justice in the 21st Century,"*, September 1-4. Cape Sounion (Greece).

Poupa, C. (2000). Electronic publication of the norms: From a monopoly to universal information service. The Swiss and French experiences. In *Pre proceedings of the IFIP 8.5 Working Conference on Advances in Electronic Government*, February 10-11, 133-147. Universidad de Zaragoza (Spain).

Poupa, C. (2000). La publication électronique des informations juridiques suisses: Vers un service universel. In Fabry, M. and Langbroek, P. (Eds.), *Management and Delivery of Justice*, 287-300. Amsterdam: IOS Press.

RS 784.103 Ordonnance du 12 avril 2000 sur les services de certification électronique (OSCert). http://www.admin.ch/ch/f/rs/7/784.103.fr.pdf.

About the Authors

Åke Grönlund is Assistant Professor in Informatics at Umeå University and Director of the Center for Studies of IT in the Public Sector (CSIPS). His research focuses on emerging uses of ICT such as electronic services in an organizational context, ICT strategies, business organization, use, and usability, most prominently electronic government and e-democracy. Current projects include regional development, local democracy and mobile work, and the recently started Democrit research program on IT and democracy. Professor Grönlund has served for many years as a consultant in international European research and development projects in the field of electronic services development, management, and evaluation. Most recent international publications include "Managing Electronic Service–A Public Sector Perspective" (Springer, 2000), "Democracy in an IT-Framed Society" (*Communications of the ACM*, January 2001), and three recent books in Swedish on electronic services, local e-democracy and electronic government. E-mail: gron@informatik.umu.se.

***

Ari-Veikko Anttiroiko is professor of Local Governance in the Department of Local Government Studies, University of Tampere, Finland. Professor Anttiroiko is one of the leading scholars in local government studies in Finland. His current research interests cover such thematic areas as globalization, information society development and strategic management of local government. He is involved in several research projects in these areas and has done related expert work in different parts of Europe. His recent publications include "The Informational Region" (1998), "The Communicative Problems and Potentials of Teledemocracy" (1998; together with Professor R. Savolainen), 'The Future of Local Government' (1999, in Finnish, with Professor P. Hoikka) and many others.

Elisabeth Davenport is Research Professor in Information Management at Napier University. She is a Fellow of the Institute for Information Scientists, a Fellow of the Centre of Social Informatics at Indiana University in the U.S. and member of the Arts and Humanities Board. She was the external assessor for the Solihull IT project, a pioneering attempt (funded by the British Library) to address issues of social inclusion by means of library-based PCs, and has managed a major EC grant for the Living memory project (DG XIII) which explored ways in which technology might enhance community. Her current areas of knowledge management research are classification in the workplace, representations of trust in digital environments and the appropriation of IT in community groups.

Brian Detlor is an Assistant Professor of Information Systems at the Michael G. DeGroote School of Business at McMaster University, Hamilton, Ontario, Canada, where he teaches courses on electronic commerce, information retrieval and intelligent agents. His research interests pertain to various issues in the areas of electronic government, information agents, enterprise portals and knowledge management. Dr. Detlor's publications include the co-authored book *Web Work: Information Seeking and Knowledge Work on the World Wide Web* published in 2000 by Kluwer Academic Publishers, as well as refereed journal articles in the *International Journal of Information Management, First Monday* and *Library Management*. He can be reached at detlorb@mcmaster.ca.

Kim Finn is a Policy Analyst with the Youth Initiatives Directorate, Department of Human Resources Development Canada, National Headquarters. She has worked for a number of departments within the Canadian civil service including Industry Canada and the Department of Agriculture and Agri-Food. Her academic and professional activities have concentrated on alternative service delivery mechanisms, public/private-sector partnerships, citizen engagement and participation in policy and decision making with an emphasis on Canadian youth, and the practical application of Web-based information products in the Canadian public sector. Ms. Finn holds a Bachelors of Environmental Studies in Urban and Regional Planning from the University of Waterloo and a Master's Degree in Public Administration from Carleton University.

Fernando Galindo is since 1982 Professor Titular of Philosophy of Law at the University of Zaragoza (Spain). Teaching on "Philosophy of Law," "Law and Computers" and "Ethics and Legislation for Engineers." Since 1984 he has been responsible for research and advice for Public Administrations, Judicial Power and Industry on "Law and Computers." Most important topics include: "Legal Databases and Artificial Intelligence" (1984-1994), "Computers, Communications and Public Administrations" (1994-96), and "Regulation of Digital Signature" (from 1997). He has served as Legal Adviser (from 1997) of the providers of certification services, SISCER and FESTE, as well as author, editor and co-editor of books, chapters of books, journals articles and recensions and news. An invited lecturer, referee of scientific conferences, journals and research programs, he has also served as panelist on the topics object of teaching and research.

William Gates is an Associate Professor of Economics at the Naval Postgraduate School. He received his PhD in economics from Yale University. In addition to is work in game theory and assignment problems, his research interests include incentives and asymmetric information, defense economics and the economics of international defense alliances. His research has been published in *International Studies Quarterly, International Public Management Journal, Defense Analysis* and *The Journal of Cost Analysis*. Before joining the Naval Postgraduate School, Dr. Gates was a economist at NASA's Jet Propulsion Laboratory.

Tom Gross holds a diploma and a doctorate degree in Applied Computer Science from the Johannes Kepler University Linz, Austria. Since 1999 he is a senior researcher in the Computer-Supported Cooperative Work research group at the German National Research Center for IT (GMD). His research interests include computer-supported cooperative work, human-computer interaction and e-democracy. He has written numerous publications, organized several scientific events and served on the committees of various conferences in these areas. Before joining GMD he was a research and teaching assistant at the Department of Applied Computer Science at the Johannes Kepler University Linz, Austria.

Lars-Erik Janlert is Professor of Computing Science at Umeå University and Director of the Umeå Center for Interaction Technology (UCIT). His research ranges from artificial intelligence and human-computer interaction to the use and impact of information technology in a wider perspective. His most recent books are *Tänkande som Beräkning* (Thinking as Computation) and *Datatyper och Algoritmer, Andra Upplagan* (Datatypes and Algorithms, 2nd ed., together with Torbjörn Wiberg). His mail address is lej@cs.umu.se.

Barb Kieley is the Managing Director of the Ottawa practice of Deloitte Consulting. As the Canadian leader of the firm's strategic IT consulting practice, Ms. Kieley specializes in IT strategic planning and in organizational transformation through information management and technology (IM/IT). Since joining the firm in 1987, she has worked primarily with public-sector clients in Canada and the U.S., implementing IT strategies within their organizations. Currently, her key area of focus is the development of e-Government strategies for federal and state level governments. Ms. Kieley is a leader in the e-Government industry and has spoken as several conferences and workshops. She has often been quoted and published in publications such as *Municipal World* and *Technology in Government*. She holds bachelor's degrees in Mathematics/Computer Science and Biology from Carleton University.

Greg Lane is Director of Business Development for Deloitte Consulting's public-sector services, working closely with all levels of Government to secure client engagements. He sits on the national board of the Canadian Information Processing Society and is the chair of the Public Sector Business Committee for the Information Technology Association of Canada. Prior to joining Deloitte Consulting in 1999, Mr. Lane held senior leadership roles at both Bell Canada and EDS. He has lectured at the University of Ottawa in the administration faculty on Governance and IT and has contributed to Lac Carling Review on the same topic. He received his undergraduate diploma in business at Algonquin College and received his MBA from Massey University in New Zealand.

Roland Leenes is Assistant Professor in the Department of Public Administration at the University of Twente. Since 1995, he is involved in the OL2000 project and has contributed to the Enschede OL 2000 pilot and co-authored two handbooks for the OL2000 task force. He received his PhD for his research on legal expert systems and dialogue games. His research interests include governance in the information age, developments in electronic public service delivery and electronic democracy.

Klaus Lenk can be reached at the Institute of Public Administration Science, University of Oldenburg, D-26111 Oldenburg; email: Lenk@uni-oldenburg.de. Since 1975, Dr. Lenk is Professor of Public Administration Science and cofounder of the field "Verwaltungsinformatik" in Germany (1974). His main areas of research are electronic government (IT use in public administration), administrative policy and reform, and political implications of the informatisation of society (for more details see http://www.uni-oldenburg.de/verwaltungswissenschaft). He is chairing the Working Committee 6.2 "Administrative Informatics" of the German Society for Informatics (GI). Professor Lenk was in charge of the "German Memorandum on e-Government" proclaimed in 2000.

Ann Macintosh is Director of the International Teledemocracy Centre at Napier University. She is actively involved with governmental, business and voluntary organisations concerned with the research and development of digital government systems in the UK, Europe and the Commonwealth of Scotland. She was a member of the Scottish Executive's Ministerial Task Force on "Digital Scotland" and also a member of the UK-Online working group to specify e-democracy services for this government portal. She is on the Advisory Council for the Commonwealth Centre for Electronic Governance.

Anna Malina is working on a project funded by the Joseph Rowntree Charitable Trust. Her remit is to monitor and evaluate e-petitioner. She is currently finalising a doctoral thesis researching community development in cyberspace. Her study analyses the background, development and societal significance of a community-based electronic network. Ms. Malina is generally interested in new relationships developing in society as a result of new ICTs and new forms of electronic communication. Specific research interests include community informatics, social shaping of technology, the operation of late capitalism and modernisation of state procedures, aspects of e-Government and e-democracy, and the nature of public participation in the [electronic] public sphere. She has published several pieces of work in these areas.

Agneta Nilsson (nilsson@informatik.gu.se) is a PhD student in the Department of Informatics at the University of Göteborg in Sweden. Her main interest is change management aspects of information systems development in the public sector. Her recent research has focused on management aspects when introducing groupware in local government in Sweden. Another theme is the use of Internet technologies within health care.

Mark E. Nissen is Assistant Professor of Information Systems and Acquisition Management at the Naval Postgraduate School and Office of Naval Research Young Investigator. His research focuses on the investigation of knowledge systems for enabling and managing change in areas such as process innovation, electronic business and knowledge flow. Recently he has been investigating knowledge systems to innovate processes in the acquisition domain, and he is currently involved with intelligent supply chain agents, as well as techniques and technologies for the capture and distribution of knowledge in very-large enterprises. Professor Nissen's publications span both the information systems and acquisition fields, with recent and forthcoming articles in journals such as *MIS Quarterly*, *Journal of Management Information Systems*, *Decision Support Systems*, *Journal of Information Technology Management*, *Acquisition Review Quarterly* and *National Contract Management Journal*. He has also recently published his first book, entitled *Contracting Process Innovation*, and he received the Menneken Faculty Award for Excellence in Scientific Research, the top research honor bestowed upon faculty at the Naval Postgraduate School. Before his information systems doctoral work at the University of Southern California, he acquired over a dozen years' management experience in the aerospace and electronics industry and served as a Supply Officer in the Naval Reserve.

Gilles Paquet studied philosophy and social sciences at Laval. He pursued graduate studies in economics at Laval, Queen's (Canada) and at the University of California, as a Postdoctoral Fellow in Economics. Professor Paquet has taught economics at Carleton University and economics and public management at the University of Ottawa. He has authored, co-authored and edited numerous publications on issues ranging from Canada's economic history, regional and industrial development, knowledge production and management, trade and technology, governance entrepreneurship and public management.

Christine Poupa is a researcher, specializing in information system management in public administration, cyberadministration and cyberdemocracy. She has been working at the Idheap (Institute for Advanced Studies in Public Administration, Switzerland) from 1994 to 2001. Her last publications have appeared in *Management and Delivery of Justice* and *Proceedings of the IFIP 8.5 Working Conference on Advances in Electronic Government.*

Agneta Ranerup (agneta@informatik.gu.se) is a Lecturer in the Department of Informatics at the University of Göteborg in Sweden. She received her PhD in informatics from the University of Göteborg in 1996. Her main research interest is democratic aspects but also change management aspects of information systems development in the public sector. Her recent research has focused on the use of on-line forums in local government politics. Another theme has been change management aspects when introducing groupware in local government in Sweden.

Andreu Riera received his BSc in Computer Science at the Autonomous University of Barcelona (Spain) in 1993. From 1993 to 2000 he was Researcher and Lecturer at that university. In 1999, he completed a PhD on cryptographic protocols for large-scale electronic elections over the Internet. During his research he participated in two government-funded research projects on e-voting and published several research papers on e-voting in international conferences and journals. He has been speaker at several seminars and conferences on e-voting organized by universities and public offices. In February 2000 he joined iSOCO, the first spin-off of the Spanish Research Council, as Research Manager. He is founder and CEO of SCYTL, a company specialized in the development of cryptographic technology to enable secure e-voting over the Internet.

Jeffrey Roy holds a PhD in Public Policy from Carleton University, a Master's of Business Administration from the University of Ottawa and a BA in Economics from the University of Waterloo. He teaches courses in corporate governance, e-Governance, public management, consultation and negotiation and regional economic development at the University of Ottawa. Professor Roy's current research includes international studies on collaborative governance, new corporate governance models of knowledge-based start-up companies, and prospects for e-Government and private-public partnerships. These initiatives involve a variety of partners including Mitel Corporation, OCRI, Government of Canada, EDS Systemhouse, Deloitte Consulting and Deloitte Touche.

Jordi Sànchez is Director of the Jaume Bofill Foundation; Professor of Political Science at the Universitat Autònoma de Barcelona (UAB) and at the Universitat Oberta de Catalunya (UOC), the first virtual university in Catalonia; and a member of the Board of Trustees of the Catalan TV Corporation (Public Broadcasting and TV Corporation), since 1996. Since 1997, he is the co-director of the first experience about Electronic Democracy in Catalonia (http://www.democraciaweb.org). He has published several articles in academic publications about political cultural, political participation, the challenge of the democracy and the impact of the new technologies to the democratic process.

Jörgen Svensson is a Lecturer in Sociology and Informatisation at Twente University in The Netherlands. He teaches courses in sociology, in welfare state development and in ICT and informatisation in the public sector. His research focuses on the application of ICT in public administration. He wrote a dissertation about the use of expert-system technology for simulating the effects of social policy.

Laia Torras holds a bachelor's degrees in Journalism (1991-96) and Political Science (1993-97) from the Autonomous University of Barcelona. She has been working at the Jaume Bofill Foundation since 1997 as the coordinator of a project on citizen participation through the Internet called Democracia.web, with the support of the Catalan Parliament. While cooperating with the Jaume Bofill Foundation, she also worked as a consultant at the Department of Peace, Human Rights, Democracy and Tolerance at UNESCO headquarters in Paris from March to December 1999. She has participated in international congresses on electronic democracy, and published several articles in specialised publications. Since January 2000 she has been taking part in coordinating all citizen participation program at the Jaume Bofill Foundation.

Roland Traunmüller can be reached at the Institute of Applied Computer Science, Johannes Kepler University Linz, A-4040 Linz, Austria; email: traunm@ifs.uni-linz.ac.at. Professor Traunmüller works in the field of Information Systems, telecooperation and applications of information technology in government. He has been a member of the steering committee "Administrative Management" at the Office of the Prime Minister since 1993 and in 1990, he also established the working group "Information Systems in Public Administration" within the International Federation of Information Processing Societies (IFIP). Currently, he serves as Deputy Chairman of the IFIP TC 8 "Information Systems" and as Vice-President of the Austrian Computer Society (OCG). Currently, he is involved in the EC IST project "eGov." For more details see http://falcon.ifs.uni-linz.ac.at/.

Mikael Wiberg is a PhD student in Informatics with a specific focus on questions concerning centralization and decentralization of work, mobile CSCW, knowledge management and knowledge-intensive organizations. Further, Mr. Wiberg has completed a lot of both practical and theoretical work related to group addressing techniques and session management models to support mobile collaboration.

Maria Wimmer can be reached at the Institute of Applied Computer Science, Johannes Kepler University Linz, A-4040 Linz, Austria; email: mw@ifs.uni-linz.ac.at. After her undergraduate studies, Dr. Wimmer worked in Italy within the EU-TMR network "OLOS" where she carried out workplace studies, specification and evaluation of system requirements, and early design prototyping of a train traffic control system. In her PhD, she developed a holistic development concept for complex safety critical systems. Her research field has now broadened to also cover distributed knowledge and e-Government. Dr. Wimmer is coordinating the annual Workshops on Knowledge Management in Electronic Government. Currently, she is involved in the EC IST project "eGov." For more details see http://falcon.ifs.uni-linz.ac.at/.

Angus Whyte is a Research Associate at the International Teledemocracy Centre. He is currently researching internet-supported democracy applications for young people. He has extensive experience of case-study research using ethnographic and action research methods in conjunction with participatory design of new media. He was previously a Senior Researcher in a European project (Living Memory, Esprit project 25621) concerned with prototype technologies for profiling and supporting the communication practices of groups and individuals in a neighbourhood of Edinburgh. His principal research interest is in the multidisciplinary field of social informatics.

Index